M000238790

Handbook on Animal-Assisted Therapy

Handbook on Animal–Assisted Therapy
Theoretical Foundations and Guidelines for Practice

Third edition

Edited by

Aubrey H. Fine
Department of Education
College of Education and Integrative Studies
California State Polytechnic University
Pomona, California, USA

AMSTERDAM • BOSTON • HEIDELBERG • LONDON • NEW YORK
OXFORD • PARIS • SAN DIEGO • SAN FRANCISCO • SINGAPORE
SYDNEY • TOKYO
Academic Press is an imprint of Elsevier

Academic Press is an imprint of Elsevier
32 Jamestown Road, London NW1 7BY, UK
30 Corporate Drive, Suite 400, Burlington, MA 01803, USA
525 B Street, Suite 1800, San Diego, CA 92101-4495, USA

First edition 2001
Second Edition 2006
Third Edition 2010

Notice
No responsibility is assumed by the publisher for any injury and/or damage to persons or
property as a matter of products liability, negligence or otherwise, or from any use or operation
of any methods, products, instructions or ideas contained in the material herein. Because of
rapid advances in the medical sciences, in particular, independent verification of diagnoses
and drug dosages should be made

British Library Cataloguing-in-Publication Data
A catalogue record for this book is available from the British Library

Library of Congress Cataloging-in-Publication Data
A catalog record for this book is available from the Library of Congress

ISBN : 978-0-12-381453-1

For information on all Academic Press publications visit
our website at www.elsevierdirect.com

Typeset by TNQ Books and Journals

Printed and bound in United States of America

11 12 13   10 9 8 7 6 5 4 3

Working together to grow
libraries in developing countries

www.elsevier.com | www.bookaid.org | www.sabre.org

ELSEVIER   BOOK AID
              International   Sabre Foundation

About the Editor

Dr. Fine has been a faculty member at California State Polytechnic University since 1981. Recipient of many awards, he earned the prestigious Wang Award in 2001, given to a distinguished professor within the California State University system, in this instance for exceptional commitment, dedication, and exemplary contributions within the areas of education and applied sciences. He was also awarded the Educator of the Year in 1990 by the Learning Disability Association of California.

Animals have been an integral part of Dr. Fine's clinical practice over the past three decades. His clinical practice primarily focuses on the treatment of children with attention, behavioral, adjustment and developmental disorders. His practice includes two therapy dogs, birds and a bearded dragon. In addition to his expertise in the area of AAT, Dr. Fine has published several academic books and video documentaries on related subjects such as parent/child relationships, learning/attention disorders, and sports psychology. His newest book *Afternoons with Puppy* is a heartwarming account about the evolving relationships and outcomes among a therapist, his therapy animals and his patients over the course of over two decades.

Contents

Part One – The Conceptualization of the Animal/Human Bond: The Foundation for Understanding Animal-Assisted Therapy

Part Two – Animal-Assisted Therapy: Conceptual Model and Guideliness for Quality Assurance

Contributors

Phil Arkow
The Latham Foundation, California, 94501, USA and The American Humane Association, Englewood, Colorado, 80112, USA

Arnold Arluke
Northeastern University, Boston, Massachusetts, 02115, USA

Frank R. Ascione
University of Denver Graduate School of Social Work, Denver, Colorado, 80208, USA

Mara M. Baun
University of Texas Health Science Center at Houston, Houston, Texas 77030, USA

Alan M. Beck
School of Veterinary Medicine, Purdue University, West Lafayette, Indiana, 47907, USA

Ann Berger, MSN
National Institutes of Health, Bethesda, Maryland, 20892, USA

Barbara W. Boat
University of Cincinnati College of Medicine; Cincinnati Children's Hospital Medical Center, Ohio, 45267, USA

Christine Bowers
California State Polytechnic University, Pomona, California, 91010, USA

Andrea Brooks
Pets Are Wonderful Support (PAWS), San Francisco, California, 94107, USA

Kris Butler
American Dog Obedience Center, LLC, Oklahoma, 73069, USA

Cynthia Chandler
University of North Texas, Denton, Texas, 76209, USA

Susan Phillips Cohen
The Animal Medical Center, New York, 10065, USA

Raymond Coppinger
Hampshire College, Amherst, Massachusetts, 01002, USA

Aubrey H. Fine
California State Polytechnic University, Pomona, California, 91768, USA

Erika Friedmann
University of Maryland School of Nursing, Baltimore, Maryland, 21201, USA

Julia Gimeno
California State Polytechnic University, Pomona, California, 91768, USA

Ken Gorczyca
Pets Are Wonderful Support (PAWS), San Francisco, California, 94107, USA

Temple Grandin
Colorado State University, Fort Collins, California, 80523, USA

Lynette A. Hart
School of Veterinary Medicine, University of California, Davis, California, 95616, USA

Jana I. Helgeson
California State Polytechnic University, Pomona, California, 91768, USA

Rebecca A. Johnson
Sinclair School of Nursing, University of Missouri, Columbia, Missouri, 65211, USA

Aaron H. Katcher
Psychiatrist—Independent Practice, Arlington, Texas, 76017, USA

Alan E. Kazdin
Department of Psychology, Yale University, New Haven, Connecticut, 06520, USA

Jane Irene Kelly
Marauder Media, Pleasant Hill, California, USA

Steven Klee
Green Chimneys Children's Services, New York, 10509, USA

Katherine A. Kruger
Center for the Interaction of Animals and Society, Matthew J. Ryan Veterinary Hospital, University of Pennsylvania, Philadelphia, Pennsylvania, 19104, USA

John Lipp
Pets Are Wonderful Support (PAWS), San Francisco, California, 94107, USA

Maureen A. Frederickson-MacNamara
Animal Systems Ltd, Asheville, North Carolina, 28805, USA

Gerald P. Mallon
Hunter College School of Social Work, New York, 10021, USA

Marie S. McCabe
American Humane Association, Human-Animal Interactions, Englewood, Colorado, 80112, USA

Patricia McConnell
University of Wisconsin, Madison, Wisconsin, 53515, USA

Richard Meadows
College of Veterinary Medicine, University of Missouri, Columbia, Missouri, 65211, USA

Gail F. Melson
Purdue University, West Lafayette, Indiana, 47907, USA

Jeffrey Mio
California State Polytechnic University, Pomona, California, 91768, USA

Laura Nelson
Pets Are Wonderful Support (PAWS), San Francisco, California, 94107, USA

Dana O'Callaghan
National University and Palomar College, California, 91730, USA

Jose M. Peralta
College of Veterinary Medicine, Western University, Pomona, California, 91766, USA

Teri Pichot
Private Practice, Denver, Colorado, USA

Allie Phillips
American Humane Association, Human-Animal Interactions, Englewood, Colorado, 80112, USA

Lori Popejoy
School of Nursing, University of Missouri, Columbia, Missouri, 65212, USA

Lisa Ross
Touro University, California, 94592, USA

Samuel B. Ross, Jr.
Green Chimneys Children's Services, New York, 10509, USA

Karen Schaffer
New Mexico State University, Las Cruces, New Mexico, 88001, USA

James A. Serpell
*School of Veterinary Medicine, University of Pennsylvania, Philadelphia,
Pennsylvania, 19104, USA*

Perry Skeath
National Institutes of Health, Bethesda, Maryland, 20892, USA

Heesook Son
University of Maryland School of Nursing, Baltimore, Maryland, 21201, USA

C. Victor Spain
Merck & Co., Inc, Philadelphia, Pennsylvania, 19146, USA

Ilana Strubel
*San Francisco Community Clinic Consortium's VET SOS, San Francisco, California,
94103, USA*

Philip Tedeschi
*Institute for Human/Animal Connection, University of Denver Graduate School
of Social Work, Denver, Colorado, 80208, USA*

Richard Timmins
Association for Veterinary Family Practice, Camano Island, Washington, 98282, USA

Chia-Chun Tsai
Yuanpei University Department of Nursing, Taiwan, R.O.C.

Dennis C. Turner
Institute for Applied Ethology and Animal Psychology, Switzerland

Stephanie Venn-Watson
National Marine Mammal Foundation, San Diego, California, USA

Cindy Wilson
*Uniformed Services University of the Health Sciences, Bethesda, Maryland,
20895, USA*

Belinda Wong
University of California, San Francisco, California, 94720, USA

Foreword

The book that you are holding is a compendium, containing data, theory and guidelines for the practice of what has come to be known as *animal-assisted therapy* (abbreviated as AAT). This is defined as a form of therapy that involves using an animal as a fundamental part of a person's treatment. Although the most common form of animal used is the dog, followed by cats, many kinds of animals have been used in therapy, mostly small animals (rabbits, birds, fish, gerbils), but some large animals have been employed (mostly horses), and some exotic species (e.g. elephants, dolphins, lizards).

The range of problems that animal-assisted therapy has addressed is quite broad. While most people are aware of assistance animals, such as guide dogs for the blind, hearing assistance dogs, handicap assistance dogs and, more recently, seizure alert and seizure assistance dogs, the general public is only slowly coming to understand that animals can be used to deal with a broad variety of psychological as well as physical problems. Most often animals are used to assist in problems involving emotional distress and/or general stress-related symptoms. When used in this context the animals are often referred to as *comfort animals*. However, some animal interventions involve treatment of cognitive functioning, social interaction problems, and even extreme conditions, such as autism. More recently, the therapeutic use of animals has been extended to educational settings, where the animal is used to improve motivation and focus the attention of children, as demonstrated by several successful programs that utilize *reading assistance dogs.*

When I see a book like this, with all of its data, theory and practice information, I must admit that I have a feeling of disbelief. This is not a disbelief in the validity of the data, or the success of animal-assisted therapeutic interventions, but rather a disbelief that this area has come to be accepted by mainstream psychological, educational and medical researchers and practitioners. This was not always so. My own first contact with this type of therapy actually led me to predict that such endeavors would never come to pass.

Before we get to my experience, it is important to know that therapeutic use of animals has a long history. In ancient Egypt, the city of Hardai became known as Cynopolis (City of Dogs) because in its many temples dedicated to Anubis, the dog-headed guide of the dead, dogs were used as offerings. However, dogs were also used in healing practices there. It was believed being licked by a dog, especially in those areas of the body containing sores or lesions, could help to heal the injury or cure the disease causing it. This practice was picked up by the Greeks, and temples dedicated to Asclepius, their god of medicine and healing, often contained dogs trained to lick wounds. In the Middle Ages, Saint Roch was said to have been cured of a plague of sores through being licked by his dog. The value of being licked by a dog is still believed by many cultures to have curative powers. There is even a contemporary French saying, "Langue de chien, langue de médecin" which translates to "A dog's tongue is a doctor's tongue." Perhaps there is some validity to this since recent research has shown that the dog's saliva actually contains a number of antibacterial and antiviral compounds, as well as some growth factors that may promote healing.

However, animal-assisted therapy today involves using animals to assist in the healing of psychological and emotional problems, rather than using them as sources of antibiotics which are better obtained from pharmacological sources. Here, again, we have historical antecedents. In the late 1600s, John Locke (who would introduce psychology to the concept of association in learning), suggested that small pet animals aided in the social development of children, including the development of empathy. In the 19th century, Florence Nightingale suggested that small pets relieved depression in patients, especially for those with chronic conditions.

Still there were little data, nor was there widespread acceptance of the fact that the presence of animals can assist and improve psychological functioning. Instead, there were many anecdotes that suggested that this might be the case. For example, during World War II, a Corporal William Wynne was recovering from wounds in an army hospital in the Philippines. To cheer him up members of his company brought his Yorkshire terrier, Smoky, to the hospital. The effect was remarkable, and not only did Corporal Wynne's mood improve, but it had a positive effect on the other injured soldiers in the ward. The degree of psychological improvement impressed the commanding officer of the hospital unit, Dr. Charles Mayo, who would later go on to head the now famous Mayo Clinic in Rochester, Minnesota. As a result, he decided to regularly take Smoky on his rounds in the military hospital to act as a living antidepressant for his patients. In effect, Smoky became a therapy dog, and as such he continued to be part of a visitation program for 12 years, well beyond the end of World War II.

This brings us to my initial contact with the idea of animal-assisted therapy. It was quite early in my career, in the 1960s, and I was attending the American Psychological Association meetings in New York. Because of my interest in dogs and their relationship to humans, I was caught by the title of a talk to be given by a child psychologist, Boris Levinson, who was at Yeshiva University. This would turn out to be the first formal presentation of animal-assisted therapy given before a national audience. Levinson was working with a very disturbed child and found, by chance, that when he had his dog Jingles with him the therapy sessions were much more productive. Furthermore, other children who had difficulty communicating seemed more at ease and actually made real attempts at conversation when the dog was present. Levinson gathered data from several such cases and this formed the basis of the paper that he presented at this APA meeting. The reception of his talk was not positive, and the tone in the room did not do credit to the psychological profession. Levinson was distressed to find that many of his colleagues treated his work as a laughing matter. One even asked him what percentage of the therapy fees he paid to the dog. This did not bode well for the future of such research and therapy, and I thought that it was likely that I would never hear about such use of animals in therapeutic interactions again.

I might have been correct, except that a savior of this concept, whose voice could not be ignored by the psychological community, essentially spoke from beyond his grave. At this point in time, it was only some 15 years after Sigmund Freud's death. Just by chance, several new biographies of Freud's life had recently been released. In addition, translations of many of his letters and journals were just being published in

English. There were also new insights into Freud's life coming from books published by people who knew him, and some even described his interactions with his household full of dogs.

From these various sources, we learned that Freud often had his chow chow, Jofi, in his office with him, even during psychotherapy sessions. The dog was originally in the room as a comfort to the psychoanalyst, who claimed that he was more relaxed when the dog was nearby. However, Freud soon began to notice that the presence of the dog seemed to help patients during their therapy sessions as well. This difference was most marked when Freud was dealing with children or adolescents. It seemed to him that the patients seemed more willing to talk openly when the dog was in the room. They were also more willing to talk about painful issues.

The positive results were not limited only to children, but also were seen in adults. The presence of the dog seemed to make adults of both sexes feel more comfortable as well. During psychoanalysis, when the patient is getting near to uncovering the source of their problem there is often a "resistance phase," as if the person was trying to defend themselves from the psychological pain and deep emotions that exposing their repressed trauma might cause. In the resistance phase the patient might become hostile, might stop actively participating in therapy, or might obviously be withholding information. Freud's impression was that the expression of this resistance was much less vigorous when the dog was in the room.

When he began to observe the effects the dog had on the therapy session, he speculated a bit as to the cause. In a psychoanalytic session the patient is asked to free associate or simply say whatever comes into their mind. To facilitate this, the patient is asked to stretch out on a couch and relax. The therapist sits behind the patient, out of his line of sight. The reason is that this keeps the patient from watching the facial expressions of the therapist which might be interpreted as disapproval or some other emotion. The idea is to let the patient freely follow their own patterns of association while they work their way toward the source of their problem, rather than taking any indirect guidance from the therapist's responses. Now, although the therapist is out of sight, the dog is quite clearly in view, usually lying calmly and quietly nearby. The dog appears to be unmoved by anything that the patient says, and nothing seems to shock the therapist's shaggy companion. Freud concluded that this gives the patient a sense of safety and acceptance. Even when the patient describes very painful or embarrassing moments, the dog does not react, except perhaps with a calm glance in the patient's direction. This gives the patient some confidence that all is well and anything can be expressed in this place. Thus the dog provides a sense of reassurance. Freud recorded this information in his notes and it would eventually encourage the systematic use of dogs in therapy.

From this newly available information it became clear that Freud had observed very much the same phenomena that Levinson described, concerning those therapy sessions when he was treating children in the presence of his dog. When Levinson and others learned about Freud's experiences with this, it seemed like a form of certification. Levinson's groundbreaking book on what he called "Pet-Oriented Child Psychotherapy" followed not long thereafter in 1969.

The climate had certainly now warmed. With evidence that Freud was willing to entertain the usefulness of animal helpers in psychotherapy, and Levinson's book collecting his case studies, the laughter stopped and some serious work began. Psychiatrists Sam and Elizabeth Corson were two of the first to formally use dogs in their treatment procedures, when they opened the first pet-assisted therapy program at a psychiatric unit at Ohio State University in 1977.

The ultimate validation of animal-assisted therapy, at least for those in the fields of mental health and behavior, would come from the public health ecologist Alan Beck and the psychiatrist Aaron Katcher. They used direct physiological measures to show that when a person interacted with, or even was simply in the presence of, a friendly dog, there were direct changes in their physiological responses. Breathing became more regular, heart beat slowed, muscles relaxed and there were other physiological changes suggesting a lowering of sympathetic nervous system activity. Since it is the sympathetic nervous system which responds to stress, this indicated that the dog was clearly reducing the stress levels of the people in its presence. There is a bias among psychological researchers, in that they tend to use physiological measures as if they are the "gold standard" for the validity of a concept. Since they could now see the direct effects that pets were having on the physiological indexes of stress, the notions associated with animal-assisted therapy became much more acceptable. This is evidenced by the fact that the number of pet-assisted therapy programs was under 20 in 1980 but, by the year 2000, over 1,000 such programs were in operation. These programs not only include dogs who are brought into the psychotherapist's office as part of treatment, but also visitation programs where dogs are brought into hospitals and homes for the elderly. There are also some rehabilitation programs where the dogs are brought in as companions to build morale and confidence, and the use of animals in educational settings.

This book documents the current status of animal-assisted therapy, its practice, and the data supporting it. It also goes well beyond Freud's initial speculations as to theoretical basis for therapeutic effects of interactions with animals. In order to do this, the basis of the human/animal bond is explored as well as the cultural significance of animals. There is even coverage of animal abuse and the welfare of assistance animals. This is likely the best collection of material covering the use of animals as an aide to therapy available at this time. It is a good starting place for anyone interested in engaging in animal-assisted therapy, and a fine resource to allow those already practicing it to update their knowledge and hone their skills.

We have come a long way from Boris Levinson's hostile reception by his psychological colleagues. Now there are dogs, cats, and other animals routinely assisting human beings through difficult emotional times, and helping to work through their psychological problems. In my more philosophical moments I often muse on the history of this burgeoning area of mental health research and practice. I still sometimes ask myself, "Could it be that animal-assisted therapy is really the unintended legacy of that reddish-brown dog who laid at the feet of the founder of psychoanalysis while he worked with his patients?"

Stanley Coren

Professor Emeritus
Department of Psychology
University of British Columbia

Preface

It has been over ten years since our first edition of this Handbook was published. Since that time, animal assisted interventions (AAI—a broad term that includes what we have traditionally either called "animal assisted therapy" or "animal assisted activities" as well as other terms) have continued to generate tremendous interest in the general sector, as well as the scientific community perhaps because of people's curiosity about the human–animal bond. Over the years several progressive changes have been made, and several scientific disciplines are beginning to look more closely at the impact of AAI. We believe that this volume will be an important contribution to the literature on animal assisted interventions in promoting a clearer understanding of the scope of practice. The contributors to the book continue to take a critical analysis of what are best practices in AAI, and provide the readers with a glimpse to what is needed in the future to develop more evidence-based practices.

Animals have been an integral part of my clinical practice for over three decades. My initial experiences were discovered serendipitously, but ever since my work with a tiny gerbil and children with learning disabilities, I have become fascinated with the genuine power of the human–animal bond. When I first accepted the editorship of this Handbook, I was excited about the opportunity because of my genuine enthusiasm about AAI; I was also compelled to put together a book that helped clarify some of the misconceptions about the topic. Furthermore, I wanted to develop a book that not only imparted a strong theoretical overview, but also provided clinicians, researchers and scholars as well as all others interested in AAI with the a clearer understanding of the value of the human–animal bond as well as potential methods for application.

There have been many changes and updates in this new addition including several new chapters. All previous chapters incorporated in this volume have been updated and there are several new contributions including chapters on applying AAI with persons with autistic spectrum disorders, the role of animals in palliative care, a chapter on what therapists need to know about animal behavior, psychiatric service animals, understanding pet bereavement as well as many other chapters.

The chapters in this book are divided into four major parts. The strength of each part relates to how the chapters are closely interrelated. It will become apparent to the reader that the therapeutic use of animals is an emerging approach that is built on a long history of our association with and curiosity about other living beings. Qualitatively, AAI demonstrate a significant contribution to the overall quality of life. Nevertheless, there is a strong need for more evidence-based research that quantifies the value of these approaches.

It is important to point out that scientific and clinical community investigating these interventions is built on interdisciplinary professions that bridge the worlds of mental and physical health professionals, with their counterparts in ethology, animal behavior and animal welfare. As it has been previously noted, one of the major weaknesses of animal AAI is the limited scientific evidence demonstrating its efficacy. It is also hoped that the contents of this book act an impetus for further empirical investigations into the therapeutic use of animals in clinical practices.

Part I consists of seven chapters that focus on the conceptualization of the human–animal bond and incorporate chapters addressing numerous topics. The book begins with a chapter by Fine and Beck that provides an overview of the human animal bond movement and clarifies a direction for the future. This chapter is followed by a chapter written by Serpell that provides a historical exploration of the value of human–animal relationships. The chapter is shadowed by one written by Kruger and Serpell which provides an excellent overview of the various definitions of AAI and the various theoretical models that have been used to explain how AAI may work. The reader will find this introductory chapter extremely helpful in conceptualizing the broad scope of AAI. Katcher and Beck provide an overview of where AAI has come from and the difficult road it continues to battle to justify its efficacy.

The section culminates with three other chapters. The chapters address the a comprehensive review of the research explaining the psychosocial benefits of animals as well as an explanation of the value of animals as social supports. The final chapter provides a comprehensive explanation of the physiological benefits found as a consequence of the human-animal bond.

Part II focuses on the conceptual models of AAI and contains three descriptive chapters providing an overview of designing and implementing AAI services. This information is invaluable in understanding how to develop institutionally based treatment programs. In the chapter by Fredrickson-MacNamara and Butler the readers will become more acquainted with models and standards to consider in selecting certain species of animals with various populations. The chapter also focuses on the factors that affect the performance of various animal species. For those readers interested in designing and implementing AAI programs in health and mental health organizations, Malon et al. have updated their previous chapter to provide the reader with a series of concerns that must be addressed for effective program intervention. The writers incorporate within their discussion various organizational, staff and client issues that must be considered. The section ends with a chapter developed from an interview with Dr. Patricia McConnell and her perceptions of what therapists need to be aware of about animal behavior and welfare.

Part III documents the therapeutic efficacy of the human animal relationship with specific populations. Chapters discuss using animals with specific populations including children, those receiving palliative care, persons with chronic disorders and AIDS, persons with autistic spectrum disorders, the elderly as well as the application of AAI in specialized settings. There are also a couple of other chapters that have been incorporated that clarify how animals can be naturally included in psychotherapy and techniques on how too incorporate animals in working with and understanding families. Readers will also find a chapter by Ascione et al. on animal abuse as well as research on the relationship between animal abuse and interpersonal violence. The section ends with a chapter written by Tedeschi et al which gives the reader a glimpse into the emerging area of psychiatric service animals..

Part IV, the final section of the book, consists of seven chapters that are more general in nature. A chapter by Cohen provides a useful overview in helping clients with the process of bereavement. Cohen's chapter is followed by a passionate section written by Arkow who describes some new strategies and alternatives for humane education. The last four chapters within this section address several current and important subjects. Serpell, Coppinger, Fine, and Peralta have prepared an updated chapter addressing the importance of safeguarding animals' welfare and discuss the ethical concerns that must be taken into consideration while engaging in AAI. The chapter promotes a better understanding by clinicians while working alongside therapy animals. Timmins, Fine, and Meadows prepared a chapter discussing the importance of developing healthy relationships with family practice veterinarians and what their contribution to AAI can be. In the final two chapters, Kazdin, Turner and Wilson, as well as Fine and Mio present various points of views on the future direction of AAI. Each of the chapters provide of glimpse to future directions in the field. All offer suggestions of what needs to occur to help AAI establish more credibility..

It is hoped that this book will become an impetus for further study and investigation. No one can forecast with accuracy the future, but I believe that after more applicable research is documented, the findings will help AAI become more commonly practiced and respected.

Acknowledgements

This book could have not been written without the support of all the contributing authors. Their insight into the field of animal assisted therapy and the human–animal bond has made this a meaningful project to steward and edit. I thank Nikki Levy and Barbara Makinster from Elsevier, who were very supportive throughout this project.

I also want to thank Ronalea Spinks, Michele Fitzgerald, Christine Bowers, and Julia Gimeno who helped gather some of the research for this updated volume. I am grateful for all their efforts and support. Finally, I want to thank my wife, Nya who has been very supportive during this entire process. Her encouragement and shared love of animals also has made this project more meaningful.

Aubrey H. Fine

February, 2010

Dedication

This edition of the *Handbook* is dedicated to the following:

To all the clinicians and scholars who have made contributions to this *Handbook* and the field of animal-assisted interventions. Without your trailblazing efforts the field would not be as respected as it is today. Thank you for your leadership!

To my wife Nya and sons Sean and Corey: our love and work with animals have strengthened our relationship and our family. I am blessed to have you all in my life. You are all the spark in my heart.

To my mother and sister Roslyn who have had such a great impact on all of my life.

Finally, this *Handbook* is especially dedicated to my dear P.J. You have been a devoted and loving companion for so many years. You have enriched my life and truly have helped me understand the power of the human/animal connection. You are fondly treasured by all for your gentleness and warmth.

Part One

The Conceptualization of the Animal/Human Bond: The Foundation for Understanding Animal-Assisted Therapy

1 Understanding our kinship with animals: input for health care professionals interested in the human/animal bond

Aubrey H. Fine*, Alan Beck[†]

* California State Polytechnic University, [†] Purdue University

Cats delight the eye by delicately walking among vases and sculpture or stalking a piece of string or exploring an empty paper bag. They are almost never self-conscious, and they do not use your direct gaze as an invitation. While walking in a park or wood, the wandering trail of the dog as it explores its environment gives our gaze a path to follow and a place to rest. The dog's form and motion provide a foreground for the confusion of natural scenes and make visual choices for us. Alternatively, the sight of a sleeping dog can induce a sense of relaxation and well-being.

Between Pets and People: The Importance of Animal Companionship
(Alan Beck and Aaron Katcher, 1996)

1.1 Introduction

This introductory chapter provides readers not only with a basic foundation to appreciate and understand this unique kinship with all living creatures but also to discover the roots to the overwhelming growing interest in animal-assisted intervention (AAI). The chapter should also help solidify and clarify how the benefits witnessed within this unique bond have prompted numerous professionals to become more curious about the advantages of animal-assisted interventions.

It is apparent that dogs have been bred to coexist with their human counterparts and have filled many roles including herding, guarding, hunting, fishing and being our best friend (Clutton-Brock, 1995). Dogs have also been widely used as service animals, supporting the quality of life of people in need. There have been increasing insights into science's current understanding of dog behavior and cognition. Perhaps one of the strongest insights that she discusses pertains to dogs' ability to understand our behaviors (Hare, 2007; Hare et al., 2002). Horowitz (2009) explains that dogs'

Handbook on Animal-Assisted Therapy. DOI: 10.1016/B978-0-12-381453-1.10001-7

strengths in communicating with humans relate to their predisposed ability to inspect our faces for critical information, for reassurance and for guidance. These traits are a definite asset for their interactions. In essence, dogs are keen observers of our reactions.

As time progresses, numerous interventions have developed employing a strong belief that relationships with animals contribute to the well-being of people. Although plagued with poor research, limited scientific evidence, animal-assisted interventions have grown, primarily on anecdotal outcomes. It is apparent that clinicians from numerous disciplines seem to have become enamored with the therapeutic roles that animals have in the lives of their patients. For some, their clinical interests stem from their personal convictions and attractions to animals, while others have been driven because of their perceived perception that animals may provide a useful alternative for clinical application.

1.2   Introduction to the human/animal bond (HAB)

The science of understanding the human/animal connection appears to have made some healthy steps forward since the National Institutes of Health (NIH) convened a workshop on the health benefits of pets in 1987 (NIH, 1987). In fact, in the fall of 2008, a similar meeting was held in Bethesda, Maryland, under the auspices of the National Institute of Child and Human Development addressing the need for clarity in research. Beck and Katcher (2003) point out that there is still a continued need to generate awareness of the importance of human/animal interactions and to truly study the specifics of the nature of this relationship. Nevertheless, some progress has been made identifying the physiological and psychological benefits that animals provide to our lives. Ever since the benchmark study by Friedmann et al. (1980) that demonstrated the health benefits of pet owners a year after being discharged from a coronary care program, the curiosity of HAB has grown steadfast. In fact, Phillips (2002) points out that, in the United Kingdom, pet ownership seems to result in savings to the national health program to the sum of about £600 million per year.

The interest in the human/animal connection has been heightened in the past few decades as a direct result of mainstream media's and the popular press's coverage of the impact of animals on humans' lives. This coverage has increased the general public's curiosity to our unique relationships with animals. It is evident that many people seem to romanticize their relationships with animals (Fine and Eisen, 2008). Although with good intentions, some treat animals as if they are part human. Jon Katz (2003) in his book *The New Work of Dogs* warns readers that pet owners use dogs to fill emotional gaps in their lives. He warns that dog owners have created exceedingly high expectations for emotional support they expect from their pets—forgetting that animals are not humans. Most scholars would argue that to consider their behavior human is an injustice and disrespectful to the animal. Although potentially harmful, anthropomorphism, and its way of thinking, does have its positives and negatives. Beckoff (2007) writes in *New Scientist Life* that he believes that while we should not impose human attributes onto animals, we may use anthropomorphisms as a strategy to identify commonalities and then use human language to communicate what we observe. According to Steven Mithen (1996) in his book *The Prehistory of the Mind: An Exchange,* without anthropomorphism, neither pet keeping nor animal domestication would ever have been possible. Serpell (2003) suggests that by enabling our ancestors to attribute human thoughts, feelings, motivations, to other species, the process and the way of thinking opened the gateway for some animals to become more readily accepted in human circles first as pets, and ultimately becoming domestic dependents. Serpell (1996) also argues in an earlier paper that most pet owners believe that their animals genuinely "love" or "admire" them. He suggests that the fact remains that without this belief system, the relationships most people have with pets would be essentially meaningless. The inheritances we share with non-human animals is the basis for all biomedical research and it is most likely the roots of behavioral processes; indeed, we have a great deal in common with the animals that share our lives (Beck, 1996). Perhaps anthropomorphizing our pets says something about our needs as humans (Fine and Eisen, 2008).

We are now entering a new crossroads in an era of scientific curiosity where there is a greater interest to define the underlying mechanisms of the bond. More scholars are now becoming curious about the underlying mechanisms that allow these interventions to be considered much more than puppy love. Although there are a wealth of testimonials documenting the significance of animals in our lives, Knight and Herzog (2009) point out that there is limited empirical research that has explored these relationships. Perhaps today's glamor found in this unique affection/connection with animals and within animal-assisted interventions is directly related to the mystique of interspecies bonding. People seem intrigued with our similarities and differences and want to better understand our relationships with domestic and exotic animals.

According to the American Veterinary Medical Association (2007), there were 72 million dogs owned in the USA in 2006. Who would have thought that the pet industry would become an annual $45 billion industry in the USA where funds are spent to make the quality of life more comfortable for our companion animals (American Pet Products Association, 2009)? Within the report estimates have been made which articulate where the money is actually spent. The following highlights the findings:

Food $17.4 billion
Supplies/OTC medicine $10.2 billion
Vet care $12.2 billion
Live animal purchases $2.2 billion
Pet services: grooming and boarding $3.4 billion

1.3 Defining the human/animal bond

Turner (2007) points out that the human/animal bond is a well-documented phenomenon that has been around since humans began domesticating animals. The strength of the human/animal connection allowed companion animals to quickly adopt roles as members of the family. Chandler (2001), Serpell (1996) and Flom

(2005) have documented that the power of the human/animal bond has been described in sources as diverse as ancient literature, modern fiction, and research reports in the professional literature. All have pointed out there is something extraordinary about our relationships, which are quite different than conventional human relationships. Ian Robinson (1995) highlights the association between people and animals and provides some insights into these relationships. He suggested that the more similar the social organization and communication systems are of the two species, the more likely that each will understand the other better. He ends his essay by suggesting that our relationships with other species fulfill human needs that are beyond simple economic needs.

Konrad Lorenz (the famous ethologist), Boris Levinson (a psychotherapist who is considered by many as the father of animal-assisted therapy) and Leo Bustad (founder of the Delta Society) were perhaps the three most influential people who pioneered the term the human/animal bond. Lorenz once stated that the wish to keep an animal usually arises from a general longing for a bond with nature. The bond with a true dog is as lasting as the ties of this earth can ever be. Bustad (1983) extended this quote by stating that this bond is similar to human functions that go hand in hand with the emotions of love and friendship in the purest and noblest forms. Beck (1999) noted that the term "bond" was borrowed from the terminology linked to the relationship cherished by parents and their children.

Although the term seems simplistic to understand, Davis and Balfour (1992) claim that there is no universally accepted definition of human/animal bond. This lack of agreement was also suggested in the writings of Bayne (2002). Although there does not seem to be universal agreement within the definition, several researchers have identified a few common specific ingredients. Tannenbaum (1995) suggested that the relationship needs to be of a continuous nature and must be bi-directional. Furthermore, he points out that the relationships should be voluntary. Russow (2002) also suggested that the relationship needs to be reciprocal and persistent. She explains that there is no true bond if the animal does not recognize you. She also suggests that the relationship involves increased trust on the animal's behalf and increased caring and understanding of the animal's needs on the part of the human. In her article, as well as others including Beck (1999), the authors all seem to highlight the mutual benefit of the bond that promotes an increase in the well-being for both parties.

Bonding is the forming of close, specialized human relationships, such as the link between parent and child, husband and wife, friend and friend. Many of these relationships are recognized by behaviors understood by all involved. Similar behaviors, often in similar settings, are seen in animals, especially birds and mammals, and we often use the same term—"bonding." Domesticated animals are invariably social species that exhibit social interaction and "bonding-like" behaviors among themselves. The humane community adopted the term because they wanted to capture the spirit and connotation of the "infant/parent bond." Those who care about animals want to imply that the relationship is healthy and natural. While some argue that the bond with animals does not emulate all the psychological implications of human/human bonding, the general public uses the term both in its literal meaning and as a metaphor for the many roles animals play in our lives.

Finally, the American Veterinary Medical Association's Committee on the Human-Animal Bond defines the human/animal bond as, "a mutually beneficial and dynamic relationship between people and other animals that is influenced by behaviors that are essential to the health and well-being of both. This includes, but is not limited to, emotional, psychological, and physical interactions of people, other animals, and the environment" (JAVMA, 1998).

1.4   Pets and people: case studies reveal the importance

Some may wonder why there is such an intense focus on people and their pets. From a purely pragmatic point of view, pets fill a void in most owners' lives. Instead of an empty house, people come home to a happy loving animal such as a dog or a cat. In 2002, the organization Pawsitive InterAction held its inaugural educational conference on the human/animal bond in Atlanta, Georgia. While at the meeting, Beck (2002) suggested that one of the growing reasons why pets are so revered is that animals offer an array of health benefits, beyond their loving companionship. He stated that "the companionship of animals decreases loneliness and stimulates conversation." He also went on to elaborate that by encouraging touch and giving humans a loving creature to care for, the interaction with animals stimulates physical reactions that are very necessary and important in humans.

Dr. Edward Creagan (2002), a professor of medical oncology at the Mayo Clinic, who also attended the meeting pointed out that he believes there is an indisputable mind/body connection that is anchored by our pets. He believes that pets create a balance between one's mind and body. Fine (2006) and Fine and Eisen (2008) also suggest that our pet companions provide a source of pleasure, connection to the outside world and for some people the promise of hope and a reason to live. The virtue of hope is a state of mind that allows people to reach deep inside to persevere. In the instance of the human/animal bond, some people may find hope in unusual places, such as puppy's big brown eyes!

Over the years, both the authors have listened to and heard numerous personal accounts on the importance of animals in the lives of people. Fine coauthored a book that highlights numerous accounts of how people have disclosed the importance of their relationship with their beloved companion animals or therapy animals (Fine and Eisen, 2008). Nevertheless, one example jumps out and is exemplary in explaining this position.

Several years ago, Rev. Delana Taylor McNac, a hospice chaplain, encountered an elderly couple, Harold and Rose, who lived in an apartment with a black and tan, rather portly Dachshund named "Stretch." Harold was on hospice for terminal heart disease. Not long after his admission, Harold's condition stabilized somewhat and he was on hospice for over a year. Unfortunately, his wife Rose began to decline. She began to have memory lapses that kept her from helping Harold take his medications properly. He was too weak to care for her and the stress on them both began to show. A decision was made to move the couple, but their children decided they would move them to a place without Stretch. The staff attempted to intervene, knowing how important the dog was to Harold, but to no avail. An out-of-state relative took the dog away the day of the move, before we could offer additional options.

When McNac next visited Harold and Rose in their new apartment, she was shocked at the change in him. He sat alone in a back room in the dark, quietly grieving. He told her that he missed his dog, and he worried about how Stretch was doing in his new home. His wife, despite her confusion, knew that he was missing his dog and she was angry at the family for taking him away.

Over the next six weeks, Harold continued to decline rapidly. He also became increasingly confused, remembering who McNac was, but not knowing why she visited him. Her last visit was one she would never forget. She explained how she observed Harold was lying on his bed, fully clothed, talking nonsensically to no one in particular, staring at the television. Beside him, where Stretch always lay, Harold petted an invisible dog over and over again. He died later that night.

The essence of this case study portrays how important animals can become in the lives of many, including those with terminal illnesses. In an upcoming chapter within this volume on palliative care, more attention will be given to explain this phenomenon. However, it is important to realize that when one is adjusting to and coping with any chronic illness, one's emotional outlook is of utmost importance, and animals may act as an important social support in these times (Fine and Eisen, 2008). Johnson (2008) in an interview discussed her research in the area of cancer. She noted that the patients who received dog visits in her study revealed that the animals helped them feel less anxious. They also disclosed that the pet visits provided them with a distraction from their grueling treatment.

1.5   Theories explaining the bond

The sense of being needed has been scrutinized by numerous scholars as one of the number of reasons why the bond is established. The theories of attachment and animals acting as social supports provide a logical explanation of why so many young and old people engage in the care of a dependent animal. In upcoming chapters, these theories will be elaborated upon in more depth, but the authors felt compelled to elaborate a bit here. Attachment theory, which was developed by Bowlby (1969), was written to explain the need for humans to protect and to be protected (Sable, 1995). Bowlby (1969, 1980) and Ainsworth (1989) suggested that attachment behavior was any form of behavior that resulted in a person attaining or maintaining proximity to some other clearly identified individual who is perceived as better able to cope with the world. The biological function attributed to the attachment is that of protection.

Beth Ellen Barba (1995) suggested that the roles of humans in relationship with their pets often parallel roles of human/human relationships, especially that of child and parent. Just as young children rely on their parents, pets must depend on their human companions for continual care, protection from dangerous situations, and explanation of things on their behalf due to lack of language (i.e. a pet owner's explanation to the veterinarian). Many pet owners are often observed playing with their pets as parents would with their children and talking to them in baby talk or what

Hirsch-Pasek and Treiman (1982) called "motherese." In fact, the intense attachment to our pets has often been witnessed in times of natural disasters and people's refusal to evacuate their homes. Recent examples of this emotional hardship would be Hurricane Katrina which hit the deep south of the USA in August of 2005 or the major fires in Southern California in 2008. Companion animals are critical in the lives of many and there is a deep sense of responsibility to safeguard their lives. Lookabaugh Triebenbacher (2000) has written extensively in regards to how humans perceive animals as significant members of their family. She reports that companion animals may play numerous roles within the family including a close friend, a confidant and an outlet of affection and support. It seems that the greatest time period when families have animals in their homes is during childhood and early adolescence. Melson (2005) and Myers (2006) have written two excellent books describing in detail the importance of animals in the lives of children and how animals foster both emotional and cognitive growth. Nevertheless, the roles of companion animals are not exclusive to children. Animals have an important place in the lives of people who are in transition (for example, those experiencing a divorce or the death of a spouse), newlyweds and the elderly.

Pet owners commonly view their relationships with animals in humanistic terms. Many seem to develop anthropomorphic attitudes towards their pets, projecting onto the animals their own human feelings, motives and qualities, and often perceiving pets as substitutes for other people (Selby and Rhoades, 1981). Beck and Katcher (2003) suggested that sharing our lives with companion animals usually leaves people feeling safer and brings more constancy in the person's daily life.

Bryant (2008) suggests that most humans seek out social support to help them adapt to difficult situations. She argues that social support is a foundation for healthy functioning and mental health. She believes that pets and animal companions are an excellent resource for people to secure social support and positively affect their physical and mental health. McNicholas and Collis (1995) pointed out that some people may become more attached to animals than to humans since they perceive their pets as always being available to meet their needs. The authors also noted that it often appears easier for humans to bond with animals than with other humans—unlike most humans, pets are typically indifferent to their human companions' material possessions, status, well-being and social skills. McNicholas and Collis (2000) also suggest that the presence of a dog facilitates social interactions with other people. Wells (2009) points out that walking with a dog results in a significantly higher number of chance conversations with complete strangers than walking alone; however, it seems dependent on the characteristics of the animal. Fine and Eisen (2008) and Serpell (1986) suggest that the more infantile the features the animals have and the more unique outward appearance that the animal displays, the more impactful the initial interaction. In every day language, people seem to be suckers for warm looking eyes and a cold nose. Bonas et al. (2000) state that the relationship between the individual and the dog is similar to human-to-human relations, where the animals provide comfort and a positive social outlet. Garrity and Stallones (1998) imply that the positive impact of dogs on humans is consistent with the literature on the benefits associated with human social support.

There has been a wealth of research that has suggested that the presence of animals may act as a buffer for stress (Allen et al., 2002). Strand (2004) developed a thesis where she argues that a healthy relationship with a pet can help buffer children from intra-parental conflicts within the home. She points out that animals could become healthy alternatives for children to seek refuge during parental arguments. On the other hand, Wells (2005) found that even viewing video recordings of fish, birds, and monkeys (rather than be surrounded by live animals) also had a buffering effect from the stress. Her findings seem to suggest that observing animals in a tranquil environment has a sedating effect on our behavior.

1.6 The biological benefits of the bond

Wells (2009) in her descriptive paper on the effects of animals on humans' health and well-being stresses that the notion that "pets are good for us" is by no means a new one. She suggested that it is only relatively recently that any scientific attention has been devoted to the relationship between companion animals and physical well-being in humans.

Before we actually address the biological benefits of the bond, it is imperative to illustrate that medical and social sciences continue to be baffled with regards to what contributes to the well-being of the ill. Follansbee (2007), past president of the San Francisco Medical Society, states that "the practice of medicine is not only about predictable outcomes with standard therapies." He elaborated in his remarks that there is more to promoting the recovery of patients than just dispensing prescriptions. His comments accurately describe a dilemma that continues to plague medical science. What are the other elements and variables that contribute to the health care of a patient?

Healing is quite complex and interfaces with numerous other dimensions. Paracelsus, a famous physician of the sixteenth century, alluded that the main reason for healing and recovery could also be attributed to love and the power found in the human spirit. Although stated several hundred years ago, many leading scientists have voiced similar comments. In fact, James Lynch (1977) suggested "that the health of the human heart depends not only on such factors as genetics, diet and exercise, but also to a large extent on the social and emotional health of the individual" (p. 13). In essence, healthier people receive and give love to others. It is amazing to realize that sometimes the simple act of being a friend and caring for another can have a significant impact on our neuro-chemistry. Over the past several decades, scientists have scrutinized and have unearthed the evidence that supports this assumption. Equally as revealing is the literature that suggests that the friendships do not have to be human/human in nature, but could be with other species.

Holtzman and Britz (1986) reported a benchmark study that investigated the effects of human relationships on the heart. William Kraus conducted the study on 5,300 intensive care unit patients. Ironically, although one would have taken for granted variables such as hospital prestige and advances in technological sophistication, the variable that impacted the patients the most seemed to be the relationship between the caregiver and the patient. In essence, holding, talking and reassuring the patients were the hospital's best factors for ICU survival rates.

Olmert (2009) argues that "contrary to the romantic myths about the unconditional love that animals and humans have for each other, there could be a strong physiological reason why we have such a strong bond with them." Numerous papers have been written over the past few decades which illustrate the unique physiological benefits that animals foster. The roots of these physiological studies go back to earlier works of Friedmann, Katcher and Lynch who have demonstrated the value of caressing an animal on cardiovascular health. Friedmann et al. (1990) also postulated that pet ownership leads to the following benefits: (a) improved fitness by providing a stimulus for exercise; (b) decreased anxiety by providing a source of physical contact; and (c) decreased loneliness by providing companionship.

Since that time, several researchers have looked at the impact on numerous neurotransmitters and being surrounded by animals. Perhaps the premier study on the relation that animals have to our biological emotional health was initiated by Odendaal (2000) and Odendaal and Meintjes (2003). Odendaal and Meintjes (2003) studied 18 subjects and the effects of gently stroking and talking to their pet dogs. Their data indicated that their level of oxytocin almost doubled and a similar outcome was found in their own animals. Their study also found a decrease in the pressure of both groups as well as a decrease in the cortisol levels. Finally, their research also seemed to indicate that there was an increase in beta endorphins and dopamine production in the humans. Touching, stroking, and holding have been shown to reduce heart rate in humans in a number of studies.

Mendelson and Baggot (2007) suggest some of the strongest evidence for the role of oxytocin in commitment and love comes from studies in prairie voles. Prairie voles often show pair bonding (commonly referred to as mating for life), whereas montane voles do not. Several elegant studies have demonstrated that a primary difference between these closely related species is the location of oxytocin receptors in the central nervous system (CNS) (Gavish et al., 1981 and Carter et al., 1995—in Olmert, 2009, p. 247). In the monogamous prairie voles, injections of oxytocin directly into specific CNS loci increase preferences for a single partner over other partners, and injections of specific oxytocin antagonists depress single-partner preference. Mendelson and Baggot (2007) summarize the research by inferring that, although the exact relationship between oxytocin release and emotion is not completely understood, it seems clear (from the available data) that circulating levels of oxytocin change in response to affiliation and intimacy.

Clearly the benchmark study by Odendaal, which has been replicated by Johnson et al. (2002), highlights the enormous physiological impact that animals have or could have on our lives. Spa treatments have often been highly regarded as a method to revitalize our souls and bodies. It is apparent that interacting with a loved pet has similar outcomes and perhaps could be considered a biological alternative to a spa.

1.7   Final remarks

A rationale has been presented describing the potential benefits to the human/animal connection. This introductory explanation should be a useful platform to conceptualize the underlying elements of AAI. It should also provide an explanation that could help all readers understand why some clients are enamored with their pets. Although growth has been witnessed over the decades, the emerging field of HAB continues to have many battlegrounds to contend with. The discipline needs a facelift of more rigorous scientific scrutiny. Research documenting the correlations and value of animals in our lives would enhance HAB's credibility. This has been an ongoing battle that must be embarked upon if the benefits are to be respected by reliable sources. On the positive side, the general public would not be surprised by the claims made about HAB. Perhaps many would not even care. Many are satisfied with the knowledge that they have been befriended by a being that they love and are devoted to. They live the miracles that the scientific and clinical communities would like to harness and understand better.

Both of these diametric positions leave us with questions to answer as we embark on tackling the future. It is inevitable that science will provide us with clearer explanations of why and how, but perhaps we may never be able to capture clearly the healing power that comes from a loving relationship—either between humans or between humans and other species. The words of the brilliant Albert Einstein echo clearly as we march to our future. Although understanding helps us persevere, we should also respect that "not everything that can be counted counts, and not everything that counts can be counted." We need to appreciate that there are elements of life that can never be fully explained but only witnessed. Perhaps we need to take heed of his wisdom, as we set forth to unearth the unique strength found within.

References

Ainsworth, M. (1989). Attachment beyond infancy. *American Psychologist, 44*, 709–716.

Allen, K. M., Blascovich, J., & Mendes, W. B. (2002). Cardiovascular reactivity and the presence of pets, friends and spouses: the truth about cats and dogs. *Psychosomatic Medicine, 64*, 727–739.

American Pet Products Association (2009). Industry statistics & trends. Retrieved August 16, 2009 from: http://www.americanpetproducts.org/press_industrytrends.asp

American Veterinary Medical Association (2007). U.S. Pet Ownership & Demographics Sourcebook (2007 ed.). American Veterinary Medical Association.

Barba, B. E. (1995). A critical review of research on the human/companion animal relationship. *Antrhozoös, 8*, 9–15.

Bayne, K. (2002). Development of the human-research animal bond and its impact on animal well-being. *Institute for Laboratory Animal Research Journal, 43*(1), 4–9.

Beck, A. M. (1996, May 17). The common qualities of man and beast. *The Chronicle of Higher Education, 42*(36), B3.

Beck, A. M. (1999). Companion animals and their companions: sharing a strategy for survival. *Bulletin Science, Technology & Society, 19*(4), 281–285.

Beck, A. M. (2002, May). *Health effects of companion animals*. Atlanta, GA: Paper presented at 1st Annual Pawsitive Interaction Conference.

Beck, A. M., & Katcher, A. H. (1996). *Between Pets and People: The Importance of Animal Companionship*. West Lafayette, IN: Purdue University Press.

Beck, A. M., & Katcher, A. H. (2003). Future directions in human-animal bond research. *American Behaviorial Scientist, 47*, 79–93.

Beckoff, M. (2007). Do animals have emotions? *New Scientist Life, 2605*, 12–13.

Bonas, S., McNicholas, J., & Collis, G. (2000). Pets in the network of family relationships: an empirical study. In A. L. Poderscek, E. S. Paul, & J. A. Serpell (Eds.), *Companion Animals and Us: Exploring the Relationships Between People and Pets* (pp. 209–234). Cambridge, UK: Cambridge University Press.

Bowlby, J. (1969). Disruption of affectional bonds and its effects on behavior. *Canada's Mental Health Supplement, 69*, 1–17.

Bowlby, J. (1980). *Attachment and Loss*. New York: Basic Books.

Bryant, B. K. (2008, Sept. 30–Oct. 2). *Social support in relation to human animal interaction*. Bethesda, Maryland: Paper presented at the NICHD/Mars meeting on Directions in Human-Animal Interaction Research: Child Development, Health and Therapeutic Interventions.

Bustad, L. K. (1983). *Symposium summary*. Vienna, Austria: Paper presented at the International Symposium on Human-Pet Relationship.

Carter, C. S., Devries, A. C., & Getz, L. L. (1995). Physiological substrates of mammalian monogamy: the prairie vole model. *Neuroscience and Biobehavioral Reviews, 19*, 303–314.

Chandler, C. (2001). *Animal Assisted Therapy in Counseling and School Settings*. Greensboro, NC: ERIC Clearinghouse on Counseling and Student Services.

Clutton-Brock, J. (1995). Origins of the dog: domestication and early history. In J. Serpell (Ed.), *The Dometic Dog: Its Evolution, Behaviour and Interactions with People* (pp. 7–20). Cambridge, UK: University of Cambridge.

Creagan, E. (2002, May). Pets, not pills. *The healing power of fur, fins and feathers*. Atlanta, GA: Paper presented at 1st Annual Pawsitive Interaction Conference.

Davis, H., & Balfour, D. (1992). *The Inevitable Bond*. Cambridge, UK: Cambridge University Press.

Fine, A. H. (2006). Animals and therapists: Incorporating animals in outpatient therapy. In A. Fine (Ed.), *Handbook on Animal Assist Therapy* (2nd ed.), (pp. 179–211) San Diego, CA: Academic Press.

Fine, A. H., & Eisen, C. (2008). *Afternoons with Puppy: Inspirations from a Therapist and His Therapy Animals*. West Lafayette, IN: Purdue University Press.

Flom, B. (2005). Counseling with pocket pets: using small animals in elementary counseling programs. *Professional School of Counseling, 8*(5), 469–471.

Follansbee, S. (2007). Another cat story. *San Francisco Medicine, 80*, 7.

Friedmann, E., Locker, B. Z., & Lockwood, R. (1990). Perception of animals and cardiovascular responses during verbalization with an animal present. *Anthrozoös, 6*(2), 115–134.

Garrity, T. F., & Stallones, L. (1998). Effects of pet contact on human well-being. In C. C. Wilson, & D. C. Turner (Eds.), *Companion Animals in Human Health* (pp. 3–22). Thousand Oaks, CA: Sage.

Gavish, L., Carter, C. S., & Getz, L. L. (1981). Further evidence for monogamy in the prairie vole. *Animal Behavior, 29*, 955–957.

Hare, B. (2007). From nonhuman to human mind what changed and why? *Current Directions in Psychological Science, 16*(2), 60–64.

Hare, B., Brown, M., Williamson, C., & Tomasello, M. (2002). The domestication of social cognition in dogs. *Science, 298*(5598), 1634–1637.

Hirsch-Pasek, K., & Treiman, R. (1982). Doggerel: Motherese in a new context. *Journal of Child Language, 9*, 229–237.

Holtzman, A. H., & Britz, W. (1986). Pet ownership and health status during bereavement. *Omega, 17*(21), 187–193.

Horowitz, A. (2009). *Inside of a Dog: What Dogs See, Smell, and Know.* New York: Scribner.

Journal of the American Veterinary Medical Association. (1998). Statement from the committee on the human-animal bond. *Journal of the American Veterinary Medical Association, 212*(11), 1675.

Johnson, R. (2008, September 30–October 2). *Physiological benefits of AAT.* Bethesda, Maryland: Paper presented at NICHD/Mars meeting on Directions in Human-Animal Interaction Research: Child Development, Health and Therapeutic Interventions.

Johnson, R., Odendaal, J., & Meadows, R. (2002). Animal-assisted interventions research: issues and answers. *Western Journal of Nursing Research, 24*(4), 422–440.

Katz, J. (2003). *The New Work of Dogs: Tending to Life, Love and Family.* New York: Villard Books.

Knight, S., & Herzog, H. (2009). All creatures great and small: new perspectives on psychology and human-animal interactions. *Journal of Social Issues, 65*(3), 451–461.

Lynch, J. J. (1977). *The Broken Heart: The Medical Consequences of Loneliness.* New York: Basic Books.

McNicholas, J., & Collis, G. (1995). The end of the relationship: coping with pet loss. In I. Robinson (Ed.), *The Waltham Book of Human–Animal Interaction: Benefits and Responsibilities of Pet Ownership* (pp. 127–143). Oxford: Pergamon Press.

McNicholas, J., & Collis, G. (2000). Dogs as catalysts for social interactions: robustness of the effect. *British Journal of Psychology, 9*, 61–70.

Melson, G. (2005). *Why the Wild Things are: Animals in the Lives of Children.* Cambridge: Harvard University Press.

Mendelson, J., & Baggot, M. (2007). Love: a chemical connection. Is there a pharmacology of love? *San Francisco Medicine, 80*(6), 10–15.

Mithen, S. (1996). *The Prehistory of the Mind: An Exchange.* London, UK: Thames and Hudson.

Myers, G. (2006). *The Significances of Children and Animals: Social Development and Our Connections to Other Species* (2nd ed., revised). Lafayette, IN: Purdue University Press.

NIH. (1987). The health benefits of pets. *Workshop summary. Sept* 10–11, Bethesda, MD: National Institutes of Health, Office of Medical Applications of Research, Technology Assessment Workshop.

Odendaal, S. J. (2000). Animal assisted therapy: magic or medicine? *Journal of Psychosomatic Research, 49*(4), 275–280.

Odendaal, S. J., & Meintjes, R. (2003). Neurophysiological correlates of affiliative behavior between humans and dogs. *Veterinary Journal, 165*, 296–301.

Olmert, M. D. (2009). *Made for Each Other.* Philadelphia: De Capo Press.

Phillips, C. (2002, Jan. 21). Does pet ownership reduce the number of GP consultations? What pets can do for patients. London, UK: Paper presented at Pets are Good for People, a meeting of the Comparative Medicine Section, Royal Society of Medicine.

Robinson, I. (1995). Associations between man and animals. In I. Robinson (Ed.), *The Waltham Book of Human-Animal Interaction: Benefits and Responsibilities of Pet Ownership* (pp. 1–8). Melton Mowbray, Leicestershire, UK: Waltham Centre for Pet Nutrition.

Russow, L. M. (2002). Ethical implications of the human-animal bond. *International League of Associations for Rheumatology, 43*(1), 33–37.

Sable, P. (1995). Pets, attachment, and well-being across the life cycle. *Social Work, 40*(3), 334–341.

Selby, L. A., & Rhoades, J. D. (1981). Attitudes of the public towards dogs and cats as companion animals. *The Journal of Small Animal Practice, 22*(3), 129–137.

Serpell, J. (1986). *In the Company of Animals: A Study of Human-Animal Relationships.* New York: Basil Blackwell.

Serpell, J. A. (1996). *In the Company of Animals* (2nd ed.). Cambridge, UK: Cambridge University Press.

Serpell, J. A. (2003). Anthropomorphism and anthropomorphic selection—beyond the "cute response." *Society & Animals, 11,* 83–100.

Strand, E. B. (2004). Interparental conflict and youth maladjustments: the buffering effects of pets. *Stress, Trauma, and Crisis, 7,* 151–168.

Tannenbaum, J. (1995). *Veterinary Ethics: Animal Welfare, Client Relations, Competition and Collegiality* (2nd ed.). St. Louis, MO: Mosby.

Triebenbacher, S. L. (2000). The companion animal within the family system: the manner in which animals enhance life within the home. In A. Fine (Ed.), *Animal Assisted Therapy: Theoretical Foundations and Guidelines for Practice* (pp. 337–375). San Diego, CA: Academic Press.

Turner, W. G. (2007). The experiences of offenders in a prison canine program. *Federal Probation, 71*(1), 38–43.

Wells, D. L. (2005). The effect of videotapes of animals on cardiovascular responses to stress. *Stress and Health, 21,* 209–213.

Wells, D. L. (2009). The effects of animals on human health and well-being. *Journal of Social Issues, 65*(3), 523–543.

2 Animal-assisted interventions in historical perspective

James A. Serpell, PhD

University of Pennsylvania

2.1 Introduction

Although every topic has its own unique history that can be explored, analyzed and interpreted, the limits of historical inquiry are inevitably bound by the quantity and quality of surviving documents and artifacts. Unfortunately, surviving historical accounts of people's relationships with animals are both unusual and sketchy, and the little documentary evidence that exists tends to refer to the lives of the rich and famous. Our knowledge of how ordinary people in the past related to animals, or made use of their companionship, remains indistinct and largely speculative. Even where the historical evidence is relatively complete, there is a danger of over-interpreting it—of attributing values, attitudes, and sentiments that make sense to us from a modern perspective, but which would not necessarily have possessed any meaning for our historical predecessors. All of this demands that we treat historical evidence with an appropriate degree of caution.

With this proviso in mind, the present chapter will attempt to provide a brief historical account of the various ways in which animals in general, and companion animals in particular, have been perceived as contributing to human mental and physical health. While attempting to set this work in historical context, the chapter will not attempt a detailed review of recent studies of animal/human therapeutic interactions, since this material has already been adequately covered elsewhere (see Kruger et al., 2004; Serpell, 1996; Wilson and Turner, 1998).

2.2 Animal souls and spiritual healing

In the history of human ideas concerning the origins and treatment of illness and disease, non-human animals play a variety of important roles. The precise charac-teristics of these roles depend, however, not only on the prevailing view of animals, but also on the particular supernatural or "scientific" belief systems in which they are imbedded.

Probably the most archaic of these belief systems, usually referred to as "Animism," involves the concept that all living creatures, as well as other natural objects and

Handbook on Animal-Assisted Therapy. DOI: 10.1016/B978-0-12-381453-1.10002-9

phenomena, are imbued with an invisible soul, spirit or "essence" that animates the conscious body, but that is able to move about and act independently of the body when the bearer is either dreaming or otherwise unconscious. According to the typical animist worldview, all manifestations of sickness or misfortune are the direct result of assaults against a person's soul or "essence" by other angry or malevolent spirits encountered during these periods of unconsciousness. In some cases, these spiritual assaults are thought to be retaliatory; the result of some deliberate or inadvertent moral transgression on the part of the person. Alternatively, the person may be the innocent victim of an attack by spirits acting on behalf of a malevolent shaman or witch. Clues to the origins of spiritual assaults are often provided by the content of the dreams or visions that immediately preceded a particular bout of illness, injury or misfortune (Benedict, 1929; Campbell, 1984; Eliade, 1964; Hallowell, 1926; Martin, 1978; Nelson, 1986; Serpell, 2005; Speck, 1977; Wenzel, 1991).

Animist belief systems are characteristic of all hunting and foraging societies, and among these societies, offended animal spirits are often viewed as the most common source of malignant spiritual influences. Many Inuit peoples believe, for example, that the spirits of hunted animals, like the ghosts of murdered humans, are capable of seeking vengeance. To avoid this happening, all animals, whether dead or alive, are treated with great respect. Otherwise, the hunter or his family can expect to suffer some misfortune: the animals will no longer allow themselves to be killed, or they may take their revenge by afflicting someone with disease, physical handicap or even death (Wenzel, 1991). As an Inuit informant once eloquently expressed it:

> *The greatest peril in life lies in the fact that human food consists entirely of souls. All the creatures that we have to kill and eat, all those that we have to strike down and destroy to make clothes for ourselves, have souls, like we have, souls that do not perish with the body, and which must therefore be propitiated lest they should avenge themselves on us for taking away their bodies.*
>
> *(Rasmussen, 1929, p. 56)*

In other hunting and foraging cultures, more specialized sets of moral relations existed between people and the animals they hunted for food. For instance, many Native American and Eurasian peoples believed in the concept of personal "guardian spirits" (Benedict, 1929; Hultzkrantz, 1987). Among the Ojibwa (Chippewa) and their Algonkian neighbors, these spirits were known as *manito* and they were commonly represented as the spiritual prototypes or ancestor figures of wild animals. All of these *manito* were thought of in highly anthropomorphic terms. They were easily offended, capricious, and often bad-tempered, but they could also be appeased and, to some extent, cajoled by ritual means. Living animals were regarded as "honored servants" of their respective *manito*, and one such spirit apparently presided over and represented all of the earthly members of its species. At the same time, animals were also viewed as temporary incarnations of each *manito* who sent them out periodically to be killed by favored hunters or fishermen. For this reason, hunters invariably performed deferential rituals upon killing an animal, so that its "essence" would return to the *manito* with a favorable account of how it was treated.

According to the Ojibwa worldview, the activities of *manito* explained nearly all the circumstances of everyday life. Every natural object, whether animate or inanimate, was charged with spiritual power, and no misfortune, whether illness, injury, death, or failure in hunting or fishing, was considered accidental or free from the personalized intent of one *manito* or another (Landes, 1968). Animal guardian spirits were also believed to vary in terms of power. Some species, especially small and relatively insignificant ones, such as the majority of insects, and such things as mice, rats or squirrels, were believed to possess correspondingly limited spiritual influence, and rarely furnished people with useful guardian spirits. In contrast, more physically impressive species, such as bears, bison, wolves or eagles, were deemed to possess extraordinary spiritual power, and were therefore eagerly sought after as patrons (Benedict, 1929; Landes, 1968).

The methods used to obtain the patronage of these kinds of guardian spirits varied from culture to culture, but they almost invariably involved some form of physical ordeal (Benedict, 1929). Among the Ojibwa, young men at puberty were expected to isolate themselves in the forest and endure long periods of fasting, sleeplessness and eventual delirium in an effort to obtain visions. Those who were successful experienced vivid hallucinations in which their "souls" entered the spirit world and encountered one or more *manito* who offered their future help and protection in return for a variety of ritual obligations. *Manito* advice or assistance could sometimes be discerned through natural portents and coincidences but, more often, guidance came indirectly through the medium of subsequent dreams and visions. At such times the person's "soul" was believed to re-enter the supernatural dimension and confer with its spiritual guardian. The content of dreams was therefore considered of primary importance as a guide to action in daily life (Landes, 1968).

In some societies, it was considered virtually suicidal to injure, kill or eat any member of the same species as one's guardian spirit. Like the Ancient Mariner's albatross, it could result in the withdrawal of spiritual patronage, and cause general misfortune, illness, and death. On the other hand, and in an equally large number of cultures, the guardian spirit specifically awarded its protégé the authority to kill members of its own species (Benedict, 1929; Hallowell, 1926).

As in most fields of individual achievement, not all men and women were equally good at obtaining the support of animal guardian spirits. Some never obtained visions and were regarded as "empty, fearful and cowardly" for the rest of their lives. A small minority, on the contrary, displayed extraordinary visionary talents and were henceforth regarded as medicine men, sorcerers or shamans (Landes, 1968).

2.3   Animal powers and shamanism

Mircea Eliade (1964) refers to shamanism as an "archaic technique of ecstasy" derived from guardian spirit belief. Both represent quests for magico-religious powers, and shamans differ from everyone else only in "their capacity for ecstatic experience, which, for the most part, is equivalent to a vocation" (Eliade, 1964, p. 107). Although shamanic power was derived from the assistance of one or more guardian spirits, the relationship between the shaman and his spiritual "helpers" or "familiars" was both more intimate and more intense than that attained by ordinary persons. In most cases, the shaman not only earned the patronage of guardian spirits but also developed the capacity to control them.

Shamans, typically, could achieve this power at will by entering a state of trance or ecstasy, usually induced by monotonous chanting, drumming and dancing, and commonly assisted by the consumption of psycho-active drugs. Such states were considered to be analogous to death – the only other time when a person's "essence" becomes truly detached from the body and capable of independent actions in time and space. According to Eliade, this ecstatic "out-of-body" experience enables the shaman to divest himself of human form and recover the situation that existed at the beginning of time when no clear distinctions separated humans from animals. As a result, he is able to re-establish friendship with animals, acquire knowledge of their language, and also the ability to transform himself into an animal as and when occasion demands. The result is a kind of symbiosis in which the person and the guardian spirit fuse to become two aspects of the same individual (Eliade, 1964).

Although they occasionally take human form, the vast majority of shamanic "familiars" are animals of one kind or another. Once he has adopted this disguise, the shaman is able to move about freely, gather information and perform magical acts at a distance from his body. It is unclear from the various anthropological accounts, however, whether the animal spirit had its own independent existence when not in the shaman's service, or whether it was simply a material form assumed by the shaman when engaging in the practice of magic. Stories and legends concerning shamans provide conflicting evidence in this respect. In some, shamans are said to be able to disappear when attacked or pursued, whereupon all that will be seen is some swift-footed animal or bird departing from the scene. If this animal is injured or killed, the shaman will experience an identical mishap wherever his or her body happens to be. On the other hand, shamans never killed or consumed the flesh of animals belonging to their familiar's species, implying that these spirits existed separately, and could easily be mistaken for ordinary animals (Speck, 1918).

Depending on their particular talents, shamans are believed to be able to foretell the future, advise on the whereabouts of game animals or predict impending catastrophes. Their ability to control the forces of nature can also be employed to manipulate the weather, subdue animals or bring them close to the hunter. Above all, since all manifestations of ill-health are thought to be caused by angry or malignant spirits, shamans possess a virtual monopoly on the treatment of sickness. Since the shaman is generally the only individual capable of visiting the spirit world at will through the agency of his animal "familiars," he provides the only reliable method of discovering and counteracting the spiritual origins of physical and mental illness (Eliade, 1964; Speck, 1918).

2.4   Animism in classical and medieval times

Although animist belief systems are particularly characteristic of hunting and foraging peoples, they have also persisted in a variety of forms in many pastoral nomadic and agricultural societies where they often coexist, through a process of synchretic fusion, with more recently imposed religious creeds and practices. An interesting contemporary example still flourishes among Central American indigenous peoples such as the Maya. Although Christianized and agricultural, the Mayan inhabitants of Chamula in the Mexican province of Chiapas believe in the existence of individual "soul animals" or *chanul* that are assigned to each person at birth by the celestial powers, and which share reciprocally every stroke of fortune that their human counterparts experience. All *chanul* are non-domesticated mammals with five digits, and they are physically indistinguishable from actual wild animals. Indeed, a person may only discover the identity of his soul animal through its recurrent appearance in dreams, or with the help of a shaman (Gossen, 1996).

The Maya believe that most illness is the result of an injury inflicted upon a person's *chanul*. These injuries may be inflicted deliberately via witchcraft, by another person mistaking one's *chanul* for an ordinary animal and hurting or killing it, or it may be "self-inflicted" in the sense that the person may allow him or herself to experience overly intense emotions, such as intense fear, rage, excitement or sexual pleasure, that can frighten or upset the *chanul*. The people of Chamula are also extremely reluctant to kill any wild mammal with five digits, since by doing so they believe they might inadvertently kill themselves, or a friend or relative.

As far as curative measures are concerned, the only traditional remedy for an illness resulting from damage to one's soul animal is to employ the services of a shaman who will use various rituals, and the influence of his own, more powerful soul animals, to discover the source of the affliction and counteract it. According to Mayan folklore, shamans and witches also possess the ability to adopt the material form of their *chanul* in order to gain access to the supernatural realm (Gossen, 1996).

The purpose of dwelling on this particular example of contemporary Amerindian belief in soul animals is that it illustrates, according to Gossen (1996), the remarkable tenacity of animistic/shamanistic ideas and practices in Central America, despite the coercive influence of nearly five centuries of imported Roman Catholicism. Similarly, in Europe and around the Mediterranean basin, it appears that vestiges of comparable belief systems survived in a number of local and regional healing cults, at least until the early modern period.

In the pre-classical period, the connection with animism was particularly obvious. In ancient Egypt, for example, the entire pantheon was dominated by distinctly shamanic images of animal-headed gods and goddesses, including the dog-headed Anubis who guided the souls of the dead on their journey through the underworld, and whose other roles included physician and apothecary to the gods, and guardian of the mysteries of mummification and reincarnation. Dogs and snakes were also the sacred emblems of the Sumerian goddess, Gula the "Great Physician," and of the Babylonian and Chaldean deity, Marduk, another god of healing and reincarnation (Dale-Green, 1966; Schwabe, 1994).

In the classical period, the animist associations are somewhat less prominent but still readily discernible. Within the Greek pantheon, the gods were less often represented as animals, but they retained the shamanic ability to transform themselves into animals in order to disguise their true identities. Dogs and serpents also played a central role in the cult of Asklepios (Aesculapius), the son of Apollo, who was known as the God of Medicine and the Divine Physician. Asklepios's shrine in the sacred grove at Epidaurus functioned as a kind of ancient health resort. Like modern day Lourdes, it attracted crowds of suppliants seeking relief from a great variety of maladies. As part of the "cure," it provided an early instance of institutional, animal-assisted therapy. Treatment involved various rites of purification and sacrifice followed by periods of (drug-induced?) sleep within the main body of the shrine. During their slumbers the God visited each of his "patients," sometimes in human form but more often in the guise of a snake or a dog that licked them on the relevant injured or ailing portions of their anatomy. It appears that the dogs that lived around the shrine may have been specially trained to lick people. It was believed that these animals actually represented the God and had the power to cure illness with their tongues (Dale-Green, 1966; Toynbee, 1973). Inscribed tablets found within the precincts of the temple at Epidaurus testify to the miraculous powers of the local dogs:

> *Thuson of Hermione, a blind boy, had his eyes licked in the daytime by one of the dogs about the temple, and departed cured.*
> *A dog cured a boy from Aigina. He had a growth on his neck. When he had come to the god, one of the sacred dogs healed him while he was awake with his tongue and made him well.*

Although evidently material in form, the healing dogs and snakes at Epidaurus clearly fulfilled much the same function as shamanic spirit helpers. Through their ability to renew themselves periodically by shedding their skins, not to mention their potentially venomous qualities, snakes have always possessed strong associations with healing, death and reincarnation (Morris and Morris, 1968). Likewise, in mythology, the dog is commonly represented as an intermediary between this world and the next. Some authors have attributed this to the dog's carrion-eating propensities, while others ascribe it to the dog's proverbial watchfulness and alertness to unseen "spiritual" threats, as well as its liminal, ambiguous status as a voluntary occupant of the boundary zone separating human and animal, culture and nature (Serpell, 1995; White, 1991).

During the early centuries of Christianity, traces of ancient shamanic ideas and practices were still prevalent throughout much of Europe. In addition to being healers, most of the early Celtic saints and holy men of Britain and Ireland were distinguished by their special rapport with animals, and many, according to legend, experienced bodily transformations into animal form (Armstrong, 1973; Matthews, 1991). St. Francis of Assisi, who appears have been influenced by Irish monastic traditions, has also been described as a "nature mystic." Among other feats, he preached sermons to rapt audiences of birds, and was able to pacify rabid wolves (Armstrong, 1973). One of his followers, St. Anthony of Padua (1195–1231), preached so eloquently to the fishes in the sea that they all lined up along the shoreline to listen to his words of wisdom (Spencer, 1993).

The particular notion that dogs could heal injuries or sores by touching or licking them also persisted well into the Christian era. St. Roch who, like Asklepios, was generally depicted in the company of a dog, seems to have been cured of plague sores by the licking of his canine companion. St. Christopher, St. Bernard and a number of other saints were also associated with dogs, and many of them had reputations as healers.

A faint ghost of older, shamanistic traditions can also be detected in the curious medieval cult of the greyhound saint, St. Guinefort. Guinefort, or so the legend goes, was unjustly slaughtered by his noble master who mistakenly believed that the dog had killed and devoured his child. Soon afterwards, however, the babe was found sleeping peacefully beside the remains of a huge, predatory serpent that Guinefort had fought and killed. Overcome with remorse, the knight threw the dog's carcass into a well, covered it with a great pile of stones, and planted a grove of trees around it to commemorate the event. During the thirteenth century, this grove, about 40 kilometers north of the city of Lyons, became the center of a pagan healing cult. Peasants from miles around brought their sick and ailing children to the shrine where miraculous cures were apparently performed (Schmitt, 1983).

Centuries later, the close companionship of a "Spaniel Gentle or Comforter"— a sort of nondescript, hairy lap-dog—was still being recommended to the ladies of Elizabethan England as a remedy for a variety of ills. William Harrison, in his *Description of England* (1577), admitted to some skepticism on the subject: "It is thought by some that it is verie wholesome for a weake stomach to beare such a dog in the bosome, as it is for him that hath the palsie to feele the dailie smell and savour of a fox. But how truelie this is affirmed let the learned judge." The learned Dr. Caius, author of *De Canibus Britannicus* (1570), was less inclined to doubt: "though some suppose that such dogges are fyt for no service, I dare say, by their leaves, they be in a wrong boxe." He was of the opinion that a dog carried on the bosom of a diseased person absorbed the disease (Jesse, 1866).

Thus, over historical time, a kind of progression occurs from a strong, archaic belief in the supernatural healing power of certain animals, such as dogs, to increasingly vague and superstitious folk practices in which the special "spiritual" qualities of the animal can no longer be discerned, and all that remains is a sort of "quack" remedy of dubious therapeutic value. In medieval Europe, this trend was associated with the Church's vigorous suppression of pre-Christian and unorthodox religious beliefs and practices. In the year 1231 AD, in an effort to halt the spread of religious dissent in Europe, the office of the Papal Inquisition was created in order to provide the Church with an instrument for identifying and combating heresy. Prior to this time, religious and secular authorities had adopted a relatively lenient attitude to the variety of pagan customs and beliefs that abounded locally throughout Europe. The Inquisition systematically rooted them out and obliterated them. Ancient nature cults, and rituals connected with pre-Christian deities or sacred groves, trees, streams and wells, were ruthlessly extirpated. Even the harmless cult of St. Guinefort was the object of persecution. A Dominican friar, Stephen of Bourbon, had the dead dog disinterred, and the sacred grove cut down and burnt, along with the remains of the faithful greyhound. An edict was also passed making it a crime for anyone to visit the place in future (Schmitt, 1983).

Although the picture is greatly distorted by the Inquisition's peculiar methods of obtaining and recording evidence, it appears that the so-called "witch craze" that swept through Europe between the fifteenth and seventeenth centuries originated as an attack on local folk healers or cunning folk; the last degenerate practitioners of archaic shamanism (Briggs, 1996; Serpell, 2002). According to the establishment view, not only did these medieval witches consort with the Devil in animal form, they also possessed the definitively shamanic ability to transform both themselves and others into animals (Cohn, 1975). In Britain and Scandinavia, witches were also believed to possess supernatural "imps" or "familiars" most of which appeared in animal form. In fact, judging from the evidence presented in contemporary pamphlets and trial records, the majority of these "familiars" belonged to species we nowadays keep as pets: dogs, cats, cage birds, mice, rats, ferrets, and so on (Ewen, 1933; Serpell, 2002; Thomas, 1971). In other words, close association or affinity with animals, once a sign of shamanic power or budding sainthood, became instead a symptom of diabolism. Animal companions still retained a certain "otherworldly" quality in the popular imagination of the Middle Ages and the Renaissance, but mainly as potential instruments of maleficium—the power to harm others by supernatural means.

All of these trends also reflected the marked medieval tendency to impose a rigid separation between human and non-human animals; a tendency that was reinforced by ideals of human conduct that emphasized self-control, civility and chastity, while at the same time rejecting what were then viewed as animal-like attributes, such as impulsiveness, coarseness and licentiousness (Elias, 1994; Salisbury, 1994; Serpell, 2005).

2.5   Animals as agents of socialization

The close of the seventeenth century, and the dawn of the so-called "Age of Enlightenment," brought with them certain changes in the public perception of animals that have been thoroughly documented by historians of the early modern period (e.g. Maehle, 1994; Thomas, 1983). These changes included a gradual increase in sympathetic attitudes to animals and nature, and a gradual decline in the anthropocentric attitudes that so characterized the medieval and Renaissance periods (Salisbury, 1994). The perception of wild animals and wilderness as threatening to human survival also decreased in prevalence, while the practice of pet-keeping expanded out of the aristocracy and into the newly emergent, urban middle classes. This change in animal-related attitudes and behavior can be plausibly attributed, at least in part, to the steady migration of Europeans out of rural areas and into towns and cities at this time. This rural exodus helped to distance growing sectors of the population from any direct involvement in the consumptive exploitation of animals, and removed the need for value systems designed to legitimize or reinforce such practices (Serpell, 1996; Serpell and Paul, 1994; Thomas, 1983).

The notion that nurturing relationships with animals could serve a socializing function, especially for children, also surfaced at about this time. Writing in 1699,

John Locke advocated giving children "dogs, squirrels, birds or any such things" to look after as a means of encouraging them to develop tender feelings and a sense of responsibility for others (Locke, 1699, p. 154). Deriving their authority from the works of John Calvin and Thomas Hobbes, many eighteenth-century reformers believed that children could learn to reflect on, and control, their own innately beastlike characteristics through the act of caring for and controlling real animals (Myers, 1998). Compassion and concern for animal welfare also became one of the favorite didactic themes of children's literature during the eighteenth and nineteenth centuries, where its clear purpose was to inculcate an ethic of kindness and gentility, particularly in male children (Grier, 1999; Ritvo, 1987; Turner, 1980).

In the late eighteenth century, theories concerning the socializing influence of animal companionship also began to be applied to the treatment of the mentally ill. The earliest well-documented experiment in this area took place in England at The York Retreat, the brainchild of a progressive Quaker called William Tuke. The York Retreat employed treatment methods that were exceptionally enlightened when compared with those which existed in other mental institutions of the day. Inmates were permitted to wear their own clothing, and they were encouraged to engage in handicrafts, to write, and to read books. They were also allowed to wander freely around the Retreat's courtyards and gardens that were stocked with various small domestic animals. In his *Description of the Retreat* (1813, p. 96), Samuel Tuke, the founder's grandson, described how the internal courtyards of the Retreat were supplied "with a number of animals; such as rabbits, sea-gulls, hawks, and poultry. These creatures are generally very familiar with the patients: and it is believed they are not only the means of innocent pleasure; but that the intercourse with them, sometimes tends to awaken the social and benevolent feelings."

During the nineteenth century, pet animals became increasingly common features of mental institutions in England and elsewhere. For example, in a highly critical report on the appalling conditions endured by the inmates of Bethlem Hospital during the 1830s, the British Charity Commissioners suggested that the grounds of lunatic asylums "should be stocked with sheep, hares, a monkey, or some other domestic or social animals" to create a more pleasing and less prison-like atmosphere. Such recommendations were evidently taken seriously. According to an article published in the *Illustrated London News* of 1860, the women's' ward at the Bethlem Hospital was by that time "cheerfully lighted, and enlivened with prints and busts, with aviaries and pet animals," while in the men's ward the same fondness was manifested "for pet birds and animals, cats, canaries, squirrels, greyhounds &c...[some patients] pace the long gallery incessantly, pouring out their woes to those who listen to them, or, if there be none to listen, to the dogs and cats" (cited in Allderidge, 1991).

The beneficial effects of animal companionship also appear to have been recognized as serving a therapeutic role in the treatment of physical ailments during this period. In her *Notes on Nursing* (1880), for instance, Florence Nightingale observes that a small pet "is often an excellent companion for the sick, for long chronic cases especially."

2.6   Animals and psychotherapy

Despite the apparent success of nineteenth-century experiments in animal-assisted institutional care, the advent of scientific medicine largely eliminated animals from hospital settings by the early decades of the twentieth century (Allderidge, 1991). For the following 50 years, virtually the only medical contexts in which animals are mentioned are those concerned with zoonotic disease and public health, or as symbolic referents in psychoanalytic theories concerning the origins of mental illness.

Sigmund Freud's ideas concerning the origins of neurosis tended to reiterate the Hobbesian idea of mankind's inherently beastlike nature (Myers, 1998). According to Freud, infants and young children are essentially similar to animals, insofar as they are ruled by instinctive cravings or impulses organized around basic biological functions such as eating, excreting, sexuality, and self-preservation. Freud referred to this basic, animal aspect of human nature as the "Id." As children mature, their adult caregivers "tame" or socialize them by instilling fear or guilt whenever the child acts too impulsively in response to these inner drives. Children, in turn, respond to this external pressure to conform by repressing these urges from consciousness. Mental illness results, or so Freud maintained, when these bottled-up animal drives find no healthy or creative outlet in later life, and erupt uncontrollably into consciousness (Shafton, 1995).

Freud interpreted the recurrent animal images that surfaced in his patients' dreams and "free associations" as metaphorical devices by means of which people disguise unacceptable thoughts or feelings. "Wild beasts," he argued, "represent passionate impulses of which the dreamer is afraid, whether they are his own or those of other people" (Freud, 1959, p. 410). Because these beastly thoughts and impulses are profoundly threatening to the "Ego," they are locked away in dark corners of the subconscious where they can be safely ignored, at least during a person's waking hours. To Freud and his followers, the aim of psychoanalysis was to unmask these frightening denizens of the unconscious mind, reveal their true natures, and thus, effectively, to neutralize them (Serpell, 2000).

Freud's concept of the "Id" as a sort of basic, animal "essence" in human nature bears more than a superficial resemblance to animistic and shamanistic ideas concerning animal souls and guardian spirits, and the "inner" or spiritual origins of ill-health (Serpell, 2000). In the works of Carl Jung, particularly his discussions of mythological archetypes in dreams and visions, and his concept of the "Collective Unconscious," this resemblance becomes more or less explicit (Cook, 1987). It is also echoed in the writings of Boris Levinson, the founder of "pet-facilitated therapy." In his book *Pets and Human Development*, Levinson states that:

> *One of the chief reasons for man's present difficulties is his inability to come to terms with his inner self and to harmonize his culture with his membership in the world of nature. Rational man has become alienated from himself by refusing to face his irrational self, his own past as personified by animals.*
>
> *(Levinson, 1972, p. 6)*

The solution to this growing sense of alienation was, according to Levinson, to restore a healing connection with our own, unconscious animal natures by establishing positive relationships with real animals, such as dogs, cats and other pets. He argued that pets represent "a half-way station on the road back to emotional well-being" (Levinson, 1969, p. xiv) and that "we need animals as allies to reinforce our inner selves" (Levinson, 1972, pp. 28–29). Levinson went beyond the Freudian idea that animals were essentially a symbolic disguise for things we are afraid to confront in the flesh to arguing that relations with animals played such a prominent role in human evolution that they have now become integral to our psychological well-being (Levinson, 1972, p. 15).

2.7 Animals, relaxation, and social support

During the last 20 years, and at least partly in response to the skepticism of the medical establishment, the theoretical emphasis has shifted away from these relatively metaphysical ideas about animals as psycho-spiritual mediators, toward more prosaic, scientifically "respectable" explanations for the apparent therapeutic benefits of animal companionship (Serpell, 2000). The primary catalyst for this change of emphasis was a single, ground-breaking study of 92 outpatients from a cardiac care unit who, statistically speaking, were found to live longer if they were pet owners (Friedmann et al., 1980). This finding prompted a whole series of other health-related studies (see Anderson et al., 1992; Friedmann et al., 2000; Garrity and Stallones, 1998), as well as stimulating a lot of discussion concerning the possible mechanism(s) responsible for the apparent salutary effects of pet ownership. Of these, at least two have stood the test of time. According to the first, animals are able to induce an immediate, physiologically de-arousing state of relaxation simply by attracting and holding our attention (Katcher et al., 1983). According to the second, companion animals are capable of providing people with a form of stress-reducing or stress-buffering social support (McNicholas and Collis, 1995; Serpell, 1996; Siegel, 1990).

Although the de-arousing effects of animal contact have been demonstrated by a considerable number of recent studies, little evidence exists at present that these effects are responsible for more than transient or short-term improvements in physiological parameters, such as heart rate and blood pressure (Friedman, 1995). In contrast, the concept of pets serving as sources of social support seems to offer a relatively convincing explanation for the more long-term benefits of animal companionship.

Cobb (1976) defined social support as "information leading the subject to believe that he is cared for and loved, esteemed, and a member of a network of mutual obligations." More recent authors, however, have tended to distinguish between "perceived social support" and "social network" characteristics. The former represents a largely qualitative description of a person's level of satisfaction with the support he or she receives from particular social relationships, while the latter is a more quantitative measure incorporating the number, frequency and type of a person's overall social interactions (Eriksen, 1994). However we choose to define it, the importance of social support to human well-being has been acknowledged implicitly throughout history. Loneliness—the absence of social support—has always been viewed as such a painful and unpleasant sensation that, since time immemorial, societies have used solitary confinement, exile and social ostracism as methods of punishment. The autobiographical accounts of religious hermits, castaways and prisoners of war provide a clear picture of the psychological effects of social isolation. Most describe feelings equivalent to physical torture which increase gradually to a peak before declining, often quite sharply. This decrease in pain is generally associated with the onset of a state of apathy and despair, sometimes so severe that it involves complete catatonic withdrawal (Serpell, 1996).

Within the last 10–15 years, an extensive medical literature has emerged confirming a strong, positive link between social support and improved human health and survival (see Eriksen, 1994; Esterling et al., 1994; House et al., 1988; Sherbourne et al., 1992; Vilhjalmsson, 1993). The precise mechanisms underlying these life-saving effects of social support are still the subject of some debate, but most authorities appear now to agree that the principal benefits arise from the capacity of supportive social relationships to buffer or ameliorate the deleterious health effects of prolonged or chronic life stress (Ader et al., 1995). In theory, this salutory effect of social support should apply to any positive social relationship; any relationship in which a person feels *cared for*, *loved* or *esteemed*. As far as the vast majority of medical researchers and practitioners are concerned, however, the only relationships that are assumed to matter are those that exist between closely affiliated persons— friends, marital partners, immediate family members, and so on. Despite the growing evidence of recent anthrozoological research, the notion that animal companions might also contribute socially to human health has still received very limited medical recognition (Serpell, 1996).

2.8   Conclusions

For most of human history, animals have occupied a central position in theories concerning the ontology and treatment of sickness and disease. Offended animal spirits were often believed to be the source of illness, injury or misfortune, but, at the same time, the assistance of animal guardian spirits—either one's own or those belonging to a "medicine man" or shaman—could also be called upon to mediate in the process of healing such afflictions.

Although such ideas survived here and there into the modern era, the spread of anthropocentric and monotheistic belief systems during the last 1–2 thousand years virtually annihilated animist belief in the supernatural power of animals and animal spirits throughout much of the world. In Europe during the Middle Ages, the Christian Church actively persecuted animist believers, branding them as witches and heretics, and identifying their "familiar spirits" with the Devil and his minions in animal form.

During the period of the "Enlightenment," the idea that pet animals could serve a socializing function for children and the mentally ill became popular, and by the nineteenth century the introduction of animals to institutional care facilities was widespread. However, these early and preliminary experiments in animal-assisted therapy were soon displaced by the rise of scientific medicine during the early part of the twentieth century. Animals continued to play a somewhat negative symbolic role in the development of psychoanalytic theories concerning the origins of mental illness, but no further medical discussion of their value as therapeutic adjuncts occurred until the late 1960s and 1970s when such ideas resurfaced in the writings of the influential child psychotherapist Boris Levinson.

Recent interest in the potential medical value of animal companionship was largely initiated by a single study that appeared to demonstrate life-prolonging effects of pet ownership among heart-attack sufferers. This study has since prompted many others, most of which have demonstrated either short-term, relaxing effects of animal contact, or long-term health improvements consistent with a view of companion animals as sources of social support. Despite these findings, the positive therapeutic value of animal companionship continues to receive little recognition in mainstream medical literature, and, as a field of research, it is grossly under-supported by government funding agencies.

Considered in retrospect, it is difficult to escape the conclusion that the current inability or unwillingness of the medical establishment to address this topic seriously is a legacy of the same anthropocentrism that has dominated European and Western thinking since the Middle Ages (Serpell, 2005). Hopefully, with the gradual demise of this old-fashioned and prejudiced mindset, we can return to a more holistic and open-minded view of the potential contribution of animals to human well-being.

References

Ader, R. L., Cohen, N., & Felten, D. (1995). Psychoneuroimmunology: interactions between the nervous system and the immune system. *The Lancet, 345*, 99–103.

Allderidge, P. H. (1991). A cat, surpassing in beauty, and other therapeutic animals. *Psychiatric Bulletin, 15*, 759–762.

Anderson, W. P., Reid, C. M., & Jennings, G. L. (1992). Pet ownership and risk factors for cardiovascular disease. *Medical Journal of Australia, 157*, 298–301.

Armstrong, E. A. (1973). *Saint Francis: Nature Mystic*. Berkeley: University of California Press.

Benedict, R. F. (1929). The concept of the guardian spirit in North America. *Memoirs of the American Anthropological Association, 29*, 3–93.

Briggs, R. (1996). *Witches and Neighbours*. London: Vicking.

Campbell, J. (1984). *The Way of the Animal Powers*. London: Times Books.

Cobb, S. (1976). Social support as a moderator of life stress. *Psychosomatic Medicine, 38*, 300–314.

Cohn, N. (1975). *Europe's Inner Demons*. New York: Basic Books.

Cook, D. A. G. (1987). Jung, Carl Gustav (1875–1961). In R. Gregory (Ed.), *The Oxford Companion to the Mind* (pp. 403–405). Oxford: Oxford University Press.

Dale-Green, P. (1966). *Dog*. London: Rupert Hart-Davis.

Eliade, M. (1964). *Shamanism: Archaic Techniques of Ecstacy*, trans. In W. R. Trask (Ed.). New York & London: Routledge.

Elias, N. (1994). *The Civilizing Process*, trans. Edmund Jephcott. Oxford, UK: Blackwell.

Eriksen, W. (1994). The role of social support in the pathogenesis of coronary heart disease: a literature review. *Family Practice, 11*, 201–209.

Esterling, B. A., Kiecolt-Glaser, J., Bodnar, J. C., & Glaser, R. (1994). Chronic stress, social support, and persistent alterations in the natural killer cell response to cytokines in older adults. *Health Psychology, 13*, 291–128.

Ewen, C. L. C. (1933). *Witchcraft and Demonianism*. London: Heath Cranton.

Friedman, E. (1995). The role of pets in enhancing human well-being: physiological effects. In I. Robinson (Ed.), *The Waltham Book of Human-Animal Interaction: Benefits and Responsibilities of Pet-ownership* (pp. 33–53). Oxford: Pergamon.

Friedmann, E., Katcher, A. H., Lynch, J. J., & Thomas, S. A. (1980). Animal companions and one-year survival of patients after discharge from a coronary care unit. *Public Health Reports, 95*, 307–312.

Friedmann, E., Thomas, S. A., & Eddy, T. J. (2000). Companion animals and human health: physical and cardiovascular influences. In A. L. Podberscek, E. S. Paul, & J. A. Serpell (Eds.), *Companion Animals and Us* (pp. 125–142). Cambridge: Cambridge University Press.

Freud, S. (1959). *The Interpretation of Dreams*, J. Strachey (Ed. and Trans.). New York: Basic Books.

Garrity, T. F., & Stallones, L. (1998). Effects of pet contact on human well-being: review of recent research. In C. C. Wilson & D. C. Turner (Eds.), *Companion Animals in Human Health* (pp. 3–22). Thousand Oaks, CA: Sage.

Gossen, G. H. (1996). Animal souls, co-essences, and human destiny in Mesoamerica. In A. J. Arnold (Ed.), *Monsters, Tricksters, and Sacred Cows: Animal Tales and American Identities* (pp. 80–107). Charlottesville: University Press of Virginia.

Grier, K. C. (1999). Childhood socialization and companion animals: United States, 1820–1870. *Society & Animals, 7*, 95–120.

Hallowell, A. I. (1926). Bear ceremonialism in the Northern Hemisphere. *American Anthropologist, 28*, 1–175.

House, J. S., Landis, K. R., & Umberson, D. (1988). Social relationships and health. *Science, 241*, 540–545.

Hultzkrantz, A. (1987). On beliefs in non-shamanic guardian spirits among the Saamis. In T. Ahlbäck (Ed.), *Saami Religion* (pp. 110–123). Åbo, Finland: Donner Institute for Research in Religious and Cultural History.

Jesse, G. R. (1866). *Researches into the History of the British Dog*, (vols. 1–4). London: Robert Hardwicke.

Katcher, A. H., Friedmann, E., Beck, A. M., & Lynch, J. J. (1983). Looking, talking and blood pressure: the physiological consequences of interaction with the living environment. In A. H. Katcher, & A. M. Beck (Eds.), *New Perspectives on Our Lives with Companion Animals* (pp. 351–359). Philadelphia: University of Pennsylvania Press.

Kruger, K., Trachtenburg, S., & Serpell, J. A. (2004). Can animals help humans heal? Animal-assisted Interventions in Adolescent Mental Health. Philadelpia, PA: Center for the Interaction of Animals & Society. http://research.vet.upenn.edu/cias/publication/tabid/1918/default.aspx.

Landes, R. (1968). *Ojibwa Religion and the Midéwiwin*. Madison: University of Wisconsin Press.

Levinson, B. (1969). *Pet-oriented Child Psychotherapy*. Springfield, IL: Charles C. Thomas.

Levinson, B. (1972). *Pets and Human Development*. Springfield, IL: Charles C. Thomas.

Locke, J. (1699). *Some Thoughts Concerning Education*. Reprinted with an introduction by F.W. Garforth (1964). London: Heinemann.

Maehle, A. H. (1994). Cruelty and kindness to the "brute creation": stability and change in the ethics of the man-animal relationship, 1600–1850. In A. Manning, & J. A. Serpell (Eds.), *Animals and Human Society: Changing Perspectives* (pp. 81–105). London and New York: Routledge.

Martin, C. (1978). *The Keepers of the Game*. Berkeley: University of California Press.

McNicholas, J., & Collis, G. M. (1995). The end of a relationship: coping with pet loss. In I. Robinson (Ed.), *The Waltham Book of Human-Animal Interaction: Benefits and Responsibilities of Pet-ownership* (pp. 127–143). Oxford: Pergamon.

Morris, R., & Morris, D. (1968). *Men and Snakes*. London: Sphere Books.

Myers, O. E. (1998). *Children and Animals*. Boulder, CO: Westview Press.

Nelson, R. K. (1986). A conservation ethic and environment: the Koyukon of Alaska. In N. M. Williams, & E. S. Hunn (Eds.), *Resource Managers: North American and Australian Hunter-gatherers* (pp. 211–228). Canberra: Institute of Aboriginal Studies.

Rasmussen, K. (1929). Intellectual life of the Iglulik Eskimos. *Report of the Fifth Thule Expedition, 7*(1), 56.

Ritvo, H. (1987). *The Animal Estate: The English and Other Creatures in the Victorian Age*. Cambridge, MA: Harvard University Press.

Salisbury, J. (1994). *The Beast Within: Animals in the Middle Ages*. London and New York: Routledge.

Schmitt, J. C. (1983). *The Holy Greyhound: Guinefort, Healer of Children since the 13th Century*, trans. M. Thom. Cambridge: Cambridge University Press.

Schwabe, C. W. (1994). Animals in the ancient world. In A. Manning, & J. A. Serpell (Eds.), *Animals and Human Society: Changing Perspectives* (pp. 36–58). London and New York: Routledge.

Serpell, J. A. (1995). From paragon to pariah: some reflections on human attitudes to dogs. In J. A. Serpell (Ed.), *The Domestic Dog: Its Evolution, Behaviour and Interactions with People* (pp. 245–256). Cambridge: Cambridge University Press.

Serpell, J. A. (1996). *In the Company of Animals* (2nd ed.). Cambridge: Cambridge University Press.

Serpell, J. A. (2000). Creatures of the unconscious: companion animals as mediators. In A. L. Podberscek, E. S. Paul, & J. A. Serpell (Eds.), *Companion Animals and Us* (pp. 108–121). Cambridge: Cambridge University Press.

Serpell, J. A. (2002). Guardian spirits or demonic pets: the concept of the witch's familiar in early modern England, 1530–1712. In A. N. H. Creager, & W. C. Jordan (Eds.), *The Animal/Human Boundary* (pp. 157–190). Rochester: University of Rochester Press.

Serpell, J. A. (2005). Animals and religion: towards a unifying theory. In F. de Jonge, & R. van den Bos (Eds.), *The Human-Animal Relationship* (pp. 9–22). Assen: Royal Van Gorcum.

Serpell, J. A., & Paul, E. S. (1994). Pets and the development of positive attitudes to animals. In A. Manning, & J. A. Serpell (Eds.), *Animals and Human Society: Changing Perspectives* (pp. 127–144). London and New York: Routledge.

Siegel, J. M. (1980). Stressful life events and use of physician services among the elderly: the moderating role of pet ownership. *Journal of Personality and Social Psychology, 58*, 1081–1086.

Shafton, A. (1995). *Dream Reader: Contemporary Approaches to the Understanding of Dreams*. Albany, NY: SUNY Press.

Sherbourne, C. D., Meredith, L. S., Rogers, W., & Ware, J. E. (1992). Social support and stressful life events: age differences in their effects on health-related quality of life among the chronically ill. *Quality of Life Research, 1*, 235–246.

Speck, F. G. (1918). Penobscot shamanism. *Memoirs of the American Anthropological Association, 6*, 238–288.

Speck, F. G. (1977). *Naskapi* (3rd ed.). Norman: University of Oklahoma Press.

Spencer, C. (1993). *The Heretic's Feast*. London: 4th Estate.

Thomas, K. (1971). *Religion and the Decline of Magic*. Harmondsworth: Penguin Books.

Thomas, K. (1983). *Man and the Natural World: Changing Attitudes in England, 1500–1800*. London: Allen Lane.

Toynbee, J. M. C. (1973). *Animals in Roman Life and Art*. London: Thames & Hudson.

Tuke, S. (1813). *Description of the Retreat*. Reprinted with an introduction by R. Hunter & I. Macalpine (1964). London: Dawsons.

Turner, J. (1980). *Reckoning with the Beast: Animals, Pain, and Humanity in the Victorian Mind*. Baltimore: Johns Hopkins University Press.

Vilhjalmson, R. (1993). Life stress, social support and clinical depression: a reanalysis of the literature. *Social Science Medicine, 37*, 331–342.

Wenzel, G. (1991). *Animal Rights, Human Rights: Ecology, Economy and Ideology in the Canadian Arctic*. London: Belhaven Press.

White, D. G. (1991). *Myths of the Dog-man*. Chicago: Chicago University Press.

Wilson, C. C., & Turner, D. C. (1998). *Companion Animals in Human Health*. Thousand Oaks, CA: Sage.

3 Animal-assisted interventions in mental health: definitions and theoretical foundations

Katherine A. Kruger, MSW, James A. Serpell, PhD

University of Pennsylvania

3.1 Introduction

As described earlier (Serpell, this volume), the advent of scientific medicine toward the end of the nineteenth century had the effect of displacing companion animals from therapeutic settings until the 1960s when the concept was revived in the writings of Boris M. Levinson. In his book, *Pet-Oriented Child Psychotherapy*, Levinson described the benefits that his dog brought to his counseling sessions with children and youth, and provided numerous examples of ways in which animals could enhance therapy (Levinson, 1969). Based largely on case studies and anecdotes, Levinson intended for this material to inform and encourage future research into the various beneficial effects that he observed. While this has occurred to some degree, more often Levinson's writings have been used to justify the implementation of animal-assisted interventions (AAIs) in the absence of valid efficacy studies.

Despite their long history, and the unequivocally positive media attention they typically receive, animal-assisted interventions are currently best described as a category of promising complementary practices that are still struggling to demonstrate their efficacy and validity. Some attempts have been made to standardize terminology and procedures, and various certificate programs are now being offered in association with colleges and universities. However, if the field is to move beyond its fringe status, it must begin to follow the path taken by other alternative and complementary therapies (e.g. psychology, acupuncture, chiropractic, etc.) that have established their credibility by means of carefully controlled clinical trials and valid efficacy studies. With that objective in mind, the goals of this chapter are to clarify the distinction between therapy and other assistive or recreational uses of animals, and then to explore some of the theories that underlie the incorporation of animals into therapeutic contexts.

3.2 Defining animal-assisted interventions

In their critical review of the literature on animal-assisted interventions, Beck and Katcher (1984) aptly state that "a clear distinction should be made between emotional

Handbook on Animal-Assisted Therapy. DOI: 10.1016/B978-0-12-381453-1.10003-0

response to animals, that is, their recreational use, and therapy. It should not be concluded that any event that is enjoyed by the patients is a kind of therapy." Although this statement was made more than 20 years ago, the term animal-assisted therapy continues to be applied to an array of programs that would not qualify as therapy in any scientific/medical sense of the word. The *Oxford English Dictionary* (1997) defines *therapy* as "the medical treatment of disease; curative medical or psychiatric treatment." In contrast, *recreation* is defined as a "pleasant occupation, pastime or amusement; a pleasurable exercise or employment." Despite the obvious distinction, there is a tendency in certain quasi-medical fields to weaken or confuse the meaning of the word therapy by linking it to experiences that may provide transient relief or pleasure, but whose practitioners cannot ethically or credibly claim to diagnose or change the course of human disease (e.g. aromatherapy, massage therapy, crystal/ gemstone therapy, etc.). Regrettably, this is also the case with many programs that are promoted as animal-assisted therapy. Just as we would not refer to a clown's visit to a pediatric hospital as clown-assisted therapy, the urge to call animal recreation and visitation programs therapy should be resisted.

In her review of the literature, LaJoie (2003) reports finding 20 different definitions of animal-assisted therapy, and 12 different terms for the same phenomenon (e.g. pet therapy, pet psychotherapy, pet-facilitated therapy, pet-facilitated psychotherapy, four-footed therapy, animal-assisted therapy, animal-facilitated counseling, pet-mediated therapy, pet-oriented psychotherapy, companion/animal therapy, and co-therapy with an animal). This multiplicity of terms and definitions creates confusion both within the field and without. In an attempt to promote the standardization of terminology, the Delta Society (n.d.), one of the largest organizations responsible for the certification of therapy animals in the USA, has published the following widely cited definitions of Animal-Assisted Therapy and Animal-Assisted Activity:

> *Animal-Assisted Therapy (AAT): AAT is a goal-directed intervention in which an animal that meets specific criteria is an integral part of the treatment process. AAT is directed and/or delivered by a health/human service professional with specialized expertise, and within the scope of practice of his/her profession. Key features include: specified goals and objectives for each individual; and measured progress.*
>
> *Animal-Assisted Activity (AAA): AAA provides opportunities for motivational, educational, recreational, and/or therapeutic benefits to enhance quality of life. AAAs are delivered in a variety of environments by specially trained professionals, paraprofessionals, and/or volunteers, in association with animals that meet specific criteria. Key features include: absence of specific treatment goals; volunteers and treatment providers are not required to take detailed notes; visit content is spontaneous.*

Although the Delta Society lists horses as being animals eligible for certification through their PetPartners® program, interventions involving the use of horses typically fall under the jurisdiction of a separate group of agencies. Prominent among these is the North American Riding for the Handicapped Association (NARHA), its subsection the Equine Facilitated Mental Health Association (EFMHA), and its affiliate-partner the American Hippotherapy Association (AHA), which provide separate definitions for the terms equine-facilitated psychotherapy (EFP) and Hippotherapy:

> *EFP is an experiential psychotherapy that includes equine(s). It may include, but is not limited to, a number of mutually respectful equine activities such as handling, grooming, longeing (or lunging), riding, driving, and vaulting. EFP is facilitated by a licensed, credentialed mental health professional working with an appropriately credentialed equine professional. EFP may be facilitated by a mental health professional that is dually credentialed as an equine professional (EFMHA, 2003). EFP denotes an ongoing therapeutic relationship with clearly established treatment goals and objectives developed by the therapist in conjunction with the client. The therapist must be an appropriately credentialed mental health professional to legally practice psychotherapy and EFP.*
>
> *(EFMHA, 2005)*

> *Hippotherapy is done by an Occupational, Physical and Speech Therapist (OT, PT, ST) who has been specially trained to use the movement of the horse to facilitate improvements in their client/patient. It does not teach the client how to ride the horse. Therapists use traditional techniques such as NDT (neurodevelopmental treatment) and SI (sensory integration) along with the movement of the horse as part of their treatment strategy. Goals include: improving balance, coordination, posture, fine motor control, improving articulation, and increasing cognitive skills.*
>
> *(AHA, 2005)*

While we include specific definitions of EFP and hippotherapy for the sake of comparison and completeness, the Delta Society definition of AAT is general enough to include these sorts of interventions. What should be emphasized is that these definitions of animal-assisted therapy, equine-facilitated psychotherapy, and hippotherapy all share the following attributes:

1. The intervention involves the use of an animal or animals.
2. The intervention must be delivered by, or under the oversight of, a health/human service professional who is practicing within the scope of his/her professional expertise.

It should be noted that the Delta Society definitions include statements about the need for participating animals to "meet specific criteria," while those utilized by the EFMHA and AHA do not. Ensuring the suitability of an animal for any type of work is of paramount importance for both the animals and the humans involved, and many facilities do require a formal behavioral evaluation prior to allowing animals to interact with clients or patients. However, the criteria by which animals are determined to be suitable for this work are highly variable and often subjective, and what particular interventions require from animals may be diverse and changeable (e.g. some practitioners see a benefit to using skittish or behaviorally challenging animals with particular clients). It is also worth mentioning that formalized behavioral screenings and certifications are not available for all species being used as therapeutic adjuncts, so while these assurances are desirable when available, their absence does not necessarily disqualify a program from being considered therapy. Questions regarding an animal's suitability for therapy work arise primarily from risk management considerations (e.g. patient safety; liability issues) and concerns about animal welfare. However, these considerations are extraneous to a general definition of therapy. Certainly, such issues should be given top priority when developing and implementing AAIs, but they do not help us to define therapy since an intervention can still achieve therapeutic goals without formal criteria being met by the participating animal(s) (see, e.g. Wells et al.'s (1997) article on the use of feral cats in psychotherapy).

While it would be preferable for this chapter to only include information from studies and programs that adhere strictly to the definition of AAT outlined above—specifically, those that are facilitated by health/human service professionals within the scope of their professional expertise and that have clear treatment goals—too few studies and programs fulfill all the necessary criteria. Therefore, for the purposes of this chapter, animal-assisted therapy, animal-assisted activities, and various equine-facilitated programs are grouped together under the more general term *animal-assisted interventions* (AAIs)—defined here as "any intervention that intentionally includes or incorporates animals as part of a therapeutic or ameliorative process or milieu." The *Oxford English Dictionary* (1997) defines *intervention* as "the action of intervening, 'stepping in', or interfering in any affair, so as to affect its course or issue." This definition provides the flexibility needed to discuss programs that can fit within a medical model and those of a more quasi-medical nature, but which still seek to "affect the course" of people's lives in a positive direction.

Guide, assistance, and service animals are purposefully excluded from the above definition of AAIs. The *Americans with Disabilities Act of 1990* (ADA) defines a *service animal* as "any guide dog, signal dog, or other animal individually trained to provide assistance to an individual with a disability" (United States Department of Justice (USDOJ), 1996). The role of the service animal, as defined by the ADA, is to perform some of the functions and tasks that the individual cannot perform as a result of their disability (USDOJ, 1996). While the use of a service animal may provide some psychological benefits to its handler (e.g. decreased feelings of loneliness and isolation, or increased socialization), and not withstanding the nascent use of Psychiatric Service Dogs (Psychiatric Service Dog Society, 2003), service animals are typically viewed as tools rather than treatments, and thus do not constitute an animal-assisted intervention as we define the term.[1, 2]

---

[1] It should be noted that because service animals are not legally considered pets, the ADA includes special provisions that allow for service animals to accompany their handlers into businesses and public places where pets are typically prohibited; the same is not true of therapy animals. While obtaining the status of "therapy animal" may provide a pet with limited entrée into places where animals are typically prohibited (e.g. hospitals, nursing homes, psychiatric facilities, etc.), therapy animals and their handlers are not granted any rights or protections under the ADA.

[2] An emerging issue in this field is the growing use of Emotional Support Animals (ESA). The role these animals play has blurred the boundaries between pet ownership, mental health treatment, and the use of service animals. Unlike guide and service animals, ESAs do not necessarily receive special training, perform specific tasks, or accompany their handlers outside the home. Though very little authoritative information has been written on the topic, it appears that in order to qualify as an ESA, a health care provider must simply prescribe the animal for a patient with an emotional disability. In many cases, this prescription is all that differentiates ESAs from pets. As of this writing, ESAs are a controversial issue, with some suggesting that ESAs are an abuse and misinterpretation of the intent of the ADA (Grubb, 2002), while others seek to characterize ESAs as bona fide service animals (Bazelon Center for Mental Health Law, n.d.).

3.3   Theoretical frameworks

The field of animal-assisted interventions currently lacks a unified, widely accepted, or empirically supported theoretical framework for explaining how and why relationships between humans and animals are potentially therapeutic. A considerable variety of possible mechanisms of action have been proposed or alluded to in the literature, most of which focus on the supposedly unique intrinsic attributes of animals that appear to contribute to therapy. Others emphasize the value of animals as living instruments that can be used to affect positive changes in patients' self-concept and behavior through the acquisition of various skills, and the acceptance of personal agency and responsibility. This section presents an overview of the theories most commonly found in the literature and, in some cases, those that seem to offer the best frameworks for future study.[3]

3.3.1   Intrinsic attributes of animals as contributors to therapy

The notion that animals possess certain inherent qualities that may facilitate therapy is widespread in the AAI literature. According to this view, the mere presence of the animal, its spontaneous behaviors, and its availability for interaction may provide opportunities and confer benefits that would be impossible, or much harder, to obtain in its absence.

Reduction of anxiety and arousal

The idea that the presence of, or interactions with, animals can produce calming effects in humans is commonly cited in the AAI literature. One popular explanation for this phenomenon is derived from E. O. Wilson's (1984) so-called *biophilia hypothesis*. This theory asserts that humans possess a genetically based propensity to attend to, and be attracted by, other living organisms (Kahn, 1997) or, as Wilson put it, an "innate tendency to focus on life and lifelike processes" (as cited in Gullone, 2000). The foundation of biophilia is that, from an evolutionary standpoint, humans increased their chances of survival through their attention to, and knowledge of, environmental cues. Clinically speaking, it is hard to imagine a better pairing of attributes—a tool that can simultaneously engage and relax the patient. To quote Melson (2001):

> [watching] animals at peace may create a coupling of decreased arousal with sustained attention and alertness, opening the troubled child to new possibilities of learning and growth. The child can then experience unconditional love and models of good nurturing, practice caring sensitively for another, and assume mastery tempered with respect.

---

[3] At this point we need to acknowledge a personal bias. Animal-assisted interventions are practiced with individuals at virtually every stage of life, and with a vast array of mental and physical diagnoses. Our previous work in this area focused largely on animal-assisted interventions in adolescent mental health (Kruger et al., 2004) and, consequently, much of what appears in this chapter is a reflection of that narrow exploration of this broad and highly diverse field. We have tried nevertheless to ensure that the information included here is relevant to interventions practiced with individuals of all ages, and with a wide variety of mental health diagnoses.

Although there are abundant references in the literature that suggest the presence of animals can sometimes exert calming or de-arousing effects on people (Bardill and Hutchinson, 1997; Brickel, 1982; Friedmann et al., 1983; Mallon, 1994a,b; Mason and Hagan, 1999; Reichert, 1998; Reimer, 1999), there are no convincing data demonstrating that these effects are due to any innate attraction to animals. Additionally, Serpell (1986) points out that "it has been known since the 1950s that any stimulus which is attractive or which concentrates the attention has a calming effect on the body," suggesting that animals may be just one means to this end. Moreover, even proponents of biophilia acknowledge that individual experience and culture play important roles in determining people's responses to animals (Kahn, 1997; Serpell, 2004).

Brickel (1985) offers learning theory as another explanation for the potential anti-anxiolytic benefits of animals in therapeutic contexts. According to learning theory, an activity that is pleasurable will be self-reinforcing, and will be more likely to occur in the future. Unpleasant or anxiety-provoking activities—e.g. enduring painful or embarrassing visits to a therapist—may result in avoidance or withdrawal behavior. Just as enjoyable activities are self-reinforcing, avoidance of pain and discomfort provides a negative reinforcement by assuring minimal exposure to the painful stimulus. Brickel (1982) suggests that animals introduced in a therapeutic context may serve as a buffer and divert attention from an anxiety-generating stimulus that the patient faces. This interference allows for self-monitored control over exposure to the stimulus instead of withdrawal and avoidance (e.g. a child may choose to reveal sexual abuse first to the therapy animal, rather than revealing it directly to the therapist). If the theory holds, repeated exposure through the animal's diverting properties, together with non-aversive consequences, should result in the reduction or extinction of anxiety. Brickel does not offer an explanation for why animals, in particular, are apparently so diverting, and it is presumably necessary to resort to other theories to account for this.

While evolutionary and learning theories have not adequately explained why some humans report feeling calmer when an animal is present, numerous researchers have attempted to examine and measure various human physiologic responses to interaction with animals. Studies that have focused on the anti-anxiolytic effects of an animal presence have typically measured heart rate and blood pressure as indicators of arousal (DeMello, 1999; Friedmann et al., 1980, 1983; Katcher et al., 1983), although a subset of studies has collected information on additional variables such as skin temperature, behavioral manifestations of stress, state/trait anxiety, and levels of cholesterol, triglycerides, and phenylethylamine in the plasma (Anderson et al., 1992; Freidmann et al., 2000; Hansen et al., 1999; Nagengast et al., 1997; Odendaal and Lehman, 2000; Wilson, 1991). As with much of the literature on AAIs, findings in this area are conflicting and, regrettably, fundamental methodological differences between the studies make it impossible to draw any firm conclusions about the impact that animals may have on human arousal, since both positive and negative effects have been reported.

Based on all of the available research, the most credible conclusion that one can draw at this stage is that the presence of certain animals can produce calming effects for some people in some contexts, but Wilson's (1991) finding that interacting with an animal was more stressful than reading quietly does highlight the need for studies that compare animal-assisted interventions with activities with similar aims but that do not incorporate animals. In other words, a finding that the presence of an animal decreases arousal does not rule out the possibility that other interventions or activities that do not include animals might be as, or more, effective.

Social mediation

The observation that animals can serve as catalysts or mediators of human social interactions, and may expedite the rapport-building process between patient and therapist, is often noted in the AAI literature. AAI practitioners and theorists have suggested that animals stimulate conversation by their presence and unscripted behavior, and by providing a neutral, external subject on which to focus (Fine, 2000; Levinson, 1969). Studies that have attempted to look at the social-facilitation effects of animals have produced similarly positive results across a range of populations (e.g. children with physical disabilities; the elderly; college students; typical dog owners; and adult and adolescent psychiatric inpatients). And, drawing from psychoanalytic theory, there are ample references in the AAI literature to patients being able to reveal or discuss difficult thoughts, feelings, motivations, conflicts, or events by projecting them onto a real or fictional animal (Mason and Hagan, 1999; Reichert, 1998; Reimer, 1999; Serpell, 2000; Wells et al., 1997). Reichert (1998) provides this example from her clinical experience with a sexually abused child:

> I told one child that Buster [a dog] had a nightmare. I then asked the child, "What do you think Buster's nightmare was about?" The child said, "The nightmare was about being afraid of getting hurt again by someone mean."

In support of the notion of expedited rapport-building, several studies conducted with college students produced evidence that people are perceived as happier, friendlier, wealthier, less threatening, and more relaxed when they appear in a picture with a friendly animal versus how they are perceived when the same picture is shown with the animal omitted (Lockwood, 1983; Rossbach and Wilson, 1992; Wells and Perrine, 2001). In three studies that examined a small number of subjects walking with and without their dogs in familiar and unfamiliar areas, all found significant increases in positive social interactions with strangers when the dogs were present (Eddy et al., 2001; Mader et al., 1989; Messent, 1983). Finally, in a seminal pilot study, Corson et al. (1977) investigated the impact of a dog-walking program on a small number of adult and adolescent psychiatric inpatients ($n = 50$, with only five subjects being studied in depth) who were considered to be socially withdrawn and unresponsive to other forms of treatment. The quantitative findings of this study included decreases in the response time to questions posed by the therapist, exponential increases in the number of words used in responses, and increases in the percentage of questions answered.

Studies of the ability of animals to alter perceptions of social desirability and increase positive social interactions between strangers have been uniformly positive. When considered alongside the large numbers of anecdotal statements attesting to the power of animals to hasten the building of rapport between patient and therapist, as well as facilitating meaningful interaction between the two, these findings have important health care implications. If the presence of an animal can make the therapist appear happier, friendlier, less threatening, and more relaxed, it seems reasonable to believe that some patients would achieve a greater sense of comfort more quickly. In addition to enhancing the patient's perception of the health care provider, the presence of an animal provides a benign, external topic of conversation on which to focus, which may further hasten and enhance the development of a working alliance. Given that compliance and retention in treatment, as well as treatment outcomes, may be strongly related to the quality of the therapeutic relationship, this particular aspect of animal-assisted interventions merits urgent investigation.

Attachment theory, transitional objects, and social needs

The AAI literature abounds with anecdotal statements concerning the loving bonds that are forged between humans and animals (Bardill and Hutchinson, 1997; Harbolt and Ward, 2001; Kale, 1992; Mallon, 1994b), with the implication that these attachments are part of what helps clients to achieve therapeutic gains. With regard to attachment, Triebenbacher (1998) writes:

> humans have an innate, biologically-based need for social interaction, and this interaction becomes increasingly focused toward specific figures. Behaviors such as following, smiling toward, holding, and touching are evident in the reciprocal relationship between child and attachment figure...These behaviors can be exhibited not only toward primary attachment figures but substitutes or supplemental figures as well.

Certainly, the behaviors that Triebenbacher describes can be observed in human interactions with animals, and there is no question that people form attachments with animals, but correlations between attachment and positive therapeutic outcomes have yet to be convincingly established in relation to AAIs. Theories related to attachment and social needs are, nonetheless, conceptually helpful in developing an understanding of the potential value of incorporating animals into therapeutic contexts.

Encompassed within the broad concept of attachment is the phenomenon of the "transitional object." While transitional objects are primarily considered the purview of very young children, the existence of a transitional effect in AAIs is alluded to sufficiently often in the literature (Katcher, 2000; Levinson, 1970, 1978, 1984; Mallon, 1994b; Reichert, 1998; Triebenbacher, 1998) to warrant further attention. The transitional object, as defined by Winnicott (1971), is an item or object, such as a blanket or soft toy that serves a comforting function for a child and helps to alleviate the normal developmental stress of separation from the primary caregiver (Cwik, 1991). In therapeutic contexts, animals are often described as alleviating the stress of the initial phases of therapy by serving a comforting, diverting role until the therapist and patient have developed a sound rapport.

While animals may serve as both attachment figures and transitional objects, it is important to note that the roles of attachment figure and that of transitional object are, by definition, mutually exclusive. Attachment implies a long-lasting emotional bond, whereas "transitional" implies a passage from one condition to another and the absence of a lasting bond. To quote Cwik (1991), "the fate of the [transitional] object is that it slowly loses meaning as transitional phenomena spread out over the child's whole cultural field." In the context of animal-assisted interventions, the role of the animal as a transitional object would appear to be more therapeutically desirable than that of attachment figure. The purpose of a transitional object is to act as a bridge to a higher or more socially acceptable level of functioning, not to serve as a substitute for failed or inadequate human relationships. This is not to say that forming emotional bonds with animals should be entirely discouraged, but that the fostering of strong attachments in the course of brief treatments may be ethically and therapeutically unsound.

Attachment is also one component of Robert Weiss' (1974) theory of "social provisions," a needs-based theory in some ways akin to Maslow's "hierarchy of needs" (1970), which assumes that some aspects of a person's psychological well-being can only be met through the medium of social relationships. In addition to attachment, Weiss included the need for social integration, reassurance of worth, reliable alliance, guidance, and opportunities for nurturance among these necessary social provisions (Weiss, 1974). Weiss's ideas permeate the AAI and "human/animal bond" literature, particularly in relation to the putative role of animals as outlets for nurturing behavior (Beck and Katcher, 1996; Enders-Slegers, 2000; Lapp and Scruby, 1982; Mallon, 1994a).

Finally, some mention should be made of the influence Carl Rogers' (cited in Allen, 2000) ideas concerning "non-evaluative empathy" and "unconditional positive regard" in studies of both pet ownership and AAIs (see, e.g. Katcher, 1983). The twin notions that companion animals are "empathic"—i.e. able to "sense" and respond to people's feelings and emotions—as well as being unconditionally loving are so often cited in the AAI literature that they have acquired the status of clichés. Nevertheless, arguing from a Rogerian perspective, the potential value of animals as non-judgemental confidantes and sources of unconditional positive regard might repay more detailed empirical investigation.

3.3.2   Animals as instruments of cognitive and behavioral change

A final set of theories relevant to this discussion concerns the use of animals as living, interactive tools that can be used to help people see both themselves and the world in new ways, and to add new skills and responses to their behavioral repertoires. Although there is some overlap between these theories and those described in the previous section, what sets them apart is their emphasis on the formation of a working relationship between the patient and the animal. Most programs that incorporate equines draw heavily from these theories, as do programs that incorporate animal training and care-taking into their protocols.

Cognitive and social cognitive theories

Cognitive and social cognitive theories are founded on the belief that there is a continuous reciprocal relationship between a person's cognitions, behavior, and the environment (e.g. if I think I'm a bad person, I will behave like a bad person, and will therefore be treated like a bad person by those around me). The goal of therapy is to bring about positive changes in a person's self-perceptions—and hence their behavior—via improvements in, for example, self-esteem, self-efficacy, internalized locus of control, and so on. Learning and change take place through observation, imitation, direct instruction, and/or association (Allen, 2000; LaJoie, 2003).

The notion of wanting clients to learn appropriate behaviors through observation is common in the literature on animal-assisted interventions (Fine, 2000; Rice et al., 1973; Taylor, 2001; Vidrine et al., 2002), and is sometimes referred to as "modeling," a term first coined by Bandura et al. (1961). Another benefit often ascribed to AAIs is the ability of animals to help people learn about appropriate social interactions, and the cause-and-effect of their behavior (Brooks, 2001; Nebbe, 1991). Animals are thought to be uniquely helpful in providing feedback on social behavior, due to their unambiguous, "honest," and immediate responses to both pleasurable and aversive stimuli. Bardill and Hutchinson (1997) provide a clear example of this phenomenon:

> Graham [a cocker spaniel that lives in a closed adolescent psychiatric unit] responds positively and affectionately to acts of kindness many times during the day. Negative behaviors toward Graham, such as teasing or rough play, are responded to by Graham's avoidance of the perpetrator and peer pressure [from the other adolescents on the unit].

Three additional and interrelated aspects of social cognitive theory appear relevant to the use of animals in therapeutic roles: "self-efficacy," "performance accomplishment," and "personal agency." Self-efficacy is a belief in one's ability to perform behaviors that will create an expected and desirable outcome, and performance accomplishment involves the successful performance of a behavior that was once feared (Allen, 2000). These two concepts are related in that Bandura (cited in Allen, 2000) theorized that performance accomplishment was the single most efficient method for increasing feelings of self-efficacy. Also related is the notion of "personal agency," a condition in which people come to believe that they can make things happen that will be of benefit to themselves and others (Allen, 2000). Animal-assisted interventions are often structured around creating enhancement in these three realms.

Cognitive theories also offer us a reason to be circumspect in our enthusiasm about the benefits of animal-assisted interventions that aim to ameliorate feelings of helplessness or inferiority. As Newman and Newman (1995) remind us, the social environment does not reward all skills and achievements equally. It is extremely difficult for a person who does not excel in culturally valued skills to compensate through the mastery of others (Newman and Newman, 1995). Thus, if an intervention aims to provide long-term and generalized increases in feelings of self-efficacy, it needs to offer the acquisition of skills that are high in social desirability, offer a convenient means for continued learning (and thus continued positive feedback) after the end of the intervention, and a high likelihood of successful mastery. To date, there have been no long-term follow-up studies of the impact or efficacy of animal-assisted interventions. Although some have attempted to determine if changes in behavior could be observed beyond the context of the intervention (generally school and home) (Katcher and Wilkins, 1998; Kogan et al., 1999), the results are conflicting, and as yet no evidence exists that longstanding benefits are derived from participation in these programs.

Role theory

Role theory is similar to social cognitive theory in that its emphasis is on the way the social environment shapes the developmental process. In this theoretical framework, a role is defined as any set of behaviors that has a socially agreed-upon function and an accepted code of norms (Biddle, Biddle and Thomas as cited in Newman and Newman, 1995). The theory holds that as people enter new roles, they modify their behavior to conform to these role expectations (Newman and Newman, 1995). Obviously, whether these changes in behavior are positive or negative depend on the role that is assumed and the context in which it is assumed.

Interventions that aim to modify behavior sometimes do so by asking clients to assume a new role that may offer opportunities for learning and positive change. This differs from role-playing in that, rather than simply acting out a role, individuals actually assume a new role (Siegel et al., n.d.). The rationale against using simple role-play is that clients may see themselves as merely performing a part, and when they step outside the role, they may also stop the behaviors associated with it. Proponents of a role assumption approach believe that it offers a greater chance for the successful assimilation of new behaviors into a patient's repertoire (Siegel et al., n.d.).

Numerous animal-assisted intervention models appear to fit within this theoretical framework and, to some extent, any program that provides individuals with an opportunity to train or care for animals allows the person to assume the role of teacher or caretaker (Brickel, 1985). Despite the compelling nature of the anecdotes that exist in the literature (Corson et al., 1975; Rochberg-Halton, 1985) no evidence has been offered to suggest that the effects of role assumption are superior to role-play, that benefits are long-lasting, or that behavioral changes persist beyond the context of the intervention.

3.4   Summary and conclusions

Based on what we have presented, it is clear that despite the longevity of the practice of including animals in therapeutic contexts, and the unvaryingly positive media attention that animal-assisted interventions receive, the field is still struggling to define itself and gain credibility as a form of complementary medicine. Recent attempts have been made to standardize terminology, but there has, as yet, been no formalized field-wide consensus on a particular set of terms, definitions, and practices. There is, however, some agreement that therapy is distinct from other types of animal-centric activities, and is set apart by the involvement of appropriately credentialed health/human services professionals, and by the need for formalized treatment plans and goals.

As we have demonstrated, animal-assisted interventions draw from an impressive variety of disciplines and perspectives (e.g. genetics, biology, developmental psychology, psychoanalytic theory, behaviorism, etc.). Theories regarding the mechanisms responsible for therapeutic benefits tend to center either on the notion that animals possess unique attributes that can facilitate and contribute to therapy, or that developing a working relationship with an animal can lead to positive changes in cognition and behavior through the acquisition of novel skills, and the acceptance of personal agency and responsibility. While impressive in their variety and scope, not a single theory that appears in this chapter has been adequately tested empirically, and most studies have returned equivocal or conflicting results when the necessary testing has been attempted.

To move the field of AAIs forward, studies must begin to focus on and answer some of the most basic research questions. With very few exceptions, the research that has been conducted to date has not been designed or controlled in ways that bring AAIs closer to becoming empirically supported treatments. Study samples have tended to be small, unrepresentative and heterogeneous, and without adequate control groups. Going forward, of utmost importance is the careful definition of the population under examination and what is to be measured, as well as a need for controlled designs and stated outcomes that are relatively impervious to expectancy and demand effects, as well as self-report or personal interest biases (for information on developing controlled clinical trials, see, e.g. the National Center for Complementary and Alternative Medicine, 2004). Additionally, most studies that have examined AAIs have reported on the positive benefits that are observed while in the context of the therapeutic milieu, but have not examined whether these effects carry over into other contexts, or if they are retained over time. Rigorous efficacy and effectiveness research conducted by individuals trained in clinical research and program evaluation is needed. In the absence of such research, and despite the many potential benefits that have been advanced in the AAI literature, the scientific and medical communities will continue to assume little or no long-term beneficial impact of these interventions.

References

Allen, B. P. (2000). *Personality Theories: Development, Growth, and Diversity* (3rd ed.). Boston, MA: Allyn and Bacon.

American Hippotherapy Association (AHA) (2005). Frequently asked questions about hippotherapy. [Online]. Available: http://www.narha.org/PDFFiles/FAQ_Hippotherapy.pdf

Americans with Disabilities Act of 1990 (ADA), Pub. L. No. 101-336, § 2, 104 Stat. 327 (1990).

Anderson, W. P., Reid, C. M., & Jennings, G. L. (1992). Pet ownership and risk factors for cardiovascular disease. *Medical Journal of Australia, 157*, 298–301.

Bandura, A., Ross, D., & Ross, S. A. (1961). Transmission of aggression through imitation of aggressive models. *Journal of Abnormal and Social Psychology, 63*, 575–582.

Bardill, N., & Hutchinson, S. (1997). Animal-assisted therapy with hospitalized adolescents. *Journal of Child and Adolescent Psychiatric Nursing, 10*(1), 17–24.

Bazelon Center for Mental Health Law (n.d.). Fair housing information sheet # 6: Right to emotional support animals. In "No Pet" Housing [Online]. Available: http://www. bazelon.org/issues/housing/infosheets/fhinfosheet6.html

Beck, A. M., & Katcher, A. H. (1984). A new look at pet-facilitated therapy. *Journal of the American Veterinary Medical Association, 184*(4), 414–421.

Beck, A. M., & Katcher, A. H. (1996). *Between Pets and People: The Importance of Animal Companionship*. West Lafayette, IN: Purdue University Press.

Brickel, C. M. (1982). Pet-facilitated psychotherapy: a theoretical explanation via attention shifts. *Psychological Reports, 50*, 71–74.

Brickel, C. M. (1985). Initiation and maintenance of the human-animal bond: familial roles from a learning perspective. *Marriage and Family Review, 8*(3/4), 31–48.

Brooks, S. (2001, Winter). Working with animals in a healing context. *Reaching Today's Youth,* 19–22.

Corson, S. A., Corson, E. O. L., & Gwynne, P. H. (1975). Pet-facilitated psychotherapy. In R. S. Anderson (Ed.), *Pet Animals and Society* (pp. 19–36). Baltimore, MD: Williams and Wilkins.

Corson, S. A., Corson, E. O. L., Gwynne, P. H., & Arnold, L. E. (1977). Pet dogs as nonverbal communication links in hospital psychiatry. *Comprehensive Psychiatry, 18*(1), 61–72.

Cwik, A. J. (1991). Active imagination as imaginal play-space. In M. Schwartz-Salant & M. Stein (Eds.), *Liminality and Transitional Phenomena* (pp. 99–114). Wilmette, IL: Chiron Publications.

Delta Society. (n.d.). About animal-assisted activities and animal-assisted therapy [Online]. Available: http://www.deltasociety.org/aboutaaat.htm

DeMello, L. R. (1999). The effect of the presence of a companion-animal on the physiological changes following the termination of cognitive stressors. *Psychology and Health, 14*, 859–868.

Eddy, J., Hart, L. A., & Boltz, R. P. (2001). The effects of service dogs on social acknowledgments of people in wheelchairs. *Journal of Psychology, 122*(1), 39–45.

Enders-Slegers, M. J. (2000). The meaning of companion animals: qualitative analysis of the life histories of elderly cat and dog owners. In A. L. Podberscek, E. S. Paul, & J. A. Serpell (Eds.), *Companion Animal and Us: Exploring the Relationships Between People and Pets* (pp. 237–256). Cambridge: Cambridge University Press.

Equine Facilitated Mental Health Association (EFMHA) (2003). What is equine facilitated psychotherapy (EFP)? [Online]. Available: http://www.narha.org/sec_efmha/default.asp.

Equine Facilitated Mental Health Association (EFMHA) (2005). *EFP efficacy.* [Online]. Available: http://www.narha.org/SecEFMHA/Efficacy.asp.

Fine, A. H. (2000). Animals and therapists: incorporating animals in outpatient psychotherapy. In A. H. Fine (Ed.), *Handbook on Animal-assisted Therapy* (pp. 179–211). New York, NY: Academic Press.

Friedmann, E., Katcher, A. H., Lynch, J. J., & Thomas, S. A. (1980). Animal companions and one-year survival of patients after discharge from a coronary care unit. *Public Health Reports, 95*, 307–312.

Friedmann, E., Katcher, A. H., Thomas, S. A., Lynch, J. J., & Messent, P. R. (1983). Social interaction and blood pressure. *Journal of Nervous and Mental Disease, 171*(8), 461–465.

Freidmann, E., Thomas, S. A., & Eddy, T. J. (2000). Companion animals and human health: physical and cardiovascular influences. In A. L. Podberscek, E. S. Paul, & J. A. Serpell (Eds.), *Companion Animal and Us: Exploring the Relationships between People and Pets* (pp. 125–142). Cambridge: Cambridge University Press.

Grubb, D. (2002). *CODA, Coalition of assistance dog partners.* [Online]. Available: http://www.gdui.org/cado.html.

Gullone, E. (2000). The biophilia hypothesis and life in the 21st century: increasing mental health or increasing pathology? *Journal of Happiness Studies, 1,* 293–321.

Hansen, K. M., Messinger, C. J., Baun, M. M., & Megel, M. (1999). Companion animals alleviating distress in children. *Anthrozoös, 12*(3), 142–148.

Harbolt, T., & Ward, T. H. (2001). Teaming incarcerated youth with shelter dogs for a second chance. *Society and Animals, 9*(2), 177–182.

Kahn, P. H. (1997). Developmental psychology and the biophilia hypothesis: children's affiliation with nature. *Developmental Review, 17,* 1–61.

Kale, M. (1992). At risk: working with animals to create a new self-image. *InterActions, 10*(4), 6–9.

Katcher, A. H. (1983). Man and the living environment: an excursion into cyclical time. In A. H. Katcher & A. M. Beck (Eds.), *New Perspectives on Our Lives with Companion Animals* (pp. 519–531). Philadelphia, PA: University of Pennsylvania Press.

Katcher, A. H. (2000). The future of education and research on the animal-human bond and animal-assisted therapy. Part B: Animal-assisted therapy and the study of human-animal relationships: discipline or bondage? Context or transitional object? In A. H. Fine (Ed.), *Handbook on Animal-assisted Therapy* (pp. 461–473). New York, NY: Academic Press.

Katcher, A. H., Friedmann, E., Beck, A. M., & Lynch, J. J. (1983). Looking, talking and blood pressure: the physiological consequences of interaction with the living environment. In A. H. Katcher & A. M. Beck (Eds.), *New Perspectives on Our Lives with Companion Animals* (pp. 351–359). Philadelphia, PA: University of Pennsylvania Press.

Katcher, A., & Wilkins, G. G. (1998). Animal-assisted therapy in the treatment of disruptive behavior disorders in children. In A. Lundberg (Ed.), *The Environment and Mental Health* (pp. 193–204). Mahwah, NJ: Lawrence Erlbaum Associates, Inc.

Kogan, L. R., Granger, B. P., Fitchett, J. A., Helmer, K. A., & Young, K. J. (1999). The human-animal team approach for children with emotional disorders: two case studies. *Child and Youth Care Forum, 28*(2), 105–121.

Kruger, K., Trachtenberg, S., & Serpell, J. A. (2004). *Can animals help humans heal? Animal-assisted interventions in adolescent mental health.* [Online]. Available. http://www2.vet.upenn.edu/research/centers/cias/pdf/CIAS_AAI_white_paper.pdf.

LaJoie, K. R. (2003). *An evaluation of the effectiveness of using animals in therapy.* Louisville, KY (University Microfilms No. 3077675): Unpublished doctoral dissertation, Spalding University.

Lapp, S. A., & Scruby, L. (1982). Responsible pet relationships: a mental health perspective. *Health Values: Achieving High Level Wellness, 6*(1), 20–25, July–Aug.

Levinson, B. M. (1969). *Pet-oriented Child Psychotherapy.* Springfield, IL: Charles C. Thomas.

Levinson, B. (1970). Pets, child development, and mental illness. *Journal of the American Veterinary Medical Association, 157*(11), 1759–1766.

Levinson, B. M. (1978). Pets and personality development. *Psychological Reports, 42,* 1031–1038.

Levinson, B. M. (1984). Human/companion animal therapy. *Journal of Contemporary Psychotherapy, 14,* 131–144.

Lockwood, R. (1983). The influence of animals on social perception. In A. H. Katcher & A. M. Beck (Eds.) *New Perspectives on Our Lives with Companion Animals* (pp. 64–71). Philadelphia, PA: University of Pennsylvania Press.

Mader, B., Hart, L. A., & Bergin, B. (1989). Social acknowledgments for children with disabilities: effects of service dogs. *Child Development, 60*, 1529–1534.

Mallon, G. P. (1994a). Cow as co-therapist: utilization of farm animals as therapeutic aides with children in residential treatment. *Child and Adolescent Social Work Journal, 11*(6), 455–474.

Mallon, G. P. (1994b). Some of our best therapists are dogs. *Child and Youth Care Forum, 23* (2), 89–101.

Maslow, A. H. (1970). *Motivation and Personality* (2nd ed.). New York: Harper Row.

Mason, M. S., & Hagan, C. B. (1999). Pet-assisted psychotherapy. *Psychological Reports, 84*, 1235–1245.

Melson, G. F. (2001). *Why the Wild Things Are: Animals in the Lives of Children*. Cambridge, MA: Harvard University Press.

Messent, P. R. (1983). Social facilitation of contact with other people by pet dogs. In A. H. Katcher & A. M. Beck (Eds.) *New Perspectives on Our Lives with Companion Animals* (pp. 37–46). Philadelphia, PA: University of Pennsylvania Press.

Nagengast, S. L., Baun, M. M., Megel, M., & Leibowitz, J. M. (1997). The effects of the presence of a companion animal on physiological arousal and behavioral distress in children during a physical examination. *Journal of Pediatric Nursing, 12*(6), 323–330.

National Center for Complementary and Alternative Medicine (NCCAM). (2004). *Applying for NCCAM clinical trials grants: points to consider*. [Online]. Available: http://nccam. nih.gov/research/instructions/poc.htm.

Nebbe, L. L. (1991). The human-animal bond and the elementary school counselor. *The School Counselor, 38*(5), 362–371.

Newman, B. M., & Newman, P. R. (1995). *Development through Life: A Psychosocial Approach* (6th ed.). New York, NY: Brooks/Cole Publishing Company.

Odendaal, J. S. J., & Lehmann, S. M. C. (2000). The role of phenylethylamine during positive human-dog interaction. *Acta Veterinaria Brno, 69*, 183–188.

Oxford English Dictionary. (1997) (2nd ed.). Oxford University Press.

Psychiatric Service Dog Society. (2003). *Psychiatric service dog tasks*. [Online]: Available: http://www.psychdog.org/tasks.html.

Reichert, E. (1998). Individual counseling for sexually abused children: a role for animals and storytelling. *Child and Adolescent Social Work Journal, 15*(3), 177–185.

Reimer, D. F. (1999). Pet-facilitated therapy: an initial exploration of the thinking and theory behind an innovative intervention for children in psychotherapy. Boston, MA: Unpublished doctoral dissertation, Massachusetts School of Professional Psychology.

Rice, S. S., Brown, L. T., & Caldwell, H. S. (1973). Animals and psychotherapy: a survey. *Journal of Community Psychology, 1*, 323–326.

Rochberg-Halton, E. (1985). Life in the treehouse: pet therapy as family metaphor and self-dialogue. *Marriage and Family Review, 8*(3–4), 175–189.

Rossbach, K. A., & Wilson, J. P. (1992). Does a dog's presence make a person appear more likable?: Two studies. *Anthrozoös, 5*(1), 40–51.

Serpell, J. A. (1986). In the Company of Animals: A Study of Human-Animal Relationships. Cambridge, UK: Cambridge University Press.

Serpell, J. A. (2000). Creatures of the unconscious: companion animals as mediators. In A. L. Podberscek, E. S. Paul, & J. A. Serpell (Eds.), *Companion Animal and Us:*

Exploring the Relationships Between People and Pets (pp. 108–121). Cambridge, UK: Cambridge University Press.

Serpell, J. A. (2004). Factors influencing human attitudes to animals and their welfare. *Animal Welfare, 13*(Suppl), 145–152.

Siegel, W.L., Murdock, J.Y. & Colley, A.D. (n.d.). Learning to train dogs reduces non-compliant/aggressive classroom behaviors of students with behavior disorders. Unpublished manuscript.

Taylor, S. M. (2001). *Equine facilitated psychotherapy: an emerging field.* Saint Michael's College, Colchester, VT: Unpublished master's thesis.

Triebenbacher, S. L. (1998). Pets as transitional objects: their role in children's emotional development. *Psychological Reports, 82,* 191–200.

United States Department of Justice. (1996). *Commonly asked questions about service animals in places of business.* [Online]. Available: http://www.usdoj.gov/crt/ada/qasrvc.htm.

Vidrine, M., Owen-Smith, P., & Faulkner, P. (2002). Equine-facilitated group psychotherapy: applications for therapeutic vaulting. *Issues in Mental Health Nursing, 23,* 587–603.

Weiss, R. S. (1974). The provision of social relationships. In Z. Rubin (Ed.), *Doing unto Others* (pp. 17–26). Engelwood Cliffs, NJ: Prentice Hall.

Wells, E. S., Rosen, L. W., & Walshaw, S. (1997). Use of feral cats in psychotherapy. *Anthrozoös, 10*(2/3), 125–130.

Wells, M., & Perrine, R. (2001). Pets go to college: the influence of pets on students' perceptions of faculty and their offices. *Anthrozoös, 14*(3), 161–167.

Wilson, C. C. (1991). The pet as anxiolytic intervention. *Journal of Nervous and Mental Disease, 179*(8), 482–489.

Wilson, E. O. (1984). *Biophilia.* Cambridge, MA: Harvard University Press.

Winnicott, D. W. (1971). Transitional objects and transitional phenomena. In D. W. Winnicott (Ed.), *Playing and Reality* (pp. 1–25). New York, NY: Basic Books.

4 Newer and older perspectives on the therapeutic effects of animals and nature

Aaron H. Katcher, Alan M. Beck

Purdue University

Before the twentieth century, human medicine treated diseases with a pharmacopoeia pieced together from personal experience, professionally accumulated lore, and custom. A physician's actions were based on whim, intuition, received wisdom or personal experience not governed by professional or scientific consensus. Now the medical profession is heading toward evidence-based medicine (Daly, 2005; Eddy, 2005), which is dependent upon the explicit and judicious use of current best evidence in making decisions about patient care, i.e. the application of the scientific method to medical practice, based on a foundation of critical studies testing the efficacy of individual and combinations of treatment. Psychiatry, with some resistance from the pharmaceutical industry, is also moving in the same direction (March et al., 2005; Jensen et al., 2005). Animal-assisted therapy (AAT) is a volunteer activity that has marginal acceptance based on the almost universal fondness for cute animals and a general belief that animals and nature are among life's good things. If AAT is to gain acceptance as a legitimate treatment modality, much more information will have to be forthcoming. It is the purpose of this chapter to outline strategies for acquiring the information necessary to ground AAT in reliable evidence so that it might have a place in clinical medicine. The authors decided to adopt this approach because there has not been any critical evidence published that would necessitate a revision of the conclusion of our other articles on the subject (Beck, 2000; Beck and Katcher, 1984, 2003) or those of other researchers (Barker and Wolen, 2008; Wilson and Barker, 2003).

The first requirement for establishing animal-assisted therapy (AAT) as an evidence-based therapeutic modality is having the evidence. Unfortunately, the field from its inception has relied upon individual case reports, poorly designed studies, "pilot" investigation, studies published in books and proceedings volumes, and even self published in book form (Beck and Katcher, 1984). This kind of publication protects papers from the stringent review afforded by refereed journals. Two of the most famous papers in the field are the budgie study (Mugford and M'Comisky, 1975) in which the number of subjects was too small to permit statistical analysis and the original, self published, evidence in support of the "Eden Alternative" (Thomas, 1994) in which the evidence consisted of four graphs with no indication of the number of subjects and no statistical

Handbook on Animal-Assisted Therapy. DOI: 10.1016/B978-0-12-381453-1.10004-2

analysis. There is a general impression that "Edenizing" a nursing home lessens medication usage and most observers believe it is a better alternative to the general nursing home facility (Thomas, 1996). In the years since Levinson's (1969) initial review of the state of the field, two specialty journals have appeared to give authors a venue for publication, but the preponderance of citations in AAT papers from these two journals, *Anthrozoös* and *Society & Animals*, still speaks to the failure of authors to find a home for their studies in the journals that influence clinicians in fields of psychology, psychiatry, nursing, social work, and education. Most articles about human/animal interactions published in more traditional medical journals have been, by and large, studies of the relationship between pet ownership and human health or review articles (e.g. Friedmann et al., 2003; Katcher et al., 1983; Ulrich, 1984; Walter-Toews, 1993).

Evidence-based medicine rests on firm pillars of epidemiological evidence and controlled studies testing the interventions suggested by the epidemiological investigation. We would not be advocating lowering of blood lipids, cessation of cigarette smoking, exercise regimens, or the Mediterranean diet if there were not unequivocal longitudinal and cross-sectional (synchronic) studies suggesting a strong relationship among cholesterol, cigarette smoking, exercise, and diet and coronary artery disease. Equally strong studies suggested that lowering cholesterol, exercising, and smoking cessation reduces risk from that disease. The epidemiological evidence for a relationship between pet ownership and overall health, or specific disease incidence is at best inconsistent (Friedmann, 2000; Nimer and Lundahl, 2007; Virués-Ortega and Buela-Casal, 2006). The literature on pets and health contrasts with the much larger body of evidence that relates social support to health (Giles et al., 2005; Ross, 2005; Schone and Weinick, 1998; Subramanian et al., 2005; Virués-Ortega and Buela-Casal, 2006; Wilkinson and Marmot, 2003). In fact, some early studies may conclude that cat ownership does not improve health and may even be detrimental (Friedmann, 2000; Friedmann and Thomas, 1995; Rajack 1997). Later studies find that cat ownership can be protective against cardiovascular diseases (Qureshi, 2009).

What is needed at this juncture, even before contemplating the difficulty of clinical trials in this area, is a firm foundation for predicting positive health benefits from pet ownership. Published results are generally positive but often only one kind of human/animal relationship is considered (Nimer and Lundahl, 2007). At the present level of our knowledge, we have to entertain the notion that some kinds of pets, cats, for example, may be significantly less beneficial than dogs (Headey, 1999; Siegel, 1990) or even have detrimental effects. Exposure to house pets decreased the risk of non-Hodgkin's lymphoma, but contact with cattle and pigs increased the risk (Tranah et al., 2008). In many cases, dogs alone may be important to the intervention by stimulating walking (Bauman et al., 2001; Ham and Epping, 2006; Messent, 1983) or improved social interaction with others (McNicholas and Collis, 2000; Thorpe et al., 2006; Wells, 2004). The impact of animal contact can be different for male and female owners (Miller et al., 1992) or be especially important for a specific age group, as dog and cat contact early in one's life protects a person from allergy in the future (Bufford et al., 2008; Ownby et al., 2002). Indeed, it may be useful to distinguish the value of animal contact apart from the benefits of human/human contact which has pronounced and well-documented effects (Giles et al., 2005; Lynch, 2000; Schone and Weinick, 1998).

Once such epidemiological evidence is at hand it would be possible to make specific recommendations for the therapeutic placement of pets. However, there is a peculiar problem with framing therapeutic interventions with pets that should be recognized.

Evidence-based medicine is absolutely dependent upon random assignment therapeutic trials for its factual base. The trials need not be double-blind; obviously a study of diet or exercise cannot be a double-blind trial. Animal contact, as an experimental variable, can be compared to a comparable control variable, like music (Voith et al., 1984). But there are some circumstances in which random assignment intervention trials present real difficulty. It is universally recognized that church attendance, even when other variables are controlled for, is usually positively associated with better health (Ferraro and Albrecht-Jensen, 1991), although the opposite as been reported (Cline and Ferraro, 2006). The effect is not trivial and much more consistent than the evidence for the relationship between pet ownership and health. However, having that information it is difficult to frame a recommendation for a therapeutic study. Do you assign people to attend church and compare them with people who read the *New York Times* on a Sunday morning? Is it possible to assign people to attend church and expect the same effects as you have in people who attend by conviction (or their spouse's conviction)? Attempts to randomize prayer could not find any impact on health, though other neotic (intuitively useful but not easily assessable) therapies such as music, imagery, and touch did have some effects (Krucoff et al., 2005). There are problems that arise when a therapeutic effect is potentially dependent upon a social relationship. For someone attending church a social relationship exists between a person and *both* God and the congregation. For the pet owner, a social relationship exists between the owner and the pet and also the people who relate to him through the pet. Can such social links be created by assignment?

Moreover, studies of pet ownership and health introduce an added moral complexity to therapeutic trials. What kind of responsibility does the experimenter have to the animal used in study? At the very least, the experimental team must monitor the health and well-being of the animal and the tensions, if any, the animal creates in the host family for the duration of the study. The team should also consider if it is incumbent upon them to remove the pet from the adoptive home if its welfare is in danger. Unfortunately, that places the investigators in an ethical dilemma. They are interested in completing the study and ending the participation of a study member by removing the pet if it threatens the integrity of the study. Without some neutral arbiter, the pet's welfare cannot be assured.

Although dogs are a major focus of people in the field—perhaps because of their own attachments (see later) or because support for studies often comes from the pet industry and dogs contribute disproportionately to that industry's income—consideration should be given to other less demanding animals, in the absence of clear indications of a clear therapeutic advantage of dogs. In our studies with children, fish, amphibians, reptiles, and small mammals elicited positive emotional responses and active caregiving responses, and signs of bonding from children and adolescents (Katcher and Teumer, 2006; Katcher and Wilkins, 2000) Many of these animals are contained in cages, and make less social demands on their caregivers than animals such as dogs and horses.

In other studies, having animals as a focus of interest can improve family dynamics. Parents who were given a bird feeder and an initial supply of birdseed identified family involvement as a particularly beneficial aspect of the program, and 90% of contacted families were still feeding birds one year after program termination (Beck et al., 2001). In general, children frequently turn to their pets as a way of mitigating life's stress, such as starting school for the first time (Melson et al., 1997). Alzheimer's disease patients, who are often too agitated to eat properly, are less agitated in a room with a fish tank. They gained weight and even expressed fewer disruptive behaviors after a fish tank was placed in their dining room (Edwards and Beck, 2002).

Even just observing animals can reduce cardiovascular stress (Wells, 2005) so there is even reason to propose the use of robotic animals, either as a control experience or as the experimental intervention (Kimura et al., 2005; Melson et al., 2005; Yokoyama, 2005). There are none of the moral concerns attendant to placement of a live animal. Problems introduced by virtue of personality differences between breeds of dogs do not arise, and the robotic animal does not place any demands on family resources (i.e. cost of food, time needed to exercise the pet, trouble in cleaning up, and effects of noise). The use of such robotic animals will be dependent upon obtaining data about the duration of interest shown by owners, frequency of interaction, and measures of interaction that go beyond the subject's recollected account (i.e. electronic modification of the robot to determine the frequency and duration of use). Robotic animals would also be useful in determining the limits of the human tendency to project individuality, personality, and emotional attachment onto animals (Kerepesi et al., 2006; Kramer et al., 2009; Shioya et al., 2005).

The second large area of activity that is subsumed under AAT is the direct use of an animal as a therapeutic tool in a patient encounter. These interactions are relatively brief in duration, they are guided by the therapist, and the client does not take permanent possession or responsibility for the animal. AAT as practiced now is not conceptualized as primary therapy (Beck and Katcher, 1996). There are no studies in which all medications are stopped and the patient is treated only with AAT and the control group given a placebo. AAT is by nature a kind of auxiliary therapy akin to art, horticultural, dance, and occupational therapies. However, AAT is a bit more peculiar than art or dance therapy. No one would teach only pottery in occupational therapy, or Balinese shadow dancing in dance therapy. Yet it is the convention of AAT therapists to work only with the animals to which they are strongly bonded. Most therapists work only with their own animals. This bonding between therapists and their pets (Katcher and Wilkins, 2000) creates problems not only because of the issue of bias, but also because choosing the best animal for a patient involves changing therapists, and there is no body of professionals who can speak to the relative merits of different kinds of animals or (see earlier discussion) animal surrogates.

Sometimes intellectual clarity can be obtained by a kind of thought experiment. We would like to have the reader imagine two pentagonal buildings a hundred yards away from each other. One has a series of rooms built about a central court with outward facing windows that overlook an encircling ring of trees, shrubs, and lawn, as well as windows looking into a central court which is illuminated by a skylight and has a fountain with a pool inhabited by koi (*Cyprinus carpio*). Each of the rooms is equipped to have a different kind of experience with animals. One is a large space that can be used for agility trials in dogs or even exotic beasts such as llamas. Another contains a collection of smaller animals in cages that can be tended, played with, and serve as a stimulus for learning. A third might be a large aviary with provision for tending plants as well. Other rooms are smaller and can be used for intense work with a single animal, or play with a robotic animal of some sort.

The other building has no outer windows, but where the windows would be, large liquid crystal screens display continually changing images of colorful geometrical shapes. There are windows that face onto the central court but the court brightly illuminated as well contains a number a sculptures of intricate inorganic shapes. Within the rooms there would be activities such as are usually part of occupational therapy—painting and working with other media, music and dance.

With those two facilities at the disposal of a research group it would be possible to randomly assign children to a type of conventional auxiliary therapy such as occupational therapy, art, dance or music as the control experience, and some form of AAT as the experimental therapy. The experimental therapy could be chosen by the diagnostic team and not be a therapist specializing in whatever animal that claims his/her affections. Observers could be chosen who are not recruited from the ranks of animal enthusiasts and hence do not have an obvious bias.

Obviously, this perfect design is not possible but it is good to have an idea of what would be ideal. Now the challenge is to design studies that more approximate the ideal than what we do now. Knowing what the perfect study could contain helps identify the failings and possible confounders, which then can be mitigated with a variety of design tools, such as controls, stratification, pilot studies, and sample size.

The focus of this volume and most of the writings in the field on animals and nature as therapy misses the most salient questions at this time in our history, culture, and social organization. Those questions revolve around the effects of subtracting nature and contact with animals from our experience as children and adults in industrialized societies. Indeed, the same questions could be asked about the huge increase in urban growth in the non-industrialized world as well. As late as 1910, more than half the population of the USA was found in farms. With the advent of the automobile and the decline in the family farm in favor of industrial farming, as well as the progressive usurpation of farm land by suburban growth, animals and uncultivated open spaces moved further and further from our daily lives. As late as 50 years ago, live animals were to be found in butchers' shops, and fish markets displayed whole fish. Now children never see an intact animal displayed in shops either dead or alive.

There is a long history documenting the importance of contact with nature for all (Ulrich, 1993) and the special roles of nature for children (Kahn, 1999; Kahn and Kellert, 2002; Melson, 2001; Rud and Beck, 2003). However, with the advent of television, and then video games, and the increasing anxiety about dangers to children if their play is unsupervised, fewer and fewer children are spending time out of doors, exploring nature and placing themselves in a position to see wild animals first hand (Louv, 2005). Organized sports are just that, "organized," and the children are ferried to play on sterile greens where vigorous mowing and poisoning hold nature back.

This secular trend toward decreasing experience with nature, and decreasing time spent out of doors, has gone along with increasing rates of ADHD (Kuo and Taylor 2004), juvenile obesity, and childhood Type 2 diabetes (Haslam and James, 2005) as more and more children spend less and less time out of doors. In a more metaphorical sense, both children and adults have developed a decreasing capacity to pay attention to what is out there in the real world and are increasingly locked into a virtual world of television, computers, computer games, iPods and cellular telephones that draws the person away from what is directly about their world.

We desperately need to know what the effects of the subtraction of nature and nature-directed activity have been in the lives of our children. If there is any general conclusion that we can carry away from what we know about AAT and the effects of animals on health and mental state, it is that these effects may be large, especially in people who are vulnerable by virtue of a predisposing genetic or environmentally acquired constitution. The importance of knowing the harm this great subtraction has accomplished outweighs the understanding of artificial contact such as occurs between patient and therapist or volunteer in AAT and the clinical significance of any limited contact between patients and AAT practitioners.

What follows is a list of questions that has considerable value in setting an agenda for human/animal relationship research:

- How much of the rapid growth of children diagnosed with ADHD and children in special education has to do with the increasing lack of experience with animals and nature as well as decreased opportunity for physical activity?
- How much of the increasing difficulty that boys experience in completing high school and college stems from unmet needs for activity, and contact with animals and nature?
- How could contact with nature and animals be used to reform our present method of schooling in which learning and physical inactivity are so strongly linked?
- How does the lack of experience with animals and nature affect our capacity for language, narration and metaphor?
- How does human and animal companionship interrelate: are they additive or competitive or both? When can one substitute for the other, and when can it not?
- What changes in our social structure can bring about a greater interaction between people and nature, if it is found that lack of such interaction has detrimental effects?

These are just some of the questions that can be asked, but they all focus on the larger problem: the decreasing level of contact with nature and animals in our society. They are also aimed at what mechanisms can be instated to create a sustained relationship between animals and people, not a temporary clinical relationship based on perhaps a misapplied medical model to what is really a societal problem.

References

Barker, S. B., & Wolen, A. R. (2008). The benefits of human-companion animal interaction: a review. *Journal of Veterinary Medical Education, 35*, 487–495.

Bauman, A. E., Russell, S. J., Furber, S. E., & Dobson, A. J. (2001). The epidemiology of dog walking: an unmet need for human and canine health. *Medical Journal of Australia, Dec. 3–17, 175*(11–12), 632–634.

Beck, A. M. (2000). The use of animals to benefit humans, animal-assisted therapy. In A. H. Fine (Ed.), *The Handbook on Animal Assisted Therapy, Theoretical Foundations and Guidelines for Practice* (pp. 21–40). New York: Academic Press.

Beck, A. M., & Katcher, A. H. (1984). A new look at pet-facilitated therapy. *Journal of the American Veterinary Medicine Association, 184*, 414–421.

Beck, A. M., & Katcher, A. H. (1996). *Between Pets and People: The Importance of Animal Companionship.* West Lafayette, IN: Purdue University Press.

Beck, A. M., & Katcher, A. H. (2003). Future directions in human-animal bond research. *American Behavioral Scientist, 47*(1), 79–93.

Beck, A. M., Melson, G. F., da Costa, P. L., & Liu, T. (2001). The educational benefits of a ten-week home-based wild bird feeding program for children. *Anthrozoös, 14*, 19–28.

Bufford, J. D., Reardon, C. L., Li, Z., Roberg, K. A., DaSilva, D., Eggleston, P. A., et al. (2008). Effects of dog ownership in early childhood on immune development and atopic diseases. *Clinical and Experimental Allergy, 38*, 1635–1643.

Cline, K. C., & Ferraro, K. F. (2006). Does religion increase the prevalence and incidence of obesity in adulthood? *Journal for the Scientific Study of Religion, 45*(2), 269–281.

Daly, J. (2005). *Evidence-based Medicine and the Search for a Science of Clinical Care.* California: Milbank Books on Health and the Public.

Eddy, D. M. (2005). Evidence-based medicine: a unified approach. *Health Affairs, 24*, 9–17.

Edwards, N. E., & Beck, A. M. (2002). Animal-assisted therapy and nutrition in Alzheimer's disease. *Western Journal of Nursing Research, 24*, 697–712.

Ferraro, K. F., & Albrecht-Jensen, C. M. (1991). Does religion influence adult health? *Journal for the Scientific Study of Religion, 30*(2), 193–202.

Friedmann, E. (2000). The animal-human bond: health and wellness. In A. H. Fine (Ed.), *The Handbook on Animal Assisted Therapy, Theoretical Foundations and Guidelines for Practice* (pp. 41–58). New York: Academic Press.

Friedmann, E., & Thomas, S. A. (1995). Pet ownership, social support, and one-year survival after acute myocardial infarction in the Cardiac Arrhythmia Suppression Trial (CAST). *American Journal of Cardiology, 76*, 1213–1217.

Friedmann, E., Thomas, S. A., Stein, P. K., & Kleiger, R. E. (2003). Relation between pet ownership and heart rate variability in patients with healed myocardial infarcts. *American Journal of Cardiology, 91*, 718–721.

Giles, L. C., Glanek, G. F. W., Luszcz, M. A., & Andrews, G. R. (2005). Effect of social networks on 10 year survival in very old Australians: the Australian longitudinal study of aging. *Journal of Epidemiology and Community Health, 59*, 574–579.

Ham, S. A., & Epping, J. (2006). Dog walking and physical activity in the United States. *Preventing Chronic Disease.* Available from: URL: http://www.cdc.gov/pcd/issues/2006/apr/05_0106.htm.

Haslam, D. W., & James, W. P. T. (2005). Obesity. *The Lancet, 366*, 1197–1206.

Headey, B. (1999). Health benefits and health costs savings due to pets: preliminary estimates from an Australian national survey. *Social Indicators Research, 47*, 233–243.

Jensen, P. S., Garcia, J. A., Glied, S., Crowe, M., Foster, M., Schlander, M., et al. (2005). Cost-effectiveness of ADHD treatments: findings from the multimodal treatment study of children with ADHD. *American Journal of Psychiatry, 162*, 1628–1636.

Kahn, P. H., Jr. (1999). *The Human Relationship with Nature: Development and Culture.* Cambridge, MA: The MIT Press.

Kahn, P. H., Jr., & Kellert, S. (2002). *Children and Nature: Psychological, Sociocultural and Evolutionary Investigation.* Cambridge, MA: The MIT Press.

Katcher, A. H., & Teumer, S. P. (2006). A 4-year trial of animal-assisted therapy with public school special education students. In A. H. Fine (Ed.), *Handbook on Animal-Assisted Therapy: Theoretical Foundations and Guidelines for Practice* (2nd ed.) (pp. 227–242). New York: Academic Press.

Katcher, A. H., & Wilkins, G. G. (2006). The Centaur's lessons: therapeutic education through care of animals and nature study. In A. H. Fine (Ed.), *he Handbook on Animal Assisted Therapy, Theoretical Foundations and Guidelines for Practice* (pp. 153–177). New York: Academic Press.

Katcher, A. H., Friedmann, E., Beck, A. M., & Lynch, J. J. (1983). Looking, talking and blood pressure: the physiological consequences of interaction with the living environment. In A. H. Katcher & A. M. Beck (Eds.), *New Perspectives on Our Lives with Companion Animals* (pp. 351–359). Philadelphia: University of Pennsylvania Press.

Kerepesi, A., Kubinyi, E., Jonsson, G. K., Magnusson, M. S., & Miklósi, Á (2006). Behavioural comparison of human–animal (dog) and human–robot (AIBO) interactions. *Behavioural Processes, 73*, 92–99.

Kimura, R., Sugiyama, Y., Ohkubo, E., Naganuma, M., Hiruma, K., Horiguchi, A., et al. (2005). *Child and pet-robot interaction in children's hospital (1) theoretical issues and procedure. SICE Annual Conference, Okayama, August 8–10, 2005.* Japan: Okayama University.

Kramer, S. C., Friedmann, E., & Bernstein, P. L. (2009). Comparison of the effect of human interaction, animal-assisted therapy, and AIBO-assisted therapy on long-term care residents with dementia. *Anthrozoös, 22*(1), 43–57.

Krucoff, M. W., Crater, S. W., Gallup, D., Blankenship, J. C., Cuffe, M., Guarneri, M., et al. (2005). Music, imagery, touch, and prayer as adjuncts to interventional cardiac care: the monitoring and actualization of neotic trainings (MANTRA) II randomized study. *The Lancet, 366*, 211–217.

Kuo, F. E., & Taylor, A. F. (2004). A potential natural treatment for attention-deficit/hyperactivity disorder: evidence from a national study. *American Journal of Public Health, 94*, 1581–1586.

Levinson, B. M. (1969). *Pet-oriented Child Psychotherapy*. Springfield, IL: Charles C. Thomas.

Louv, R. (2005). *Last Child in the Woods: Saving our Children from Nature—Deficit Disorder*. Chapel Hill, NC: Algonquin Books.

Lynch, J. J. (2000). *A Cry Unheard: New Insights into the Medical Consequences of Loneliness*. Baltimore, MD: Bancroft Press.

March, J. S., Silva, S. G., Compton, S., Shapiro, M., Califf, R., & Krishnan, R. (2005). The case for practical clinical trials in psychiatry. *American Journal of Psychiatry, 162*, 836–846.

McNicholas, J., & Collis, G. M. (2000). Dogs as catalysts for social interactions: robustness of the effect. *British Journal of Psychology, 91*, 61–70.

Melson, G. F. (2001). *Why the Wild Things Are: Animals in the Lives of Children*. Cambridge, MA: Harvard University Press.

Melson, G. F., Kahn, P. H., Jr., Beck, A. M., Friedman, B., Roberts, T., & Garrett, E. (2005). Robots as dogs?—Children's interactions with the robotic dog AIBO and a live Australian shepherd. In *Extended Abstracts of CHI 2005*. New York, NY: ACM Press. (Peer reviewed.).

Melson, G. F., Schwarz, R. L., & Beck, A. M. (1997). Importance of companion animals in children's lives—implications for veterinary practice. *Journal of the American Veterinary Medical Association, 211*, 1512–1518.

Messent, P. R. (1983). Social facilitation of contact with other people by pet dogs. In A. H. Katcher & A. M. Beck (Eds.), *New Perspectives on Our Lives with Companion Animals* (pp. 37–46). Philadelphia: University of Pennsylvania Press.

Miller, D., Staats, S., & Partlo, C. (1992). Discriminating positive and negative aspects of pet interaction: sex differences in the older population. *Social Indicators Research, 27,* 363–374.

Mugford, R. A., & M'Comisky, J. G. (1975). Some recent work on the psychotherapeutic value of cage birds with old people. In R. S. Anderson (Ed.), *Pet Animals and Society* (pp. 54–65). London: Baillière Tindall.

Nimer, J., & Lundahl, B. (2007). Animal-assisted therapy: a meta-analysis. *Anthrozoös, 20,* 225–238.

Ownby, D. R., Johnson, C. C., & Peterson, E. L. (2002). Exposure to dogs and cats during the first year of life and the risk of allergic sensitivity at six to seven years of age. *Journal of the American Medical Association, 288,* 963–972.

Qureshi, A. I. (2009). Cat ownership and the risk of fatal cardiovascular diseases. Results from the Second National Health and Nutrition Examination Study Mortality Follow-up Study. *Journal of Vascular and Interventional Neurology, 2*(1), 132–135.

Rajack, L. S. (1997). Pets and human health: the influence of pets on cardiovascular and other aspects of owners' health. Doctoral dissertation, University of Cambridge.

Ross, N. (2005). Health, happiness, and higher levels of social organization. *Journal of Epidemiology and Community Health, 59,* 614.

Rud, A. G., Jr., & Beck, A. M. (2003). Companion animals in Indiana elementary schools. *Anthrozoös, 16,* 241–251.

Schone, B. S., & Weinick, R. M. (1998). Health-related behaviors and the benefits of marriage for elderly persons. *The Gerontologist, 38,* 618–627.

Shioya, M., Ohkubo, E., Sasaki, T., Kimura, R., & Naganuma, M. (2005). *Evaluation of temporal change of patient concentration during Robot Assisted Activity by means of eye contact analysis, SICE Annual Conference, Okayama, Aug. 8–10, 2005.* Japan: Okayama University.

Siegel, J. M. (1990). Stressful life events and use of physician services among the elderly: the moderating role of per ownership. *Journal of Personality and Social Psychology, 58,* 1081–1086.

Subramanian, S. V., Kim, D., & Kawachi, I. (2005). Covariation in the socioeconomic determinants of self rated health and happiness: a multivariate multilevel analysis of individuals and communities in the USA. *Journal of Epidemiology and Community Health, 59,* 664–669.

Thomas, W. H. (1994). *The Eden Alternative: Nature, Hope and Nursing Homes.* Sherburne, NY: Eden Alternative Foundation.

Thomas, W. H. (1996). *Living Worth Living: The Eden Alternative in Action.* Acton, MA: VanderWyk and Burnham.

Thorpe, R. J., Jr., Simonsick, E. M., Brach, J. S., Ayonayon, H., Satterfield, S., Harris, T. B., et al. (2006). Dog ownership, walking behavior, and maintained mobility in late life. *Journal of American Geriatrics Society, 54,* 1419–1424.

Tranah, G. J., Bracci, P. M., & Holly, E. A. (2008). Domestic and farm-animal exposures and RISK of non-Hodgkin's lymphoma in a population-based study in the San Francisco bay area. *Cancer Epidemiology, Biomarkers and Prevention, 17*(9), 2382–2387.

Ulrich, R. S. (1984). View through a window may influence recovery from surgery. *Science, 224,* 420–421.

Ulrich, R. S. (1993). Biophilia, biophobia, and natural landscapes. In S. R. Kellert & E. O. Wilson (Eds.), *The Biophilia Hypothesis* (pp. 73–137). Washington DC: Island Press.

Virués-Ortega, J., & Buela-Casal, G. (2006). Psychophysiological effects of human-animal interaction: theoretical issues and long-term interaction effects. *Journal of Nervous and Mental Disease, 194*(1), 52–57.

Voith, V. L., Glickman, L. T., Smith, S., Hamilton, G., Ryer, E., Shofer, F., et al. (1984). *Comparison of the effects of companion animals and music on nursing home residents: a controlled intervention study: a report to the AVMA Foundation.* Schaumburg, IL: American Veterinary Medical Association.

Walter-Toews, D. (1993). Zoonotic disease concerns in animal assisted therapy and animal visitation programs. *Canadian Veterinary Journal, 34*, 549–551.

Wells, D. L. (2004). The facilitation of social interactions by domestic dogs. *Anthrozoös, 17*, 340–352.

Wells, D. L. (2005). The effect of videotapes of animals on cardiovascular responses to stress. *Stress and Health, 21*, 209–213.

Wilkinson, R., & Marnot, M. (2003). *Social Determinants of Health: The Solid Facts* (2nd ed.). Copenhagen: WHO Publications.

Wilson, C., & Barker, S. (2003). Challenges in designing human-animal interaction research. *American Behavioral Scientist, 47*(1), 16–28.

Yokoyama, A. (2005). *The trial of RAA/RAT in the clean room at the pediatrics ward. SICE Annual Conference. Okayama, Aug. 8–10, 2005.* Japan: Okayama University.

—

5 Positive effects of animals for psychosocially vulnerable people: a turning point for delivery

Lynette A. Hart

University of California

5.1 Introduction: factors affecting the human/animal relationship

The positive psychosocial effects of human/animal relationships engage our interest, arising from our own firsthand experiences with pet animals and our scientific curiosity, as well as the practical questions concerning how best to include pets as an adjunct for treatment for an autistic child or a paraplegic veteran, or to enhance the quality of life of an elderly person in an assisted-living facility. Despite the ever-growing research literature on the psychosocial effects of animals, a significant gap remains between that knowledge base and implementing it into treatment or support services for psychosocially vulnerable people. This chapter first reviews the research-based information about the benefits of pets, especially for the most vulnerable people, and then addresses the practical implementation of this expanding research.

5.1.1 Background and definitions

Typically, animal-assisted interventions (AAI), including animal-assisted activities (AAA), medically directed animal-assisted therapy (AAT), and uses of animals in animal-assisted education (AAE) are arranged in settings where the contact with the animal and the handler is scheduled for residents in a facility. These settings generally do not take into account the specific needs or interests of the person being assisted. Full-time exposure to animals is not usually provided, and the handler differs from the person being served the intervention.

This chapter suggests that to enjoy the positive effects, a relationship with an animal should be individually tailored to the psychosocial characteristics of the person. For example, full-time contact sometimes offers greater potential than a part-time relationship to impact the person's life. Therapeutic psychological relationships with animals arise with assistance animals, working animals, and companion animals, where a special handler of the animal may or may not be involved. Early uses of assistance dogs emphasized them helping in specific utilitarian tasks, such as aiding

Handbook on Animal-Assisted Therapy. DOI: 10.1016/B978-0-12-381453-1.10005-4

those with visual, hearing, or ambulatory disabilities, but by now their provision of psychologically therapeutic benefits, contact comfort, or as a social lubricant, also is highly valued (Hart, 2003). Dogs now fulfill a growing number of therapeutic roles, perhaps most notably including assisting people with mental illness.

The breeding and methods for training assistance dogs also are more varied than in the past. While no standardized certification criteria have been legislated or regulated in the USA pertaining to assistance animals, leaders in the various types of equine therapy have developed their own certification programs. In the USA, providers associated with therapeutic horseback riding programs generally affiliate with the North American Riding for the Handicapped Association (NARHA, 2010), a centralized professional organization which offers three levels of certification for instructors. In addition, specialty certification is available for instructors on carriage driving and gymnastics on a horse, termed vaulting. As a reflection of the fact that horses make a growing contribution to the mentally ill, a subsidiary section of NARHA focuses on mental health and is called the Equine Facilitated Mental Health Association (EFMHA, 2010).

5.1.2   Can pets be prescribed?

The positive results that have been reported for health effects of pets have spurred some mental health practitioners, aware of the tendency to "prescribe pets," to formulate standardized techniques for offering contact with companion animals for people with disabilities or special needs. The role of pets is often assessed among individuals who have chosen to keep pets, such as populations of vulnerable individuals with disabilities, autism, Alzheimer's disease, AIDS, or the elderly. However, profiling pets as though their effects for people of such groups are uniform has proven to be not useful when attempting to assess and predict which individuals would be likely to benefit from periodic or sustained contact with companion animals. Community-based epidemiological studies of pet keeping produce useful results for analyzing the geographic context and demographic factors that may be significant. To be able to effectively "prescribe" pets, we will need to become knowledgeable about those cases where pets are not associated with health benefits or may even add to the burden of vulnerable individuals or be harmful, as well as the cases where the animals are associated with positive effects.

5.1.3   Subcultures and psychosocial effects of pets

Epidemiological studies of entire communities identify subcultures where certain individual circumstances, neighborhoods, geographical features, or special situations are associated with beneficial or adverse health parameters. One classic epidemiological study by Ory and Goldberg (1984) revealed that pets were associated with negative indicators for elderly women living in rural settings, but with positive indicators for women in suburban and urban settings, suggesting a varying role of the pet with geographic location. The combination of higher socioeconomic status and pet ownership was associated with more positive indicators of happiness for women

(Ory and Goldberg, 1983); however, pet ownership was more typical among less affluent women. Weak attachment to a pet was associated with not being in a confidant relationship with the spouse and was also associated with unhappiness, when compared with non-owners and attached owners whose spouses more often were confidants.

A fairly recent community-based, longitudinal study examined over a one-year period whether attachment to companion animals was associated with changes in health among older people (Raina et al., 1999). Non-owners showed greater deterioration in their activities of daily living than pet owners, but the pet owners as a group were younger, more likely to be married or living with someone, and more physically active. Pet ownership was a positive factor associated with the change in psychological well-being of participants over the one-year period.

5.1.4 The type of pet matters

Selection of the type of pet is important in the outcome. For example, people who are burdened in their personal circumstances or health status, as is common for the elderly, can benefit from pets despite the pet's care required, especially if they select a low-care cat rather than a dog or horse. Benefits were associated with cat companionship for men with AIDS (Castelli et al., 2001) and middle-aged women giving care to family members with Alzheimer's disease (Fritz et al., 1996); in contrast, having a dog was more problematic in these two studies.

The term *pet* covers a wide range of animals and relationships, as families seek out pets to fill different roles. The pet's treatment depends on the family's context, traditions, and expectations. A study of residents in Salt Lake County revealed that pet-keeping practices vary with neighborhood and community (Zasloff and Hart, unpublished results). Zip code areas predicted the sources residents used in acquiring their pets with some showing high levels of pet adoptions from shelters. Other neighborhoods favored purebred animals; still other areas were associated with high adoptions of feral cats.

Employing epidemiological methods with statistical representation of the entire community offers a view of the context, including the community's affluence, geography, age, gender, and ethnicity of pet-owning participants. By examining microneighborhoods and subcultures, we can more accurately profile the range of styles of pet ownership characteristic in our diverse societies, as well as identifying additional questions that need to be clarified.

5.1.5 Focus on the elderly

Considering age, the *elderly* are a growing population where animals can play a special supportive role. However, as mentioned above, the animal must be highly individualized to match the person with respect to personal history, living situation, and general health. As people age, they can be swamped in losses. Their former social networks shrink as they leave the workplace, move into smaller homes, lose friends and family members who have moved away or died, and/or experience chronic health problems or disabilities. The Activities of Daily Living that are used in assessing a person's active-life status are portrayed in Table 5.1, showing basic activities, as well as instrumental ones required for fully independent living. To put this into clear perspective, Figure 5.1 shows the years of life expectancy for men and women at ages 70, 80, and 90 years; also indicated is the able-bodied portion of their life expectancy,

Table 5.1 Activities of Daily Living: lists of activities that are commonly used by medical professionals, usually with the elderly, to assess their fundamental functioning (left side) and ability to live independently (right side).

Activities of Daily Living: Basic	Activities of Daily Living: Instrumental
☐ Personal hygiene	☐ Doing light housework
☐ Dressing and undressing	☐ Preparing meals
☐ Eating	☐ Taking medications
☐ Transferring from bed to chair, and back	☐ Shopping for groceries or clothes
☐ Voluntarily controlling urinary and fecal discharge	☐ Using the telephone
☐ Elimination	☐ Managing money
☐ Moving around (as opposed to being bedridden)	☐ Using technology

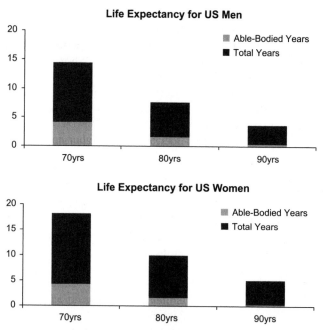

Figure 5.1 Although the number of years of life expectancy for women at 70, 80, and 90 years of age exceeds that of men, the expected period of disability is also greater for women than men and from the age of 70 is a majority of the remaining years of life, for both men and women (from Crimmins et al., 1996). Being unable to perform essential tasks in the Activities of Daily Living was defined as a disability.

revealing that most people experience a substantial period of disability at the end of their lives when they are unable to perform all the activities of daily living without assistance, representing further losses (Crimmins et al., 1996). Further, the person's cohort shrinks over time as the like-aged counterparts die at a growing rate. Among a person's counterparts in the USA, 76% remain alive at 70 years of age, 53% at 80 years, 21% at 90 years, and 2% at 100 years. Having a companion animal can offer a source of reliable and accessible companionship. In one study of elderly dog owners, a majority said their dog was their only friend and believed their relationship with their dog was as strong as with humans (Peretti, 1990).

Understanding how best to optimize contact with animals for elderly people to increase benefit for them but not create a burden in their varied circumstances is an urgent question for society today, and one that is touched on several times in this chapter. Bridging the gap between the research results and the practitioners' needs for specific and practical information requires evidence-based tailoring of the animal contact for effective therapeutic assistance with patients.

5.2   Goals of this chapter

This chapter is intended to present some highlights from the research literature, while also addressing the gap between research and practice and pointing the way toward an integrated translation of knowledge into helpful programs and practice. It also points to the importance of considering the specific roles of different animal species, dogs, cats, and horses, birds and fish, in enhancing the quality of human lives. Some related recent reviews of relevance to this theme are those by Wells (2007, 2009) on the health effects of dogs, and the intriguing roles of companion animals in detecting medical conditions, such as the presence of emerging cancer or predicting an impending seizure attack. Another paper, by Barker and Wolen (2008), reviews over 100 studies on the health benefits of human/animal interactions.

5.3   The potential of pets to enhance the quality of life

An important point to emphasize is that while companion animals offer potential enhancements to a person's quality of life that can stem an unraveling decline into disability or disease, they only rarely offer a pathway to curing disease. As an unconditional support system, pets can be recruited for contact at any time of day or night. Essential comfort, relaxation, and entertainment are near at hand. The conflicts with the non-verbal animal are few as long as the person avoids behavior problems through careful pet selection and management.

Human relationships, or a lack of them, can promote health, or produce stress. Increased mortality rates are associated with decreased social connections (Berkman and Breslow, 1983). Despite family, friends, and other support services, at times of challenge and heartbreak, some vulnerable people will be without the social relationships they need for a reasonable quality of life. Persons who are facing hearing, visual, or mobility disabilities, living alone in later years, or experiencing the onset of serious medical problems, may be at particular risk. Even temporary crises can be paralyzing in their impact.

Anyone who is socially isolated, and possibly experiencing an increase in medical problems, may begin to feel profoundly alone. The high costs of loneliness and a lack of social support to human health are well documented (House et al., 1988). While the link of loneliness and depression with cancer and cardiovascular disease has long been recognized (Lynch, 1977), depression is now considered to be a central etiologic factor of these diseases (Chrousos and Gold, 1992).

Recognizing that some elderly individuals are seriously challenged with their health problems and inability to perform activities of daily living, one community program over two decades ago placed animals, usually dogs, with elderly and provided some support for their care (Lago et al., 1989). Cats require less effort than dogs, and may be more appropriate companions for some elderly persons. While the effects of cat ownership are not well studied in this context, an Australian study found better scores on psychological health among cat owners than non-owners (Straede and Gates, 1993). Cat-owning women rate their cats highly in providing affection and unconditional love (Zasloff and Kidd, 1994a). A study by Karsh and Turner (1988) found that long-term cat owners were less lonely, anxious, and depressed than non-owners; the study even found that the pet owners reported improvements in blood pressure.

Permanent institutional living almost always curtails the person's quality of life, and reduces contact with the world at large, along with increasing the cost of living. And it is widely recognized that for some people in residential retirement communities, companion animals can contribute to their psychosocial health, and help extend by months, or even a few years, the period of living independently.

But what about precarious persons or the elderly who still live at home? Animal-assisted activities (AAA) or therapy (AAT), and other types of support related to pets, generally are not offered to precarious individuals who still live at home. An obvious gap exists in finding approaches to filling this need and testing the various approaches.

Finally, in introducing this section, it should be emphasized that a well-documented area is for children with mental or neuromuscular disabilities that benefit greatly from the extraordinary experience of therapeutic horseback riding, an occasion that affords joyous human social support as well as the unique sensation and physical challenge of riding the horse (Hart, 1992). Even the families of the afflicted child seem to benefit.

In short, a wide array of animals, and different contexts, give rise to a variety of psychosocial effects. These are organized as four main categories and reviewed in the section below.

5.3.1 Effects on loneliness and depression

Most people that are caregivers of pets value companionship most in their relationships with pets. However, for those who are isolated, the lack of companionship, depression, and lack of social support are major risk factors that can impede a person's well-being and even increase the likelihood of suicide or other maladaptive behaviors. Individuals experiencing adversity are more vulnerable and subject to feelings of loneliness and depression.

The concept of social support creating both main and buffering effects against stress is well known in discussions of human social support (Thoits, 1982), and pets seem to, at times, substitute for human companions in fulfilling this role. A study by Siegel (1993) showed that animals offer their elderly human companions a buffer of protection against adversity, as manifest in fewer medical visits during a one-year period.

In a notable review paper, psychological, social, behavioral, and physical types of well-being, pertaining to benefits of pets, were examined with regard to social support (Garrity and Stallones, 1998). Pet association frequently appeared beneficial, both directly and as a buffering factor during stressful life circumstances, but did not occur for everyone.

Descriptive, correlational, experimental, and epidemiological research designs have been used to assess the effects of contact with companion animals on human well-being. Correlational studies, whether of a cross-sectional or longitudinal type, often assess just whether or not a pet is present and have not taken into account the wide differences in individual variation of the target population, type of pet, and environment. These issues will be addressed in this section.

Elderly people

Among elderly people in one study who were grieving the loss of their spouses within the previous year and who lacked close friends, a high proportion of individuals without pets described themselves as depressed; low levels of depression were reported by those with pets (Garrity et al., 1989).

One of the unexplored confounding aspects in the analysis of the potential beneficial effects of pets for the elderly is that people who seek out animal companionship may be more skilled in making choices that maintain their own well-being than non-pet owners. The traits of dependability, intellectual involvement, and self-confidence are strong characteristics that are established at a young age and continue throughout life; individuals who as young people express this planful competence seem able to take adverse life events in their stride and take effective actions to keep their lives on track (Clausen, 1993). A decision to live with an animal could be one aspect of taking effective action in one's life. Individuals keeping pets may also have acquired social skills and abilities that were reflected in the decision to have a pet.

It is tempting to ascribe the beneficial effects of pets for grieving elderly (Garrity et al., 1989) to the constant responsibility to nurture another individual, the loving devotion of a pet, and even the laughter that a pet inevitably brings into everyday life. Living alone is common in elderly people, and this lifestyle itself may be inherently stressful. Loneliness is associated with various diseases. Elderly women living alone were found in one study to be in better psychological health if they resided with an animal: less lonely, more optimistic, more interested in planning for the future, and less agitated than those women who lived without a pet (Goldmeier, 1986). In contrast, women living with other relatives did not show an extra boost with a pet.

Women graduate students who lived alone also showed a protective effect of a pet: those living with a companion animal, a person, or both, rated themselves as less lonely than those living entirely alone (Zasloff and Kidd, 1994b).

However convincing the above findings are, the psychosocial benefits, such as lowered risk of depression, are not necessarily accompanied by general differences in health status. No differences in health status were found among a large group of people (21 to 64 years of age) with and without pets (Stallones et al., 1990). The same finding was reported in a large study on just the elderly (Garrity et al., 1989).

People with mental illnesses

In the area of disabilities, we have traditionally thought of service dogs as being employed in the service of the blind, deaf, or hearing-impaired, and those who must rely on the use of wheelchairs. A new development is the contribution of service dogs for the mentally impaired or disabled. For this new area employing psychiatric service dogs, the formalized tasks of the dog include providing companionship, contact comfort, and affection, all of which contribute to the stabilization of mental health for someone suffering from mental illness (Psychiatric Service Dogs Society, 2010). For a syndrome very much in the public eye, post-traumatic stress disorder following war experiences, the syndrome is being treated at some centers by the warmth and acceptance dogs offer when providing tactile contact and calming the patient.

The use of psychiatric service dogs is broadening the concept of service dogs. Persons being treated work with dog training specialists and peers in training their own dogs. Clearly, professionals working in this new field recognize that the dog is just one aspect of treatment, along with pharmaceutical treatment and counseling assistance from human health professionals, as well as intervention with veterinarians when indicated.

The use of birds in residential facilities is an interesting sideline of this field. Depressed community-dwelling elderly in one study were less negative psychologically after prolonged exposure to pet birds (Mugford and M'Comisky, 1975). Depressed elderly men at an adult day health care program exposed to an aviary, and who ended up actually using the aviary, had a greater reduction in depression than those that did not interact with the aviary. In fact, the latter group showed no overall difference in depression (Holcomb et al., 1997). Those seeking out the aviary also apparently were more interactive with family and staff members. Along the same lines, lonely elderly people in a skilled rehabilitation unit who were given a budgerigar in a cage for a period of 10 days showed decreased depression (Jessen et al., 1996).

People who are mentally ill have also been a recent focus of the therapeutic equine advocates who now have an organization, the Equine Facilitated Mental Health Association (EFMHA, 2010). One difference between dogs and horses is that whereas a dog can be available 24 hours a day to provide companionship and comfort, equine-assisted therapy requires a significant infrastructure and human organization in order to provide treatments, even once a week. The equine therapists point out, however, that the power, beauty, and strength of a horse compel the attention of the rider. For some patients the horse is uniquely effective in motivating the person and facilitating treatment.

Many communities have an equine-facilitated program operating nearby and if not currently utilized some of the horses could be cross-trained perhaps to provide not only the physical rehabilitation, but some mental therapy to a different set of patients. Green Chimneys (2010) is an example of a comprehensive residential treatment center for mentally disturbed children where equine-facilitated therapy is one of the important treatment modalities that are available.

People with a disability or requiring clinical care

The third topic in this section on depression and loneliness concerns benefits of pets for people in long-term treatment facilities, where irreversible disabilities like deafness and diseases such as Alzheimer's disease are common. While a full-time therapeutic pet might seem best in terms of reducing loneliness, the pet can be just an occasional friend. AAT provided once or three times a week to elderly people in long-term facilities can result in a significant reduction of loneliness (Banks and Banks, 2002).

One important and common disability, loss of hearing, limits communication and predisposes people to feeling isolated and lonely, even when others may be nearby. In these circumstances, a hearing dog can offer ameliorative benefits aside from alerting the caregiver to the phone ringing. A dog, being a full-time companion, ends up being a conversational partner that responds behaviorally to the statements and moods of other people nearby, facilitating the person to socialize within the community. People with impaired hearing and a hearing dog rated themselves as less lonely after receiving their dogs, and also were less lonely than those who were slated to receive a hearing dog soon (Hart et al., 1996).

Alzheimer's disease is one of the most challenging conditions for both the patient and the caregivers, and one that will increase with the changing demographics and growing aging population in much of the Western world. As noted, a cure is not to be expected from a pet, but some specific and important aspects of quality of life and patient management may be helped with strategic employment of animals. Another study of nursing home residents with dementia found that they had improved orientation to the days of the week based upon the presence or absence of a Canine Companion who participated at a day program on Tuesdays and Fridays (Katsinas, 2000). Dogs were used to join the patient for short walks within the facility; in the case of wandering a bit, the dog could be called back and the patient would also return.

Another study of a closed psychiatric ward for persons with dementia found in recordings of the general ward noise with a sound level meter that the noise levels were substantially decreased in the experimental ward during the dog's two 3 hour visits each week, but not in the control ward (Walsh et al., 1995). Fewer loud spontaneous vocalizations and aggressive verbal outbursts resulted in a significantly lower intensity of noise levels in the experimental ward during the presence of the dog.

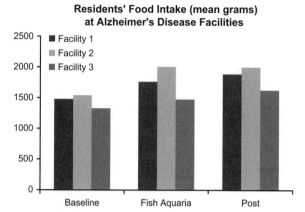

Figure 5.2 A virtually unexplored treatment for patients' disinterest in food and lack of appetite that is common in Alzheimer's disease and cancer may be exposure to animals. Elderly residents in facilities for Alzheimer's patients, when provided a fish aquarium in their dining room, increased their nutritional intake and also had a weight gain (from Edwards and Beck, 2002). The increased intake persisted for some weeks after the aquarium was removed.

Here again, the pet does not have to be a dog or even a cat. Introducing fish aquaria into three residential facilities for people with Alzheimer's disease resulted in an increased average nutritional food intake as shown in Figure 5.2, with weight gains for the residents who previously had been losing weight (Edwards and Beck, 2002). Residents remained at the dining table longer and were more attentive in the presence of the aquaria, eating the prepared food and requiring significantly less nutritional supplements such as Ensure (a 25% reduction).

These three studies involving patients with Alzheimer's disease highlight the opportunities to consider less-conventional benefits of animals contributing to the person's quality of life, by increasing their engagement in living, such that they eat more nutritiously, are more aware of days of the week, and express less distress in aggressive and loud outbursts. These outcomes—appetite, awareness of time, and aggressive outbursts—involve issues that regularly challenge caregivers and family members who assist in the management of patients with Alzheimer's disease and some other diseases as well.

Summary

Despite some refinements that could be made in methodology by taking individual differences into account and the common use of cross-sectional or correlational studies, the numerous reports of positive effects for the comforting and calming effects of animals in alleviating loneliness and depression are impressive. The reliability of the conclusions of these studies is shown. One such meta-analysis evaluated studies of AAA and AAT for reducing depressive symptoms in humans. The studies included had to show random assignment of a treatment and a comparison or control group, use a patient self-report measure of depression, and report sufficient information to calculate effect statistical strength of the treatment effect (Souter and Miller, 2007). The five studies meeting the criteria showed a significant effect of moderate magnitude, indicating that AAA and AAT are associated with fewer depressive symptoms. A broader meta-analysis, of AAT studies in general, identified 49 out of 250 studies that met the inclusion criteria (Nimer and Lundahl, 2007). Moderate significant effects were found in four areas: autism-spectrum symptoms, medical difficulties, behavioral problems, and emotional well-being.

5.3.2 Socializing effects

Somewhat linked to the effects of alleviating depression and loneliness in specific groups is the socially lubricating effect of pets, especially dogs. Such effects are strongly supported by empirical data. AAA visits in institutional environments improved social interactions among residents and staff in two separate studies, one in a psychiatric facility for elderly women (Haughie et al., 1992) and the other in a residential home (Francis et al., 1985). Along the same lines, social interactions were shown to improve in association with visits by animals to nursing homes for patients with Alzheimer's disease (Beyersdorfer and Birkenhauer, 1990; Kongable et al., 1989).

It is broadly recognized that the absence of a supportive network of social companionship leads to loneliness, depression, and stress, as well as at times suppression of the immune system, with predisposition to some disease states. With the substantial buffering effects for stress and anxiety that social companionship by animals provides (Serpell, 1986/1996), it is tempting to speculate that companionship of animals could result in a reduced likelihood or reduced severity of certain diseases for certain people.

As any dog, cat, and even horse owner knows, people almost inevitably speak to their animals. Apparently, animal companions make great conversational partners! If you need documentation, you are referred to the studies by Rogers et al. (1993) and Beck and Katcher (1989). Conversational dogs can be such a strong component of walking, for those that at least occasionally walk their dogs, that they talk about their dogs to other people they meet on walks when the dog is not present (Rogers et al., 1993). And it is not just dogs, cats, and horses. Most people with birds even talk to their companions (Beck and Katcher, 1989). Animals do not just provoke people to talk to them, but provoke people to speak with one another, stimulating friendly conversations and providing a comfortable topic of conversation. People may start conversations, laugh, and exchange stories more when a dog is present than when the person is alone (Messent, 1984).

Among people using assistance dogs, social facilitation, social support, and affection correlate with the person's self-perceived health (Lane et al., 1998). The dog creates social opportunities with people while also serving as an essential family member and friend. Dogs may have an edge over cats in this respect because they stay closer to a person than cats, and seem to more easily provoke social interactions

(Miller and Lago, 1990). That said, a rabbit, or even a turtle can stimulate people to socialize with other people, talking about the animal (Hunt et al., 1992).

The powerful socializing effect of dogs, while evident to almost any dog owner, is a primary benefit for people with hearing dogs, even overshadowing the hearing loss contribution (Hart et al., 1996). The socializing effect extends to adults or children using wheelchairs who have a service dog (Eddy et al., 1988; Mader et al., 1989). People will stop and talk to the person in the wheelchair, and smile more than when the dog is absent. The dog normalizes the social environment for the person with a disability who might otherwise be ignored or treated awkwardly.

Investigators have yet to reach the limits on the types of mental illness that may be benefited by therapeutic animals. An impressive study of a clinical population of elderly schizophrenic patients in a controlled, clinical trial, found that exposure to AAT was associated with a significant improvement in interpersonal socialization, as well as some enhancement of activities of daily living and general well-being (Barak et al., 2001).

5.3.3   Motivating effects of pets

A third identifiable effect of animals, becoming more apparent, is their effect in motivating people to engage in constructive activities. This may be in taking walks, a necessary responsibility for dogs in restricted living quarters. For others, it inspires them to bring animals into a nursing home, school, or hospital on a regular basis, where they can see firsthand the valuable effect on others.

From the 1980s, the practice of taking pets on a regular basis to nursing homes became widespread and is now referred to as animal-assisted activities (AAA). If an aspect of an integrated overall treatment plan for the patient, the nursing home visits may be known as animal-assisted therapy (AAT). Volunteers who do engage in AAA or AAT find it rewarding to share their animals with others. The motivation to volunteer their time usually would not occur if the person were visiting the nursing home without an animal. The animal partner is the essential participant inspiring the volunteer.

Animals provide significant motivation for children in learning environments and can range from learning about nature and conservation to how to care for a pet and as a bridge to learning about biology. The popular programs for children reading to dogs capture the motivational magic of pets that reduces the child's self-consciousness about reading (Reading Education Assistance Dogs: R.E.A.D., 2010). Extending to pervasive developmental disorders, children with a dog present were found in one study to be more focused, more aware of their social environments, and more playful (Martin and Farnum, 2002). While the dog garnered its share of the attention, the effects extended beyond the dog.

A recent area of serious, health-related research, reflecting the known health benefits of physical activity, is that dogs motivate people to take walks. After adopting a dog, people sharply increased their daily walking in one of the first studies in this area (Serpell, 1991). In a related finding, elderly people in southern California who kept dogs reported spending 1.4 hours per day outdoors with the animal (Siegel, 1990). Exactly what influences dog owners to engage in walking their dogs is a specific current focus of epidemiologic inquiry, since several studies show that most dog owners do not gain the health benefits of exercise. As shown in Figure 5.3, elderly people who do regularly walk have a more rapid walking speed than non-walkers in one study, and maintained their advantage over non-walkers during a 3-year period (Thorpe et al., 2006). This edge in walking speed of dog walkers was seen whether or not the dog was with them. A study of California adults found the dog owners walked 18.9 minutes more per week than non-owners, and they engaged in more recreational walking than others (Yabroff et al., 2008). A study in Australia reports that while most dog owners did not engage in dog walking *per se*, they did average 18 minutes' more walking per week than non-owners (Bauman et al., 2001). The percentage of owners and non-owners that met the criterion of 150 minutes' walking per week did not differ between study groups, so the gain was in walking above the minimum criterion. In another Australian cross-sectional study, only 23% of dog owners walked at least five times a week, but still the owners had better odds of sufficient activity than non-owners (Cutt et al., 2008a). The finding that only a minority of dog owners walks regularly seems consistent across many large studies and settings. The message that comes through from these various studies is that dogs somehow lead to social support to be more active and may promote in their caregivers an intention to walk aside from meeting the dog's eliminative needs (Cutt et al., 2008b).

5.3.4   Physiologic and calming effects

The final topic under the section on the potential of pets to enhance the quality of life concerns the measurable physiological and calming effects. One of the early studies on this topic dealt with fish. Looking at fish in an aquarium relaxes and relieves anxiety as was indicated for dental patients in a waiting room (Katcher et al., 1984).

The calming effects of fish, of course, go beyond the dental office with the sound of drills in the background. Individuals with Alzheimer's disease, and who still live at home, are calmer with a companion animal around (Fritz et al., 1995). A calmer

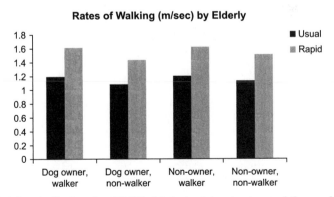

Figure 5.3 A longitudinal study of 2,533 elderly participants measured the usual and rapid walking rates of participants at the beginning of the study and three years later. With this method, the authors documented the decline in walking speed for all groups, and substantiated that fast walkers retained their advantage (from Thorpe et al., 2006)

patient is undoubtedly less distressing and exhausting to the caregiver, who is at risk for burnout in this challenging situation.

Similar calming effects for patients have been reported in therapeutic residential settings. During group therapy with dissociative patients, a therapy dog provided a calming influence and also alerted the therapist to distressed patients (Arnold, 1995). On the psychiatric ward, substantial reduction in noise levels brought about by a therapy dog's visit benefits both the patients and staff in the ward (Walsh et al., 1995). In a clinical population of hospitalized psychiatric patients, exposure to AAT was associated with reduced state anxiety levels for patients with a variety of psychiatric diagnoses, especially patients, but also for those with mood and other disorders; this was in contrast with a recreation session that was associated with reduced anxiety only for patients with mood disorders (Barker and Dawson, 1998).

The calming effects of animals are especially valuable with children exhibiting attention deficit/hyperactive disorder. During therapeutic interventions in a learning setting, animals captured and held children's attention and directed their attention outward (Katcher and Wilkins, 1997). Calming the children was a first essential step toward creating a learning environment. Behavioral improvements generalized somewhat beyond the classroom but did not carry over to all contexts. In a classroom study of children with Down's syndrome, a real dog provided a more sustained focus than an imitation dog for positive and cooperative interactions with the nursing staff (Limond et al., 1997).

Evidence for animals calming people is well documented for dogs assisting people who have frequent seizures. A person who never knows when a seizure will occur suffers ongoing anxiety. Providing trained service dogs to assist persons who have seizures also gave them a feeling of calmness, and led to the discovery that the dog often was alerting prior to the seizure, providing advance notice for the person to get situated for the seizure (Strong et al., 1999). Using specially trained seizure-alert dogs, a research team found not only were seizures reliably predicted, but over time there was a reduction in the frequency of seizures to around half the previous rate (Brown and Strong, 2001; Strong et al., 2002). In looking for a mechanism, the investigators thought that this reflected the person being calm, more relaxed, and less anxious.

The ability of some pet dogs to alert to impending epileptic seizures in their human owners has expanded into an area of respected clinical research. One study reported that for dogs living with epileptic children, 40% showed anticipatory behavior prior to the seizures (Kirton et al., 2004). Similar results were found by another team of investigators, reporting that 33% of dogs living with a person that had seizures alerted prior to seizure onset (Dalziel et al., 2003). Interestingly, the phenomenon of seizure detection, which so far goes beyond any instrument that medical investigators have yet to devise, frequently occurs spontaneously with no intentional training of the responding dog. As mentioned above, dogs can also be trained as seizure alert dogs. One caution to be noted is the potential for seizures to possibly provoke fear, avoidance, or even aggression in pet dogs if they are not specially trained or habituated to seizures (Strong and Brown, 2000).

One of the intriguing sets of physiological effects from contact with animals comes from recent studies from Japan, on the autonomic and oxytocin responses of people to

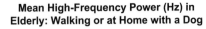

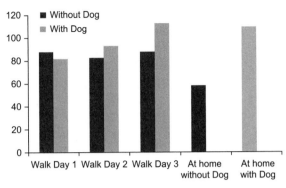

Figure 5.4 Using mean high-frequency power as a measure of autonomic nervous activity, increases occurred when the elderly were with the dog that was used in the study. In walks on successive days with the dog, the mean high-frequency power increased each day, but not when the person walked alone. When relaxing at home, the score when with the dog was about double that found when the person was alone (from Motooka et al., 2006)

animals. Motooka and colleagues (2006) used mean high-frequency power as a measure of autonomic nervous activity and found a strong response when elderly were at home with a dog, and an increasing response at a lower level when walking a dog over successive days. Their dramatic results partially shown in Figure 5.4 bear replication and further study.

Several studies now have examined human changes in oxytocin levels as a function of interactions with a dog. Oxytocin is known for its calming effects. Thus, it is interesting to examine some research that seems to delve into the mechanism by which canine contact, or even the gaze, may bring about a feeling of calmness. An increase in oxytocin following a dog gazing at the bonded owner was reported recently (Nagasawa et al., 2008). In another study shown in Figure 5.5, being with a dog resulted in significantly increased oxytocin levels for women, compared with reading, which resulted in falling oxytocin (Miller et al., 2009). The oxytocin levels of men are not necessarily so easily boosted and, in the study just cited, the levels were lowered in the reading scenario and were not boosted by having the companion dog around. One cannot help but think that the effect on women in some way relates to the potential for maternal behavior.

5.4 Personalized normalizing of the environment for people with special needs

The foregoing sections reviewed the compelling evidence for the strong impact of animals with regard to the socializing, motivating, and calming effects in the alleviation of loneliness and depression for the elderly, those with mental illness, and

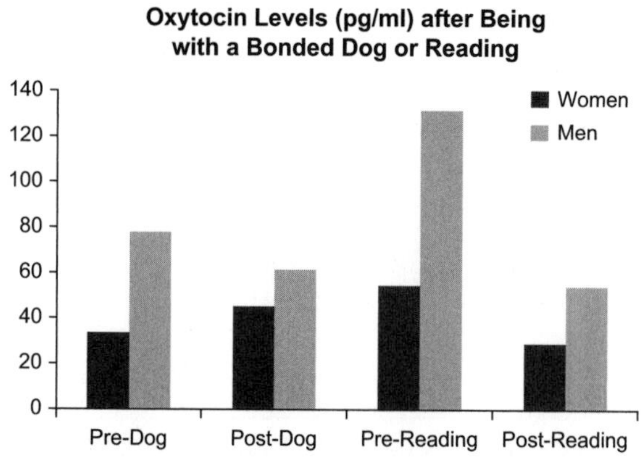

Figure 5.5 Measures of oxytocin levels in participants before and after being with a bonded dog or reading were somewhat opposite for men and women. Men showed declines after both the dog and the reading treatments, whereas women's levels significantly increased after being with their dogs, but declined after reading. Participants showed wide variability in their responses (from Miller et al., 2009)

people in institutional care facilities. This data-based evidence raises the question of how all of this works. The discussion of physiological aspects addresses one end of this question. The other is the psychological framework that mediates the effects, resulting basically in normalizing the environment, especially with people with special needs.

Several theoretical and somewhat overlapping perspectives have been proposed which can be useful in thinking about some of the results reviewed above. Attachment theory asserts that emotional well-being is affected by personal relationships; pets are included among significant attachment figures for promoting general mental health, offering unconditional love such as the perfect love of the ideal mother (Hanselman, 2002). Some adult owners turn to their dogs in times of emotional distress, as an attachment figure or safe haven; dogs are chosen over relatives and friends except romantic partners (Kurdek, 2009).

Pet ownership can be placed in the construct of self-psychology, in which the animal reflects back to the person as a mirror, representing an idealized partner who carries wished-for traits, or is a twin duplicate in perfect agreement with the person (Brown, 2004, 2007).

Coming from a sociological perspective, identity and self-concept are proposed as being of central importance by Sanders (2000). In his ethnographic exploration of people's association with guide dogs, the dog shapes interactions with the public; the involvement in the owner/dog team extends the person's self-definitions and social identities.

Another model is the stress-coping model (Spence and Kaiser, 2002). This was implied in a study of adaptation in chronically ill children. Chronic illness can impose demands on the child and family, drawing down individual and family resources. This affects the perceived demands which determine the amount of stress experienced by the individual or family. Cognitive and behavioral coping to the perceived demands in order to restore stability leads to adaptation. The stress coping model conceives of companion animals as a source of social support in which petting the animal, and the acceptance by the animal, helps in coping with stress. These various theoretical frameworks discussed above can be used to develop new hypotheses, and offer some possible explanations for observed behaviors.

The psychosocial and normalizing effects described here are not indications to prescribe companion animals to individuals who are lonely or depressed in an across-the-board fashion. Contact with a particular animal can lead to positive or negative effects, varying with the person and the context. The effects depend on the person's previous experience with animals, the person's current health and responsibilities, and the species and breeds of animals. At the outset, it is useful to consider the suitability of species and the specific challenges and problems that can arise in a particular context (Sachs-Ericsson et al., 2002; Schuppli and Fraser, 2000). As an example, many hospice patients who would be keen to keep a companion animal are too frail to provide care, especially for a dog, or they live in a residence where pets are not allowed (Phear, 1996). Some of the nursing home residents in a facility simply do not want assistance animals around (Banks and Banks, 2003). An important consideration is that in middle and older age, people tend to be drawn to the species and even breed they had enjoyed previously (Kidd and Kidd, 1989). However, medical, economic, and housing situations may limit the practicality of acquiring the most favored species and breed. A woman who has always kept a German shepherd is likely to retain that strong preference, even in her eighties when she weighs less than the dog. Offering her a bird or a cat, although safer, may not be helpful.

Paradoxically, old age is the period when people are most strongly and deeply attached to their animals, yet this also is the age where the fewest people keep animals. Those likely to gain the greatest benefit from companion animal ownership are the least likely to have companionship with animals (Poresky and Daniels, 1998).

One often cited reason why people who could benefit from a pet do not have one is a concern about what will happen to the beloved pet when the elderly caregiver dies. Some veterinary schools have offered a long care guarantee for a pet of a deceased elder, but the costs would be prohibitive for many. On the negative side of companion or assistance animals, one focus group of elderly described both emotional and pragmatic reasons for no longer keeping pets (Chur-Hansen et al., 2008). Convenience, negative opinions about companion animals, and competing demands on time or energy were among the pragmatic reasons. Emotional reasons included not needing additional social support, not wanting another "child," and not wanting either the pet or themselves to go through a grieving process.

A message that comes across repeatedly is that the psychosocial benefits of companion animals are more likely when the person is strongly attached to the animal (Garrity et al., 1989). People who were relatively compatible with their pets reported better mental health overall and fewer physical symptoms. The fit between the animal and the owner on physical, behavioral, and psychological dimensions is key to enjoying the benefits (Budge et al., 1998).

Harking back to the preferred species, optimal attachment and compatibility are more likely when the animal is of the person's preferred species and breed. In a study addressing this issue, dogs were more salient for participants than cats in maintaining morale in the family (Albert and Anderson, 1997). Yet, cats may elicit attachment as strongly as dogs (Zasloff and Kidd, 1994a). These studies indicate that psychosocial benefits of pets relate to the companionship they offer, not usually to the instrumental or physical assistance they provide.

While most uses of animal assistance are directed toward psychosocially vulnerable people with little prospect of full recovery, all people are likely to experience periods in their lives of heightened vulnerability due to severe illness or disability or suffering through the illness or death of family members. Anyone living long enough sustains some adverse consequences of aging. These experiences can create a precarious vulnerable state, particularly if the person lacks a strong network of social support. Whether a precipitating problem represents an onset of an entrenched or a temporary period of vulnerability, companion animals can buffer and normalize a stressful circumstance, offering engaging and accepting interactions without reflecting back the discomfort, concern, and agitation of the difficult situation. An animal communicates a message such as "It's not as bad as it seems; everything is fine" and thus helps put people more at ease in coping with the situation. For friends visiting someone with a disability, an animal offers a pleasant focus of attention that is apart from the difficult medical circumstance. Elderly people with companion animals, especially dogs, differ from others in not increasing their medical visits during times of life stress events (Siegel, 1993).

The nurturing of a small child and/or an animal is an important part of human development. For children in large families, the older ones experience nurturing as they care for younger siblings. The youngest siblings, or children who have no siblings, can gain the benefits of nurturing by giving the attention and time spent with their animals (Melson, 1988).

Much has been said in this chapter about patients with Alzheimer's disease. For those still living at home with family caregivers, regular contact with companion animals can normalize the home social environment, reducing aggressive outbursts and episodes of anxiety (Fritz et al., 1995). The time when the patient has to be placed in an institutional facility may even be delayed. The model for these effects is that animals play a role as a stress buffer that softens the impact of stressful events.

Among people with a service dog maintained primarily for utilitarian purposes such as to pull a wheelchair or provide visual guidance for someone who is blind, there is clearly a value of the dogs' psychosocial contributions above the instrumental assistance. A service dog can even normalize and calm social interactions at home and work (P. Knott, personal communication).

The same concept of psychosocial contributions holds for police canines. Officer companions of police dogs generally value the dog's psychosocial contributions to interacting with the public over and above the instrumental assistance (Hart et al., 2000).

Therapeutic horseback riding is another area inviting a reference to specific mechanisms by which the therapeutic effects are brought about. A meta-analysis of 11 studies on gross motor function in children with cerebral palsy showed that

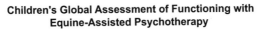

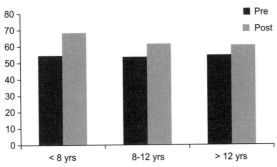

Figure 5.6 Equine-assisted psychotherapy for victims of family violence resulted in increased scores for children on the Global Assessment of Functioning scale. The positive effect was most marked among the youngest children, under 8 years of age (from Schultz et al., 2007). The global scale measures psychological, social, and school functioning for children aged 6–17 years of age.

horseback riding induces normalized pelvic movement, resembling normal ambulation, improvement in joint stability, improved weight shift management, and better dynamic postural stabilization (Sterba, 2007). Other work, not surprisingly, shows that riding horses is more effective than riding a barrel (Benda et al., 2003) or sitting astride a rocker board or other inanimate sitting device (Lechner et al., 2007). At the other extreme, vaulting, a type of structured dancing or gymnastics on a horse, is an ideal modality for offering group psychotherapy to some women (Vidrine et al., 2002). As an aside there is evidence of improvements in insulin sensitivity in elder diabetic patients following 12 weeks of exercise using horseback riding therapeutic equipment (Kubota et al., 2006).

Finally, under the topic of equine-assisted psychotherapy used for children who have suffered violence, it appears that this is particularly effective in normalizing the behavior of the young children involved (Figure 5.6; Schultz et al., 2007). Selby (2009) has provided a general review of equine-assisted psychotherapy.

5.5 For the health professions: leadership in implementing animals as treatment or social support

The above sections document the role that companion animals play in people's quality of life, be it in the life of a so-called normal person or in the life of a psychosocially vulnerable person. While the contributions of animals can enhance anyone's life, they can be crucial for persons whose network of social support is limited or absent. Research literature on human social support documents the essential role of relationships for avoiding early mortality and morbidity; undoubtedly relationships with animals offer social support and are efficacious for some people. By offering meaningful love and comfort, animals provide support that can, for some, be health sustaining when human companionship is lacking.

Emphasized above is that to play a major positive role in people's lives, the animal needs to be well suited to the person's living situation; the person should be able to manage care for the animal, and to do so in a way in which behavior problems in the animal can be avoided. Health professionals have an opportunity to provide leadership both by assisting in individualized pet placements with follow-ups to increase the rate of success and anticipating problems before they become serious.

A new area that is overdue for the benefits of companion animals is that of precarious individuals still living within their homes; health professionals can play an important role to address this gap. As an example, the organization Pets Are Wonderful Support in San Francisco (PAWS, 2010) has a long track record of recruiting and managing volunteers who provide whatever instrumental assistance is required in supporting people with the auto-immune disorder syndrome (AIDS) and other disabling diseases, compromising their ability to keep their animals. Changing litter boxes, delivering pet food, taking animals to the veterinarian, and walking dogs are a few of the tasks regularly fulfilled by the PAWS volunteers. PAWS can serve as a model for delivering assistance to the elderly, or people with disabilities, who cannot perform all the tasks required in keeping a companion animal.

Leadership from the health professional community is also needed to develop creative solutions for offering more flexible means of providing people continued contact with animals in later life, but without burdensome responsibilities. A wide range of types of exposure with varying levels of caregiver responsibility are available. Working with very disturbed young children in long-term residential care, Green Chimneys (2010) employs many methods for children building relationships with animals and can serve as a model for community efforts to serve both the elderly and people with disabilities. Some city council programs, such as those that oversee senior citizen centers, often include representatives from the human and animal health professions. They would be well positioned to begin tackling these challenges of the elderly living at home who could profit psychosocially from the companionship of the appropriate animal.

Precautions are in order with regard to assuring professional oversight and guidance in selecting and placing dogs in new settings. A case in point is the new use of specially trained dogs to calm abused children during forensic or child-abuse interviews and in court hearings. Rather than inviting volunteers to participate in this complex legal situation, this role requires that the animal use be conducted with legal, mental health, and animal behavior professionals providing vigilance in assuring that essential requirements for confidentiality and well-trained dogs for this task are employed (Courthouse Dogs, 2010).

With so many documented contributions from animals to the quality of life for both the psychosocially vulnerable as well as the rest of us, the primary challenge now is the translational phase, to apply the knowledge we have about human/animal interactions, to practical programs that enhance health-giving aspects of relationships with animals. Continuing education and formal education on human/animal inter-actions for health professionals are not as yet generally available.

However, this situation is being addressed by the new organization, International Society for Animal-Assisted Therapy (ISAAT, 2010), which has outlined an essential list of curricular topics and course of study. Educational institutions that recruit an appropriate group of faculty and lay out the details of a full curriculum for animal-assisted interventions can apply to ISAAT for certification in offering a two-year course for preparing individuals already in the health, legal, or veterinary profession for involvement in this area. Institutes that already have been accredited are: Institute for Social Learning with Animals, Germany; I.E.T., Institute for Applied Ethology and Animal Psychology, Switzerland; and the Magid Institute of the Hebrew University of Jerusalem, Israel.

This new development will spearhead the creation and availability of curricular resources and enhance the number of people prepared to provide leadership in the area of human/animal interaction, bringing research into practice. Undoubtedly, new institutes will be developed in the near future in the USA and Japan. A structured curriculum and accreditation process will accelerate filling the gap between research findings and practical application and provide useful guidelines to assist health professionals who seek to make informed, evidence-based decisions when assisting patients regarding interactions with companion animals.

References

Albert, A., & Anderson, M. (1997). Dogs, cats, and morale maintenance: some preliminary data. *Anthrozoös, 10*, 121–124.

Arnold, J. C. (1995). Therapy dogs and the dissociative patient: preliminary observations. *Dissociation, 8*, 247–252.

Banks, M. R., & Banks, W. A. (2002). The effects of animal-assisted therapy on loneliness in an elderly population in long-term care facilities. *Journal of Gerontology: Medical Sciences, 57A*, M428–M432.

Barak, Y., Savorai, O., Mavashev, S., & Beni, A. (2001). Animal-assisted therapy for elderly schizophrenic patients: a one-year controlled trial. *American Journal of Geriatric Psychiatry, 9*, 439–442.

Barker, S. B., & Dawson, K. S. (1998). The effects of animal-assisted therapy on anxiety ratings of hospitalized psychiatric patients. *Psychiatric Services, 49*, 797–801.

Barker, S. B., & Wolen, A. R. (2008). The benefits of human-companion animal interaction: a review. *Journal of Veterinary Medical Education, 35*, 487–495.

Bauman, A. E., Russell, S. J., Furber, S. E., & Dobson, A. J. (2001). The epidemiology of dog walking: an unmet need for human and canine health. *Medical Journal of Australia, 175*, 632–634.

Beck, A. M., & Katcher, A. H. (1989). Bird human interaction. *Journal of the Association of Avian Veterinarians, 3*, 152–153.

Benda, W., McGibbon, N. H., & Grant, K. L. (2003). Improvements in muscle symmetry in children with cerebral palsy after equine-assisted therapy (hippotherapy). *Jounral of Alternative and Complementary Medicine, 9*, 817–825.

Berkman, L., & Breslow, L. (1983). *Health and Ways of Living: Findings from the Alameda County Study.* New York: Oxford University Press.

Beyersdorfer, P. S., & Birkenhauer, D. M. (1990). The therapeutic use of pets in an Alzheimer's unit. *American Journal of Alzheimer's Care and Related Disorders and Research, 5,* 13–17.

Brown, S. W., & Strong, V. (2001). The use of seizure-alert dogs. *Seizure, 10,* 39–41.

Brown, S. E. (2004). The human-animal bond and self psychology: toward a new understanding. *Society and Animals, 12,* 67–86.

Brown, S. E. (2007). Companion animals as self objects. *Anthrozoös, 20,* 329–343.

Budge, R. C., Spicer, J., Jones, B., & St. George, R. (1998). Health correlates of compatibility and attachment in human-companion animal relationships. *Society and Animals, 6,* 219–234.

Castelli, P., Hart, L. A., & Zasloff, R. L. (2001). Companion cats and the social support systems of men with AIDS. *Psychological Reports, 89,* 177–187.

Chrousos, G. P., & Gold, P. W. (1992). The concepts of stress and stress disorders: overview of physical and behavioral homeostasis. *Journal of the American Medical Association, 267,* 1244–1252.

Chur-Hansen, A., Winefield, H., & Beckwith, M. (2008). Reasons given by elderly men and women for not owning a pet, and the implications for clinical practice and research. *Journal of Health Psychology, 13,* 988–995.

Clausen, J. A. (1993). *American Lives: Looking Back at the Children of the Great Depression.* New York: Free Press.

Courthouse Dogs (2010) Retrieved Feb. 10, 2010 from http://www.courthousedogs.com/

Crimmins, E. M., Hayward, M. D., & Saito, Y. (1996). Differentials in active life expectancy in the older population of the United States. *Journal of Gerontology: Social Sciences, 518,* S11–S120.

Cutt, H. E., Knuiman, M. W., & Giles-Corti, B. (2008a). Does getting a dog increase recreational walking? *International Journal of Behavioral Nutrition and Physical Activity, 5,* 10.

Cutt, H., Giles-Corti, B., Knulman, M., Timperio, A., & Bull, F. (2008b). Understanding dog owners' increased levels of physical activity: results from RESIDE. *American Journal of Public Health, 98,* 66–69.

Dalziel, D. J., Uthman, B. M., McGorray, S. P., & Reep, R. L. (2003). Seizure-alert dogs: a review and preliminary study. *Seizure, 12,* 115–120.

Eddy, J., Hart, L. A., & Boltz, R. P. (1988). The effects of service dogs on social acknowledgements of people in wheelchairs. *Journal of Psychology, 122,* 39–45.

Edwards, N. E., & Beck, A. M. (2002). Animal-assisted therapy and nutrition in Alzheimer's disease. *Western Journal of Nursing Research, 24,* 697–712.

Equine Facilitated Mental Health Association (2010). Retrieved Jan. 15, 2010 from http://www.narha.org/SecEFMHA/WhatIsEFMHA.asp

Francis, G., Turner, J. T., & Johnson, S. B. (1985). Domestic animal visitation as therapy with adult home residents. *International Journal of Nursing Studies, 22,* 201–206.

Fritz, C. L., Farver, T. B., Hart, L. A., & Kass, P. H. (1996). Companion animals and the psychological health of Alzheimers patients' caregivers. *Psychological Reports, 78,* 467–481.

Fritz, C. L., Farver, T. B., Kass, P. H., & Hart, L. A. (1995). Association with companion animals and the expression of noncognitive symptoms in Alzheimer's patients. *Journal of Nervous and Mental Disorders, 183*(8), 359–363.

Garrity, T. F., & Stallones, L. (1998). Effects of pet contact on human well-being. In C. C. Wilson & D. C. Turner (Eds.), *Companion Animals in Human Health* (pp. 3–22). Thousand Oaks, CA: Sage Publishers.

Garrity, T. F., Stallones, L., Marx, M. B., & Johnson, T. P. (1989). Pet ownership and attachment as supportive factors in the health of the elderly. *Anthrozoös, 3,* 35–44.

Goldmeier, J. (1986). Pets or people: another research note. *Gerontologist, 26,* 203–206.

Green Chimneys (2010) Retrieved Jan.15, 2010 from www.greenchimneys.org/

Hanselman, J. L. (2002). Coping skills interventions with adolescents in anger management using animals in therapy. *Journal of Child and Adolescent Group Therapy, 11,* 159–183.

Hart, L. A. (1992). Therapeutic riding: assessing human versus horse effects. *Anthrozoös, 5,* 138–139.

Hart, L. A. (2003). Pets along a continuum: response to "What is a pet?" *Anthrozoös, 16,* 118–122.

Hart, L. A., Zasloff, R. L., Bryson, S., & Christensen, S. L. (2000). The role of police dogs as companions and working partners. *Psychological Reports, 86,* 190–202.

Hart, L. A., Zasloff, R. L., & Benfatto, A. M. (1996). The socializing role of hearing dogs. *Applied Animal Behavior Science, 47,* 7–15.

Haughie, E., Milne, D., & Elliott, V. (1992). An evaluation of companion pets with elderly psychiatric patients. *Behavioral Psychotherapy, 20,* 367–372.

Holcomb, R., Jendro, C., Weber, B., & Nahan, U. (1997). Use of an aviary to relieve depression in elderly males. *Anthrozoology, 10,* 32–36.

House, J. S., Landis, K. R., & Umberson, D. (1988). Social relationships and health. *Science, 241,* 540–545.

Hunt, S. J., Hart, L. A., & Gomulkiewicz, R. (1992). Role of small animals in social interaction between strangers. *Journal of Social Psychology, 133,* 245–256.

International Society for Animal-Assisted Therapy (2010). Retrieved Jan. 15, 2010 from www. aat-isaat.org/

Jessen, J., Cardiello, F., & Baun, M. M. (1996). Avian companionship in alleviation of depression, loneliness, and low morale of older adults in skilled rehabilitation units. *Psychological Reports, 78,* 339–348.

Karsh, E. B., & Turner, D. C. (1988). The human-cat relationship. In D. C. Turner & P. Bateson (Eds.), *The Domestic Cat: The Biology of its Behaviour.* Cambridge, UK: Cambridge University Press.

Katcher, A., & Wilkins, G. G. (1997). Animal-assisted therapy in the treatment of disruptive behavior disorders in children. In A. Lundberg (Ed.), *The Environment and Mental Health: A Guide for Clinicians* (pp. 193–204). Mahwah, NJ: Lawrence Erlbaum Associates.

Katcher, A., Segal, H., & Beck, A. (1984). Comparison of contemplation and hypnosis for the reduction of anxiety and discomfort during dental surgery. *American Journal of Clinical Hypnosis, 27,* 14–21.

Katsinas, R. P. (2000). The use and implications of a Canine Companion in a therapeutic day program for nursing home residents with dementia. *Adaptation Aging, 25,* 13–30.

Kidd, A. H., & Kidd, R. M. (1989). Factors in adults' attitudes toward pets. *Psychological Reports, 65,* 903–910.

Kirton, A., Wirrell, E., Zhang, J., & Hamiwka, L. (2004). Seizure-alerting and -response behaviors in dogs living with epileptic children. *Neurology, 62,* 2302–2305.

Kongable, L. G., Buckwalter, K. C., & Stolley, J. (1989). The effects of pet therapy on the social behavior of institutionalized Alzheimer's clients. *Archives of Psychiatric Nursing, 3,* 191–198.

Kubota, M., Nagasaki, M., Tokudome, M., Shinomiya, Y., Ozawa, T., & Sato, Y. (2006). Mechanical horseback riding improves insulin sensitivity in elder diabetic patients. *Diabetes Research and Clinical Practice, 71,* 124–130.

Kurdek, L. A. (2009). Pet dogs as attachment figures for adult owners. *Journal of Family Psychology, 23,* 439–446.

Lago, D., Delaney, M., Miller, M., & Grill, C. (1989). Companion animals, attitudes toward pets, and health outcomes among the elderly: a long-term follow-up. *Anthrozoös, 3,* 25–34.

Lane, D. R., McNicholas, J., & Collis, G. M. (1998). Dogs for the disabled: benefits to recipients and welfare of the dog. *Applied Animal Behavior Science, 59,* 49–60.

Lechner, H. E., Kakebeeke, T. H., Hegemann, D., & Baumberger, M. (2007). The effect of hippotherapy on spasticity and on mental well-being of persons with spinal cord injury. *Archives of Physical Medicine and Rehabilitation, 88,* 1241–1248.

Limond, J. A., Bradshaw, J. W. S., & Corrnack, K. F. M. (1997). Behavior of children with learning disabilities interacting with a therapy dog. *Anthrozoös, 10,* 84–89.

Lynch, J. J. (1977). *The Broken Heart: The Medical Consequences of Loneliness.* New York: Basic Books.

Mader, B., Hart, L. A., & Bergin, B. (1989). Social acknowledgements for children with disabilities: effects of service dogs. *Child Development, 60,* 1528–1534.

Martin, F., & Farnum, J. (2002). Animal-assisted therapy for children with pervasive developmental disorders. *Western Journal of Nursing Research, 24,* 657–670.

Melson, G. F. (1988). Availability of and involvement with pets by children: determinants and correlates. *Anthrozoös, 2,* 45–52.

Messent, P. R. (1984). Correlates and effects of pet ownership. In R. K. Anderson, B. L. Hart, & L. A. Hart (Eds.), *The Pet Connection: Its Influence on our Health and Quality of Life* (pp. 331–340). Minneapolis, MN: University of Minnesota.

Miller, M., & Lago, D. (1990). The well-being of older women: the importance of pet and human relations. *Anthrozoös, 3,* 245–251.

Miller, S. C., Kennedy, C., DeVoe, D., Hickey, M., Nelson, T., & Kogan, L. (2009). An examination of changes in oxytocin levels in men and women before and after interaction with a bonded dog. *Anthrozoös, 22,* 31–42.

Motooka, M., Koike, H., Yokoyama, T., & Kennedy, N. L. (2006). Effect of dog-walking on autonomic nervous activity in senior citizens. *Medical Journal of Australia, 184*(2), 60–63.

Mugford, R., & M'Comisky, J. (1975). Some recent work on the psychotherapeutic value of cage birds with old people. In R. S. Anderson (Ed.), *Pet Animals and Society* (pp. 54–65). London: Bailliere Tindall.

Nagasawa, M., Kikusui, T., Onaka, T., & Ohta, M. (2008). Dog's gaze at its owner increases owner's urinary oxytocin during social interaction. *Hormones and Behavior, 55,* 434–441.

Nimer, J., & Lundahl, B. (2007). Animal-assisted therapy: a meta-analysis. *Anthrozoös, 20,* 225–238.

North American Riding for the Handicapped Association (n.d.). Retrieved Jan. 15, 2010 from www.narha.org/

Ory, M. B., & Goldberg, E. L. (1983). Pet possession and life satisfaction in elderly women. In A. H. Katcher & A. M. Beck (Eds.), *New Perspectives on Our Lives with Companion Animals* (pp. 303–317). Philadelphia, PA: University of Pennsylvania Press.

Ory, M. B., & Goldberg, E. L. (1984). An epidemiological study of pet ownership in the community. In R. K. Anderson, B. L. Hart, & L. A. Hart (Eds.), *The Pet Connection: Its Influence on Our Health and Quality of Life* (pp. 320–330). Minneapolis, MN: University of Minnesota.

Peretti, P. O. (1990). Elderly-animal friendship bonds. *Social Behavior and Personality, 18,* 151–156.

Pets Are Wonderful Support (2010). Retrieved Jan. 15, 2010 from www.pawssf.org

Phear, D. N. (1996). A study of animal companionship in a day hospice. *Palliative Medicine, 10,* 336–338.

Poresky, R. H., & Daniels, A. M. (1998). Demographics of pet presence and attachment. *Anthrozoös, 11*, 236–241.

Psychiatric Service Dog Society (2010) Retrieved Sept. 2, 2009 from http://www.psychdog. org

Raina, P., Waltner-Toews, D., Bonnett, B., Woodward, C., & Abernathy, T. (1999). Influence of companion animals on the physical and psychological health of older people: an analysis of a one-year longitudinal study. *Journal of the American Geriatric Society, 47*, 323–329.

Reading Education Assistance Dogs (2010). Retrieved Jan. 15, 2010 from http://www. therapyanimals.org/R.E.A.D.html

Rogers, J., Hart, L. A., & Boltz, R. P. (1993). The role of pet dogs in casual conversations of elderly adults. *Journal of Social Psychology, 133*, 265–277.

Sachs-Ericsson, N., Hansen, N. K., & Fitzgerald, S. (2002). Benefits of assistance dogs: a review. *Rehabilitation Psychology, 47*, 251–277.

Sanders, C. R. (2000). The impact of guide dogs on the identity of people with visual impairments. *Anthrozoös, 13*, 131–139.

Schultz, P. N., Remick-Barlow, G. A., & Robbins, L. (2007). Equine-assisted psychotherapy: a mental health promotion/intervention modality for children who have experienced intra-family violence. *Health and Social Care in the Community, 15*, 265–271.

Schuppli, C. A., & Fraser, D. (2000). A framework for assessing the suitability of different species as companion animals. *Animal Welfare, 9*, 359–372.

Selby, A. (2009). A systematic review of the effects of psychotherapy involving equines. *M.S. Social Work Thesis.* University of Texas at Arlington.

Serpell, J. (1986/1996). Health and friendship. In *In the Company of Animals: A Study of Human-Animal Relationships* (pp. 108–126). Cambridge, UK: Cambridge University Press.

Serpell, J. (1991). Beneficial effects of pet ownership on some aspects of human health and behavior. *Journal of the Royal Society of Medicine, 84*, 717–720.

Siegel, J. (1990). Stressful life events and use of physician services among the elderly: the moderating role of pet ownership. *Journal of Personality and Social Psychology, 58*, 1081–1086.

Siegel, J. M. (1993). Companion animals: in sickness and in health. *Journal of Social Issues, 49*, 157–167.

Souter, M. A., & Miller, M. D. (2007). Do animal-assisted activities effectively treat depression? A meta-analysis. *Anthrozoös, 20*, 167–180.

Spence, L. J., & Kaiser, L. (2002). Companion animals and adaptation in chronically ill children. *Western Journal of Nursing Research, 24*, 639–656.

Stallones, L., Marx, M. B., Garrity, T. F., & Johnson, T. P. (1990). Pet ownership and attachment in relation to the health of U.S. adults, 21 to 64 years of age. *Anthrozoös, 4*, 100–112.

Sterba, J. A. (2007). Does horseback riding therapy or therapist-directed hippotherapy rehabilitate children with cerebral palsy? *Developmental Medicine and Child Neurology, 49*, 68–73.

Straede, C. M., & Gates, G. R. (1993). Psychological health in a population of Australian cat owners. *Anthrozoös, 6*, 30–42.

Strong, V., & Brown, S. W. (2000). Should people with epilepsy have untrained dogs as pets? *Seizure, 9*, 427–430.

Strong, V., Brown, S., Huyton, M., & Coyle, H. (2002). Effect of trained seizure alert dogs on frequency of tonic-clonic seizures. *Seizure, 11*, 402–405.

Strong, V., Brown, S. W., & Walker, R. (1999). Seizure-alert dogs: fact or fiction? *Seizure, 8*, 62–65.

Thoits, P. (1982). Conceptual, methodological, and theoretical problems in studying social supports as a buffer against life stress. *Journal of Health and Social Behavior, 23*, 145–159.

Thorpe, R. J., Jr., Simonsick, E. M., Brach, J. S., Ayonayon, H., Satterfield, S., Harris, T. B., Garcia, M., & Kritchevsky, S. B. (2006). Dog ownership, walking behavior, and maintained mobility in late life. *Journal of the American Geriatric Society, 54,* 1419–1424.

Vidrine, M., Owen-Smith, P., & Faulkner, P. (2002). Equine-facilitated group psychotherapy: applications for therapeutic vaulting. *Issues in Mental Health Nursing, 23,* 587–603.

Walsh, P. G., Mertin, P. G., Verlander, D. F., & Pollard, C. F. (1995). The effects of a "pets as therapy" dog on persons with dementia in a psychiatric ward. *Australian Occupational Therapy Journal, 42*(4), 161–166.

Wells, D. L. (2007). Domestic dogs and human health: an overview. *British Journal of Health Psychology, 12,* 145–156.

Wells, D. L. (2009). The effects of animals on human health and well-being. *Journal of Social Issues, 65,* 523–543.

Yabroff, K. R., Troiano, R. P., & Berrigan, D. (2008). Walking the dog: is pet ownership associated with physical activity in California? *Journal of Physical Activity and Health, 5,* 216–228.

Zasloff, R. L., & Kidd, A. H. (1994a). Attachment to feline companions. *Psychological Reports, 74,* 747–752.

Zasloff, R. L., & Kidd, A. H. (1994b). Loneliness and pet ownership among single women. *Psychological Reports, 75,* 747–752.

6 The animal/human bond: health and wellness

Erika Friedmann*, Heesook Son*, Chia-Chun Tsai [†]

*University of Maryland, [†] Yuanpei University, Department of Nursing

6.1 Introduction

Health comprises the integration of psychological, physical, social, environmental, and spiritual aspects of an individual into a functional whole (Audy, 1971; Thomas et al., 2003, 2002; Sterling, 2003). Maximal health and wellness is life lived to its fullest. Individuals achieve optimal functioning along their personal continuums from minimal to optimal individual capacity. Individuals with personal, environmental, or physical limitations can achieve a high degree of health and wellness by living to their maximal capacities in a combination of these spheres (Audy, 1971). Healthy individuals live in harmony with themselves, others, and their environments.

Animal-assisted therapy (AAT) and animal-assisted activities (AAA) are two of several ways that animals can enhance or compromise individuals' health. While this chapter focuses on physical indicators of health, it is important to remember the interconnections between the physical, social, and psychological components of health. Thus the psychological and social impact of friendly animals reported in Dr. Hart's chapter will also impact the physical aspects discussed here. Psychosocial factors either promote health by moderating or promote disease by enhancing pathological processes (Audy, 1971). Psychosocial as well as physiological challenges play important roles in the pathogenesis of chronic disease (Thomas et al., 1997).

Animal-assisted activities refers to a general category of interventions without a common protocol. In general, AAA involves introduction of a companion animal to an individual who does not own that animal with the expectation that the introduced animal will provide short-term benefits to the individual at least while the animal is present. The benefits demonstrated from AAA are important components of benefits that can be derived from AAT. The impact of an animal on any one aspect of health will have effects on and affect other aspects. There is a great deal of variety in the implementation of AAA. It can involve the introduction of one or more animals of the same or different species to an individual in a private or group setting. The introduced animal(s) are accompanied by an individual responsible for the safe introduction and interaction of the pair.

The focus of most research addressing benefits of pet ownership or interaction with friendly animals stems from their potential to decrease loneliness and depression,

Handbook on Animal-Assisted Therapy. DOI: 10.1016/B978-0-12-381453-1.10006-6

reduce stress and anxiety, and provide a stimulus for exercise (Friedmann and Thomas, 1985). Stress, anxiety, and depression are associated with the hyperactivity of the sympatho-adrenal-medulla (SAM) system, the hypothalamic-pituitary-adrenal axis (HPA), and abnormal platelet reactivity (Musselman et al., 1998; Rozanski et al., 1999). Chronic stimulation of these responses increases likelihood of chronic disease morbidity and mortality (McEwen, 1998). SAM hyperactivity results in increased catecholamine release (Louis et al., 1975; Veith et al., 1994; Wyatt et al., 1971), reduced HR variability/increased sympathetic tone (Musselman et al., 1998), decreased myocardial perfusion and ventricular instability (Corbalan et al., 1974; DeSilva et al., 1978; Julius and Nesbitt, 1996; Skinner, 1985, 1981). In response to stress and depression, the HPA system initiates a series of neurohormonal responses and releases corticosteroids into the blood stream (Arato et al., 1986; Banki et al., 1992; Nemeroff et al., 1984; Pasic et al., 2003; Rozanski et al., 1999). The combination of stress, and anxiety and/or depression and the physiological components of these responses enhance the risk of cardiac mortality (Lampert et al., 2000; Rozanski et al., 1999). Excessive stress and psychological distress contribute to diseases of the skin, respiratory tract, as well as disruption in immune function and cardiovascular disease.

The presence of or interaction with friendly animals is conceptualized as a means of alleviating distress caused by loneliness and depression as well as decreasing physiological stress responses. The physiological outcomes studied as indicators of distress/stress include elevated blood pressure (BP), heart rate (HR), peripheral skin temperature and cortisol (Baun et al., 1991), in addition to risk factors for and mortality among patients with coronary heart disease.

Many applications of AAA are designed to benefit individuals by reducing stress and loneliness and inducing attention to and interaction with the outside world. Many of the studies that were designed to evaluate AAT would be evaluating AAA under more current nomenclature. In this chapter they will be termed AAA.

6.2   Stress-reducing health benefits from AAA

Within the past 15 years, several studies have directly addressed the impact of AAA on physiological indicators of health or stress/distress. The mixed results of the studies highlight the importance of considering the method of introduction of the animal and the way the AAAs are conducted in developing interventions to meet specific goals.

6.2.1   Individual AAA

Evidence for the success of an individual AAA at decreasing physiological indicators of stress is largely derived from studies using dogs with children and adults. In these studies, one animal interacts with each person in an individually oriented session.

The presence of a friendly dog was effective at reducing BPs and HRs of 2–6-year-old children undergoing simulations of routine physical examinations compared with the same children without a dog (Nagengast et al., 1997). Although the presence of a friendly dog was effective at reducing behavioral signs of distress in 2–6-year-old children undergoing actual physical examinations when compared with other children without a dog present, the physiological anti-arousal effects of the AAA were not replicated (Hansen et al., 1999).

Asking children to interact with a dog during a stressful activity was somewhat successful at reducing stress indicators. Havener et al. (2001) used AAA to reduce anxiety of 7–11-year-old children ($N = 20$) who were undergoing a dental surgical procedure. The children were encouraged to touch, pet, and talk to a dog that was lying beside them. There were no differences in peripheral skin temperature responses to the dental procedure between children with and those without a dog present during the procedure. A subgroup of 17 of the children indicated that they were stressed by coming to the dentist. In this group of stressed children, the dog's presence moderated the stress response; there was less of a decrease in peripheral skin temperature between baseline and midpoint of the dental procedure in the children who had the dog present during the dental procedure.

Hospitalized patients also experience reduced stress when they interact with or watch companion animals. In a recent study, heart failure patients ($n = 76$) were randomly assigned to a 12-minute animal-assisted interaction (AAI) with a volunteer and therapy dog, a 12-minute interaction with a volunteer only, or usual care. The AAI group had significantly greater reductions in epinephrine and norepinephrine levels during and after the intervention compared with the volunteer group and significantly greater reductions in systolic pulmonary artery pressure and pulmonary capillary wedge pressure during and after AAI compared with the usual care group (Cole et al., 2007). Having an aquarium in their hospital rooms reduced stress levels of adult patients awaiting heart transplants (Cole and Gawlinski, 2000).

The stress-reducing effects of the presence of an animal extend to adult outpatients as well. Oncology patients who chose to have chemotherapy in a room with dogs present had significantly more improvement in oxygen saturation than those who did not have dogs present. Oxygen saturation actually decreased in the latter group (Orlandi et al., 2007).

Evidence from Holter monitoring of healthy older adults in their homes suggests cardiovascular benefits of the presence of pets. Four older adults who participated in a study of dog walking also agreed to have the dog spend time with them at their homes. During the 6 hours of home monitoring they spent two, 30-minute periods specifically interacting with the dog. Their cardiac function, as indicated by higher heart rate variability (HRV), was better when they were interacting with the dog than when the dog was not present (Motooka et al., 2006)

Attitudes toward an AAA animal influence its effectiveness. Playing with a friendly dog appeared to mute physiological arousal during play activities of pediatric cardiology inpatients who developed rapport with the dog during individual AAA. Heart rate, BP, oxygen saturation, and respiratory rate were recorded before, during and after 10–20 minutes of interacting with dogs by the patients and at least one parent. The increase in the child's respiratory rate was negatively correlated with rapport with the dog. The better the rapport, the smaller the increase during inter-action. Decreases in respiratory rate were most frequent during physical contact between the dog and the patient (Wu et al., 2002). Including the child's physical exertion level in the analysis would strengthen the evidence.

Physiological stress indicator levels among health care professionals indicate that they also can benefit from AAA. Interacting with a therapy dog for 5 minutes led to decreased serum and salivary cortisol. The magnitude of the decreases in cortisol during 5 minutes of AAA was similar to decreases during 20 minutes of rest or 20 minutes of AAA (Barker et al., 2005).

While most of the studies of stress indicator reduction during AAA utilize a dog, other animals can provide similar benefits. Blood pressure and HR were lower during a moderately stressful activity after viewing videos of birds, primates, or fish than after control conditions, indicating the potential for many species to reduce stress responses (Wells, 2005).

6.2.2   Group AAA

The physiological effects of an AAA group and a child-life therapy group were similar for 70 children (mean age 9.9 years) hospitalized for an extended time, mostly for chronic diseases (Kaminski et al., 2002). In both groups, children were able to move around freely and choose activities of their choice with parents and/or staff and volunteers. Salivary cortisol, HR, and BP did not change significantly from before to after AAA or group child-life therapy or differ between the participants in the two therapies, despite observations of a more happy affect after AAA.

An aquarium in the dining room provided group AAA in a unique study of food intake among nursing home residents with dementia. The weight loss typically experienced in this population is due to failure to eat rather than changes in metabolic state. The introduction of an aquarium to the group dining room led to increased nutritional intake and weight gain. The aquarium held residents' attention and encouraged them to spend more time eating (Edwards and Beck, 2002).

Individual AAA, in which a companion animal, usually a dog, was present during a stressful activity, was beneficial for reducing physiological indicators of distress in children and adults. The benefits of individual AAA were documented for the time the animals were present, but extension of the effects beyond the time of interaction was not documented. Group AAA did not improve physiological indicators of distress, but did encourage nursing home residents with dementia to remain in the dining room and eat.

AAA were demonstrated to be effective for reducing stress indicators and in situations where the individual's response with and without the animal present were compared, but not when different individuals participated and did not participate in AAA. Inconsistencies of the results of investigations of the effectiveness of AAA highlight the importance of methodological design in evaluating its effectiveness. It is important to consider the appropriateness of the specific implementation of AAA to obtain the desired outcome. Schwartz and Patronek (2002) provide excellent insight into many of the methodological issues to be considered in design and interpretation of studies assessing the anxiety-reducing effects of AAA.

A larger and ever-increasing body of research provides a theoretical basis for positive impact of AAA and AAT on human health. Some of the research relies on epidemiological research methods that study groups of people in their natural environments while other research relies on experiment data from studies over short durations in laboratory or home conditions. Two intervention studies examined the physiological impact of acquiring pets.

6.3   Epidemiological evidence for health benefits

Epidemiological methods allow non-manipulative investigation of the association between specific characteristics or exposures and health outcomes by examining large groups of subjects in their natural settings. Single epidemiological studies provide evidence of association but are not conclusive with respect to causation. The combined evidence from several epidemiological studies provides strong support for causation of health outcomes, usually mortality or morbidity.

The integrative aspect of the various components of health is demonstrated by the combined contributions of social, psychological, environmental, and physical factors to chronic diseases. Coronary heart disease was among the first chronic diseases for which the contribution of social and psychological factors was demonstrated (Jenkins, 1976b,a). Pets were conceptualized as a contributor to the social aspect of health. The cardiovascular system was a logical starting point for evaluating the possible effects of owning pets on human health (Friedmann et al., 1980).

Several case control studies demonstrate the association of owning a pet with cardiovascular health. In the first study of this type, pet ownership was associated with survival among patients who were hospitalized for heart attacks, myocardial infarctions, or severe chest pain, angina pectoris (Friedmann et al., 1980). Only 5.7% of the 53 pet owners compared with 28.2% of the 39 patients who did not own pets died within one year of discharge from a coronary care unit. The relationship of pet ownership to improved survival was independent of the severity of the cardiovascular disease. That is, among people with equally severe disease, pet owners were less likely to die than non-owners. Owning a pet did not appear to substitute for other forms of social support such as being married or living with others. This study was replicated and extended to a larger number of subjects with improved measures of cardiovascular physiology and psychosocial status (Friedmann and Thomas, 1995). Among 369 patients who had experienced myocardial infarctions and had ventricular arrhythmias, followed by life threatening irregular heartbeats, both owning pets and having more support from other people tended to predict one-year survival. As in the previous study, the association of pet ownership with survival could not be explained by differences in the severity of the illness, psychological or social status, or demographic characteristics between those patients who owned pets and those who did not.

The possibility that some species of animals might provide distinct benefits to their owners while others might not, gained limited support from epidemiological evidence. In Friedmann and Thomas's (1995) study, dog owners were approximately 8.6 times more likely to be alive in one year as those who did not own dogs. The effect of dog ownership on survival did not depend on the amount of social support or the severity of the cardiovascular disease. In contrast, cat owners were more likely to die than people who did not own cats. The relationship of cat ownership to survival was confounded by the effect of social support, which was low among cat owners and among those who died, and by the over-representation among cat owners of women, who were almost twice as likely to die as men. A subsequent study of 6-month survival among 454 patients who were admitted to a hospital for myocardial infarction also suggested that cat ownership might have different health impacts than dog ownership (Rajack, 1997). Cat owners were more likely to be readmitted for further cardiac problems or angina than people who did not own pets. However, in contrast to the previous studies, pet ownership was not related to 6-month survival, or to other indicators of health. The one difference between dog and cat owners' cardiovascular health must be interpreted cautiously; one significant difference among many comparisons raises the possibility of a chance effect.

Pet ownership may protect people from developing coronary heart disease or slow its progression in addition to influencing the survival of individuals who have experienced myocardial infarctions. Several cross-sectional studies and one longitudinal descriptive epidemiological study addressed the differences between pet owners and non-owners in health indicators. Among 5,741 people attending a screening clinic in Melbourne, Australia, risk factors for coronary heart disease were significantly greater among the 4,957 pet non-owners than among the 784 pet owners. For men, plasma levels of cholesterol and triglycerides, and systolic BP were higher among pet non-owners than pet owners. For women, differences in risk factors between pet owners and non-owners occurred only for those women who are most susceptible to coronary heart disease, women in the menopausal and post-menopausal age groups (Anderson et al., 1992). A study of senior citizens ($n = 127$) also indicated that pet owners have lower serum triglyceride levels than non-owners (Dembicki and Anderson, 1996). In contrast, a random sample of 5,079 adults from Canberra and Queanbeyan, New South Wales, Australia, interviewed in 2000 and 2001—approximately 57% of whom were pet owners—revealed no significant reduction in cardiovascular risk factors for pet owners or in use of health services (Jorm et al., 1997; Parslow and Jorm, 2003). In fact, pet owners had higher diastolic BP after controlling for age, sex, and education than those without pets (Parslow and Jorm, 2003). When the older group—those 60 to 64 years old—was examined separately, there was no evidence for a health benefit (Parslow et al., 2005). Differences in patterns of pet ownership may be responsible for the apparent discrepancies. Pet ownership was considerably more common in the New South Wales survey than in Melbourne survey. Types of pets were not evaluated in the New South Wales survey.

In several surveys, owning a pet was related to proxies for physiological health such as medical visits, number of health problems, or functional status. In large representative sample surveys of the populations of Germany and Australia, after taking into account demographic predictors of health status, people who owned pets made fewer medical visits than those who did not (Headey et al., 2002). In the USA, pet owners ($n = 345$) among the 938 Medicare enrollees in an HMO reported fewer medical visits including both fewer total doctor contacts and fewer respondent-initiated medical contacts over a one-year period than non-owners (Siegel, 1990). Further analyses of the data indicated that pet ownership was a significant moderator of the impact of psychological distress on doctor contacts, independent of the effects of health status, depressed mood, and other demographic factors. For individuals who did not own pets, psychosocial distress, as assessed by stressful life events, was directly correlated with doctor contacts; the higher the stress level, the more contacts. However, for pet owners increased stress levels did not predict more physician contacts. There was also evidence for differences in the effects of dogs and other pets on health as assessed by health behavior. For individuals who did not own dogs, doctor contacts increased as life events increased. In contrast, among dog owners, life events were unrelated to respondent initiated doctor contacts.

A Canadian longitudinal telephone survey of adults 65 years and older also supported a positive impact of pet ownership on respondent's ($n = 995$) ability to complete activities of daily living at study entry and one year later. After controlling for physical activity, age, and living situation, the ability to complete activities of daily living decreased more in one year for people who did not own pets than for people who kept them (Raina et al., 1999).

One of the major questions arising in studies finding an association of pet ownership with health status is whether the data are due to people with better health status choosing to own or interact with pets. If so, the better health could predate the pet exposure. Thus, the causal relationship would begin with better health status and end with pet ownership. The question of which came first, pet ownership or better health was addressed in a novel longitudinal study. A cohort of 343 people entered into a population study in 1921 was asked in 1977 about their history of playing with pets; this was then followed for 15 years. In 1977, there was no relationship of pet-related behavior to long-term survival. This was true even when looking separately at individuals with low social support (Tucker et al., 1995). These data do not support the supposition that better health predates or causes more interaction with pets.

Introduction of an animal into a living situation can lead to improved health status. Adopting a pet was associated with improved health status for the adopters (Serpell, 1991). People who adopted dogs or cats from an animal shelter ($n = 71$) experienced significant reductions in minor health problems including headaches, hay fever, painful joints, one month after adopting the pet. Dog adopters ($n = 47$) maintained the decrease in minor health problems over the 10-month duration of the study; cat owners did not. In this study, dog owners both appeared to walk slightly more at baseline and reported increased frequency and duration of walking at 10 months. This suggests the possibility that adoption of a cat could have encouraged the owner to spend additional time at home and thus forego walks. The physiological benefits associated with acquiring a dog could have been the result of increased physical activity engendered in walking the animal. In fact, the absence of long-term benefits for cat owners supports this possibility. However, those who adopted dogs already tended to walk more at baseline than those who adopted other animals and the control group. The differences in walking may have been a reflection of other differences in lifestyle and availability of time for walking and caring for a dog. Differences in the health experience of those who adopted dogs and cats also may be confounded by differences in stressful life events. Introducing pets and plants into nursing homes similarly was associated with improvement in minor health problems as evidenced by reduction in amount spent on medications (Montague, 1995).

Dog and cat ownership might have different associations with health status as evidenced by two case control studies (Friedmann and Thomas, 1995; Rajack, 1997) and two longitudinal studies (Serpell, 1991; Siegel, 1990). Too few pet owners own only other species in these studies to begin to explore differences in health among them. The mechanisms for differences in health status of dog and cat owners as well as which aspects of health might be affected by each species remains to be evaluated. Apparent difference in health benefits of dog and cat ownership, with the exception of exercise-related benefits, many be reflections of differences between people who choose to own different species (Serpell, 1991).

6.4   Experimental or quasi-experimental research

In an attempt to understand how, from a physiological perspective, pets provide the benefits detailed above, a number of researchers have investigated the short-term effects of companion animals on people. These short-term effects, measured on the time scale of minutes rather than months or years, may be the bases for the long-term effects demonstrated in epidemiological studies as well as for other more subtle effects of pet ownership.

The vast majority of the studies of the effect of animals on human physiology utilize experimental techniques in which the physiological effect of an image of an animal or an animal stimulus is measured. Although the epidemiological studies cited above include pets of all types, a majority of the studies of the short-term impact of animals on human physiology are limited to the effects of dogs. This is largely a matter of convenience because dogs are kept as pets so frequently and they are easy to handle. In the research investigating the short-term stress-reducing effects of animals, two types of potential health benefits were investigated: direct effects on physiological indicators of stress and stress moderating or buffering effects. The experimental and quasi-experimental studies investigate whether explicitly and/or implicitly observing animals is associated with direct effects on people's physiology or associated with moderating people's stress responses. Researchers have evaluated people's responses to three different exposures to animals: (1) people explicitly looking at or observing animals or pictures of animals, (2) people implicitly observing or being in the presence of animals, and (3) people touching or interacting with animals.

6.4.1   Effects of explicitly looking at or observing animals or pictures of animals

Studies of the impact of looking at or observing animals document the direct impact of animals on people's responses to scenes and the people in them (Lockwood, 1983; Rossbach and Wilson, 1992) and examine the physiologic indicators of parasympathetic nervous system arousal while and/or immediately after watching animals (i.e. Eddy, 1996, 1995; Globisch et al., 1999; Katcher et al., 1983). Only one research group (Katcher et al., 1983) addressed the effect of explicitly looking at or observing animals on people's responses to stressors.

Friendly domestic animals have been used effectively in the advertising and publicity industries to impute safety, believability, and trustworthiness to people who accompany them (Lockwood, 1983). Research supports the positive influence of looking at animals on some of people's moods and perceptions. Young adults rated scenes and the people depicted in pictorial scenes were rated as significantly more friendly (Lockwood, 1983), less threatening (Lockwood, 1983), happier (Lockwood, 1983; Rossbach et al., 1992) and more relaxed (Rossbach et al., 1992). In contrast pictures of animals culturally associated with fear elicited negative feelings and physiological arousal (Globisch et al., 1999).

Physiological indicators of parasympathetic nervous system arousal also indicate that looking at or observing domestic animals is associated with relaxation. Blood pressures of normotensive and hypertensive adults decreased progressively while watching fish swim in an aquarium (Katcher et al., 1983). The duration of the decreases was greater when observing an aquarium with fish than when looking at an aquarium with plants and moving water but without fish and than when looking at a wall.

Looking at familiar non-domestic animals can lead to decreases in physiologic arousal. The BPs and HRs of a chimpanzee's caretaker and research assistants who assisted with the chimpanzee ($n = 9$) tended to be lower while watching the chimps than during a relaxation period (Eddy, 1995). In a single case report, the BP and HR of a 26-year-old male snake owner was lower during a six-minute period of watching his pet than during the preceding six minutes when he sat alone and relaxed (Eddy, 1996).

The potential stress response-moderating effects of watching animals first were in a study of the physiological impact of watching fish swim in an aquarium (Katcher et al., 1983). Blood pressure increases in response to reading aloud were less pronounced after watching fish than after watching other stimuli.

The studies of people observing fish and chimpanzees indicate that observing animals from a safe position often encourages people to relax. The constant motion of the animals studied in this context characteristically attracts the observer's attention. The evidence presented through the comparison of the fish in the aquarium with the fishless aquarium and the wall support the contention that this attraction might be a prerequisite for continued relaxation over a longer time span (Katcher, 1981). Katcher suggested the biophilia hypothesis as one reason for people's extended attention to the fish swimming in the tank compared with other stimuli. The data obtained during observation of loud, rambunctious chimpanzees suggest that profound tranquility and serenity might not be prerequisites for the decreased parasympathetic nervous system arousal while watching animals (Friedmann et al., 2000).

6.4.2   Effects of implicitly observing or being in the presence of an animal

Observing or being in the presence of animals without being instructed to attend to them impacts both indicators of physiological arousal (Friedmann et al., 1983) and moderates the stress response. This situation contrasts with the previous group of studies where individuals were directed explicitly to focus on the animals.

The presence of a dog accompanying a researcher had direct impact on cardio-vascular and psychological indicators of arousal. In a study of BPs in the home setting, children's ($n = 38$) BPs during the entire experiment were lower among those who had the dog present for the first half of the experiment than those who had the dog present for the second half of the experiment (Friedmann et al., 1983).

The effect of the presence of a friendly dog on the stress response to several stressors has been evaluated. The presence of a friendly dog attenuated the cardio-vascular stress responses of 38, 9- to 15- year-old children to reading aloud (Fried-mann et al., 1983). In a similar study conducted among college students ($n = 193$), the presence of a dog caused significant moderation of HR, but not BP responses (Locker, 1985). In a group of 11 community-living older adults with slightly elevated BP, during a social stressor, talking about their normal daily activities, were 7/2 mmHg lower with a companion animal present than without a companion animal present (Friedmann et al., 2007).

The presence of a dog moderated responses to cognitive stressors in some situations but not others. Neither BP nor HR responses to two cognitive stressors, mental arithmetic and oral interpretation of drawings, differed between dog owning college students accompanied by their dogs and those who were not accompanied by their dogs (Grossberg et al., 1988). In contrast, in a study of women's ($n = 45$, mean age $= 39$ years) cardiovascular stress responses, the presence of a dog led to reduced cardiovascular reactivity compared with the presence of another person, even when the person was chosen by the subject to provide support (Allen et al., 1991). Extending this study, the cardiovascular reactivity of married couples ($n = 240$) to stressors while one member of the couple was alone, with a pet or friend, with their spouse, or with their spouse and their pet was examined. People who owned pets had lower resting BPs and experienced less of an increase in BP during cold pressor tests and mental arithmetic than non-owners. Among pet owners, their smallest responses to the stressful tasks was when the pet was present (Allen et al., 2002). The authors concluded that the non-judgmental aspect of the support afforded by the pet was responsible for decreasing the stress response. This is consistent with other research indicating greater stress responses in the presence of more judgmental or authoritative individuals (Long et al., 1982).

A study of the effects of the presence of an animal on women's cardiovascular responses to a number of everyday stressors in the normal home environment led to different results (Rajack, 1997). There were no differences in the cardiovascular responses of dog owners with their dogs present ($n = 30$) and non-owners ($n = 30$) to running up and down the stairs, and reading aloud. Dog owners tended to have greater HR responses to hearing the alarm clock sound. On the basis of the research summarized above, the presence of an animal has the potential to influence stress responses but does not do so uniformly.

Attitudes toward animals impact the stress buffering effects of the presence of an animal; not all individuals respond similarly. Recognizing that there is variability in individuals' responses to the presence of animals, researchers addressed the role of attitudes toward animals in the anti-arousal effects of animals of the same type (Friedmann et al., 1990). Cardiovascular stress responses in the presence of a dog were significantly lower for people with a more positive attitude toward dogs than for those with a more negative attitude toward dogs (Friedmann et al., 1990).

The research addressing the effects of implicitly watching or being in the presence of animals suggests that several factors may contribute to the effects of the presence of an animal on the stress response. These include the type and familiarity of the setting, type of stressor, perceptions about the type of animal, and relationship with the animal. For example, the stresses associated with either the setting itself or the nature of the task may overwhelm the stress moderating effects of the presence of the pet.

Based on the data presented, pet ownership is not necessary for individuals to receive stress-moderating benefits from the presence of a friendly animal. Positive perceptions of dogs promote their effectiveness at reducing people's stress responses (Friedmann et al., 1990). Since attitudes toward species are related to choice of pets (Serpell, 1981), particular effort will be required to separate the contributions of attitudes toward species and pet ownership itself to the stress moderating effects of animals.

6.4.3 Effects of interacting with animals

Interacting with a friendly animal, not necessarily one's own pet, leads to direct anti-arousal effects, but not necessarily to the stress moderating effects. Interacting with a pet by talking to and touching it were less stress inducing than talking or reading to other people (Baun et al., 1984; Jenkins, 1986; Katcher, 1981; Wilson, 1987). Blood pressures of dog owners ($n = 35$) recruited from a veterinary clinic waiting room were measured while they rested without their pets in a private consultation room, interacted with their pets, and read aloud without their pets in the same room (Katcher, 1981). Similarly, BPs and HRs were measured while self-selected undergraduate students ($n = 92$) read aloud, read quietly, and interacted with a friendly but unfamiliar dog (Wilson, 1987) or pet owners ($n = 20$) read aloud or interacted with their pets (Jenkins, 1986). In all three studies, none of the cardiovascular levels increased while interacting with a pet; however, they did increase significantly while reading aloud. The physiological effects of petting one's own pet and someone else's pet were compared (Baun et al., 1984). Blood pressures decreased significantly from the first to the final assessment when dog owners ($n = 24$) petted their own dogs but not when the same individuals petted the unfamiliar dog. These differences disappeared if the initial greeting response when the owner's own dog entered the room was omitted.

The direct physiological consequences of touching animals that are uncommon pets or zoo animals were addressed in studies of touching snakes (Alonso, 1999; Eddy, 1996) and chimps (Eddy, 1995). In a case study of one snake owner, BP during six minutes of touching his pet were lower than in the periods of relaxing and looking at the snake that preceded it (Eddy, 1996). In a study of snake non-owners who were not fearful of snakes ($n = 5$), BPs and HRs were not different when holding the snake, watching the snake, or relaxing (Alonso, 1999). BPs and HRs were higher when a chimpanzee's caretaker and assistants touched/tickled the chimps through a barrier than when they rested or observed the chimps through a barrier (Eddy, 1995). This occurred despite the subject's reported fondness for and lack of fear of the animals.

The stress moderating effect of touching animals has been investigated in one study to date (Straatman et al., 1997). After a baseline rest period, an unfamiliar small dog was placed in the laps of the men preparing and presenting a four-minute televised speech. There were no significant differences in cardiovascular stress responses between these men and men without a dog in their lap. Having a dog on the lap did not reduce the arousal associated with the tasks presented in this study.

The differences in arousal during interaction with animals suggest strongly that the individual's attitude toward an animal is of prime importance in determining whether touching that animal will enhance relaxation. The non-judgmental aspect of interacting with an animal compared with the demands of interacting with other people is frequently cited as a possible reason for the difference in physiological arousal during human/human and human/animal interactions (Allen et al., 1991, 2002; Friedmann et al., 1990; Katcher, 1981; Locker, 1985).

The variety of ways of physically interacting with animals and the difficulty of standardizing interactions and responses also inhibit research in this area. It is particularly difficult to evaluate the relative contributions of the physical movement and exertion during interaction and the contributions of the calming influences of the interaction with animals. During vigorous interaction, the arousal-moderating effects of the animal may be more than counteracted by the effects of the exertion on BP and HR.

Results of the one study addressing the stress moderating effect of interacting with animals (Straatman et al., 1997) highlight the possibility that the demands of the stressor might counteract the stress moderating effect of interaction with animals. A crucial factor appears to be the type of task the human/animal interaction was expected to moderate. Interaction with an animal may interfere with task completion and thus potentiate physiological arousal rather than relieving it.

6.5 Comparison of effects of presence of and interaction with animals

A final study specifically compared the stress responses of normotensive adults ($n = 50$) when a friendly animal (dog or goat) was present but the participants did not interact with it to when the animal was present and the participants were permitted to pat it. A third condition had no animal present. Blood pressure and HR increased during the cognitive stressor. Systolic BP, diastolic BP, and HR decreased more after the stressor if an animal was present, than if it was not. The reduction was greater in the situation where the person observed the animal than when interaction with the animal was permitted (DeMello, 1999).

As with other areas of research, the outcomes of studies addressing the physiological impact of friendly animals on cardiovascular status are influenced by the design of the studies. In studies of the effects of implicitly watching animals and those of evaluation of AAA, those with crossover research designs, in which the same individuals are exposed to both the animal present and animal absent condition, revealed stress moderating effects from the presence of friendly animals (Allen et al., 1991, 2002; Friedmann et al., 1990; Locker, 1985; Nagengast et al., 1997) and those without crossover designs did not (Grossberg et al., 1988; Hansen et al., 1999; Havener et al., 2001; Rajack, 1997). The ability of crossover designs, in which the same procedure is repeated both with and without an animal present, to evaluate both within subject and between subject variability is particularly important for dependent variables such as BP and HR, which vary tremendously from minute to minute and from person to person (Friedmann et al., 2000; Moody et al., 1996). This variability presents a significant challenge when moving to the natural setting. The combination of large variability and small sample size can make it very difficult to draw meaningful conclusions from studies, particularly those that appear to show that AAA, observing an animal, or interacting with an animal has no effect on the outcome of interest.

6.5.1 Clinical trials of pet interventions

When people hear about the effects of pet ownership on health, they frequently ask whether they should obtain a pet. The gold standard for evaluating the effectiveness of interventions is the randomized double blinded clinical trial in which individuals are randomly assigned to an intervention or a control/usual care group. In the case of "prescribing a pet," a double blind trial is not possible, because the participant knows whether a pet has been prescribed. It is, however, possible to conduct randomized trials. Two small studies gave pets to elderly individuals and observed changes in health without random assignment of pets. Although both showed improvements in health status among those who received a pet, the results could be related to differences between those individuals choosing to have a pet bird (Mugford and M'Comisky, 1975) or an aquarium rather than to obtaining a pet (Riddick, 1985). More recently, Allen et al. (2001) conducted a randomized trial of dog ownership. Men in a high stress occupation who were willing to keep dogs were randomly assigned to obtain dogs (therapy) or not (control/usual care). All patients received usual medication, an ACE inhibitor. Cardiovascular responses to mental stress were measured before the assignment of therapy and after 6 months of therapy. Resting BPs for all participants were lower after therapy than before. While the cardiovascular responses to mental stress did not differ before intervention in those men assigned to the two groups, after intervention the responses were lower in those who received pets.

6.6   Exercise-related health benefits from AAA and AAT

Several recent studies provide evidence that AAA have the potential to improve physical fitness and function. Physical activity is one of the strongest predictors of health and well-being throughout the life course and remains a major protective factor for morbidity and mortality in late life (Bean et al., 2004; Lollgen et al., 2009; Netz and Jacob, 1994; Resnick et al., 2006; Sundquist et al., 2004). Walking a dog addresses important barriers to people's physical activity (Ham and Epping, 2006). In focus groups, dog owners reported that their dog was a strong source of motivation, companionship and social support that encouraged them to walk with their dog (Cutt et al., 2008a). Furthermore, walking with a dog may provide greater cardiovascular benefit than walking alone. Older adult participants ($n = 13$) wore a portable electrocardiograph monitor to measure heart rate variability (HRV) while they walked for 30 minutes alone and for 30 minutes with an unfamiliar dog. The order of walking activities was varied randomly. Heart rate variability, which is associated with lower cardiac mortality, was significantly higher while walking with the dog than while walking alone (Motooka et al., 2006).

Large, national surveys indicate that dog owners exercise more than owners of other pets or pet non-owners (Anderson et al., 1992; Bauman et al., 2001; Dembicki et al., 1996). Among 5,741 people attending a screening clinic in Melbourne, Australia (Anderson et al., 1992), and Japanese adults completing an internet survey ($n = 5,177$) (Oka and Shibata, 2009), dog owners exercised more than other study participants. While dog owners were more likely to exercise than owners of other pets, there were no systematic differences in other health-related behaviors between pet owners and non-owners or between dog and cat owners (Dembicki et al., 1996). However, not all dog owners walk their dogs. Dog walking is related to meeting national recommendations for moderate to vigorous physical activity (Coleman et al., 2008). In one US national survey, among the 1,282 individuals who reported walking for pet care, 59% took two or more walks per day and 80% took at least one 10-minute daily walk (Ham and Epping, 2006).

In China in 1992, after decades of prohibiting pet ownership, a natural experiment in pet ownership provided an excellent opportunity to evaluate the impact of obtaining a pet on health-related behaviors and health. In a population-based survey of women residing in three cities in China, dog owners exercised for 20 minutes or more 36% more often than non-owners even after taking into account the effects of age, education, income, and other health-related variables on walking behavior (Headey et al., 2008). Two longitudinal studies indicated that acquiring a dog led to significant increases in walking (Cutt et al., 2008b; Serpell, 1991). Acquiring a dog led to significant increases in exercise within one month compared to acquiring a cat or not acquiring a pet. The improvement continued through to the end of the 10-month study (Serpell, 1991). In a longitudinal survey of a community sample among the people who did not own dogs ($n = 773$), those who acquired a dog in a one-year period also experienced a significant increase in recreational walking which was significantly greater than the increase in that same time period for people who did not acquire a dog (Cutt et al., 2008b).

Not only can exercising a dog increase walking, it can also increase the impact of the walking on cardiovascular health. For older adults, walking a dog improved cardiac function compared with walking alone (Motooka et al., 2006).

Dogs contribute to increased adherence with exercise. Long-term maintenance of exercise programs is notoriously poor, averaging about 50% (Morgan, 2001). One reason for low long-term adherence is that typical programs to promote physical activity do not promote purposeful activity (Morgan, 2001). Walking a dog has a purpose and thus can increase adherence. In addition to providing purposeful activity, dog walking may create a form of social support that has been identified as an effective behavioral strategy for increasing physical activity (Ham and Epping, 2006).

6.7   Discussion

Animal-assisted therapy is a promising intervention for improvement of people's physical health. A recent meta-analysis concludes that AAT provides a medium-sized beneficial effect for health outcomes. The lack of difference in effect size between studies that included control groups and those that did not was interpreted as strong evidence for the validity of the estimated effect size (Nimer and Lundahl, 2007). The most extensive documentation of the positive impact of animals on physical health comes from epidemiological studies that support long-term health effects of pet ownership, from experimental and quasi-experimental studies that support short-term impact of people explicitly looking at or observing animals, people implicitly observing or being in the presence of animals, and people touching or interacting with animals as well as from trials directly evaluating the impact of assignment to receive a pet. Large pets, especially dogs, provide an impetus for exercise and promote physical fitness through exercise. Animal-assisted therapy with dogs can provide motivation for physical activity and lead to enhanced physical fitness and health.

As the evidence for AAA affecting physiological aspects of human health increases, a number of broad issues about factors that might influence the appropriateness of AAA or AAT for a specific person or in a specific situation remain to be investigated. Issues arising in reference to each category of human/animal interaction are addressed within the section devoted to that topic. Broader questions, which require further research, include: (1) Do the effects of different types of animals on people's health or health indicators differ and if so what are the cultural, experiential and attitudinal bases for these differences? (2) What is the optimal duration of each session and frequency of sessions of AAA or AAT for specific health benefits? (3) Are the short-term direct or stress moderating physiological responses to animals the basis for the differences in health status found in the longer-term epidemiological studies? (4) Are there differences on the basis of sex or other demographic characteristics in the direct or stress moderating short term or the long-term differences in the health effects of animals? (5) Are animals more effective at moderating the effects of certain types of stressors than others? The final and perhaps most important theme is the necessity for optimal research design in studies attempting to address these issues.

We are not aware of studies directly comparing the effectiveness of different species for use in AAA or AAT. Behavioral studies of interactions of animals with people indicate that people respond differently to different animals. These data provide a concrete basis for testing a long-held assumption that individuals will have different physiological responses to different animals. Evidence from several epidemiological studies (Friedmann et al., 1995; Rajack, 1997; Serpell, 1991) demonstrates that different types of pets might have different impact on people's health and its underlying physiology. Furthermore, different groups of individuals may have different physiological responses to AAA as suggested by Miller's study of oxytocin responses of men and women (Miller et al., 2009).

The studies conducted to date focus primarily on the effects of friendly animals, and dogs in particular, on individuals' physiology. The effects of specific animals on individuals' physiology are likely based on individuals' previous direct and indirect experiences with as well as their beliefs, desires, and fears about specific species or even breeds (Friedmann et al., 2000). The interpretation of an animal as safe or unsafe might depend on early learning and/or personal experiences, even for animals that are culturally or innately defined as dangerous. The data presented suggest that individuals' responses to AAA with various species or even breeds are likely to differ according to individuals' perceptions of different animals.

Even within species, compatibility with a specific animal can affect health outcomes. For example, among pet owners ($n = 176$) those who are more compatible with their pets report fewer illness symptoms and better psychological well-being. This was not the case for attachment; pet attachment was associated with worse physical health (Budge et al., 1998). In a small survey of older Latino pet owners ($n = 24$) who indicated they were in good or excellent health, there was no relationship of pet attachment to self-perceived health or functional ability (Johnson and Meadows, 2002). Additional research directly addressing perceptions of and responses to a variety of animals and compatibility with specific animals would facilitate understanding in this area.

The physiological benefit from AAA will also depend on the recipient's psychological and health status at a specific time. A terminally ill cancer patient refused a pet visit because "I've always had animals in my life. I love them. But I don't want one now because I would want to take it home with me and I'm not going home" (Muschel, 1984, p. 456).

The research investigating the short-term effects of animals on human health included investigation of two types of potential health benefits: direct effects on physiological stress indicators and stress moderating or buffering effects. The experimental and quasi-experimental studies provide evidence that explicitly and implicitly observing animals can lead to both direct and stress moderating effects. Interacting with a friendly animal, not necessarily one's own pet, also leads to direct anti-arousal effects (Baun et al., 1984; Katcher, 1981; Wilson, 1987, 1991) but not to stress moderating effects (Straatman et al., 1997). Studies conducted to date have not addressed the likely effects from different types of human/animal interaction in a systematic comparative manner. Too many variables have been varied between studies to draw meaningful conclusions.

Additional research evidence supports both direct anti-arousal and stress moderating effects of explicitly looking at or observing animals and of implicitly observing animals. Research supports direct anti-arousal effects but not stress moderating effects of interaction with animals. Many of the studies examining direct or stress moderating benefits of animals differ from each other on the basis of two or more factors. Thus, while these studies provide important evidence that human/animal interactions have direct and stress moderating effects, it impossible to attribute the observed effects to specific variables. Systematic research delimiting the mechanisms for and factors contributing to both short- and long-term health benefits from these types of human/animal interactions and the mediators of these effects is sorely needed.

Animals may be unpleasant or stressful to some individuals. These individuals are routinely and appropriately excluded from studies of the health benefits of companion animals through the informed consent process or through activity selection.

Addition of an animal to a stressful situation may increase distress rather than alleviate it. Exacerbation of the stress response would exacerbate the negative health effects of stress rather than ameliorate them. Two studies support the importance of attending to this possibility (Craig et al., 2000; Straatman et al., 1997).

Dogs, among the more traditional pets, provide the special benefit of encouraging exercise. Older adults are among the most sedentary in the American population with those 65 and older most likely to engage in no leisure time physical activity at all and least likely to meet the current Surgeon General's recommendations for physical activity (Centers for Disease Control and Prevention, 2010; Matthews et al., 2008). Walking dogs has beneficial physiological effects. The combination of the physiological health benefits and the motivational aspects of walking with a dog make interventions using dog walking prime candidates for successful health benefits from interactions with animals.

Contact with animals or their refuse can also have severe detrimental physiological effects. Even small common companion animals can transmit infectious diseases, cause allergies, and inflict injuries such as bites and scratches (Morrison, 2001; Plaut et al., 1996). Several case reports indicate that pets may have negative health consequences for elderly owners including rotator cuff injuries and falls (Nair et al., 2004). The potential for physical injuries is generally minimized in AAT and AAA programs. There are few if any reports of zoonoses due to AAT or AAA. The dearth of reports could be due to a lack of such injuries, the lack of a central registry for making such reports, or poor recognition of the diseases. According to Brodie et al. (2002), the risks associated with zoonoses in the controlled environment of most medical or long-term care facilities are minimal. As AAT and AAA become more common and the number of immuno-compromised individuals increases, infection control policies and procedures geared toward management and prevention of zoonotic illnesses are crucial for all facilities that employ AAT (Guay, 2001; Robinson and Pugh, 2002).

6.7 Conclusion

A growing body of research supports the effectiveness of individual but not group AAA for reducing stress. Research addressing the effects of animals on human health and indicators of physiological arousal conducted to date provides intriguing evidence that animals can provide physiological benefits, particularly for cardiovascular health. Epidemiological studies indicate that owning pets is associated with better one-year survival of patients after myocardial infarctions, fewer health complaints, reduced use of medical resources, and fewer risk factors for cardiovascular disease. Owning or acquiring dogs may be more beneficial than having cats only. Dogs are associated with increased walking and exercise, which are linked with better health. Animal-assisted activities and AAT are differentially effective based on individual goals and characteristics. Additional evidence is required to understand the effective targeting of individuals for AAA or AAT.

References

Allen, K., Blascovich, J., & Mendes, W. (2002). Cardiovascular reactivity and the presence of pets, friends and spouses: the truth about cats and dogs. *Psychosomatic Medicine, 64*, 727–739.

Allen, K., Shykoff, B. E., & Izzo, J. L. (2001). Pet ownership, but not ACE inhibitor therapy, blunts home blood pressure responses to mental stress. *Hypertension, 38*, 815–820.

Allen, K. M., Blascovich, J., Tomaka, J., & Kelsey, R. M. (1991). Presence of human friends and pet dogs as moderators of autonomic responses to stress in women. *Journal of Personality and Social Psychology, 61*, 582–589.

Alonso, Y. (1999). Effect of pets on human health: is there a correlation? *Gesundheitswesen, 61*, 45–49.

Anderson, W., Reid, C., & Jennings, G. (1992). Pet ownership and risk factors for cardio-vascular disease. *Medical Journal of Australia, 157*, 298–301.

Arato, M., Banki, C. M., Nemeroff, C. B., & Bissette, G. (1986). Hypothalamic-pituitary-adrenal axis and suicide. *Annals of the New York Academy of Sciences, 487*, 263–270.

Audy, J. R. (1971). Measurement and diagnosis of health. In P. Shepard & D. McKinley (Eds.), *Environmental Essays on the Planet as Home* (pp. 140–162). Boston, MA: Houghton Mifflin.

Banki, C. M., Karmacsi, L., Bissette, G., & Nemeroff, C. B. (1992). CSF corticotropin-releasing hormone and somatostatin in major depression: response to antidepressant treatment and relapse. *European Neuropsychopharmacology, 2*, 107–113.

Barker, S. B., Knisely, J. S., McCain, N. L., & Best, A. M. (2005). Measuring stress and immune response in healthcare professionals following interaction with a therapy dog: a pilot study. *Psychological Reports, 96*, 713–729.

Bauman, A. E., Russell, S. J., Furber, S. E., & Dobson, A. J. (2001). The epidemiology of dog walking: an unmet need for human and canine health. *Medical Journal of Australia, 175*, 632–634.

Baun, M. M., Bergstrom, N., Langston, N. F., & Thoma, L. (1984). Physiological effects of human/companion animal bonding. *Nursing Research, 33*, 126–129.

Baun, M. M., Oetting, K., & Bergstrom, N. (1991). Health benefits of companion animals in relation to the physiologic indices of relaxation. *Holistic Nursing Practice, 5*, 16–23.

Bean, J. F., Vora, A., & Frontera, W. R. (2004). Benefits of exercise for community-dwelling older adults. *Archives of Physical Medicine and Rehabilitation, 85*, S31–S42.

Brodie, S. J., Biley, F. C., & Shewring, M. (2002). An exploration of the potential risks associated with using pet therapy in healthcare settings. *Journal of Clinical Nursing, 11*, 444–456.

Budge, R. C., Spicer, J., Jones, B., & St. George, R. (1998). Health correlates of compatibility and attachment in human-companion animal relationships. *Society and Animals, 6*, 219–234.

Centers for Disease Control and Prevention. (2010). U.S. Physical Activity Statistics. http://apps.nccd.cdc.gov/PASurveillance/DemoCompareResultV.asp?State=0&Cat=1&Year=2007&Go=GO#result [Online] Dec. 5, 2009.

Cole, K. M., & Gawlinski, A. (2000). Animal-assisted therapy: the human-animal bond. *AACN Clinical Issues, 11*, 139–149.

Cole, K. M., Gawlinski, A., Steers, N., & Kotlerman, J. (2007). Animal-assisted therapy in patients hospitalized with heart failure. *American Journal of Critical Care, 16*, 575–585.

Coleman, K. J., Rosenberg, D. E., Conway, T. L., Sallis, J. F., Saelens, B. E., Frank, L. D., et al. (2008). Physical activity, weight status, and neighborhood characteristics of dog walkers. *Preventive Medicine, 47*, 309–312.

Corbalan, R., Verrier, R. L., & Lown, B. (1974). Psychological stress and ventricular arrhythmia during myocardial infarction in the conscious dog. *American Journal of Cardiology, 34*, 692–696.

Craig, F., Lynch, J. J., & Quartner, J. L. (2000). The perception of available social support is related to reduced cardiovascular reactivity in phase II cardiac rehabilitation patients. *Integrative Physiological and Behavioral Science, 35*, 272–283.

Cutt, H. E., Giles-Corti, B., Wood, L. J., Knuiman, M. W., & Burke, V. (2008a). Barriers and motivators for owners walking their dog: results from qualitative research. *Health Promotion Journal of Australia, 19*, 118–124.

Cutt, H. E., Knuiman, M. W., & Giles-Corti, B. (2008b). Does getting a dog increase recreational walking? *International Journal of Behavioral Nutrition and Physical Activity, 5*, 17.

Dembicki, D., & Anderson, J. (1996). Pet ownership may be a factor in improved health of the elderly. *Journal of Nutrition for the Elderly, 15*, 15–31.

DeMello, L. R. (1999). The effect of the presence of a companion-animal on physiological changes following the termination of cognitive stressors. *Psychology and Health, 14*, 859–868.

DeSilva, R. A., Verrier, R. L., & Lown, B. (1978). The effects of psychological stress and vagal stimulation with morphine on vulnerability to ventricular fibrillation (VF) in the conscious dog. *American Heart Journal, 95*, 197–203.

Eddy, T. J. (1995). Human cardiac responses to familiar young chimpanzees. *Anthrozoös, 4*, 235–243.

Eddy, T. J. (1996). RM and Beaux: reductions in cardiac activity in response to a pet snake. *Journal of Nervous and Mental Disease, 184*, 573–575.

Edwards, N. E., & Beck, A. M. (2002). Animal-assisted therapy and nutrition in Alzheimer's disease. *Western Journal of Nursing Research, 24*, 697–712.

Friedmann, E., Katcher, A. H., Lynch, J. J., & Thomas, S. A. (1980). Animal companions and one-year survival of patients after discharge from a coronary care unit. *Public Health Report, 95*, 307–312.

Friedmann, E., Katcher, A. H., Thomas, S. A., Lynch, J. J., & Messent, P. R. (1983). Social interaction and blood pressure: influence of animal companions. *Journal of Nervous and Mental Disease, 171*, 461–465.

Friedmann, E., & Thomas, S. A. (1985). Health benefits of pets for families. *Marriage and Family Review, 4*, 191–203.

Friedmann, E., & Thomas, S. A. (1995). Pet ownership, social support, and one-year survival after acute myocardial infarction in the Cardiac Arrhythmia Suppression Trial (CAST). *American Journal of Cardiology, 76*, 1213–1217.

Friedmann, E., Thomas, S. A., Cook, L. K., & Picot, S. J. (2007). A friendly dog as potential moderator of cardiovascular response to speech in older hypertensives. *Anthrozoös, 20*, 51–63.

Friedmann, E., Thomas, S. A., & Eddy, T. J. (2000). Companion animals and human health: physical and cardiovascular influences. In A. L. Podberscek, E. Paul & J. A. Serpell (Eds.), *Companion Animals and Us: Exploring the Relationships between People and Pets* (pp. 125–142). Cambridge, UK: Cambridge University Press.

Friedmann, E., Zuck Locker, B., & Lockwood, R. (1990). Perception of animals and cardiovascular responses during verbalization with an animal present. *Anthrozoös, 6,* 115–134.

Globisch, J., Hamm, A. O., Esteves, F., & Ohman, A. (1999). Fear appears fast: temporal course of startle reflex potentiation in animal fearful subjects. *Psychophysiology, 36,* 66–75.

Grossberg, J. M., Alf, E. F., Jr., & Vormbrock, J. K. (1988). Does pet dog presence reduce human cardiovascular responses to stress? *Anthrozoös, 2,* 38–44.

Guay, D. R. (2001). Pet-assisted therapy in the nursing home setting: potential for zoonosis. *American Journal of Infection Control, 29,* 178–186.

Ham, S. A., & Epping, J. (2006). Dog walking and physical activity in the United States. *Preventing Chronic Disease, 3,* A47.

Hansen, K. M., Messenger, C. J., Baun, M., & Megel, M. E. (1999). Companion animals alleviating distress in children. *Anthrozoös, 12,* 142–148.

Havener, L., Gentes, L., Thaler, B., Megel, M. E., Baun, M. M., Driscoll, F. A., et al. (2001). The effects of a companion animal on distress in children undergoing dental procedures. *Issues in Comprehensive Pediatric Nursing, 24,* 137–152.

Headey, B., Grabka, M., & Kelley, J. (2002). Pet ownership is good for your health and saves public expenditure too: Australian and German longitudinal evidence. *Australian Social Monitor, 4,* 93–99.

Headey, B., Na, F., & Zheng, R. (2008). Pet dogs benefit owners' health: a "Natural Experiment" in China. *Social Indicators Research, 87,* 481–493.

Jenkins, C. D. (1976a). Medical progress. Recent evidence supporting psychologic and social risk factors for coronary disease (first of two parts). *New England Journal of Medicine, 294,* 987–994.

Jenkins, C. D. (1976b). Recent evidence supporting psychologic and social risk factors for coronary disease. *New England Journal of Medicine, 294,* 1033–1038.

Jenkins, J. (1986). Physiological effects of petting a companion animal. *Psychological Reports, 58,* 21–22.

Johnson, R. A., & Meadows, R. L. (2002). Older Latinos, pets, and health. *Western Journal of Nursing Research, 24,* 609–620.

Jorm, A. F., Jacomb, P. A., Christensen, H., Henderson, S., Korten, A. E., & Rodgers, B. (1997). Impact of pet ownership on elderly Australians' use of medical services: an analysis using Medicare data. *Medical Journal of Australia, 166,* 376–377.

Julius, S., & Nesbitt, S. D. (1996). Sympathetic nervous system as a coronary risk factor in hypertension. *Cardiologia, 41,* 309–317.

Kaminski, M., Pellino, T., & Wish, J. (2002). Play and pets: the physical and emotional impact of child-life and pet therapy on hospitalized children. *Children's Health Care, 31,* 321–335.

Katcher, A. H. (1981). Interactions between people and their pets: form and function. In B. Fogle (Ed.), *Interrelationships between People and Pets* (pp. 41–67). Springfield, IL: Charles C. Thomas.

Katcher, A. H., Friedmann, E., Beck, A. M., & Lynch, J. J. (1983). Talking, looking, and blood pressure: physiological consequences of interaction with the living environment. In A. H. Katcher & A. M. Beck (Eds.), *New Perspectives on Our Lives with Animal Companions* (pp. 351–359). Philadelphia, PA: University of Pennsylvania Press.

Lampert, R., Jain, D., & Burg, M. M. (2000). Destabilizing effects of mental stress on ventricular arrhythmias in patients with implantable cardioverter-defibrillators. *Circulation, 101,* 158–164.

Locker, B. Z. (1985). *The cardiovascular response to verbalization in type A and type B individuals in the presence of a dog.* New York University. PhD.

Lockwood, R. (1983). The influence of animals on social perception. In A. H. Katcher & A. M. Beck (Eds.), *New Perspectives on Our Lives with Animal Companions* (pp. 64–71). Philadelphia, PA: University of Pennsylvania Press.

Lollgen, H., Bockenhoff, A., & Knapp, G. (2009). Physical activity and all-cause mortality: an updated meta-analysis with different intensity categories. *International Journal of Sports Medicine, 30,* 213–224.

Long, J. M., Lynch, J. J., Machiran, N. M., Thomas, S. A., & Malinow, K. L. (1982). The effect of status on blood pressure during verbal communication. *Journal of Behavioral Medicine, 5,* 165–172.

Louis, W. J., Doyle, A. E., & Anavekar, S. N. (1975). Plasma noradrenaline concentration and blood pressure in essential hypertension, phaeochromocytoma and depression. *Clinical Science and Molecular Medicine Supplement, 2,* 239s–242s.

Matthews, C. E., Chen, K. Y., Freedson, P. S., Buchowski, M. S., Beech, B. M., Pate, R. R., et al. (2008). Amount of time spent in sedentary behaviors in the United States, 2003–2004. *American Journal of Epidemiology, 167,* 875–881.

McEwen, B. S. (1998). Stress, adaptation, and disease. Allostasis and allostatic load. *Annals of the New York Academy of Science, 840,* 33–44.

Miller, S. C., Kennedy, C., DeVoe, D., Hickey, M., Nelson, T., & Kogan, L. (2009). An examination of changes in oxytocin levels in men and women before and after interaction with a bonded dog. *Anthrozoös, 22,* 31–42.

Montague, J. (1995). Continuing care—back to the garden. *Hospitals and Health Networks, 69* (58), 60.

Moody, W. J., Fenwick, D. C., & Blackshaw, J. K. (1996). Pitfalls of studies designed to test the effect pets have on the cardiovascular parameters of their owners in the home situation: a pilot study. *Applied Animal Behaviour Science, 47,* 127–136.

Morgan, W. P. (2001). Prescription of physical activity: a paradigm shift. *Quest, 53,* 366–382.

Morrison, G. (2001). Zoonotic infections from pets. Understanding the risks and treatment. *Postgraduate Medicine, 110,* 24–30, 35.

Motooka, M., Koike, H., Yokoyama, T., & Kennedy, N. L. (2006). Effect of dog-walking on autonomic nervous activity in senior citizens. *Medical Journal of Australia, 184,* 60–63.

Mugford, R. A., & M'Comisky, J. G. (1975). Some recent work on the psychotherapeutic value of cage birds for old people. In R. S. Anderson (Ed.), *Pet Animals and Society* (pp. 54–65). London: Bailliere Tindall.

Muschel, I. J. (1984). Pet therapy with terminal cancer patients. *Journal of Contemporary Social Work,* Oct., 451–458.

Musselman, D. L., Evans, D. L., & Nemeroff, C. B. (1998). The relationship of depression to cardiovascular disease: epidemiology, biology, and treatment. *Archives of General Psychiatry, 55,* 580–592.

Nagengast, S. L., Baun, M., Megel, M. M., & Leibowitz, J. M. (1997). The effects of the presence of a companion animal on physiological arousal and behavioral distress in children during a physical examination. *Journal of Pediatric Nursing, 12,* 323–330.

Nair, B. R., Flynn, B., & McDonnell, M. (2004). Pet owners and risk factors in cardiovascular disease. *Medical Journal of Australia, 180,* 144.

Nemeroff, C. B., Widerlov, E., Bissette, G., Walleus, H., Karlsson, I., Eklund, K., et al. (1984). Elevated concentrations of CSF corticotropin-releasing factor-like immunoreactivity in depressed patients. *Science, 226,* 1342–1344.

Netz, Y., & Jacob, T. (1994). Exercise and the psychological state of institutionalized elderly: a review. *Perceptual and Motor Skills, 79*, 1107–1118.

Nimer, J., & Lundahl, B. (2007). Animal-assisted therapy: a meta-analysis. *Anthrozoös, 20*, 225–238.

Oka, K., & Shibata, A. (2009). Dog ownership and health-related physical activity among Japanese adults. *Journal of Physical Activity and Health, 6*, 412–418.

Orlandi, M., Trangeled, K., Mambrini, A., Tagliani, M., Ferrarini, A., Zanetti, L., et al. (2007). Pet therapy effects on oncological day hospital patients undergoing chemotherapy treatment. *Anticancer Research, 27*, 4301–4303.

Parslow, R. A., & Jorm, A. F. (2003). Pet ownership and risk factors for cardiovascular disease: another look. *Medical Journal of Australia, 179*, 466–468.

Parslow, R. A., Jorm, A. F., Christensen, H., Rodgers, B., & Jacomb, P. (2005). Pet ownership and health in older adults: findings from a survey of 2,551 community-based Australians aged 60–64. *Gerontology, 51*, 40–47.

Pasic, J., Levy, W. C., & Sullivan, M. D. (2003). Cytokines in depression and heart failure. *Psychosomatic Medicine, 65*, 181–193.

Plaut, M., Zimmerman, E. M., & Goldstein, R. A. (1996). Health hazards to humans associated with domestic pets. *Annual Review of Public Health, 17*, 221–245.

Raina, P., Waltner-Toews, D., Bonnett, B., Woodward, C., & Abernathy, T. (1999). Influence of companion animals on the physical and psychological health of older people: an analysis of a one-year longitudinal study. *Journal of the American Geriatric Society, 47*, 323–329.

Rajack, L. S. (1997). *Pets and human health: the influence of pets on cardiovascular and other aspects of owners' health.* Cambridge, UK: University of Cambridge. PhD.

Resnick, B., Ory, M., Hora, K., Rogers, M., Page, P., Lyle, R., et al. (2006). Screening for and prescribing exercise for older adults. *Geriatrics and Aging, 9*, 174–182.

Riddick, C. C. (1985). Health, aquariums, and the non-institutionalized elderly. In M. B. Sussman (Ed.), *Pets and the Family* (pp. 163–173). New York: Haworth Press.

Robinson, R. A., & Pugh, R. N. (2002). Dogs, zoonoses and immunosuppression. *Journal of the Royal Society of Health, 122*, 95–98.

Rossbach, K. A., & Wilson, J. P. (1992). Does a dog's presence make a person appear more likeable? *Anthrozoös, 5*, 40–51.

Rozanski, A., Blumenthal, J. A., & Kaplan, J. (1999). Impact of psychological factors on the pathogenesis of cardiovascular disease and implications for therapy. *Circulation, 99*, 2192–2217.

Schwartz, A., & Patronek, G. (2002). Methodological issues in studying the anxiety-reducing effects of animals: reflections from a pediatric dental study. *Anthrozoös, 15*, 291–299.

Serpell, J. A. (1981). Childhood pets and their influence on adults' attitudes. *Psychological Reports, 49*, 651–654.

Serpell, J. A. (1991). Beneficial effects of pet ownership on some aspects of human health and behaviour. *Journal of the Royal Society of Medicine, 84*, 717–720.

Siegel, J. M. (1990). Stressful life events and use of physician services among the elderly: the moderating role of pet ownership. *Journal of Personality and Social Psychology, 58*, 1081–1086.

Skinner, J. E. (1985). Regulation of cardiac vulnerability by the cerebral defense system. *Journal of the American College of Cardiology, 5*, 88B–94B.

Skinner, J. E. (1981). Blockade of frontocardial-brain stem pathway prevents ventricular fibrillation of ischemic heart. *American Journal of Physiology, 240*, 156–163.

Sterling, P. (2003). Principles of allostasis: optimal design, predictive regulation, pathophysiology and rational therapeutics. In J. Shulkin (Ed.), *Allostasis, Homeostasis, and the Costs of Adaptation*. Cambridge, MA: MIT Press.

Straatman, I., Hanson, E. K. S., Endenburg, N., & Mol, J. A. (1997). The influence of a dog on male students during a stressor. *Anthrozoös, 10*, 191–197.

Sundquist, K., Qvist, J., Sundquist, J., & Johansson, S. E. (2004). Frequent and occasional physical activity in the elderly: a 12-year follow-up study of mortality. *American Journal of Preventive Medicine, 27*, 22–27.

Thomas, S. A., Friedmann, E., Khatta, M., Cook, L. K., & Lann, A. L. (2003). Depression in patients with heart failure: physiologic effects, incidence, and relation to mortality. *AACN Clinical Issues, 14*, 3–12.

Thomas, S. A., Friedmann, E., Wimbush, F., & Schron, E. B. (1997). Psychological factors and survival in the cardiac arrhythmia suppression trial (CAST): a reexamination. *American Journal of Critical Care, 6*, 16–26.

Thomas, S. A., Liehr, P., DeKeyser, F., Frazier, L., & Friedmann, E. (2002). A review of nursing research on blood pressure. *Journal of Nursing Scholarship, 34*, 313–321.

Tucker, J. S., Friedman, H. S., Tsai, C. M., & Martin, L. R. (1995). Playing with pets and longevity among older people. *Psychology and Aging, 10*, 3–7.

Veith, R. C., Lewis, N., Linares, O. A., Barnes, R. F., Raskind, M. A., Villacres, E. C., et al. (1994). Sympathetic nervous system activity in major depression. Basal and desipramine-induced alterations in plasma norepinephrine kinetics. *Archives of General Psychiatry, 51*, 411–422.

Wells, D. L. (2005). The effect of videotapes of animals on cardiovascular responses to stress. *Stress and Health, 21*, 209–213.

Wilson, C. C. (1987). Physiological responses of college students to a pet. *Journal of Nervous and Mental Disease, 175*, 606–612.

Wu, A. S., Niedra, R., Pendergast, L., & McCrindle, B. W. (2002). Acceptability and impact of pet visitation on a pediatric cardiology inpatient unit. *Journal of Pediatric Nursing, 17*, 354–362.

Wyatt, R. J., Portnoy, B., Kupfer, D. J., Snyder, F., & Engelman, K. (1971). Resting plasma catecholamine concentrations in patients with depression and anxiety. *Archives of General Psychiatry, 24*, 65–70.

Part Two

Animal-Assisted Therapy: Conceptual Model and Guidelines for Quality Assurance

7 Animal selection procedures in animal-assisted interaction programs

Maureen Fredrickson-MacNamara MSW, CEIP *,
Kris Butler†

* Animal Systems, Ltd, † American Dog Obedience Center, LLC

7.1 Introduction

Today's animal-assisted interaction programs now place animal/handler teams into close relationship with people and into settings never imagined by the crafters of standards and selection procedures developed over 15 years ago. While the changing role of animals and the settings in which they work does not mean that previous work is irrelevant, these changes require taking a step back to reassess the objectives of selection procedures in light of new information and considerably more experience.

One of the primary changes in the practice of animal-assisted interactions is the mounting recognition of the value of animal contact by providers in the fields of human health, development, and education. The increased recognition is due, in part, to findings revealing that the incorporation of animals may result in positive progress toward human physical, cognitive, psychosocial, communication, and educational goals (Barker et al., 2003; Cole and Gawlinski, 2000; McGibbon et al., 1998; Marr et al., 2000; Odendaal, 2000). Concurrently, a dramatic increase in the expectations of animals and the handlers involved in animal-assisted interaction programs has occurred as health care and education providers must demonstrate a value to participants in order to justify any risk associated with animal contact (Beck, 2000). The skills and aptitude required of animals engaged in participant-specific medical, psychological, and educational applications is a role that is new, specific, and profound.

It is, therefore, imperative that selection procedures be based on the realities of the job that the animals are asked to perform. This chapter provides a brief overview of the development of selection procedures for animal/handler teams engaged in animal-assisted interactions. Additionally, the extent to which current procedures truly assess the specific behavioral repertoire and skills required of the animals and whether these practices provide an accurate picture of the animal's "fit" with participant specific applications is examined. Next, the chapter will compare and contrast the selection and training practices of animals engaged in animal-assisted interactions with the selection and training practices of other animal functions such as police work and

Handbook on Animal-Assisted Therapy. DOI: 10.1016/B978-0-12-381453-1.10007-8

competition. Finally, the chapter recommends the development of selection procedures that accurately reflect the role of the animal in moving adults and children
across the lifespan toward increased functional capacity. Throughout the chapter the
authors will focus primarily on the selection of dogs and horses as these two species
are most commonly encountered in animal-assisted interactions; however, it should
be noted that the selection of other animals most often follows either similar
procedures to dogs and horses or are included but lack specific procedures.

7.2   Description of terms

In order to consider carefully animal selection requirements, it is important to
understand how programs including animals in the delivery of services are defined,
with providers and volunteer organizations differing in how they characterize these
activities (Fredrickson, 2003). Animal-assisted interactions is a term which includes
two types of human/animal interactions: animal-assisted activities (AAA), or animal
visits, with spontaneous content, volunteer implementation, and no participant-
specific goals, and animal-assisted therapy (AAT), a specified interaction, implemented by a trained human health, welfare or education professional to meet explicit
participant-specific goals (Delta Society, 1996).

While no definition is perfect, the distinction between these two types of human/
animal interactions is by no means utilized with any regularity or predictability. This
chapter will utilize the term animal-assisted interactions to refer to these activities in
general and the term animal-assisted *applications* to refer to those interactions
meeting the definition of animal-assisted therapy as described above for the following
reasons.

First, many programs focus on the delivery of educational applications such as
reading improvement. Even though these programs may meet the animal-assisted
therapy criteria of explicit participant-specific goals, specified interactions, and
implemented by an education professional, labeling these applications as "therapy" is
confusing and misleading. Second, volunteer handlers and volunteer handler organizations often view the terms animal-assisted activities and animal-assisted therapy
from a hierarchical perspective,[1] perceiving animal-assisted activities as less than or
not as important as animal-assisted therapy (Fredrickson, 2003). Thus, the names of
animal/handler registries and in the titles given to animals involved in these programs
are most often associated with animal-assisted therapy (i.e. Therapy Dogs Inter-
national®). Third, most, if not all animals engaged in human/animal interaction
programs are referred to as a therapy animal (i.e. therapy horse, therapy dog) whether
the animal interaction consists of a volunteer implemented, spontaneous interaction
with no participant-specific goals or consists of specified interactions, implemented

---

[1] As past Vice President of Programs for the Delta Society, the first author facilitated terminology
discussions at national conferences of the Delta Society and North American Riding for the Handicapped
Association. Volunteers consistently stated that activities not meeting the criteria of specified interaction,
implemented by a trained human health, welfare or education professional to meet explicit participant-specific goals, were *therapeutic*, thus fitting the definition of animal-assisted therapy.

by a trained human health, welfare or education professional to meet explicit participant-specific goals. Finally, the majority of animal-assisted interaction programs are referred to as animal-assisted therapy even when the human/animal interaction lacks explicit participant-specific goals and specified interactions and is implemented by a volunteer rather than a trained human health, welfare or education professional (Katcher, 2000). This is an important point when considering the factors relevant to selecting animals for work directly with a medical, psychological or educational provider in a participant-specific application.

7.3   Animal selection procedures; a brief overview

In the 1970s, a majority of animal-assisted intervention programs incorporating companion animals were implemented by animal welfare organizations that encouraged volunteers to take animals in the shelter to visit people in nursing homes and other residential settings. The focus of the programs was to provide a recreational activity and a break from the monotony and isolation of residential living (Corson et al., 1975). However, by the 1990s, concerns about health risks associated with animals, fleas, ticks, bacterial diarrhea, a propensity to bite or scratch or jump on people when startled, and any number of other hazards had greatly reduced this practice. In addition, concerns for the welfare and health of the animals themselves were raised. The A.S.P.C.A. reported that, "visiting strange settings with unpredictable people and unusual noises stresses the animals, especially young animals that are awaiting adoption" (*Shelter Animals*, 1992). Therapeutic riding programs provided riding lessons as a recreational activity for adults and children with physical or cognitive disabilities who were excluded from other types of recreation. These programs had no structured approach to help guide the development of the animal-assisted interactions (Beck, 2000; Spink, 1993).

The programs of this era, primarily, utilized selection procedures intended to reduce the risk of contact with animals. For example, early dog selection procedures focused on public health risks such as species-specific diseases, parasites, injuries caused by bites or scratches, and injuries from a dog's interference with equipment or people (i.e. scratching, tripping someone or jumping on people). Similarly, horses were selected based on a steady nature, and their tractability around people with limited physical control and unusual equipment. Thus, the minimum selection criteria for the animals in these early programs included documentation of some form of animal behavioral screening by a veterinarian, evidence of routine veterinary care such as annual vaccinations, and internal and external parasite control (NARHA, 1994; New and Strimple, 1988).

During the 1980s, a number of studies carried out in a variety of institutional settings reported improvement in human functioning in a number of areas such as improved affect, decreases in aggression and better attendance in psychiatric sessions (Banziger and Roush, 1983; Brickel, 1984; Francis et al., 1985; Hendy, 1984; Kongable et al., 1989; Robb, 1983). The findings propelled the trend for long-term care facilities to acquire resident animals with risk management as the primary concern.

In 1983, *Guidelines: Animals in Nursing Homes* (Hines et al., 1983) recommended that prior to placing animals in the facility a full assessment should be performed including assessment of the social needs of residents, evaluation of the layout of the facility, and consideration of the role of the animals in the facility. The *Guidelines* did not address selection of animals that accompanied a non-professional volunteer or a staff member's pet which stayed during a particular shift. Health care providers, experienced volunteers and animal care and welfare professionals created recommendations for companion animals which continued to focus primarily on the medical and physical safety of the participants. The minimum selection criteria for animals included medical screening, temperament/behavioral evaluation, and methods to monitor the animals over time (New and Strimple, 1988). Visiting animals were most frequently screened by using puppy temperament tests and other breed-specific temperament evaluations.

At the same time, the appeal of integrating horses to benefit people with disabilities seemed to be greater to horsemen and riding instructors than to professionals in medicine, special education, and mental health. For volunteer providers in these programs, risk management remained the primary concern of selection procedures. Conversely, in a small number of equine-assisted applications in which the goal was the pursuit of specific clinical and remedial applications (i.e. hippotherapy), horses were also evaluated in terms of the quality of the gaits as the horse's movement directly affects the rider's posture, balance and coordination (Glasow and Spink, 1992).

By the 1990s, a plethora of not-for-profit organizations were launched by pet owners (rather than professionals in medical, psychological or educational fields) to identify volunteers and their pets that had passed generalized screening procedures are were considered safe to visit. Approved animal/volunteer teams visited any number of different institutions. Volunteers included people who visited, handling their own pets (dogs, cats, rabbits), and those who handled resident animals that participants could visit within farm and therapeutic riding programs. Thus it became important not only to determine risk of contact with animals but also to identify the ways in which the handler influenced the animal. Screening procedures once designed with the animal as its exclusive focus now began to explicate the expectations of the person presenting the animal (i.e. the handler) (Hines and Fredrickson, 1998).

Concurrently, the first standards for human/animal interactions were published. *Standards of Practice for Animal-Assisted Therapy and Animal-Assisted Activities* (Delta Society, 1996) combined recommendations made in guidelines for placing resident animals with public health concerns. Thus the Standards not only defined the different types of human/animal interactions but also described animal selection procedures based on broad criteria, such as reliability, predictability, controllability, and suitability, in order to address the majority of risk management concerns encountered in a variety of facilities (Fredrickson and Howie, 2000). The Standards provided a framework to shift the focus of selection procedures from an exclusive concern for the medical and physical safety of participants to considerations for handler skill and concerns for the impact of the facility on the animal. This was also true for standards for therapeutic riding programs or farm programs.

Since the advent of the twenty-first century, high profile events such as school shootings and the terrorist attacks of 9/11 fueled the desire of a variety of individuals to share their pets with others. As a result, animal-assisted interactions implemented through non-professional, volunteer organizations expanded into increasingly chaotic and unpredictable settings such as schools and mental health treatment facilities. To justify the increased risk and secure acceptance within the health care and education industry, national companion animal and equine organizations recommended expanded selection procedures to identify the ways in which a number of variables within the whole environment, not just a particular facility, influenced animal behavior (Fredrickson-MacNamara and Butler, 2006).

These recommendations left plenty of room for community-based organizations to develop selection procedures tailored to determine the degree to which the animal/ handler team possessed the skills and aptitude needed in a specific environment. Few, if any, organizations have taken this step; instead crafting selection procedures that use a single procedure that attempts to determine the appropriateness of an animal/ handler team in any type of environment with little or no regard for the different applications that might be utilized within any given environment.

In addition, most selection procedures are carried out at two-year intervals with the animal considered appropriate for work during the length of this time but without consideration for events that may alter the animal's behavior or health. In a study of horse temperament tests, researchers concluded that only a small number of behavioral parameters were consistent beyond the first year (Visser et al., 2001). This raises concerns regarding current testing practices as many require retesting at a variety of intervals ranging from only once in the animal's life to every two years.

Currently, the perception that animal-assisted applications are a valid modality for improvement in participant functioning among providers of health, mental health, and education services has increased significantly. However, along with the increased acceptance of animal-assisted applications has come a heightened requirement for these interactions to result in progress toward participant-specific goals. Choosing the best animal for a specific participant for a given medical, psychological or educational application requires more information than is provided by selection procedures designed for interactions that consist of spontaneous content and no participant-specific goals. Thus, an activity such as walking a dog must result in improvement in *measurable* goals identified in the participant's individual treatment or education plan. It is also important to understand the attributes of an animal that are most likely to positively impact the health and well-being of people of different cultural backgrounds and histories. Without this knowledge, generalizations may be made that lead to false expectations and failure in animal-assisted applications.

Similarly, therapeutic riding programs have traditionally used retired performance horses due to convenience, availability or the belief that a simple change of equipment can convert the horse to a different behavioral orientation. Spink (1993) writes that, "using a substandard mount to work toward highly specialized therapeutic objectives is analogous to playing a beautiful piece of classical music on a honkytonk piano. If the horse can be likened to an instrument (albeit one with feelings and personality), the instrument used in treatment-oriented programs must be highly refined and calibrated to a precise standard" (p. 95).

7.3.1 Mythology of selection procedures

Despite selection procedures' evolution from a risk management and risk reduction focus to an animal/handler team and environmental perspective, the fact remains that most selection procedures do not identify the specific ways in which the team is expected to interact with participants in animal-assisted applications. Current selection procedures were developed to identify people and socialized pets most likely to be safe enough to visit—somewhere. Approval of animal/handler teams by community organizations is, most often, predicated upon the principle that a test of the animal's trained basic obedience skills and, in some cases, a demonstration of willingness to interact with people is a reflection of the animal's future reactions and responses to unfamiliar people and unfamiliar circumstances. Unfortunately, few events are substantively comparable to animal-assisted applications. Nevertheless, from a single test, often administered at a training center familiar to the animal, "somewhere" translates to "anywhere."

Yet, a number of studies have found that an animal's behavior is governed by context. In tests of grazing animals, studies have found that behavior was predictive of only certain types of behavior such as shying and that specific behaviors were related, primarily, to the context in which the animals were evaluated (Boissy, 1995; Lanier et al., 2000; Stephen et al., 2001). In a study of the inter-relationship between various dog behaviors, Goodloe and Borchelt (1998) found only a limited link between obedience training and desirable behaviors. The author suggested that owners willing to spend more time with their dogs may behave differently with their dogs and therefore reduce the dog's fear in new and unusual situations.

Moreover, in a study of dogs' play behavior, Svartberg and Forkman (2002) reported that the behavior of family dogs was influenced more by the type of the game (and to a certain extent by the level of fear) than by their familiarity to the play partner or their willingness to retrieve and tendency for being possessive. The authors found that dogs do not generalize these behavior routines to other, functionally different situations. And, similar to the findings of Goodloe and Borchelt (1998), this study found that dogs that received more playful interaction with their owner were less likely to show fear during play in an unfamiliar place. It would seem from these two studies that a relevant question for handlers would be the amount of time they spend with their dog.

Moreover, a real concern is the fact that few evaluation procedures regularly include children and yet many dogs are involved in programs that bring unpredictable children and dogs together. This is particularly disturbing in light of the fact that most dog bites in the USA involve children and a dog that is familiar to them (Beck and Jones, 1985). A study of the importance of dogs having contact with children during puppy socialization periods found that dogs have difficulty getting along with children if they have not been socialized as puppies to children (Arai and Ohta, 2009; Tóth et al., 2008).

Another concern regarding the use of selection procedures developed for animal-assisted interactions is the fact that the evaluator tests animals without a clear idea of the skills expected of the animal during animal-assisted applications. In order to accurately assess the animal's and handler's appropriateness, the context of the situation must be clear to the evaluator. Prior to assessing aptitude or skills, it is critical first to know what outcome is expected (De Becker, 1997). When the outcome of the selection procedure is unclear, the reliability of the test is no better than mere chance. In the case of most animal-assisted applications, a better degree of prediction than chance is needed to provide participants and sponsors with confidence in the viability of the program.

The majority of selection procedures are conducted by individuals who volunteer their time to administer a particular test developed by national or local organizations. The individual conducting the selection procedure may meet training and experience criteria of a national human/animal interaction organization or may be an animal professional such as a veterinarian or animal trainer. This factor brings into question the degree to which various evaluators understand the dynamics of animal-assisted applications. Understanding the unique interplay of the animal's and the handler's abilities and aptitude in relation to participant-specific goals can be a crucial element. For example, an evaluator who shows dogs in competition obedience, and is unfamiliar with the ways in which a social worker may incorporate a dog in work with a participant to improve personal boundaries, might reject a dog unless it demonstrated precision obedience skills. However, these skills may not be relevant to the participant with whom the dog will work.

Recommendations for evaluators involved in selecting horses for animal-assisted applications suggest that such evaluations be carried out by a team. The team should be comprised of two people who are highly qualified in horse training, behavior and riding. At least one of the people involved in the selection procedure should be skilled in the specific application in which the horse will work (Spink, 1993).

Katcher (2000) writes that as long as animal-assisted applications remain a volunteer activity implemented by handlers dedicated to one particular species or breed of companion animal, the factors which influence participant outcomes will remain elusive. This brings up an important point in terms of the degree to which animal-assisted applications are a suitable fit for volunteer handlers and their pets.

There is a strong social and emotional connection between handlers and their animals. For example, researchers in Japan (Nagasawa et al., 2009) found that interactions with dogs, especially those initiated by the dogs' gazing at their owners, can increase hormones associated with human attachment (i.e. oxytocin). The animals, after all, often hold the admission tickets to activities their handlers enjoy very much. It is understandable that some handlers measure a degree of their worth based on the recognition they receive from their animal-related services (Butler, 2004a).

A study of family members' perception of the pet dog's temperament conducted by Ledger and Baxter (1996) found that family members varied considerably in their report of the dog's temperament. As such, it is a rare dog or horse owner who willingly acknowledges that their animal is inappropriate for an application or may be ineffective in certain situations. The handler who knows that golden retrievers make the best therapy dogs cannot be objective enough to believe that both outcomes are possible.

Sometimes handlers want to keep the team intact, even when the animal is ready to break up the act (Butler, 2004a). Dodging this phenomenon is not simply unfortunate, it can be also abusive. How the animal interacts toward participants and within the specific environment is often indicative of the animal's comfort level. An animal consistently placed in untenable situations may eventually retaliate. Here is another example of how critical the handler's skills are. If a handler is not sensitive to and respectful of the needs of the animal, the handler can inadvertently place his/her needs over those of the animal. This may result in illness for a submissive animal, or aggression in the case of an assertive or fearful animal. When denial keeps handlers from accepting the unwanted reality that their animals are not appropriate for the work, handlers may offer excuses—rationalizations, minimizations, and justifications—to remove any blame from a behavior.

In the foreword to *Therapy Dogs Today* (Butler, 2004b), Fredrickson-MacNamara wrote that effective handlers are capable of sublimating their own egos during animal-assisted application sessions. Although handlers who work with animals in competitions or the performance of specific management tasks are congratulated for their skill and expertise, handlers who work within animal-assisted applications must be able to sublimate themselves to the developing intimacy between the participant and the animal. Those handlers who understand that the focus and purpose of interactions is the participant struggling to heal and not to their animal or themselves have reached a significant level of maturity and expertise in this work. Without this understanding, the handler remains in competition with the participant for reward and recognition.

This may contribute to the current trend for handlers to select animals as potential partners in animal-assisted interaction programs based on a perceived metaphorical connection between the animal and participants. For example, handlers may select a dog that needs a home, a dog that surely was abused rationalizing that the dog should be a therapy animal so he can share his story. Some handlers have been known to select animals with amputations with the notion that participants will identify with the dog's loss without consulting mental health staff as to participant goals.

Concerns regarding this practice are two-fold. First, handlers who decide that an abused or neglected animal may be appropriate for work in animal-assisted applications *before* the animal has been rehabilitated may ignore the needs of the animal in terms of its own healing. Many animals with abuse histories remain distrustful of strangers and unpredictable places for the rest of their lives. Second, the use of metaphor is not a technique that should be implemented by a volunteer. Selecting an animal based on a similarity to participant histories may interfere with the process and focus determined as most appropriate by mental health or medical professionals.

7.4 Selection based on outcome vs settings

In general, animal-assisted interactions incorporate animals in ways that can be loosely categorized; implicitly observing or being in the presence of animals, explicitly looking at or observing animals, and interacting with animals. These parameters provide a context from which to consider participant interaction. The greater the degree of contact between animal and participant the greater the demand for clear definitions of optimum animal behavioral and skill capacities.

In sessions that incorporate animals by creating opportunities for participants to observe or be in the presence of animals, there may be little need for evaluation of individual animals. For example, in residential centers for patients with Alzheimer's disease, an aviary built along hallways can help residents focus externally. While it is important to select the appropriate animals (birds as opposed to sedentary reptiles), evaluating each finch for specific behaviors is less important. The expected outcome of the interaction between participants and animals requires a passive role for the animal.

Animal-assisted applications require the most rigorous definition of outcomes and the relationship of the selection procedure to actual interaction with the participant. Animal-assisted rehabilitation applications provide an excellent example of situations in which it is critical to determine the most appropriate species as well as important to determine the performance expectations of the individual animal. A participant who has head injuries may work with a dog during inpatient rehabilitation sessions. Once discharged, the same participant may be referred to a hippotherapy program to continue to work on balance and coordination needs with a physical or occupational therapist.

In this case, participant goals must first be clearly defined. While the participant is an inpatient, goals may be standing balance and speech improvement. A quiet dog or even a cat or rabbit may be appropriate in this setting. It is possible that, once discharged, intervention goals for the participant will change. Goals could be directed more toward social interactions and less focused on physical rehabilitation. A therapeutic riding program that enables the participant to learn riding skills with the help of volunteers and a quiet, well-behaved horse has different performance expectations from the hippotherapy program that focuses on rhythmic balance changes and may require a horse that moves with more spark and energy.

More explicit participant goals may be defined in a rehabilitation program in which the participant is specifically directed to look at a particular animal and describe it. The same role may be required in a mental health program for children with emotional disorders. A therapist may ask the participant to identify non-verbal behavior. In these types of interventions, the goals of each program will demand more specificity in terms of the individual animal's behavior. A dog incorporated in the rehabilitation program may be required to lie quietly on a table while a horse incorporated in the mental health program would be more effective if it was highly interactive with other horses in the environment.

In another example, consider a psychotherapy application in which a therapist works with a mentally ill adult regarding the effects his aggressive behavior has on others. The therapist may choose to work with a horse that will move away from the adult unless the adult speaks in a softer tone, moves more slowly, and minimizes gesturing. For this application to be effective as well as safe, the handler must have a clear understanding of the performance expectations for the horse and must not interfere with the horse's natural instinct to retreat or the therapeutic value is greatly diminished, if not lost. However, it is critical that the handler ensures that the interaction does not become too stressful for the horse.

Imagine the effectiveness of a plumber whose only tool is a pipe wrench, or a carpenter with only a hammer, or, more importantly, a physician who caries only one drug. The effectiveness of any of these professionals would be severely limited if not totally impossible if their tools were limited to a few items or a single type of tool. This is essentially the situation encountered in the field of animal-assisted applications. Applications are most frequently developed around the availability of animals and handlers. These animals are then incorporated into programs not necessarily because they are the best suited to the task at hand but because they are at the door.

While this situation may not be a cause for concern in animal-assisted interaction programs designed for spontaneous content and generalized motivational or recreational impact, this practice can severely limit development of effective and efficient animal-assisted applications. To date, animal-assisted interactions are driven by the preferences of the handler, or community organization, not the goals of the participant. For example, the majority of screening procedures are targeted toward dogs. Indeed, a number of volunteer animal-assisted interaction organizations such as Therapy Dogs International and Therapy Dogs, Inc. restrict their programs to dogs.

This aspect of volunteer-driven programs has resulted in the majority of animal-assisted interactions incorporating only dogs or horses. While these species are highly interactive, trainable and predictable, the behavioral repertoire of different species can offer significant opportunities to improve the therapeutic capacity of individual sessions.

Consider, for example, an animal-assisted educational application designed to improve adolescent boys' reading scores. Boys of this age may be more motivated to read about reptiles and arachnids than common household pets. Selecting dogs for this group because the organization only works with dogs may reduce progress toward participant-specific goals. Furthermore, including a toy poodle in this application because the volunteer available at that time or the educator has a toy poodle can result in an equally ineffective application.

Human capacity to realistically assess the specific content of animal/participant interactions and to respond ethically to the continued engagement of those animals has not kept pace with these new applications. Providers are increasingly required to demonstrate a direct connection between participant-specific goals and animal contact; nevertheless, there has been relatively little attention paid to how to create or alter the animal interactions for the betterment of the participants (Katcher, 2000). Take for example, an incident that occurred when an alternative high school contracted with a local therapeutic riding center to conduct a vaulting[2] program for eight adolescent boys to reduce aggression. This mental health application failed to meet participant goals in large part because the participants were identified to participate in the vaulting program rather than identifying the animal-assisted interactions based on participant goals.

More specifically, social workers contracted with the riding center because of its availability. In turn, the largest horse available at the riding center was the vaulting horse. The boys, however, were an average of 100 to 150 pounds overweight, and were inner city youth who represented a number of different ethnic backgrounds. None of the boys had ever seen a horse nor were they interested in learning to vault. In

---

[2] In vaulting, movements such as those found in men's gymnastics on a stationary horse are carried out on a moving horse.

considering the goals of the participants as well as cultural and historical connections for the participants, one can see that animal interaction consisting of gymnastics on horses was not an appropriate match to the needs of the participants. The development of a canine weight pulling program may have been more successful because it would have provided the boys with dogs that modeled the stature needed in their neighborhood and weight training is a relevant activity within their world.

From this perspective, it can be seen that the practice of utilizing available animals and volunteer handlers for animal-assisted applications results in the preselection of animals based on factors that may have nothing to do with the most effective and efficient approach to the participants' goals. It is crucial, therefore, to examine and compare how the innate behaviors of animals can be effectively harnessed to support and improve application goals.

Behavior patterns are vastly different between carnivorous and non-carnivorous animals. The fact that rabbits and guinea pigs need to eat more frequently than dogs may actually enhance their role in a setting with a goal of increasing patients' nurturing skills. In the same way, these animals require handling and techniques that can accommodate the animal's frequent need to eliminate.

Innate behaviors such as the degree of physical contact, engagement with humans, and eye contact can be present in animals that do not possess high levels of performance skill. Likewise, these innate behaviors do not necessarily exist in every well-behaved animal that performs well for people other than its owner/handler. These specific skills and intrinsic behaviors relate to *application* and must be defined and considered in animal selection processes. An accurate assessment of species, breed, and individual capacity for work in animal-assisted applications can make a significant difference in participant outcomes.

This form of task analysis is common to other animal "occupations." Take, for example, the canine "occupation" of tactical dogs. "Tactical dog" refers to dogs that work with military, law enforcement, and support personnel in a professional capacity. Within the realm of tactical dogs, there are many applications, such as narcotics detection, trailing, wilderness search and rescue, among others. The National Tactical Police Dog Association (NTPDA) has developed specific detailed behavioral expectations for dogs working within each application as well as a detailed process for evaluating tactical dogs and handlers. After meeting prerequisites, each handler and dog team must demonstrate specific tasks relating to specific goals in a reality-based test in an environment designed to include the unpredictable elements a team will likely encounter. There are specific behaviors relating to each task, and specific tasks relating to each job description.

In an interview with the second author, Brice Cavanaugh, a member of the board of directors for NTPDA, the importance of reality-based evaluations to introduce the elements of unpredictability in the work in which the dogs and their handlers will be engaged was emphasized. Cavanaugh noted that dogs work without equipment while being evaluated to assess the behaviors they are likely to revert to in stressful situations. Cavanaugh feels strongly that animal selection is the key to success and believes selection should first relate to a dog's capacity for a specific job, with initial training emphasizing capacity and then reining in drive with control.

He looks to different breeds of dogs with different intrinsic talents for different aspects of tactical work and suggests that people should embrace what makes different breeds of dogs different. For example, he stated his dog of choice to train for free ranging explosives detection would be a German Shorthaired Pointer, but his dog of choice to train for tasks involving bite work would be a Belgian Malinois.

Furthermore, one commonality, he feels, between dogs currently selected for animal-assisted interactions and tactical canine selection made by volunteers is a lack of understanding of ways in which (human) job needs relate to the activities of the dogs. Cavanaugh referred to people who volunteer with their *pets* (his term within this context) in search and rescue efforts as *hobbyists*. A second commonality Cavanaugh suggested is that hobbyists often try to make their pet into something it isn't. Rather, Cavanaugh explains, dogs should be trained within their capacity by manipulating their natural drives and desires, and then they are reined in with control. Through manipulation of nature, dogs do not consider their tasks to be "work." Thus, stress caused by time should not become an issue if the dog has a strong internal desire to perform its task. If tasks are inherent, working lives of dogs are long. For example, the successful dog for explosives detection work is the dog that is inherently driven to hunt and range. For this dog, job success is more likely because it can be given something (different) to hunt and then it can be taught range work to find it. Furthermore, dogs and their handlers are evaluated annually because court cases depend on annual recertification.

In the same way, Jan Spink, founder of the New Harmony® Institute, developed the Equine Behavioral Profile System (EBPS)—a system to test for baseline performance objectives for horses engaged in animal-assisted applications. Spink writes that fundamental performance objectives must be identified in order to fairly assess the performance of potential and active therapy horses. She notes that this practice helps "minimize the influence of arbitrary or subjective preferences or discrepancies that have occurred" through the use of donated horses (p. 139). She further notes that performance objectives can be systematically or sequentially arranged and defined in terms of replicable tasks and subtasks to enhance selection accuracy.

The EBPS selection procedure consists of three parts, which include Objects, Position Changes, and Backriding. Each part includes a behavioral screening scale that rates the horse's ability to cope with the real-life challenges presented in the course of the test. Most importantly, the EBPS defines and ranks the horse's response to each item and to the overall test. Thus, evaluators have a clear understanding of what behavior from the horse is acceptable for work in specific participant-specific applications.

7.5   Development of a job description for animal-assisted applications

As animal-assisted applications expand to address a widening range of participant-specific goals it will be imperative to develop clear, measurable performance objectives for the handlers and animals engaged in this work. Effective selection procedures will require more than value judgments. In other words, by considering specific performance criteria, medical, psychological, and educational professionals can best determine the fit between the team and participant-specific goals.

Measurability requires clarity and specificity of an outcome. Determining whether or not a rabbit will be a good therapy animal is more difficult than scoring the length of time a rabbit will stay in its basket while being passed between two people. The performance objective requiring the rabbit to stay in the basket for a specified amount of time despite movement of the basket is not only clearer than a more fluid notion of a "good" therapy rabbit; it also tests an expectation of the real-life application.

Weiss and Greenberg (1997) recently found that a dog's success in most commonly used selection test items for service work did not predict later success as a service dog. Success as a service dog is less obvious and is a value-laden judgment rather than predicting whether or not a dog will learn certain commands to a prescribed level of accuracy and response time. In addition, Serpell and Hsu (2001) reported on a new method to test dogs for service dog work; however, the applicability of this evaluation to therapy dogs has not been investigated.

In a process similar to the selection procedures employed for tactical dogs are the ways in which many service/assistance dogs are trained and developed to perform tasks specific to the individual with whom they will be partnered, before going to live and work with that person. A dog that guides a person with a visual impairment does not have the same job description as a dog that alerts a mother with limited ability to hear her baby crying. Beyond training that targets specific tasks, these animals must demonstrate the capacity to perform their *jobs*.

Applying this approach requires the identification of performance outcomes expected in at least broad categories. Similar to the EBPS medical, psychological and educational applications could identify the most critical skills required by animals working in a particular application. While the specific details of the performance outcomes will vary with the specific setting, defining such task expectations enables the handler and professional to determine whether or not the task can be managed. By defining how the animal's presence or interactions will result in progress toward participant-specific goals, selection procedures can be targeted toward identifying the characteristics or behaviors that have a likelihood of affecting the stated outcomes.

Central to any job description for animal-assisted applications is a clear performance outcome related to the duration, response, and type of physical contact expected of the animal. This is a task routinely expected but rarely defined in selection procedures.

7.6 Capacity for work

Proxemics is the study of personal space and the degree of separation that individuals maintain between each other in social situations. Each species has its own rules relating to personal territory. Animals participating in animal-assisted interactions are no exception. Within each personal territory, there are zones (Figure 7.1). The zone at which an individual is first aware of another is the public zone. From there one enters the social zone. Although it is permissible to be in another's social zone, it is the non-verbal communication between the individuals that will make the situation either

Proxemics
Personal Territory

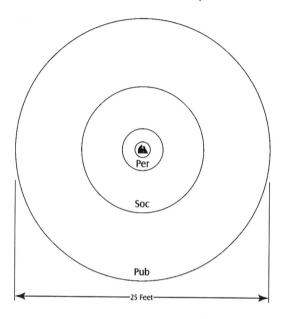

    🐾 – Intimate Zone – 18 inches to contact
    Per – Personal Zone – 4 feet to 18 inches
    Soc – Social Zone – 12 feet to 4 feet
    Pub – Public Zone – 25 feet to 12 feet

Figure 7.1 Personal territory zones. Graphic and corresponding text first published in *Therapy Dogs Today: Their Gifts, Our Obligation.* © 2004. Reprinted with permission of Kris Butler and Funpuddle Publishing Associates.

intimidating or acceptable. Moving still closer brings an individual into another's personal zone, which can be read either as a sign of favor or manipulation. Closer than the personal is the intimate zone, which includes contact. An individual is overwhelmingly aware of another within one's intimate zone. Species maintain rigid rules of communication within this proximity. Ignoring or being unaware of those rules can be perceived as disrespect or intimidation. It is crucial to note that the great majority of animal-assisted interaction programs encourage participants to interact with animals in this zone yet rarely define how differences in terms of the animal's response may affect participant outcomes.

Whenever the barrier of an intimate zone is crossed, animals respond by signaling. These signals are obvious announcements of respect, appeasement, fear, defensiveness or aggression; yet animals in animal-assisted applications are routinely required to work with people for whom their language is completely foreign. The handler's ability to interpret and respond to each animal's important communiqués is a critical factor in the outcome of an interaction.

Touching is the most intimate act of communication. Touching is an integral part of almost every animal-assisted interaction and, while no one would suggest that people stop petting animals during animal-assisted interactions, it is crucial that the animals are allowed to seek out this intimate contact. Animals that obediently tolerate an invasion of their intimate space may become overwhelmed or stressed.

Particularly for small animals such as rabbits, guinea pigs, and tiny dogs, there are unique intrinsic vulnerabilities associated with being prey. Predators often hover over, swoop in, and grab their prey, carrying it off for consumption. Nature has endowed small prey animals with an intuitive sense of the seating arrangement at nature's dinner table. Animal-assisted interactions routinely place a person or groups of people physically over an animal, in positions that suggest hovering, swooping, and grabbing at the animal. Warranted or not, animals' bodies respond to their intuition and signal their levels of discomfort.

Body language enables any species to send messages, note reception of messages, break through defenses, and avoid conflict. The process of communication is complicated and becomes even more so when different species have different interpretations for the signals included in their vocabulary. Often humans do not recognize the signaling of an animal or misinterpret the signals as disinterest or disobedience; yet each signal is part of a message an animal might be trying to convey about personal territory. During animal-assisted interactions, people may behave in ways that inadvertently signal tension to animals.

A further advantage to developing precise performance expectations for animals involved in animal-assisted applications is that it encourages the development of a professional relationship with the animal. Again, the models used by law enforcement and military agencies in assessing dogs for tactical professional roles are instructive. In these roles, dogs are selected primarily for their abilities to perform specific tasks. Dogs that detect drugs in vehicles do not have the same job descriptions as dogs that search for explosives in buildings or dogs that search for people. The question of whether the dog is the handler's favorite breed or makes a good companion for the handler's children is a secondary consideration and in actuality has nothing to do with the dog's performance of its "professional" duties.

In a similar vein, Rebecca O'Connor (2003) describes the relationship involved in working with a hunting hawk as a professional relationship much like the relationship that exists between a senior employee and employer. The commonality here is that like the tactical dog handler, there are specific expectations of the bird in terms of job performance. In both scenarios, the animal may be brilliantly successful in its career, a steady and consistent worker or one that needs constant supervision and correction.

The need for the development of a professional relationship between the handler and/or the medical, psychological or educational professional can alleviate the problems caused by the tendency for handlers to interpret animal behavior anthropomorphically. Handlers are frequently heard to exclaim that their dog "understands" the child's fear of doctors or that horses always know what is best for people. While anthropomorphic interpretation may be a good strategy for some animal-assisted interactions, it is less useful in selecting animals working in animal-assisted applications.

Renowned paleo-biologist Stephen J. Gould noted, "We cannot avoid the language and knowledge of our own emotional experience when we describe a strikingly similar reaction observed in another species." According to Marc Bekoff (2009), "Anthropomorphism endures because it is a necessity, but it also must be done carefully, consciously, empathetically, and from the point of view of the animal, always asking, 'what is it like to be that individual.' We must make every attempt to maintain the animal's point of view. We must repeatedly ask, 'What is that individual's experience?'" (p. 42).

To ensure quality, respectful programs it is critical that animals are never "used" in animal-assisted interactions, but treated as partners in a mutually respectful relationship. The needs of animals must always be considered, accommodated, and balanced with the needs of participants within the scope of animal-assisted interactions. The challenge is to accept and appreciate each animal for what it is designed by nature to be and not project our human images of "success" onto them. When people humanize the animal, it strips from the animal the very reason we love them. By cultivating the relationship with the animal first based on in its capacity as a professional and second as a pet or favorite horse, questions about job performance, health requirements and retirement can be met with less emotional challenge and more ethical consideration.

Today, one of the most important challenges facing the ethical incorporation of animals in medical, psychological and educational applications is a lack of awareness on the part of the people that work with them of the complex, stressful situations in which the animals are being expected to participate. Many of today's animal-assisted interactions are stressful to animals, perhaps for no other reason than the huge shift from people and settings that would be normal for the species. The key is in determining whether an animal has the capacity to recover from the encroachment of strangers, cope comfortably in the environment, and respond appropriately to interactions. Animal-assisted interactions are not appropriate if the emotional or activity levels of targeted participant(s) are overwhelming to available animals. Spink (1993) remarks that the tester should be perceptive enough to avoid overwhelming the horse with too much or improperly presented stimuli as this may elicit a strong fight or flight response and teach the horse that these situations or objects are dangerous.

7.7 Handler recommendations

Effective interactions consist of handlers who appropriately present animals and animals that appropriately receive the participants with whom they are interacting. Animals that possess and demonstrate unique behaviors have a talent or capacity for animal-assisted interactions. Animal contact may facilitate participant goals by contributing to feelings of safety, comfort, and connection. The behaviors that are required to make people feel safe, comfortable, and connected to animals that interact with them remain consistent. However, animals' and handlers' abilities to demonstrate specific behaviors depend on environmental factors, as well as team skills and talents.

The handler's role in animal-assisted interaction is to present the animal. Presenting an animal involves preparation (training, veterinary care, grooming), assessments prior to every intervention, moment-to-moment assessments, and actively working as the animal's advocate. Presentation skill includes a handler's knowledgeable and proactive handling to enhance the animal's ability to meet formal or informal participant or program goals, and a basic knowledge of communication skills to enhance human-to-human interactions. Components of the handler's role include the ability to:

• demonstrate appropriate treatment of people and animals
• demonstrate appropriate social skills (eye contact, smiles, confident posture, conversation) needed for interacting with people in animal-assisted interaction
• prepare for, conduct, and conclude a visit
• demonstrate handling methods that encourage participant-specific goals
• maintain confidentiality
• demonstrate pleasant, calm, and friendly reaction to and attitude towards animals during various tasks and scenarios
• demonstrate proactive (rather than reactive) animal handling skills
• act as animal's advocate in all situations, protecting and respecting the animal's needs
• effectively read the animal's cues (stress, excitement, etc.) and act accordingly.

During animal-assisted interactions, the animal's role is to "receive" the person or people with whom the animal is interacting. The process of being received is what gives people the perception that there is a connection or bond between themselves and the animal. It is primarily that perception which motivates people to participate in therapy, learning, discussion, or other targeted activities. Animals that initiate physical contact, remain engaged, make eye contact, respect personal boundaries, and allow their behaviors to be redirected convey that a connection exists (Butler, 2004b). Simply being able to cause an animal to make eye contact by saying its name is enough to create a sense of connection.

Animal behaviors that reduce the perception of a connection include disinterest, reluctance to engage, disregard for personal boundaries, and any conduct that might be interpreted as aggressive or stress related. The reasons behind an animal's behavior are never as important as the effects of that behavior on the people being visited. For example, some animals vocalize when they are excited, but the issue is not so much what the animal means as whether the specific participant feels threatened by the behavior. While friendliness and confidence are necessary qualities for animal-assisted interactions, animals must also respect personal boundaries. Jumping, pawing, and licking (beyond the few quick and respectful face-to-face calming licks) can seem intrusive to participants.

Animals must be confident enough in their interactions with people to accept occasional rough handling due to arthritic joints or spastic muscles, they must be able to tolerate uncontrolled vocalizations from strangers, and they must be focused on people with whom they are working. This special relationship expands the handlers' responsibility for the animals' safety and comfort.

Author Kris Butler writes in her book *Therapy Dogs Today: Their Gifts, Our Obligation* (2004b) that animal-assisted interactions can be viewed within the context

The Balance Scale

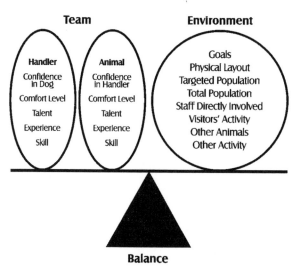

Figure 7.2 The balance scale. Graphic and corresponding text first published in *Therapy Dogs Today: Their Gifts, Our Obligation.* © 2004. Reprinted with permission of Kris Butler and Funpuddle Publishing Associates.

of balance and compensation (Figure 7.2). This concept of balance can inform animal-assisted interactions. As children, we learned about balance and compensation on the playground. With a teeter-totter for a teacher, young children quickly figure out that it is not just size and strength that matter. The key to success on a teeter-totter lies in the ability and willingness of participants to compensate to achieve balance.

Participants in animal-assisted interactions include the animal and handler as a team on one end of the scale, and the environmental factor on the other. When teams and environments are in balance, interactions can reasonably be expected to succeed.

Compensation can be viewed as either adding an equivalent to one side or decreasing/eliminating an undesired effect on the other. A dog might possess a talent for receiving young children, and feel completely at ease listening to one child at a time reading out loud. Yet it is possible for the same dog to be uncomfortable walking through the crowded, noisy halls of the school in which it works. The other students will make their presence known if given a chance, and so the students and their unsupervised (and so highly unpredictable) behavior must be considered on the environmental side of the balance scale. An example of compensation would be for the handler to walk the dog through the school only after the students were already in class or, if the dog were small, to use a carrier to transport the dog through the school.

Butler also points out that although they work together as a team, each handler and animal comes with individual levels of comfort, talent, skill, experience, and confidence in each other. Each team performs its own balancing act between the animal and handler on its "team" end of the balance scale.

Comfort levels are dependent on each team member's individual ability to cope with the environment. Comfort is mostly an animal-related issue, simply because handlers do not repeatedly take the team into environments where the handler feels uncomfortable.

The most essential element an animal and handler possess is talent, yet it is often overlooked. Talent is a natural endowment. Some people are talented piano players; others simply play the piano. Talented handlers are able to deal with the reality of their current situation and act as their animals' advocates. Talented animals are able to demonstrate behaviors previously described as being therapeutic.

Skill refers to a team's trained or acquired behaviors. High levels of skill never compensate for absence of talent. Some animals can be trained to persevere in spite of distractions and sensory bombardment. Just because some animals are willing to tolerate overwhelming environments does not mean people have license to exploit the animals. Sometimes an environment imposes too much upon an animal.

The perception of a strong moment-to-moment connection between the handler and the animal increases everyone's confidence in the team. Handlers who talk in normal everyday tones and who make contact, either by touching or speaking, with their animals frequently, demonstrate the bond that exists between themselves and their animals. Handler skill should reflect a loving partnership with the animal, while subtly suggesting that the handler is indeed in control and can easily redirect the animal's behavior when necessary (Butler, 2004a).

For example, a participant might not be able to identify that the handler kept a gentle hand on the dog, scratching behind the ears, during most of the animal-assisted interaction, but the result is that the participant is left with a positive feeling about a strong, respectful relationship between the animal and handler. When a handler physically places the animal into position and then does not touch the animal again except to reposition, it leaves an entirely different impression. Both gruff tone of voice and physical pushing/pulling can be distracting and create negative judgments about the relationship between handler and animal.

Together, an animal and a handler create a uniquely balanced team; but they do not visit in a vacuum. Within each facility are environmental elements that affect each team's talent and comfort levels, test each team's skill level, and draw from each team's experiences differently. An animal's and handler's abilities to demonstrate specific behaviors depend on environmental factors, as well as team skills and talents. The best way to determine if teams are appropriate for specific environments is by assessing their behaviors within those environments.

No matter where teams work, each environment includes a targeted population, specific goals for that population, a specific number of staff people involved, a total population, and perhaps visitor activity, other animals, and other activity. Assessments made through careful observation, not necessarily a formal process, will best determine whether an animal and handler team can remain in balance within a specific environment.

Staff participation carries more weight than any other element on the environmental side of the balance scale. Effective staffing mitigates risks associated with unpredictable populations and enables teams to address complex goals. Skill becomes an important issue when goals are complex and specific. Team skills must be adequate to meet the goals of the program. Gentle, talented animals without high levels of trained skill can provide effective opportunities for communication and socialization.

Some participants are not appropriate for hands-on animal-assisted interaction with available animals, no matter how tolerant or talented the animals might be. Animal-assisted interaction is not appropriate for people who might harm the available animals or handlers, even inadvertently. Staff's role includes screening to determine which participants are appropriate for animal-assisted interactions. For example, individual children who sit in chairs or on the floor are less threatening to small animals than groups of children who are playing throughout the environment. Sometimes balance is achieved through selection of larger species of animals to compensate for more reactive populations.

Environments that facilitate animal-assisted interaction often include other animals, including residential animals, multiple visiting animals, visiting family pets, or service dogs. Some animals are, at best, unable to maintain focus in the presence of other animals and, at worst, aggressive toward or fearful of other animals. Balance is dependent upon the working animal's ability to disregard other animals in the environment, or staff's ability to limit the access of other animals to selected areas of the facility.

Medical, psychological or educational professionals may play different roles in the process of delivering animal-assisted applications depending on the delivery model used. Brooks (2006) names these the diamond and triangle models. In the diamond model, the medical, psychological or educational professional works in partnership with the animal handler. This creates an interactive structure in which the handler and the professional must be sure of professional and communication boundaries and pathways in order to ensure smooth interactions. This model is most often utilized when large animals are involved such as horses or when the animal may be working at a distance from the participant.

In the second model, the triangle model, the medical, educational or psychological professional works without the assistance of an animal handler. Also referred to as dual-role handlers, these professionals most often work with their own animals, within their professional environment. The triangle model requires the professional to assume the roles and responsibilities on both sides of the balance scale. This delivery model of animal-assisted applications is most often used when the nature of the session requires maximum privacy and confidentiality (i.e. disclosure of incest or childhood sexual assault) or when the animal's role is primarily passive in nature such as helping an individual child improve their reading skills. The animals working in this delivery model must be skilled to the degree that they behave appropriately even in the absence of direct handler attention. Length of workdays and workweeks are huge comfort-level issues for these animals. This model can put more pressure on the animal and requires careful consideration of the selection, training, and scheduling of animals who will work in this model.

Sometimes there is no capacity for balance. Ethical handlers will remove their animals any time the environment is stacked against them. When it becomes impossible for an animal to work comfortably within the environment(s) available to the animal, it is the handler's responsibility to retire the animal from animal-assisted interactions. When animals that live in the therapeutic setting such as resident pets or animals living on therapeutic farms are unable to cope with the environment in which they live, it is imperative that the handler or advocate rehome these animals or, if rehoming is not realistic, consider euthanasia.

Handlers make up 50% of working animal-assisted interaction teams, but carry 100% of team responsibility for the process. The significance of adequate handler training and screening cannot be overemphasized. Handlers' experience, skill, and health are equally as important as animal assessment to minimize risk to all who participate in animal-assisted interactions. Handler competence and understanding ways in which the animal's capacity relates to the human participant's goals directly affect the degree of effectiveness within animal-assisted applications.

7.8 Summary

Today, animal-assisted interactions are never alike. Therefore, it is critical to go beyond training methods and one-time approaches developed years ago to screen animal/handler teams for the brief nursing home and hospital visiting programs. Typical animal-assisted interaction programs go beyond merely offering participant's opportunities to have contact with animals. Animals have been moved to the front-lines of successful treatment and education plans because of their capacity to motivate participants to engage in a wide range of physical, cognitive, psychosocial, communication, and educational applications.

It is clear that there is much more to learn about the selection, training, and care of animals involved in animal-assisted interactions. Expectations for animals involved in these settings have changed dramatically in the last ten years. However, the failure of providers to define precise expectations of the specific content of interactions or what the animal is expected to *do* in animal-assisted applications continues to limit the acceptance of these applications by the health and education industries.

Animal-assisted applications are still considered by the majority of professionals as non-traditional interventions that do not conform to the long-established or inherited way of thinking or acting. In the professional ethics and legal fields, approved practice is generally based on prevailing standards of conduct engaged in by ordinary, reasonable, and prudent practitioners with the same or similar training (Reamer, 2006).

Innovations are vitally important to every profession. Advances in knowledge, based on an integration of precise conceptualization and the results of evaluative research, are essential elements in professionals' efforts to refine and enhance their ability to help people. Innovations such as animal-assisted applications, however, also carry risks (Schantz, 1990; Walter-Toews, 1993). In order to justify any risk associated with animal-assisted applications, health care and education providers must demonstrate that measurable value has occurred as a result of these innovations. Merely providing anecdotal reports will not satisfy the need to support these applications by research and evaluation data (Beck and Katcher, 2003).

To do this it will be necessary to create precise descriptions of the role of the animal and the tasks expected of the animal within different applications. In this process, the handlers' emotional connection with the animal must be moved to the background and the participant's connection to the animal must be brought to the foreground through the use of objective measures and observation. In order to realistically determine the effect of animal contact on participants in a variety of medical, psychological, and educational applications, the participant animal relationship must be prioritized. In other words, it is time to select animals for work in animal-assisted applications where their professional role is primary. Whether or not these animals are then invited to live within their human partners' families is a secondary consideration. Cavanaugh stated it well when he recommended that in selecting animals for work in animal-assisted applications providers should "choose animals with the thought that lives depend on the choice." Do we owe the animals or participants anything less?

References

Arair, S., & Ohta, M. (2009). The importance of dogs having contact with children during the canine socialization period. *Journal of Veterinary Behavior, 4*(2), 94–95.

Barker, S. B., Rogers, C. S., Turner, J. W., Karpf, A. S., & Suthers-McCabe, H. M. (2003). Benefits of interacting with companion animals: a bibliography of articles published in refereed journals during the past 5 years. *American Behavioral Scientist, 47*(1), 94–99.

Banziger, G., & Roush, S. (1983). Nursing homes for the birds: a control-relevant intervention with bird feeders. *The Gerontologist, 23*(5), 527–531.

Beck, A. M. (2000). The use of animals to benefit humans, animal-assisted therapy. In A. H. Fine (Ed.), *The Handbook on Animal Assisted Therapy: Theoretical Foundations and Guidelines for Practice* (pp. 21–40). San Diego, CA: Academic Press.

Beck, A. M., & Jones, B. A. (1985). Unreported dog bites in children. *Public Health Reports, 100*(3), 315–321.

Beck, A. M., & Katcher, A. A. (2003). Future directions in human-animal bond research. *American Behavioral Scientist, 47*(1), 79–93.

Bekoff, M. (2009). *Wild Justice: The Moral Lives of Animals*. Chicago: University of Chicago Press.

Boissy, A. (1995). Fear and fearfulness in animals. *Quarterly Review of Biology, 70*(2), 165–191.

Brickel, C. M. (1984). Depression in the nursing home: a pilot study using pet-facilitated therapy. In R. K. Anderson, B. L. Hart & L. A. Hart (Eds.), *The Pet Connection* (pp. 407–415). Minneapolis: University of Minnesota.

Brooks, S. (2006). Animal assisted psychotherapy and equine facilitated psychotherapy with children who have trauma histories. In N. Boyd (Ed.) *Working with Traumatized Youth in Child Welfare*. New York: Guilford Press.

Butler, K. (2004a). *Therapy Dogs: Compassionate Modalities*. Book and DVD. Norman, Oklahoma: Funpuddle Publishing Associates.

Butler, K. (2004b). *Therapy Dogs Today: Their Gifts, Our Obligation*. Norman, Oklahoma: Funpuddle Publishing Associates.

Cavanaugh, B., personal communication, CAVK9 • 1619 Hwy 11 • Hazel Green, WI 53811 • 888.SWAT.K9S (792.8597) • www.CAVK9.com

Cole, K. M., & Gawlinski, A. (2000). Animal-assisted therapy: the human-animal bond. *Advanced Practice in Acute and Critical Care, 11*(1), 139–149.

Corson, S. A., Corson, E. O., & Gwynne, P. H. (1975). Pet-facilitated psychotherapy. In R. S. Anderson (Ed.), *Pet Animals and Society* (pp. 19–36). London: Baillière Tindall.

De Becker, G. (1997). *The Gift of Fear: Survival Signals that Protect Us from Violence*. New York: Little, Brown and Company.

Delta Society. (1996). *Standards of Practice for Animal-assisted Activities and Animal-assisted Therapy*. Renton, WA: Delta Society.

Francis, G., Turner, J. T., & Johnson, S. B. (1985). Domestic animal visitation as therapy with adult home residents. *International Journal of Nursing Studies, 22*, 201–206.

Fredrickson, M. A. (2003). Assisted vs facilitated, role or terminology in equine facilitated mental health programs. *Equine Facilitated Mental Health Newsletter*. Denver: NARHA.

Fredrickson, M. A., & Howie, A. R. (2000). Methods, standards, guidelines and considerations in selecting animals for animal assisted therapy. Part B: Guidelines and standards for animal selection in animal-assisted activity and animal-assisted therapy programs. In A. Fine (Ed.), *Handbook on Animal-assisted Therapy: Theoretical Foundations and Guidelines for Practice*. San Francisco, CA: Academic Press.

Fredrickson-MacNamara, M. A., & Butler, K. (2006). The art of animal selection for animal-assisted activity and therapy programs. In A. H. Fine (Ed.), *Handbook on Animal-assisted Therapy: Theoretical Foundations and Guidelines for Practice* (2nd ed.). San Francisco, CA: Academic Press.

Glasow, B., & Spink, J. A. (1992). *Therapeutic Riding in the United States*. Hamburg, West Germany: Report presented to the 4th International Congress on Therapeutic Riding.

Goodloe, L. P., & Borchelt, P. L. (1998). Companion dogs temperament traits. *Journal of Applied Animal Welfare Science, 1*(4), 303–338.

Hendy, H. M. (1984). Effects of pets on the sociability and health activities of nursing home residents. In R. K. Anderson, B. L. Hart & L. A. Hart (Eds.), *The Pet Connection* (pp. 430–437). Minneapolis: University of Minnesota Press.

Hines, L. M., Lee, R. L., Zeglen, M. E., & Ryan, T. (1983). *Guidelines: placement of animals in nursing homes*. Irvine, CA: Paper presented at the Conferences on the Human-Animal Bond, University of Minnesota, Minneapolis, MN and University of California.

Hines, L. M., & Fredrickson, M. A. (1998). Perspectives on animal-assisted therapy. In C. C. Wilson & D. C. Turner (Eds.), *Companion Animals in Humans Health*. Thousand Oaks: Sage Publications.

Katcher, A. H. (2000). The future of education and research on the animal-human bond and animal assisted therapy. In A. H. Fine (Ed.), *The Handbook on Animal Assisted Therapy: Theoretical Foundations and Guidelines for Practice* (pp. 461–473). San Diego: Academic Press.

Kongable, J. G., Buckwalter, K. C., & Stolley, J. M. (1989). The effects of pet therapy on the social behavior of institutionalized Alzheimer's clients. *Archives Psychiatric Nursing, 3*, 191–198.

Lanier, J. L., Grandin, T., Green, R. D., Avery, D., & McGee, K. (2000). The relationship between reaction to sudden, intermittent movements and sounds and temperament. *Journal of Animal Science, 78*, 1467–1474.

Ledger, R., & Baxter, M. (1996). A validated test to assess the temperament of dogs. In I. J. H. Duncan, T. M. Widowski & D. B. Haley (Eds.), *Proceedings of the 30th International Congress of the ISAE, Guelph, Canada. Col* (pp. 111). Canada: C.K. Centre for the Study of Animal Welfare.

Marr, C. A., French, L., Thompson, D., Drum, L., Greening, G., Mormon, J., et al. (2000). Animal-assisted therapy in psychiatric rehabilitation. *Anthrozoös, 13*(1), 43–47.

McGibbon, N. H., Andrade, C. K., Widener, G., & Cintas, H. L. (1998). Effect of an equine-movement therapy program on gait, energy expenditure, and motor function in children with spastic cerebral palsy: a pilot study. *Developmental Medicine and Child Neurology,* *40*(11), 754–762.

Nagasawa, M., Kikusui, T., Onaka, T., & Ohta, M. (2009). Dog's gaze at its owner increases owner's urine oxytocin during social interaction. *Hormones and Behavior,* *55*(3), 434–441.

New, J. C., & Strimple, E. (1988). *Therapy dog criteria: minimum medical criteria. Paper presented at the seventh annual Delta Society Conference, People, Animals and the Environment.* Orlando, FL: Exploring Our Interdependence.

North American Riding for the Handicapped Association. (1994). *How to start a NARHA center.* NARHA. [Online]. http://www.NARHA.org.

O'Connor, R. (2003). *Lift.* Santa Barbara, CA: Red Hen Press.

Odendaal, J. S. (2000). Animal-assisted therapy: magic or medicine? *Journal of Psychosomatic Research, 49*(4), 275–280.

Reamer, F. G. (2006). Nontraditional and unorthodox interventions in social work: ethical and legal implications. *Families in Society: The Journal of Contemporary Social Services, 87* (2), 191–197.

Robb, S. S. (1983). Companion animals and elderly people: a challenge for evaluators of social support. *The Gerontologist, 23,* 277–282.

Schantz, P. M. (1990). Preventing potential health hazards incidental to the use of pets in therapy. *Anthrozoös, 4,* 14–23.

Shelter Animals (1992). American Society for the Prevention of Cruelty to Animals.

Serpell, J. A. and Hsu, Y. (2001). A novel approach to evaluating performance-related behavior in prospective guide dogs. Reprinted from Garner, J. P., Mench, J. A., and Heekin, S. P. (Eds.), *Proceedings of the 35th Congress of the ISAE.* Center for Animal Welfare, UC Davis, USA.

Spink, J. (1992). *The Therapy Horse: A Model for Standards and Competencies.* San Antonio: Therapy Skill Builders.

Spink, J. (1993). *Developmental Riding Therapy.* San Antonio: Therapy Skill Builders.

Stephen, J. M., Ledger, R. A., & Stanton, N. (2001). Comparison of the perceptions of temperament in dogs by different members of the same household. In J. P. Garner, J. A. Mench & S. P. Heekin (Eds.), *Proceedings of the 35th International Congress of the ISAE, Davis, California, USA* (p. 113). Center for Animal Welfare, UC Davis.

Svartberg, K., & Forkman, B. (2002). Personality traits in the domestic dog (Canis familiaris). *Applied Animal Behaviour Science, 79,* 133–155.

Tóth, L., Gácsi, M., Topál, J., & Miklósi, A. (2008). Playing styles and possible causative factors in dogs' behaviour when playing with humans. *Applied Animal Behaviour Science, 114,* 473–484.

Visser, E. K., van Reenen, C. G., Schilder, M. B. H., Knaap, J. H., and Blokhuis, H. J. (2001). Can behavioral parameters in young horses be used to quantify aspects of temperament? Reprinted from: Garner, J. P., Mench, J. A., and Heekin, S. P. (Eds.), *Proceedings of the 35th Congress of the ISAE.* Center for Animal Welfare, UC Davis, USA.

Walter-Toews, D. (1993). Zoonotic disease concerns in animal assisted therapy and animal visitation programs. *Canadian Veterinary Journal, 34,* 549–551.

Weiss, E., & Greenberg, G. (1997). Service dog selection tests: effectiveness for dogs from animal shelters. *Applied Animal Behaviour Science, 53,* 297–308.

8 Designing and implementing animal-assisted therapy programs in health and mental health organizations

Gerald P. Mallon*, Samuel B. Ross, Jr. [†], Steve Klee[†], Lisa Ross[‡]

[*] Hunter College School of Social Work, [†] Green Chimneys Children's Services, [‡] Touro University

8.1 Introduction

Although health and mental health systems continually examine fresh and original approaches to serve their client constituents, new proposals are seldom greeted with enthusiasm within organizational structures (Bolman and Terrance, 1991; Brager and Holloway, 1978; Dutton, 1992; Kets de Vries and Miller, 1984; Morgan, 1986; Moss-Kanter, 1982, 1988). One relatively new approach that utilizes a variety of animals including companion animals, farm animals, and injured wildlife as adjuncts in the treatment of various populations, has, or soon may receive, greater acceptance and consideration by health or mental health organizations (Brooks, 2001; Hanselman, 2001; Mallon, 1994a,b, 1999). Utilizing animals in health and mental health organizations is a proposal that has engendered both the regard and the ire of administrators.

The emerging breadth of its applications and the involvement of skilled professionals from diverse disciplines have made animal-assisted therapy (AAT) more than a "therapeutic" intervention. Although AAT is beginning to be recognized as a treatment modality much like dance, music, art, and poetry therapy (Beck and Katcher, 1984), it is also important to note that the main difference between AAT and other adjunctive therapies is that the central "tools" in this intervention are living, breathing, interacting creatures. This is an important element because when animals are introduced into a health or mental health delivery system, unique organizational issues must be considered.

Utilizing a predominantly social work and psychological approach to organizational administration, this chapter contains advice to help organizations discern whether or not to utilize AAT and to aid implementation. What can be considered are equine experiential learning, equine facilitated psychotherapy and therapeutic riding

Handbook on Animal-Assisted Therapy. DOI: 10.1016/B978-0-12-381453-1.10008-X

as part of a program offering. In addition, horticultural activities should be considered as part of the introduction of the activities. Clarity as to whether the program is to provide therapy or psychotherapy must be part of any planning. Today, dog training by students, school gardens, mini-zoos, visiting animals and handler and nature therapy combine elements which are seen in animal-assisted therapy and activity programs. With Green Chimneys Children's Services (see Ross, 1999) as our organizational model of choice, the authors, who are among the principal administrators of this program, focus on rules and principles that guide program development.

8.2   Animal-assisted therapy

Boris M. Levinson (1962) was the first professionally trained clinician to formally introduce and document the way in which companion animals could hasten the development of a rapport between therapist and patient and increase patient motivation (Mallon, 1994c). First termed *pet therapy* by Levinson, this approach is now known as animal-assisted therapy. Originally ridiculed by his colleagues for presenting such a "preposterous" technique, Levinson continued to research, write, and speak about the efficacy of this novel intervention throughout his life.

Levinson initially advocated utilizing animals with children in residential treatment and wrote extensively about it (Levinson, 1968, 1969, 1970, 1971, 1972; Levinson and Mallon, 1996). In an attempt to gather data on the utilization of animals in organizations, Levinson conducted the first survey documenting the use of pets in residential schools (Levinson, 1968). With a sample of 160 residential and day schools identified from the *Directory for Exceptional Children*, a response rate of 75.6% ($n = 121$) was obtained. Levinson found that 40.7% did not permit pets in the schools. State regulations, fear of diseases, the labor-intensive nature of caring for pets, and potential mistreatment by the children were all cited as reasons for barring animals in organizational settings. In the 1970s, the American Humane Education Society commissioned a survey to determine how many institutions in the country were using animals in facilitating the treatment of clients. The survey indicated results (48%) similar to those found earlier by Levinson. Several of the institutions surveyed reported disadvantages as well as advantages (Arkow, 1982). In many cases, these programs were developed in a surge of enthusiasm, by well-meaning, but overzealous and inexperienced individuals (Daniel et al., 1984).

By the 1980s, then, the necessity of careful program design became clear. Although many other AAT programs are rapidly emerging both in this country and abroad, one organization that has thoughtfully and carefully crafted an animal-assisted program for children is Green Chimneys Children's Services, located in Brewster, New York, 60 miles outside of New York City.

8.3   The Green Chimneys model

The main campus of Green Chimneys Children's Services is a year round residential treatment center and special education program for children and youth with special needs. Green Chimneys serves 102 children and adolescents in residence and 96 in the day program. The students share the rural environs of the campus with barnyard animals, domestic companion animals, and wildlife. But the healing power of human/ animal interactions has been an active component in this organizational therapeutic milieu for more than 60 years.

This former dairy farm was purchased in 1947 by the Ross family, and the organization was originally designed as an independent boarding school for very young children. Operating as Green Chimneys School for Little Folk, the educationally based facility incorporated the dairy farm into the children's daily lives. Initially, the staff did not know or appreciate the therapeutic part of this alliance. The staff saw the animals as merely providing companionship, socialization, pleasure, and education for the students. They soon realized, however, that they were providing much more.

In the early 1970s, the school evolved into a residential treatment center that specialized in the care of children with emotional and behavioral needs. Children came with histories of severe neglect; sexual, physical, and emotional abuse; homelessness; family substance abuse; and behavioral and educational difficulties. Many had learning disabilities and had experienced very limited success in school. Most were hospitalized for aggressive behaviors, suicide attempts, or chronic depression. The majority lived in poverty. Most had experienced significant psychosocial stressors at home, in school, and in their communities.

Although many changes occurred as the organization changed its program to meet the needs of a new population, the human/animal interactions component remained intact. The staff realized that these special children and youth, mostly from urban environments, could truly benefit from interactions with animals.

As part of the program, students are involved in a client focused survey so that it is clear what experiences the student has had with animals before entering the program. Green Chimneys Longitudinal Assessment Scales (GLAS) were developed by Myra Ross for use in the program; measurable treatment outcomes are monitored by clinical program staff and are maintained in the case record. Non-licensed personnel deliver animal-assisted activities so that their work is distinguished from licensed professionals who are licensed as therapists and as such provide animal-assisted therapy.

There has been a tremendous growth in programming at Green Chimneys with environmental education clearly in mind. New initiatives include: work in animal welfare; youth enrichment; Wildlife activities—Green Chimneys was issued a permanent license from the US Fish and Wildlife in 2009; training of assistance dogs—students are involved in training assistance dogs; and opportunities for Green Chimneys' staff to bring their own companion animals to the workplace provided that the dog has a role in the program and is approved after a test of behavior.

Many youth whom we serve have been turned off by their families and their communities and Green Chimney's goal is to reintroduce them to the world around them. The animals cannot speak for themselves so students have to anticipate their needs. Since they cannot protect themselves, the students protect them. Peer relationships develop as a result. Staff trust students to do their very best and students rise to the occasion. Everything we do has a value to humans and animals. In a real sense we all learn from "daily" happenings.

Being that Green Chimneys is in the New York City watershed area, careful control of manure, food waste, water run-off and trash storage and removal including whatever is recycled must be planned for. Learning to assume responsibility for one's living space both indoors and out is extremely important for the health and welfare of humans and animals. As we move into the twenty-first century, Green Chimneys maintains its focus on growing "green" and going "green."

8.4   Organizational issues

The eventual success or failure of a proposed organizational innovation is a consequence of the interplay of power and politics at numerous levels—individual, intra-organizational, interorganizational, and societal (Frost and Egri, 1991). The Performance Improvement Committee, which is a board and staff committee, meets monthly. The Executive Council of Green Chimneys, which consists of the agency's executive director, the organization's founder, the clinical director, the clinical coordinator, the director of treatment, the chief fiscal officer, director of education, and the director of fund development, meets on a weekly basis to monitor/review agency practices and procedures and to ensure that all parts of the organization are functioning at optimal efficiency. This council provides leadership and direction, and acts as a sounding board on major organizational issues, including the utilization of animals in the treatment programs.

Other health and mental health organizations that wish to implement an animal-assisted program component must consider the level of support that the innovation can amass on multiple levels. The following questions represent areas that the Green Chimneys' Executive Council recommends as important considerations to be discerned by other organizational administrators who wish to implement an AAT program:

- Is there administrative support for the idea?
- Does the idea have board support and will it need board approval?
- Does the innovation have staff that will support the idea?
- Will new staff have to be trained and hired?
- Has anyone asked the clients if they think this is a good idea?
- How will the innovation be funded, and what costs will be incurred throughout the process?
- What are the salient issues with respect to infection control?
- What are the issues with respect to safety and humane treatment of animals?
- What liability issues need to be considered?
- Is there family support for the program?
- Do the clinical staff accept and support the program?

And, in the age of managed care:

- Are there measurable outcomes that will enable the organization to document and evaluate the program's effectiveness?
- How can this intervention be monitored for continuous quality improvements?

8.5   Program design issues

8.5.1   Staff issues

Because animals have always been a part of the Green Chimneys approach to working with children and families, we have always enjoyed the support of our organization's board of directors and agency administrators. But as the agency has grown, we have often had to find ways to ensure that our animal focus is maintained.

Knowledgeable, experienced, and enthusiastic personnel greatly influence a program and ensure programmatic longevity. A consistent group of core staff make management easier. After a great deal of experimentation and trial and error logic, Green Chimneys has found that an animal-assisted program can be staffed by licensed and credentialed personnel (social workers, nurses, psychologists, physicians, occupational therapists, physical therapists, vocational therapists, teachers, certified therapeutic riding instructors, licensed wildlife rehabilitation staff) and other staff (child care workers, school personnel, recreation workers, nurses aides, therapy aides); and volunteers can provide animal-assisted activities (AAAs). It has been an ongoing challenge for our organization to determine which staff positions or responsibilities should be filled by professionals, which should be staffed by trained personnel, and which are suited for volunteers. Over the years we found that many of the staff currently employed by the agency came forward to fill roles in working with both children and animals. Staff may bring animals to work if there is a therapeutic purpose. Two key factors were their desire to incorporate animals into their work with people and their commitment to designing innovative approaches to working with people in need. An additional essential element was whether or not they had the support of their supervisors in this endeavor. Green Chimneys has historically recognized that those helping professionals who work with both people and animals need to be flexible, but there is also a need for structure, consistency, and limits. Many different philosophies are represented by those who are interested in developing approaches to working with animals and humans. Before any new program can be developed, it will need to be approved by the organization's board of directors and administrative staff. The first question that most boards of directors and administrators will want an answer to is this: How does this project relate to the organization's mission, vision, values, goals, and needs? On a secondary level, both bodies will want to know about costs, about maintaining the program, about agency personnel and client support, and about liability. At Green Chimneys, we receive many calls and e-mails asking about insurance coverage and names of agents and carriers. When interviewing for positions, administrative staff must seek out the candidate's specific beliefs and personal stance. Know where the candidate stands on issues that may come up in the workplace. Staff surveys may be another important step that can permit their voices to be heard when considering a new intervention.

8.5.2   Client issues

Although it has been written that the human/animal bond is universal (Mallon, 1992; Senter, 1993, p. 1), the reality is that not all people like animals. Some clients may be allergic to specific animals, some may have a phobia about a particular animal, and others may just not have had positive experiences with animals. At Green Chimneys many of these issues are immediately addressed at intake, when the client first arrives for services. Clients are screened for allergies and asked about fears or dislikes for particular animals. It should be noted that there is evidence that youngsters with pets are less likely to develop allergies. At Green Chimneys we have a high number of children diagnosed with asthma but we have not had any child hospitalized as a result of an asthma attack. The allergy information is integrated into the client's initial prospective treatment plan. Although Green Chimneys would like all of its clients to have a positive experience with animals, the organization respects the fact that not all children respond the same way to animal-assisted approaches to treatment.

Another means for assessing patient satisfaction or dissatisfaction is to conduct a survey of the clients' likes and dislikes about their treatment. This is more or less standard practice in most health and mental health organizations in today's managed care environment. A client-focused survey soliciting patient response toward animals is an important place to begin the process. In addition, it may be important to do a thorough assessment of any history of animal abuse. Most surveys to children, families and staff give approval to animals, working at the farm and gardening.

Concern for the physical well-being of the clients is a major priority in health and mental health care-related organizations. Cleanliness, infection control, and risk of illness related to zoonotic conditions claim a central focus in most health and mental health care systems. Organizations interested in adopting an AAT approach must research federal, state, and local regulations early in the planning process to consider possible limitations for such an intervention. It can be very disappointing for those interested in designing an AAT program to discover that rigid local health laws prohibit such techniques.

8.6   Animal selection

Choosing animals at Green Chimneys to be part of our AAT program is an exciting endeavor, but animal selection can also be an imposing task. Again, we would caution that those wishing to introduce animals into an existing organization should start small. Zoning and health regulations will undoubtedly affect the location, nature, and size of programs incorporating animals. Geography also plays a large role in the selection of animals. Organizations in urban environments obviously need to consider restricting the program to smaller companion animals (see Senter, 1993, Chapters 4 and 5 and Serpell et al., 2000). Some programs may choose to have a visiting AAA program, rather than having animals in residence. Rural programs, such as our Green Chimneys program, utilize a wide variety of animals including farm animals and captive wildlife. Our wildlife program is coordinated by an individual who is a licensed wildlife rehabilitator (see Senter, 1993, Chapters 2 and 3). Most of our wild animals have sustained injuries and are only temporarily placed at the farm for rest, medical care, and eventual release. The size of the physical space needed for each animal is determined by the animal's physical size and need for space. An administrative policy should also be in place that ensures that all animals are healthy, have up-to-date vaccinations and a record kept on file of their health status.

Research and courses at colleges and universities have helped provide evidence of the value of such programs. Accrediting bodies have looked at the programs and have approved their place in hospitals, agencies and schools. Foundations, corporations and individuals have shown a real interest and are providing funding as it relates to the human/animal bond and related topics.

8.7 Cost effectiveness

Initial start-up and continued financing, in any organization, play a large role in the decision to develop or not develop a new program. This is particularly true for non-profit organizations. Regardless of how useful an AAT program is deemed to be for an organization, the bottom line for most agency administrators and boards is how much it is going to cost and how will it be funded? Our Green Chimneys founder, Dr. Sam Ross, and our organization's development staff spend a great deal of time and energy on fundraising efforts to keep all of our programs fiscally sound. Although this process can be a time-consuming enterprise, the good news is that incorporating animals does not have to be an expensive undertaking. There are many ways to raise money for programs. Innovative thinking and creativity are the keys.

All new programs have start-up costs, dictated by the size and nature of the innovation. "Start small" is a good maxim. Funds for animal upkeep and maintenance refer to the day-to-day expenses of keeping animals. These costs will vary from program to program, but generally include food, shelter, veterinary costs, grooming costs, and staff salary costs.

At Green Chimneys we have found five ways to support an animal-assisted program: (1) use of present funds, (2) foundation or corporate support, (3) fee for service, (4) outright donations, and (5) sale of items. Where costs are minimal and programs are small, using present funds may be a quick-start solution. Many foundations or corporations, especially those with an obvious interest in animals, can provide possible seed money to start a program. Fees for services can be generated through visiting animal programs or by offering specialized training. Donation from the community and sales in the community not only help support the program, but bring the organization's name out into the community. Linking the community to the program's efforts to help its constituents can be useful in many ways.

Since introducing the Farm-on-the-Moo-ve program, a mobile program of providing animal contact with students as caregivers, the program has been replicated at many other places and has quite literally brought the farm into the community, in many cases to an urban community which is largely estranged from human/animal connections.

8.8 Liability

All organizations are concerned about the potential for liability issues. Obviously there are risks inherent in having animals on site in a health or mental health organization. Green Chimneys has developed a documented safety plan for both clients and animals, and we would recommend that such a plan be considered a necessity for every organization. In the sections that follow, we discuss our Green Chimneys protocols for minimizing risk. These should be carefully considered and followed by organizational staff. The first place that organizations should start when considering liability issues is by reviewing their current insurance carrier's policies about animals. If animals are included in the policy coverage and the organization's carrier is clear that the organization is launching a new initiative then there is no need for further coverage. If animals are not included in the current coverage then the organization must obtain coverage for staff, clients, and visitors.

8.9   Outcomes

The widespread ardor about the almost universal efficacy of animal-assisted programs has for many years all but obscured any serious questioning of its possible risks. In the age of managed care, health and mental health organization administrators must evaluate the effectiveness of their interventions. Any program evaluation of a health or mental health organization must also include a review of the effectiveness of an organization's animal-assisted programs (Anspach, 1991; LaJoie, 2003). Although organizational administrators must develop stringent criteria used for what constitutes a therapeutic gain, they must also develop criteria for what constitutes an effective programmatic intervention. Some suggested questions that should be assessed include these: Is this intervention cost effective? Are there other interventions that are equally clinically appropriate and useful, but more cost effective? How many clients are utilizing this service in a given cycle? What are the instruments used by program evaluators to determine clinical or program effectiveness with respect to this intervention? Therefore, guidelines for the implementation of an animal-assisted program need to identify conditions necessary to preserve the health and safety of both the animals and clients, and to ensure that the intervention is programmatically effective. Administrators should resist the attempt to rationalize the implementation of such programs solely as a kind of therapy that has universal benefits solely because of its appeal. Outcome studies are equally important in order to prevent outright rejection of the plan considering it unimportant or non-therapeutic. It is important to keep careful records on the children involved in the program.

8.10   Infection control issues

Even in the best AAT programs, there is an element of risk. At Green Chimneys we have been aware of and respond to these risk factors on a daily basis. A medical services committee has the responsibility of including human and animal infection control. Animals bite, some produce allergic reactions, and some pass on zoonotic diseases. Therefore, an AAT program must develop infection control policies that address the need for some animals to avoid contact *with* certain people, and to develop surveillance procedures and responses. Every setting where pets or animals of any type are located must have some rules in place. At Green Chimneys we maintain a health record on each animal and we recommend this task as an essential component of any planned AAA/T program.

8.11   Rules that guide animal-assisted therapy programs

Following Lewis's (1982) advice, rules that guide an intervention to action specify the practice. The Performance Improvement Committee and the Executive Council at Green Chimneys have focused a great deal of attention on the development of rules to guide practice in our AAT approaches to treatment. These rules are enumerated for all Green Chimneys staff as a part of the agency's initial formal orientation process and are codified in writing in our organization's literature. We have found the following rules to be useful and we believe they are adaptable for other organizations:

1. House animals are to be approved by the organization's administrator or designee.
2. Appropriate animals include dogs, cats, birds, fish, hamsters, gerbils, guinea pigs, rabbits, and, where appropriate conditions exist, farm animals such as goats, sheep, ducks, chickens, cows, and horses.
3. Wildlife are not permitted in the program unless they are cared for under the supervision of a licensed individual and then only in a rehabilitative circumstance, a previously injured status or are permanently injured.
4. At the time of admission, a medical record is started on each animal and is kept up to date as long as the animal remains in the organization.
5. Animals are to have up-to-date vaccinations by a licensed veterinarian.
6. Animals are to have an annual physical by a qualified veterinarian.
7. Animals who are ill are to be treated by a qualified veterinarian.
8. Aggressive animals will be removed immediately.
9. Dogs or cats are to be altered or spayed.
10. The administrator or designee is responsible for acceptable animal husbandry practices.
11. Animals are to be controlled by leash, command, or cage.
12. Animals are not permitted (except assistance dogs) in the following areas: areas where food is cleaned, stored, or prepared; vehicles used for the transportation of food; patient/ staff toilet, shower, or dressing rooms; and drug preparation areas, nursing stations, and sterile and cleaning supply rooms.
13. All pet utensils, food, and equipment used for maintenance of pets are to be kept in an area separate from clients' food preparation areas and are to be kept cleaned.
14. Animals are to be fed according to a schedule posted where the animals live and are cared for.
15. Animals are not to be fed human food.
16. Freshwater is to be made available for the animals at all times.
17. Food handlers are not to be involved in animal care, feeding, or cleanup of animal food or waste.
18. Dogs and cats are to be effectively housebroken.
19. Animal waste is to be picked up and disposed of in a trash receptacle made available for this purpose.
20. Any animal that bites a staff member or patient is to be quarantined for 10 days.

21. Animals who die on the premises are to be disposed of in accordance with the established organizational procedure.
22. Animals from outside the agency are permitted to visit the premises through a prearranged agreement under rules for visiting pets.
23. Animals are to be groomed daily.
24. All staff (except for kitchen workers, for sanitary reasons) are encouraged to be involved in actively caring for the animals.
25. Clients are to be involved in caring for the animals.
26. Animals are to be part of weekly sessions with the clients.
27. Issues related to death and dying must be appropriately handled.
28. Animal abuse issues need to be handled therapeutically and on a case by case basis.

8.12   Principles that guide animal-assisted therapy programs

If a worker is "lacking a rule," the worker will search his or her own memory for a principle. This practice principle tells the worker what to do. Rules are clear cut and therefore can be more rapidly recalled from memory. The principle that is more abstract requires a more time-consuming and complex mental undertaking to recover from memory (Lewis, 1982, pp. 57–58). Principles are expressions of goals and permit staff to have leeway regarding the means by which they are carried out.

In identifying principles for the AAT practitioner, we offer the following, which are used at Green Chimneys:

1. All animals will be carefully selected and subject to behavioral assessment to determine their aptitude for working with people.
2. At time of hire, staff will be surveyed to determine allergies, fears, or dislike of animals. Attitudes of workers will be measured to evaluate former relationships with animals.
3. As part of screening at the time of intake or admission, clients will be surveyed to determine allergies, fears, dislike, or past abusive behavior toward animals. Attitudes of clients will be measured to evaluate former relationships with animals.
4. The rights of individuals who do not wish to participate in the program will be considered first and off-limits areas for animals will be maintained for this purpose.
5. Companion animals should not pose a threat or nuisance to the clients, staff, or visitors.
6. Workers should integrate the patient interactions with animals into their comprehensive treatment plan, with specific and relevant goals.
7. The worker will strive to assure the patient the opportunity to choose his or her own goals in work with the animals and assist him or her in identifying and achieving this end.
8. Sessions that involve animal-assisted therapy must be documented in the weekly progress notes.
9. The worker will document any and all interactions that may be novel behavior as a result of the human/animal bonding.
10. The worker will closely supervise and monitor any patient who has a past history of animal abuse.
11. The worker will closely supervise and monitor the temperament of all animals that are utilized with patients. Animals will be permitted to rest every hour and a half and not be permitted to work more than 5 hours per day.
12. The worker should process animal-assisted activities to assist the patient in exploring new or possibly previously unexplored issues.

13. The worker should encourage the patient to work with her or him in settings other than the offices, that is, conduct a session while taking the dog for a walk.
14. The worker should utilize the animals with the patient to explore areas that can be seen as dress rehearsal for life, that is, birth, death, pregnancy.
15. The worker should utilize the animal-assisted interaction to aid the patient in mastering developmental tasks.
16. The worker should utilize the animal to promote feelings of self-worth in the patient whenever possible.
17. The worker should utilize the animal to promote responsibility and independence in the patient.
18. The worker should utilize the animal to teach the patient the need to sacrifice or undergo inconvenience for the sake of a loved one.
19. The worker should make every effort to utilize the animal to promote companionship, warmth, and love with the patient.
20. The worker should remember that utilizing an animal is not an "open sesame" or a panacea to working with or uncovering the "inner world" of the troubled patient.
21. The worker should work to maintain the "therapy" component in animal-assisted therapy.
22. The worker should utilize the animal to teach lessons in life, thereby promoting and nurturing appropriate emotional responses from clients.
23. The worker should help the individual who has made a contact and interest in the animals share this experience with a peer as a means of establishing peer relationships.
24. AAT needs to be integrated into the larger therapeutic milieu and to fit with the other adjunctive therapies the child is receiving as per their individualized treatment plan.

8.13 Conclusions

Encouraging well-designed, carefully evaluated interventions is essential to responsible current and future AAT program development. A diverse array of helping professionals is often in search of ways to improve the quality of life of persons who have overwhelming obstacles to overcome. To those clients who could benefit from an animal companion, a health or mental health care professional may be able to facilitate a new or support a long-established relationship by being sensitive to what is occurring in the field and by knowing which resources are available (Netting et al., 1988, pp. 63–64). Our challenge is for health and mental health organizations to look for meaningful ways to incorporate animals into our human services organizations in mutually beneficial partnerships.

While what has been offered here is not, as Levinson pointed out, the panacea to the world's ills, it is a beginning. Animals can fulfill an important role for many people, but organizations that wish to set in motion such interventions must be careful to also initiate rules and principles to guide this practice. There is an ever growing body of knowledge, information and research which can help prepare interested persons to initiate a human/animal interaction program. Courses, workshops and seminars are being held all over this country and in the global community. Although the labor-intensive nature of integrating animals into a health or mental health system may at first seem a daunting task, the organizational benefits of such an intervention are numerous (Mallon, 1994a). The introduction of animals into a human service system will not produce additional competitiveness or alienation, but can, instead, provide that calming, unqualified attention and love that are needed to help some clients flourish, moving away from illness and toward health. As health and mental health organizations struggle to find their niche in an ever expanding network of diverse services, we must be alert to novel and creative approaches to helping our clients, including in some cases where indicated, utilizing an array of diverse animals as adjuncts in the treatment of various populations.

References

Anspach, R. R. (1991). Everyday methods for assessing organizational effectiveness. *Social Problems, 38*(I), 1–19.

Arkow, P. (1992). *Pet Therapy: A Study of the Uses of Companion Animals*. Colorado Springs, CO: Human Society of the Pikes Peak Region.

Beck, A. M., & Katcher, A. H. (1984). A new look a pet-facilitated therapy. *Journal of American Veterinary Medicine Association, 184*(4), 414–420.

Bolman, L., & Terrance, D. (1991). *Reframing Organizations*. San Francisco: Josey-Bass.

Brager, G., & Holloway, S. (1978). *Changing Human Service Organizations: Politics and Practice*. New York: Free Press.

Brooks, S. (2001, Winter). Working with animals in a healing context. *Reaching Today's Youth* 19–22.

Daniel, S., Burke, J., & Barke, J. (1984). Educational programs for pet-assisted therapy in institutional settings: an interdisciplinary approach. *Veterinary Technician, 5*(2), 394–397.

Dutton, J. E. (1992). The making of organizational opportunities: an interpretive pathway to organizational change. *Research in Organizational Behavior, 15*, 195–226.

Frost, P. J., & Egri, C. P. (1991). The political process of innovation. *Research in Organizational Behavior, 13*, 229–295.

Hanselman, J. L. (2001). Coping skills interventions with adolescents in anger management using animals in therapy. *Journal of Child and Adolescent Group Therapy, 11*(4), 159–195.

Kets de Vries, M. F. R., & Miller, D. (1984). *The Neurotic Organization*. New York: Harper Business.

LaJoie, K. R. (2003). *An evaluation of the effectiveness of using animals in therapy. Unpublished doctoral dissertation*. Louisville, KY: Spalding University. (University Microfilms No. 3077675).

Levinson, B. (1962). The dog as co-therapist. *Mental Hygiene, 46*, 59–65.

Levinson, B. (1968). Household pets in residential schools. *Mental Hygiene, 52*, 411–414.

Levinson, B. (1969). *Pet-oriented Child Psychotherapy*. Springfield, IL: Charles C. Thomas.

Levinson, B. (1970). Nursing home pets: a psychological adventure for the clients (part 1). *National Humane Review, 58*, 15–16.

Levinson, B. (1971). Household pets in training schools serving delinquent children. *Psychological Reports, 28*, 475–481.

Levinson, B. (1972). *Pets and Human Development*. Springfield, IL: Charles C. Thomas.

Levinson, B., & Mallon, G. P. (1996). *Pet-oriented Child Psychotherapy* (2nd ed.). Springfield, IL: Charles C. Thomas.

Lewis, H. (1982). *The Intellectual Base of Social Work Practice*. New York: The Lois and Samuel Silberman Fund and Haworth Press.

Mallon, G. P. (1992). Utilization of animals as therapeutic adjuncts with children and youth: a review of the literature. *Child and Youth Care Forum, 21*(1), 53–65.

Mallon, G. P. (1994a). Some of our best therapists are dogs. *Child and Youth Care Forum, 23* (2), 89–101.

Mallon, G. P. (1994b). Cow as co-therapist: utilization of farm animals as therapeutic aids with children in residential treatment. *Child and Adolescent Social Work Journal, 11*(6), 455–474.

Mallon, G. P. (1994c). A generous spirit: the work and life of Boris Levinson. *Anthrozoös, 7* (4), 224–231.

Mallon, G. P. (1999). Animal-assisted therapy interventions with children. In C. E. Shaefer (Ed.), *Innovative Psychotherapy Techniques for Children and Adolescents* (pp. 415–434). New York: Wiley and Sons.

Morgan, G. (1986). *Images of Organization*. Newbury Park, CA: Sage Publications.

Moss-Kanter, R. (1982). Dilemmas of managing participation. *Organizational Dynamics, 3*, 5–27.

Moss-Kanter, R. (1988). When a thousand flowers bloom: structural, collective and social conditions for innovation in organization. *Research in Organizational Behavior, 10*, 169–211.

Netting, F. E., Wilson, C., & New, J. C. (1988). The human-animal bond: implications for Practice. *Social Work, 39*(1), 60–64.

Ross, S. B. (1999). Green Chimneys: we give troubled children the gift of giving. In F. R. Ascione & P. Arkow (Eds.), *Child Abuse, Domestic Violence, and Animal Abuse: Linking the Circles of Compassion for Prevention and Intervention* (pp. 367–379). Indiana: Purdue University Press.

Senter, S. (Ed.). (1993). *People and Animals: A Therapeutic Animal-assisted Activities Manual for Schools, Agencies and Recreational Centers*. Brewster, NY: Green Chimneys Press.

Serpell, J., Coppinger, R., & Fine, A. H. (2000). The welfare of assistance and therapy animals: an ethical comment. In A. H. Fine (Ed.), *Handbook on Animal-assisted Therapy* (pp. 415–431). New York, NY: Academic Press.

9 Understanding the other end of the leash: what therapists need to understand about their co-therapists

Patricia McConnell*, Aubrey H. Fine[†]

*University of Wisconsin-Madison, [†] California State Polytechnic University

During the summer of 2009, Dr. Patricia McConnell and Aubrey Fine talked to discuss her impressions of what therapists should be aware of while partnering with a therapy animal. The following is a synopsis of their conversation and some of the conclusions that were formulated.

Patricia McConnell, PhD, CAAB, is an Ethologist and Certified Applied Animal Behaviorist who has consulted with cat and dog lovers for over 22 years. She combines a thorough understanding of the science of behavior with years of practical, applied experience. Her nationally syndicated radio show, *Calling All Pets*, played in over 110 cities for 14 years. She is the behavior columnist for *Bark* magazine ("the New Yorker of Dog Magazines") and Adjunct Associate Professor in Zoology at the University of Wisconsin-Madison, teaching "The Biology and Philosophy of Human/ Animal Relationships." She is the author of 12 books on training and behavioral problems, as well as the critically acclaimed books *The Other End of the Leash, For the Love of a Dog* and *Tales of Two Species*.

AHF: In your book *The Other End of the Leash*, you discuss dog owners' needs to understand how their dogs think. What insights can you give our readers about dog behavior as it relates to animal-assisted therapy?

Patricia: In one sense, I'd say to people who are going into this field the same things that I would tell any owner, which is that so often our dogs are basically confused! After all, they're individuals of one species trying to translate the communications of another species. And so, there are some general principles that are equally relevant in the field of animal-assisted therapy and intervention, as they are with any dog owner. First, it's important to keep in mind that dogs primarily communicate with visual signals. Yes they vocalize, and yes, of course, they can respond to verbal cues and listen to what we say. Sound is truly an important part of our interactions with dogs. But vision trumps sound in both species (remember "a picture is worth a thousand words"?). I did some research on this issue in the early 90s, showing that, when asked to sit to the simultaneous production of a movement and a sound, puppies performed at much higher levels when presented with the movement by itself rather than just the sound. Every trainer will tell you that dogs are

Handbook on Animal-Assisted Therapy. DOI: 10.1016/B978-0-12-381453-1.10009-1

watching you all the time, and that yes, they can learn verbal cues, but that your movements are even more important.

That's especially relevant to people with therapy dogs because so many human actions are misconstrued by dogs. A movement can mean one thing to a person, and something else to a dog. Hugging is a perfect example. One of the reasons why many dogs are not good prospects for being a therapy dog is that they appear to interpret a hug as a kind of a threat or a challenge for social status. At the least, it is something that makes them uncomfortable, whereas we give hugs to express affection. In this case it is easy for dogs and humans to miscommunicate. Therapy dog owners need to be on guard for that kind of miscommunication.

Not only can hugs can be threatening to dogs, but direct approaches or direct eye contact can be threatening to some as well. That's why we need to condition and train our dogs to become comfortable with hugs and stares, and also to choose dogs with a personality that allows them to tolerate and even enjoy some of that. It also emphasizes why handlers need to be informed about canine ethology.

Another general principle for assistance dog owners to remember is the importance of reinforcing our dogs for doing what *we want them to do*, rather than focusing on what we *don't want them to do*. The latter, regrettably, seems to be our default! Our tendency seems to be to wait for an animal to do something we don't want and then correct it, rather than proactively teaching a dog what we *do* want them to do. Positive reinforcement for good behavior is much more successful and so much more communicative. For example, when we say "no" to a dog for jumping up, we haven't told her what we want her to do. There are at least 20 other things she could do that would be wrong: she could chew on the wheelchair, urinate in the hallways or bark when she shouldn't. How is she supposed to know what we want? The word "no" provides little information, and that's what dogs need to be well behaved. Once you take the perspective of "I need to focus on teaching my dog what I do want her to do," everything changes. Your whole relationship changes with your dog, because now you have a dog who can trust you to help her be right. If you have a working dog who desperately needs you to communicate clearly, then it is especially important. Always ask yourself: "what do I want?" when your dog does something you don't want her to do. It's your job to teach it to your dog, not hers to figure out on her own.

AHF: Do you have any suggestions on how you can prepare a therapy animal to greet various clients in a positive manner?

Patricia: The best approach is to set up training situations in which the dog could be reinforced for learning the correct behavior. If the dog, for example, is greeting too enthusiastically, then we should teach the dog that if he sits and lets the child come to him, keeping all four paws on the ground, wonderful things are going to happen. It's not hard to train that, although of course it's more difficult with some dogs than it is with others. Training polite greeting behavior requires knowing what the dog wants to work for and using that as reinforcement. Perhaps it's a treat, or playing with a ball, or even being allowed to be petted by the visitor. In this case, for example, first teach the dog to sit in a situation with no distractions, and provide lots of reinforcement for it. Gradually start to ask the dog to sit when slightly distracted, but not overwhelmed with excitement. Next, start asking the dog to sit when there is somebody in view, and provide lots of high-quality reinforcement for a good response. Eventually, ask the person to approach you, and have them ask the dog to sit. If he does, instantly give the dog reinforcement. If the dog doesn't sit and jumps up, the visitor (who should be a good friend who is "in" on the training) should immediately turn and walk away.

AHF: You seem to be emphasizing the critical importance of training as well as the use of successive approximation to shape behaviors of the dog and our own expectations. It seems logical that the animal needs to be well trained before being engaged as a therapy animal.

Patricia: You have hit the nail on the head! The key is to do the training in a step-by-step fashion just as we teach children to learn and perform anything new. Nobody puts a child down on a piano bench for the first time and expects them to play Beethoven's fifth!

AHF: I agree whole-heartedly.

Patricia: We start training the kinds of responses we want *outside* of the situation in which we want them performed. Think of therapy or assistance work as an Olympic performance that requires hours and hours of practice. The key to success is starting *outside* of the therapy situation in a step-by-step way that increasingly approximates the kind of situation the dog will be in once he's working.

AHF: Thank you for clarifying. We all need to respect our differences and realize that dogs respond differently than humans. Understanding the other end of the leash leads to a more reliable and enhanced relationship. Dogs aren't humans with four legs. When you wrote that book *The Other End of the Leash*, what prompted you to write it?

Patricia: What prompted me to write *The Other End of the Leash* was two-fold. First, my life-long motivation has been to improve the relationship between people and animals. To me that relationship is a biological phenomenon that is one of our greatest blessings. It's an amazing gift that we can either cherish or abuse. So one of my goals was to improve the relationship in a very general way between people and animals.

The other motivation relates to my desire to be a bridge between the scientists who study behavior and people who love animals, because it seems to me that there is a bit of a gap. There are many people in academia who study behavior, and learn so many amazing things about it, but yet there is still a bit of a black hole between that world and people who live with and love animals. I have always wanted to be a bridge between those two worlds. One way to do that is to observe communication (and miscommunication!) between people and dogs. So much of our miscommunication is based on our genetic predispositions to behave in certain ways. A good example of this, mentioned earlier, is hugging. Young children hug at a very early age, and all of the higher apes hug, for that matter—it's just something we do; part of who we are inherently as a species. Of course there are cultural influences in affiliative behavior, but nonetheless, it's a strong genetic predisposition. Having studied communication as an ethologist, I couldn't help but notice how often there was a species difference in basic behaviors like hugging and greeting behavior, or play behavior and the expression of affection. *The Other End of the Leash* was written to help people understand how their behavior influences their dog's behavior, in order to improve their relationship.

AHF: I think that this is an important topic because once we respect the differences and similarities of our species we truly can relate more effectively.

Patricia: Agreed! Absolutely.

AHF: What would be the key behaviors you would want to see in a dog that you would consider ready to work as a therapy animal?

Patricia: Good question. Perhaps the two most important aspects of behavior important in therapy dogs are as much related to personality as to training. Without question, the most important behavior in a good therapy dog is based on a personality trait we could call being affiliative to people. All of us who have had or worked with a lot of dogs know that, starting at a very early age, there are dogs that just seem to adore people. You know the ones I mean—they see a person walking down the street and go all gooey, wagging from the shoulders back, apparently thrilled to meet another human being. I have a Border Collie like that. When he sees an approaching person it's as though he's thinking "OH BOY! Look, there's another one!"

However, I also see dogs that may be polite to strangers, but are not particularly happy to see them. What they really want is to meet another dog. They will run up to a group of dogs and people and greet the dogs but ignore their owners. There are actually quite a few dogs like that, and there is nothing wrong with it. Most of these dogs have strong bonds with their owners, but they're not necessarily good prospects for therapy or assistance work, because they are not that interested in interacting with people outside of their own family. You can influence a dog's interest in people through training and experience, but in my experience it is hard to overcome a dog who is born primarily interested in other dogs.

AHF: There are always dogs that are more compatible with others and I think that's what you're alluding to. But in fact, dogs still have a canine instinct to be around dogs as well. Are you stating that certain dogs would favor being around their own species?

Patricia: They do. I see dogs who love their owners, but really don't care very much about other people. I've met hundreds of them in consultations and training classes, who greet you quickly, if at all, and then leave to interact with other dogs. That's in contrast to the dogs who seem absolutely thrilled to meet another person. I was just talking recently to someone involved in animal-assisted activities who said that one of the common problems they encounter is dogs who are so bonded to their owner that they ignore the patient and they don't really want to interact with other people that much. I think that speaks to this personality trait that I'm talking about, about this strong affiliation to humans, that is essential in a good therapy dog

The second trait, perhaps more obvious but still deserving attention, is the importance of dogs that are friendly but not overly reactive or active. I suspect that category actually includes a number of traits and behaviors which might be sorted independently, including general energy levels (from high or low) to overall confidence (from overally pushy to calmly secure to downright fearful). Certainly we know that shyness, or the fear of unfamiliar things, is strongly influenced by genetics as well as environment. Energy levels can also be altered substantially through training and maturity, but they have a genetic component as well. Thus, this category of "reactivity" is a big one, and requires a thoughtful evaluation of both breeding and experience in therapy work.

Figure 9.1 Here's a lovely example of two very relaxed and happy individuals! Notice that their mouths are relaxed and open, and their eyes a showing true smiles ("Duchenne smile"), in which the smile moves upward and causes the eyes to close into a "happy squint." The perfect faces to see on a therapy dog and its client!

AHF: One of the strengths of using dogs in therapy, which may be poorly understood by many, is the fact that dogs seem to have a keen ability to understand our behaviors. Some believe that dogs' strengths in communicating with humans pertain to their predisposed ability to inspect our faces for critical information, for reassurance and for guidance. I believe that these are crucial traits that many dogs have developed to become keen observers of our reactions. I feel that these skills make dogs, especially therapy dogs, more responsive to our actions. Can you comment on this?

Patricia: That's an excellent point, Aubrey. There is research showing that if a domestic dog is unable to solve a problem, she is quick to turn and look at her owner, as if for assistance. Wolves, on the other hand, do not, even if they have been hand raised by people and spend a great deal of time with them. There is no question that dogs are especially attuned to accepting humans as social partners...one great big multi-species pack as it were.

AHF: The next question has several elements integrated. At what age do you feel a dog is ready to work in therapy? How much training do you think an animal would need to be ready for this work so that we can protect the animal's and patient's welfare?

Patricia: I'm glad you asked because it's a critical question. I suspect, although I don't have any data, that at least some dogs are being asked to do this kind of work when they're not ready for it. Keep in mind that dogs aren't emotionally mature until they're about three years of age. I think that is often forgotten. I've talked to a number of people who have had their dogs tested as therapy prospects and be rejected, but the dog was only a year and a half old!

There's a lot of training that's involved in a good working dog, and that takes time. Think of what we are asking of these dogs—it's more than we would expect from most people. The dogs who can pull this off are amazing; we should be building statues in honor of them! Given how much we expect from them, it's only fair to give them the kind of training that you would want if you were asked to do something that was difficult. And good training takes time.

We also need to give dogs time to develop emotional maturity. Good working dogs need time to develop emotional control and to be able to self handicap themselves. As an example, I was once lucky enough to watch the international herding dog trials in Scotland. This is the crème de la crème of Border Collie herding dogs in which they're being asked to work under extreme pressure. It's physically and emotionally demanding and the average age of the dogs competing was seven years old. That means that the average age of a dog who's competing in the equivalent of the Olympics was a middle aged dog! I think that's because the older dogs had the experience and the emotional maturity to know when to act and when to inhibit themselves. Therapy dogs have to make a lot of decisions as well, so, in a very general sense, I would suggest that dogs not be asked to do this kind of work until they're older. Of course there are exceptions, I know of a dog who did an amazing job with one particular person when he was only a year and half old, but in general we need to let our dogs develop and mature before we expect too much of them.

AHF: Unfortunately, this is one of the mishaps that happens frequently. Some people want to start working with their dogs too early. Sometimes younger dogs with their zest and their sort of puppy features seem to be more intriguing and attractive for people. But I agree with you that many young dogs aren't ready for the stressors that they will be placed in while working with a diverse group of individuals. Therapists, clinicians and those who volunteer with their animals need to realize that this isn't about our love and admiration for our pets. We need to think of what is in the best interest of the patient and the therapy animal. We are talking about our trained co-therapists that need to be safeguarded from the stressors of their working environment. Safety for all involved must be of outmost importance! What specific things should clinicians look for in a good therapy dog? Are some breeds better than others? Would you suggest a certain gender over another, or to make decisions on an individual basis?

Patricia: I would love to see some research on the effect of sex on performance, but I anecdotally I haven't seen any evidence of any effect.

Not long ago, I was asked by the editor of *Bark* magazine if males or females were easier to train, so I did some research and I put that question out on my blog. There is little to no research on the topic, but I got some fascinating answers from readers. They said: "females are easier," and "males are easier," and "females are smarter," and "males are smartest!" No consensus there! The only real data we really have is that males tend to be more successful at high performance events like herding and retrieving. But we don't know why, because there are many factors that go into that statistic. After all, females go into heat and have puppies, so they can't work part of the year. In addition, professionals make more money if their male is successful than if their female is, so there may be a bias to putting more effort into training males than females. We simply don't know if it has anything to do with the sex of the dog.

I can tell you that the people I've talked to locally who have therapy or assistance dogs have varying experiences. One person has had 4 males and 4 females and the males have been much better, but you can hear the opposite depending on who you talk to. In my area, the assistance dogs are half males, half females. My guess is that if sex has an effect, it's relatively small. I suspect that personality, training and experience are much more important.

I think that might be true of a breed effect as well. I would guess that if somebody did the research, personality and training would come out as the most important factors. I wouldn't be surprised if there wasn't some breed effect, after all, some breeds are inherently more people oriented and some are designed to be hyper-reactive, but I think it primarily goes back to the individual dog. I love that you mentioned your 7 or 8 year old dog earlier, again, because I think so many people try out with their year and a half old puppy when their dog might be just perfect at 6 or 7 or 8. When one of my best herding dogs, Cool Hand Luke, was young, he'd sometimes lose his cool while working sheep, and cause trouble in some situations. But by the time he was 7 or 8, he developed an incredible sense of finesse and maturity that made him invaluable.

AHF: If you were getting a puppy, how do you evaluate early temperament traits that could be used as indicators for future therapy animals?

Patricia: Oh you asked the $64,000 dollar question! If someone could answer that question they could either be very happy or very wealthy—or both!

AHF: Sorry.

Patricia: No, its okay…it's the question that everybody asks. And it's the question we don't have an answer to right now. My best answer is that all you can do is create a probability statement. You can get a puppy that has a higher probability of working out than another puppy. But it's like the weather…just because there's a likelihood of showers, doesn't mean there's going to be rain, right?

AHF: No, I think that's a very good point, because it is all about probability and possible predictability. You often see breeds such as Golden and Labrador Retrievers, but I want to also highlight that you also see mixed breed dogs and other breeds of dogs becoming wonderful candidates. You shouldn't have preconceived assumptions. I often have people calling and asking what breed you would recommend. Will you give a general answer or do you think there are certain species that are more aligned to becoming therapy animals?

Patricia: There are certain breeds of dogs that seem to be more common as assistance and therapy dogs. I think one of the reasons that Golden Retrievers are so popular, for example, is because so many of them have that high level of human affiliation that I was talking about earlier. In contrast, I see dogs of other breeds who are a bit more reserved, perhaps an example might be an Anatolian Shepherd, who was bred to be a bit cautious around strangers. So, again, it goes back to a probability statement. Some breeds will have a higher number of individuals who might be good therapy dogs, but even within breeds that are commonly used for assistance work, like Labradors and Goldens, for example, there are plenty of good dogs that aren't right for the work. We all know individuals in those breeds who have super high energy levels and are too rambunctious. Or perhaps they're fearful, or maybe they don't have a lot of emotional control.

I do think that one of the reasons that Goldens and Labradors are so popular is that they appear to be what scientists call "neotenized," or animals who still behave a bit like puppies even when they are grown up. You might think of them as "Peter Pan" dogs, who maintain that youthful joy and exuberance, even when they are middle aged. But again, we're back to that probability statement, because it really is always about each dog as an individual.

AHF: Very good. Where does obedience training intersect with temperament and the individual quirks of the animal? We don't want all the animals to be the same but we do want consistent behavioral reactions. To what extent can we enable an individual dog's personality to work with AAT beyond some of the issues that we've talked about?

Patricia: This is an important question for everybody who is interested in having a therapy dog. Temperament is a critical factor, because no matter how good a trainer you are, it is not possible to change an individual's temperament. After all, temperament is defined as behavioral predispositions that you are born with. Of course, you can influence how temperament affects behavior: that's what personality is—personality is temperament plus experience. So you can certainly shape an animal's behavior, but you can't turn an animal who is genetically predisposed to be shy and fearful into a bold, confident animal. This, Aubrey, this is the biggest problem that I've seen with people who come to me and say "Help! I got this puppy to be a therapy dog and he's terrified of the nursing home and I want you to fix it." I had a psychologist come in once as a client, explaining that he had "an amazing dog that worked with troubled children, autistic children, and children with severe behavioral disabilities. The dog was virtually bomb proof and absolutely wonderful and I want you to help me find another one." He stated repeatedly that his previous dog was "one in a million." I wrote a column in *Bark* magazine reminding us all that "one in a million" means that they are...

AHF: One in a million

Patricia: Exactly! One in a million, as in: rare, hard to find, and difficult to replicate! I say this as a reminder that not all dogs can be therapy dogs, no matter how good a trainer you are.

That said, training and experience can have a profound effect on an individual's behavior. And so it is crucial to socialize a puppy appropriately, to condition a puppy to enjoy different situations, and to help healthy neural connections form at an early age (even in utero, by the way—we've learned that in utero experiences can have a profound effect on how a dog reacts to stress). And so, both genetics and experience and training act as partners to create a dog who, we all hope, becomes a brilliant therapy dog who helps lots of people.

AHF: That's an extremely good point. Although we have our personal admirations for our own animals, we need to put their work into a realistic perspective. The bottom line is that clinicians need to recognize that their animals need to be prepared to take on their very difficult roles.

Patricia: To add to that excellent point, I think it is critical for all of us to be on guard against projecting our own feelings onto the patient, or onto the therapy animal. You know just because we felt good about an interaction doesn't mean the patient did.

I've talked to people who were involved in some kind of animal-assisted activity and left glowing, just so happy to have done a good thing. Except, sometimes when you analyze the dog's or the patient's responses, they weren't enjoying themselves as much as the owner. Years ago, when the Delta Society was first forming, I heard a talk at one of their conferences in which a survey was done after animal-assisted activities. The dog owners evaluated their interactions as overwhelmingly positive and useful. However, the patients were nowhere near as positive as the handlers in their response. Some of them enjoyed it; some of them did not, often because they felt that they didn't have any choice in the timing of the visit or who came to see them.

I know that since then many of these issues have been discussed at length, including in your book, about how important it is to have patient acceptance and control. However, the main point stands that it's critical not to project your feelings and your desires onto the patient or your dog. Some patients may not want the interaction, and some dogs may not enjoy the work. I've seen quite a few clients who came to me saying "I want this dog to be a therapy dog" and in five minutes I thought, oh dear, but the dog doesn't want to be. It sounds like you have had similar experiences.

I think it is understandably hard for people to accept that the dog that they love so much may not be the perfect dog for this kind of work. This is true in other fields as well. People come to me and say "I want this dog to be an agility dog" and I'll go watch the dog in an agility trial, and the dog looks miserable. He might be looking back at the car, tongue flicking, yawning, or other signs of stress. It can be hard for any of us to step back and be objective, but the more you know, the easier it is. And I think that's why you, Aubrey, can look at your dog and say, "I love this dog, but this is not the right dog." And I can look at my young 3-year-old Border Collie and say, "I love this dog so much I could just get teary-eyed talking about him and he's a brilliant sheep herding dog at the farm…but he will never be a brilliant performing dog at a herding dog trial." That's just not who he is. It doesn't mean I love him any less, and in a way, it allows me to love him more, by honoring who he is and not trying to make him something he's not.

AHF: I think that's really crucial. What are the signs that dogs may be stressed in doing any of the animal-assisted interventions that we're talking about? For example, a colleague once shared with me an outcome she witnessed while her therapy dog was working with children with terminal illnesses. The dog seemed to demonstrate traits of being tired, which I believe could have been signs of stress. What do you recommend for therapists or clinicians to be aware of when trying to determine stress in their therapy while working? What provisions would you recommend to ameliorate or avoid these significant challenges for the animals involved?

Patricia: It's a great question. I think everybody who does any kind of animal-assisted work should be a working ethologist, a Jane Goodall in the hospital or the clinic so that they know the signs of stress in their dogs. It's true that some of them are relatively subtle. Everyone who does assistance work should look for behaviors like tongue flicks, where the tongue comes straight out the front of the dog's mouth. Often that is a sign of low level anxiety. Yawning can also be a sign of low level anxiety. Of course, dogs yawn sometimes just like we do when they're waking up, but a dog that is wide awake and yawning is often an uncomfortable dog. Sometimes dogs will turn their head and look away. Perhaps you ask them to get up on a bed or to greet somebody, and they stand still and turn their head in another direction. That's often a sign of a dog saying I just can't do this, I don't want to interact.

We also should attend to any change in energy, whether it's an increase or a decrease. It's easiest for people to notice when their dog starts to look physically tired and becomes slower and less enthusiastic. But I think that it's often easy to misinterpret dogs that start acting as if they had an overabundance of energy, or what I would call frantic energy. Dogs who are uncomfortable or nervous can seem wildly friendly or enthusiastic, when in reality they are the equivalent of someone babbling foolishly at a party because they are nervous. So it's important to look at changes in energy level either way.

Every handler should know the general signs of tension and stress in dogs and also know his or her own dog, knowing their "baseline" behavior and what changes if they become agitated or less enthusiastic, for example. That requires being a really good observer, like a scientist in the field. You can train yourself to improve your observational skills by starting to watch for one individual behavior at a time. Perhaps one session you'll notice tail position, and another you'll focus on tongue flicks. Go to a vet clinic and sit in the lobby and look for tongue flicks so that your brain is programmed to notice them.

There's an excellent video, by the way, by Suzanne Hetts and Daniel Estepp, on reading dog postures and expressions. It's titled *Canine Behavior: Observing and Interpreting Canine Body Postures*. It's the best video I've seen on helping people read the signs of discomfort in dogs. And no matter how much you already know, remember that the learning should never stop. Make sure that you stay up to date with the current changes in our understanding of animal behavior so that you can continue to enhance your relationship with your assistance animal.

AHF: Absolutely. Do you have any guidelines for the amount of time a dog should work on a given day?

Patricia: I don't have a generic guideline, because it depends so much on each individual dog. I guess the only general guideline I have is to stop working before you think you should! One of the guidelines in any kind of animal training, when you're training a new behavior or you're counter conditioning a dog who has a behavioral problem, that is the second you stop and ask yourself, "Should I stop now...?"

AHF: You're too late!

Patricia: Exactly! Or at least it is time to stop before going any further.

AHF: So it's a way of thinking. It's a prescription that if you're going to do animal-assisted interventions you have to be cognizant or aware of the therapy animal that you're working with. You must take into account how best you safeguard the integrity, the quality of life, the health, both physical and mental, of that animal.

Patricia: That's right. That's why another generic guideline is to always be cognizant of what you and I see as hard work for our dogs. Working dogs have so many decisions to make, and must always be self-inhibiting while dealing with new experiences and new people. Even if they love every single second of it, it's still hard work. After all, I love my work too, and I know Aubrey that you do too, but it doesn't

Figure 9.2 This dog's face is the opposite of those in Figure 9.1. Notice that the mouth is closed, the eyes are rounded and the muscles between the eyebrows are contracted. This is the face of an anxious dog who is nervous or uncomfortable. A therapy dog with this expression on its face should immediately be removed from the situation.

Figure 9.3 Who looks happier here? The young girl is showing the same relaxed mouth and "squinty" eyes of the happy individuals in Figure 9.1, but the dog's face is showing signs of discomfort. The mouth is closed, the eyes are rounded and are showing what trainers call "whale eye", with the whites on the side of the dog's eye showing. This is a perfect illustration of our different reactions to hugs—people love them and dogs often don't!

mean we're not tired at the end of the day. That's one reason why it's critical for the handler and owner to schedule some down time for the dog. Let the dog safely off leash, let them sniff and roll and run around somewhere just being a dog, not being asked to do anything for anyone else. If they need to sleep, let them sleep. And don't schedule a day where you have 4 or 5 therapy sessions, then come home and have company coming for dinner who can't wait to pet the therapy dog! Think of it in terms of how much work and how much play is right for my dog.

AHF: The critical issue is that we all must consider a healthy balance, between the animals, their work and the patients and individuals they support.

Patricia: Yes, that's the word! Dogs need a balance between work and play just like we do.

AHF: Do you have guidelines or suggestions for our readers on optimal dog training methods? Are there models that you'd recommend?

Patricia: There are (at least!) two separate things people need to be looking at: one is training and the other is socializing, and those can get confounded and confused. First of all training, which starts the day you get a puppy. People often ask: "When should I start training? At what age?" The answer is that you are always training your dog, from the first second that you get him! Every single second that you're with anybody, whether human or dog, you're training them, they are learning something, about you, about the world and about how to behave.

I would argue that the first job of any owner is to learn how to use positive reinforcement and how to train dogs to do what you want in ways that are effective, fun and don't damage your relationship. We need to throw away the archaic model of "getting dominance over your dog" and use science and the psychology of learning to train our dogs That doesn't mean spoiling dogs with cookies by the way, it means rewarding dogs for good behavior and helping them figure out what that is, as if we were coaches trying to help them, rather than waiting for a chance to punish them.

Beyond using the right methods, people with assistance dogs would do well to think 5 or more years ahead and ask: What do I want this dog to do to be a successful working dog? Certainly you want your dog to be able to walk politely on a leash, you want your dog to be able to sit or lie down and stay when asked, you want your dog to not snatch food out of the hands of children and you want your dog to be polite when they greet people. So beyond socializing and exposing dogs to things like wheelchairs and oxygen tanks, it would be smart to come up with a short list of the things that are critical to success. Work on having your dog master those things in any context. Don't feel like you have to teach your dog 30 or 40 different cues—you're much better off using your time to teach your dog to master a smaller number of things that truly matter.

By mastering, I mean sitting when asked at the door when company comes instead of only sitting when asked while you hold the dinner bowl in your hand! Mastering gets back to that step-by-step process we talked about earlier, where you start in different contexts where there's no distractions and gradually work your way up to bigger and bigger distractions. Of course, it's important to remember that little puppies don't have the emotional control to stay on a long stay or to "leave it" until they've had maturity and practice.

Training as described above is a crucial part of preparing a working dog, but, as I mentioned earlier, the socializing and conditioning part is critical also. That can actually start before a dog is born: We know that female mammals who are extremely stressed during certain stages of pregnancy give birth to young who are born with, and maintain, dysfunctional reactions to stress as they mature. Keep that in mind if you're going to get a puppy—do as much as you can to understand how the mother has been treated during pregnancy and what the life of the puppies was like in the first weeks after they were born. You want to ensure that the developing puppy receives different kinds of stimuli—varying temperatures, different kinds of substrates to walk on once they are paddling around, and that they are well socialized as they get older.

Be careful with the concept of socialization, it is often misunderstood. Socialization does not mean taking a 7 week-old puppy to a noisy and raucous state fair and overwhelming her with too much stimuli! I mention this because trainers and behaviorists hear all too often of dogs who have been traumatized instead of "socialized." You want to do these things thoughtfully and carefully. Get your puppy out and about to a friend's quiet house, and then out to meet another socially polite dog. Slowly and gradually create situations in which a new dog who you've just started working with becomes familiar and comfortable around wheelchairs or people who walk with a different gait, or children whose arms flail. You can start conditioning your dog to be comfortable around somebody moving a little strangely or seeing somebody flail their arms by giving him a treat when he sees something out of the ordinary. However, always be careful not to overdo it.

AHF: Good answer. A therapist recently asked me a question that I thought the readers would be interested in hearing. In training her dog, the animal became very accustomed to responding to the clinician's directions but was not as responsive when the requests were made by others. She often looked to the therapist for clarification. What would be your suggestions for this?

Patricia: I'm glad you asked, because it brings up an issue that both relates to the specific problem of having your dog respond to unfamiliar people, and also to training in general. It's very common for dogs not to "listen" and respond to other people for a couple of reasons...one is that we basically teach them not to. Think about it: How often have you been in a conversation with a person in the presence of your dog, while you concentrate on your conversation and pay no attention to the words your dog might interpret as cues? Perhaps your friends say: "Come on in and sit down!" but you didn't expect your dog to "sit down" when she heard the word "Sit," did you?

Even more importantly, we're often not conscious of what the relevant cue is to the dog. For example, when we ask a dog to do something simple like sit when asked, we usually do more than say the word "sit." We change the way our face looks. We move our bodies by moving our arm or leaning forward, but when we're interacting with other people, we often just use the word "sit." But the dog has learned to sit to a hand movement or a forward lean. So, if you want your dog to listen to other people, your number one job is to know precisely what cues are truly relevant to your dog. Many of us move our bodies without any awareness of it, but believe me, your dog knows exactly what you are doing! Just the smallest movement from you can have a big effect on your dog.

AHF: Right, just like we have learned from Clever Hans.

Patricia: Yes, That's a wonderful example. Clever Hans was a horse who was brilliant—but not in the way his owner thought. His owner spent years teaching him mathematics, and believed that he had successfully trained Clever Hans to add, subtract, multiply. It turned out, through a long period of study by a scientist named Pfungst, that Clever Hans could only get the right answer if he had visual access to somebody who knew the answer himself.

AHF: Right.

Patricia: Clever Hans was using movements of the person to tell him when he was close to the right answer—a raise of the eyebrows or a tip of the head, which it turns out to be what we do when we're anticipating the right number (Clever Hans would paw the ground: one, two, three, etc. until he got to the right number). So he really was a brilliant horse, not because he could do math, but because he was such a great observer of human behavior.

Our dogs are brilliant observers too. The equivalent example in dog training is when we say sit; we usually cock our head or lift our hand. From your dog's perspective, why wouldn't that be the relevant cue? So if you're going to have your dog listen to somebody else, then you need to be aware of all the things *you* do to get your dog to respond, and teach them to another person. One of the biggest challenges for dogs is compensating for not *what* people say, but *how* they say it. You may say "Paws Up!" in a rising pitch while someone else says it in a low, descending voice, which sounds completely different to your dog. By the way, working on this is a great process for anyone interesting in having a well-trained dog—the more you are aware of all the cues you use, whether consciously or not, the more life will make sense to your dog and the more likely she is to listen to you!

AHF: Very important. Thank you for that answer. Besides aggression, and possibly fearful animals, are there any other traits that you would highly discourage in both a handler and a potential therapy animal?

Patricia: I'd say that the first thing that comes to mind in addition to the problems you mention is a lack of ability to read social signals. The handler has to be able to read the patient and the dog both, and that's a lot to attend to. You know, Aubrey, both of us have spent a lifetime working with both species, and it is just patently obvious that some people are better than others at being sensitive to social signals. A psychologist named Paul Ekman looked at people's ability to read emotional expressions on the faces of others and he found some people are much, much better than others at reading subtle signs of fear or boredom or irritation. Interestingly, there was no sex difference, disproving the stereotype that women are better than men at reading facial signals, but people varied widely in their ability to pick up on another's internal affect. By the way, you can learn to get better at it by studying facial expressions, and I would encourage everyone to work on it. Working dog handlers need to be especially good at being able to both read the patient and the dog.

Certainly some dogs seem to be exceptionally keyed in to expressions of emotion in people, while other dogs are a bit oblivious. You know the ones I mean! The ones who are so beside themselves with exuberance that they miss the look of apprehension on the patient's face. I do think that's why some dogs flunk out—I hear you laughing

Aubrey, because you know I'm talking about some of those Goldens you've told me about who are semi-hysterical with happiness when they meet any new human at all! My Border Collie Willie would flunk out in seconds right now, because he seems mind boggled every time he meets a new person. I imagine his brain to be saying "OH! Oh look! I can't believe I found ANOTHER human! Another one! Can you believe it?!" He's joyful and crazed with happiness and truly funny—and completely inappropriate right now as an assistance/therapy dog!

AHF: It really does sounds like it! We talked earlier about older dogs. My question for you is what suggestions can you give therapists working with animals, who are now aging?

Patricia: My pleasure. As we discussed before, I think a lot of dogs actually get better at their job as they mature. But once they do get past a "certain age" into their senior years, it's critical to remember that dogs are like us—they tire more easily. It's not being problematically anthropomorphic to be aware that age can make a dog's life more difficult. Thus, it's important to be aware that you may have had a dog who was a brilliant therapy dog for many years, but who can't necessarily keep up with the same kind of schedule that she had before. Perhaps it might be best to work halftime, decreasing the number of sessions or making them shorter, with a longer rest period in between. As they get older I think that's really, really important. Of course what's "older" depends on the breed; old age for a St. Bernard is 8 or 9, while for a terrier it is going to be much later.

It's also important to remind ourselves that older dogs lose their physical abilities as well as their energy levels. A dog might have leapt up on beds for years, but suddenly stopped responding to the owner's cue to do so. That might be as much about physical ability or pain as anything else. We need to be sensitive to changes that occur faster than we might expect, given our long life spans compared to that of dogs.

Figure 9.4 Which dog is slightly uncomfortable in this photo? A good assistance dog handler would notice right away that the white dog's mouth is closed—often a sign of discomfort or nervousness.

AHF: Can dogs become depressed? Perhaps we can focus our discussions toward our awareness of emotions of dogs.

Patricia: That's certainly a rich topic! I'd say that the bottom line is that, when comparing the emotions of dogs with those of people, it's a glass half empty and a glass half full. There's no question that there's a lot that's different between our emotional life and that of dogs. Brain structures that mediate emotions are larger and more active in people than in dogs. These areas integrate the rational decision-making part of our brain, the associational areas they're called, and the more primitive emotional part of our brain.

So we know there are substantial differences, that's the "glass half empty" part. But we also know that the glass is half full—that the basic emotions like fear and anger and happiness are primal, primitive emotions that live in very old parts of our brain and that appear to work in very similar ways in all mammals, not just dogs. By the way, it does seem that dogs are particularly expressive—their faces are remarkably good at expressing emotions. I believe that's one of the reasons why we have this miraculously remarkable relationship with them.

But in terms of the basic emotions, I think it's critical for people to remember how easy it is for our dogs to be frightened. Fear is a primal emotion that is designed to keep you alive so that you can pass your genes on to the next generation. It is also important to be aware that fear and anger are both primal emotions, and are tightly linked in the brain. One of the changes I see sometimes in older dogs, replicating those in people, is that sometimes dogs have less patience when they're older. Maybe their hips hurt; maybe they just get tired more easily. I can't tell you how many clients I've seen who've told me "He's always been so wonderful with children, he lets them do anything, but now he's snapped at one and I can't understand why!" Well, perhaps because he is now 11 years old and he's put up with all this stuff until now, but now he's older and a tad tired and can get a little grumpy when his hips hurt!

That's another reason why it is so important to be able to read your dog. I just had an incident with one of my young Border Collies that is a good reminder of that. I had asked him to sit and stay while I chatted with some friends. There were other dogs not on sit/stays, but Willie is excellent at these kinds of stays, and normally would have behaved beautifully. However, he kept breaking his stay and walking away. Now, he's not perfect but that wasn't typical behavior at all. Finally, the third time I looked at him and I said Willie, "what is wrong?" Aubrey, he gave me a look that could bring tears to your eyes it was so intense with pleading. I interpreted it anthropomorphically as "Please, please, please let me get out of here." I said "Where do you want to go?" and he ran to the car and looked desperate for me to open the door. I put him in the car and as I walked back I realized that 2 years before he'd been attacked by one of the dogs he was standing beside in that very place, in that very context. I had forgotten, and he hadn't. He was afraid and he was trying to tell me. It's critical for people to not look at their dogs as being just "obedient" or "disobedient," but as sentient animals with a rich stew of emotions that influences their behavior.

That's a long answer to your first question! The short answer is that yes, I do think that dogs can get depressed. It might feel different to them than depression does to us, but surely something of the feeling of sadness is shared between dogs and people.

AHF: The other side to this position of course is that dogs are trying to communicate something to us that we don't understand, because we speak different languages.

Patricia: That's right. And I think it's up to us to be as good a translator as we can.

AHF: Absolutely. I'd like to end just with final thoughts or words of wisdom that you would like to conclude with. What final words of wisdom would you like to leave our readers with?

Patricia: Well, we've touched on it earlier, but I'd like to emphasize it again that this work is very challenging. I'm not saying that lots of dogs don't love it, but I do think that the dogs who are good at this deserve silver chalices and big blue ribbons. I know there are a lot of them out there and I wish I could thank every single one of them in person.

But this is not work for every dog, so don't feel disappointed if a prospect doesn't work out. We are asking dogs to be absolutely bomb proof around other dogs, around a vast variety of people in a multitude of conditions, in stressful circumstances with weird, strange noisy machinery. The dogs who are great at it are one in a million dogs. Don't be disappointed in a dog who can't do this—give him some years to mature, and try again, or love him for what he *can* do. You know there are not a lot of us who could win the Tour de France! And there's not a lot of us who could win an Olympic gold medal in ice skating. It's true that it takes a lot of practice, but it's also what you're born with. Aubrey, you and I could swim until we grew gills but we would never be Michael Phelps. So if you have a great assistance or therapy dog, you are one lucky person! I salute you and the team your dog completes. If you don't have one yet, remember that this is challenging work and that not all dogs are suited for it.

In summary, here's my gratitude and admiration for all the good work done by working teams everywhere, and my love and sloppy kisses for all of the dogs who are better suited to other work!

Part Three

Best Practices in Animal-Assisted Therapy: Guidelines for Use of AAT with Special Populations

10 Incorporating animal-assisted therapy into psychotherapy: guidelines and suggestions for therapists

Aubrey H. Fine EdD

California State Polytechnic University

10.1 Introduction

Aaron came to his social skill's group early each week so he could get Sasha's undivided attention. "Can I bring in the cage and hold Sasha for a while? She is so cute," bellows Aaron as I entered the building. "Sure, why not," I replied. What he did not realize is that my eyes never left him as he carried in my small gerbil, sat down in the classroom and let her out of the cage. Here is a ten-year-old child diagnosed with ADHD, sitting and giggling and smiling, as Sasha crawls over his legs. So as not to frighten her, he sits calmly—something that is hard for him to do. He eventually begins to stroke her and tells her how beautiful she is. "You are a sweetheart, Sasha. I love you," he whispers, with a proud smile.

At these times, Aaron acts like a different child. Around Sasha he slows down, and she has a calming effect on him. Her nature seems to transform him. Perhaps it is her size. He does not want to overpower her, so he moves slowly and talks gently. She reciprocates, by snuggling and allowing his tender touch. Over the course of the program, I often brought Sasha to Aaron so that he can learn to gage his own activity level and perhaps be in more control (Fine and Eisen, 2008, p. 7).

This case study occurred over 30 years ago. Sasha eventually was to become my first therapy animal. Those preliminary observations helped develop my early understanding of the value of animal-assisted interventions. In particular, I began to appreciate how the integration of an animal into therapy promoted a more nurturing and safer environment for clients.

As has been articulated throughout this book, the value of the human/animal bond has been seriously investigated over many decades. Furthermore, popular culture reflects the bond between humans and animals as is seen in the popular press and the film industry. Most recently, various films in our pop culture have portrayed the importance of the human/animal bond as well as the impact of the bond. There has also been a proliferation of books focusing on the importance of wildlife to humans as

Handbook on Animal-Assisted Therapy. DOI: 10.1016/B978-0-12-381453-1.10010-8

a recognition of the positive impact that animals have on the lives of people: Olmert (2009) *Made for each Other*; Becker et al. (2005) *Chicken Soup for the Dog Lover's Soul*; Chernak-McElroy (1996) *Animals as Teachers and Healers*; Von Kreisler (1997) *The Compassion of Animals*; and Grogan (2005) *Marley and Me*. It seems a logical next step that mental health professionals try to incorporate the human/ animal bond connections, when applicable, into their practices where applicable. As Bern Williams once stated: "There is no psychiatrist in the world like a puppy licking your face."

10.2   The need for research

Despite positive anecdotal examples, the reader needs to recognize that there is limited empirical support and research validating the overall effectiveness of AAT (Fine, 2002, 2003, 2008; McCulloch, 1984; Serpell, 1983). Voelker (1995) noted that the biggest challenge facing advocates of animal-assisted therapy can be summed in two words. "Prove it" (p. 1,898). Voelker (1995) stresses that the major difficulties in obtaining outcome data in animal-assisted therapy is that many of the professionals applying these strategies do not see the necessity of conducting outcome research or, possibly, they do not take the time to validate outcomes. This lack of documentation and thorough investigation leaves a large void in demonstrating the efficacy of this approach. It seems that most clinicians persevere and incorporate the modality primarily on qualitative impressions that have been observed or heard about. However, a lack of empirical evidence may continue plaguing the acceptance of AAI, especially as many become more concerned about evidence-based forms of psychotherapy.

Barak et al. (2001) notes that research is also needed to identify the underlying mechanisms of AAT that produce therapeutic changes. The findings from these studies would be valuable to understand how the interventions work, so that the best practice procedures can be implemented. Unfortunately, many outsiders have a limited awareness of how AAI is applied and there is a need to demystify the process. In addition, there also needs to be a more appropriate bridge between clinical practice and best practice research. Practitioners are encouraged to pay closer attention to the need for program evaluation and documentation. All of these efforts should assist the scientific community with the needed research priorities.

Many have pointed out that although the utilization of animals may be highly appealing, it needs to be understood that just because an interaction with an animal is enjoyable, does not imply that the procedure is therapeutic (Katcher, 2000; Serpell, 1983).

Fine, in an interview with Kale (1992), pointed out that animals could have a therapeutic impact on children when the approach was integrated with other strategies. "To say that the therapeutic changes occur solely in isolation would perhaps be quite misleading." Fine (2005) explains that it is important to understand how animal-assisted interventions can be integrated alongside traditional psycho-therapeutic approaches. Attention in future research must address this concern.

Therefore, it is strongly emphasized that over the next decade a concentrated effort be initiated to demonstrate the efficacy of this modality. The findings from quality designed studies will help clinicians as well as researchers answer a variety of questions, including:

1. Under what conditions are animal-assisted interventions (AAI) most beneficial?
2. With what special groups do AAI appear to work the best?
3. Under which theoretical orientation (e.g. humanistic, cognitive, behavioral) does the incorporation of animals seem the most therapeutically effective?

10.2.1 Objective of the chapter

The objective of this chapter is to provide the reader with practical insight into how animals may be incorporated into a therapeutic practice. Within this context, the author will also provide suggested guidelines to assure quality control for the client's and animal's safety. Case studies will be incorporated to illustrate how the interventions can be applied logically.

10.3 The role of animal-assisted therapy in psychotherapy: is there such a thing as an AAT Rx?

As previously discussed, one of my greatest reservations in recommending AAT has been the lack of published protocols. There is a definite lack of clarity of how a treatment regime can be replicated. Unfortunately, this lack of clarity makes it difficult to develop a clear cut Rx for AAT. One should not look at AAT in isolation, but rather how the animals support and augment the clinician's ability to work within his/her theoretical orientation (Fine, 2005, 2008). Fine (2005) has suggested that there are several basic tenets to consider when one incorporates animals into therapeutic practice. Therapists should consider utilizing a simple problem-solving template as they plan on applying AAT interventions with their various patients. The following three questions should be considered:

1. What benefits can AAT/AAI provide this client? The clinician needs to consider the benefits animals will have in the therapy. What benefits will the animals provide in the clinical intervention? Should therapists only expect the animals to act as social lubricants to promote a safer environment, or can the animal's involvement be more deeply integrated within the clinical efforts?
2. How can AAT strategies be incorporated within the planned intervention? A clinician must begin to conceptualize the vast array of opportunities that the therapy animals can provide. Several of these alternatives will be discussed later in the chapter. A plan must be formulated so the outcome will not be purely serendipitous.
3. How will the therapist need to adapt his/her clinical approach to incorporate AAT? This perhaps is the most critical aspect to consider. A clinician must take into account how incorporating animals into therapy may alter his/her clinical orientation. Therapists must also mull this over (even if being an animal lover) if they are comfortable practicing psychotherapy co-jointly with their animals. If the animal's presence does not match the style of therapy practiced, it may cause more dissidence and become ineffective.

In a similar vain, Chandler (2005) points out that the therapist should design inter-ventions to involve a therapy animal in ways that will move a client toward treatment goals. The decisions regarding if, when and how a therapy animal can or should be incorporated into counseling depends on: (1) the client's desire for AAI along with the appropriateness of the client for AAI (which may be prohibited by such things as animal allergies, animal phobias, or client's aggressive tendency); (2) the counselor's creative capacity to design AAI consistent with a client's treatment plan; and (3) the therapy animal's ability to perform activities that assist in moving a client in a direction consistent with treatment goals (Chandler, 2005).

To assist in better understanding how to apply AAT in traditional clinical practices, the following section briefly describes basic foundation strategies that should be considered.

10.4   Consideration 1—why clinicians may find animals therapeutically beneficial

10.4.1   Animals as a social lubricant for therapy

Parish-Plass (2008) suggests that AAT is based on the very strong emotional connection and evolving relationship between the therapist, client and animal. She points out that an animal's presence in the environment contributes to the perception of a safe environment. She also believes that the client's perceptions that the therapist makes the therapy animal feel safe contribute to the client's impression that s/he will feel safe as well. Early research investigating the incor-poration of animals within outpatient psychotherapy was somewhat limited. Nevertheless, Rice (1973) conducted a study to evaluate the extent to which animals were used by psychotherapists in the USA as a whole. The study also attempted to classify the ways in which animals served in psychotherapeutic roles. One hundred and ninety members (64% of the sample) of APA Division 29 (Division of Psychotherapy) responded to the survey. The findings of the study suggested that 40 clinicians (21%) indicated that they used animals or animal content in conjunction with their psychotherapy.

The most powerful finding from this study pertained to the specific uses of the animal within the therapeutic setting. The researchers reported that some therapists found some utility in actually having animals present in therapy, while others utilized animals in a conceptual manner. Common commentaries about the utilization of real animals pertained to employing an animal as a vehicle for cultivating or modeling the positive nature of interpersonal relationships. Most of the responders pointed out that animals were used to ease the stress of the initial phases of therapy to establish rapport. The researchers also reported isolated uses of animals such as suggesting that a patient obtain a pet as a means of introducing practical caretaking responsibilities. The conceptual use of animals by most reporting clinicians was most frequently symbolic. Therapists often incorporate animal content to formulate interpretations of patient's fantasies or underlying themes in their discussions.

Mallon (1992) points out that the animals should not be considered as substitutes for human relationships but as a complement to them. It has been noted that animals appear to decrease the initial reservations that may develop from initially entering therapy. Arkow (1982) suggested that the animal may act as a link in the conversation between the therapist and the client. He called this process a rippling effect. Others such as Corson and Corson (1980) describe this process as a social lubricant. It appears that the presence of the animal allows the client a sense of comfort, which then promotes rapport in the therapeutic relationship.

Box 10.1 Case study

Fine and Eisen (2008) described how a gentle golden retriever aided a young girl with selective mutism into feeling more comfortable in therapy. "For years Diane's parents had told themselves their daughter was shy. But after her first week at kindergarten, the teacher called the parents into school for a conference where they were told that Diane needed professional help. In school she was not only unwilling to speak, but she cowered with fright when approached or spoken to. Diane's parents, concerned and upset by this evaluation, tried to work with Diane to overcome her selective mutism and fear when away from her home. Yet, nothing they said or did made any impression on Diane. She refused to talk and, at times, seemed incapable of speech, as though she physically either could not hear or speak.

I first met Diane and her parents on a weekday in the afternoon. When I introduced Puppy and myself, Diane didn't respond. She gave no indication that she had even heard me. Instead, like Charles, she began to pet Puppy's head, running her hands over Puppy's ears, nose and muzzle. Although she never changed her body posture, she was smiling and enjoying her interaction with Puppy.

I turned towards the girl and called Puppy's name quietly. When Puppy looked up at me, I gave her a hand signal to come towards me and then continued back into the inner office. As Puppy walked away, I watched Diane's face fall and her eyes take on a sad and disappointed look. I told her, "Oh, I'm sorry. I didn't realize you wanted Puppy to stay with you. All you have to do for her to come back is to say, 'Puppy, come.'"

Diane's parents stared at me, with a look of skepticism on their faces. Then, in a low voice, she called, "Puppy, come, please come, Puppy." The parents in awe gazed at their daughter. I gave Puppy the signal to go and she ran over to Diane, who slid off of her chair and began hugging Puppy tightly.

Sitting on the floor beside Puppy and Diane, I began to talk to her. I told her that I knew how hard it was for her to talk to people she didn't know and how happy I was that she was brave enough to call for Puppy. Hoping to build on this small first step, I asked her what she liked about Puppy. She hesitated a moment and then answered, "She is so soft and cuddly." As we talked, Puppy sat beside Diane who leaned against her and laced her fingers through Puppy's fur.

(Continued)

Box 10.1 Case study—*cont'd*

When the session ended, I asked Diane to say goodbye to Puppy. She hugged the dog again and said, "Goodbye." Her voice was soft, but it was clear. Puppy reciprocated with a head nudging and a huge lick on her arm. She had made a remarkable breakthrough and was about to begin her journey towards interacting with the world outside her home.

Over the course of the next five months, Diane, Puppy and I developed a wonderful relationship. Our simple first session eventually changed her life. For Diane, her whole world opened up and she eventually developed the confidence to talk and interact with others (p. 9).

Kruger et al. (2004) and Beck et al. (1986) suggested that a therapist who conducts therapy with an animal being present may appear less threatening and, consequently, the client may be more willing to reveal him/herself. A gentle animal helps a client view the therapist in a more endearing manner. This perception was also found by Peacock (1986), who reported that in interviews in the presence of her dog, children appeared more relaxed and seemed more cooperative during their visit. She concluded that the dog served to reduce the initial tension and assisted in developing an atmosphere of warmth. There have been numerous studies which have elicited similar findings. Odendaal and Meintjes (2003) suggested that animals appear to have a calming effect on humans and reduce arousal. In their study, the data linked tactile contact with a dog with experimentally induced low blood pressures.

10.4.2 The benefits of animals as an extension to a therapist: a method for rapport building

Animals are known for the zealous greetings they provide to visiting clients they encounter. Levinson (1965), in a seminal article on the use of pets (in the treatment of children with behavior disorders), implies that bringing in the animal at the beginning of therapy assisted frequently in helping a reserved client overcome his/her anxiety about therapy. Many therapy dogs are more than willing to receive a client in a warm and affectionate manner. Imber-Black (2009) points out that animals in therapy provide healthy support for spouses being yelled at by their partners and shy children who are anxious to attend therapy.

For example, in most cases, animals can become an extension of the therapist. Personally, the animals that work with me are very responsive to greeting visitors. Children look forward to seeing and interacting with Fine's therapy animals (PJ and Magic—golden retrievers, Tikvah—a bare eyed cockatoo and Ozzy—a bearded dragon). The dogs eagerly walk over to the children encouraging attention. These initial encounters ease the tension at the beginning of every meeting. The animals are instrumental in regulating the emotional climate.

Boris Levinson (1964), a pioneer of utilizing animals in therapeutic relationships, suggested that the animals may represent a catalyst in helping a child make more progress in a clinician's setting. It seems evident that the animals' presence may make the initial resistance easier to overcome. Furthermore, as suggested by Fine and Mio (2006) (and in an updated chapter later in this volume) as well as by Parish-Plass (2008), the AAI acts as an adjunctive therapy that supports the clinicians' abilities to work on the client's cognitive, social and behavioral issues. As Parish-Plass (2008) states, "the animal is the tool, and the client is the focus" (p. 12).

Box 10.2 Case study

Several years ago, a 15-year-old boy, who was diagnosed as being depressed, was referred to my office. When he entered the waiting room he became very intrigued with the fish tanks. It seemed that over the years he had developed a strong interest in tropical fish. This common interest appeared to enhance our therapeutic rapport quickly. Over the next six months, our common interest went beyond talking about and observing the fish to a higher level of involvement. After careful consideration and planning, we both believed that putting together a 60-gallon salt water tank would be therapeutically beneficial for him. Indirectly and directly, his involvement and efforts in helping select the fish, plants, scenery, and rocks not only enhanced our bond but definitely appeared to uplift his sense of demoralization. Jeff had something to look forward to. His drive to fight off his lethargy and helpless thoughts seemed to be impacted by the sight of a new environment which he helped design and build. He frequently stopped at the office to check on the fish, taking pride in his accomplishments. Although Jeff continued to battle with his depression, he continued to find refuge and support in the tank he established. The partnership we established in developing the tank was a definite asset to our working relationship.

10.4.3   A therapeutic benefit of animals in therapy: a catalyst for emotion

Fine and Beiler (2008) point out that, for many clients, the mere presence of an animal in a therapeutic setting can stir emotions. Simply interacting with an animal in a therapeutic setting can lighten the mood and lead to smiling and laughter. Animals may also display emotions or actions that may not be professionally appropriate for therapists to display. For example, the animal might climb into a client's lap or sit calmly while the client pets him. Holding or petting an animal may soothe clients and help them feel calm when exploring difficult emotions in treatment that might be overwhelming without this valuable therapeutic touch.

Animals within therapeutic settings can also elicit a range of emotions from laughter to sorrow. Often in the literature on animal-assisted therapy more attention has been given to the softer emotions, which the human/animal bond instills. Nevertheless, recognition that animals can exhibit humorous behaviors is relevant. Norman Cousins (1989) in his premier writing of *Head First: The Biology of Hope* has emphasized for decades that humor was not only beneficial in improving an individual's mental state, but also his/her physical constraints. Laughter and joy are two ingredients which positively impact a person's quality of life. It seems apparent that not only do animals promote warmth within a relationship, but they may also bring joy and a smile.

There are numerous examples that can be applied to illustrate this phenomenon. For example, a playful cockatoo or a puppy getting itself into mischief can always garner a smile. There have been numerous occasions where the animals incorporated therapeutically get themselves in comical/playful situations. It seems that when this occurs, the laughter generated has therapeutic value.

Selectively, animals are in a unique situation to display emotions and behaviors that may not be deemed professionally appropriate for a human service provider. For example, in difficult periods within therapy, a client may be in need of comforting and reassurance. The presence of an animal may become that catharsis. The holding of an animal or the petting of an animal (be it a cat, dog, or a bunny) may act as a physical comforter and soothe many patients. The touching of the animal and the proximity to the animal may also represent an external degree of safety within many clients.

Moreover, an additional benefit of the animals may be their contribution in helping clients gage excessive emotion and reactive behavior. On numerous occasions, the author has witnessed that when a dispute would take place, the animal's presence seemed to lend some comfort and stability to the environment. The adults seemed to regulate their reactiveness, possibly because they were aware of the animal's presence. Furthermore, in working with children who are quite active and impulsive, it is amazing to observe how large birds (cockatoos and macaws) seemed to help promote a decorum for what is or is not considered acceptable behavior. It seems that most children gave tremendous respect to the birds' presence (possibly some unconscious intimidation) and the reduction to their disruptiveness was evident. Most children seemed to realize that their escalated behaviors would cause uneasiness in the birds, which they did not want to cause. In addition to this one benefit, as a follow-up to the child's outbursts and the bird's ability to help reduce the tension, discussions on self-control and behavioral regulation were introduced.

10.4.4   Animals acting as adjuncts to clinicians

Mallon (1992) emphasizes in his paper that the animals must be considered as adjuncts in the establishment of a therapeutic relationship and bond. Hoelscher and Garfat (1993) suggest that when relating to a therapist with an animal, people with difficulties sometimes find the animals the catalyst for discussion, which previously may have been blocked. For example, several years ago, an eight-year-old girl visited the office. She was very intrigued with the birds she saw and wanted to hold a few of the small lovebirds. Without asking if she could hold the bird, she eagerly put her hand towards the animal. To her dissatisfaction, the bird hissed at her. Shortly after this experience, I explained to the girl that she needed to ask the bird's permission (and mine) to touch the animal. Ironically, this was followed by a powerless response of "I know what you mean." Her response to my statement piqued my attention, since she was referred for depressive symptoms. I picked up the lovebird and began to scratch her head. I told the girl that the bird was very sensitive to touch, and there were certain spots that she did not like to be touched. At this point, the girl became very teary eyed and responded by saying once again (very sadly this time) "I know what you mean." Shortly after, she began to reveal a history of sexual abuses by one of her grandparents. It was apparent the serendipitous use of the bird acted as a catalyst to promote a discussion on feelings that she had buried. Over the course of her treatment, we used the example of the bird to help her gain insight on the importance of giving people permission to embrace you, and how you have the right to tell people that your body is private.

10.4.5 The use of the relationship with animals vicariously—role modeling

A valued benefit of incorporating animals clinically is the vicarious outcomes that a client may develop as a consequence of the interaction between the clinician and the animals. For example, the loving relationship between the animal and the therapist may explain by example to the client some of the caring traits of the clinician. This outcome may enhance the development of the therapeutic relationship and alliance. Personally, over the years, this writer has been amazed with the comments he has received from clients observing his interaction with the animals. The most common response pertains to the interaction with the animals and how some clients compare these interactions with their own child/parent relationships (since most of his clients are children and their parents). Other clients comment on how well the animals are treated, including the elements of compassion, consistency, firmness, and love. These scenarios can be used to demonstrate to the client appropriate interactions and responses to behaviors.

Experienced clinicians will attest to the numerous occasions (during sessions) that boundaries need to be placed on the animals. This demonstration of limit setting should be a valuable teaching tool for the clients. The therapist can use these episodes as opportunities to model specific discipline or problem-solving strategies. For example, within my office, one of the many therapy birds that I use is an umbrella cockatoo. She periodically has a tremendous need for attention, and one approach that she uses is to screech. Parents are always amazed with my approach and the explanation that I give to them. The most common approach applied is extinction, and the eventual reinforcement of the appropriate behavior when it is demonstrated (verbal praise and petting the bird). The outcome to this interaction eventually leads to an informal discussion on behavior management, which may have implications to their own child rearing practices.

As can be seen, there are numerous episodes that a clinician could draw upon. It is of utmost importance that the therapist takes advantage of teachable moments and learning opportunities. Discussions with adults on boundary setting, the need to be loved and admired and appropriate ways of interacting are all relevant.

10.5 Consideration 2—the therapeutic environment: animals as an aspect of milieu therapy

Modifications to the work environment may also be considered a valuable contribution which animals can influence. The perceived environment appears to be more friendly and comfortable to incoming clients. Barnard (1954) pointed out that it was Ernst Simmel's pioneering work that gave serious thought to the manipulation of the environment to meet the unconscious needs of clients. In her paper, Barnard (1954) reported that in ancient times even pagan temples (which promoted healing) provided an atmosphere of encouragement and hope. She noted that in an ancient institution in Cairo patients were entertained daily with musical concerts as one source of their therapy. The underlying force within milieu therapy is recognizing the "climate" within the environment and its impact on the client. Sklar (1988) points out that there is a constant interaction between the client and the therapist that is impacted by the physical and emotional environment that is created in the clinician's office. Sklar's writings as well as Langs' (1979) suggest that the development of an effective therapeutic alliance may actually begin with the creation of a proper therapeutic environment. Sklar (1988) reports on how many outpatient clinics neglect giving attention to the physical environment in which the therapeutic process unfolds. Goldensohn and Hahn (1979) report that a client's readiness for psychotherapy could be disturbed by the simplicity of a clinic's decor and perhaps by its disorder.

Sklar (1988) also reported that many facilities that provide mental health services appear to be proud of the happy, affectionate family atmosphere that the clinic attempts to create. He suggested that one must not only focus on the client's internal dynamics for treatment to become successful, but in addition, the therapists also must address the clinical space within which treatment is ongoing.

As the research suggests, little attention appears to be given by most therapists to the elements which enhance their therapeutic environment. Light music, lighting and climate control have always been intuitively associated with a more comfortable environment. These ingredients seem to promote a sense of security and comfort. It seems obvious that living beings could also be utilized to complement the work environment by making it more appealing and relaxing. Of utmost value is that the animals appear to bring a certain sense of security and warmth into the environment. For example, Katcher et al. (1983) reported, in their study on anxiety and discomfort before and during dental surgery, that subjects viewing the aquarium appeared more comfortable and less anxious than those subjects in a control group not viewing an aquarium. Watching a school of fish swim harmoniously can be quite relaxing for some. With proper lighting and an attractively designed tank, clients could feel more at ease when they enter an office or while undergoing a therapy session. Over the years, I have found fish tanks to be extremely enticing. The gentleness of the fish and the ambiance developed can be truly beneficial to a therapy session.

Unfortunately, when schools in a fish tank are not properly selected, the outcome can make people feel uncomfortable, especially if the fish incorporated are aggressive and hyperactive. For example, early in my own personal utilization of fish tanks for the ambiance they promote, my selection of fish was not appropriate. Two fish in the school were quite active and aggressive. They would often be observed fighting and chasing each other. Rather than finding the fish tank to be relaxing and comforting, many of the clients noted that they felt uneasy watching the fish. One adult was overheard saying that the activity level of the fish reminded her of the chaos that she witnesses within her own home, especially with her children. Although this event serendipitously led to a discussion about her concerns with her children, it did not put her at ease.

With the importance of a therapeutic environment now established, it is notable to appreciate how animals can be viewed within this dimension. Beck and Katcher (1983) suggest that animals have the capacity to modify a person's environment. Friedmann et al. (1983) have demonstrated that people appear to exhibit lower blood pressure and verbally express feelings of relaxation in the presence of a dog, while Beck and Katcher (1983) have been able to correlate a similar phenomenon in the presence of viewing a tank of fish. Lockwood (1983) hypothesizes that this outcome may occur because people perceive most situations with animals as safer and perhaps more benign.

Very few studies have been implemented investigating the impact that animals have in altering the therapeutic effects of an environment. Beck et al. (1986) initiated a study in Haverford, Pennsylvania, where the initial hypothesis speculated that the animals would alter the therapeutic environment and make it less threatening to patients with various mental illnesses. These patients (who met in a room containing birds) attended sessions more faithfully and became more active participants in comparison to a control group. The researchers' findings reported that the experimental group (who conducted their therapy in the presence of the birds) had a greater rate of attendance and demonstrated more frequent participation than did the non-bird group. In addition, their findings from the Brief Psychiatric Rating Scale identified a reduction in hostility scores in clients within the experimental milieu. The researchers believed that this outcome was enhanced due to the impression the clients had about the birds (that the animals were perceived by the patients as less hostile, and, therefore, the clients felt more at ease in the presence of the animals).

Not only can animals be used to enhance the milieu as well as enhance the relationship between the client and the therapist, but also the therapist can also observe how the client relates and interacts with the animal. The client may unconsciously be overbearing and controlling to the animal or, for that matter, may act coldly and unresponsively. These experiences may provide the therapist with an alternate diagnostic window to view his/her client.

10.6 Consideration 3—incorporating theory into practice: animal-assisted therapy from a life stage perspective

A clinician's theoretical orientation will have a strong bearing on the incorporation of animals within his/her therapeutic approach. An explanation that seems to naturally align itself is developmental psychologist Erik Erikson's theoretical orientation. Erikson views development as a passage through a series of psychosocial stages, each with its particular goals, concerns, and needs. Although the themes may repeat during a lifecycle, Erikson noted that certain life concerns were more relevant during specific eras. For example, as people age and experience new

Table 10.1 Erik Erikson's eight stages of development

Stage 1: Basic Trust vs. Basic Mistrust (1st Year)
Virtue—Hope
Estrangement, Separation, and Abandonment

Stage 2: Autonomy vs. Shame and Doubt (2nd Year)
Virtue—Will

Stage 3: Initiative vs. Guilt (3–5 Years Old)
Virtue—Purpose

Stage 4: Industry vs. Inferiority (6th Year to Puberty)
Virtue—Competence (Workmanship)

Stage 5: Identity vs. Identity Confusion (Adolescence)
Virtue—Fidelity

Stage 6: Intimacy vs. Isolation (Young Adulthood)
Virtue—Love
Elitism

Stage 7: Generativity vs. Stagnation (Middle Adulthood)
Virtue—Care
Generational (Parental Responsibilities towards the Youth)

Stage 8: Integrity vs. Despair (Older Adulthood)
Virtue—Wisdom—Integration of Life Experiences
Ritual—Integration
Perverted Ritual—Sapientism (Pretense of being Wise)

situations, they confront a series of psychosocial challenges. This author recommends that clinicians should consider the various eight stages of psychosocial development and reflect on how the application of animals may be appropriate. To articulate the various stages, I have incorporated Table 10.1 to illustrate the major elements found within each stage. This will be followed by an interpretation of how Erikson's theory can be applied to animal-assisted therapy.

10.6.1 Suggested developmental goals and treatment purposes for children

Within the first series of life stages, the primary goals that need to be achieved pertain to a child's need to feel loved, as well as developing a sense of industry and competence. In a practical sense, animals can assist the clinician in promoting unconditional acceptance. Bowers and MacDonald (2001) point out that children over the age of five turn to their beloved companion animals when they feel stressed and are in need of unconditional love. Children may also use their relationships with pets as an emotional buffer to help cope with a stressful environment or emotional discord (Strand, 2004). It seems that the animal's presence allows the child to have something to turn to for emotional support during times of conflict. This position may hold true in a therapy environment. The animal's presence in therapy (as discussed previously) may assist a child in learning to trust. Furthermore, the animal may also help the clinician demonstrate to the child that he is worth loving. Unfortunately, for some children, their reservoirs of life successes are limited and they feel incompetent. This sense of incompetence may be acted out aggressively towards others or internally against oneself. A therapist may utilize an animal to help a child see value in his life. Gonski (1985) further suggests that the presence of a therapy animal "enables the child to initially begin to trust in a safer, nonjudgmental object prior to placing their confidence in the worker or other significant adult" (p. 98).

The animal-assisted therapy can eventually go beyond the office visits. A clinician may suggest to a family the value of having a pet within the home. The animal may help a child in developing a sense of responsibility as well as importance in life. Triebenbacher-Lookabaugh (1998) points out that children perceive their pets as special friends and important family members. In her study, she points out that 98% of the participants viewed their pets as important family members. She also noted that children may use their pets as transitional objects. Results from the study support the position that pets may offer children emotional support and a strong source of unconditional love.

Therapists may use the experience of the interaction between the child and the therapy animal as an opportunity to observe and assess if a child may psychologically benefit from having a pet within the home. Levinson (1965) reported that a pet within the home may be an excellent extension to therapy. The pet could provide the child with constant solace and unconditional joy and warmth.

Fine et al. (in press) point out that boys and girls describe companion animals as siblings and cast them in a sibling role. The language used by the children to describe interactions with and time spent with the pet was very similar to what was used to describe interactions with and time spent with peers and siblings (Melson, 2001). Children often use their pets as confidants, beginning at a very early age and continuing on into adolescence and adulthood. Children confide many different feelings to their pets, ranging from anger and sadness to happiness and sharing deep secrets. They recognize that their pet is able to handle full disclosure while remaining an uncritical and accepting audience capable of listening intently and keeping a secret. Additionally, it has been shown that children who are significantly involved with their pets show more empathy and are more skilled at predicting the feelings of others in certain situations (Daly and Morton, 2009; Melson et al., 1992).

Bryant (1990) reports of how animal companions have been cited as providing important social support for children. Bryant reports that animals within a home may assist children in developing a greater sense of empathy for others. Further studies, such as Poretsky et al. (1988) and Covert et al. (1985), both have documented similar outcomes. These researchers suggest that pet ownership may be extremely valuable in enhancing a child's self-esteem and social skills, as well as a sense of empathy. Although Paul and Serpell (1996) are in agreement with these findings qualitatively, they indicated that most of the research conducted has not demonstrated any firm causal relationship between childhood pet ownership and alterations in the psychological well-being of children. It is interesting to note that many researchers seem to agree that there appears to be qualitative support for the value of the animal/human bond but that there are difficulties in quantifying this value. Perhaps some of the challenges that researchers are being confronted with pertain not only to quality research protocols presently under investigation, but also to a possible measurement problem.

However, there have been some studies, such as Bryant (1990), which do demonstrate some promise in promoting the therapeutic benefit of pets for children. In her study, Bryant (1990) studied the potential social-emotional benefits and liabilities of children having pets. Although the study and its implications were based on children, it is important for clinicians to consider some of the findings as being pertinent for adolescents and adults. Two hundred and thirteen children were surveyed as part of the sample under investigation. The outcome of the study identified four potential psychological benefits for children to have animals. Furman's (1989) "My Pet" Inventory was utilized to assess the subjects' interests. A factor analysis of Furman's inventory indicated that, from a child's perspective, there are four factors in which the child/pet relationship can be viewed as potentially beneficial. The factor of mutuality was defined by Bryant (1990) as having to do with the experience of both giving and receiving care and support for the animal.

Furman (1989) originally identified these variables as companionship and nurturance. The enduring affection factor identifies the child's perception of the lasting quality of their relationship with their pet. This factor focuses on the child's perception of the permanence of the emotional bond between the child and the animal. The third factor, which was entitled enhanced affection, identifies the perception from the child that the child/pet relationship makes him/her feel good, as well as important. This factor is a crucial element that clusters the admiration and affection between the animal and the child. Finally, the factor of exclusivity focuses on the child's internal confidence in the pet as a confidant. This factor appears to be extremely crucial for therapists to underscore.

It is within this factor that a child may rely on the pet companion to share private feelings and secrets. This may be an important outlet, especially when there are limited friends and supports within the community or the home. Mallon (1994a) also points out that there is evidence that a child may use an animal as a confidant. In his study on the effects of a dog in a therapeutic setting treating children with behavior disorders, the staff observed that the children would often utilize the dog as a sounding board or a safe haven to discuss their problems and troubles.

Bryant (1990) suggests that the viewing of the child/pet relationship may be extremely valuable in understanding the dynamics within the family. Negative relationships may also be indicative of existing or impeding crises within the family.

On the other hand, within the study, Bryant (1990) also pointed out some of the limitations to the child/pet relationship. Some of the constraints included distress associated with taking care of the pet, the unfair grief of a pet acting mean, or the rejection of the child by the pet. These data are in agreement with other researchers such as Kidd and Kidd (1980, 1985) who point out that the choice of the animal with the child has to be a proper match. Different breeds of animals (dogs, cats, and birds) may offer unsuitable physical and psychosocial benefits to their owners. Unfortunately, if the wrong animal or breed is selected as a pet for the child, there may not be the effective bond which was described earlier. Finally, the research of Wedl and

Kotraschal (2009) suggest that girls were more likely to want to have a pet and seem to develop stronger emotional relationships than boys.

10.6.2 Suggested developmental goals and treatment purposes for adolescence

Erikson views adolescence as a time where the teenager must achieve a sense of identity. The teen goes through many physical and mental changes in his/her quest to secure an adult-like status. The developmental period appears to be the first time that there is a conscious effort in defining a sense of self. During this period, the teen begins to organize drives, beliefs, and ambitions toward a consistent and clear image of self. It is at this time frame that the emotional stability of the youth may be extremely fragile. Some teens may be unable to cope with the many physical, social, and developmental expectations that come with this passage. Their strong need for affiliations and the need to be wanted and to fit in with peers may become the primary goals within therapy. A clinician may find an animal's presence valuable in making the teen feel more at ease during his/her visit. The teen may be more willing to take down some of the barriers, if she/he feels more comfortable. Furthermore, although a teen may project the need to be adult-like, the teen may appreciate the free spirit of an animal. The comfort the youth may receive may allow him/her to feel more appreciated.

The value identified earlier in regards to the psychosocial benefits of having a pet as a child may also be pertinent to a teenager. A therapist may strongly suggest to a family that having a pet may aid a teen in experiencing some social isolation. Kidd and Kidd (1990), in their study on high school students and pets, suggested that pet ownership may be beneficial both to adolescents who are having challenges in personal independence as well as mature inter-familial relationships. Walsh (2009a) also points out the value for teens in taking responsibility for an animal's daily care and well-being. She discusses how the experiences are an excellent opportunity to form a bond as well as learning to express affection and empathy.

10.6.3 Suggested developmental goals and treatment purposes for adults

Therapists who focus more on adults may also find Erikson's insight beneficial. With young adults, their need to recognize that they can also take care of others may become a great starting point for discussion. A therapist may use a therapy animal as a starting point to discuss decisions about having children or, for that matter, child-rearing practices. It is not uncommon for some therapists to suggest to young couples that they try to rear a pet as a precursor to deciding if they are ready for children. The animal's presence may be an ideal introduction to this topic. Furthermore, adults experiencing parenting challenges and couples who are experiencing marital dysfunction may find the metaphors and the stories related to bringing up children and learning to share one's life with another person as all appropriate topics. The presence of animals, and examples incorporating animals, may give some clarity to the subject of generativity versus self-absorption. Finally, Walsh (2009b) points out that much can be learned about relation patterns in a family by asking the adults about their companion animal. The stories can reveal a great deal about the family dynamics and how the family lives with one another.

10.6.4 Suggested developmental goals and treatment purposes for the adults

Finally, animals may tremendously impact a clinician's ability to interact with elderly clients. Similar to the role that an animal may have in treating a child, a therapist may find an animal extremely useful in securing a positive relationship with an elderly client. Clients who have had a history of animals within their lives may find the animal's presence extremely advantageous in reminiscing past life events. Raina et al. (1999) have found that the daily activities for seniors who had pets were dramatically increased in comparison to the elderly who did not live in the company of animals. Barak et al. (2001) believes that AAT "reawakens both memories of a former life" and a "need to continue interacting with animals" among seniors. It is astonishing how a lifetime of growing up with animals may make it easier, for some people, to reminisce and think about major milestones in their lives. Reflections of the past may become more apparent as a consequence of compartmentalizing specific life events, which may have revolved around or included pets. A clinician may ascertain that the presence of the animal may act as a catalyst for reliving past events.

Furthermore, the clinician may also recommend to an elderly patient that he or she consider purchasing a pet. Research such as Ory and Goldberg (1983), Friedman et al. (1980), Kidd and Kidd (1997), Jenkins (1986), and Garrity et al. (1989), as well as the information noted in the chapter on aging, all suggest the inherent value of seniors having pets. A client's sense of value could be tremendously enhanced as a consequence of feeling needed once again. In addition, many individuals will thrive from the positive attention they will receive from their companion animal. In some cases, the animal/human relationship may become the necessary ingredient which alleviates a perceived sense of loneliness and isolation. Findings from research by Hunt et al. (1992) suggested that unobtrusive animals evoked social approaches and conversations from unfamiliar adults and children. It is apparent that the presence of an animal may become a social lubricant for spontaneous discussions with passing strangers. Furthermore, the walking of pets would also possibly enhance an individual's physical health and stamina. Kidd and Kidd (1997) point out that since dogs require considerable energy in care, their survival rate might be associated with the greater physical activity on behalf of their owners.

10.7 Practical suggestions for clinician's applying animals

10.7.1 Training and liability

Therapists considering incorporating animals within their practice must seriously think about the factors of liability, training, as well as the safety and welfare of both the animal and the client. Hines and Fredrickson (1998) and the Delta Society's Pet

Partner Program strongly advocate that health care professionals must have training on techniques of AAT. Clinicians also need to be aware of best practice procedures ensuring quality, as well as safety, for all parties. Table 10.2 identifies some of the basic guidelines that clinicians should consider when instituting an AAI intervention. Those clinicians living in North America should register through the Delta Society for a one-day workshop or a home study course. In an effort to achieve the best possible qualitative results, Hines and Frederickson (1998) strongly suggest that health care staff receive training. They point out that without adequate training on how to apply AAT, therapists may inappropriately incorporate animals and get poor results. The Pet Partners Program developed by the Delta Society includes in-service training on a variety of areas, including an awareness of health and skill aptitude of the animals, as well as strategies to incorporate the animals with the clients. The Pet Partner

Table 10.2 Guidelines for incorporating animals in AAT

Basic requirements

- All dogs must have excellent temperament
- The animals need to be calm and gentle and enjoy being around people
- As therapy animals, the animals will be exposed to unusual sights, sounds, and smells. The therapist needs to be confident that the animals are prepared for these unusual circumstances
- All therapy animals need to be obedient and follow directions of the therapist.
- Able to regain self-control after play or excitement
- Able to sit quietly for extended periods
- Able to navigate through crowded environments
- Attentive to the handler

Preparation

All therapy dogs should have some certification in obedience training such as meeting the standards of the American Kennel Club's Canine Good Citizens Test. The test requires the dog to master the following skills:

- Be comfortable with a friendly stranger
- Walk comfortably in a heel position on a leash
- Sit, stay, come, and lie down on command
- Be able to ignore a neutral dog
- Practice self-control
- Refrain from any aggressive responses

Safety and comfort guidelines to consider

- Major rule to follow—Always protect your therapy animal. Remove the animal from all stressful situations. Over time, you can continue to train the animal to overcome situations which were previously considered stressful
- Give the animal constant breaks, providing walks and play breaks will allow the animal to be less stressed throughout the day
- Always have fresh water available all day. On break times, have some of the animal's favorite toys available
- On a daily basis have a pleasant grooming session
- In the therapy environment, establish a safe space away from any stimulation. Within that area have the animal's favorite bed or cage

Program should be considered as a valuable introductory course. All of the training will aid practitioners in gaining appropriate guidelines for quality practice (Hines and Fredrickson, 1998).

There are numerous references that therapists should consider reading to help them understand dog behavior and possible training techniques. *At the Other End of the Leash* by Patricia McConnell (2002) and *The Power of Positive Dog Training* by Pat Miller (2001) are two excellent guides. There are many other good books on this area including the many books written by Stanley Coren. Dr. McConnell's chapter (Chapter 9) also has some wonderful insights to consider.

Finally, it is imperative that an animal's well-being is preserved and safeguarded. Several chapters earlier in this book identify some of the behaviors that animals can display when they feel stressed, especially while in the work setting. The readers are encouraged to review those chapters for more details. Additionally, Chapter 23 examines the ethical issues in utilizing animals in therapeutic settings. These issues are to be considered strongly to safeguard the quality of life of the involved therapy animals.

10.7.2   Precautions for the clients

Therapists must make wise choices in selecting animals for their practice. Not all pets make good adjunct therapists. A clinician who is considering incorporating animals within his/her psychotherapy must strongly consider what animals will serve the best purpose. This may mean further studying, and purchasing animals that best suits his/her needs. Unfortunately, a good home pet may not be suitable for therapy.

Wishon (1989) points out that an underestimated problem that may occur in the animal/human bond is the pathogens that can be transmitted from animals to human beings. This process is now known as "zoonoses." Wishon (1989) reports that most cats and dogs carry human pathogens which, along with those carried by other animals, have been associated with more than 150 zoonotic diseases. However, Hines and Fredrickson (1998) point out that the data regarding the transmission of zoonotic diseases in any AAT programs have been minimal. Practitioners are advised to work closely with veterinarians and other public health specialists to ensure the safety of the animals as well as the clients involved.

Brodie et al. (2002) suggest that, although the potential to suffer some harm from AAI may exist, it can be minimized by taking simple precautions. These precautions include the careful selection of therapy animals, rigorous health care and monitoring for the animal and informed consent by all those involved. When following good medical practices for both the animals and the patients, the risks for allergies, zoonoses and potential injuries can be tremendously reduced. Finally, the clinician should be aware of any fears of animals or allergies before utilizing animals adjunctively with specific clients. This will ensure that the addition of the animal will not complicate the therapy.

10.7.3   Additional concerns

There are numerous other concerns which a clinician should consider prior to introducing animals into his/her practice. Although some of the concerns cannot be completely planned for, the therapist must be aware of them. For example, a clinician should consider how to handle explaining an illness of the animal to his/her clients and how to explain the death of a beloved animal. Both of these variables are realistic concerns which will have to be considered seriously. Over the years, concerned attached clients have had difficulties accepting these inevitable problems. Furthermore, the introduction of new animals into a practice will also need attention. A suggestion is to transition gradually all new animals, so that you are comfortable with the behavior. At times, young animals (specifically rambunctious young puppies) will need significant attention until they are capable of being more actively involved.

10.8 Conclusions

With thought and planning, animals can make a major contribution to a therapist's arsenal in treating clients. Animals can enhance the therapeutic environment by making the milieu more emotionally and physically accessible to clients. Some clinicians may still be skeptical of the therapeutic value of the animal/human bond, and may initially underestimate the clinical utility of animals as an adjunct to therapy. It is understood, as was discussed at the outset of this chapter, that the lack of documentation and thorough investigation of outcome research leaves a large void on the efficacy of this approach. Interested clinicians may initially incorporate animals solely to develop rapport with clients. Nevertheless, after reading this chapter, a skilled and well-informed clinician should be able to recognize a multitude of benefits which animals can fulfill. A therapist may have to make some adjustments to his/her practicing philosophy to ease the incorporation of animals into one's professional repertoire.

Those clinicians who craft a place (for animals) into their therapeutic regime will not be disappointed with their efforts. Their therapeutic milieu and approach will be richer as a consequence. As George Eliot (1857) writes in *Mr. Gilfil's Love Story*, "Animals are such agreeable friends. They ask no questions and they pass no criticism." The unconditional love and devotion that an animal will bring to a therapeutic practice will be an asset that may never be thoroughly understood but should be appreciated and harnessed.

References

Arkow, P. (1982). *Pet Therapy: A Study of the Use of Companion Animals in Selected Therapies.* Colorado Springs, CO: Humane Society of Pikes Peak Region.

Barak, Y., Savorai, O., Mavashev, S., & Beni, A. (2001). Animal-assisted therapy for elderly schizophrenic patients: a one-year controlled study. *American Association for Geriatric Psychiatry, 9*(4), 439–442.

Barnard, R. (1954). Milieu therapy. *Menninger Quarterly, 8*(2), 21–24.

Beck, A., Hunter, K., & Seraydarian, L. (1986). Use of animals in the rehabilitation of psychiatric inpatients. *Psychological Reports, 58*, 63–66.

Beck, A., & Katcher, A. H. (1983). *Between Pets and People: The Importance of Animal Companionship*. New York: G.P. Putnam's Sons.

Becker, M., Kline, C., & Shojai, A. D. (2005). *Chicken Soup for the Dog Lover's Soul*. Deepfield Beach, FL: Health Communications, Inc.

Bowers, M. J., & MacDonald, P. (2001). The effectiveness of equine-facilitated psychotherapy with at risk adolescents. *Journal of Psychology and Behavioral Sciences, 15*, 62–76.

Brodie, S., Biley, F. C., & Shewring, M. (2002). An exploration of the potential risks associated with using pet therapy in healthcare settings. *Journal of Clinical Nursing, 11*, 444–456.

Bryant, B. (1990). The richness of the child-pet relationship: a consideration of both benefits and costs of pets to children. *Anthrozoös, 3*, 253–261.

Chandler, C. K. (2005). *Animal Assisted Therapy in Counseling*. New York: Routledge.

Chernak-McElroy, S. (1996). *Animals as Teachers and Healers*. New York: Ballantine Books.

Corson, S. A., & Corson, E. O. (1980). Pet animals as nonverbal communication mediators in psychotherapy in institutional settings. In S. A. Corson & E. O. Corson (Eds.), *Ethology and Nonverbal Communication in Mental Health* (pp. 83–110). Oxford: Pergamon Press.

Cousins, N. (1989). *Head First: The Biology of Hope*. New York: E. P. Dutton.

Covert, A. M., Nelson, C., & Whiren, A. P. (1985). Pets, early adolescents and families. *Marriage and Family Review, 8*, 95–108.

Daly, B., & Morton, L. (2009). Empathic differences in adults as a function of childhood and adult pet ownership and pet type. *Anthrozoös, 22*, 371–382.

Eliot, G. (1857). *Mr. Grifil's Love Story*. Whitefish, MT: Kessinger.

Fine, A. H. (1992, July). *The flight to inner freedom: utilizing domestic animals and exotic birds in the psychological treatment of children with unhealthy self-esteem*. Montreal, Canada: Paper presented at the Sixth International Conference on Human-Animal Interactions.

Fine, A. H. (1993). *Pets are Loving Project. A Manual and Resource Guide for Supporting Children*. Pomona, CA: California State Polytechnic University Graphics.

Fine, A. H. (1999). *Fathers and Sons: Bridging the Generation*. South Bend: Diamond Communications.

Fine, A. H. (2003, Nov. 1). *Animal assisted therapy and clinical practice*. Seattle, WA: Psycho-Legal Associates CEU meeting.

Fine, A. H. (2005, May 2). *Animal assisted therapy and clinical practice*. San Francisco, CA: Psycho-Legal Associates CEU meeting.

Fine, A. H. (2008, Sept. 30–Oct. 2). *Understanding the application of animal assisted interventions*. Bethesda, MD: National Institute of Child and Human Development meeting on the Impact of Animals in Human Health.

Fine, A. H., & Beiler, P. (2008). Therapists and animals: demystifying animal assisted therapy. In A. Strozier (Ed.), *The Handbook of Complementary Therapies*. New York: Haworth Press.

Fine, A. H., & Eisen, C. (2008). *Afternoons with Puppy: Inspirations from a Therapist and his Animals*. West Lafayette, IN: Purdue University Press.

Fine, A. H., & Mio, J. S. (2006). The role of animal assisted therapy in clinical practice: The importance of demonstrating empirically oriented psychotheraphies. In A. Fine (Ed.), *Handbook on Animal Assisted Therapy* (2nd ed.). (pp. 513–523) San Diego: Academic Press.

Fine, A. H., Lindsey, A., & Bowers, C. (in press). Incorporating animal assisted interventions in therapy with boys at risk. In C. Haen (Ed.), *Engaging Boys in Treatment: Creative*

Approaches to Formulating, Initiating, and Sustaining the Therapy Process. New York: Routledge.

Friedmann, E., Katcher, A. H., Lynch, J. J., & Thomas, S. A. (1980). Animal companions and one-year survival of patients after discharge from a coronary care unit. *Public Health Reports, 95*, 301–312.

Friedmann, E., Katcher, A. H., Thomas, S. A., Lynch, J. J., & Messent, P. R. (1983). Social interaction and blood pressure: Influence of animal companions. *Journal of Nervous and Mental Disease, 171*(18), 461–465.

Furman, W. (1989). The development of children's social networks. In D. Belle (Ed.), *Children's Social Networks and Social Supports* (pp. 151–172). New York: Wiley.

Garrity, T. F., Johnson, T. P., Marx, M. B., & Stallones, L. (1989). Pet ownership and attachment as supportive factors in the health of the elderly. *Anthrozoös, 3*, 35–44.

Goldensohn, S., & Haan, E. (1974). Transference and countertransference in a third party payment system (HMO). *American Journal of Psychiatry, 83*, 255–260.

Gonski, Y. (1985). The therapeutic utilization of canines in a child welfare setting. *Child and Adolescent Social Work Journal, 2*(2), 93–105.

Grogan, J. (2005). *Marley & Me.* New York: Harper Collins.

Hines, L., & Fredrickson, M. (1998). Perspectives in animal assisted therapy and activities. In C. Wilson & D. Turner (Eds.), *Companion Animals in Human Health.* Thousand Oaks, CA: Sage.

Hoelscher, K., & Garfat, T. (1993). Talking to the animals. *Journal of Child and Youth Care, 8* (2), 87–92.

Hunt, S. J., Hart, L., & Gomulkiewics, R. (1992). Role of small animals in social interactions between strangers. *Journal of Social Psychology, 10*, 32–36.

Imber-Black, E. (2009). Snuggles, my cotherapist, and other animal tales in life and therapy. *Family Process, 48*, 459–461.

Jenkins, J. L. (1986). Physiological effects of petting a companion animal. *Psychological Reports, 58*, 21–22.

Kale, M. (1992). How some kids gain success, self-esteem with animals. *InterActions, 10*(2), 13–17.

Katcher, A. H. (2000). Animal assisted therapy and the study of human-animal relationships: discipline or bondage? Context or transitional object? In A. Fine (Ed.), *Handbook on Animal-assisted Therapy.* San Diego: Academic Press.

Katcher, A. H., Friedmann, E., Beck, A. M., & Lynch, J. J. (1983). Looking, talking, and blood pressure: The physiological consequences of interaction with the living environment. In A. Katcher & A. Beck (Eds.), *New Perspectives on Our Lives with Companion Animals* (pp. 351–359). Philadelphia, PA: University of Pennsylvania Press.

Kidd, A. H., & Kidd, R. M. (1980). Personality characteristics and preferences in pet ownership. *Psychological Reports, 46*, 939–934.

Kidd, A. H., & Kidd, R. M. (1985). Children's attitudes toward their pets. *Psychological Reports, 57*, 15–31.

Kidd, A. H., & Kidd, R. M. (1990). High school students and their pets. *Psychological Reports, 66*, 1391–1394.

Kidd, A., & Kidd, R. (1997). Changes in the behavior of pet owners across generations. *Psychological Reports, 80*, 195–202.

Kruger, K., Trachtenberg, S., & Serpell, J. A. (2004). *Can animals help humans heal? Animal-assisted interventions in adolescent mental health.* Retrieved from. http://www2.vet.upenn.edu/research/centers/cias/pdf/CIAS_AAI_white_paper.pdf.

Langs, R. (1979). *The Therapeutic Environment.* New York: Jason Aronson.

Levinson, B. M. (1965). Pet psychotherapy: use of household pets in the treatment of behavior disorder in childhood. *Psychological Reports, 17*, 695–698.

Lockwood, R. (1983). The influence of animals on social perception. In A. H. Katcher & A. M. Beck (Eds.), *New Perspectives on Our Lives with Companion Animals* (pp. 351–362). Philadelphia: University of Pennsylvania Press.

Mallon, G. P. (1992). Utilization of animals as therapeutic adjuncts with children and youth: a review of the literature. *Child and Youth Care Forum, 21*(1), 53–67.

Mallon, G. P. (1994a). Cow as co-therapist: utilization of farm animals as therapeutic aides with children in residential treatment. *Child and Adolescent Social Work Journal, 11*, 455–474.

Mallon, G. P. (1994b). Some of our best therapists are dogs. *Child and Youth Care Forum, 23* (2), 89–101.

McCulloch, M. J. (1984). Pets in therapeutic programs for the aged. In R. K. Anderson, B. L. Hart, & L. A. Hart (Eds.), *The Pet Connection* (pp. 387–398). Minneapolis: Center to Study Human-Animal Relationships and Environment.

McConnell, P. (2002). *At the Other End of the Leash.* New York: Ballantine Books.

Melson, G. (2001). *Why the Wild Things Are: Animals in the Lives of Children.* Cambridge: Harvard University Press.

Melson, G., Peet, S., & Sparks, C. (1992). Children's attachment to their pets: links to socioemotional development. *Children's Environmental Quarterly, 8*, 55–65.

Miller, P. (2001). *The Power of Positive Dog Training.* New York: Hungry Minds.

Odendaal, S. J., & Meintjes, R. (2003). Neurophysiological correlates of affiliative behavior between humans and dogs. *Veterinary Journal, 165*, 296–301.

Olmert, M. D. (2009). *Made for Each Other.* Philadelphia: De Capo Press.

Ory, M. G., & Goldberg, E. L. (1983). Pet possession and life satisfaction in elderly women. In A. H. Katcher & A. M. Beck (Eds.), *New Perspectives on Our Lives with Companion Animals.* Philadelphia: University of Pennsylvania Press.

Parish-Plass, N. (2008). Animal assisted therapy and children suffering from insecure attachment due to abuse and neglect: a method to lower the risk of intergenerational transmission of abuse? *Clinical Child Psychology and Psychiatry, 13*, 7–30.

Paul, E. S., & Serpell, J. A. (1996). Obtaining a new dog: effects on middle childhood children and their families. *Applied Animal Behavior Science, 47*, 17–29.

Peacock, C. (1986, Aug.). *The role of the therapeutic pet in initial psychotherapy sessions with adolescents.* Boston: Paper presented to Delta Society International Conference.

Poretsky, R. H., Hendrix, C., Mosier, J. E., & Samuelson, M. L. (1988). Young children's companion animal bonding and adults' pet attitudes: a retrospective study. *Psychological Reports, 62*, 419–425.

Raina, P., Waltner-Toews, D., & Bonnett, B. (1999). Influence of companion animals on the physical and psychological health of older people: an analysis of a one-year longitudinal study. *Journal of the American Geriatric Society, 47*(3), 323–329.

Serpell, J. A. (1983). Pet psychotherapy. *People–Animal–Environment* 7–8.

Sklar, H. (1988). The impact of the therapeutic environment. *Human Sciences Press, 18*(2), 107–123.

Strand, E. B. (2004). Interparental conflict and youth maladjustment: the buffering effect of pets. *Stress, Trauma, and Crisis, 7*, 151–168.

Triebenbacher-Lookabaugh, S. (1998). Pets as transitional objects: their role in children's emotional development. *Psychological Reports, 82*, 191–200.

Voelker, R. (1995). Puppy love can be therapeutic, too. *Journal of the American Medical Association, 274*, 1897–1899.

Von Kreisler, K. (1997). *The Compassion of Animals*. Rocklin, CA: Prima Publishing Co.

Walsh, F. (2009a). Human-Animal Bonds I: The relational significance of companion animals. *Family Process, 48*, 462–480.

Walsh, F. (2009b). Human-Animal Bonds II: The role of pets in family systems and family therapy. *Family Process, 48*, 481–499.

Wedl, M., & Kotraschal, K. (2009). Social and individual components of animal contact in preschool children. *Anthrozoös, 22*, 383–396.

Wishon, P. M. (1989). Disease and injury from companion animals. *Early Child Development and Care, 46*, 31–38.

11 Application of animal-assisted interventions in counseling settings: an overview of alternatives

Aubrey H. Fine*, Dana O'Callaghan,
Cynthia Chandler†, Karen Schaffer‡, Teri Pichot§,
Julia Gimeno*

*California State Polytechnic University, †University of North Texas,
‡New Mexico State University, §Jefferson County Department of Health and Environment

An overview of AAI as an aspect of therapy

Aubrey H. Fine, Dana O'Callaghan, Cynthia Chandler, Teri Pichot

11.1 Introduction

The primary purpose of this chapter is to provide the reader with a better understanding of the multitude of therapeutic options on how animals can be incorporated effectively. The chapter is divided into three major themes. The first section of the chapter provides an overview of the applications of animal-assisted interventions (AAI) in various disciplines and provides a discussion highlighting the numerous ways in which AAI can be integrated and applied. The second section builds on this information and provides useful techniques and strategies for AAI with children and adults. Finally, the chapter concludes with specific information on the application of equine therapy.

In the course of the past 40 years, the utilization of therapy animals in health care has increasingly gained much attention. Originally AAI were incorporated sporadically by a few professionals; AAI is now becoming more recognized as a potential alternative in numerous health care disciplines. Professionals in various mental health disciplines, speech and language therapists, psychotherapists, occupational therapists, physical therapists, and nurses are but a few of the disciplines incorporating animals as part of their therapeutic regime. Fine (2008) and Fine and Mio (2006) point out that the greatest challenge that advocates for AAI now face is to document not only how

Handbook on Animal-Assisted Therapy. DOI: 10.1016/B978-0-12-381453-1.10011-X

AAI makes a difference, but also the specific protocols that are followed. It is clear that the interventions are in need of a stronger set of evidence-based findings. Protocols need to be evaluated and articulated so there will be more opportunities for replication. For AAI to advance as a more reputable intervention there needs to be more rigorous research to document its efficacy.

Unfortunately, the literature on AAI is filled with glamorous anecdotal comments on the value of AAI, but many questions continue to be left unanswered. Regrettably, the methods of how one applies AAI with various populations are very poorly understood and best practice options have not been readily established and clarified. One of the earliest studies examining the use of animals in psychotherapeutic settings identified some of the therapeutic purposes for utilizing animals. Rice et al. (1973) found that respondents included animals as a source of comfort, as a reward in behavior modification framework and, in addition, from a gestalt perspective as a way of exploring the meaning of touch, smell, and warmth. Rice's study, however, did not identify specific techniques utilized with animals in psychotherapy. O'Callaghan (2008) investigated the various animal-assisted interventions incorporated by mental health professionals as part of their therapeutic regime as well as the various therapeutic purposes intended with each technique. Participants were recruited nationally from various AAI/AAT for mental health providers. O'Callaghan postulated from a review of the literature that there were about 18 animal-assisted therapy techniques and ten therapeutic intentions that were identified as the primary reasons why clinicians utilized AAI. Results from O'Callaghan's study did explore how mental health professionals incorporated a variety of animal-assisted techniques for various therapeutic intentions. She found that the vast majority of mental health counselors reported using AAT to *build rapport in the therapeutic relationship.* They often did this by reflecting on the client's relationship with the therapy animal, encouraging the client to interact with the therapy animal, and sharing information about the therapy animal. O'Callaghan also found that therapy animals provided therapeutic benefits solely from their presence and without any direct intervention from the mental health professional. For instance, therapists did not encourage or guide an interaction between client and therapy animal. The animal's existence in a therapy environment provided benefits. This finding seems consistent with much of the literature describing the use of animal-assisted therapy interventions. Corson and Corson (1980) were also early pioneers in the study of AAT. They performed one of the first controlled studies involving animals as adjuncts in the therapeutic process. They reported that patients in a hospital setting displayed increased verbalization when therapy animals were included in psychotherapy treatment. Corson and Corson noted that the therapy animal was included in a non-directive fashion. Participants indicated that *enhancing trust* and *facilitating feelings of safety* in the therapeutic environment were also some of the therapeutic benefits of incorporating therapy animals. Table 11.1 describes the findings from O'Callaghan's study reviewing the top five reported therapeutic techniques and reported intentions of each technique of the subjects involved in her research.

Given this diversity within AAI approaches, it would seem that an understanding of how therapy animals are incorporated into the therapeutic regime of a clinician is

Table 11.1 (From O'Callaghan, 2008)

Top five techniques	Top intention for each technique, reported by respondents
1. Therapist reflects or comments on client's relationship with therapy animal	building rapport in the therapeutic relationship
2. Therapist encourages client to interact with therapy animal by touching or petting therapy animal	building rapport in the therapeutic relationship
3. Information about therapy animal's family history (breed, species, and so forth) is shared with client	building rapport in the therapeutic relationship
4. History related to therapy animal is shared with client	building rapport in the therapeutic relationship
5. Animal stories and metaphors with animal themes are shared with client by therapist	facilitating insight

critical in elevating the status of AAI as a complementary treatment modality. LaJoie (2003) in her dissertation proposed a classification system in order to better organize the literature in this field. She noted that to complicate matters worse, various terms were used to describe the roles of animals as therapeutic tools.

11.2   Understanding the magnitude of AAI from an interdisciplinary perspective

11.2.1   The role of AAI in speech and language, occupational and physical therapy and education

Over the past 40 years, numerous health care disciplines have incorporated AAI into their work place. It is apparent that, to most practitioners, AAI on a superficial level uses the animals to captivate their clients and to enhance their rapport. Disciplines such as physical therapy, occupational therapy, speech therapy, nursing, mental health, and education are some of the disciplines where animals are now being used as an aspect of treatment. For example, during a hospital physical therapy session, the act of petting or grooming the dog can be used to target muscles in the hand, arm, or shoulder. Patients frequently are willing to engage in a repetitious task for longer periods of time when they are engaged with a dog (Pichot, 2009). The dog's presence takes the patient's mind away from the discomfort of the exercise and adds a more casual feel (Fick, 1993; Steed and Smith, 2002).

In reviewing the literature, it is apparent that AAI has also been adopted by various speech and language therapists. However, there is little research or information describing how AAI is incorporated into the treatment process. Macauley (2006) cited six studies investigating the effects of AAT in speech and language treatment, all of the studies involved children as the recipients of treatment. One pilot study involved the incorporation of canines in speech and language treatment with preschoolers with speech delay (Macauley et al., 2002). An additional case study (Adams, 1997) examined the enhancement of speech therapy by also involving canines. The remaining studies incorporated the use of hippotherapy as a treatment modality in the field of speech and language treatment.

Macauley (2006) investigated the effectiveness of AAI in speech and language therapy for persons with aphasia. Although no significant differences were found in Macauley's study, participants noted some of the differences during AAT speech and language sessions. Participants reported more motivation when the therapy dog was incorporated into the session. In some cases, participants were asked to direct their statements to the dog, resulting in more effort in their conversations according to outside observers. In addition, participants also stated they felt less tension in their visit when the therapy dog was present. Oftentimes when therapy animals were part of a therapy session, the animals may have engaged in spontaneous moments undirected or unscripted by the therapist. According to Macauley (2006), participants spontaneously verbalized statements directed toward the therapy dog more so during AAT speech and language sessions compared to traditional speech and language sessions.

On the other hand, Mullett (2008) described a unique application of utilizing an animal in therapy. Mullett (2008) noted how a therapy dog named Pita would respond with a bark when she heard the words "cow" and "squirrel." For one patient, witnessing Pita's response provided motivation for that patient to verbalize these words more easily. Mullett explains that, for some patients, a therapy dog can offer the right amount of entertainment, distraction and pleasure to the therapy process, which seems to motivate the clients to work harder. Fine (2006, 2008) has also observed similar outcomes in mental health and occupational therapy.

AAI is now quite commonly practiced in the field of occupational therapy as an adjunct to therapy. The United States Department of Labor describes the role of occupational therapists as helping patients improve their tasks in living and working environments (Bureau of Labor and Statistics, 2009). Occupational therapists apply treatments to develop, recover, or maintain the daily living skills and work skills of their patients. For example, the occupational therapists at St. Mary's Hospital for Children, in Bayside New York, developed an animal-assisted therapy occupational therapy program in the winter of 1998 (Oakley and Bardin, n.d.). Oakley and Bardin describe animal-assisted occupational therapy as a process where the "occupational therapist conducts the therapy session using the dog as a modality to facilitate the development of skills needed by the child to achieve independent functioning in the areas of self-help, play and learning." As a child learns or relearns daily tasks such as grooming, a therapy dog can become part of that learning process. Oakley and Bardin describe a possible technique:

> For example, a child recovering from a traumatic brain injury experiences considerable difficulty dressing and grooming him/herself due to the loss of function in one arm. The therapist may ask the child to reach out with the weak arm to pet, brush or even feed the dog. The therapist may add a wrist weight to the weak arm in order to develop strength, or use an adapted brush with a special

handle to assist the child in holding the brush. The child becomes motivated and
excited to participate in treatment; thus helping to achieve treatment goals quicker
and easier.

As has been witnessed in many disciplines, the therapy animal acts as a catalyst of discussions including motivating the patients to talk about previous pets they owned. This seems to be a simple bridge to the therapy animal and perhaps the patient's personal interest in animals. In a paper by Velde et al. (2005), they described how occupational therapists may incorporate therapy animals into their practice. Velde et al. examined three different qualitative case studies utilizing animal-assisted therapy in occupational treatment. Each case study revealed different themes that emerged when incorporating a therapy animal into treatment. Ferrese et al. (1998, as cited in Velde et al.) reported that patients were able to tolerate treatment for longer periods of time when a therapy animal was present, as well as increasing patient's positive affect. They observed more smiles and increased verbalizations from the patients. Specifically related to occupational treatment goals, Ferrese et al. also noted that therapists report patients' physical benefits such as increased range of motion. The second case study investigated the incorporation of therapy animals with hospice patients. Garland et al. (1997, as cited in Velde et al.) also reported similar results, themes related to remotivation, and cognition including memory as well as tolerance for activities. In both case studies, reports indicated that the animals' presence seemed to distract the patients from the arduousness of the tasks and motivated them to work harder. Herbert and Greene (2001) found similar results when a therapy animal accompanied senior citizens in their walking program, compared to times when the senior citizens walked alone. They suggested that the dogs had the potential to improve physical conditioning for senior citizens at an assisted living facility. This perception has also been documented by Johnson in her work with the elderly.

Finally, it is also clear that AAI has found a role in the education of children. The presence of a therapy animal has the possibility to provide a calming and supportive atmosphere to children in the classroom, thus influencing children's performance in academic settings. Jalongo et al. (2004) stated that "Animal-assisted therapy is founded on two principles: children's natural tendency to open up in the presence of animals and the stress-moderating effect of an animal's calm presence" (p. 10). Within San Diego's Unified School District in San Diego, California, a therapy dog named Sunny assists students through adaptive physical education (ARAcontent, n.d.). Teacher Andrea Bazer co-works with Sunny and about 45 preschool to sixth grade children with disabilities at five different schools. Part of Sunny's role is to play fetch and other interactive games. While some school districts are welcoming therapy animals onto campuses, other therapy animal teams are finding alternative ways of bringing animal-assisted therapy to school children. Therapy Dogs United (2008), a non-profit organization based in PA, has created a traveling program bringing therapy dogs to various schools. Therapy Dogs United's ACE (Animal Care for Exceptional Children and Adults) program is designed to help children and young adults with social, emotional, physical and developmental challenges achieve positive outcomes. Their weekly visits are conducted with a therapy animal, handler, and counselor or trained therapist.

The authors will now address how various philosophically trained mental health providers utilize AAI in their practices. This dialogue will be followed with a more lengthy discussion of the various clinical applications of AAI by various disciplines.

11.2.2 Integrating AAI into psychotherapy

When psychotherapists are contemplating adding a therapy animal as a tool in their practice, it is most helpful to begin by making a list of key principles upon which their underlying guiding theory relies. By becoming clear regarding one's theoretical approach, therapists can determine if incorporating a therapy animal is compatible. Once this crucial step is in place, the therapy animal then becomes a valuable tool in the work prescribed by the guiding approach.

Chandler et al. (n.d., under review) demonstrate the versatility of AAT as various techniques are applied in ways consistent with several different counseling theories, including person-centered, cognitive-behavioral, behavioral, psychoanalytic, gestalt, and solution-focused brief therapy (see Tables 11.2 and 11.3).

General AAI techniques for children and adults

Aubrey H. Fine, Dana O'Callaghan, Karen Schaffer, Teri Pichot, Julia Gimeno

In the previous chapter, several general tenets of the various applications of AAI were discussed in great detail. These tenets appear to be the strongest reasons why most clinicians apply animals in their work regardless of their professions and theoretical orientation. Before we add to this list and discuss some unique approaches, a brief review will be incorporated. Table 11.4 lists the four major tenets that Fine discusses in the previous chapter. The readers are encouraged to review these principles as a foundation for the information discussed within this chapter.

Many benefits of AAI have been demonstrated in AAT research and some of the most notable benefits include, but are not limited to: (a) increasing client motivation to attend sessions (Lange et al., 2006/2007); (b) contributing to unconditional acceptance of a client and facilitating client/therapist rapport and trust (Lange et al., 2006/2007; Reichert, 1994, 1998); (c) increasing client focus and attention during sessions (Fick, 1993; Heindl, 1996; Limond et al., 1997; Martin and Farnum, 2002; Richeson, 2003); and (d) providing nurturance, growth and healing of a client through client/therapy animal play, petting and other appropriate interactions (Cole et al., 2007; Fine, 2006; Friedmann et al., 1983; Odendaal, 2000; Wilkes et al., 1989).

When therapists initially learn about the power of integrating a therapy animal into a psychotherapy session, an exciting chapter in the clinician's professional life unfolds. Once the nascent excitement begins to fade and reality begins to set in, therapists soon begin to wonder, "What do I do with the therapy animal in the session? What is the animal's role?" The therapist is the one who must decide if, when and how a therapy animal is to be incorporated into the therapy process. The therapy animal can best be described as an "adjunct tool" (Chandler, 2005, p. 89; Fine, 2006) in therapy, meaning the therapy animal works as an assistant to the therapist.

Table 11.2 Sample psychotherapeutic animal-assisted interventions (briefly summarized from Chandler et al., n.d., under review)

Psychotherapeutic theory	Animal-assisted intervention (AAI)*	AAI intention	Case scenario
Person-centered	Therapist reflects upon client's feelings while client pets and hugs therapy dog during spontaneous client therapy/animal interaction	Increase client's sense of safety and trust	After a spontaneous intervention with a counselor and her therapy dog a female adolescent lowers her defenses and becomes much more cooperative in an initial intake interview with a probation officer in a juvenile detention facility
Cognitive-behavioral	Therapist facilitates clients performing tricks with a therapy animal	Challenge client's irrational beliefs, enhance frustration tolerance, and increase self-confidence	An adolescent male in a juvenile detention facility tried unsuccessfully a few times to get a therapy dog to do a trick and then gave up quickly out of frustration stating he could not do it. Following processing of self-defeating thoughts with a therapist and some brief coaching and encouragement the juvenile tried again until after several more attempts he and the dog succeeded with the trick
Behavioral	Therapist facilitates clients teaching obedience commands to therapy animals	Experiential lessons for clients on impulse control, behavioral learning, behavioral modification, and generalization (from dogs to juveniles) of positive benefits of change in behaviors	A group of adolescent males in a juvenile detention facility learn to modify their own behaviors while teaching unadoptable dogs good manners and obedience so the dogs can be adopted into good homes instead of being euthanized

(*Continued*)

Table 11.2 Sample psychotherapeutic animal-assisted interventions (briefly summarized from Chandler et al., n.d., under review)—*cont'd*

Psychotherapeutic theory	Animal-assisted intervention (AAI)*	AAI intention	Case scenario
Psychoanalytic	Therapist facilitates client insight from client interaction with a therapy animal serving as a transitional object	Uncover unconscious anxiety of client to make it conscious so the client can better resolve an anxiety	Ten-year-old male described by school counselors as at risk for academic and social failure begins group equine therapy and experiences his horse to be very nervous and anxious around him but the horse is not this way around his same age and gender therapy partner. The therapist learns from the client that the client believes the horse acts this way because the horse does not like him. The therapist encourages him to spend the next week pondering why he thinks the horse does not like him. The following week the client exclaims that he has figured it out—that the horse does not like him because he does not like himself. After processing why he does not like himself the client achieves new personal insight and support and encouragement from the therapist and other members of the therapy group. The client is now able to approach and interact with the therapy horse without the horse becoming nervous or anxious around the client

Gestalt	Therapist facilitates client group to achieve a task together with a therapy animal	Uncover self-defeating personal beliefs, limited thinking styles, and dysfunctional communication and interaction patterns that impair authentic living	Clients must cooperate together to move a horse over a low obstacle in a large arena. The only rules are: during the task clients may not speak words out loud or touch or bribe the horse. But, clients may speak to one another during infrequent timeouts called by the therapist. Though not revealed to the group until the end of the task, success relies on (1) how well the group works together in respectful ways, and (2) clients' ability to initiate creative problem solving
Solution-focused brief therapy	Therapist changes the client's therapeutic environment and activities to include equine-assisted therapy	To provide the type of therapeutic environment and activities that will facilitate client personal growth and development	An adolescent male in a juvenile detention facility was withdrawn and introverted for many months until he participated in group therapy with horses, a therapy environment where he thrived though he had no previous exposure to horses. Successes with the horses brought him out of his shell and he developed self-confidence. The support from his therapist and the respect he received from his peers in his equine group facilitated his development as a compassionate leader of his group

*The sample AAI are not meant to suggest that certain AAI are limited only to certain theories, rather it is meant to demonstrate that AAI is versatile enough to be incorporated into a variety of theoretical approaches.

Table 11.3 Principles of solution-focused based therapy and AAI (Pichot and Dolan)

1. If something is working, do more of it	When working with a therapy dog, it becomes immediately clear who likes dogs and who is interested in receiving a visit. A solution-focused therapist using a therapy dog is always cognizant of these moments, and takes the time whenever possible to allow the clients to have the desired interaction
2. If it is not working, do something different	Adding a therapy dog as a tool can be just the something "different" that works. A therapy dog can provide just the needed distraction to allow client and therapist alike to discover a different path that might be more effective
3. Small steps lead to large changes	When observing a therapy dog and professional in action, it soon becomes clear that each tiny act adds upon another, building upon something special deep within the client, resulting in something powerful
4. The solution is not necessarily directly related to the problem	This approach believes that the clients' solutions to their problems oftentimes have nothing to do with what originally caused the clients' problems. In the end, the therapy dogs make a difference to each client in very different ways
5. The language requirements for solution development are different than those needed to describe a problem	Because animals do not speak, clients are forced to use a different way of communicating when interacting with a therapy dog
6. No problem happens all the time. There are always exceptions that can be utilized	Solution-focused therapy suggests helping the clients change their focus onto times in which the problem is not occurring or is not as severe. Animals excel at this technique, for they do not analyze problems

Table 11.4 Tenets of animal-assisted therapy

Tenet 1: Animals acting as a social lubricant
Tenet 2: A catalyst for emotion
Tenet 3: Animals as teachers
Tenet 4: Adjuncts to clinicians and animals changing the therapeutic environment

11.3   General therapeutic approaches for children and adults

11.3.1   Therapeutic use of metaphors and stories

Mallon (1994) discovered that animals have been symbols of power and nurturance. The metaphors of flight with birds and strength of horses can be used therapeutically by therapists to help their clients uncover internal concerns. McMullen (in press), McMullen and Conway (1996), Close (1998), Battino (2003), Barker (1996) and Argus (1996) point out that metaphors are extensively utilized by clients in their conversations with therapists. Their research suggests that the incorporation of metaphor themes throughout the course of therapy may actually represent a productive indicator of the therapeutic relationship. Kopp (1995) pointed out that metaphors are similar to mirrors in their ability to reflect inner images within people. Metaphor therapy resides on the position that people, in general, structure their reality metaphorically. Both the client and the clinician can apply metaphors as a method of discovering and understanding client's concerns. The imagery generated from the metaphors can be used to help the client uncover how s/he is coping or feeling. For example, a client could be talking to a therapist about feeling overwhelmed about her daily life. When asked what she plans to do about it, the client responds quickly by stating "I really don't want to open that can of worms right now." The metaphor of the "opening of the can of worms" may represent the client's unwillingness to scramble and try to clean up the mess that she is in right now (rushing around trying to prevent the mess that would be made when the worms squirm out). She does not want to face the formidable task of putting her life in order. The metaphor helps to accentuate that position.

Probably the most effective metaphors and stories about birds pertain to their grace in flight. Therapeutic discussions range from the majestic eagle soaring freely to the beauty in the flight of a flock of birds. Equally as beneficial are the sad metaphors that can be applied to a clipped (wings) or grounded bird.

Additional metaphors may include feeling chained or leashed, smothered or being in a cocoon. Clients may develop therapeutic gains when the metaphors applied may also suggest a resolution. For example, the entire process of metamorphosis is an excellent example, which illustrates a transformation. The caterpillar goes through the arduous task of spinning its cocoon that initiates the metamorphosis from its present state to the magnificent butterfly. For months the caterpillar leads its sheltered existence as its body is transformed. Therapeutically, the process of metamorphosis can be valuable in explaining two challenges. Numerous insightful dialogues can be developed on either of these two themes. Some clients will benefit from a discussion of the process of transformation, while others may gain some insight into themselves while discussing the sheltering of a being in a protective environment. Furthermore, the short-lived life of a butterfly can also be related to the price that some will take for the outcome.

11.3.2   Storytelling

Deshazer (1994) and Combs and Freedman (1990) imply that embellishing a client's thoughts through storytelling stems from the narrative psychotherapy tradition. From this approach, insights suggest that meaning is given to our lives and movement occurs in therapy when we have transformational stories which help put our lives in a new context. The narrative approach to therapy suggests that some clients appear to be stuck in their lives and the new stories generated help them gain a better understanding of their life conditions. Furthermore, the various stories may also lend credible approaches and insight for possible resolution. It seems that for some clients, the previous stories they rehearse in their heads to cope with their challenges are not effective any longer or lose their meaning. Therapeutic storytelling that takes advantage of thematic concerns can integrate narratives that directly pertain to the client's concerns.

Experientially, since the author's practice incorporates animals, he also applies metaphors and uses stories with animals to help clarify certain positions to his clients. Freeman (1991) points out that stories are appropriate in different manners at all stages of life. A clinician's ability to care for and maintain effective communication between his/her patients can be augmented and enhanced by the stories we hear and share. The use of tales can be utilized as a source of support and expression as a child or an adult works through a specific concern. The story may reflect a specific dilemma that the individual is attempting to confront and provide some insight on methods for resolution. Fine et al. (in press) suggests that stories help us see the world from the inside perspective of other people. Through stories, outcomes and consequences of decisions are illustrated. Stories of events concerning people or animals can be an inspiring approach to apply with our clients. The stories can therapeutically illustrate and uncover specific concerns and issues, and also help our clients unravel their concerns from other perspectives.

11.3.3   Walking therapy

Biophilia is a fundamental human need to affiliate with other living organisms (Kahn, 1997). The Kahn (1997) research reveals that children have an abiding affiliation with nature. Combining the therapeutic usage of animals along with nature exploration could be a powerful approach with some clients. A natural outcome of having a therapy animal is to walk the animal. While walking, one has the opportunity not only to engage in discussion, but also to experience the surroundings. At times, the serendipitous observations may enhance or stimulate the ongoing conversation between the clinician and the client. Fine (2006) has found walking a productive part of therapy in some cases. When working with clients whose concerns are non-threatening, the walk may put the client at ease. While working with children, most do not appear to become distracted while on a walk, but rather engage in discussions freely. While taking a walk, many life examples may be illustrated. For example, if the dog needs to relieve itself, the client must learn to be patient and understanding. Furthermore, the clinician can model responsible behavior and bring materials to clean up the mess.

While walking, children seem to display a great sense of pride leading the animal. In fact, on numerous occasions I stop the walk and make a point out of how important the child appears leading the animal. This redirection emphasizes the importance of the special bond. They are periodically stopped by a pedestrian who may ask them a question about the animal, and in most cases, the interactions are quite pleasant. Combining utilizing the natural environment, along with the animals, seems to be an added benefit in strengthening the rapport with the child.

11.3.4 Clinical applications

Over the years, walking therapy has been applied with many of my clients. A population which seems to have had the greatest gains is children with selective mutism and those with separation and social anxiety. By using the walk as an excuse to leave the office, children who experience separation anxiety begin to practice leaving their parents. The ventures beyond the office can be used as true experiences for separation. The client can be instructed to develop alternative cognitive structures that promote optimal thinking.

In the several cases of treating children with selective mutism, the walks with the dogs are initially utilized as an opportunity to get the child to talk louder. While walking, there may be many competing sounds, which may impede our ability to hear each other. Requesting that the child speak louder is simply a reality of the environment. Amazingly, as the children become more comfortable with the animals, and begin to enjoy their walks, their comfort and confidence seem to be increased. Bowers and MacDonald (2001) noted similar findings. They point out that affectionate animals have been found to elicit verbalizations in clients who refuse to speak or who are very withdrawn.

A natural occurrence during the walk is the occasional interruption from another pedestrian walking by. The animal seems to stimulate greetings from passers-by. This outcome may eventually be a planned goal for the walk. Early in treatment, a clinician may select a route where there likely will not be any people on the road. However, as the client's confidence seems to build, a clinician may plan to take a route where interaction will be generated. A clinician may use some time prior to the walk to prepare the client with strategies in the event that a civilian may try to start up a conversation. The walk then could represent a true test to assess progress. The client then can return to the office and with the clinician's support, evaluate the outcome.

The walks through the community or in the park may be useful for some clinicians. This option not only helps clients feel more relaxed, but also the milieu may enhance their willingness to talk and reflect.

It is important that clinicians have the client sign a waiver consenting to go on walks with the animals. Table 11.5 is an example of potential forms that can be used.

Table 11.5 Consent form for taking walks with the animals: an aspect of AAT

I hereby give my consent that my child may go on therapeutic walks in the surrounding area with the therapist as an aspect of the animal-assisted therapy. I have been informed (by the therapist) of the purpose of such walks and also realize that a potential consequence of the walks is that my child's anonymity may be discovered (by a bystander walking by). All attempts will be made to keep the walks private, and no information about our visits will be disclosed on these walks.

I will always be informed of when a walk will be taken, as well as the route and duration. I have the right to refuse having my child take a walk with the animals at any given time period.
Signature_____
Client's name_____
Date_____/_____/_____

11.4   Application of AAI with children: selected approaches

11.4.1   Play therapy

Play therapy incorporates the value of play as a treatment modality, most notably when working with children. The Association for Play Therapy (APT) offers the following definition for play therapy: "the systematic use of a theoretical model to establish an interpersonal process wherein trained play therapists use the therapeutic powers of play to help clients prevent or resolve psychosocial difficulties and achieve optimal growth and development" (APT, 2009). Play is a child's language; play therapy allows a trained therapist to help children express and work through emotional difficulties in their natural language of play. Although approached by many theoretical orientations, play therapists have begun to incorporate therapy animals into their practice. VanFleet, a psychotherapist and author, incorporates canines into her practice. VanFleet (personal communication, December 30, 2009) offers the following information regarding canine-assisted play therapy.

> *Canine Assisted Play Therapy: The focus of Canine-Assisted Play Therapy (CAPT) is to build relationships based on reciprocity and play, and because this represents a process, it can be used with a wide range of presenting difficulties. CAPT is typically used in conjunction with other play therapy and Filial Therapy work. In particular, there are five major, and somewhat overlapping, goal areas in which we focus our CAPT efforts. When clients have goals in these areas, then we consider using CAPT as part of the comprehensive treatment plan.*

Table 11.6 describes the five major goals in CAPT.

There are three major forms of play therapy in which CAPT is typically used.

In ***non-directive play therapy***, the child chooses which toys to play with and how to play with them. The therapist follows the child's lead and helps the CAPT dog do the same. Sometimes the child involves the dog, and sometimes not. The therapist ensures that the dog is treated appropriately and that the dog has the chance to "opt out" of activities at any time. This requires a highly trained dog that is tolerant of many things that can occur in play sessions and that is relatively calm by nature. At no time, however, are dogs expected to do things they do not like.

In ***directive play therapy***, the therapist suggests basic activities designed to meet the child's goals or needs. Again, dogs are not asked to do things they do not enjoy. Many different activities are included under this category and are outlined in more detail below.

Some examples of activities used during directive play therapy work are listed below:

- how to meet and greet a dog safely and properly
- how to conduct positive, force-free dog training (including free shaping, lure-reward, and clicker training)
- how to teach a dog new tricks, such as jumping through a hoop, hiding in a box, roll-over, etc.
- helping the dog overcome "problems" similar to the child's (asking children's advice or conducting a pretend call-in television show for children to respond to animal-related problems not unlike their own)

Table 11.6 The five major goals in CAPT

Attachment/ Relationship	Children learn healthy ways to be cared *for* (basic trust); how to relate to others; the importance of reciprocity in relationships; essentially, what healthy attachment relationships are like…we help children and adolescents learn how to transfer what they have learned about relationships with the therapy dogs to companion animals at home and then to their human relationships
Empathy	Children learn about appropriate caregiving, how to consider and behave in ways that respect the welfare of another. CAPT is used to help children develop empathic responses by attuning to the dogs' communications and feelings
Self-regulation	Children learn to have patience when the dogs do not do as the children wish, when teaching new tricks or behaviors to the dogs, or when they are jointly learning new tasks or games. Emphasis is placed on learning canine communication signals and responding appropriately to them
Problem-resolution	CAPT process can be applied in the resolution of a variety of specific problems, such as anxiety reduction, appropriate expression of anger, development of frustration tolerance, the handling of aggressive impulses, reduction of distractibility and impulsiveness, elimination of animal maltreatment, the overcoming of trauma-reactive behaviors (e.g. lying or stealing), increases in healthy attachment, and increases in overall adjustment
Self-efficacy	Clients develop safety and self-protection abilities, a sense of competence (through canine skill building) and confidence

- storytelling involving the dog directly or indirectly
- how to recognize and adjust to canine communication signals (e.g. yawns, nose licks, whale eye, tucked tail, play invitations)
- managing arousal games, such as rope tug with a long rope, ball games, frisbee
- reacting to playful activities that the dog offers! Dogs often suggest new activities that if therapist and child are attending to, can be very helpful in terms of the therapeutic work

Part of the skill of CAPT involves turning various activities into therapeutically meaningful interactions. Some of this is accomplished by the use of creative cues for the dog. For example, a dog learns basic targeting to the cue "kiss me." The dog touches its nose to the child's hand. This can be useful in attachment work. The main thing for all CAPT activities is that they must be mutually enjoyable for child and dog! This helps children learn the importance of reciprocity in relationships and typically leads to greater empathy in their interactions.

11.4.2   Bibliotherapy

According to Riordan and Wilson (1989), bibliotherapy is "the guided reading of written materials in gaining understanding or solving problems relevant to a person's therapeutic needs." The term was originally coined by Samuel Crothers in 1916 when he recognized the poignant therapeutic benefits of literature (Ludwig, 2009; Olsen, 2007). Olsen (2007) points out that bibliotherapy can be employed by nearly every helping profession, with almost every age group and population. As an adjunct to therapy, bibliotherapy allows children reading or listening to stories to identify with the significant characters. The process aids the child in experiencing an emotional catharsis as the characters in the story express themselves. The benefits of bibliotherapy for children are vast, including instilling moral values, shaping behavior, improving and enabling the growth of critical thinking skills, and overall strengthening personal character (Ludwig, 2009).

With an effective clinician, bibliotherapy can help children gain some insight into themselves and their situations (McMillen and Pehrsson, 2004). The medium can be applied in several ways. One can hear a story, read a story, or even watch a story via a movie or a documentary. Hearing the story may support the therapeutic relationship between the listener and the storyteller, and allows the listener to take a passive role. Ludwig (2009) suggests that in addition to discussing the book, activities such as role-playing, using puppets, drawing out Venn diagrams and writing out essays about their personal experiences and how the book affected them enhance the overall efficacy of the approach.

There are numerous books that can be utilized. Readers are encouraged to look at the American Guidance Service's BookFinder for some specific books or can also search various websites that identify appropriate books. The authors highly recommend that one should personally review books or stories before recommending them. This way, one can assure their appropriateness. Table 11.7 lists several animal theme books that would have value in bibliotherapy. The books were highly recommended by Deanne Ginns-Gruenberg at selfesteemshop.com

Gladding and Gladding (1991) point out that there are two distinct forms of bibliotherapy. The first form dates back to the 1930s when any written material was used to assist in the modification and expression of a person's thoughts, feelings or behaviors (Rubin, 1978). More recently, bibliotherapy has emphasized the interaction between a therapist and a client and has focused more on the dialogue that occurs following the reading as opposed to the act of reading the material itself. The authors believe that this form of interactive bibliotherapy is the most valuable to apply in AAI.

In regards to AAI, the use of animals as the main characters has proven to be valuable in helping children absorb difficult information. Burns (2001) suggests that many of the outcomes in stories that highlight animals often can parallel similar challenges that children faced. The stories became segues to therapeutic conversations between himself and his clients. Ultimately, stories that emulated the animal's ability to successfully problem solve challenges led to more effective problem solving and personalization.

Table 11.8 developed by Fine (1996) illustrates the factors that should be taken into consideration when applying bibliotherapy with children in an AAI environment.

Table 11.7 ■

Topic	Title	Author
AD/HD	*Shelley the Hyperactive Turtle*, Second Edition	Moss, Deborah M.
Anger	*Llama Llama Mad at Mama*	Dewdney, Anna
Blame	*It's Not My Fault*	Carlson, Nancy
Bullies	*Bye-Bye, Bully! Kid's Guide for Dealing with Bullies*	Jackson, J. S.
Bullies	*Mookey the Monkey Gets Over Being Teased*	Lonczak, Heather
Bullies	*Tale of Sir Dragon: Dealing with Bullies for Kids (and Dragons)*	Pendziwol, Jean E.
Divorce	*Charlie Anderson*	Abercrombie, Barbara
Divorce	*Dinosaurs Divorce*	
Emotions and feelings	*Why Do You Cry?*	Klise, Kate
Friendship and bullying	*How to Be a Friend*	Laurie and Marc Brown
Health	*Dinosaurs Alive and Well!*	Laurie and Marc Brown
Impulsivity	*Me First*	Lester, Helen
Loss	*When Dinosaurs Die*	
Loss	*Badger's Parting Gifts*	Varley, Susan
Loss	*Brave Bart*	Sheppard, Caroline H.
Loss of friend	*Chester Raccoon and the Acorn Full of Memories*	Penn, Audrey
Manners	*Beartrice Doesn't Want To*	Numeroff, Laura
Manners	*Dear Miss Perfect: Beast's Guide to Proper Behavior*	Dutton, Sandra
Manners	*Do Unto Otters: Book About Manners*	Keller, Laurie
Moving	*Kiss Goodbye*	Penn, Audrey
Nightmare	*Little Rabbit and the Nightmare*	Klise, Kate
Perfectionism	*Wallace's Lists*	Bottner, Barbara and Kruglik, Gerald
Perseverence	*Alexandra Keeper of Dreams*	Baumgardner, Mary Alice
Self-esteem	*Giraffes Can't Dance*	Andreae, Giles
Self-esteem	*Hippo-Not-Amus*	Tony and Jan Payne
Self-esteem	*I Like Me*	Carlson, Nancy
Self-esteem	*I Wish I Were a Butterfly*	Howe, James
Self-esteem, friendship	*Rainbow Fish*	Pfister, Marcus
Separation anxiety	*Kissing Hand*	Penn, Audrey
Separation anxiety	*Llama Llama Misses Mama*	Dewdney, Anna
Separation anxiety	*Stellaluna*	Cannon, Janell
Separation anxiety	*When Fuzzy was Afraid of Losing His Mother*	Maier, Inger
Sibling rivalry	*Pocket Full of Kisses*	Penn, Audrey

(*Continued*)

Table 11.7 ∎—*cont'd*

Topic	Title	Author
Trauma	*Terrible Thing Happened*	Holmes, Margaret M.
Adoption	*A Mother for Choco*	Kasza, Keiko
Emotions, friendship	*Ready for Anything*	Kasza, Keiko
Friendship	*Charlotte's Web*	White, E. B.
Lessons about treating people with kindness	*Black Beauty*	Sewell, Anna
Perseverance and self-esteem	*The Tortoise and the Hare*	Aesop
Hard work, tenacity and preparation	*The Ant and the Grasshoper*	Aesop
Bullying and self belief	*The Ugly Ducking*	Hans Christian Andersen

Table 11.8 Factors for bibliotherapy

Child factors	Book factors
Child's age	Type of book
Sex	Plot
Why bibliotherapy is being applied	Difficulty level
Reading abilities	Appropriateness for child
Reading preferences	

11.4.3 Puppetry

In addition to simple storytelling, the use of puppets to act out the stories seems to strengthen this process. For example, Fine and Fine (1996), suggested that animal puppet characters appear to provide a basis for identification but, at the same time, allow a disguise so that a child has less of a need to be guarded. Linn et al. (1986) and Linn (1977) identify several attributes of puppetry that may contribute to its efficacy. Both articles advocate that the process of puppetry is immediately involving, active and quite intimate. Puppets may serve as a catalyst for a child's interaction as s/he manipulates the puppet. Puppets can also be used to directly talk with the child, and the child does not assume any other character. Therapists, who have therapy animals within their practice, could find puppets of the same breed as the animals. These puppets could act as "a talking extension" for the animal the child has bonded with. The author has found this approach very valuable with his younger primary school-aged clients.

Irwin (1975) points out that although there is a wealth of qualitative writing in regards to the diagnostic and therapeutic value of puppetry with children, there is little research on how it can be effectively applied in clinical settings. He does suggest that puppetry, because of its stimulating qualities and manipulative material, readily stimulates children in revealing both private symbols and thoughts. The scenarios applied and the fantasies acted out may provide the clinician with a clearer picture of the child's inner world and how s/he copes. The process may also be therapeutic in its release of expression and emotion, without the child having to take personal responsibility for what has been said. As stated earlier, the animated animals could be viewed as an extension of the live animals and could make discussing hard subjects an easier option.

The content of the puppet therapy sessions could be loosely focused on the recurring themes identified in previous therapy sessions. Themes for the puppetry should relate to the client's goals but could include scenarios that act out behavioral control, anger, fear, rejection, social skills, as well as abandonment. The therapist should be observant of the types of animals the child selects in the puppet sessions. Diagnostically, this can shed a great deal of insight, i.e. does the child select timid or aggressive animals? Furthermore, the therapist can observe the child's interaction with the puppets and assess how the child is reacting to the topic. For example, if the puppet scenario were open-ended, the child would have a choice of developing a fantasy that demonstrated either a nurturing, caring personality or an aggressive style. The style in which the child interacts with the puppets may shed tremendous clinical insight. Finally, a clinician could use the puppetry sessions as an opportunity to help the child develop problem-solving alternatives for various challenges.

11.5   Application of AAI with adults

While there are many similarities with the use of AAI and minors, there are some unique adaptations in applying AAI techniques given the therapeutic needs of adults. The very psychological and physical factors that make the use of animals so effective with children (e.g. social lubricant, increase comfort, decrease stress, anxiety, and depression) are in play with adults as well (Barker and Dawson, 1998; Brubaker et al., 2004; Chasnetski et al., 2004; Fick, 1993; Folse et al., 1994; Friedman et al., 1983, 1993; Katcher, 1985; Marr et al., 2000; Mcvarish 1995; Odendaal, 2000; Wilson, 1987, 1991). It appears that the results of the majority of studies support the integration of AAI as an adjunct to the therapy services provided to adults as a worthwhile endeavor if done appropriately.

11.5.1   Introducing an adult client to AAI

A primary difference when using a therapy animal during a formal psychotherapy session is in the explanation to the client as to why the animal is present. Children simply enjoy having an animal present, and they most often do not seek any explanation as to the role the animal will play. Adults on the other hand tend to be very pragmatic and will oftentimes see an animal's role as superfluous. Since adult clients are frequently the ones paying for the services, they want to get on with the session and may marginalize the role a therapy animal can play. While many understand the healing properties of pets, they frequently believe they could simply interact with their own family pet and receive the same benefit, and therefore do not want to use such an intervention during a purchased service. Because of this, the presentation of animal-assisted interventions and being sensitive to the way the client thinks are pivotal to successfully integrating therapy animals into a psychotherapy session with an adult.

It is important always to ask and never assume that a dog's presence is helpful or even appropriate. Not everyone likes dogs, and it is common place for many adult clients not to view a therapy dog as something that would help them solve their problems. Most have never been exposed to animal-assisted interventions and are surprised when the option of having a therapy dog join the session is offered.

11.5.2 Relationship building between an adult client and therapy animal

A therapist using a therapy dog is always cognizant of moments where an adult client and therapy animal exchange contact, the therapist takes the time whenever possible to allow the clients to have the desired interaction, for it is through these client-initiated interactions that the therapist will learn the most about the clients and what motivates them. This is especially true when working with externally motivated clients. These moments in which clients disclose a desire or what touches their hearts are those precious moments in which their guard is lowered, if only for a moment. Noticing this and creating similar moments in the future betters the odds of the therapist making inroads with the clients' therapeutic issues. Being ever vigilant to what works is key to knowing what to do in the future. Dogs are experts at this. They can tell immediately who likes them and who to visit. For example, I have found that my therapy dog, Rocky, immediately recognizes clients who have shown in the past that they enjoy a visit. He gives his relaxed doggy smile and lowers his head in happy recognition combined with a gentle tail wag when he sees these clients in the waiting room. These moments become the opener we need to begin a casual, yet effective conversation that later leads to therapeutic work in future sessions.

11.5.3 Relationship questions

Relationship questions allow the client to think from the perspective of another person or being. While I am aware that my therapy dog does not think in human terms and am careful not to anthropomorphize my canine partner in my own mind, asking my clients to think about how their behaviors might be perceived by my therapy dog can be a very therapeutic intervention, for it teaches them empathy, the ability to notice small behavioral changes, and the ability to think before they act. So, when working with an adult client during an individual session, the following dialogue might occur:

Therapist (T): So, you mentioned you would like to be more confident.

Client (C): Yeah.

T: So, I'm wondering if we could imagine that it was the end of our session, and somehow you became more confident as a result of our conversation. What would Rocky see as you walked past his gate on your way out that made him think, "Wow! That session must have gone really well! Something is different about Patty."

C: Well, that I was walking with my head up high.

T: Would that be different?

C: Yeah! I usually look at the ground.

T: OK, What would be different that resulted in you walking with your head high?

C: That I believe I can do this.

T: And would that be different for you to believe you can do this?

C: I think so!

T: What is letting you know when you leave here that this is something you can do?

C: Well, I know I can do it, I just allow myself to get discouraged.

T: So, how on this day are you able to keep yourself from getting discouraged and stay focused on the fact that you know you can do this?

This is an excellent example of how animal-assisted therapy can be used when the therapy dog is not actually in the room with the client. In this case, the therapist is asking relationship questions through the eyes of the therapy dog to encourage the client to imagine what others might see once the desired change has taken place. It becomes a powerful tool to assist the client in discovering small behavioral cues that will be different when she is thinking differently.

11.5.4 Interventions with adult clients

Exceptions

Exceptions are anytime that the problem does not exist or is a little bit better. Animals are experts at creating situations in which clients are more relaxed and more themselves; bettering the odds of the symptoms decreasing during a session. The following is from an interaction with a client who came for services due to depression.

Therapist (T): Hi, Sam. How are you? [Asking while I approach the waiting room with Rocky in tow.]

Sam (S): Hi, Rocky. Hi, old boy. [The client leans forward in his chair and lowers his head toward Rocky, as Rocky reciprocates with a lick on the nose. The client smiles as he ruffles Rocky's fur and stands to walk with me back to the office.]

T: Rocky looks happy to see you.

S: Yeah. He's a good boy. [The client again smiles as he looks down at Rocky walking with us.]

T: It's good to see you smiling.

S: Well, it's been a tough week.

T: Wow! So even though it has been a tough week, Rocky was still able to find two smiles in you.

S: Well, it's hard to be sad around Rocky.

T: What is different about Rocky that lets you set aside your troubles if even for a moment?

It would have been tempting for many therapists to follow the verbal path of, "It's been a tough week." However, by highlighting times in which the symptoms are just a little better, the client's focus shifts away from the problem. This helps the client to explore how he created this exception, thereby increasing the client's ability to choose to create additional exceptions in the future.

11.5.5   Applications of AAI with adult clients

Private practice setting

Clients who seek services through a therapist's private practice are many times quite different from those who come to a publicly funded agency setting. They frequently have identified a specific problem that they would like to be resolved, and they are paying for the service themselves, making efficiency and professionalism key characteristics on their list of things they require from their therapists. While remaining purposeful of when to include an animal in a therapy session is always key to effective animal-assisted therapy, it becomes a public relations issue as well when working with clients in a private practice setting.

Agency setting

While the necessary policies and procedures required to implement an animal-assisted intervention program within an agency setting can initially be quite daunting, it can be well worth it. Information is now readily available that provides sample policies and procedures and identifies key elements that must be addressed to minimize liability (e.g. Pichot and Coulter, 2007). Once these important elements are addressed, the presence of therapy dogs can have a profound impact not only with the agency clients, but with the staff members as well. When a therapy dog is used in an agency setting such as a public health department, there are three general ways in which the work can be done: (1) change the general environment of the agency, (2) work directly work with clients, and (3) healing for staff members.

University setting

The university counseling center has the potential to be an ideal setting for the integration of animal-assisted interventions in the therapy session. Given that many are coming from homes where companion animals were a part of the family, students are often missing their companion animals when they relocate to the college environment. As a result, a number of universities are now permitting companion animals to live with students on campus for many of the same reasons that make human/animal interactions helpful—to ease the transition to college and alleviate homesickness, reduce stress, facilitate social interaction with other students, and to provide comfort and support (Bliss, 2008; Jan, 2008; Mott, 2008).

Many students are dealing with multiple stressors related to environmental factors such as: poverty, being a war veteran, financial concerns, working full time as well as going to school, experiencing multiple losses, or being in a variety of roles (parent, spouse, student) which adds to a student's sense of being overwhelmed and may serve as a catalyst for seeking psychological services in the first place. Consequently, a practitioner in the university counseling center will be working with a wide range of client interpersonal styles, presenting concerns, and diagnostic concerns. As stated in the beginning of the section integrating AAI with adult clients, there are a number of studies that were specifically conducted with college students that indicate that AAI, if applied appropriately, may be effective in decreasing physiological indicators of stress and anxiety (e.g. heart rate, blood pressure) as well as depressive symptoms. Given that many college student presenting problems are often related to stress, anxiety and depression, the integration of AAI as an adjunct to their therapy may be beneficial.

For many student clients, having a therapy animal in session is beneficial in that its presence alone contributes to the establishment of a home-like atmosphere that is conducive to helping students quickly feel comfortable enough to engage in self-disclosure. This is particularly advantageous for the student client who has never been in therapy before and is ambivalent about seeking psychological help or for a client who might be shy and withdrawn. The therapy animal provides a means of connecting with the therapist in that the animal becomes a momentary topic of conversation and provides an opportunity for the client to "warm up" to beginning the work that will be done in the therapy hour. For male college students in particular, the therapy animal presence can make quite a difference in facilitating relaxation and greater levels of comfort in being in a setting that might be rather foreign or intimidating for one who typically might not seek such help. In initial group therapy sessions, the therapy animal facilitates interaction between group members who are beginning to know one another and are dealing with the awkwardness and uncertainty about being in this type of treatment modality.

This writer (KS) has found that therapy animals have been extremely powerful when working with clients who were survivors of childhood trauma, abuse, and family violence. Often college students are young adults who are dealing with issues related to identity development, separation from home, autonomy, and the development of committed, intimate relationships (Kenny and Rice, 1995). According to attachment theory, the college student who came from secure and supportive relationships with parents will most likely have a positive internal representation of self (e.g. sees self as worthy, loveable) as well as view others equally positively—as being trustworthy and responsive to their needs (Bowlby, 1980) and consequently have coping strategies for dealing with the transition to college. But for those students who came from homes where family violence or abuse and neglect was occurring, levels of risk for having a negative internal representation of self (e.g. sees self as unworthy) and a negative view of others as being untrustworthy or unresponsive to their needs might be greater. With a negative internal representation of self or others, the student may experience greater levels of stress and difficulty coping with the developmental challenges that will invariably come their way as they deal with the adjustment to college and the transition to adulthood (Kenny and Rice, 1995). It has been hypothesized that internal self representations may be amenable to change based upon experiences in current relationships (Bowlby, 1988; Kenny and Rice, 1995). While the focus of these authors has been on current relationships with human beings, it might also be the case that being attached to an animal could assist in being better able to adjust and cope with the stress associated with transition. It equally seems plausible that the development of a relationship with a being from another species could carry significance in that it is an opportunity to develop a safe attachment, particularly for those clients who have had their trust in humans "stomped on" by those who abused them. It also seems reasonable to consider that the presence of a therapy animal might facilitate attachment behaviors in survivors of abuse, particularly in the development of the therapeutic relationship. Assuming that the therapy animal provides some sense of security and comfort, it might assist the survivor in taking greater interpersonal risks with the therapist. Having a therapy animal present encourages these clients to have the experience of trusting another being (therapist and therapy animal) and experiencing unconditional love that permits the development of a safe attachment.

Because so many trauma survivors, particular those with a history of sexual and/or physical abuse, have experienced touch that has been hurtful, the presence of a therapy animal can provide opportunities for safe touch. While a psychologist or counselor might be hesitant to offer physical comfort to a client (and the client might be reluctant to ask) by hugging them, a therapy animal does not have to attend to such boundaries. When talking about past traumatic events, the opportunity to pet or hold the therapy animal can be extremely comforting and soothing and/or provide a momentary distraction while discussing emotionally intense events. Having a therapy animal present can provide a sense of safety when describing such experiences. Often adult survivors of childhood abuse have described how, when they were being abused, they turned to their own companion animals as a source of comfort, security, and support. These animal/human interactions are often critical as a coping strategy for the abused child or adolescent which makes the presence of a therapy animal all the more significant as the adult survivor heals from the past trauma.

Box 11.1 is a brief case study highlighting the incorporation of AAI with a university student.

Box 11.1 Case study

Carla (a pseudonym) was struggling with severe depression that was impacting her academic functioning. She sought therapy because she was having suicidal thoughts. Initially, the primary goals of therapy were to lessen the depressive symptoms so Carla would no longer be suicidal and be better able to function academically.

Carla was engaged from the moment she met "Elsa" the Newfoundland therapy dog. She would often hug or briefly speak to her during the sessions. Gradually, because of her increased sense of comfort, Carla disclosed her childhood history of sexual abuse by a babysitter that occurred over a period of four years. The abuse continued to impact Carla in her adult life, most notably in her relationships with others and the lack of empowerment she often experienced.

Carla and her boyfriend decided to adopt a small adult male dog from the local shelter. Carla reported that the dog had started to bite other pedestrians when they were walking him. Carla began professional dog training sessions and reported that she and the trainer worked on reducing aggressiveness. In one of her sessions, she reported that the dog trainer had become perturbed with Carla because she was verbally disciplining the dog with a very weak and timid voice. In exacerbation, the trainer yelled at Carla that she needed to become more self-assured and firm with the dog. After some exploration, it became apparent that the trainer was trying to tell Carla that if she were unable to be the "leader" with her dog, the dog would take over this role and rule her life and home. Carla and I (KS) then performed through role play how she might speak assertively and confidently with the dog by having her give obedience commands to Elsa, the therapy dog.

After leaving the session, Carla took her own dog for a walk, without her boyfriend, and practiced saying "no" whenever the dog started to bark at people. Carla continued to practice this with her dog over the next few weeks. In finding her own voice with her dog, Carla also found her voice in her relationship with her boyfriend. She began asserting limits in how she was willing to be treated by her boyfriend. When this led to an escalation in his efforts to control and abuse her, Carla voiced her decision to end the relationship—something she had never done in the past. It was clear that the opportunity to practice assertiveness and boundary setting with Elsa and with her own dog enabled her to become the "leader" of her own life.

11.6 Concluding remarks

AAI has entered a crossroad from being a misunderstood therapeutic approach to becoming a more respected therapeutic alternative. As AAI continues gaining professional acceptance, more extensive research is needed to document its efficacy, for it to be recognized more favorably. Additionally, attention must also be given to clarify the scope of interventions and to document and explain how various AAIs can be applied.

Throughout this chapter, the authors provided some insights into how AAI can be integrated into various professional disciplines, especially those in mental health. Attention was also given to highlighting some specific applications for children and adults as well as a how one could apply equine therapy. As previously noted, although progress has been made clarifying the various applications of AAI, more research and evaluation continues to be needed to assess the impact of various AAI techniques. This scrutiny will help advance the field so its value as a complementary intervention will be more received.

John Abernethy, a famous English surgeon, once stated that "there is no short cut, nor 'royal road' to the attainment of medical knowledge. The path which we have to pursue is long, difficult, and unsafe." Our quest in this crossroad of time is to advance a field that continues to have growing pains. We need to bridge science with practice to reduce the chasm that is in between. During this new era, we must caution against the overexaggerated claims of the curative value of the human/animal bond and strive to legitimize and document the therapeutic benefits derived from our bond and curiosity with animals. Our job will be arduous, but with concentrated efforts to pursue knowledge, we will move beyond rhetoric and establish a stronger foothold for the future of this field.

References

Adams, D. L. (1997). Animal-assisted enhancement of speech therapy: a case study. *Anthrozoös, 10*(1), 53–56.

American Psychological Association. (2002). Ethical principles of psychologists and code of conduct. *American Psychologist, 59*, 236–260.

American Veterinary Medical Association (n.d.). Therapy animals prove "man's best friends" hold healing power. Retrieved Feb. 13, 2010 from http://www.nbc26.com/Global/story. asp?S=11756142&nav=menu1454_11_6

ARAcontent. Therapy animals prove "man's best friends" hold healing power. Dogs online magazine. Courtesy of ARAcontent, copyright 2008–2010.

Argus, L. (1996). An intensive analysis of metaphor themes in psychotherapy. In J. Mio & A. Katz (Eds.), *Metaphor: Implications of Applications* (pp. 73–85). Mahwah, New Jersey: Lawrence Erlbaum Associates.

Association for Play Therapy (n.d.). Play therapy defined. Retrieved Nov. 2, 2009 from: http://www.a4pt.org/ps.playtherapy.cfm?ID=1158

Barker, S., & Dawson, K. (1998). The effects of animal-assisted therapy on anxiety ratings of hospitalized psychiatric patients. *Psychiatric Services, 49*(6), 797–801.

Barker, P. (1996). *Psychotherapeutic Metaphors: A Guide to Theory and Practice.* New York: Brunner/Mazel.

Barnard, R. (1954). Milieu therapy. *Menninger Quarterly, 8*(2), 21–24.

Battino, R. (2003). *Metaphoria: Metaphor and Guided Metaphor for Psychotherapy and Healing.* New York: Crown Publishers.

Beck, A. M. (2000). The use of animals to benefit humans: animal assisted therapy. In A. Fine (Ed.), *Animal Assisted Therapy* (pp. 21–40). San Diego, CA: Academic Press.

Benton, S., Benton, S. L., Tsing, W. C., Newton, F. B., Robertson, J. M., & Benton, K. L. (2003). Changes in client problems: contributions and limitations from a 13-year study. *Professional Psychology: Research and Practice, 34*, 66–72.

Berg, I. K. (1994). *Family Based Services: A Solution-focused Approach.* New York: Norton.

Bliss, S. (2008). Man's best friend being phased into dorm life. CNN.com/living. Retrieved from: http://www.conn.com/2008/LIVING/wayoflife/09/24/dorm.life.pets/index.html

Bowers, M. J., & MacDonald, P. (2001). The effectiveness of equine-facilitated psychotherapy with at risk adolescents. *Journal of Psychology and Behavioral Science, 15*, 62–76.

Bowlby, J. (1980). *Attachment and Loss, Vol. III: Loss, Sadness and Depression.* New York: Basic Books.

Bowlby, J. (1988). *A Secure Base: Parent-Child Attachment and Healthy Human Development.* New York: Basic Books.

Brubaker, A. S., Lau, J. K., San Miguel, M., & Geisler, M. W. (2004). Frontal midline theta activity as an index of the efficacy of animal-assisted therapy in cases of math anxiety. *International Journal of Psychophysiology, 54*, 158–159.

Bureau of Labor Statistics, U.S. Department of Lab. *Occupational Outlook Handbook, 2010–2011 edition, Occupational Therapists.* Available at http://www.bls.gov/oco/ocos078.htm (accessed May 18, 2010).

Burns, G. W. (2001). *101 Healing Stories: Using Metaphors in Therapy.* New Jersey: John Wiley and Sons Inc.

Chandler, C. K. (2005). *Animal Assisted Therapy in Counseling.* New York: Routledge.

Chandler, C. K., Portrie-Bethke, T. L., Minton, C. B, Fernando, D. M., & O'Callaghan, D. M. (n.d., under review). Matching animal assisted techniques and intentions with counseling guiding theories.

Charnetski, C. J., Riggers, S., & Brennan, F. X. (2004). Effect of petting a dog on immune system function. *Psychological Reports, 95,* 1087–1091.

Close, H. R. (1998). *Metaphor in Psychotherapy: Clinical Applications of Stories and Allegories.* San Luis Obispo, CA: Impact Publishers.

Combs, G., & Freedman, J. (1990). *Symbol Story and Ceremony using Metaphor in Individual and Family Therapy.* New York: Norton.

Cole, K. M., Gawlinski, A., Steers, N., & Kotlerman, J. (2007). Animal-assisted therapy in patients hospitalized with heart failure. *American Journal of Critical Care, 16,* 575–585.

Coren, S. (2000). *How to Speak Dog: Mastering the Art of Dog-Human Communication.* New York: Fireside.

Corson, S., & Corson, E. (1980). Pet animals as nonverbal communication mediators in psychotherapy in institutional settings. *Ethology and Nonverbal Communication in Mental Health,* 83–110.

Davis, K. D. (2002). *Therapy Dogs: Training Your Dog to Reach Others* (2nd ed.). Wenatchee, WA: Dogwise.

DeJong, P., & Berg, I. K. (2008). *Interviewing for Solutions* (3rd ed.). Belmont, CA: Thomson Brooks/Cole.

De Shazer, S. (1984). *Words were Originally Magic.* New York: Norton.

Ferrese, L., Forster, B., Kowalski, R., & Wasilewski, L. (1998). *Occupational therapists: perspectives on using animal assisted therapy with an elderly population.* Unpublished master's project. Dallas: College Misericordia.

Fick, K. (1993). The influence of an animal on social interactions of nursing home residents in a group setting. *American Journal of Occupational Therapy, 47*(6), 529–534.

Fine, A. (2008). *Understanding the application of animal assisted interventions. National Institute of Child and Human Development meeting on the Impact of Animals in Human Health.* Bethesda, MD. Sept. 30–Oct. 2.

Fine, A., & Beiler, P. (2008). Therapists and animals: demystifying animal assisted therapy. In A. Strozier (Ed.), *The Handbook of Complementary Therapies.* New York: Haworth Press.

Fine, A., Lindsay, A., & Bowers, C. (In press). Incorporating animals-assisted interventions as an adjunct to therapy with boys at risk. In C. Haen (Ed.), *Engaging Boys in Treatment: Creative Approaches to Formulating, Initiating, and Sustaining the Therapy Process.* New York: Routledge.

Fine, A. H., & Eisen, C. J. (2008). *Afternoons with Puppy: Inspirations from a Therapist and his Animals.* West Lafayette, IN: Purdue University Press.

Fine, A. H. (2006). Incorporating animal-assisted therapy into psychotherapy guidelines and suggestions for therapists. In A. H. Fine (Ed.), *Handbook on Animal-assisted Therapy: Theoretical Foundations and Guidelines for Practice* (2nd ed.). (pp. 167–206) San Diego: Academic Press.

Fine, A. H., & Mio, J. S. (2006). The future of research, education, and clinical practice in the animal-human bond and animal-assisted therapy. Part C: The role of animal-assisted therapy in clinical practice: the importance of demonstrating empirically oriented psychotherapies. In A. H. Fine (Ed.), *Handbook on Animal-assisted Therapy: Theoretical Foundations and Guidelines for Practice* (2nd ed.). (pp. 167–206) San Diego: Academic Press.

Fine, A. H., & Fine, N. (1996). *Therapeutic Recreation and Exceptional Children.* Springfield, IL: Charles C. Thomas.

Folse, E. B., Minder, C. C., Aycock, M. J., & Santana, R. T. (1994). Animal-assisted therapy and depression in adult college students. *Anthrozoös, 7*, 188–194.

Freeman, M. (1991). Therapeutic use of storytelling for older children who are critically ill. *CHC, 20*(4), 208–213.

Frederickson, M. (in press). Methods, standards and guidelines in selecting animals for animal assisted interventions. In A. H. Fine, (Ed.), *Handbook on Animal-assisted Therapy: Theoretical Foundations and Guidelines for Practice.* San Diego, CA: Academic Press.

Friedman, E., Katcher, A., Thomas, S., Lynch, J., & Messent, P. (1983). Social interaction and blood pressure: influence of companion animals. *Journal of Nervous and Mental Disease, 171*, 543–551.

Friedman, E., Locker, B., & Lockwood, R. (1993). Perception of animals and cardiovascular responses during verbalization with an animal present. *Anthrozoös, 62*, 115–133.

Gallagher, R. P. (2008). *National Survey of Counseling Center Directors 2008.* Washington, DC: International Association of Counseling Services.

Gladding, S. T., & Gladding, C. (1991). *The ABC's of bibliotherapy for school counselors. School Counselor, 39*(1), 7–13.

Heindl, B. A. (1996). The effectiveness of pet therapy as an intervention in a community-based children's day treatment program. *Dissertation Abstracts International, 57*(4-A), 1501.

Herbert, J. D., & Greene, D. (2001). Effect of preference on distance walked by assisted living residents. *Physical and Occupational Therapy in Geriatrics, 19*, 1–15.

Irwin, E. C., & Shapiro, M. I. (1975). Puppetry as a diagnostic and therapeutic technique. *Tracult. Aspects Psychistr. Art, 4*, 86–94.

Jalongo, M. R., Astorino, T., & Bomboy, N. (2004). Canine visitors: the influence of therapy dogs on young children's learning and well-being in classrooms and hospitals. *Early Childhood Education Journal, 32*(1), 9–16.

Jan, T. (2008). MIT students take on some furry roommates. The Boston Globe. Retrieved from: http://www.boston.com/news/education/higher/articles/2008/09/09/mit_students_take_on_some_furry_roommates/

Kahn, P. H. (1997). Developmental psychology and the biophilia hypothesis: Children's affiliation with nature. *Developmental Review, 17*, 1–61.

Katcher, A. H. (1985). Physiologic and behavioral responses to companion animals. In J. Quackenbush & V. Voith (Eds.), *The Human Companion-Animal Bond. The Veterinary Clinics of North America: Small Animal Practice, 15(2)* (pp. 403–410).

Kenny, M. E., & Rice, K. G. (1995). Attachment to parents and adjustment in late adolescent college students. *The Counseling Psychologist, 23*, 433–456.

Kopp, R. R. (1995). *Metaphor Therapy.* New York: Brunner/Mazel.

Lab, D. D., Feigenbaum, J. D., & De Silva, P. (2000). Mental health professionals' attitudes and practices toward male childhood sexual abuse. *Child Abuse and Neglect, 24*, 391–409.

LaJoie, K. R. (2003). *An evaluation of the effectiveness of using animals in thearpy. Unpublished doctoral dissertation.* Louisville, KY: Spalding University.

Lange, A., Cox, J., Bernert, D., & Jenkins, C. (2006/2007). Is counseling going to the dogs? An exploratory study related to the inclusion of an animal in group counseling with adolescents. *Journal of Creativity in Mental Health, 2*(2), 17–31.

Langs, R. (1982). *Psychotherapy: A Basic Text.* New York: Jason Aronson.

Limond, J., Bradshaw, J., & Cormack, K. (1997). Behavior of children with learning disabilities interacting with a therapy dog. *Anthrozoös, 10*(2–3), 84–89.

Linn, S. (1977). Puppets and hospitalized children: talking about feelings. *Journal of the Association for the Care of Children in Hospitals, 5*(4), 5–11.

Linn, S., Beardslee, W. R., & Patenaude, A. F. (1986). Puppet therapy with pediatric bone marrow transplant patients. *Journal of Pediatric Psychology, 11*, 37–45.

Ludwig, T. (2009). *Relational Aggression and Bibliotherapy: Using Children's Literature to Address Emotional Bullying, Foster Empathy and Create a Safer Social and Learning Environment in Schools.* Phoenix, Arizona: IRA Conference.

Macauley, B. L. (2006). Animal-assisted therapy for persons with aphasia: a pilot study. *Journal of Rehabilitation Research and Development, 43*(3), 357–366.

Macauley, B. L., Tanner, A. K., & Laing, S. P. (2002). The effectiveness of animal-assisted therapy for preschoolers with language delay: a pilot study. Unpublished observations.

Mallon, G. P. (1994a). Some of our best therapists are dogs. *Child and Youth Care Forum, 23* (2), 89–101.

Mallon, G. P. (1994b). Cow as co-therapist: utilization of farm animals as therapeutic aides with children in residential treatment. *Child and Adolescent Social Work Journal, 11*, 455–474.

Mallon, G. P., Ross, S. B., & Ross, L. (in press). Designing and implementing animal-assisted therapy programs in health and mental health organizations. In A. H. Fine, (3rd ed.). *Handbook on Animal-assisted Therapy: Theoretical Foundations and Guidelines for Practice.* San Diego, CA: Academic Press.

Marr, C., French, L., Thompson, D., Drum, L., Greening, G., Mormon, J., et al. (2000). Animal-assisted therapy in psychiatric rehabilitation. *Anthrozoös, 13*(1), 43–47.

Martin, F., & Farnum, J. (2002). Animal assisted therapy for children with pervasive developmental disorders. *Western Journal of Nursing Research, 24*(6), 657–671.

McMillen, P., & Pehrsson, D. E. (2004). A bibliotherapy evaluation tool: grounding counselors in the therapeutic use of literature. *The Arts in Psychotherapy, 3*(1), 47–59.

McMullen, L. M. (in press). Putting it in context: metaphor and psychotherapy. In R. W. Gibbs, Jr. (Ed.), *The Cambridge Handbook of Metaphor and Thought.* New York: Cambridge University Press.

McMullen, L., & Conway, J. (1996). Conceptualizing the figurative expressions of psychotherapy clients. In J. Mio & A. Katz (Eds.), *Metaphor: Implications and Applications* (pp. 59–73). Mahwah, New Jersey: Lawrence Erlbaum Associates.

McNicholas, J., & Collis, G. M. (2000). Dogs as catalysts for social interactions: robustness of the effect. *British Journal of Psychology, 91*, 61–70.

Mcvarish, C. A. (1995). The effects of pet facilitated therapy on depressed institutionalized inpatients. *Dissertation Abstracts International, 55*(7-B), 3019.

Mott, M. (2008). Pets at college can ease homesickness. Petside.com. Retrieved from: http://www.petside.com/pets-at-college-can-ease-homesickness.html

Mullett, S. (2008). A helping paw. RN, 39-44. Retrieved Sept. 15, 2009 from ModernMedicine.com

Oakley, D., & Bardin, G. (n.d.). The potential benefits of animal assisted therapy for children with special needs. Retrieved Sept. 15, 2009 from: http://www.kidneeds.com/diagnostic_categories/articles/animalassistedtherapy.htm

O'Callaghan, D. (2008). *Exploratory study of animal assisted therapy interventions used by mental health professionals. Unpublished doctoral dissertation.* Denton: University of North Texas.

Odendaal, J. S. J. (2000). Animal-assisted therapy—magic or medicine? *Journal of Psychosomatic Research, 49*(4), 275–280.

Olsen, M. A. (2007). Bibliotherapy: school psychologists' report of use and efficacy. *Department of Counseling Psychology and Special Education.*

Pichot, T. (2009). *Transformation of the Heart: Tales of the Profound Impact Therapy Dogs have on their Humans*. Bloomington, IN: iUniverse.

Pichot, T., & Coulter, M. (2007). *Animal Assisted Brief Therapy: A Solution-Focused Approach*. Binghamton, NY: Haworth.

Pruitt, J. A., & Kappius, R. E. (1992). Routine inquiry into sexual victimization: a survey of therapists' practices. *Professional Psychology: Research and Practice, 28*, 474–479.

Read, J., & Fraser, A. (1998). Abuse histories of psychiatric inpatients: to ask or not to ask? *Psychiatric Services, 49*, 355–359.

Reichert, E. (1994). Play and animal-assisted therapy: a group treatment model for sexually abused girls ages 9–13. *Family Therapy, 21*(1), 55–62.

Reichert, E. (1998). Individual counseling for sexually abused children: a role for animals and storytelling. *Child and Adolescent Social Work Journal, 15*(3), 177–185.

Rice, S., Brown, L., & Caldwell, H. S. (1973). Animals and psychotherapy: a survey. *Journal of Community Psychology, 1*, 323–326.

Richeson, N. E. (2003). Effects of animal-assisted therapy on agitated behaviors and social interactions of older adults with dementia. *American Journal of Alzheimer's Disease and Other Dementias, 18*, 353–358.

Riordan, R. J., & Wilson, L. S. (1989). Bibliotherapy: does it work? *Journal of Counseling and Development, 67*(9), 506–508.

Rubin, R. J. (1978). *Using Bibliotherapy: A Guide to Theory and Practice*. Phoenix: Oryx.

Schaefer, K. D. (2007). Cruelty to animals and the short- and long-term impact on victims. *Journal of Emotional Abuse, 7*, 31–57.

Shiloh, S., Sorek, G., & Terkel, J. (2003). Reduction of state-anxiety by petting animals in a controlled laboratory experiment. *Anxiety, Stress and Coping: An International Journal, 1477–2205, 16*(4), 387–395.

Steed, H. N., & Smith, B. S. (2002). Animal assisted activities for geriatric patients. *Activities, Adaptation and Aging, 27*(1), 49–61.

Starker, S. (1988a). Do-it-yourself therapy: the prescription of self-help books by psychologists. *Psychotherapy: Theory, Research, Practice, Training, 25*(1), 142–146.

Straatman, I., Hanson, E. K. S., Endenburg, N., & Mol, J. A. (1997). The influence of a dog on male students during a stressor. *Anthrozoös, 10*, 191–197.

Sussman, M. B. (Ed.). (1985). *Pets and the Family*. New York: Haworth.

The Israeli Association of Animal Assisted Psychotherapy Code of Ethics (n.d.). Retrieved from: http://www.iaapsytherapy.org/image/users/84580/ftp/my_files/IAAAP%20Code%20of%20Ethics.pdf

Therapy Dogs United. (2008). ACE program. Retrieved Feb. 12, 2010 from http://www.therapydogsunited.org/program/facility%20therapy%20dog/

Velde, B. P., Cipriani, J., & Fisher, G. (2005). Resident and therapist views of animal-assisted therapy: implications for occupational therapy practice. *Australian Occupational Therapy Journal, 52*, 43–50.

Watsh, P. G., & Mertin, P. G. (1994). The training of pets as therapy dogs in a women's prison: a pilot study. *Anthrozoös, 7*(2), 124–128.

Wilkes, C., Shalko, T., & Trahan, M. (1989). Pet therapy: implications for good health. *Health Education, 20*, 6–9.

Wilson, C. C. (1987). Physiological responses of college students to a pet. *Journal of Nervous and Mental Disease, 175*, 606–612.

Wilson, C. C. (1991). The pet as an anxiolytic intervention. *Journal of Nervous and Mental Disease, 179*, 482–489.

12 Animals in the lives of children

Gail F. Melson*, Aubrey H. Fine[†]
*Purdue University, [†]California State Polytechnic University

12.1 Introduction

All therapeutic interventions involving animals rest on a powerful assumption: there is something about animals that powerfully attracts and motivates humans. This assumption seems particularly compelling when children are involved. In this chapter we examine this assumption closely. First, we document the pervasiveness of animals, both real and symbolic, in children's lives. Second, we ask what the presence of such animals might mean for development. As a guide, we draw on four helpful conceptual approaches—psychodynamic, relational and self psychologies, ecological psychology and the biophilia hypothesis. We consider how existing research might support and also challenge hypotheses drawn from these approaches. In the 2006 edition of the *Handbook*, we noted the paucity of well-conducted research studies. Although the empirical base of human/animal interaction (HAI) studies continues to grow, there remain many gaps in knowledge (Melson, in press). Hence, a review of research on HAI and children's development still raises more questions than provides answers.

We use both conceptual frameworks and existing research to suggest implications for therapeutic practice with children and their families. (In doing so, we draw on case examples from the clinical practice of the second author, AHF, and of other clinicians.) Throughout this essay, we emphasize the importance of considering both children and animals within family systems and when AAT occurs, within therapeutic systems. As children develop, they are embedded within complex social systems, the most important of which is the family. When animals are added, both child and animal become part of a dynamic system which almost always includes at least one adult (Melson, 2007). We must consider the entire system when we ask: What is the significance of animals in children's lives?

12.2 Where are animals in children's lives?

The world of childhood in contemporary Western societies is "peopled" with animals. Overall in the USA, pet ownership rates are high; 62% of American households had one or more resident animals in 2008 (APPMA, 2009). According to the 2009/2010 National Pet Owners Survey, 71.4 million US households own a pet. In 1988, the first year the survey was conducted, 56% of US households owned a pet as compared to 62% in 2008.

Dogs and cats are found in at least one out of every three households. Among families with children under 18 years of age, 38% were pet owners in 2008, and most families report more than one pet (APPMA, 2009). Moreover, based on surveys, most parents acquire animals "for the children," in the belief that pets teach lessons of responsibility and nurturing while providing companionship and love (Melson, 2001). According to parents, children maintain high levels of daily involvement in caring for and playing with family pets as the children grow from preschoolers to teens, even though children's (human) family time decreases as they age (Melson and Fogel, 1996). While children's own attachments to pets vary depending on many factors, in general, children report a strong bond with at least one resident animal.

The demographics of pet ownership become more striking when juxtaposed against the changing demographics of human family structure. Since the Baby Boom generation, within-home family size has been shrinking, as declining birth rates and rising divorce rates strip away additional children and adults from the household. To be sure, children have been adding "sometime" family ties—non-custodial parents, half-siblings, stepparents, longer living grandparents—but they often juggle commitments within and outside the family. When we search for affective bonds present 24/7 to children within their homes, pets may well be the most available. Thus, in 2003, 68% of family groups with children under 18 years of age were in married couple families, with both father and mother present (Fields, 2004); however, in the same time period, an estimated 75% of households with children reported at least one pet present during the time the child is growing up (AVMA, 2003). As noted earlier, that rate has held steady for several years, but it seems to have declined in the most recent survey by APPMA (2009). That survey reported a total of 77.5 million dogs and 93.6 million cats in American homes.

Beyond pets in the home, children encounter animals in their classrooms, especially in the early years of school. For example, a survey of 431 Indiana public elementary school teachers found that over a quarter (26.1%) had resident pets in their classrooms, while an additional 46% had animal "visitors" (Rud and Beck, 2003). Teachers who incorporate animals in their classrooms echoed pet-owning parents in extolling the benefits of fish, rabbits, gerbils, hamsters, and other "pocket pets" in teaching children responsibility and caring, providing enjoyment, and generally enhancing children's psychological well-being. Given the pervasiveness of pets in children's homes, it's not surprising that teachers view animals as lending their classroom a more "homey" atmosphere. A year-long observational study of preschoolers' responses to animals in their classroom revealed that observing and interacting with animals stimulated children's development in wide-ranging ways (Myers, 1998). These animal encounters stimulated children's language, sense of self, connection with others, imagination, and play.

Children's encounters with animals are not limited to those species kept as pets. Although children's everyday contact with wildlife has been shrinking as Western societies become more urbanized, what one might call *intentional wildlife experiences* persist. Families and schools set up bird feeders, take children to zoos and aquariums, and organize nature walks in parks. An estimated 63 million individuals in the USA feed wild birds at home-based outdoor bird feeders (Dickenson and Edmondson, 1996). Zoos and aquariums draw millions of visitors who are disproportionately families and groups with children.

The animal world of children extends beyond direct contact with living animals to encompass mediated exposure, through print, audio and visual media such as Animal Planet. This involvement at a remove is gaining in importance; for many children, it is the dominant mode of gaining knowledge about wild animals. For example, in one study of rural 8–14 year olds living next to a national park and protected wilderness, over 60% said they had seen more animals on television and in the movies than in the wild (Nabhan and Trimble, 1994).

Finally, anyone who remembers childhood is likely to recall fanciful animal characters—Peter Rabbit, Barney the dinosaur, Curious George, or Nemo the damselfish. Children's picture books, stories, toys, games, and media are saturated with animal symbols, reflecting, in part, the cultural assumption that animals and children naturally go together. Thus, when Swedish, Hungarian and Chinese researchers wanted to examine how six and seven year olds in their cultures made up stories, they asked each child to tell a story about a dog (Carlsson et al., 2001). There is also ample evidence from children themselves of interest in animals. For example, in a study of 8–13-year-old Dutch children's Internet use, "seeking information about animals" was one of the four most common descriptions of positive experiences with the Internet (Valkenburg and Soeters, 2001). In sum, wherever one looks, animals, particularly those species kept as pets, are an integral part of children's lives.

12.3   What do animals mean in children's lives?

The pervasiveness of animals—pets, wildlife, story characters—raises the question of their significance for children. Scholars have considered theory and research on the possible role of animals in children's lives: (a) nurturance and caring for others, including empathy; (b) coping with stress; (c) emotion regulation, self-control and positive adjustment; (d) reduction of maladaptive outcomes, such as conduct disorder symptoms; (e) theory of mind; (f) social support; and (g) physical activity, among other outcomes. Parents cite increased responsibility, companionship, and "fun" as benefits that companion animals confer on their children (Melson, 2001). To understand *why* and *how* interactions with animals might impact child development, a theory-driven approach is needed. Such an approach is essential for guiding AAT with children as well.

12.3.1   Psychodynamic theories

Freud (1965) was struck by children's fascination with animals, noting how frequently animals appeared in the dreams of children (and adults). For him, animal figures represented projections of powerful adults, usually parents, who were too threatening to the child to pop up undisguised in the dream world. From a psycho-analytic perspective, children and animals shared a natural kinship, since biological urges rather than human reason held sway over both of them. Even more than Freud, Jung stressed that animal symbols often expressed facets of the self. As one Jungian psychologist argued, "The Self is often symbolized as an animal, representing our instinctive nature and its connectedness with one's surroundings" (von Franz, 1972).

Such was the frequency of animal imagery in children's dreams and associations that psychoanalytically oriented psychologists developed a variety of projective tests using animal images for children and even for the purported "inner child" of adult patients. A recent version is the Animal Attribution Story-Telling Technique (Arad, 2004), in which family members assign an animal counterpart to each member of the family and then tell a short story about the animal protagonists. The technique has been applied to family therapy with families that have a child diagnosed with conduct disorder or ADHD, and according to its developer, "the animal name attribution to family members creates a fun, non-threatening atmosphere that helps to promote the description of personality traits and interpersonal relationships through the various animal counterparts" (p. 249).

Play therapists often advocate the use of animal toys. A therapeutic technique, "My Family as Animals," was designed "to interest and maintain the attention of children so that therapists will become more comfortable with the presence of young ones in the room" (Rio, 2001).

There are many therapists who employ animal puppets in their work with children. It appears that most children relate more easily to animal puppets than to other types of puppets, including those with human features. Children seem to interact more calmly and open up more naturally. Perhaps this is because children do not see animal puppets as an extension of themselves. Fine (2005) and Fine and Lee (1996) recommend that clinicians using puppets therapeutically consider incorporating animal puppets in their work because such puppets could be considered less threatening than human representations. It appears that children can act out their conscious and unconscious feelings more freely with animal versus human figures (Fine, 2005).

Fine (2005) reports that animal puppetry can be quite clinically revealing, especially as it relates to observing how clients select their puppets and how they act with them. Specific themes can be played out that directly relate to the challenges a child is experiencing. Fine and Lee (1999) point out that while observing the child during puppet play, the clinician can develop a clearer diagnostic understanding of the child. The medium of puppetry can help the child verbalize certain conscious-associated feelings or act out unconscious feelings, thereby relieving underlying tensions. For example, Adam (all client names have been changed to protect confidentiality) is a six-year-old boy who has a mild learning disability. He was referred for therapy because of being constantly bullied by others and feeling left out. An aspect of his cognitive therapy was AAT. He responded well to the animals in the office, especially the young golden retriever. At times puppets were also integrated, and he felt very comfortable when the therapist presented a group of animal puppets. In fact, several of the puppets had been purchased because of their similarities to the therapy animals within the practice.

Clinically, it was diagnostically fascinating to observe how Adam selected specific animal puppets. Although traditionally gentle in nature in the office, when the medium of puppetry was applied, he acted out aggressively towards the therapist's puppets. Growls and hostile tone accompanied his actions. It soon became apparent that his behavior in the play session was cathartic, allowing him to vent his frustrations in a constructive manner. Outside the therapy context, in his classroom, playground and other settings, he was always being picked on. Within this session, he was rebelling against his victimization by acting out. When the therapist redirected the session, he had his puppet reveal hurt feelings and beg the other puppet to exhibit kindness. Immediately, Adam's puppet acted more compassionately and became more accepting. The puppet session led to a discussion of how to handle bullies. The medium provided an excellent entry into this discussion, allowing Adam to feel less threatened about confronting his feelings.

Bibliotherapy, especially books about animals, also can be an effective adjunct to traditional AAT (Fine and Lee, 1996). In Chapter 11, several therapeutic approaches are discussed in detail; bibliotherapy is one of the approaches. Readers are encouraged to review that material. Briefly, reading materials may serve as a springboard for discussing sensitive issues "while at the same time giving the child an opportunity to explore these issues in an indirect and more comfortable manner" (Fine and Lee, 1999, p. 261). There are many books on subjects ranging from topics of death, trauma, bullying, and divorce that have animals as their main characters. The indirect use of animals as stand-ins for the self and other humans makes these books easy to read and follow without arousing the child's defenses. Appropriate books can be found through a variety of sources including by searches on the Internet and resource books such as the *Bookfinder*, published by the American Guidance Services.

Implications for AAT

Because animals slip under the radar of human defense mechanisms, animal presence in the therapeutic setting, either direct or indirect (e.g. as a story character), may help open a window into the person's or family's underlying issues. However, a skilled therapist is required to help the client make sense of this "unleashed" (if one may permit the pun) material. Moreover, psychodynamic theory cannot specify the forms of animal contact considered most helpful in various circumstances. Would a therapist's dog in the therapy room be preferred to a storytelling exercise involving animal characters? When, and under what circumstances?

Clinically, the answers to these questions are complex. Parish-Plass (2008) advocates living animals for preverbal and non-verbal children and also for traumatized or highly anxious children who lack the emotional ability for symbolization. For some children, the live animal will be an appropriate therapeutic choice, while for other children, storytelling or perhaps puppetry or animal figures will be a powerful alternative. Fine (2005) suggested that both alternatives—living animals and symbolic representations—fit naturally in a practice centered on AAT or AAI. Clinical experience suggests that child clients readily accept approaches that involve animals, but the specific modality and approach must be individualized.

Another implication of the psychodynamic approach for AAT stems from the view that children are instinctively drawn to animals because both are subject to the sway of id, biological urges untamed by the strictures of civilization. As Freud (1980) put it: "The child unhesitatingly attributes full equality to animals; he probably feels himself more closely related to the animal than to the undoubtedly mysterious adult, in the freedom with which he acknowledges his needs." Thus, Boris Levinson (1997), the great pioneer of animals within child therapy contexts, liked to observe child clients as they watched Jingles, the dog Levinson dubbed his "co-therapist." Jingles went about being a dog, therapy or no therapy—shedding fur, taking a nap, licking his genitals, slopping up water from his dish. How children responded to this essential dogginess gave Levinson clues to the internal struggles being fought.

Having several animals in my practice (AHF), Levinson's comment is particularly evocative. On various occasions, all of the animals have acted in ways that generate a smile, laughter, or an endearing feeling. For example, when the birds begin to talk to the clients, it often catches them off-guard. Snowflake, an Umbrella cockatoo, tends to greet clients when they enter the room with a soft "hi." The greeting usually prompts children to head toward the bird and begin a conversation. The cockatoos frequently act in mischievous ways. Periodically, they sneak off their perches and wander to a near-by computer. When not closely monitored, they have pecked off all the keys of the computer keyboard, while the therapy dogs sat and watched. (Surprisingly, the keyboards were not destroyed, and could be reassembled quite easily.) Children have been easily amused by the behaviors of the birds. Such incidents illustrate the role that animal behavior can play in providing moments of humor and distraction. What appears to be animal "misbehavior" can provide an opening for discussion of a child's feelings of "badness.'

Parish-Plass (2008) suggests that AAT provides avenues for treating children with insecure attachment. She suggests from her work with animals and children with attachment disorders that the presence of the animal provides a calm and less threatening atmosphere for therapy. She believes that AAT serves as a catalyst because it takes place in a "twilight area" within the mind that can be interpreted both in the play world and the real world of a child. She identifies several goals that animals can help with while treating children with insecure attachment due to abuse and neglect. The most critical benefit is that the therapy animal can assist a child who has little reason to trust adults as well as enabling a working client/therapist connection. The animals also seem to facilitate change in the child's mental representations and help the child work through salient and threatening issues concerning his/her difficult life situation. Parish-Plass also suggests that the animal's presence or as a subject matter can be used as a valuable assessment tool. For example, exploration of pet history in the family can provide information concerning the type of environment the child was raised in because of the proven link between animal abuse, domestic abuse, and child abuse. Finally, she suggests that clinicians can utilize the interactions as a window into a child's daily life. Clinicians can use these observations to provide a better understanding about the child's reaction to social situations.

12.3.2   Relational and self psychologies

Social connections were of paramount importance for psychologists, such as George Herbert Mead and Charles H. Cooley, who argued that a child's sense of self and indeed all thought and emotion emerge through relationships with others, called "objects" by object psychologists, like Margaret Mahler and Heinz Kohut. Cooley coined the term "looking glass self" to capture how the self is built from the qualities seen reflected in the eyes of others. Among the interpersonal experiences that these relational and self psychologists contended were building blocks for a cohesive and balanced sense of self were the following: mirroring (feeling recognized and affirmed), merging (feeling one with another), adversary (being able to assert oneself against an available and responsive other), efficacy (feeling able to elicit a response from the other), and vitalizing (feeling the other is attuned to one's shifting moods) (Wolf, 1994). It was assumed that only other humans were eligible to provide such relationship benefits. However, human/animal interaction (HAI) research finds that many children report these building blocks in their relationships with their pets (Melson, 2001). Thus, the range of "self object" experiences now includes other species, not just human/human bonds.

An important relationship is that of caregiver/cared for, or nurturer/nurtured. Wild bird feeding (Beck et al., 2001) and even exposure to wild animals (Myers and Saunders, 2002) has been shown to prompt children to think about themselves as caregivers and conservers. There is evidence that children engage in caregiving, nurturing relationships with pets, along with play and companionship (Melson and Fogel, 1996). Given the high incidence of pet ownership and relatively lower incidence of younger siblings and dependent elderly living in households with children, pets may well be the most frequent opportunity to observe, learn and practice nurturing others. This opportunity, unlike the nurture of young children, is not perceived as gendered; that is, children do not identify pet care with the feminine role, but consider it gender neutral, equally appropriate for males and females (Melson and Fogel, 1989). By contrast, children as young as three years of age view the care of infants and young children as "female" (Melson and Fogel, 1988), and gender differences in observed nurturing behaviors toward babies appear by age five (Melson et al., 1986; Melson and Fogel, 1982).

Attachment theory singles out one type of relationship as particularly significant. In the secure attachment relationship, another individual provides the child with a sense of security and safety, particularly under conditions of perceived threat. The founding father, John Bowlby (1969), and mother, Mary Ainsworth (1979), of attachment theory began with the assumption that mothers were the primary attachment figures, but since then, attachment theory and research gradually have expanded the list of potential "attachment objects" to fathers, older siblings, grandparents and child care providers, among others. Human/animal interaction researchers have suggested that pets often function as attachment "objects" for children (Melson, 2001), by giving them a sense of reassurance, calm, and security.

Because secure attachments in childhood are predictive of concurrent and later adjustment, resilience and coping with stress, it is possible that children's attachments to their pets may be linked to these positive outcomes as well. As we discuss later, there is growing evidence that pets do function as supports when children are feeling distressed or going through difficult transitions (Melson, 2001). The possible role of animals as coping "mechanisms" has implications for children in therapy.

Pets can also help children by acting as an emotional buffer for children coping with a stressful environment or emotional discord. According to Strand (2004), children who have pets in their home often turn to them for comfort during high stress situations such as parental disputes. She has found evidence that children who use their pet interaction as a "buffer" or as a self-calming technique may exhibit fewer behavioral problems because they have an outlet to help them regulate reactions to environmental stressors. The companion animal's presence allows the child to have something to turn to for emotional support during times of high internal or external conflict. Additionally, the pet provides the constant nurturing and acceptance needed to facilitate healthy coping skills, even in difficult times (Strand, 2004).

Implications for AAT

A cornerstone of relational and self psychologies is that only *relationships*, as contrasted to interactions or contacts, contribute to the self. Thus, children must develop an ongoing relationship with a specific individual animal before these "building blocks" of self can be activated. The ingredients of relationship involve commitment over time. Moreover, specific qualities of a relationship predict which building blocks can come into play. For example, children are most likely to develop a secure attachment bond to another when, over an extended period, that individual has been promptly responsive to the child's needs (Ainsworth, 1979). It is unclear how long, broad, and deep contacts with another individual need to be for a therapeutic relationship to emerge. This poses challenges for AAT, which generally lasts for a limited period per session over a limited number of sessions. The more limited the contact with an individual animal, or the more different animals participate interchangeably, the less likely building blocks of self will emerge.

Some self-object experiences—merging, vitalizing, secure attachment—may be more likely with animal species like dogs that are highly responsive to humans (and within species, individual animals who are most responsive). However, the well-known human propensity to anthropomorphize animals—think of a child looking at a fish in an aquarium and exclaiming: "He likes me!"—might make self-object experiences at times *more* likely with animals than with humans. Moreover, because animals are especially suited for children to experience and re-enact nurturer/nurtured interactions, HAI lends itself to exploring themes of neglectful or abusive parenting, feelings of abandonment, and examples of being well cared for (Parish-Plass, 2008).

12.3.3   Ecological systems psychology

This perspective emphasizes the importance of contexts of development, radiating outward from the most intimate—the family—to neighborhood, school, region, and culture (Bronfenbrenner, 1979). In this view, nuanced, multi-layered depiction of children's environments is as essential as a detailed anatomy of a child's internal physiology and psychology. In other words, ecological systems emphasize that we understand children "from the outside in" as well as "from the inside out." Like relationship psychologists, ecological systems view relationships as important within all the settings of a child's many contexts. But relationships themselves do not tell the whole story. Detailed description of physical contexts also is needed.

The term "systems" signifies that contexts are interrelated, so that one context affects every other, forming a system of interacting parts. For example, families are affected by (and contribute to) the neighborhood crime rate, which city and regional law enforcement policies also influence. While the immediate family is of primary importance as a context for child development, ecological approaches also focus on school, peer groups, neighborhood play groups, religious settings, after-school activities, and extended family members. From these contexts, individuals draw their *social network*, all those with whom they regularly interact (Cochran et al., 1990). This social network, in turn, provides the potential for *social support*, the provision of material, psychological, informational, and practical assistance (Cohen and McKay, 1984). Hundreds of studies have documented the power of social support to help both adults and children weather stress. Social support strongly predicts a wide range of positive health outcomes, from adults' recovery from stroke, cancer, and heart attack to children's risk of abuse and their success in school (Lynch, 2000).

Why is social support so potent? Researchers believe that when we receive social support, we feel loved, unconditionally accepted, esteemed, and interconnected. These feelings, more than practical assistance—for example, a loan—or information—for example, a recommended pediatrician's phone number—are the "magic bullet" of social support in ameliorating stress.

Social support research studies typically measure social support in ways that presuppose only human support. For example, an assessment might ask about "the people in your life who support you." When question format is broadened, there is evidence that many children turn to pets for reassurance and a sense of emotional support during stress. In interviews with German fourth-graders, 79% said that when they were sad, they sought out their pets (Rost and Hartmann, 1994). A study of Michigan youngsters, 10 to 14 years old, found that when they were upset, 75% turned to their pets (Covert et al., 1985). Pet-owning preschoolers in Indiana about to enter public school were less likely to be anxious and withdrawn during that transition if they turned to their pets for support when they were feeling sad or angry (Melson and Schwarz, 1994). Some children in residential therapeutic settings with animals report that when they need comforting, they seek out resident animals to talk to, touch, or just be nearby (Mallon, 1994).

Animals may play the most crucial role within the family microsystem, since children tend to view their pets as a peer or family member (Nebbe, 1991). Because companion animals are readily available and non-judgmental, they can provide a feeling of support and compassion when humans are unavailable, unable, or unwilling. In one study (Furman, 1989), elementary school-age children rated pets above parents or friends as the relationship most likely to last "no matter what" and "even if you get mad at each other."

Because pets generally have shorter lifespans than humans, children are likely to witness important lifecycle events, such as birth, serious illness and death, through experiences with family pets. Several surveys report that the majority of children experience pet loss, through death or disappearance, by adolescence (Stewart, 1983; Robin et al., 1983). Children also report worrying about their pet's health and eventual death, even when the animal is well (Bryant, 1990).

Helping children cope with animal loss

Recently, the second author spoke with one of his graduate students named Jose. He shared his tender memories of his beloved childhood dog named Boy. His sensitive portrayal is illustrative of the outcome experienced by many children who lose their beloved pet. Jose recalls:

> My first dog was a pug named Boy. I loved that dog. Boy was a gift from a man that would end up becoming the only man that I ever called Dad. His name was Eugene and he met my mom when I was eight and my brother was four. My mother had just left my brother's father after five years of physical and emotional abuse. After months of pursuing, begging, and bargaining, my mother finally gave my Dad a chance and that changed the course of my entire life. After months of gifts, pizza parlor tokens, and carnival tickets, I wouldn't accept him as anything but another man that was trying to date my mother. When we moved in with him, he gave me my space and I took full advantage of it. I never wanted to get even near him but my brother was already sold on him. He had already started to call Eugene dad.
>
> One evening I was helping my mother prepare dinner and Eugene came home from work with a cardboard box. He placed the box on the carpet, opened the lid, and out comes the cutest black face dog you have ever seen. With big eyes, a wild stub of a tail, and a beautiful tan coat, I fell in love instantly and we became best friends. Though it took many months before I every told Eugene, that night he became my Dad.
>
> When I got Boy at the age of 8, I never thought that my pre high school years would be filled with so much uncertainty. I went to seven different elementary schools, lived in multiple places including apartments, mobile homes, car garages, and RV's. Needless to say, within this time span, I had to give up Boy. My aunt had a large home and so when I was 10, Boy went to live with her. I was devastated, but I recognized that he needed a better place to live. I got to visit him often and I would play all day with him. When my home life finally stabilized, we bought a home in a nearby community in my freshman year in high school and I couldn't wait to get Boy back. However, there was a huge problem: my aunt was now so attached that she didn't want to give Boy back to us. Although it hurt me greatly, I agreed that she needed to keep my buddy. I never got him back.
>
> One summer day between my freshman and sophomore year, we received a phone call to my house. My mother answered and when she hung up the phone, she turned to me and calmly told me that Boy was dead. He had been playing in the front yard of my aunt's house when a group of guys drove by and took him and put him in the back of

their truck. Struggling to get away, Boy was able to free himself from one of the young men and leapt out of the truck, but unfortunately landed head first in the asphalt. I was devastated. I was 15 years old; a solid football player, and I cried passionately. I had lost my first best friend and I didn't even get to say goodbye.

Although the death and loss of a beloved pet may be experienced differently by people, the outcome may be the same for many; a sense of emptiness and pain. In most cases, animals live shorter lives than most humans. Clinicians agree that the animal's illness or eventual death should be explained to children truthfully and sensitively. Therapists and parents should allow children to share their feelings about their loss, including grief, anger and confusion, and help them realize their emotions are natural (Kurdeck, 2008; Nieburgh and Fischer, 1996).

Sharkin and Knox (2003) provide an excellent discussion of pet loss throughout the lifespan. They point out that, not surprisingly, people with a deeper attachment to their pets seem to experience more intense grief (Podrazik et al., 2000). According to Brown and Richard (1996), this is true for most children as well. In their research, girls reported more intense grief than boys, a finding that may reflect the greater willingness of females to self-report emotions. However, both boys and girls may be reluctant to share feelings such as grief over pet loss if they perceive they will be misunderstood by others (Brown and Richard, 1996).

The feelings associated with the death of a pet can differ depending on the circumstances. When a pet has been fortunate enough to live for a long time, the pet understandably begins to show signs of aging. Some families with pets in declining health due to aging begin to prepare for the end of life by saying their goodbyes both formally and informally. Talking about the prospect of death and preparing for it seems to soften the emotional blow but in no way guarantees that it will make it easier for a child to accept the inevitable. On the other hand, some children find it difficult to understand the death of a pet, especially when the death is not of natural causes but rather when the animal is euthanized or dies unexpectedly (Butler and Lagoni, 1996; Clements et al., 2003). Over the years, the second author has treated many children who have had difficulty dealing with the loss of their pet, especially when they felt the death was due to their own negligence. Having parents who are supportive and help the child work through the sense of guilt is critical to their well-being. Parents can also act as a reality check for children, reassuring them that the pet's death was not their fault.

Unfortunately, some parents try to hide information about an animal's illness and death, particularly when the pet is euthanized, out of desire to "protect" their child from an upsetting loss. Clinically, this isn't desirable. Nieburgh and Fischer (1996) point out that children's active imaginations may lead them to fantasies about the death of their pet that are more disturbing than what really happened. Clinicians dealing with animal loss strongly recommend that parents answer children's questions, using simple, clear and accurate information geared to the development stage of the child. Phrases such as "putting to sleep" can confuse young children, and even scare them as they prepare to go to bed at night.

We agree with Kaufman and Kaufman (2006) that it is important to allow children to grieve. Parents can help their child by allowing them to express themselves in different ways, from discussions with close family and friends, to reading books, drawing pictures and writing poetry (Brown and Richards, 1996; Kaufman and Kaufman, 2006).

There are many other therapeutic interventions appropriate for families who experience a loss of an animal. Table 12.1 lists several children's books on pet loss. Additionally, databases such as the Bookfinder or other bibliographic searches are useful in order to find other resources. Art activities and other media such as scrap booking or journaling are also dynamic and sensitive techniques to help support children. Finally, within many communities throughout the country, humane societies offer support groups for pet loss. Some universities also have "hotlines" to call for guidance and emotional support. Readers are also encouraged to review Dr. Cohen's chapter (Chapter 21) detailing the process of bereavement and various approaches that will support children and adults.

Animals in the family system

A tenet of ecological systems psychology holds that within a single context, all relationships and elements interact in what is called a "dynamic system." Thus, a child's relationship with a parent is affected by (and affects) the mother/father tie, sibling bonds, and the child's relationship with the other parent. Because of this web of mutual influence, family systems therapy considers a child entering therapy as the "presenting problem" of the family system, and generally insists on working with all family members, since therapeutic intervention must be at the level of the family system. Most systems therapists, however, assume that all members of the family system are human beings.

With few exceptions, descriptions of children's ecologies or their family systems remain restricted to an inventory of human/human ties, despite the prevalence of pets in households with children, the ubiquity of animals in children's lives, and the evidence that animals often function as social support. In part, these blinders derive from a persistent "humanocentric" perspective that recognizes only intra-species

Table 12.1 Books for Children on Death of a Pet (Corr, 2004)

I'll Always Love You (Wilheim, 1988)
Goodbye, Mitch (Wallace-Brodeur, 1995)
Lifetimes (Mellonie, 1983)
Dog Heaven (Rylant, 1995)
Cat Heaven (Rylant, 1997)
Not Just a Fish (Hemery, 2000)
The Tenth Good Thing about Barney (Viorst, 1971)
Remember Rafferty: A Book about the Death of a Pet…for Children of All Ages (Johnson, 1998)
The Black Dog Who Went Into the Woods (Hurd, 1980)
Charlotte's Web (White, 1952)
Give a Dog Your Heart: Love will Come Your Way (Fine, in Press)

contacts as significant. Melson (2001) has argued that a paradigm shift to a "bio-centric" approach, which encompasses other species and the natural world, is needed.

With such a biocentric perspective, one notes that the majority of pet owners say they consider their animals to be "family members." This does not (usually) mean that parents value the family gerbil, bird, or cat as much as their children, but their use of "family member" to describe the animal is not just a figure of speech either. It is likely that pets are drawn into the web of intersecting relationships that make up a family system. In a pioneering study, Cain (1983) reported frequent use of "triangling" with pets in the family systems of 60 pet-owning families. Triangling occurs when two family members transfer intense interpersonal feeling onto another family member. Thus, a father might yell at the dog when he was angry with his wife, a mother might say something to the cat that her daughter would overhear, or two pets would begin fighting when family members are distant or tense.

Animals in schools and neighborhoods

Ecological systems theory holds that beyond the family, the environments of school, neighborhood and community are important influences on children's development. As noted earlier, animals—living and symbolic—are found in many schools, espe-cially in the preschool and elementary school years. Research remains limited on the significance of such animal involvement, however. Myers (1998) observed a class of 25 three to five year olds over a school year, focusing on their engagement with animals—regular residents, such as a toad, guinea pig, goldfish and two diamond doves; "visitors" (including a dog, box turtles, ferrets, tarantulas, a spider monkey and pythons); and playground wildlife (birds and squirrels). He documents in rich detail how the children explored ideas about self and other identities, learned how to relate to distinctly different beings appropriately and thought about the moral claims of others. His work showed how classroom animals stimulated language, imagination and self-reflection.

Another, equally rich account of the role animals play outside the family comes from Bryant's (1985) detailed analysis of seven- and ten-year-old children's social life within their neighborhoods. She documented how on average, children named at least one neighborhood animal (not their own) as a "special friend" and reported having "intimate talks" with the animals. To understand better the roles that animals play in the microsystems beyond the family—school, neighborhood, community, peer group, etc.—we need more in-depth research, building on the foundation that Myers and Bryant have laid.

Implications for AAT

Therapeutic interventions from a family systems perspective would do well to follow Cain (1983)'s lead and consider family pets or other animals as part of that system. Where possible and appropriate, home observation might reveal patterns ripe for therapeutic interpretation. When the animals in the therapy room are similar to those a child has at home, these animals may "trigger" associations to themes involving the family pet and other (human) family members.

For example (from a clinical case in AHF's practice), a client with a language processing disorder was frequently overheard saying, "I wish my dog would listen as well as yours." This became a springboard for future discussions about why he felt his dog did not listen as well. He eventually explained that his father was not as friendly with the dog as the boy wished. He would describe how his father gave very little attention to the family dog and only "barked" out orders when convenient to him. When children recount episodes such as this about their animals at home, they also may reveal information about their relationships with other family members or the climate within the home. Returning to the previous example, it was common for this young man to disclose similarities between himself and the dog in relation to his father. It appeared that his dad frequently ignored him and gave both him and the dog limited attention. Once the boy disclosed these feelings, I (AHF) spent time reflecting how he felt and talked about his desire to get his father's approval and positive attention. At the end of one session the client looked at one of the golden retrievers who sat next to him and stated, "When you give them love and attention, they grow up stable and loving like your dogs."

As the above example illustrates, a systems approach prevents us from considering the child in isolation. Whatever we learn about a child's relationships with animals must be integrated with knowledge about human/human ties. It is still unclear whether a close bond with a pet functions as a compensatory relationship when human bonds are frayed. Another possibility is that inter-species and intra-species ties tend to be positively correlated. This would mean that children with strong parental bonds and good peer relations would be *more* not less likely to respond positively to animals, whether their own or a therapy animal. A child's sense of support from a pet's presence or behavior may be a reflection, not a cause, of the child's social skills, empathy, or social adjustment.

12.3.4   The biophilia hypothesis

This idea, first advanced by the biologist E. O. Wilson, suggests that a predisposition to attune to animal life is part of the human evolutionary heritage, a product of our co-evolution as omnivores with the animals and plants on which our survival depends (Kellert and Wilson, 1993; Wilson, 1984). Biophilia implies not a love of animals, but rather an innate interest in living things. During human evolution, this interest was fueled not only by the need to use animal and plants for food and clothing, but also because animals served as sentinels of the environment. Some animals (poisonous snakes, lions, bears) might pose a direct danger to humans, or compete with humans for food and use of an environment (Barrett, 2005). Animal behavior also was diagnostic of environmental conditions: birds circling lazily in the sky or cows grazing contentedly, like clear blue skies, tell us that environmental threats are absent. Like darkening clouds, the alarm cries of other animals communicate a nearby danger.

As with other aspects of evolutionary psychology, the biophilia hypothesis recognizes that environmental and cultural influences—the "nurture" of the "nature/nurture debate"—shape and channel biophilia's expression (Kahn, 1997, 1999). Thus, the biophilia hypothesis is consistent with evidence of children's abuse of, fear of, and dislike for animals, as well as children's attachment to their pets and fascination with wildlife and dinosaurs.

Biophilia's suggestion that we evolved to respond to animals as environmental sentinels of danger or safety implies that friendly, calm animals are likely to have a calming effect upon human mood, while agitated aggressive animals are likely to have the opposite effect. There is some evidence to support this view. Watching, for only ten minutes, tropical fish swimming in an aquarium was shown to be as effective as hypnosis in reducing the anxiety and discomfort of adult patients about to undergo dental surgery (Beck and Katcher, 1996). Children aged 9 to 16 who sit quietly next to a friendly dog have lower heart rates and blood pressure than when sitting alone. When the child is asked to read aloud some poetry, heart rate and blood pressure predictably rise, but when the dog is present, the increase is significantly lower than when reading alone (Friedmann et al., 1983). Healthy children who undergo a simulated physical medical examination in the presence of a friendly dog (versus without an animal present) have less behavioral distress (Nagergost et al., 1997).

Implications for AAT

The biophilia hypothesis provides a powerful rationale for including animals in a therapeutic context. If the hypothesis is correct, children are more likely to notice and respond to animals and animal symbols than other items, such as toys or dolls. In other words, animals are predicted to be an attention grabber that may help engage the child.

A second implication of the biophilia hypothesis is that friendly animal presence may convey that the therapeutic setting is a safe place. A child may feel calmer and therefore more open to therapeutic intervention. Both the attention-getting and calming components of AAT were documented in a well-controlled "cross-over" design study conducted by Aaron Katcher, called the "Companionable Zoo" (Katcher and Wilkins, 2000). The intervention targeted 12- to 15-year-old boys with severe conduct disorder who were in residential treatment. Half the boys were randomly assigned to the "Zoo," and half to an Outward Bound nature program. At the Zoo program, boys attended five hours of classes weekly. They first learned how to hold and care for the resident rabbits, chinchillas, guinea pigs, iguanas, turtles, doves, finches, cockatiels, goats, and Vietnamese pot-bellied pigs. Only after mastering the biology, characteristics, and care requirements of an animal could a child adopt it as a pet and name it. The child then could earn "skill cards" by learning more about the animal. Field trips to special education classes and rehabilitation hospitals allowed the children to show their animals and demonstrate their expertise in public settings. Two cardinal rules reigned at the Zoo: speak softly and be gentle with the animals, and respect the animals and each other.

After six months, "Zoo" staff found that remarkably, not a single incident requiring physical restraint occurred. (On the basis of the boys' histories, the staff expected that these boys would have to be physically restrained because of conduct disorder 35 times over a six-month period.) Behaviors at the Zoo—nurturing, affection, play, lowered aggression, peer cooperation, accepting responsibility, teaching others, and responding to adult authority—were in sharp contrast to the boys' problematic profiles. For the boys who were attending the Outward Bound program, however, aggression did not diminish, and rates of physical restraint held steady. Katcher reports that in subsequent replications over a six-year period at three other treatment centers, staff members have never reported an incident requiring physical restraint (Katcher and Wilkins, 2000). Thus, this intensive, supervised animal care experiment produced greater focused attention and calming in these boys with severe emotional and behavioral disorders.

Fine and Eisen (2008) discuss several case examples of how trained therapy animals help cultivate a more accepting environment. These case narratives describe how therapy animals acted as catalyst for comfort in difficult periods; for example, when clients disclose self mutilation or abuse, or when they express feelings of loneliness and incompetence.

The following is one example of how a black Labrador, Hart, acted as a social catalyst. On Sarah's first office visit back to the office (Dr. Fine's) after her release from the hospital, she was more at ease but still reserved. As we sit and talk, Hart sat close to her chair. At one point in the session, Sarah's reserve finally crumbles. Pushing up her left sleeve, she shows both of us her scars. As she lowers her arm, Sarah noticed that Hart's eyes were fixed on that arm. At that moment, Hart lifts her gaze from the arm and connects with Sarah's eyes. With an expression on her face that I can only call puzzled, Hart looks back at Sarah, and then Hart lowers her head and begins to lick the healed scars. Sarah is startled for a moment but then sits quietly as Hart continues to lick the wounds. Finally, she bends over Hart and holds her close (Fine and Eisen, 2008, p. 43).

Fine, in Chapter 10, discusses a variety of ways in which the presence of animals alters a therapeutic environment. From a clinical standpoint, fish tanks, vivariums, terrariums and plants are all ingredients that promote a sense of relaxation. Although discussed in the context of milieu therapy, the biophilia orientation contributes to understanding why these alternatives work. All of these options introduce elements of the living environment into the built environment of an office, thereby making it more appealing. This "greener" milieu may help generate conversations about birth, the food chain, gentleness or aggression because of the presence of animals and other living things.

However, the biophilia hypothesis sounds a cautionary note to those who hope that contact with animals will generalize to positive changes when children are in other contexts. Biophilia predicts only transient mood changes when in the presence of animals and other living things, but does not predict long-term changes, particularly when animals are no longer there. In the Companionable Zoo experiment discussed earlier, boys attending the "Zoo" continued to struggle with aggression and conduct disorder in their dorms, classrooms and other activities. Only toward the end of the six-month program did regular classroom teachers (who did not know the boys' group assignments) note lowered aggression in that context, and dorm counselors found that episodes of out-of-control behavior in the dorms began to decline. Thus, generalization to contexts where animals were not present was slow to happen, even while children were participating in the intervention. Moreover, the "cross-over" design switched the groups after six months; those who had been at the "Zoo" now entered the Outward Bound program, while those who had been in Outward Bound began attending the "Zoo." Once out of the AAT environment of the "Zoo," the symptoms of the former "Zoo boys" began to worsen. Because of this, Katcher and Wilkins (1998) speculate that any beneficial therapeutic outcomes of AAT may require continuing "doses" of animal presence to maintain children's positive mood and behavior changes.

In addition, biophilia does not give priority to animals, but sees them as part of the fabric of life, including trees and plants. Therapists who integrate AAT into their practice often also provide a "greener" environment, including houseplants, flowers, and artwork, that depicts nature. From a research perspective, changes in the child in such an environment cannot be traced solely to the animals. From the biophilia perspective, there may be multiple routes to attunement to life, with some children more responsive to flora and others to fauna.

Biophilia posits that distressed animals will convey "messages" that the environment is *not* safe, and hence may even increase a child's discomfort. This makes the animal's own behavior and temperament all the more important and places special responsibility on the animal's owner (and therapist) to monitor the animal. Of course, animal welfare concerns mandate vigilance against stressing therapy animals.

Animal analogues

In recent years, there has been a proliferation of technologies—robotic pets, virtual pets, Animal Planet, virtual gardens—that are designed to mimic aspects of living things, such as animals and plants. The theory of biophilia is not specific enough to yield predictions about precisely which aspects of a living being, such as a dog, are critical to engage attention and convey safety. Emerging research (Melson et al., 2009a,b) on how children understand and respond to robotic pets, such as AIBO, helps shed light on both the promise and limitations of technological analogues to living animals as companions or therapeutic tools for children. In a free play, non-clinical setting, 7–15-year-old children considered the robot dog more as a complex artifact and judged its potential as a social companion to be much lower than that of a living dog (Melson et al., 2009a,b). However, most of these children still considered the robot dog to have elements of a biological being, not just a machine, to be able to think, to be a friend, and to be deserving of moral regard (i.e. having the right not to be harmed). When behaviors toward the robot dog were observed, children talked, tried to play ball, and generally engaged the robot socially, although less so than with a living dog. The children were more likely to explore the robot as if it were an artifact—poking and rotating it to see how it "worked"—than to explore the dog in that way. They petted the live dog nearly five times as much as they did the robot dog (Melson et al., 2009a,b).

Clinical use of robot dogs, in comparison to living ones, shows similar results. Fine (2005) reported incorporating a robotic dog in his practice (an Icybe) to assess how children would respond to the robot in comparison to his therapy dogs. Although the children were initially very curious about the robotic dog, all of them considered it a toy rather than an animal. The robot did not seem to have any calming effects and in fact, when it seemed to wander around the office, some of the clients became more active but in an unfocused way. Most clients found it as interesting to watch how the therapy dogs and birds reacted to the Icybe's movements as it was to watch the robot move. In most cases, the animals did not know what to make of the robot, and seemed uncomfortable with its random movements.

12.4   Best practices in AAT with children

AAT rests on the foundation of animal welfare. Responsible clinicians give equal priority to the welfare of participating animals *and* children. Animal welfare is not limited to issues of good medical care, proper training, and certification as an assistance animal. In addition, as any therapist knows, anyone who has sustained contact with highly stressed populations is at risk of stress and burn-out. This makes AAT animals at risk, by definition. When therapists are also owners and enthusiastic about the therapeutic benefits of their animals, the therapist/owner may not always pick up early signs of stress.

As the field of AAT matures and moves toward "best practices," more attention to individual differences is warranted. The first source of individual difference is the therapy animal. Assuming all animals are certified and not at risk for stress, there remain individual differences in temperament, activity level, size, etc. that may make a particular animal a good or poor choice to interact with a particular child or family. There is currently more art than science to the task of matching animal to client, in terms of maximizing AAT treatment benefits.

The second source of individual difference is the child and family. Biophilia recognizes individual differences, as personal history, culture and upbringing shape our innate interest in life forms. Some children and family members do not respond to animals, have had negative experiences with animals, or are afraid of animals. We can probably locate any human on an approach-avoidance gradient with respect to animals in general or particular animal species. It is likely that individuals who come into AAT with positive predispositions toward animals, especially those similar to the therapy animal, will be more responsive in therapy and will have better outcomes.

Results of the Companionable Zoo study and other data support this hypothesis. Erika Friedmann (2000) found that adults with more positive attitudes toward dogs experienced significantly lower blood pressure when reading aloud in the presence of an unfamiliar dog than did adults with more negative attitudes toward dogs. Similarly, among boys who completed the Zoo experience, there was variation in learning and behavior change. Zoo personnel identified "high performers," boys who showed especially high motivation, lots of learning about animals and particularly gentle, responsive treatment of the animals, as well as "low performers," who were minimally engaged in the Zoo. Although both high and low performers had completed the intervention, the high performers maintained lower aggression in their regular classrooms six months after the Zoo ended, while the low performers had returned to the high pre-intervention rates of classroom disruption (Katcher and Wilkins, 2000). Thus, the same AAT intervention will have different effects on different children, in part because of the predispositions they bring into the therapy at the outset.

In another study (Melson et al., 2009a), children who were more attached to their pets at home and who were less involved with technology—using computers for fewer hours on a regular basis, for example—were more likely to view an unfamiliar, friendly dog as a being who had a psychology (could think and feel) and who deserved moral regard (should be free from harm). In short, children's home experiences with animals were "brought into" the research setting as the child encountered an unfamiliar dog. Similarly, one expects that children's home experiences, including with animals, will come into the therapy session.

Cultural differences remain poorly understood. Although cultures vary greatly in their views about animals and keeping animals—and within culture, there is wide variation—we know little about how cultural background and beliefs interact with therapeutic outcomes using AAT. Since AAT is being implemented in many countries across diverse cultures, future research is needed to make AAT culturally relevant and sensitive.

The final individual difference to consider is that of the therapist. Beyond the usual variations in training, experience, and skill level, therapists who incorporate AAT may differ in their enthusiasm and commitment to this therapy. Like clients of AAT, therapists who are more motivated are likely to achieve better outcomes. However, one caution that highly motivated AAT therapists might consider: enthusiasm for AAT, particularly with a "wonderful" therapy animal, perhaps the therapist's own pet, may make it difficult to recognize clients who are unresponsive to AAT, better suited to another type of intervention, or perhaps most difficult for the therapist, simply dislike the therapist's animal. Like everything else that occurs in the therapy room, the therapist's reactions to both positive and negative client behavior toward the therapy animal should be material for therapy supervision. Therapists working in the psychodynamic tradition should be attentive to counter-transference processes triggered by clients' treatment of the therapy animal.

12.5 Guidelines for best practices of AAT with children and concluding remarks

The following briefly highlights some guidelines that AAT and AAI practitioners may find useful:

- Match the animal to the child's needs
- Integrate the animal experience with the therapeutic goals for the child
- Understand the complex dynamic of therapist, child and animal
- Explore the role of family animals and other family members
- Be sensitive to potential for child aggression or harm toward animals
- Consider animal experiences broadly; include animal representations (puppetry, books, stories, toys, stuffed animals, art) as appropriate.

- Make animal welfare and child welfare paramount at all times
- Take cultural attitudes and family history with animals (for example, dog bites) into account
- Consider which children if any are contra-indicated for AAT and which might particularly benefit.

In sum, diverse theoretical frameworks provide conceptual underpinning for AAT with children and their families. These frameworks see animals as freeing up repressed thoughts and feelings, providing an affirming and supportive relationship, reflecting the dynamics of the family system, and focusing and calming the child and family in the therapeutic context. However, each framework also suggests cautions and limitations, which may inform the development of "best practices" as AAT continues to expand and become institutionalized.

References

Ainsworth, M. (1979). Attachment as related to mother-infant interaction. In R. Hinde & J. Rosenblatt (Eds.), *Advances in the Study of Behavior*. New York: Academic Press.

American Pet Products Manufacturers Association. (2009). *2008–2009 APPMA national pet owners survey*. Greenwich, CT: APPMA. Retrieved Nov. 12, 2009. http://americanpetproducts.org/press_industrytrends.asp

American Veterinary Medical Association. (2003). *The Veterinary Service Market for Companion Animals*. Schaumberg, IL: Center for Information Management.

Arad, D. (2004). If your mother were an animal, what animal would she be? Creating play-stories in family therapy: the animal attribution story-telling technique. *Family Process, 43*, 249–263.

Barrett, H. C. (2005). Cognitive development and the understanding of animal behavior. In B. J. Ellis & D. F. Bjorklund (Eds.), *Origins of the Social Mind: Evolutionary Psychology and Child Development* (pp. 438–467). NY: Guilford Press.

Beck, A. M., & Katcher, A. H. (1996). *Between Pets and People: The Importance of Animal Companionship* (revised edition). West Lafayette, IN: Purdue University Press.

Beck, A. M., Melson, G. F., daCosta, P. L., & Liu, T. (2001). The educational benefits of a ten-week home-based wild bird feeding program for children. *Anthrozoös, 14*, 19–28.

Bowlby, J. (1969). *Attachment*. New York: Basic Books.

Bronfenbrenner, U. (1979). *The Ecology of Human Development*. Cambridge, MA: Harvard University Press.

Brown, B., & Richards, H. (1996). Pet bonding and pet bereavement and adolescents. *Journal of Counseling and Development, 74*, 505–509.

Bryant, B. K. (1985). The neighborhood walk: sources of support in middle childhood. *Monographs of the Society for Research in Child Development, 50*(3), 1–122.

Bryant, B. K. (1990). The richness of the child-pet relationship: a consideration of both benefits and costs of pets to children. *Anthrozoös, 3*, 253–261.

Butler, C., & Lagoni, L. (1996). Children and pet loss. In C. Corr & M. Donna (Eds.), *Handbook of Childhood Death and Bereavement* (pp. 179–200). New York: Springer Publishing Co.

Cain, A. O. (1983). A study of pets in the family system. In A. H. Katcher & A. M. Beck (Eds.), *New Perspectives on Our Lives with Companion Animals* (pp. 72–81). Philadelphia, PA: University of Pennsylvania Press.

Carlsson, M. A., Samuelsson, I. P., Soponyai, A., & Wen, Q. (2001). The dog's tale: Chinese, Hungarian and Swedish children's narrative conventions. *International Journal of Early Years Education, 9*, 181–191.

Clements, P., Benasutti, K., & Carmone, A. (2003). Support for bereaved owners of pets. *Perspective in Psychiatric Care, 39*, 49–54.

Cochran, M., Larner, M., Riley, D., Gunnarsson, L., & Henderson, C. R., Jr., (Eds.), (1990). *Extending Families: The Social Networks of Parents and their Children*. New York: Cambridge University Press.

Cohen, S., & McKay, G. (1984). Social support, stress, and the buffering hypothesis: a theoretical analysis. In A. Baum, J. E. Singer, & S. E. Taylor (Eds.), *Handbook of Psychology and Health* (pp. 253–267). Hillsdale, NJ: Erlbaum.

Corr, C. (2004). Pet loss in death-related literature for children. *Omega, 48*, 399–414.

Covert, A. M., Whirren, A. P., Keith, J., & Nelson, C. (1985). Pets, early adolescents and families. *Marriage and Family Review, 8*, 95–108.

Dickinson, R., & Edmonson, B. (1996). Golden wings. *American Demographics, 18*(12), 47–49.

Field, J. (2004). *America's families and living arrangements: 2003 Current Population Report*. Washington, DC: United States Census.

Fine, A. H. (in press). *Give A Dog Your Heart: Love Will Come Your Way*. Oxnard, CA: Manadoob Corp.

Fine, A. H. (2005, May 2). *Animal Assisted Therapy and Clinical Practice*. San Francisco CA: Psycho-Legal Associates CEU Meeting.

Fine, A. H., & Eisen, C. J. (2008). *Afternoons with Puppy: Inspirations from a Therapist and His Animals*. West Lafayette, IN: Purdue University Press.

Fine, A. H., & Lee, J. (1996). Broadening the impact of services and recreational therapies. In A. Fine & N. Fine (Eds.), *Therapeutic Recreation for Exceptional Children* (pp. 243–269). Springfield, CT: Charles C. Thomas.

Freud, S. (1965). *The Interpretation of Dreams*. New York: Avon/Basic.

Freud, S. (1980). Totem and Taboo *(J. Strachey, Trans.)*. New York: Norton. (Original work published 1913.).

Friedmann, E. (2000). The animal-human bond: health and wellness. In A. Fine (Ed.), *Handbook on Animal Assisted Therapy* (pp. 41–56). NY: Academic Press.

Friedmann, E., Katcher, A., Thomas, S., Lynch, J., & Messent, P. (1983). Social interaction and blood pressure: influence of animal companions. *Journal of Nervous and Mental Disease, 171*, 461–465.

Furman, W. (1989). The development of children's social networks. In D. Belle (Ed.), *Children's Social Networks and Social Supports* (pp. 151–172). New York: Wiley.

Hemery, K. (2000). *Not just a Fish*. Omaha, NE: Centering Corporation.

Hurd, E. (1980). *The Black Dog Who Went into the Woods*. New York: Harper and Row.

Johnson, J. (1998). *Remember Rafferty: A Book about the Death of a Pet...for Children of All Ages*. Omaha, NE: Centering Corporation.

Kahn, P. H., Jr. (1997). Developmental psychology and the biophilia hypothesis: children's affiliation with nature. *Developmental Review, 17*, 1–61.

Kahn, P. H., Jr. (1999). *The Human Relationship with Nature: Development and Culture*. Cambridge, MA: MIT Press.

Katcher, A. H., & Wilkins, G. G. (2000). The centaur's lessons: therapeutic education through care of animals and nature study. In A. Fine (Ed.), *Handbook on Animal Assisted Therapy* (pp. 153–178). NY: Academic Press.

Katcher, A. H., & Wilkins, G. G. (1998). Animal-assisted therapy in the treatment of disruptive behavior disorders in children. In A. Lundberg (Ed.), *The Environment and Mental Health: A Guide for Clinicians* (pp. 193–204). Mahwah, NJ: Erlbaum.

Kaufman, K., & Kaufman, N. (2006). And then the dog died. *Death Studies, 30,* 61–76.

Kellert, S. R. & .Wilson, E. O. (Eds.), (1993). *The Biophilia Hypothesis.* Washington, DC: Island Press.

Kurdeck, L. (2008). Pet dogs as attachment. *Journal of Social and Personal Relationships, 25,* 247–266.

Levinson, B. (1997). *Pet-oriented Child Psychotherapy* (2nd ed. revised by G. Mallon). Springfield, IL: Charles C. Thomas Pub.

Lynch, J. J. (2000). *A Cry Unheard: New Insights into the Medical Consequences of Loneliness.* Baltimore, MD: Bancroft Books.

Mallon, C. P. (1994). Some of our best therapists are dogs. *Child and Youth Care Forum, 23,* 94.

Mellonie, B. (1983). *Lifetimes.* NY: Bantam.

Melson, G. F. (2001). *Why the Wild Things Are: Animals in the Lives of Children.* Cambridge, MA: Harvard University Press.

Melson, G. F. (2007). Children in the living world: Why animals matter for children's development. In A. Fogel & S. Shanker (Eds.), *Human Development in the 21st Century: Visionary Ideas from Systems Scientists* (pp. 147–154). New York: Cambridge University Press.

Melson, G.F. (in press). Child development and human-animal interaction: directions for research. In P. McCardle, S. McCune, J. Griffin, & V. Maholmes, (Eds.), *Directions in Human-animal Interaction Research: Child Development, Health, and Therapeutic Interventions.* Washington, DC: American Psychological Association.

Melson, G. F., & Fogel, A. (1982). Young children's interest in unfamiliar infants. *Child Development, 53,* 693–700.

Melson, G. F., & Fogel, A. (1988). Research review: the development of nurturance in young children. *Young Children, 43,* 57–65.

Melson, G. F., & Fogel, A. (1989). Children's ideas about animal young and their care: a reassessment of gender differences in the development of nurturance. *Anthrozoös, 2,* 265–273.

Melson, G. F., & Fogel, A. (1996). Parental perceptions of their children's involvement with household pets. *Anthrozoös, 9,* 95–106.

Melson, G. F., Fogel, A., & Toda, S. (1986). Children's ideas about infants and their care. *Child Development, 57,* 1519–1527.

Melson, G. F., Kahn, P. H., Jr., Beck, A. M., & Friedman, B. (2009a). Robotic pets in human lives: implications for the human-animal bond and for human relationships with personified technologies. *Journal of Social Issues, 65,* 545–567.

Melson, G. F., Kahn, P. H., Jr., Beck, A. M., Friedman, B., Roberts, T., Garrett, E., & Gill, B. (2009b). Children's behavior toward and understanding of robotic and living dogs. *Journal of Applied Developmental Psychology, 30,* 92–102.

Melson, G. F., & Schwarz, R. (1994). Pets as social supports for families with young children. New York city: Paper presented to the annual meeting of the Delta Society.

Myers, G. (1998). *Children and Animals: Social Development and Our Connections to Other Species.* Boulder, CO: Westview Press.

Myers, O. E., & Saunders, C. D. (2002). Animals as links toward developing caring relationships with the natural world. In P. H. Kahn & S. R. Kellert (Eds.), *Children and Nature: Psychological, Sociocultural, and Evolutionary Investigations* (pp. 153–178). Cambridge, MA: MIT Press.

Nabhan, G. P., & Trimble, S. (1994). *The Geography of Childhood: Why Children Need Wild Places*. Boston: Beacon Press.

Nagergost, S. L., Baun, M. M., Megel, M., & Leibowitz, J. M. (1997). The effects of the presence of a companion animal on physiologic arousal and behavioral distress in children during a physical examination. *Journal of Pediatric Nursing, 12*, 323–330.

Nebbe, L. (1991). The human-animal bond and the elementary school counselor. *The School Counselor, 38*, 362–371.

Nieburg, H., & Fischer, A. (1996). *Pet Loss*. New York: Harper Perennial.

Parish-Plass, N. (2008). Animal-assisted therapy with children suffering from insecure attachment due to abuse and neglect: a method to lower the risk of intergenerational transmission of abuse. *Clinical Child Psychology and Psychiatry, 13*, 7–30.

Podrazik, D., Shackford, S., Becker, L., & Heckert, T. (2000). The death of a pet. Implications for loss and bereavement across the lifespan. *Journal of Personal and Interpersonal Loss, 5*, 361–395.

Rio, L. M. (2001). My family as animals: a technique to promote inclusion of children in the family therapy process. *Journal of Family Psychotherapy, 12*, 75–85.

Robin, M., ten Bensel, R., Quigley, J. S., & Anderson, R. K. (1983). Childhood pets and the psychosocial development of adolescents. In A. H. Katcher & A. M. Beck (Eds.), *New Perspectives on Our Lives with Companion Animals* (pp. 436–443). Philadelphia, PA: University of Pennsylvania Press.

Rost, D., & Hartmann, A. (1994). Children and their pets. *Anthrozoös, 7*, 242–254.

Rud, A. G., & Beck, A. M. (2003). Companion animals in Indiana elementary schools. *Anthrozoös, 16*, 241–251.

Rylant, C. (1995). *Dog Heaven*. NY: The Blue Sky Press.

Rylant, C. (1997). *Cat Heaven*. NY: The Blue Sky Press.

Sharkin, B., & Knox, D. (2003). Pet loss; issues and implications for the psychologist. *Professional Psychology, Research and Practice, 34*, 414–421.

Stewart, M. (1983). Loss of a pet—loss of a person: a comparative study of bereavement. In A. H. Katcher & A. M. Beck (Eds.), *New Perspectives on Our Lives with Companion Animals* (pp. 390–404). Philadelphia, PA: University of Pennsylvania Press.

Strand, E. B. (2004). Interparental conflict and youth maladjustment: the buffering effect of pets. *Stress, Trauma, and Crisis, 7*, 151–168.

Valkenburg, P. M., & Soeters, K. E. (2001). Children's positive and negative experiences with the internet: an exploratory survey. *Communication Research, 28*, 652–675.

Viorst, J. (1971). *The Tenth Good Thing about Barney*. NY: Atheneum.

Von Franz, M. L. (1972). The process of individuation. In C. G. Jung & L. M. von Franz (Eds.), *Man and His Symbols* (pp. 158–229). NY: Dell.

Wallace-Brodeur, R. (1995). *Goodbye, Mitch*. Morton Grove, IL: Albert Whitman.

White, E. B. (1952). *Charlotte's Web*. New York: Harper and Row.

Wilhelm, H. (1988). *I'll Always Love You*. NY: Dragonfly Books.

Wilson, E. O. (1984). *Biophilia*. Cambridge, MA: Harvard University Press.

Wolf, E. (1994). Selfobject experiences: development, psychopathology, treatment. In S. Kramer & S. Akhtar (Eds.), *Mahler and Kohut: Perspectives on Development, Psychopathology, and Technique* (pp. 65–96). Northvale, NJ: Jason Aronson.

13 The use of therapy animals with individuals with autism spectrum disorders

Temple Grandin PhD *, *Aubrey H. Fine EdD* †, *Christine M. Bowers BA* †

* Colorado State University, † California State Polytechnic University

13.1   Introduction

Walter is now eight years old. He has been visiting the office for over a year. He sits on the floor with his legs crossed as he feeds a treat to his canine co-therapist. "Here you go, girl," he says as he flaps his hands in excitement.

It was not too long ago that Walter would just rock, shriek and simply ignore the warm hearted golden retriever as she approached. If she got too close, he would stiffen to demonstrate his displeasure. Walter has autism.

According to the Autism Society of America, autism is a "complex developmental disability that typically appears during the first three years of life and affects a person's ability to communicate and interact with others." Autism spectrum disorders (ASD) lie on a spectrum that ranges from mild to very severe. Asperger's syndrome is a milder variant on the autism spectrum. There has been a dramatic increase in the identification of persons with ASD over the past few decades (Autism Society of America, 2006). For example, 40 years ago, it was estimated that one out of every 2,500 children born was diagnosed with autism. The latest figures reported estimate prevalence rates to be one in 150 children born (Centers for Disease Control and Prevention (CDC), 2007) with autism currently affecting between 1 and 1.5 million people in America (United States Census Bureau, 2000). The CDC (2009) acknowledges the recent data released by the Health Resources and Services Administration which places ASD prevalence rates at about one in 91 children ages 3 to 17, and is currently preparing an updated prevalence rate report. Additionally, autism is four times more likely to be diagnosed in boys than girls.

In general, persons with ASD are broadly recognized as having impairments in social functioning and communication, as well as displaying repetitive or stereotyped behaviors (American Psychiatric Association, 2000). ASD are extremely variable and can vary in degrees of impairment. Some persons classified with ASD have profound challenges and will remain non-verbal, while others will demonstrate traits of brilliance. For example, it has been long accepted that Einstein and Mozart would

Handbook on Animal-Assisted Therapy. DOI: 10.1016/B978-0-12-381453-1.10013-3

probably have been diagnosed with either high functioning autism or Asperger's syndrome. Science suggests that ASD are due to abnormalities in brain development and formation (Courchesne, 2004).

Some of the major symptoms of ASD are limited or perhaps abnormal speech, impairments in reciprocal social interactions, lack of eye contact, sensory over-sensitivity, and repetitive behaviors. Often persons with ASD have a markedly con-strained repertoire of activities, which can also be developmentally inappropriate. The key to understanding the disorder is recognizing the variability that may be observed. Impaired social functioning appears to be one of the most salient characteristics within the disorder. Symptoms may include weak or no eye contact, failure to develop peer relationships, and lack of social reciprocity. When interacting with someone with ASD, they are aware of another's presence, but often will not acknowledge that person. Communication impairments within this population include slow or limited verbal language, mimicking language, echolalia, and delays in pragmatics. Many persons with ASD have the inability to initiate and sustain conversations. Finally, several persons who have disorders within the spectrum have repetitive and stereotyped behavior. These behaviors are most often recognized through repetitive motor movements, preoccupa-tion with certain objects, and inflexible adherence to routines (APADSM-IV-TR, 2000).

The most functional variation of ASD is Asperger's syndrome. Individuals with Asperger's syndrome are verbal, but generally have difficulties with social pragmatics, social interaction skills, eye contact and reading non-verbal behavior and gestures. Many persons with Asperger's syndrome also have a strong need for sameness and may have limited interests. On the other hand, there are large groups of persons with ASD who have also been diagnosed with mental retardation. These individuals usually do not develop verbal language, and have pervasive developmental delays that tremendously impact their functional self-help or social skills (Kutscher, 2006).

It is important to note that the Neurodevelopmental Disorders Work Group for the DSM-V is suggesting some possible changes for the new edition concerning ASD. There are currently three major suggestions. The first suggestion includes utilizing a single diagnosis for ASD, thus eliminating the separate categories of autism, Asperger's syndrome, and PDD-NOS. A second recommendation is changing the current three-symptom domain to two: social communication deficits and fixated interests/repetitive behaviors. The third suggestion is to define ASD symptoms along a continuum that includes normal traits, subclinical symptoms, and three different severity levels for the disorder (Swedo, 2009). Although final decisions have not been made for the upcoming DSM-V, clinicians need to realize that ASD will undergo categorical changes, which will have an impact on how we define the disorder. Nevertheless, our general understanding of the symptoms will remain the same and should not change how we problem-solve the roles that animals have in these individuals' lives.

At this time there is not a cure for those with ASD, but there is some evidence of certain therapies that have promise in helping to treat the disorder. The scientific community is in agreement that early intervention can help foster growth and development. Within this chapter, the authors will provide an argument for how animals may be incorporated with this population. Attention will be given to understanding why persons with ASD may or may not relate to animals. Suggestions will also be given to help the reader to better understand the underlying processes that impact persons with ASD in their relations with various species of animals. Significant attention will also be given to the roles that service animals and therapeutic riding may have.

13.2   Animals and individuals with ASD

For some children or adults with ASD or other developmental disorders, either a service dog or other animal-assisted interventions (AAI), including therapeutic riding, can have great benefits. Nevertheless, the first author has discovered, through conversations with parents of children with ASD, that there are several variables that need to be considered. The use of animals as part of a therapy or activities program may be very beneficial for some with ASD, but may not be beneficial for others.

It is clear that there has been a recent interest in the roles that animals have in the lives of persons with ASD. Several trade books and scholarly articles have been written attempting to document the value of animals in the lives of a person with ASD. Martin and Farnum (2002) suggest that animals may be extremely valuable to the cognitive and social lives of children as a whole. Katcher and Wilkins (2000), in a previous edition of this *Handbook*, reports that children may, at times, use animals as initial transitional objects that may eventually lead to relationships with others. Since many persons with ASD struggle with sustaining and developing relationships, animals may act as an initial catalyst to support social interactions. This position has been often documented in the literature (Fine, 2006). It appears that animals may act as a social catalyst and seem to engage the person in becoming more comfortable within the therapeutic environment.

On the other hand, there have been a handful of studies in the last decade that have demonstrated that AAI could be useful in supporting persons with ASD with many of their developmental needs. Ming-Lee Yeh (2008) suggested several interesting outcomes from her three years of research on evaluating a canine animal-assisted therapy (AAT) treatment for children with ASD in Taiwan. The study followed 33 paired autistic children, whose ages averaged 5.89 years old. Children in the control group were observed in regular living activities, while those in experimental treatment were treated with AAT activities in semi-structured small groups (5–8 persons), lasting 40 minutes, twice a week. Her study followed the impact on the clients after the 8-week study was concluded. All canine animals in this research were trained and qualified therapeutic dogs. The Vineland Adaptive Behavior Scale (VABS, Chinese version) and individual treatment goal attainment scales (GAS) were used for evaluating the effectiveness of the AAT. Ming-Lee Yeh (2008) reported significant improvements for the children who received the AAT treatment on the social skills subscale and total score on the VABS. She also reported that after playing with dogs, children revealed significant improvements on GAS in various dimensions of communication and language as well as increasing their on-task behavior. She concluded by suggesting that her findings supported that AAT was helpful to the children in recognizing their environments as well as practicing higher level interpersonal skills.

Celani (2002) in another study found that children with ASD appeared to prefer drawings of animals to those pictures illustrating humans and interpersonal interactions. Additionally, Martin and Farnum (2002) noted several improvements in children with ASD when they interacted with therapy dogs. They observed improvements in their playful moods, and better attentiveness as a direct consequence of being around the dogs.

Several popular press books, such as a Rupert Isaacson's (2009) *The Horse Boy* and Nuala Gardner's (2008) *a friend like henry*, have chronicled the unique relationships that have been established with their children with ASD and various animals. Isaacson (2009) in his book *The Horse Boy* describes how his young son Rowan diagnosed with severe autism related to horses. *The Horse Boy* traces Rowan's early difficulties with severe behavioral deficits and speech delays, and highlights the discovery of the innate value of horseback riding. On horseback, Isaacson reported that his son was calm, gave verbal directives to the horse and expressed joy. Both riding and interaction with horses on the ground was beneficial. On the other hand, Gardner (2008) recounts how the strong relationship between her son Dale and a golden retriever named Henry seemed to produce the strong breakthroughs needed in helping her son open up to the world around him. Both authors emphasize the strong bond that was established between their sons and the animals.

13.3   Why people with autism relate with animals

Grandin and Johnson (2005) hypothesize that one of the reasons why some children and adults with ASD relate really well to animals is due to sensory-based thinking. They suggest that animals do not think in words. Both their memories and their experiences are filled with detailed sensory information. A dog's world is filled with pictures, little smells, sounds and physical sensations instead of words.

The first author often gets asked, "How do you know that animals think in pictures and other sensory information?" The things that animals become afraid of are one indication that they store memories as pictures or sounds. The first author met a horse that was terrified of black cowboy hats. White cowboy hats caused no reaction. The horse's fear of black cowboy hats developed after a veterinary procedure where alcohol was thrown in his eyes. When this occurred, he was looking right at the person's black cowboy hat. Animals often associate frightening or painful experiences with something that they were seeing or hearing the moment it occurred. Often, it is a large visual feature on a person, such as a beard or a lab coat. Specific sounds may also trigger a fear reaction. For example, one elephant was known to fear diesel powered engines, but gas powered engines caused no reaction. The distinctive sound of a diesel engine was associated with a frightening past experience. In non-verbal individuals with ASD, similar "fear memories" that are linked to sensory stimuli may occur. Scientific studies have also shown that animals store information as either pictures or sounds. Birds are able to remember where they stored food and migrating birds remember visual landmarks (Grandin and Johnson, 1995). Even ants remember visual images (Judd and Collett, 1998).

There is neurological evidence that language may cover up the sensory-based thinking which is present in all people. In some cases, frontal-temporal lobe dementia (a type of Alzheimer's disease) destroys the frontal cortex and the language areas of the brain. In some patients, artistic and musical abilities will emerge in an individual who had no previous interest in art or music (Miller et al., 1998).

13.4 Sensory oversensitivity

One of the reasons why AAT is successful for some children and adults with ASD and not successful for others is due to sensory oversensitivity. A person with ASD may not be able to tolerate the smell of a dog. Another may have auditory oversensitivity and the sound of a dog barking may hurt his/her ears. When the first author was a child, the sound of a school bell felt like a dentist drill hitting a nerve. Even if the dog is trained not to bark, the individual may fear the dog will bark. Sensory oversensitivity is extremely variable. One may gag when s/he smells a dog and another may like the smell. A dog barking will not bother some and others will run screaming away from it. Persons with ASD who actively avoid dogs often do so because they have extreme sensitivity to either sound or smell.

For years, autobiographies by people with ASD have reported problems with hypersensitivity. Grandin (1995) in her book, *Thinking in Pictures*, quotes many of the early self reports. One person reported that rain sounded like gunfire. Researchers have now documented that problems with sensory oversensitivity are real (Crane et al., 2009; Davis et al., 2006; Gomes et al., 2008; Leekam et al., 2007; Wiggins et al., 2009). Both reports in the scientific literature and practical experience have shown that individuals with many other diagnoses such as ADHD, dyslexia, learning problems, and head injuries may also have problems with sensory oversensitivity (Ghanizadeh, 2009; Romanos et al., 2008; Shochat et al., 2009). Grandin (2008) reviewed additional research on sensory oversensitivity. Some children and adults with ASD cannot tolerate fluorescent lights. They can see the 50 or 60 cycle flicker. This makes them feel like they are in a disco with a strobe light. The small compact fluorescent light bulbs that screw into a lamp may also flicker and cause problems. One study showed that children with ASD had more repetitive behaviors in a room with fluorescent lights (Coleman et al., 1976). Some individuals on the spectrum have problems with fluorescent lights and others do not. If a person with ASD was introduced to a therapy dog in a room that caused sensory overload, s/he may not have a good reaction to the dog simply because of the room. To accurately judge how a person with ASD will react to a dog, the individual needs to be in a quiet place away from fluorescent lights or other sensory distractions.

13.5 Factors that worsen sensory problems

Sensory problems often get worse when an individual with ASD gets tired. A child who can tolerate a crowded supermarket in the morning when they are rested may not be able to tolerate it when they are tired. When the individual gets tired, they may feel like they are inside the speaker at a rock concert. People with ASD call this sensory overload. When sensory overload occurs, the individual may start screaming or they may just shut down and not respond. No learning can occur when overload happens. To recover, the individual has to get away from the overstimulation and calm down in a quiet place. One of the difficulties when doing research on sensory oversensitivity is its variability. This is because one person with ASD may react badly to a stimulus when others do not.

13.6   People with autism and sensory-based thinking

Many people with ASD are sensory-based thinkers. Grandin (1995), in an earlier publication, revealed that she thinks in pictures. Words narrate the pictures that pop up into her imagination. She suggested that her mind works like the Google Internet search engine for Images. She explained that all her thoughts are in photo realistic pictures (Grandin, 1995). This really helped her in her work with animals. For example, she explains that in her early work with cattle, she got in the vaccinating chute to see what the animals were seeing. She did this to determine why they often balked and refused to move through the chute. She discovered that they were afraid of shadows, dangling chains, reflections, and other distractions (Grandin, 1980; Grandin and Johnson, 2005). When she first started doing this, many feedlot managers could not understand what she was looking for. It was difficult for them to understand because they thought in words, instead of detailed visual, auditory, tactile, and smell sensations. The first author believes that for herself, vision is her preferred sense. For different individuals with ASD, the other sensory systems may be used as they perceive the world. Tito Mukhopadhyay, in his book *How Can I Talk if my Lips Don't Move?* and Donna Williams in her numerous books, describe how they are auditory thinkers. Hearing is their preferred sense because their visual system provided unreliable and distorted information. Williams (1996) described walking through a yellow kitchen that had fluorescent lights. She stated, "I saw shapes and colors as it whooshed by."

Some non-verbal individuals are tactile and smell thinkers. The circuits in the brain that process sight and hearing may be providing them with distorted information. Several individuals have reported that their hearing would fade in and out (White and White, 1987). It may be like trying to use a mobile phone with a really weak signal that keeps "breaking up." Professionals who work with individuals with ASD who are non-verbal have told the first author they believe that smell and touch may be the only senses that provide their clients with accurate and reliable information. Even though these people are not blind and are not deaf, their brain may process tactile sensations and smells more clearly than auditory or visual ones. The first author has observed that some non-verbal individuals may tap many objects and smell things. For example, she recently watched one non-verbal teenager tap everything around him. His motions were similar to a blind person who is really skilled with the white cane. He tapped and smelled objects in order to perceive them. This would explain why some non-verbal individuals, when they are first introduced to a therapy animal, may want to explore it through smell and touch. One individual with very severe visual processing problems told the first author that he had to touch every part of a dog and its leash to fully determine what it was. He had to feel the entire leash and feel how it was attached to the dog to understand what the leash was for. He also had to touch the collar and unfasten it to determine that the leash and the collar were not a permanent part of the dog.

Prothmann et al. (2009) initiated a study to assess the preference for and the responsiveness to dogs by persons with ASD. The researchers concluded that animals, specifically dogs, might make their behavioral intentions more easily understandable to persons with ASD because they do not communicate both verbally and non-verbally. They inferred that one of the major deficits in persons with ASD is their inability to combine the coordinated and parallel understanding of verbally transmitted emotion-related information and non-verbally transmitted emotion-related information. In essence, a dog's communication is not bundled with verbal and non-verbal intricacies. Dogs communicate non-verbally and portray their intentions with their body language. This is why it may be much easier for persons with ASD to understand them.

Over twenty years ago, Baron-Cohen et al. (1985) introduced the theory of mind hypothesis to explain the main symptoms that characterize the neurodevelopmental deficiencies that accompany autism. Baron-Cohen furthered the work on theory of mind in his book *Mindblindness* (Baron-Cohen, 1995). According to Lantz (2009):

> *Theory of mind is the ability to attribute [these] mental states to self and others in order to understand and predict behavior. It involves making the distinction between the real world and mental representations of the world. Individuals with autism spectrum disorder tend to be less proficient "mind readers" compared to people who are typical.*

Deficits in acquisition of theory of mind may provide a plausible explanation for the major symptoms of ASD (Tager-Flusberg, 2010). People with ASD have great difficulty understanding the point of view or the thoughts and feelings of someone else. This may be a key element to why persons with ASD relate more comfortably with animals. The understanding of theory of mind and perceptual processing may be critical in understanding why animals may be easier for people with ASD to relate to (Papp, 2006).

The authors want to stress to professionals incorporating various AAI that they consider and remember sensory problems in the autism spectrum are very variable. One individual may prefer to experience the world through vision, another may prefer auditory and another may prefer touch or smell. Depending upon severity, either the visual system or the auditory system may be scrambling sensory input, making it important to try to accommodate the individual's preferred way of perceiving the world.

13.7 Choosing animal-based interventions: suggestions for service animals and other forms of AAI

Multi-disciplinary professionals who are interested in applying AAI with persons with ASD need to integrate several of the key variables that have been discussed thus far with this population. In review, these are the critical variables that need to be considered when developing a therapeutic regimen:

1. Children and adults with ASD relate really well to animals because they use sensory-based thinking.
2. Sensory oversensitivity may have a tremendous impact on the outcome. This process is extremely variable. Some individuals may not be able to tolerate smells or sudden sounds from an animal. Many others will have no sensory problems with animals and will be attracted to them.
3. Animals, specifically dogs, may communicate their behavioral intentions more easily to persons with ASD.
4. Individuals with ASD tend to be less proficient "mind readers" compared to non-ASD people. The understanding of theories of mind and perceptual processing may be critical in understanding why animals may be easier for people with ASD to relate to.

Utilizing the previous points, we will now return to the case study of Walter, who was initially introduced at the onset of this chapter. Walter's level of impairment was moderate, and as was indicated earlier, he struggled greatly with his communication, on-task behavior, and behavior regulation. His vast therapeutic interventions, which incorporated AAI, also included behavior therapy, occupational therapy and speech and language interventions. Initially, the therapy animal was introduced to foster rapport and camaraderie. To assure that the most viable therapy animal was selected, attention was given to selecting a therapy dog that was extremely calm, was not intrusive, and followed directions explicitly. This was done to insure that there would be a higher probability that Walter would be more receptive to his new co-therapist. Over the course of treatment, Walter seemed to become more at ease in the company of the dog. Initially, he was quite resistant to her proximity, but gradually became more relaxed. What is critical to realize is that the therapist used the therapy dog's presence for a variety of purposes. For example, Walter was encouraged to play ball with the dog and to use some language when they were playing. He often would brush her and help prepare her water bowl and a small treat. Perhaps one of the activities that Walter seemed to enjoy working on the most was getting the dog to follow through a maze activity and to complete simple requests such as shaking hands, lying down and rolling over. In many ways, the dog's role was to act as a catalyst for compliance in activities that perhaps were not as desirable to complete without the animal. Attention was given to the therapy dog's appearance, making sure she was always well groomed and clean. The therapist made sure there were no noxious odors that would be aversive to him. Additionally, beyond grooming, Walter provided the lead on when he wanted to cuddle and hug the dog.

In an additional case, Fine and Eisen (2008) report the use of a young golden retriever and her interactions with a child with a dual diagnosis, which included an ASD diagnosis. The 12-year-old girl, who will be known as Sally, had numerous behavioral challenges and was often openly hostile and potentially physically aggressive. Over the course of her habilitation, effective therapies had been hard to find. However, it was noticed by her caregivers that Sally had a fondness for animals.

Her mom did not seem to understand the significance of her daughter's developmental disability. The major obstacles that she experienced at home were Sally's poor communication skills, her insistence for sameness, and her reactive aggressive behaviors. Sally would often spit at any adult that came near her when she was angry. Her limited language made matters worse even though it was also apparent that she needed to express herself.

In Sally's case, three well-trained therapy dogs were applied. Although she seemed intrigued when she was introduced to each (one at a time) she was very reluctant to touch or pet them. She would rock and curl up but when the dogs would leave, she would call for their presence. Eventually, the youngest of the three dogs was the animal that seemed to have the greatest breakthrough with her. With coaching, Sally became the dog's trainer and this new sense of perceived competence seemed to be what she needed to interact and become gentler. Over the course of the next six months, Sally brushed the therapy dog, worked on taking walks and also writing letters and drawing pictures for her.

Her family and social work staff noted that the dog and her therapy visits were Sally's favorite topic. Whenever she returned home, she seemed calmer and wanted to tell anyone who would listen about the "the girls" at Dr. Fine's office. The staff used this new interest to defuse potential conflicts, reminding Sally that she was her dog's role model.

Her lead residential therapist kept a log of the behavioral outcomes from the AAT she was receiving. The following is a brief citation from this digest (Fine and Eisen, 2008):

> *Each visit her autonomic reaction has decreased – initially her hand was ice cold and pulse rapid through the walk until returning to the parking lot. Her eyes would dart around, glassy, and huge. She looked petrified. She had limited eye contact with both Dr. Fine and any of the dogs she walked. She looked hyper-vigilant and easily distracted by all the sights and sounds of the environment, looking past the dogs instead of at them. Now she is so much more relaxed with everything! There has been a steady increase in her language abilities. I have been impressed with her ability to identify some emotions and state them to us as she walks. No longer does she spit or lose attention immediately upon encountering new adults. Now she relates to adults much better. Sally seems to have more self-awareness. She seems more content when she leaves. She does not fall asleep after visits (i.e. they do not seem so emotionally exhausting anymore; they are more therapeutic).*
>
> *She seems to want to talk about the visits, Dr. Fine, and the dogs when she is at home. She doesn't seem to want to disappoint the dogs. She recognizes all the dogs in pictures. Recently, I gave her a beanie toy dog that was a golden retriever, and she immediately called it PJ. We no longer have to take pictures during visits because she is more interested in what we are doing. She is excited and anticipates coming. She knows the route, and when I am not driving, she tells the other driver where to turn. She is making progress and that is all that counts.*

On the other hand, AAI can also be applied with individuals who have a milder version of ASD. Perhaps the most beneficial aspect that has been witnessed has been how the animals have supported conversation around metaphors for some of life's challenges that have been mutually experienced by both the animal and the client. Perhaps one of the greatest benefits has been how the animals have supported companionship and friendship in the lives of people who have felt very isolated and lonely. In *Afternoons with Puppy*, Fine and Eisen (2008) discuss the cases of two teenagers who had Asperger's syndrome and the roles that animals had in their lives. Both of these young men were so intrigued with the therapy animals that their families eventually got them their own trained pets. Although they continued to struggle with human friendships and personal interactions, the animals became a positive social outlet for both of them. In fact, with the support of the animals, one of the young men became involved with an animal social group. Although he was a bit awkward at the start, the animal acted as a social catalyst and got him to become more accepted in the group. Companionship and camaraderie may be a key ingredient to life satisfaction. In fact, it was Aristotle who once said, "What is a friend? A single soul dwelling in two bodies."

Much has been written about the psychosocial benefits of pets for persons with various disabilities. A great deal of attention has been given in the past decade to the roles that service dogs may have in families of persons with ASD. The following section will briefly identify the benefits and what therapists should be aware of in recommending this alternative.

13.8   Service animals

According to Burrows et al. (2008b) the use of service dogs to support children with ASD is a relatively new application. They note the primary purpose of getting a service animal for a person with autism is safety. The animal's presence is used to slow small children on command and to prevent the child from running into ongoing traffic or getting lost in a crowd (Burrows et al., 2008b). When the purpose of the service animal is to protect the child from danger, the dog and child are attached to each other through a belt and tether system. The belt on the child has a bungee tether attached to the dog's harness. The parent or guardian, who actually is giving the commands to the dog, is the individual holding the leash (Burrows et al., 2008b). In essence, the belt and tether system serves to prevent the child from bolting or running in the other direction, and allows the parent time to react to the child. Reports also suggest improvements in overall motor functioning as well as learning to walk at a more controlled pace (as a consequence of being attached to the dog).

Perhaps one of the side benefits of having a service dog for a person with ASD is companionship; similar to the young boys that we previously discussed. Generally, it seems that the person with ASD who gets a service animal more for companionship is traditionally higher functioning and perhaps a bit older. It has been reported that the animals have been found to have a calming effect on the individual as well. In a study by McNulty (2009), she interviewed several families that had acquired a service animal for their child with ASD. All parents reported that the service dog had a significant impact on the lives of their children and their families. McNulty (2009) reported that all families recognized additional benefits of having a service dog beyond providing safety for their child. However, they all agreed that the animals had a tremendous impact on their child's safety while walking in the community. The parents reported that the service dog made it possible for the family to partake in numerous outside activities that they previously were not eligible for because of the constant diligence required in supervising the ASD child. Families in the project reported that the service dog also acted as a social catalyst for conversations and interactions in the public. Parents also revealed that the service dog "provided the benefits of a companion animal both to the child with autism and his/her siblings by playing with the children in the family" (p. 46).

These are only a few of the benefits reported by families. Parents also reported that they found themselves getting out more and exercising as a consequence of having the dog. Interestingly, the service animal appeared to have an analgesic effect on the parents, helping reduce the stressors of having a child with ASD in their family. The service animal can provide emotional comfort and safety for the child, as well as serving as a transitional multi-sensory stimulus which can aid in the sensory and affective levels of the ASD children, as the authors elaborated on earlier.

Service animals have been found also to be beneficial to the child because of the dog's close proximity working with the child for elongated periods of time. This opportunity allows the child to build a closer and stronger bond with the animal because of the time spent together. However, precautions need to be put into place that the animal does not become a victim of tantrum behavior and overwork. This will cause tremendous stress to the animal.

McNicholas and Collis (2006) point out that animals do not seem as selective to their human companions as long as they are kind. Additionally, one of the benefits of relationships with animals is the fact that there is no need for well-developed social and communication skills. The social skills necessary to sustain a friendship with a human counterpart are more demanding than with a companion animal. Thus an additional benefit could be derived from this association.

Parents report a further sense of relief with having the service animal in the home. They admit that the dog serves as an "extra set of eyes" to monitor the movements of the autistic child, even when not in their working vest (Burrows et al., 2008a). However, it is imperative for the welfare of the animals that down time is permitted and to allow the dog some time for play, rest and relaxation. One of the side effects of the bond is that it seems that the dogs traditionally relate more with the parents instead of with the child (Burrows et al., 2008a). These findings were concurred in the McNulty (2009) study. Attention needs to be given in future research to help support opportunities for the child with ASD to foster and enhance the bond with the service animal.

13.9 Suggestions to consider before obtaining a service dog

The authors suggest that prior to recommending to families the use of a service animal, several questions need to be addressed. Perhaps the first question to be considered is does the child like dogs. Some children with ASD relate really well with dogs while others do not. It is easier to see the benefits from a service animal if a child is more comfortable with animals. Nevertheless, the authors suggest that if the child has had no previous experience with dogs, that the family considers introducing them to a friendly Labrador retriever. When a child with ASD is first being introduced to a dog s/he will fall into one of three different categories.

1. Bonds with the dog—this child is attracted to the dog and interacts with it. The child will naturally bond with dog and the dog responds in a really positive way to the child. These are the children that have a real bond with animals and would be excellent candidates for a service dog.
2. Initially fearful then bonds—this child may initially be fearful to approach the dog because it is big and novel. New things are sometimes frightening to children with ASD. The dog may have to be introduced to the child several times before the child bonds with it. This child may also be a good candidate for a service dog.
3. Dog avoider—this child may actively avoid the dog or scream when s/he sees the dog. This child is likely to be a poor candidate for a service dog. This is usually due to sensory oversensitivity to the sound of barking or to the smell of the dog.

Large, calm dogs such as Labradors are often a better choice than small dogs because they are sturdy and the child is less likely to accidentally hurt them. Labradors have two basic personality types—a heavy set calm type which is less active, and the slender "field" lab, which is hyperactive. A hyperactive Labrador would probably be a poorer choice for a non-verbal child with severe ASD.

Selecting the appropriate service dog for the child with ASD is vital for success. Parents are encouraged to not rush into the process and to work with the trainers at a selected training site to ensure a successful match. For instance, a more active child might be paired with a stoic Labrador to counterbalance the child's constant movement. On the other hand, a shy child might be paired with an outgoing golden retriever to encourage participation. The most common dogs used are Labrador retrievers and golden retrievers, although other breeds are used too, such as the standard poodle in cases where a child might be allergic to a dog with fur (Gross, 2006). Families must go to a reliable source so they can be assured of the health of the animal.

Gross (2006) provides a comprehensive description on the early training and selection of these service animals beginning with puppy rearing in the homes of volunteers. Once the dog is about 20 months of age, it returns to a formal program to undergo intensive public access training, as well as training specifically for working with persons with ASD (Gross, 2006). Before releasing the dog to a potential family, time is spent training the family with the dog. Attention is also given to help the parent consider the welfare of the animal, so its quality of life is ensured. Most of the settings provide opportunities for follow-up training at the family's home to help assimilate the dog into its new environment.

There are some programs that allow the family to select their own puppy, and help the family raise and train the puppy to become a service animal. The benefit of this is that the puppy bonds with the family from the beginning. However, this is an arduous responsibility and it is not appropriate for all (Gross, 2006).

13.10   Benefits of horseback riding

Horses and horseback riding as they are used in the therapeutic setting are divided into three divisions: (1) sport/recreational, (2) medical (also known as hippotherapy), and (3) educational (Stoner, 2002). Hippotherapy is potentially even more beneficial for people with ASD because it specifically addresses the vestibular system

(Mason, 2004). This stimulation can then lead to other benefits such as increased sensory integration. Therapeutic horseback riding is a broad definition, which can be used to describe all three divisions, and all three have overlapping qualities. However, the actual act of riding the horse may be just a part of the overall therapy in which the horse is used. Depending on the functional skills of the person with ASD, they may be encouraged to groom the horse, lead it to and from its stall, help in feeding or giving treats, and even saddle the horse before they ride. This additional contact with the horse aside from sitting astride it provides many of the same therapeutic benefits offered through interaction with more traditional therapy animals such as dogs.

Four or five parents have told the first author that their young autistic child said his/her first words when they were riding a horse. A study on the effects of riding on children with ASD, done by Bass et al. (2009), found additional benefits for the child while riding. These researchers found that riding improved social motivation and there was less inattention and distractibility. An additional study conducted by Mason (2004) found that a therapeutic riding program tailored towards children with ASD promoted improvements in muscle tone/strength/posture, musculo-skeletal flexibility, balance/coordination, language facilitation, self-esteem, and social skills. These improvements are largely associated with the actual riding of the horse. However, Mason (2004) points out that the interaction between horse, child, instructor, and other people present during the therapy session may impact the child's pro-social behaviors because of the relationships developed in the therapy setting. In a study done by Foxall (2002), it was found that the presence of the horse during therapy positively impacted the ASD person's communication skills.

There are several reasons why riding may be so therapeutic. The first is that riding is a fun activity and gets the child out doing an activity that involves interaction with both the horse and other people. Two other reasons why riding may be beneficial is that it requires the person with ASD to keep their balance, and it is rhythmic. Occupational therapists have known for years that activities that stimulate the vestibular system are often beneficial. Slow swinging on a swing stimulates the vestibular system and may help stimulate the production of speech sounds (Ray et al., 1988). Other studies have shown that swinging and other vestibular stimulations were beneficial too (Bhatara et al., 1981; Slavik et al., 1984). Sitting on an exercise ball or sitting on a T stool requires constant balancing. Horseback riding combines all of these aspects into one, while also allowing the individual to interact with the horse and the instructors. The horse's gait has been discovered to simulate the pace at which a human walks, making the pelvic position and swaying experienced when riding a horse very similar to the sway one experiences when walking (Reide, 1988). Even though the horse has a smooth gait at the walk, the horse's stride is so long that one must constantly work on balance and posture while astride the horse. The constant stimulus to the vestibular system while also responding to requests given by the instructor acts as a form of sensory integration similar to forms many occupational therapists employ, but it also incorporates the additional effect of AAT.

It is also important to note that occupational therapists have learned from experience that most interventions are largely effective if done for no longer than 20 minutes without a break. If the intervention is done for longer than 20 minutes, the nervous system may habituate. This same principle may apply to riding. To make the therapy session most effective, the child could ride for 20 minutes and then do some other activity such as grooming the horse. After the grooming break, the child could get back on the horse for another 20-minute session of riding.

13.11 Animal welfare issues

As has been discussed in various chapters in the book and extensively in the Serpell et al. chapter later in this volume, the area of animal welfare must be assessed and addressed with this population. There needs to be a balance between the needs of the child and his/her family and the needs of the dog. As can be seen throughout this chapter, there may be specific welfare concerns that must be taken into consideration when dealing with individuals with ASD. Some individuals with ASD may have a special connection with animals while others do not. Some individuals may fail to relate with animals even though they have no sensory issues (such as smell or auditory oversensitivity) related to the animal. These individuals may be rough with animals and may treat the animal as if it were an inanimate object. This problem may be more likely to occur in children and adults with severe ASD. It is in these situations that the welfare of a therapy animal must be carefully monitored.

There are two basic ways that a service dog could be used with children and adults with autism: (1) protect the individual with autism from dangers such as traffic in the streets, and (2) as a companion for an individual with autism (Burrows et al., 2008b).

In the first scenario, where a dog is used to protect a child with ASD from danger, there is the greatest potential for welfare problems. In this situation, the child may be harnessed to the dog to prevent dangerous behavior such as running out into the streets. If the child gets into sensory overload and has a huge tantrum s/he may hit the dog. To insure that the dog is protected and does not become stressed, the dog needs time where it is unleashed from the child and allowed to play and interact with the parents and other family members.

In the second scenario, an individual with ASD gets a service dog as a companion and friend. This interaction can help open up social doors and social opportunities. Other people will be attracted to the dog, which may, in turn, encourage interaction with the person with ASD. The use of the dog in this role would be mostly with children and adults on the higher functioning end of the autism spectrum. If the individual with ASD really bonds with animals the dog should have excellent welfare.

Davis et al. (2006) point out that the workload of the service animal must be carefully monitored. Wojciechowska and Hewson (2005) provide a list of variables that need to be considered to ensure quality of life in dogs. This list includes opportunities for social interaction and minimal distress. The challenge for families and therapists employing service or therapy animals is to achieve the balance that is needed in the animal's life. The dog needs respite so that s/he does not become really tired and stressed. Additionally, safeguards need to be built into ensure that the animal is safe, especially at times when a child is prone to behavioral meltdowns. The dog needs to be protected and be allowed to leave situations where there is perceived stressors placed upon it. Burrows et al. (2008b) suggest several variables to consider ensuring protection of all parties. They stated that there is a need to identify potential stressors and the importance of allowing the dogs down time for rest and recreation. Families must be aware that the dog also must be given routine breaks to urinate and/ or defecate. The dog is trained not to relieve itself while wearing the work vest. Thus, if attention is not given to this area, behavioral challenges could arise because the dog needs to relieve itself. They concluded in their paper that dogs used for this specialized service with this population might be more likely to have poorer welfare compared to other service animals. These issues need to be considered and instruction must be given to families so that these challenges are avoided.

Pavlides (2008) discusses the concerns about being aware of when a dog should eventually need to retire as a service animal. Fine (2008) has also discussed this position, and believes that a working plan needs to be formulated. Most service animals cannot work all of their lives, as arthritis or other health complications make it difficult for them to continue their work effectively. One must be able to recognize when the animal is struggling, and provisions must be made for the animal's welfare after it has retired.

13.12   Horse welfare

During visits to many therapeutic riding stables, the authors have observed that in some stables, horse welfare may be at risk from either lameness or boredom from always doing the same thing. Also, riders with handicaps often have balance problems that may put added strain on the horses. Horses that do the same thing, such as walk in a circle in the same direction around a ring all day, are at risk for becoming bored. Much like smaller animals such as cats and dogs that are often used for AAT, horses need to have variation in their routine, and stimulation to avoid the development of problematic behaviors. It is often overlooked that horses need just as much enrichment and stimulation as other animals commonly used for therapy. Another important note is that horses need a lot of room, and are a lot of work to care for and provide for. Therapeutic horseback riding is a relatively new field, and so research is needed to determine the best ways to maintain good animal welfare at therapeutic riding centers. The first step is as simple as stable managers being observant and making sure that their horses do not become overworked or bored.

Just like when selecting any other therapeutic animal, therapeutic riding centers need to obtain horses with the right temperament. The authors would recommend getting horses that have a very calm, placid temperament. A therapeutic riding stable which has a lot of highly strung horses picked for their appeal to the managers and not the individuals with ASD will most likely result in the riders being bucked off or having other unpleasant encounters. The best horses for therapeutic riding are extremely calm and steady. When the professional rider rides the perfect therapy horse it may seem like a boring old plug. A therapy horse does not need to be able to win the Kentucky Derby; it just needs to be a reliable animal so that the best therapy can be provided. Just like any other animal, all horses are individuals, each with a unique personality. This, as much as correct care of the horse, must be taken into account when selecting a good therapy horse.

13.13   Conclusions

Throughout this chapter arguments have been made highlighting the roles that animals may have in the lives of persons with ASD. As the literature points out, it is clear that for some persons with ASD, animals can provide strong social supports both as companions and as service animals. Clinicians must appreciate that persons with ASD process information differently than others. These processing differences often have an impact on the way these individuals may relate to others, including animals. For those clinicians who serve a population of children and adults with ASD, they may consider learning more about resources in their community that could help provide opportunities for the families outside the therapeutic environment (e.g. equine therapy, service animals, etc.). They should also consider some of the guidelines for incorporating animals in their therapeutic regime as was discussed in this chapter and throughout this volume.

A challenge within the clinical community has always been to focus on the things people with ASD cannot do and the significant differences these individuals possess. Nevertheless, persons with ASD can lead and live fulfilling and productive lives. Mark Van Doren once stated that the art of teaching is the art of assisting discovery. The role of AAI may be to help in this discovery and to enable persons with ASD in leading more independent and fulfilling lives.

References

American Psychiatric Association. (2000). *Diagnostic and Statistical Manual of Mental Disorders* (4th ed., text revision). Washington, DC: APA.

Autism Society of America. (2009). Website: www.autism-society.org

Baron-Cohen, S. (1995). *Mindblindness: An Essay on Autism and Theory of Mind*. Cambridge, MA: The MIT Press.

Baron-Cohen, S., Leslie, A. M., & Frith, U. (1985). Does the autistic child have a "theory of mind?" *Cognition, 21*, 37–46.

Bass, M. M., Duchowny, C. A., & Liabra, M. M. (2009). The effect of therapeutic horseback riding on social functioning in children with autism. *Journal of Autism and Developmental Disorders*. (Epub).

Bhatara, V., Clark, D. L., Arnold, L. E., Gunsett, R., & Smeltzer, D. J. (1981). Hyperkinesias treated with vestibular stimulation; an exploratory study. *Biological Psychiatry, 61*, 269–279.

Burrows, K. E., Adams, C. L., & Millman, S. T. (2008). Factors affecting the behavior and welfare of service dogs for children with autism spectrum disorder. *Journal of Animal Welfare Science, 11*, 42–62.

Burrows, K. E., Adams, C. L., & Spiers, J. (2008b). Sentinels of safety: service dogs ensure safety and enhance freedom and wellbeing for families with autistic children. *Quality Health Research, 18*, 1642–1649.

Celani, G. (2002). Human beings, animals and inanimate objects? What do people with autism like? *Autism, 6*, 93–102.

Centers for Disease Control and Prevention. (2007). Website: http://www.cdc.gov/ncbddd/autism/faq_prevalence.htm

Centers for Disease Control and Prevention. (2009). Website: http://www.cdc.gov/ncbddd/autism/data.html

Coleman, R. S., Frankel, E., Rituoc, E., & Freeman, B. J. (1976). The effects of fluorescent and incandescent illumination upon repetitive behavior in autistic children. *Journal of Autism and Developmental Disorders, 6*, 157–162.

Courchesne, E. (2004). Brain development in autism: early overgrowth followed by premature arrest of growth. *Mental Retardation and Developmental Disabilities Research Review, 10*, 106–111.

Crane, L., Goddard, L., & Pring, L. (2009). Sensory processing in adults with autism spectrum disorders. *Autism, 13*, 215–228.

Davis, R. A., Bockbrader, M. A., Murphy, R. R., Hetrick, W. P., & O'Donnell, B. F. (2006). Subjective perceptual distortions and visual dysfunction in children with autism. *Journal of Autism and Developmental Disorders, 36*, 199–210.

Fine, A. H. (2006). Animals and therapists: Incorporating animals in outpatient psychotherapy. In A. Fine (Ed.), *Handbook on Animal Assisted Therapy* (2nd ed.) (pp. 179–211). San Diego: Academic Press.

Fine, A. H. (2008). Understanding the application of animal assisted interventions. National Institute of Child and Human Development meeting on the Impact of Animals in Human Health, Bethesda, MD.

Fine, A. H., & Eisen, C. J. (2008). *Afternoons with Puppy: Inspirations from a Therapist and His Animals*. West Lafayette, IN: Purdue University Press.

Foxall, E. L. (2002). *The use of horses as a means of improving communication abilities of those with autism spectrum disorders: an investigation into the use and effectiveness of the horse as a therapy tool for improving communication in those with autism. Unpublished manuscript*. Coventry, UK: Coventry University.

Gardner, N. (2008). *a friend like henry*. Naperville, IL: Sourcebooks, Inc.

Ghanizadeh, A. (2009). Screening signs of auditory processing problem: does it distinguish attention deficit hyperactivity subtypes in a clinical sample of children. *International Journal of Pediatric Otorhinolaryngology, 73*, 81–87.

Gomes, E., Pedroso, F. S., & Wagner, M. B. (2008). Auditory hypersensitivity in the autism spectrum disorder. *Pro Fono, 20*, 279–289.

Grandin, T. (1980). Observations of cattle behavior applied to the design of cattle handling facilities. *Applied Animal Ethology, 6*, 19–31.

Grandin, T. (1995). *Thinking in Pictures*. New York, NY: Vintage Press (Random House).

Grandin, T. (2008). *The Way I See It*. Arlington, TX: Future Horizons.

Grandin, T., & Johnson, C. (2005). *Animals in Translation*. New York, NY: Scribner.

Gross, P. D. (2006). *The Golden Bridge: A Guide to Assistance Dogs for Children Challenged by Autism or Other Developmental Disabilities*. West Lafayette, IN: Purdue University Press.

Isaacson, R. (2009). *The Horse Boy*. New York, NY: Little Brown Company.

Judd, S. P. D., & Collett, T. S. (1998). Multiple stored views and landmark guidance in arts. *Nature, 392*, 710–714.

Katcher, A. H., & Wilkins, G. G. (2000). The centaur's lessons: Therapeutic education through care of animals and nature study. In A. Fine (Ed.), *Handbook on Animal Assisted Therapy* (pp. 153–178). New York: Academic Press.

Kutscher, M. L. (2006). *Kids in the Syndrome Mix of ADHD, LD, Asperger's, Tourette's, Bipolar, and More!: The One Stop Guide for Parents, Teachers, and Other Professionals*. London: Jessica Kingsley.

Lantz, J. (2009). *Theory of mind in autism: development, implications, and intervention*. Retrieved June 22, 2009. Indiana Resource Center for Autism. Website. http://www.iidc.indiana.edu/irca/education/TheoryofMind.html

Leekam, S. R., Nieto, C., Libby, S. J., Wing, L., & Gould, J. (2007). Describing the sensory abnormalities of children and adults with autism. *Journal of Autism and Developmental Disorders, 37*, 894–910.

Martin, F., & Farnum, J. (2002). Animal assisted therapy for children with pervasive developmental disorders. *Western Journal of Nursing Research, 24*, 657–670.

Mason, M. A. (2004). *Effects of therapeutic riding in children with autism. Unpublished dissertation*. Minneapolis, MN: Capella University.

McNicholas, J., & Collis, G. (2006). Animals as supports: Insights for understanding animal assisted therapy. In A. Fine (Ed.), *Handbook on Animal Assisted Therapy* (2nd ed.) (pp. 49–71). San Diego: Academic Press.

McNulty, L. (2009). Service animals and children with autism. Unpublished thesis. Institute of Technology, Sligo, Ireland.

Miller, B. L., Cummings, J., Mishkin, F., Boone, K., Prince, F., Ponton, M., & Cotman, C. (1998). Emergence of art talent on frontal temporal lobe dementia. *Neurology, 51*, 978–981.

Ming Lee Yeh, A. (2008). *Canine AAT model for autistic children*. Tokyo Japan: At Taiwan International Association of Human-Animal Interaction International Conference. 10/5–8/2008.

Mukhopadhyay, T. R. (2008). *How can I Talk if My Lips don't Move: Inside My Autistic Mind*. New York, NY: Arcade Publishing.

Papp, S. (2006). A relevance-theoretic account of the development and deficits of theory of mind in normally developing children and individuals with autism. *Theory Psychology, 16*, 141–161.

Pavlides, M. (2008). *Animal-assisted Interventions for Individuals with Autism*. London: Jessica Kingsley Publishers.

Prothmann, A., Ettrich, C., & Prothmann, S. (2009). Preference for, and responsiveness to, people, dogs and objects in children with autism. *Anthrozoös, 22*, 161–173.

Ray, T. C., King, L. J., & Grandin, T. (1988). The effectiveness of self-initiated vestibular stimulation in producing speech sounds. *Journal of Occupational Therapy Research, 8*, 186–190.

Reide, D. (1988). *Physiotherapy on the Horse*. Madison: Omnipress.

Romanos, M., Renner, T. J., Schecklmann, M., Hummel, B., Roose, M., Von Meving, C., Pauli, P., Reichmann, H., Warnke, A., & Gerlach, M. (2008). Improved odor sensitivity in attention deficit hyperactivity disorder. *Biological Psychiatry, 64*, 938–940.

Shochat, T., Tzischinsky, G., & Engel-Yeger, B. (2009). Sensory hypersensitivity as a contributing factor in the relation between sleep and behavioral disorders in normal school children. *Behavioral Sleep Medicine, 7*, 53–62.

Slavik, B. A., Kitsuwa-Lowe, J., Danner, P. T., Green, J., & Ayres, A. J. (1984). Vestibular stimulation and eye contact in autistic children. *Neuropediatrics, 15*, 33–36.

Stoner, J. B. (2002). *The efficacy of therapeutic horseback riding as a treatment tool for selected children with autism. Unpublished thesis*. New Haven, CT: Southern Connecticut State University.

Swedo, S. (2009). *Report of the DSM-V neurodevelopmental disorders work group*. Retrieved Oct. 4, 2009 from website. www.psych.org.

Tager-Flusberg, H. (2010). Evaluating the theory-of-mind hypothesis of autism. In K. A. Dodge (Ed.), *Child Psychopathology* (pp. 159–166). Boston: Pearson.

United States Census Bureau (2000). Website: www.census.gov

Wiggens, L. D., Robins, D. L., Bakeman, R., & Adamson, L. B. (2009). Brief report: sensory abnormalities as distinguishing symptoms of autism spectrum disorders in young children. *Journal of Autism and Developmental Disorders*. (Epub).

White, D. B., & White, M. S. (1987). Autism from the inside. *Medical Hypothesis, 24*, 223–229.

Williams, D. (1996). *Autism: An Inside Out Approach*. London: Jessica Kingsley.

Wojciechowska, J. I., & Hewson, C. J. (2005). Quality-of-life assessment in pet dogs. *Journal of the American Veterinary Medical Association, 226*(5), 722–728.

14 Understanding the role of animals in the family: insights and strategies for clinicians

Barbara W. Boat

University of Cincinnati College of Medicine; Cincinnati Children's
Hospital Medical Centre

14.1 Introduction

It has long been recognized by clinicians who work with children and adolescents that the entire family of the "identified patient" is relevant to the intervention whether or not the family members are actually present in the room. Only recently, however, are clinicians becoming aware that animals, especially companion animals, are an integral and important part of the family system as well. As a result, clinicians are beginning to ask about relationships with animals and incorporate aspects of these relationships into their interventions. In most cases, there is no direct contact by the clinician with the animal but the animal is, nonetheless, "present" and acknowledged in many ways. Companion animals may be spontaneously described when the child is talking about daily routines or events ("I was late because my dog, Bitsy, hid my shoe," "Mom was mad because I forgot to change my gerbil's litter," "My cat scratched me"). Companion animals may be invoked by children to describe an aspect of themselves ("I'm a real cat lover," "I hate yippy little dogs. My dog is really big").

Frequently, however, the child's experiences that are relevant to the well-being of both the child and the animal go undetected by clinicians because we do not ask specific questions about animal-related experiences. Typical "screening" questions among mental health providers are often as follows: "Do you have any pets? Oh—you have a dog. That's nice. What is your dog's name? Snoopy? That's a nice name." Thus ends the exploration and conversation about pets in the child's life. Asking focused questions can provide very useful information about the environments that the child and the animal share and contribute to developing more effective interventions.

I work in the area of childhood trauma and maltreatment. Not surprisingly, my focus is on early detection of settings where children are at risk for abuse or neglect. Adding the questions about animal-related experiences to the assessment and treatment of children and families has been invaluable in fostering awareness and

Handbook on Animal-Assisted Therapy. DOI: 10.1016/B978-0-12-381453-1.10014-5

developing interventions that prevent further victimization of both the child and the pet. In this chapter, I will discuss the following:

- Why it is important for clinicians to routinely assess the child's animal-related experiences.
- Use of a questionnaire to assess animal-related experiences.
- Clinical examples of interventions that have addressed the animal-related experiences of children and adolescents in the larger context of therapy.

14.2   Why it is important for clinicians to routinely assess the child's animal-related experiences

14.2.1   Most children have pets or live in homes where there are pets

A recent survey reports that pets are found in approximately 62% of homes in the USA (American Pet Products Manufacturers Association, 2009–2010). Pet ownership rose from 1998 to 2005 with 90 million cats and 74 million dogs as companion animals, an increase of 17% and 18%, respectively (APPMA, 2005–2006). The number of companion animal cats and dogs has continued to rise and now totals 93.6 million cats and 77.5 million dogs (APPMA 2009).

Nearly 75% of American families with school age children have at least one companion animal (Humane Society of the United States, 2004) and the majority of pet-owning households contain children. Indeed, one study found that families with children present were the most likely to own pets (Bulcroft, 1990). In another report, approximately 90% of school children had pets (Kidd and Kidd, 1985). Thus, clinicians who work with children will frequently encounter children who have had experiences with pets.

14.2.2   Pets share the daily lives of household members

Pets often are considered to be members of the family (Bonas et al., 2000; Cain, 1983; Enders-Slegers, 2000; McNicholas and Collins, 2001; Sable, 1995). In a 2005 survey, 84% of American pet owners regarded their animals as family members. Forty-one percent of dogs share their owners' beds as do up to 51% of cats. Americans spent a record $34 billion on pet products and services according to Census Bureau tracking of retail sales, exceeding spending on hardware and jewelry (American Pet Products Manufacturers Association, 2005–2006).

Holidays are celebrated by giving pets presents or treats. Birthdays and funerals of pets are memorialized (Davis, 1987; Dresser, 2000; Serpell, 1986). Pet owners have photographs of their pets and, frequently, children are photographed with the family pet. The environment in which the pet lives is usually the same environment in which the child lives. As a result, the clinician is afforded a valuable opportunity to obtain relevant information about the family setting by asking a series of questions about the pets in the household. Thus, I recommend that clinicians seek information from children and teenagers about their experiences with pets and other animals as routinely as we ask about their experiences with siblings, parents or friends.

14.2.3   Children often will talk about their pets' experiences before they disclose their own experiences

Children's animal-related experiences are a bonus for the clinician because often children will talk about what happens to pets in their homes more willingly than they will share what happens to other family members or, especially, to themselves. Because children are less likely to censor the information they give about their pets, they inadvertently reveal incidents or settings that put them at risk for abuse or neglect. A 15-year-old boy was asked if there was a stressful time when his favorite dog had been a source of comfort to him. He replied, "Yeah. After my stepdad beats me my dog jumps up and licks my tears." The clinician had no idea that the boy's stepdad was beating him.

Sharing the experiences of a pet can become a window on the world that the child inhabits. For example, during a school-based presentation on domestic violence and safety, fourth grade students were asked only one animal-related question: "Do you think your pet is safe at home?" One boy volunteered that he and his older brother each had a cat. He became teary as he shared that his older brother would tease and hurt the younger boy's cat, sometimes strangling it and often throwing the cat at the boy. Then the fourth grader went on to reveal that the older brother would hit and strangle him when their mother was not home. The teacher reported these concerns to the school counselor. Clinicians who do not inquire about animal-related experiences are missing potentially critical information about a child's environment and experiences that place their clients at risk for abuse or neglect (Boat et al., 2008).

14.2.4   The behavior that harms the animals is the same behavior that harms the human

Since the mid-1990s, the links among animal cruelty, child abuse and domestic violence have received important attention both in professional literature and in the media. Anecdotal and research evidence link acts of cruelty to animals with acts of cruelty to humans (Arkow, 1996; Felthous and Kellert, 1987; Kellert and Felthous, 1985). One study noted that in homes where children were physically abused, pets were significantly more likely to be abused. Furthermore, and importantly, inhabitants of these physically abusive homes were 11 times more likely to be bitten by the family dog (DeViney et al., 1983). Clinicians must be aware of these data on dog bites because dog bites to children aged five to nine have been designated as a major public health problem in the USA (Centers for Disease Control, 2000). The statistics on dog bites in the USA are alarming! Fifty percent of dog bite victims are children under the age of 12 and 70% of fatal dog bite attacks involve children (American Veterinary Medical Association, 2001). The important point for clinicians is that when children are bitten in their own home, this may be an indicator of a physically abusive or otherwise chaotic household. When children are bitten in a friend's or neighbor's home, we need to wonder about issues of abuse, supervision and safety in that household.

Knowing the breed of the dog that a family has chosen has implications for risk assessment and intervention. Recent research demonstrates that ownership of high-risk dogs is a significant marker for general deviance as measured by number of convictions in a court of law (Barnes et al., 2006). For example, owners of dogs that were unlicensed and cited as vicious by breed or behavior had an average of 5.9 criminal convictions compared to an average of 0.6 convictions for owners of dogs that were licensed and not deemed vicious by breed or behavior. Failure to license a dog was predictive of child endangerment, harm to a juvenile, violation of safety restraint of a child and contributing to juvenile unruliness convictions. Both failure to license a dog and owning a high-risk breed of dog should be included in professional assessments of risk to children and other vulnerable individuals.

Because the behavior that harms the animal is the same behavior that harms the human, it is not surprising that research documents that both children and animals are at risk in homes where there is domestic violence (Ascione, 1998; Ascione et al., 2004). The majority of pets in homes where battering occurred were threatened with harm or actually killed by the batterer and the majority of children witnessed the abuse to the pet. Children continued to be exposed to potential harm because their mothers remained in the home to protect the pet rather than seek safe shelter for themselves and their families. Twelve independent studies report that between 18 and 48% of battered women have delayed their decision to leave, or have returned to their batterer, out of fear for the welfare of their pets or livestock (Ascione, 2007).

Clinicians, including medical personnel, who treat children should routinely screen for domestic violence and the safety of pets (Boat, 2000). The following questions can be useful:

1. Parent screening (interview the parent alone)
   a. "Do you ever feel unsafe at home?"
   b. "Has anyone at home hit you or tried to injure you in any way?" (Questions a and b have a sensitivity of 71% and a specificity of 85% in detecting domestic violence, Eisenstat and Bancroft, 1999.)
   c. "Has anyone ever threatened or tried to control you?"
   d. "Have you ever felt afraid of your partner?"
   e. "Has your partner ever hurt, or threatened to hurt, any of your children?"
   f. "Do you have pets? If so, has your partner ever hurt or said that he/she would hurt your pets?"
   g. "Where are the guns kept in your house?" (This question is deliberately phrased as a presumptive question. The respondent can always deny that there are guns in the house.)
2. Child screening (interview the child alone)
   a. "What happens in your house when your mother and (father figure or partner) get angry with each other?"
   b. "Is there any hitting in your house?"
   c. "Have you or (siblings) ever been hurt?
   d. "Do you have any pets?" "Has anyone ever hurt or threatened to hurt your pet?"
   e. "Do you ever worry about bad things happening to your pet?"

Just as the majority of children in violent families witness domestic violence, the majority of children in violent pet owning homes also witness pet abuse (Ascione, 1998). Exposure to animal cruelty can have a significant impact on the developing child, including promoting desensitization and decreasing empathy, reinforcing the idea that the child, like the pet, is expendable, damaging the child's sense of safety and confidence in the ability of adults to protect him or her from harm, accepting physical harm as part of allegedly loving relationships, fostering the seeking of empowerment by inflicting pain and suffering and leading to the imitation of abusive behaviors.

Again, clinicians must take into account that some of the disturbed and disturbing behaviors exhibited by children may be related to their witnessing cruelty to animals. A particularly pernicious and vicious form of child and animal abuse is forcing the child to kill or maim a pet. In a poignant video titled *Both Sides of the Coin* (1991), a man who is in treatment for his violent temper describes getting his first dog, Lassie, when he was three years old. Lassie was his best friend. Each year Lassie would have puppies and each year, when the puppies began to be noisy and move around, his brutal uncle would kill them. The man recalls that when he was 12 years old, his uncle made him kill the puppies himself. The man describes holding the puppies underwater until they quit moving, then putting their bodies in a gunny sack and hiding them in the barn. He says, with a breaking voice, that he will never forget the pain and the guilt he felt. He could no longer relate to being a child and began burning down grain elevators and derailing trains. "I started acting out my pain!"

Exposure to pet abuse in the context of domestic violence can also contribute to neurobiological deficits occurring in children who witness domestic violence. One result is that the brains of children exposed repeatedly to traumas such as witnessing domestic violence are significantly smaller, resulting in serious problems in social, emotional and intellectual functioning (DeBellis, 1999; DeBellis et al., 1999). As clinicians we cannot afford to miss these important animal-related connections that place our clients at greater risk for abuse or neglect.

14.2.5   Attachment to a pet is both a positive and a potentially negative experience for a child

The child's experience of attachment to a companion animal provides important information to the clinician. When a child reveals that he or she has a favorite pet, we know that this is a positive sign of an ability to connect with another living creature. However, clinicians must be aware that caring about a pet can make the child more vulnerable to loss. Bulcroft (1990) describes an interview with a 70-year-old man in a senior center, an interview that was assessing intellectual functioning, not targeting animal-related experiences. The author asked the man to recall one of his most vivid childhood memories. With tears in his eyes, the man related that when he was eight years old, he saw his dog, Ben, killed by a stray bullet while they were hunting. Attachment to, and loss of, pets can have a lasting impact.

A teenager described how her beloved dog was killed by her stepfather after the dog tried to protect her from this man who was raping her. Another child had to give his dog away when he was moved into foster care. Sometimes the story includes threats of harm or harming the pet in order to coerce the child to comply "If you tell anyone what I did, I will kill your kitty." "If you don't have sex with me, I will sell your horses." "You have been a bad boy and to punish you, one of your puppies must die. You choose the puppy that I will kill or I will kill all of them."

In the aftermath of the Gulf Coast's Hurricane Katrina in September 2005, we have been poignantly reminded of the intensity of attachment and the fear of losing a pet. Many survivors endangered their own lives by refusing to evacuate unless they could take their pets. This reality led to the passage of the Pets Evacuation and Transportation Standards Act (PETS, 2006). This law requires that state disaster plans include provisions for household pets and service animals in major disasters in order to apply for FEMA funding.

Attachment is good. Clinicians can build on the caring feelings that a child has for a favorite pet and promote empathy and gentleness. But clinicians must also be aware about the downside of attachment and assess whether the child has experienced loss of a pet or threats of loss of a pet. Sometimes the loss, especially if it is repeated, overwhelms the child's coping abilities and the child may detach from any investment in animals in order to protect him- or herself from feeling such pain again.

14.2.6 Use of a questionnaire to assess for animal-related experiences

The Childhood Trust Survey on Animal-Related Experiences

It is useful to have a set of questions available to guide the assessment of the child's experiences with animals. The Childhood Trust Survey on Animal-Related Experiences (CTSARE) is a 10 item screening questionnaire for children, adolescents and adults that asks about experiences of ownership, attachment, loss, cruelty and fears related to pets and other animals (see Appendix A; also see Boat et al., 2008; Boat, 2002). A longer version of the CTSARE has been adapted for use in several studies (Baker et al., 1998; Flynn, 1999; Miller and Knutson, 1997) and is available in a chapter by Boat (1999). The validity and reliability of CTSARE have not been established. This instrument should be used as an interview guide and administered orally so the interviewer can use follow-up questions to obtain additional information as appropriate. The questions that are found in the CTSARE are described below:

- Questions 1 and 2 inquire about past and present ownership of pets. Data support that pets rarely survive more than two years in homes that have few resources and several risk factors for child abuse or neglect (DeViney et al., 1983). Frequently, the inhabitants of these homes list many pets and a high mortality and turnover rate. When asked what happened to all the pets he had listed, one teenager shrugged and said "I don't know. Either grandma got rid of them or they're dead." When several pets have "just disappeared," a caution flag should be raised that the family may be in need of help. Inability to care for pets adequately may indicate that resources are lacking to care for other family members.
- Question 3 seeks information about whether the child has, or has had, a favorite pet as an indicator of attachment. Lack of any special relationship with a pet may signal a child who is divested from, or never formed, close relationships.
- Question 4 asks about a difficult or stressful time when a pet was a source of comfort or support. Children often readily disclose situations where they felt vulnerable, sad or frightened when they are focused on their pet (Doyle, 2001).
- Questions 5 and 6 address issues of the pet having been hurt, worries about something bad happening to the pet and losing a pet. Responses to these questions can offer a window into the child's home environment and assist in focusing the intervention.

- Question 7 focuses on the training and discipline approaches used with the pet. Look here for harsh methods of behavior management.
- Questions 8 and 9: seeing someone hurt an animal can have a significant impact on witnesses. Sometimes a child or adult is prevented from helping a sick or injured animal. This is a potentially devastating experience. It may be important to question others to get adequate information about the child himself hurting animals or pets. Parents, neighbors, or teachers with classroom pets may observe harsh treatment of an animal. Teachers may overhear a child talking about seeing or committing cruel acts, or read about worrisome behaviors around animals in the writings of their students.
- Question 10 underscores the need to know if a child has ever been badly frightened or hurt by a pet or other animal. The trauma of being chased, pinned or bitten by a dog can shape a life-long negative response to dogs. This question also can reveal a home or neighborhood where a child may be at greater risk to be harmed by an animal. Examples include the child having access to dogs that are chained outdoors, dogs that are running freely and the presence of higher risk dogs.

14.3   Clinical examples of interventions that address the animal-related experiences of children and adolescents in the larger context of therapy

Effective interventions for both children and animals can be informed by knowing and understanding the impact of the child's animal-related experience. Effective interventions use knowledge of the child's animal-related experiences with the aim of reducing risk, addressing loss and creating safe ways for the child to attach to another living being.

14.3.1   *Foster care placements: preserving the child's connection to the pet*

One difficult adjustment for children who must go into foster care is the loss of their companion animal. Many adults who were in foster care as children describe this loss as very difficult, especially if the only place their pet could go was the local animal shelter where it would be euthanized if not adopted. A wonderful program in Florida, a collaboration between the Hurlburt Field Family Advocacy Office and the Humane Society and Adoption Center at PAWS (*Safe People, Safe Pets*) cares for the pets of foster children, including their "pocket pets" (hamsters, guinea pigs, etc.). The children can visit, see photos and otherwise stay connected to their pets. If reunion is not possible, the program facilitates the adoption of the pet and the child is usually reassured that the pet is safe and receiving good care.

Unfortunately, such foster care programs for children's pets are rare. More often the clinician's role is to support the child's feelings of loss and help the child preserve mementos and positive memories of the pet. If no photos of the pet are available, often children will find pictures in magazines that look somewhat like the pet or draw pictures. They can write about what made the pet so special and in other ways memorialize the positive aspects of their attachment (Raphael et al., 1999). Similar approaches can be used with all family members together when they share the loss of a companion animal.

Sometimes an adult learns about a child's attachment to a pet because the adult is tuned in and "hears" the child's concerns about a pet. A moving example is portrayed in the video *Battered Hearts: A Story of Family Violence* (1995). A taped 911 call to report domestic violence is played. The caller is a terrified six-year-old girl who says that her mother's old boyfriend is trying to hurt her mother. Her next sentence to the dispatcher is, "I think my cat's scared!" During the call her mother is shot by the boyfriend and the child sobs into the phone, "My mommy's dead." One can only hope that the professionals who intervened were aware of the child's concern about her cat and made sure that her cat was included in the plan of care. Preserving the girl's attachment to her cat in the aftermath of the trauma of her mother's death would be an important therapeutic intervention, even if the child and cat needed to be housed separately.

14.3.2   Domestic violence: the realities of finding shelter for pets and for families

Asking about experiences with animals is especially important when working with children or adults who have histories of trauma or maltreatment. We know that it is not uncommon for pets to be harmed in families where there is battering, and that witnessing brutal abuse of pets can be a terrifying event that contributes to feelings of helplessness and guilt. Some battered mothers and children who must leave pets behind to seek shelter have an option to put their pets in foster care (see Ascione (2000) *Safe Havens for Pets*; AHA (2009) PAWS Program). Realistically, however, many mothers and children may not be able to reclaim their pets because they cannot find pet-friendly housing after leaving the battered women's shelter. The clinician must help frame their decision to put their pet up for adoption as an act of caring and kindness. Sometimes the children will be able to have a different pet or a "pocket pet" in the new setting, a recommendation that the clinician can make if the children are invested in pets, are gentle with pets (the clinician can observe this if the pet comes for a visit), and have adequate supervision. Based on responses to the Childhood Trust Survey of Animal-Related Experiences (CTSARE), the clinician should note any instances of cruelty by the children or other adults and gage the appropriateness of animals living in this household at this time. For some very stressed families there is neither the energy nor the resources to care for themselves, much less another living creature. Failure to thoroughly assess and advise the family at this point can contribute to another round of battered pets and subsequent guilt and hopelessness.

14.3.3   Empowering youth to protect their pets

Empowering youth to protect animals, even if those animals belong to others, is another intervention strategy. Kathy, 15, had witnessed severe domestic violence for years. She remembered her parents drinking and then having terrible fights. Kathy recalled that during the fights, when she was five years old, she would grab her little sister from her high chair and flee to a closet. In tears, Kathy confessed that it was her fault that her parents fought because if she had hidden the liquor bottles her parents would not have drunk and subsequently fought. Kathy revealed on the Childhood Trust Survey of Animal-Related Experiences (CTSARE) that she loved cats. Kathy had recently moved after she had been severely beaten by her father. She could not take her cat with her so it was left with her father. She worried about the safety of her beautiful white cat as well as the neglected wolf-dog mix that lived on a short chain in her father's back yard. Soon after she left, Kathy found out that her cat was dead. Unable to prove that her father had been the one to break her cat's leg, leading to the cat being euthanized, she focused on trying to help the dog. Kathy decided to ask her local humane society to investigate the dog's living conditions. This call was empowering as the humane officer responded immediately and the dog subsequently was removed to a new home. Kathy was so relieved. She had one less creature to worry about. Later Kathy was able to move to a setting where she could have a kitten. She brought the kitten to therapy, a kitten that was as powerless to care for itself as she had been to care for herself and her sister when she was little. Now Kathy was older and able to intervene to keep animals safe. In addition, her sense of empathy and caring for animals could be reinforced as there was little else positive happening in her current life that could promote empathy and caring for people. One essential point about Kathy's case: the clinician knew about her animal-related experiences because the clinician asked about her animal-related experiences. Remember, if we don't ask, we will never know.

14.3.4 Proactive interventions when working with abused and neglected children and their caregivers

Physically and sexually abused children have a higher incidence of abusive behavior to animals (Ascione, 2001) which can involve several different motivations including their lack of boundaries, witnessing and imitating violence towards animals, or desire for revenge. Animal cruelty in childhood appears to be a marker for a host of maladaptive behaviors (McPhedran, 2009) and youth should be screened for animal cruelty in clinical and other service settings.

Some sexually abused children are sexually reactive and seek sexual stimulation. They may masturbate excessively, fondle other children or adults, or they may seek stimulation from the family pet. Sometimes the sexual abuse of the child has involved being sexual with an animal, especially a dog. If the clinician knows that a child is sexually reactive, it is imperative to talk about the possibility that the child may use the family pet in a sexual way. Creating a safety plan for both the pet and the child may avert the tragedy that occurred in this example:

A five-year-old girl had recently disclosed prolonged and significant molestation by a man who had been a trusted neighbor and friend to her family. Naturally, her mother was extremely upset by this revelation. One day the mother was walking by the closed door of her child's bedroom and heard moaning sounds inside. Upon opening the door the mother discovered that her daughter had the family pet cat between her legs and the cat was licking the child's genitals. The mother was so distraught and enraged by this scene that she grabbed the cat and slammed it against the wall, killing the cat. Clinicians who discuss these potentially abusive situations with caregivers can ensure that neither child nor pet is harmed further. A first step in preventing such a sad occurrence is to screen the family for animal-related experiences.

14.3.5   Management of cruel behaviors towards animals

Cruel behaviors toward animals may not be the primary referral concern. Unless we routinely ask about animal-related experiences, we may miss this important target for an intervention. Consider the following case.

A divorced mother of an almost four-year-old boy called me after the Head Start teacher became concerned about his aggressive behaviors toward the other preschoolers. Josh would hit, try to strangle and even tackle a peer unexpectedly. He was rough and tough and his placement in Head Start was in jeopardy.

Josh lived with his mother and his older half brother during the week and spent most weekends with his father. The mother's concern focused on his aggressive behavior with other children. However, asking about pets in the family revealed additional troubling behaviors. Josh's mother disclosed that she had a cat that had recently given birth to three kittens. She went on to state that when Josh was just three years old he had stomped on the back of a kitten from the last litter and the kitten had died. Recently she caught him holding a kitten by the neck over the toilet, ready to drop it in the water.

Further inquiry revealed that Josh's father "loved to play rough." During his weekends with Josh he would pretend to strangle him, engage Josh in very physical wrestling and expose Josh to videos depicting scary violence. The father stated that he was training Josh to be tough and not cry, no matter how much he was hurt. Josh's older brother was also very rough with him.

The intervention in this home was two-pronged and focused on protecting both the child and the cats. The parents agreed to participate in Parent-Child Interaction Therapy, a relationship enhancement, evidence-based intervention that taught them effective play and disciplinary skills (Eyberg, 1988; Hembree-Kigin and McNeil, 1995). In addition, the mother agreed to institute a safety plan for the mother cat and her kittens until she found homes for the kittens. In this case, she had a locked room where they could be safe if the mother was not home to supervise Josh. The mother also agreed to have her cat spayed, understanding that it was unfair to put Josh in a position where he could harm vulnerable pets such as kittens until his aggressive behavior was under control. Josh's behaviors improved as his parents learned new management skills—and the cats were now safe as well.

14.3.6   Community service for youths adjudicated for cruelty to animals

There are several ways in which clinicians may find knowledge of animal-related experiences useful in assisting the court in assessment and disposition of cases involving children and families. Children who have been charged with animal cruelty should be evaluated by a clinician. Depending on several factors (see Lewchanin and Zimmerman, 2000), the severity of the cruelty can be determined and appropriate interventions ordered by the judge or magistrate.

A teenager who has been adjudicated for cruelty to animals may be remanded by the courts to perform community service at a humane society. However, clinicians should insist that no child or adolescent be in a humane society unless first screened for animal-related experiences. Charles was adjudicated for animal cruelty after setting fire to a kitten. Charles was 13 and in the sixth grade. His history included witnessing many episodes of domestic violence, a substance abusing father, intense physical punishment, a larceny charge and school failure. Charles had "closed down" his feelings in the manner of many traumatized children and he felt no empathy for the kitten. He stated, "It was just a cat" and "I thought the cat was a stray." On the Childhood Trust Survey of Animal-Related Experiences (CTSARE), Charles related that his family had many pets in the past including 14 dogs and numerous rabbits, gerbils and birds. They had no cats because his father "hated cats." However, Charles did describe having two dogs that were special and a source of comfort to him. Clinically, this admission of attachment to a companion animal was useful. Charles might be an appropriate candidate for supervised community service in an animal shelter where his attachment to dogs could be used to bridge positive interactions with the feline community at the shelter.

Under no circumstances should children who have been adjudicated as cruel to animals be assigned only to cleanup jobs at shelters. They need positive supervised interactions with the animals such as learning to clicker train dogs in "good shelter dog manners" (Pryor, 1999). Children who are fearful of dogs or cats or report no attachments to a pet or other animal are usually inappropriate for this type of community service. Most importantly, clinicians involved in treatment recommendations for adjudicated youth must remember that humane societies are short staffed and often unable to provide the mentoring and supervision these referrals require.

14.3.7   Management of dog bites to children

Epidemiological data indicate that 4.5 million people are bitten by dogs each year with a total of 885,000 needing medical attention (CDC, 2009). Children are twice as likely to be hospitalized than adolescents or adults (Ozanne-Smith et al., 2001). Younger children are more often injured in the face, neck and upper torso regions (Schalamon et al., 2006) leading to life threatening medical conditions.

Dog bites can be traumatizing to both the child and the caregiver (Bernardo et al., 1998, 2000; Rossman et al., 1997). The sequelae are often more severe than is recognized in the medical and mental health communities. In addition to medical problems, dog bites can cause extreme fear and anxiety. Other negative outcomes related to dog bites that are potential stressors for caregivers include problems with medical, insurance and legal systems.

In developing therapeutic interventions with children who have been bitten and with their caregivers, clinicians need to obtain a thorough history of the child's and the caregiver's experiences with animals. Dealing with the pain, fears and physical recovery of the child can be very difficult for families. In addition, if the companion animal in the home has done the biting, difficult decisions must be made about the fate of the pet. Finally, the trauma of the bite may be an ongoing concern in the family if the child develops severe avoidance reactions to dogs as a consequence of being badly frightened and injured. The child may develop post-traumatic stress disorder (PTSD). Unrecognized and untreated symptoms of PTSD in children can lead to impairment in brain development, cognitive, behavioral and social skills (DeBellis et al, 1999; Van der Kolk, 1994).

Joey was almost four when he was bitten by the neighbor's dog. According to Joey's father, when Joey was outdoors the dog came into their yard and attacked Joey. The father was unaware of the attack until he heard his son scream and come running in the house. Joey suffered 21 bites to his head and arm and spent five days in the hospital. Two months later Joey and his parents were referred for therapy. Joey exhibited classic symptoms of post-traumatic stress disorder: waking frequently during the night, clinging to adults, regressing to baby talk, refusing to go outside to play and avoiding all contact with dogs. The neighbor who owned the Akita was aggressive and combative, threatening to go to court to avoid having his unlicensed dog euthanized. The parents had to hire an attorney with money they could not spare and felt extremely guilty for being unable to spare their son this trauma.

In my office, Joey played out his fears, aggressively growling and grabbing a toy bear in his teeth, shaking it furiously while I described his behavior and his desire to be big and strong and do back to the dog what the dog had done to him. We made a book about the bite incident and coping skills he could use and he also put in pictures of lots of "nice dogs." Joey and his parents learned the rules about how to be safer around dogs. As advocated in dog bite safety programs (American Academy of Pediatrics Dog Bite Prevention Pamphlet; Doggone Safe), we practiced standing still like a tree if a strange dog approached him or crouching like a rock if a dog jumped on him. He practiced approaching a toy dog on a leash and asking "Is your dog friendly? May I pet your dog?" Joey's grandmother had an old, almost blind, little dog. The parents noted how much Joey had liked that dog, especially putting it on a leash and tugging it all over the yard. We discussed the importance of modeling gentleness to all animals and providing constant supervision.

Perhaps the hardest thing for the parents was the amount of time it took until some of Joey's fears began to diminish. They needed substantial education about the impact of a life-threatening trauma on Joey's nervous system. His hypervigilant responses would take considerable time to abate.

Currently, we are engaged in a study at Cincinnati Children's Hospital Pediatric Emergency Department, a Level I Trauma Center that treats over 350 children with dog bites annually. Our goal is to estimate the need for supportive services for these children and their caregivers including interventions to address (1) post-bite behavioral and/or medical symptoms in the child; (2) relevant legal, insurance and animal control issues; (3) training children and family members on how to be safe around dogs; and (4) training dog owners and family members to manage dog behaviors effectively. Clinicians play an essential role in highlighting the range of issues faced by families when a child is a dog bite victim.

14.3.8   Participating in programs such as SHIP (Strategic Humane Intervention Program)

Clinicians and clients may have opportunities to participate in programs that use animal-assisted interventions. Lynn Loar developed SHIP as an intervention for children and caregivers living in high risk settings, including homeless shelters (Loar and Colman, 2004). Lynn works with groups of four to five families where the children are eight years or older, the parents/guardians, two shelter dogs and two animal behaviorists who are skilled clicker trainers. The families teach the dogs—and each other—good manners and behaviors exclusively by using positive reinforcement. SHIP seeks to improve relationships within the family at the same time that it increases the dogs' chances of adoption. The eight sessions generally run once a week for two hours.

We have been offering SHIP for five years as a collaboration among our SPCA Cincinnati, the Greater Cincinnati YWCA and the Childhood Trust of Cincinnati Children's Hospital. We have worked with mothers and children from our battered women's shelter programs and with families where teens have been adjudicated for domestic violence (Boat, 2005). The program is a novel, non-verbal approach to teaching relationship and empathy skills and is really engaging and fun!

14.3.9   Bringing family pets to the clinician's office

How fortunate is the clinician who can say to a family "Bring your dog or cat or gerbil or rat or guinea pig when you come for the next appointment. I would love to meet it!" Hearing family members talk about their pets and observing their pet interactions are additional venues for gathering valuable information. Obviously, this is not an option for many clinicians or families. But if the opportunity is present, I urge clinicians to invite companion animals to the therapy session.

Families can bring a pet to my office. I do not have any office pets, but I do have pigeons (rock doves) outside a window that can be opened. It only takes a few safflower seeds to convince a pigeon that he or she should visit regularly. For some of my clients an integral part of coming to see me is to feed—and name—the pigeons. For one traumatized and highly dissociative teenager, every therapy session began with her feeding the pigeons. This contact with the pigeons helped her make the transition into my office. She later told me that knowing she could feed the pigeons made it possible for her to come to my office when she was feeling particularly distressed and confused.

14.4   Conclusion

Routinely asking about animal-related experiences can provide important and useful information that clinicians can incorporate in their therapeutic interventions with children, adolescents and their caregivers.

References

American Academy of Pediatrics Dog Bite Prevention Pamphlet. http://www.aap.org/ advocacy/releases/dogbiteprevention.pdf

American Humane Association. (2009). *Pets and Women's Shelters (PAWS) Program.* www. americanhumane.org

American Pet Products Manufacturers Association. (2005–2006). *National Pet Owners Survey.* http://www.appma.org/press_releasedetail.asp?v=ALL&id=52.

American Pet Products Manufacturers Association. (2009–2010). *National Pet Owners Survey.* http://www.appma.org/press_releasedetail.asp?v=ALL&id=52.

American Veterinary Medical Association. (2001). http://www.avma.org/

Ascione, F. R. (1998). Battered women's reports of their partners' and their children's cruelty to animals. *Journal of Emotional Abuse, 1*(1), 119–132.

Ascione, F. R. (2000). *Safe havens for pets.* http://www.vachss.com/guest_dispatches/safe_ havens.htmlne

Ascione, F. R. (2001). Animal abuse and youth violence. *OJJDP Juvenile Justice Bulletin.* Washington, DC: US Department of Justice.

Ascione, F. R., Friedrich, W. N., Heath, J., & Hayashi, K. (2004). Cruelty to animals in normative, sexually abused, and outpatient psychiatric samples of 6- to 12-year-old children: relations to maltreatment and exposure to domestic violence. *Anthrozoös, 16*(3), 194–212.

Ascione, F. R. (2007). Emerging research on animal risk as a risk factor for intimate partner violence. In K. Kendall-Tackett & S. Giacomoni (Eds.), *Intimate Partner Violence* (pp. 3–1-3–17). Kingston, NJ: Civic Research Institute.

Arkow, P. (1996). The relationship between animal abuse and other forms of family violence. *Family Violence and Sexual Assault Bulletin, 12*(1–2), 29–34.

Baker, D., Boat, B. W., Grinvalsky, M. D., & Geracioti, T. (1998). Interpersonal and animal-related trauma experiences in female and male military veterans: implications for program development. *Military Medicine, 163*(1), 20–25.

Barnes, J. E., Boat, B. W., Putnam, F. W., Dates, H. F., & Mahlman, A. (2006). Ownership of high-risk ("vicious") dogs as a marker for deviant behaviors: implications for risk assessment. *Journal of Interpersonal Violence, 21*(12), 1616–1634.

Battered Hearts: A Story of Family Violence (1995). S.A.F.E. Place, P.O. Box 199, Battle Creek, MI, 49016.

Bernardo, L. M., Gardner, M. J., & Amon, N. (1998). Dog bites in children admitted to Pennsylvania trauma centers. *International Journal of Trauma Nursing, 4*, 121–127.

Bernardo, L. M., Gardner, M. J., O'Conner, J., & Amon, N. (2000). Dog bites in children treated in a pediatric emergency department. *Journal for the Society of Pediatric Nurses, 5*, 87–95.

Boat, B. W. (2005). The strategic humane interventions program (SHIP). *The Latham Letter,* XXVI, 3. Alameda, CA: Latham Foundation. 6–9.

Boat, B. W., Loar, L., & Phillips, A. (2008). Collaborating to assess, intervene and prosecute animal abuse: a continuum of protection for children and animals. In F. Ascione (Ed.), *International Handbook of Theory, Research and Application on Animal Abuse and Cruelty* (pp. 393–422). West Lafayette, IN: Purdue University Press.

Boat, B. W. (1999). Abuse of children and abuse of animals: using the links to inform child assessment and protection. In F. R. Ascione & P. Arkow (Eds.), *Child Abuse, Domestic Violence and Animal Abuse: Linking the Circles of Compassion for Prevention and Intervention* (pp. 83–100). West Layfayette, IN: Purdue University Press.

Boat, B. W. (2000). Children exposed to domestic violence. In R. C. Baker (Ed.), *Pediatric Primary Care: Well-Child Care* (pp. 236–239). Philadelphia, PA: Lippincott, Williams & Wilkins.

Boat, B. W. (2002). Links among animal abuse, child abuse and domestic violence. In I. Neighbors (Ed.), *Social Work and the Law: Proceedings of the National Organization of Forensic Social Workers 2000* (pp. 33–45). Binghamton, NY: Haworth Press.

Bonas, S., McNicholas, J., & Collis, G. M. (2000). Pets in the network of family relationships: an empirical study. In A. L. Podberscek, E. S. Paul, & J. A. Serpell (Eds.), *Companion Animals and Us: Exploring the Relationships between People and Pets* (pp. 209–237). New York: Cambridge University Press.

Both Sides of the Coin (1991). Varied Directions International. 18 Mt. Battle Street, Camden, ME, 04843.

Bulcroft, K. (1990). Pets in the American family. *People, Animals, Environment, 8*(4), 13–14.

Cain, A. O. (1983). A study of pets in the family system. In H. Katcher & A. M. Beck (Eds.), *New Perspectives on Our Lives with Companion Animals* (pp. 72–81). Philadelphia, PA: University of Pennsylvania Press.

Centers for Disease Control (2000). Healthy people 2010: animal control. www.healthypeople.gov

Davis, J. H. (1987). Preadolescent self-concept development and pet ownership. *Anthrozoös, 1*(2), 90–94.

De Bellis, M. D. (1999). Developmental traumatology: neurobiological development in maltreated children with PTSD. *Psychiatric Times, 16*, 11.

De Bellis, M. D., Keshavan, M. S., Clark, D. B., Casey, B. J., Giedd, J. N., Boring, A. M., Frustaci, K., & Ryan, N. D. (1999). Developmental traumatology part II: Brain development. *Society for Biological Psychiatry, 45*, 1271–1284.

DeViney, E., Dickert, J., & Lockwood, R. (1983). The care of pets within child abusing families. *International Journal for the Study of Animal Problems, 4*, 321–329.

Doggone Safe. http://www.doggonesafe.com/about%20be%20a%20tree.htmgone Safe Be A Tree Program.

Doyle, C. (2001). Surviving and coping with emotional abuse in childhood. *Clinical Psychology and Psychiatry, 6*, 387–402.

Dresser, N. (2000). The horse barmitzvah: a celebratory exploration of the human-animal bond. In A. L. Podberscek, E. S. Paul, & J. A. Serpell (Eds.), *Companion Animals and Us: Exploring the Relationships between People and Pets* (pp. 90–107). New York: Cambridge University Press.

Eyberg, S. (1988). Parent child interaction therapy: Integration of traditional and behavioral concerns. *Child and Family Behavior Therapy, 10*, 42–51.

Eisenstat, S. A., & Bancroft, L. (1999). Domestic violence. *New England Journal of Medicine, 341*(12), 886–892.

Enders-Slegers, M. (2000). The meaning of companion animals: qualitative analysis of the life histories of elderly cat and dog owners. In A. L. Podberscek, E. S. Paul, & J. A. Serpell (Eds.), *Companion Animals and Us: Exploring the Relationships between People and Pets* (pp. 237–256). New York: Cambridge University Press.

Felthous, A. R., & Kellert, S. R. (1987). Childhood cruelty and later aggression against people: a review. *American Journal of Psychiatry, 144*(6), 710–717.

Flynn, C. P. (1999). Exploring the link between corporal punishment and children's cruelty to animals. *Journal of Marriage and Family, 61*, 971–981.

Hembree-Kigin, T., & McNeil, C. (1995). *Parent-Child Interaction Therapy*. New York: Plenum Press.

Humane Society of the United States, Animal Cruelty and Family Violence: Making the Connection (2004). www.hsus.org.

Kellert, S. R., & Felthous, A. R. (1985). Childhood cruelty toward animals among criminals and noncriminals. *Human Relations, 38,* 1113–1129.

Kidd, A. H., & Kidd, R. M. (1985). Children's attitudes toward their pets. *Psychological Reports, 57*(1), 15–31.

Lewchanin, S., & Zimmerman, E. (2000). *Clinical Assessment of Juvenile Animal Cruelty.* Brunswick, ME: Biddle Publishing Company and Audenreed Press.

Loar, L., & Colman, L. (2004). *Teaching Empathy: Animal-Assisted Therapy Programs for Children and Families Exposed to Violence.* Alameda, CA: Latham Foundation.

McPhedran, S. (2009). Animal abuse, family violence, and child wellbeing: a review. *Journal of Family Violence, 24,* 41–52.

McNicholas, J., & Collins, G. M. (2001). Children's representations of pets in their social networks. *Child: Care, Health & Development, 27*(3), 279–294.

Miller, K. S., & Knutson, J. F. (1997). Reports of severe physical punishment and exposure to animal cruelty by inmates convicted of felonies and by university students. *Child Abuse and Neglect, 21,* 59–82.

Ozanne-Smith, J., Ashby, K., & Stathakis, V. Z. (2001). Dog bite and injury prevention: analysis, critical review and research agenda. *Injury Prevention, 7*(4), 321–326.

Pets Evacuation and Transportation Standards Act of 2006 Section 51 House of Representatives Sept. 20, 2006. Accessed Dec. 8, 2009. http://www.govtrack.us/congress/record.xpd?id=109-h20060920-51&bill=h109-3858

Pryor, K. (1999). *Clicker Training for Dogs.* Boston, MA: Sunshine Press.

Raphael, P., Loar, L., & Colman, L. (1999). *Teaching Compassion: A Guide for Humane Educators, Teachers, and Parents.* Alameda, CA: Latham Foundation.

Rossman, B. R., Bingham, R. D., & Emde, R. N. (1997). Symptomology and adaptive functioning for children exposed to normative stressors, dog attack, and parental violence. *Journal of the American Academy of Child and Adolescent Psychiatry, 36,* 1089–1096.

Sable, P. (1995). Pets, attachment, and well-being across the life cycle. *Social Work, 40*(3), 334–341.

Safe People, Safe Pets, Hurlburt Field Family Advocacy Office, 113 Lielmanis Avenue, Bldg. 91020, Hurlburt Field, Florida, 850-881-5111.

Schalamon, J., Aindhofe, H., Singer, G., Petnehazy, T., Mayr, J., Kiss, K., & Hollwarth, M. E. (2006). Analysis of dog bites in children who are younger than 17 years. *Pediatrics, 117,* 374–379.

Serpell, J. (1986). *In the Company of Animals: A Study of Human-Animal Relationships.* New York: Basil Blackwell Ltd.

Van der Kolk, B. (1994). The body keeps the score: memory and the evolving psychology of post-traumatic stress. *The Harvard Review of Psychiatry, Jan.–Feb.,* 250–260.

Appendix A

*(CTSARE) CHILDHOOD TRUST SURVEY ON ANIMAL-RELATED EXPERIENCES**
10 Screening Questions for Children, Adolescents and Adults

1. **Have you or your family ever had any pets?** .... **Y N**

	How many?			**How many?**
a. Dog(s)	_____			
b. Cat(s)	_____	**f.** Turtles, snakes, lizards, insects, etc.	_____	
c. Bird(s)	_____	**g.** Rabbits, hamsters, mice, guinea pigs, gerbils	_____	
d. Fish	_____	**h.** Wild animals (describe) _____	_____	
e. Horse(s)	_____	**i.** Other (describe) _____	_____	

2. **Do you have a pet or pets now?** .... **Y N**

	How many?			**How many?**
a. Dog(s)	_____			
b. Cat(s)	_____	**f.** Turtles, snakes, lizards, insects, etc.	_____	
c. Bird(s)	_____	**g.** Rabbits, hamsters, mice, guinea pigs, gerbils	_____	
d. Fish	_____	**h.** Wild animals (describe) _____	_____	
e. Horse(s)	_____	**i.** Other (describe) _____	_____	

3. **Do/did you ever have a favorite or special pet?** .... **Y N**
What kind? _____
What made the pet special? _____
_____

4. **Has a pet ever been a source of comfort or support to you—even if you did not own the pet? (e.g. when
you were sad or scared?)**.. **Y N**

How old were you? _____

Tell me about the pet _____
What happened? _____
_____

5. **Has your pet ever been hurt?**... **Y N**

What happened? _____
_____
_____

       a. Accidental? (hit by car, attacked by another animal, fell, ate something, etc.)
       b. Deliberate? (kicked, punched, thrown, not fed, etc.)

Have you ever felt afraid for your pet or worried about bad things happening to your pet? (describe) .... **Y N**
_____
_____

Are you worried now? .... **Y N**

6. **Have you ever lost a pet you really cared about? (e.g. was given away, ran away, died or was somehow
killed?)** .... **Y N**

If your pet died, was the death:

a. Natural	**b.** Accidental	**c.** Deliberate	**d.** Cruel or violent
(old age, illness, euthanized)	(hit by car)	(strangled, drowned)	(e.g. pet was tortured)

       What happened?
_____
_____
_____

7.   **How do you teach your pet(s) to "be good"? (example)** _____
      _____
      _____

      What happens when your pet misbehaves? (example) _____
      _____
      _____

8.   **Have you ever <u>seen</u> someone hurt an animal or pet?** .... **Y N**
      What happened? _____
      _____
      _____

      Have you ever seen an organized dog fight? .... **Y N**
      How old were you? _____
      Tell me about it _____
      _____
      _____

9.   **Have <u>you</u> ever hurt an animal or pet?** .... **Y N**
      How old were you? _____
      Tell me about it _____
      _____
      _____

      What kind of animal? _____
      Were you alone when you did this? .... **Y N**
      Did anyone know you did this? .... **Y N**
      What happened afterwards?_____
      _____

10.   **Have you ever been frightened, really scared or hurt by an animal?**... **Y N**
      What happened? _____
      _____

      Are you still afraid of this kind of animal or other animals? .... **Y N**
      (Describe)_____
      _____

Barbara W. Boat, Ph.D.
Director and Associate Professor
The Childhood Trust
University of Cincinnati
(513)558-9007
barbara.boat@uc.edu

* See chapter for instructions on how to use the survey.

15 Human/animal interaction and successful aging

Mara Baun*, Rebecca Johnson†

* University of Texas, † University of Missouri

15.1 Introduction

Human/animal interactions (HAI) have become an important part of the lives of many people of all ages. While many who engage in HAI believe in its usefulness, only in the last two decades have there been numerous studies that provide research data to support its beneficial effects, both physiological and psychosocial.

The increasing numbers of elderly and their longevity are supported by census data in many countries. While people are living longer and are in better health than in previous centuries, a number of elderly persons may be living at least part of their lives alone, having lost the companionship of spouses, children, other family members, and friends for a variety of reasons. While it is not suggested that animals can replace human family and friends, there are now data to support the fact that HAI can lessen the loneliness, reduce physiologic arousal, increase health behaviors, such as walking and other exercise, and improve the psychosocial status of many elderly persons. In addition, HAI has improved the lives of institutionalized elderly, both those who are cognitively intact and those with impaired cognitive ability.

15.2 Human companion/animal interactions and successful aging

Research has demonstrated that physiologic arousal lowers in response to human/companion animal interaction. Early research showed lowering of blood pressure when people interacted with dogs to which they were attached (Baun et al., 1984). More recently, Odendaal (2000) found that stress hormone (cortisol) levels decreased most when people quietly interacted with their own pet dog. Cortisol levels also decreased (but less) when people interacted with an unfamiliar, but friendly dog. Elevated cortisol levels have been linked with memory loss (Greendale et al., 2000) and as one component of "allostatic load," in which the body develops cumulative effects of repeated adaptations to stressors (Seeman et al., 1997). Allostatic load has been associated with overall physical and cognitive decline in older adults (ibid.)

Handbook on Animal-Assisted Therapy. DOI: 10.1016/B978-0-12-381453-1.10004-2

Interacting with a companion animal may be one way to reduce allostatic load. Allen et al. (2002) found that people had significantly smaller increases in blood pressure and heart rate when a dog was present while they completed arithmetic tasks and that pet owners had significantly lower blood pressure and heart rate levels than non-pet owners to begin with. Hertstein (1995) found that pet saliency or importance was a significant predictor of physical health in older adults.

Walking is one exercise in which many elderly persons participate. In a study of 394 elderly, dog walkers were more likely to achieve more time walking and at a faster pace than non-dog walkers (Thorpe et al., 2006). Dembicki and Anderson (1996) found that older adult pet owners walked longer and also had lower triglyceride and cholesterol levels than non-pet owners. Also, during dog walking, elderly volunteers were able to increase the high-frequency power values of heart rate variability, a measure of parasympathetic neural activity which potentially has a greater health benefit as a buffer against stress, than walking without a dog and that this benefit was sustained during dog walking (Motooka et al., 2006). But even more important was that this relaxation response was cumulative over additional dog walks.

Recently, dog ownership and dog walking were associated with having and maintaining over a three-year period, faster normal and rapid walking speeds in older adults (Thorpe et al., 2006). Based on these findings, dog walking may have an impact on preventing disability and functionally limiting effects of chronic illnesses.

Commitment to pets—particularly dogs—involves exercising them, and thus may lead to healthier exercise patterns among dog owners, but these patterns may differ across ethnic groups. For example, Johnson and Meadows (2002) found that while Latino elders expressed a very strong bond with their pet dogs, they did not necessarily exercise with them.

Other investigators have found that pets influence older adults' health indirectly by improving morale (Lago et al., 1989). This mind/body connection has been well established in research and can be a factor in maintaining older adults' health and preventing or minimizing disability. There is reason to believe that older adults' interaction with companion animals may activate this connection and be a powerful tool for health care providers, family members and older adults themselves in promoting successful aging by preventing chronic illnesses, or when they do occur, by minimizing their disabling effects. For example, elderly women having a pet to which they were attached were more likely to report higher levels of happiness than those who either did not have a pet or were not attached to their pets (Ory and Goldberg, 1983). This effect of pets, however, was related to the socioeconomic status (SES) of the women with those of higher SES having higher levels of happiness than those of lower SES.

In health care settings, companion animals have been found to be beneficial in many ways. For example, animal-assisted therapy in an oncology day hospital with elderly patients undergoing chemotherapy resulted in decreased depression compared with control subjects who did not have a dog present (Orlandi et al., 2007). In a study of the utility of a pet animal in the treatment of clinical depression in a nursing home, a significant reduction in depression was found in both the pet therapy and conventional therapy groups but not in the control no therapy group (Brickel, 1984). Likewise, elderly persons hospitalized for short-term rehabilitation experienced less depression when a caged bird was placed in their rooms for 7 days (Jesson et al., 1996).

Among the institutionalized elderly, animals have also been found to be therapeutic. Residents of two long-term care facilities showed significant positive changes in mood for those receiving visits from volunteers with a dog as compared to those without a dog (Lutwack-Bloom et al., 2005). Likewise, residents in long-term care facilities had less loneliness when receiving animal-assisted therapy (AAT) than those not receiving AAT (Banks and Banks, 2002).

The presence of therapy animals has been particularly useful in reducing agitated behaviors (Churchill et al., 1999, Richeson, 2003), in decreasing episodes of verbal aggression and anxiety (Fritz et al., 1995) and in increasing social interaction (Fick, 1993; Kongable et al., 1989) in institutionalized elderly with dementias, including Alzheimer's disease. Even visiting with a robotic dog has been found to be beneficial to well-being among nursing home residents (Banks et al., 2008).

Aquariums have had interesting effects on persons with Alzheimer's disease. Edwards and Beck (2002) demonstrated significant increases in nutritional intake among residents of specialized Alzheimer's units by simply placing aquariums in the dining rooms. The increases in nutrition were accompanied by significant weight gain among the residents.

Using "Living Habitat," in which plants and animals were introduced to a nursing home, a sample of residents had higher cognitive status and became more positively engaged with their environment but with a decreased sense of control after six months. Residents who had greater affinity for pets also became more positively engaged with their environment (Ruckdeschel and Van Haitsma, 2001).

While many areas of companion/animal interaction with elderly need further research to substantiate their effectiveness, there are studies to support positive benefits from this intervention. These interventions, however, need to be planned carefully considering not only characteristics of the elderly themselves but also of their environment. We present in Box 15.1 a case study of dog visitation to newly admitted nursing home residents.

Box 15.1 Effects of Dog Visitation on Newly Admitted Older Adult Nursing Home Residents (conducted by R. Johnson)

The purpose of this research was to conduct a case study of one nursing home in which a three-group, delayed treatment, pre-test post-test design was used to test the effectiveness of a dog visit protocol (DVP) on mood, social support, sense of coherence, and stress (measured via salivary cortisol). Fifteen older adults who had relocated to a nursing home in the preceding four weeks for long-term residence and scored 3 or higher on the Short Mini Mental State Exam (SMMSE) were included in the study. Participants who were moving from another nursing home were not included. Three groups were created: an experimental group who received dog visits ($n = 5$), an experimental group who received friendly person visits ($n = 5$), and a control group who received standard care ($n = 5$).

The first five residents to consent were assigned to the control group and were given the usual admission procedures of the facility, the next five were assigned to the dog visit group, and the final five were assigned to the human visit group. Experimental group participants received either 18 visits from a trained, certified visitor dog and its handler, or 18 visits from a human visitor, over a six-week period (three visits per week). Each visit consisted of a 20-minute session in the participant's room.

The dog used for the study was certified by the University of Missouri-Columbia College of Veterinary Medicine's Pet Assisted Love and Support (PALS) program. The dog handler was fully oriented to the study protocols. The handler was instructed to discuss only the dog during the visits. At the initial visit, handlers explained that visits could involve combing, petting, and talking to the dog. No lively play (e.g. throwing a ball, wrestling, etc.) was permitted.

After informed consent, all participants completed the Short Mini Mental State Exam (SMMSE), a Demographic Questionnaire (DQ), the Profile of Mood States (POMS), the UCLA Loneliness Scale (UCLA), the Social Provisions Scale (SPS), the Daily Hassles and Uplifts Scale (DHUS), and the Orientation to Life Questionnaire, a measure of sense of coherence (OTLQ). Saliva samples were collected at 8 am and 4 pm by having the older adults spit into a prepared collection tube. Post-protocol data collection occurred within one week after the experimental group participants completed their 18th dog visit or human visit. This data collection occurred during the seventh week of residence for the control group. All participants then completed the POMS, UCLA, SPS, DHUS, and OTLQ once again. Saliva samples were again collected from all participants at 8 am and 4 pm using the same method as in the pre-test. Experimental group participants also completed the Exit Questionnaire. Table 15.1 shows demographic characteristics of the sample.

For each group, T-tests were performed to detect significant differences between pre-test and post-test scores. Results (shown in Table 15.2) are reported in terms of difference scores (pre-post) and indicated that the control group had fewer uplifts and less social integration after the six-week study period. The human visit group had less depression and lower cortisol levels after the six-week study period. The dog group had no significant changes in any outcome measures. However, results were in expected directions including less loneliness, tension, depression, anger, and confusion.

Using the Kruskall-Wallis test, group mean cortisol am, pm, and the daily averages were compared for the three groups. At alpha level of 0.05 there were no statistically significant differences in cortisol levels between groups. However, the human visit group had a significantly higher post-pm cortisol level, indicating a greater level of stress after the six weeks.

The Kruskal-Wallis test was used to compare sense of coherence and mood across the three groups. Displayed results (shown in Table 15.3) indicated that at the pre-test, the dog visit group had a significantly higher sense of coherence, and stronger reassurance of worth pre score than the control group. The dog group had significantly less anger than the control group. The human visit group had a stronger sense of coherence and reassurance of worth, and less anger than the control group.

However, on the post-test scores, both the human and the dog visit group had significantly more uplifts than the control group. The dog visit group had more uplifts and less anger. The human visit group had more uplifts and less depression than the control group. There were no significant differences between the dog and human visit groups.

Table 15.1 Demographic characteristics

	Total ($n = 15$)	Control group ($n = 5$)	Dog visit group ($n = 5$)	Human visit group ($n = 5$)
Age	78.3	83.8	74.8	76.4
	(s.d. $= 12.4$)	(s.d. $= 10.0$)	(s.d. $= 13.7$)	(s.d. $= 13.9$)
Male	7 (46.7)	1 (20)	4 (80)	2 (40)
White	14 (93)	4 (80)	5 (100)	5 (100)
Marital status				
Married	1 (7)	0	1 (20)	0
Single	1 (7)	0	1 (20)	0
Divorced	4 (28)	1 (20)	1 (20)	3 (60)
Separated/widowed	8 (57.1)	4 (80)	2 (40)	2 (40)
Education no H.S.	3 (20)	1 (20)	1 (20)	1 (20)
Some H.S.	4 (26.7)	1 (20)	2 (40)	1 (20)
H.S. graduate	3 (20)	0	1 (20)	2 (40)
Some college	2 (13.3)	0	1 (20)	1 (20)
Bachelor's	2 (13.3)	2 (40)	0	0
Graduate work	1 (6.7)	1 (20)	0	0

Note: Percentages in parentheses.

Table 15.2 Within group mean difference scores

	Control group	Dog visit group	Human visit group
Hassles	3.80	1.60	0.80
Uplifts	4.00*	−1.80	−1.40
POMS			
Tension	−1.80	3.80	1.80
Vigor	−1.80	1.20	0.20
Fatigue	2.80	2.40	0.80
Confusion	0.80	0.20	1.4
Mood	−8.80	7.40	5.00
Depression	3.60	1.60	1.00*
Anger	4.00	0.60	0.20
Social provisions			
Attachment	−0.40	0.20	0.20
Social integration	0.60	0.60	−0.60
Reassurance of worth	−1.00	1.00	−0.20
Reliable alliance	0.40	0.40	0.80
Guidance	0	0	0.40
Opportunity	0.60	0	0.20
UCLA Loneliness Scale	0.20	0.20	0
Orientation to life	−2.60	0	0.40
Difference between a.m. scores (post-pre)	−0.03	0	0
Difference between p.m. scores (post-pre)	0.02	0.01	0.01*
Difference between p.m-a.m.	−0.01	0.01	0

*Note: $p < 0.10$.

Table 15.3 Between group differences: pre scores and post scores: means and standard deviations

	Pre			Post		
	Control	*Dog visit*	*Human visit*	**Control**	**Dog visit**	*Human visit*
Hassles	8.60	14.40	13.40	4.80*	12.80*	12.60
	(6.42)	(4.50)	(0.54)	(3.34)	(1.64)	(1.81)
Uplifts	15.60	18.00	17.80	11.60*	19.80*	19.20
	(9.28)	(3.74)	(3.11)	(7.43)	(1.30)	(3.83)
POMS *Tension*	6.00	5.00	4.40	7.80	1.20	2.60
	(4.06)	(6.36)	(3.04)	(6.37)	(0.83)	(2.70)
Vigor	14.20	3.20	1.60	5.60	1.600	0.60*
	(11.34)	(3.34)	(1.51)	(7.82)	(1.94)	(1.34)
Fatigue	8.80	0.60*	0.40*	3.40	0.0	0.20
	(7.29)	(1.34)	(0.54)	(4.44)		(0.44)
Confusion	5.00	22.60	17.40	16.00	21.40	17.20
	(3.80)	(2.96)	(5.02)	(11.93)	(3.71)	(4.76)
Mood	2.20	3.00	1.60	6.00	0.60	0.80
	(30.78)	(4.52)	(1.67)	(8.68)	(1.34)	(0.83)
Depression	9.20	2.80	3.20	4.20	2.60	1.80
	(9.57)	(0.83)	(0.83)	(3.76)	(1.81)	(1.30)
Anger	7.40**	−8.00	−6.20	11.00	−15.40	−11.20
	(7.43)	(16.21)	(9.67)	(3.94)	(8.64)	(8.95)
Social provisions	6.20	7.60	8.20	6.60	7.40	8.00
Attachment	(3.56)	(2.30)	(1.09)	(3.78)	(0.89)	(0.00)
Social integration	4.80	6.40	6.00	4.20	5.80	6.60
	(2.77)	(1.14)	(0.70)	(2.48)	(0.83)	(1.34)
Reassurance of worth	3.80**	7.80*	6.40	4.80	6.80	6.60
	(2.38)	(1.48)	(0.89)	(3.03)	(1.30)	(0.54)
Reliable alliance	5.60**	6.40	6.40	5.60	6.00	5.60
	(3.57)	(0.89)	(0.89)	(3.20)	(0.00)	(0.89)
Guidance	4.80	6.40	6.40	4.80	6.40	6.00
	(2.94)	(0.54)	(1.14)	(2.68)	(0.89)	(0.00)
Opportunity	5.40	4.00	4.00	4.80	4.00	3.80
	(3.20)	(1.22)	(0.70)	(2.77)	(0.70)	(1.09)
UCLA Loneliness Scale	3.40	4.20	4.00	3.20	4.00	4.00
	(2.07)	(0.44)	(0.00)	(2.16)	(0.00)	(0.00)
Orientation to life	5.60*	9.40*	9.80*	8.20	9.40	9.40
	(3.57)	(1.14)	(0.83)	(4.76)	(0.54)	(0.54)

*Note: $p < 0.10$,
**$p < 0.05$. Standard deviations in parentheses.

While we must use caution in the interpretation of findings from such a small case study, some results were in predicted directions. Perhaps because of the small sample, our findings are not similar to those of Banks and Banks (2005) who found that a dog visit reduced loneliness in nursing home residents.

The current study shows trends in the predicted direction for many of the variables examined. For example, the control group had higher levels of depression and anger and lower levels of attachment and reassurance of worth.

One other finding of note from the current study is the higher anger score of the control group over both the dog and human visit groups. This finding is not surprising. Previous studies have shown that newly admitted nursing home residents often report a variety of mental health issues due to relocation, including sadness, anxiety, stress, depression, powerlessness, anger, betrayal, social withdrawal, and decreased life satisfaction. The lack of significant differences between the human and dog visit group suggests that further comparison of these visits is warranted.

Participants in the dog visit group expressed that seeing the dog was "fun," "enjoyable," "something to do in a new place," and that the visit "cheered me up." Participants in the human visit group reported that the visitor "helps you feel welcome to a new place," is "fun," and was "a new friend, even if it was just for a study and would only be for a few weeks." Given these comments, it may be useful to conduct a qualitative study to fully describe the nature of both human and dog visits and what each may mean to newly admitted nursing home residents. In particular, the nature of the relationships formed, and how they are formed during the visits may be of interest.

15.3 Facilitating relationships between pets and older adults

15.3.1 "Aging in place"

The notion of "aging in place" is not a new concept. Most investigators and others who work with older adults routinely hear their participants/clients express a desire to remain living "in my own home." Often older adults want to remain in their own homes so that they can keep their pets. Staying in their own homes can present particular challenges given the rapidly expanding demographic group that older adults constitute and their needs for health care services. Approximately one-third of all older adults need some form of supportive care and services to remain living in the community. This care can range from homemaker services to assist with housework and bathing to professional services, such as medication management, regular monitoring of health conditions, and full-scale coordinating of many health care providers. Aging in place aims, as an alternative to relocation to a nursing home, to provide needed care and prevent relocation-associated trauma.

As the aging in place movement has grown, so have the number of options for these types of places in which to live. A wide variety of alternatives exist including subsidized apartments designed for older adults, where care and services are not provided, retirement communities, assisted living facilities where older adults may have their own room or apartment with limited services typically including congregate meals and housekeeping, or a combination of these. These models provide only partial versions of aging in place. The fear of having to move, even to a different part of the building, can be so intense for older adults that they may attempt to hide their growing needs and thus do not receive care that could facilitate their health and functioning.

A group of faculty at University of Missouri Sinclair School of Nursing whose expertise is in gerontology recognized the need for a new model of aging in place in which the threat and stress of relocation would not impede proper care provision for older adults. This Aging in Place project was formulated with two components: first, a home health agency, Senior Care, was formed to provide care coordination and direct care to older adults. The second component required a corporate partner to build and manage TigerPlace, a 32 apartment residential facility. The partnership was formed with Americare Systems, Inc., of Sikeston, Missouri. Americare is the "landlord" of the facility and provides meal service, housekeeping, and concierge-type activity planning. At TigerPlace, a resident need not relocate when even advanced levels of care are needed. The facility is equipped with sensors to detect and report falls and monitoring devices for those with dementia that are used to insure their safety. Staff of a home health agency monitor the residents' health and care needs and implement treatment plans within the facility.

TigerPlace features efficiency, one- and two-bedroom apartments, a large community room, classroom, congregate and private dining rooms, hair salon, sports bar, exercise room, theatre, and clinic space for resident use with health care providers. Situated on several acres, the facility includes walk trails and outside exercise areas.

TigerPlace has a strong relationship with the University of Missouri, and is host to students from nursing, physical therapy, social work, occupational therapy, medicine, law, journalism, engineering (who were heavily involved in developing the building with state of the art technology), and education. TigerPlace residents are encouraged to participate in the myriad of activities, lectures, concerts and exhibits that the university has ongoing, and transportation is provided.

TigerPlace is a pet-inclusive, pet-encouraging facility. This philosophy is based on research showing that human/pet interaction provides visual, auditory, olfactory and tactile stimulation, and that this interaction may stimulate well-being through chemical processes. For example, Odendaal (2000) found that in response to a quiet petting interaction with a dog, people had significant improvements in serum oxytocin, prolactin, and beta-endorphin, norepinephrine, phenylethylamine, dopamine, and cortisol levels. These neurochemicals are believed to enhance feelings of well-being, mood, and relaxation. Knowing that pets are beneficial for older adults, pets were considered throughout the design and construction of the TigerPlace facility. Each apartment has a screened porch, wide windowsills, an outside entrance, and tile entry to accommodate pet needs. But perhaps the most unique and compelling feature is the veterinary clinic within the building, specially designed to provide care for the pet residents of TigerPlace.

15.3.2 TigerPlace Pet Initiative (TiPPI)

TiPPI is a cross-disciplinary, collaborative program between the MU Sinclair School of Nursing and the MU College of Veterinary Medicine. The underlying principle of

TiPPI is the belief in the health benefits of human/animal interaction and the human/animal bond for older adults and pets. This belief is based on research showing that older adults live longer, healthier and happier lives when they own or regularly interact with pets.

TiPPI aims to:

- Foster a pet-inclusive environment at TigerPlace. An admission and periodic screening process is in place for residents' pets, and residents who do not have pets are assisted to adopt pets as they would like. As of this writing, there were four dogs and three cats residing with their owners at TigerPlace. A student "Pet Assistant" is paid to the help dog owners with walking the dogs, cleaning cat litter boxes, delivering pet food, giving medication to the pets and transporting the pets as needed.
- Facilitate excellent veterinary care of TigerPlace residents' pets, while simultaneously providing an invaluable learning experience for veterinary students to work with older adult clients. The facility features a fully equipped veterinary exam room with equipment enabling preventive health care and treatment for non-critical illnesses. Residents need only walk down the hallway with their pets to visit the veterinarian. An MU College of Veterinary Medicine faculty veterinarian makes monthly house calls to all pet owners at TigerPlace. This enables an assessment of the pets in their home environment. He provides education and suggestions for preventive care of the pets. If minor procedures are needed, the animal is taken to the onsite exam room. For more intense treatment, pets are transported (either by the pet owner or TigerPlace staff) to the Veterinary Medical Teaching Hospital, or to a local veterinarian of the owner's choosing.
- Promote human/animal contact for the residents of TigerPlace. This is done through the "PAWSitive Visits" program. Weekly the TigerPlace residents have the opportunity to interact with and learn about a particular species during this animal visitation program. An MU student coordinates a variety of animals to be brought by their owners or handlers. During these sessions the "PAWSitive Visits" Coordinator and/or the animal's owner provide a brief tutorial which stimulates discussion and reminiscence about animal experiences in the residents' lives. A recent highlight was a visit by "Cookie" and "Tuffy," two miniature horses. A wide variety of animals have visited including an assortment of dogs and cats, pot-belly pigs, alpacas, Missouri mules, birds of prey, ferrets, rabbits, and a coatamundi.
- Promote research into the benefits of human/animal interaction and the human/animal bond. TigerPlace provides an ideal place to study the role of pets in older adults' lives.
- Provide foster care and adoption services for bereaved pets. An endowment is in place so that when a TiPPI pet's owner is deceased or can no longer care for the pet, funds are available to support the pet's care in a foster home with another resident of TigerPlace, or if this is not possible, in a foster home in the community. The funds support food and medical care of the pet until it is placed in a permanent home. Recently, a pet dog was orphaned through the death of its owner. Another TigerPlace resident readily adopted the dog.

Taken in total, TigerPlace offers a remarkable change in the usual model of aging in place. It eliminates mandatory relocation as older adults' care needs increase and thus minimizes the fear associated with this. TigerPlace residents enjoy meals bordering on the gourmet prepared by a formally trained executive chef, regular activities and excursions, and most importantly they can bring their pets and know that these beloved companions will also be cared for.

15.4   Pet selection

15.4.1   Community-dwelling elderly persons

Recommending a pet for an elderly person is a challenging opportunity. Even though a number of studies have demonstrated that pets can be beneficial to the elderly, for example in alleviating depression and in increasing socialization, finding the right pet for a particular person can be difficult. The primary consideration is the health and safety of the person.

Many older adults have mobility difficulties. It is not uncommon for them to walk with canes or walkers and to be somewhat unsteady on their feet. While a young dog can provide much affection and entertainment, it may be too strong for the older adult to walk on a leash or it might be able to cause a fall by jumping against the legs or tripping the person. Older adults may not be able to move quickly enough to get a puppy house broken. Thus, an older dog, particularly one who has been obedience trained, socialized, and housebroken, may be a good alternative. Often dog breeders, especially those who show their dogs, have adult dogs who are still young but are no longer going to be shown and whom they would like to place in loving homes. These purebred dogs usually are excellent examples of the breed and have been bred for good temperament, have been socialized to dog shows where they had to perform in front of hundreds of people and dogs, and thus make excellent pets.

Other sources of well-trained dogs are the agencies who train dogs as service dogs, for example seeing eye, hearing, and assistance dogs for people with handicaps. At present, there is a 75% dropout rate for these dogs, that is, three-quarters of the dogs who have been specially reared do not succeed in their formal training program. Generally, they make excellent pets because they have had systematic socialization and obedience training since they were young puppies. There are, however, long lists of people waiting to adopt these dogs, and the puppy raisers generally have the first option to adopt the dog if it is rejected during the formal training program.

Many humane societies have adopt-a-pet programs, some designed specifically for the elderly. While there are many animals at Humane Society shelters who can become excellent pets, careful consideration needs to be given to the elderly person's abilities and the pet's needs. If the animal was brought to the shelter for behavior problems, an elderly person may not be able to provide the appropriate behavior modifications. On the other hand, sometimes wonderful pet animals are available for adoption.

Older adults seeking to acquire a dog will have individual needs and likes and dislikes. Sometimes, as individuals age, their self-concept does not change as their bodies become more limited, and they may be unrealistic in assessing what they can and cannot do. Their memories of a loved dog may not include the difficulties encountered during puppyhood, and they may only remember the docile, well-behaved older dog in the last years of its life. Thus, seeking advice on the type of dog to be acquired from an experienced dog owner or trainer and health care provider may be very useful in matching the individual with the right dog.

Most major cities have one or more kennel clubs and dog training clubs. Often these clubs provide public service through maintaining a telephone to assist persons with dog-related questions. Some purebred dog clubs participate in rescue programs where they take unwanted dogs of their breed, rehabilitate them if necessary, and place them in good homes. Some of these rescued dogs may make excellent pets for older adults. Also, veterinarians can provide advice about the care requirements of various breeds. Another avenue of information on purebred dogs is the American Kennel Club, which has an excellent website (http://www.akc.org) and can refer inquiries to the national breed clubs. In addition, there are numerous home pages on various breeds of dogs and other dog-related activities that can be accessed through one of the search engines on the Internet. Most libraries have sections on dogs.

It is a good idea for anyone, particularly older adults, not to be impulse driven in the acquisition of a pet. Besides the monetary investment, there may be a 10-to15-year commitment involved. A few weeks of investigation and planning can be a good investment in making sure that the acquisition of the pet is a positive experience. Sometimes, it is useful if an adult child partners with the older adult in the process of pet adoption. The adult child then hopefully will have some commitment to assisting their parent throughout the process. Older adults need to recognize their current and potential limitations that could occur during the life of the pet. If there is a strong potential that the person will not be able to care for the pet throughout its entire life, an arrangement might be made with a family member or other responsible person to take the pet if the older adult becomes unable to provide care either temporarily or permanently. In Houston and other cities, there are groups of volunteers who will care for pets of low income hospitalized or incapacitated older adults (http://www.pawshouston.org/).

A few retirement homes allow older adult residents to bring their pets with them, but the pet owner must be able to care for the pet, and there may be restrictions on the size and species of the pets allowed. Few of these facilities have support systems in place to the extent that TigerPlace does. Hopefully, the number of facilities allowing personal pets will increase in the future. Most nursing homes do not have facilities for personal pets. One of the greatest sources of distress for the institutional elderly can be the loss of their beloved pets. Many nursing homes do have pet visitation programs and allow individuals' pets to visit on a regular basis. Family members or friends can keep the pet and bring it to see its owner. A particularly sad occurrence is for the pet to be taken to the local Humane Society and then euthanized or placed with strangers when its owner is institutionalized so that the elderly person experiences not only the loss of personal independence but also the loss of their beloved pet significant other.

Sometimes, the choice of a pet other than a dog is ideal for an older adult. Cats, for example, require less personal care than dogs. Nonetheless, the older adult needs to be mobile enough to change the litter box and responsible enough to feed and care for the cat. Eyesight needs to be good enough to avoid tripping over any pet that has access to the floor.

Sometimes, a caged animal, such as a bird, might be a better choice if the elderly person has difficulty with mobilization. Birds can be excellent companions. Most domestic birds can be hand trained thus providing physical contact but also can be kept in cages. The elderly person needs to be able to provide food and water and clean the cage regularly.

Many other small animals could provide touch and affection for elderly persons. Gerbils, guinea pigs, mice, rats, rabbits, hamsters, turtles, and snakes are but a few of the potential small animals that could be wonderful pets. Sometimes it is not possible to predict to which animals strong bonds can develop. Physical contact with the animal is extremely important in the choice of a pet for some people but is not a strong consideration for others. For example, some older adults may find that watching fish in a tank can provide many hours of intense enjoyment.

A major consideration in the acquisition of pets by older adults is access to veterinary medical care. Frequently, elderly persons are no longer able to drive. Finding someone to take the pet to the veterinarian's office may be problematic. Even though there are many ways for the elderly to get transportation for their own health care appointments, there are no similar services for animal health care. In addition, many older adults live on fixed incomes and may not be able to afford the additional costs of health care for pets. A few cities provide low-cost clinics for animal health care, some particularly for animals belonging to older adults, but the pet owner has to find transportation to the clinics. Some veterinarians practice in mobile vans. The availability of such a veterinarian for older adults' pets would be of great assistance in allowing the elderly persons to maintain pets in their homes. Provision for the animal's health care needs to be a critical part of the planning that takes place prior to the acquisition of a pet. Sometimes, if it is not feasible for older adults to have personal pets, wild animals, such as birds and squirrels, can fill the gap. Older adults may get many hours of enjoyment from watching birds and squirrels at feeders.

15.4.2 Pets in long-term care facilities

A variety of animals can be used in institutions either as residents or as regular visitors. The most common are dogs, cats, rabbits, small rodents, birds, and fish. Dogs, cats, and rabbits generally visit on a regular basis, although some institutions have acquired them as residents.

The success of a resident animal in a long-term care facility depends on a number of factors. Probably the most important is careful planning prior to the acquisition of the animal. The first step is to review the regulations of review boards and accrediting organizations about resident or visiting animals. If there is no contradiction to the acquisition of an animal, the next step is to decide which animal is best for that facility.

Staff members need to consider who will be responsible for the animal. It is generally overly optimistic to assume that the elderly will care for resident animals. Responsibility needs to be assigned to staff members. If some aspects of care can occasionally be done by elderly residents, this care needs to be accomplished under the supervision of staff members. Thus, staff members need to be willing to assume additional duties in relation to a resident animal. The nature of the animal to be acquired, therefore, has implications for staff workload. A dog, for example, needs food, toileting, and exercise on a regular schedule 24 hours a day seven days a week.

Thus, staff working during all shifts every day will need to make provision for its care. It is possible for the day shift staff to be excited about the acquisition of a resident animal and the night shift staff to resent the added responsibilities. In such a facility, a caged bird which requires less care that can be given on only one shift might be a good choice.

Part of the planning for the acquisition of a resident pet is to consider potential allergies among residents and staff. It may be necessary to specially treat the animal to reduce the disbursement of allergens, for example dander, that can trigger allergic reactions. Also, toenails need to be kept well trimmed and blunt to prevent injury to frail skin. Likewise, a plan needs to be in place for flea and other parasite prevention.

The potential for zoonotic infections, that is, infections that can be transmitted between species, needs careful consideration. Any animal brought into a long-term care facility should be given a complete examination by a licensed veterinarian prior to introduction. There should be a plan for regular examinations to ensure that it remains free of parasites and infections, that immunizations are current, and that preventive medications, such as heart worm pills, are administered appropriately.

There may be some older adult residents who should not interact with the pet such as those who are immunocompromised or allergic to the animal. The plan for the resident animal needs to include provisions for protecting these residents. However, as Johnson et al. (2002) report, there is little if any research evidence reporting zoonotic infections in such situations. The risks to older adult residents are minimal and potentially outweighed by the benefits if facilities adhere to published guidelines (Centers for Disease Control and Prevention Healthcare Infection Control Practices Advisory Committee, 2001).

Another consideration in acquiring a resident animal is the location of the facility. Residents coming primarily from rural settings often have very different views of animals than those who have been city dwellers all of their lives. Even animals traditionally regarded as companions, such as dogs and cats, may be considered as appropriately living outside and performing some instrumental function. Retired farmers may prefer interactions with farm animals, such as sheep and chickens, than with dogs and cats. They can get a great deal of satisfaction watching these animals through the window as opposed to petting or cuddling companion animals.

The age of the animal also is a significant factor to be considered in planning. Puppies, although cute and appealing, need housebreaking and training. Older animals have the potential to have training completed before placement. One important consideration is that the animal needs to be temperament tested to ensure that it is suitable for interaction with older adults. Most cities have animal trainers who can perform this function.

Another consideration is that the animal needs time away from constant interaction with humans. While staff are not expected to work 24 hours a day, neither should such "work" be expected from the resident animal. In some instances, resident animals have actually developed stress-related illnesses in response to overstimulation. Planning for a place where the animal can be away from people for part of each day and get its proper rest is essential. Such planning requires an understanding of the behavior of the species. Dogs, for example, generally are most active in the morning and evening and sleep a great deal in between. Planning for a resident dog might include an enclosure with a shelter on the grounds where the dog can be placed in the middle of the day as well as for the night. An alternative might be for the dog to have a resting place designated within the building, which is kept free from other activities and purposes.

Some institutions have found that a more satisfactory arrangement for having a therapy animal, particularly animals such as dogs and cats, is to have the animal reside with one of the staff. Then, the animal comes to "work" with the staff member and goes home at the end of the shift to a more normal living arrangement where it can get its own needs met. Such an arrangement also negates the need for staff to provide 24-hour, seven-days-a-week care for the animal.

The need for careful planning prior to the acquisition of an animal for a long-term care facility cannot be overemphasized. It would be well to have a committee of stakeholders formed to consider aspects of acquisition of the animal and to generate a written set of guidelines that would become part of the facility's policies and a budget for care of the animal. Such careful planning should result in a happy and therapeutic relationship between the animal, staff, and residents.

15.5 Guidelines for animal-assisted therapy with older adults

Many institutions for older adults have resident pets, and many have regular pet visitation programs. While many studies have demonstrated the beneficial effects of contact with pets for a variety of persons, including the elderly, the long-term effects of resident pets and pet visitation programs have not been examined. Nonetheless, the idea of bringing pets into contact with institutionalized elderly people has become quite popular in the United States and elsewhere.

There is no doubt that the presence of pets in a setting such as a nursing home where one ordinarily does not expect to see them provides a source of distraction and novelty. All one has to do is witness the attention a dog gets as it walks into a facility. Residents, staff, and visitors descend on the dog almost like it is a magnet. Yet, the question of what the long-term effects of contact with a companion animal for the institutionalized elderly are has yet to be answered.

Distraction from one's ordinary daily life in a nursing home is not without merit. Also, pets provide a source of affectionate physical contact that often is lacking in an institutional setting. Perhaps these effects are enough to justify the cost of maintaining these programs. There are important areas to consider in instituting an animal-assisted therapy program

1. Choice of animal. Most pet visitation programs utilize companion animals such as dogs, cats, rabbits and Vietnamese pot-bellied pigs. These animals can be transported easily to the institution and walked or carried to interested residents. One criterion for animals being included as regular visitors is that they be tested for their suitability to interact with strangers. Many pet therapy groups have established their own testing programs. National organizations such as the Delta Society (http://www.deltasociety.org/) have standardized

testing that can be done by a local person who is certified. Once the animal has passed the test, it receives a certificate that it can be an institutional visitor. Often it is eligible to wear some sort of symbol of this certification so that persons who see it in the institution know that it has been tested.

2. Orientation of pet handlers. The persons bringing the animals to the institution need to have an orientation to that institution. They need to know in which sections of the building, generally eating areas, animals are not allowed. Also, they should be informed about the characteristics of persons they will encounter and how to deal with problems if they should arise. The safety both of the residents and of the persons and animal visiting is of utmost importance. It is possible for cognitively impaired older adults to behave in surprising ways and to attempt to injure animals and their handlers. Animals visiting an institution should be under the direct physical control of the handler at all times

Many persons who participate in animal visitation programs continue to do so for many years because it is so personally rewarding for them to be a part of the human/animal team. One has only to see the delight and interest on so many otherwise sad or blank elderly faces when allowed to interact with a companion animal to be "hooked" forever and convinced that animals truly are good for the elderly!

References

Allen, K., Blascovich, J., & Mendes, W. (2002). Cardiovascular reactivity and the presence of pets, friends and spouses: The truth about cats and dogs. *Psychosomatic Medicine, 64*, 727–739.

Banks, M. R., & Banks, W. A. (2005). The effects of group and individual animal-assisted therapy on loneliness in residents of long-term care facilities. *Anthrozoös, 18*(4), 396–408.

Banks, M. R., & Banks, W. A. (2002). The effects of animal-assisted therapy on loneliness in an elderly population in long-term care facilities. *Journal of Gerontology, 57*(7), 428–432.

Banks, M. R., Willoughby, L. M., & Banks, W. A. (2008). Animal-assisted therapy and loneliness in nursing homes: use of robotic versus living dogs. *Journal of the American Medical Directors Association, 9*(3), 173–177.

Baun, M., Bergstrom, N., Langston, N., & Thoma, L. (1984). Physiological effects of human/companion animal bonding. *Nursing Research, 33*(3), 126–129.

Brickel, C. M. (1984). *Depression in the Nursing Home: A Pilot Study using Pet-facilitated Psychotherapy* (pp. 407–415). Minneapolis, Minnesota: Center to Study Human-Animal Relationships and Environments.

Centers for Disease Control and Prevention Healthcare Infection Control Practices Advisory Committee. (2001). *Draft guideline for environmental infection control in healthcare facilities*. Retrieved from: http://www.cdc.gov/ncidod/hip/envior/env_guide_draft.pdf

Churchill, M., Safaoui, J., McCabe, B. W., & Baun, M. M. (1999). Using a therapy dog to alleviate the agitation and desocialization of people with Alzheimer's disease. *Journal of Psychosocial Nursing, 37*(4), 16–22.

Dembicki, D., & Anderson, J. (1996). Pet ownership may be a factor in improved health of the elderly. *Journal of Nutrition for the Elderly, 15*(3), 15–31.

Edwards, N. E., & Beck, A. M. (2002). Animal-assisted therapy and nutrition in Alzheimer's disease. *Western Journal of Nursing Research, 24*(6), 697–712.

Fick, K. M. (1993). The influence of an animal on social interactions of nursing home residents in a group setting. *American Journal of Occupational Therapy, 47*(6), 529–534.

Fritz, C. L., Farver, T. B., Kass, P. H., & Hart, L. A. (1995). Association with companion animals and the expression of noncognitive symptoms in Alzheimer's patients. *Journal of Nervous and Mental Disease, 183*(7), 459–463.

Greendale, G. A., Kritz-Silverstein, D., Seeman, T., & Barrett-Connor, E. (2000). Higher basal cortisol predicts verbal memory loss in postmenopausal women: Rancho Bernardo Study. *Journal of the American Geriatrics Society, 48*(12), 1655–1658.

Hertstein, V. (1995). *The relation between pet ownership and physical, psychological, and functional health disorders among community-based elderly residents.* Columbia University Teachers College: New York: Unpublished doctoral dissertation.

Jessen, J., Cardiello, F., & Baun, M. M. (1996). Avian companionship in alleviation of depression, loneliness, and low morale of older adults in skilled rehabilitation units. *Psychological Reports, 78*, 339–348.

Johnson, R. A., & Meadows, R. L. (2002). Older Latinos, pets and health. *Western Journal of Nursing Research, 24*(6), 609–620.

Johnson, R. A., Odendaal, J. S., & Meadows, R. L. (2002). Animal-assisted interventions research: issues and answers. *Western Journal of Nursing Research, 24*(4), 422–440.

Kanamori, M., Suzuki, M., Yamamoto, K., Kanda, M., Matsui, Y., Kojima, E., Fukawa, H., Sugita, T., & Oshiro, H. (2001). A day care program and evaluation of animal-assisted therapy (AAT) for the elderly with senile dementia. *American Journal of Alzheimer's Disease and Other Dementias, 16*(4), 234–239.

Kongable, L. G., Buckwalter, K. C., & Stolley, J. M. (1989). The effects of pet therapy on the social behavior of institutionalized Alzheimer's clients. *Archives of Psychiatric Nursing, 3*(4), 191–198.

Lago, D., Delaney, M., Miller, M., & Grill, C. (1989). Companion animals, attitudes toward pets, and health outcomes among the elderly: a long-term follow-up. *Anthrozoös, 3*(1), 25–34.

Lutwack-Bloom, P., Wijewickrama, R., & Smith, B. (2005). Effects of pets versus people visits with nursing home residents. *Journal of Gerontological Social Work, 44*(3/4), 137–159.

Motooka, M., Koike, H., Yokoyama, T., & Kennedy, N. (2006). Effect of dog-walking on autonomic nervous activity in senior citizens. *Medical Journal of Australia, 184*, 60–63.

Odendaal, J. S. J. (2000). Animal-assisted therapy: medicine or magic? *Journal of Psychosomatic Research, 49*(4), 275–280.

Orlandi, M., Trangeled, K., Mambrini, A., Tagliani, M., Ferrarini, A., Zanetti, L., Tartarini, R., Pacetti, P., & Cantore, M. (2007). Pet therapy effects on oncological day hospital patients undergoing chemotherapy treatment. *Anticancer Research, 27*, 4301–4304.

Ory, M. G., & Goldberg, E. L. (1983). Pet possession and well-being in elderly women. *Research on Aging, 5*(3), 389–409.

Raina, P., Waltner-Toews, D., Bonnett, B., Woodward, C., & Abernathy, T. (1999). Influence of companion animals on the physical and psychological health of older people: an analysis of a one-year longitudinal study. *Journal of the American Geriatric Society, 47* (3), 323–329.

Richeson, N. E. (2003). Effects of animal-assisted therapy on agitated behaviors and social interactions of older adults with dementia. *American Journal of Alzheimer's Disease and Other Dementias, 18*(6), 353–358.

Ruckdeschel, K., & Van Haitsma, K. (2001). The impact of live-in animals and plants on nursing home residents: a pilot longitudinal investigation. *Alzheimer's Care Quarterly, 2* (4), 17–27.

Seeman, T., Singer, B., Rowe, J., Horwitz, R., & McEwen, B. S. (1997). The price of adaptation: allostatic load and its health consequences: the MacArthur Studies of Successful Aging. *Archives of Internal Medicine, 157,* 2259–2268.

Siegel, J. (1990). Stressful life events and use of physician services among the elderly: the moderating role of pet ownership. *Journal of Personality and Social Psychology, 58,* 1081–1086.

Thorpe, R., Simonsick, E. M., Brach, J. S., Ayonayon, H., Satterfield, S., Harris, T. B., Garcia, M., & Kritchevsky, S. B. (2006). Dog ownership, walking behavior, and maintained mobility in late life. *Journal of the American Geriatrics Society, 54*(9), 1419–1424.

16 Increasing the effectiveness of palliative care through integrative modalities: conceptualizing the roles of animal companions and animal-assisted interventions

Perry Skeath*, Aubrey H. Fine†, Ann Berger*

*National Institutes of Health, †California State Polytechnic University

16.1   Introduction

This chapter discusses how palliative care is being extended to relieve the disease symptoms, side effects, and associated burdens that can beset a patient at many points along the course of an illness. The addition of integrative modalities has been particularly helpful in enabling palliative care to be very successfully applied well beyond its historical roots in end-of-life care.

Part one (Extending palliative care through an integrative approach) presents a successful demonstration of how the principles and practices of integrative palliative care can outperform palliative care that lacks integrative modalities in terms of both the range of service provided and the degree of patient satisfaction. We present an example of how a growing number of pain and palliative care services are very successfully incorporating integrative care into their routine practice and delivering better service. This approach has not only given us more tools to perform our service, but has extended our practice far beyond its traditional boundary of end-of-life comfort (as illustrated in the account above) into comprehensive health care starting at the early stages of any serious illness and continuing on through the disease trajectory. The take-home message is that not only can an integrative approach to health care be welcomed and provide very substantial improvements of service within traditional medical settings, but an integrative approach can enable a health care consulting service to expand far beyond its original boundaries.

Part two (Meeting the challenges of research on healing in palliative care) addresses the special challenges facing medical researchers when designing experiments to understand subjective human responses to caring—either from animals, from other humans, or from one's self. What provides the strongest evidence to document the outcomes of animal-assisted intervention (AAI) programs, or palliative care services, or any program aimed at improving people's subjective experience of living? The caring stimulus, the variety of situational factors, and the subjective response are all complex, and the research strategy must be designed to capture complex data. We discuss why combined methodologies—both qualitative and quantitative—provide much stronger evidence from complex data than quantitative assessments alone. Two examples of highly successful research program strategies that made excellent use of both qualitative and quantitative methodologies are described, along with the application of combined methodologies in our current research on psycho-socio-spiritual healing.

Part three (The role of pet companions in supporting persons with chronic disease or terminal illness) discusses in theory and in practice how animal companions and animal-assisted therapy may be applied in palliative care. We describe research and integrative clinical programs that utilize or are relevant to animal companionship or animal-assisted intervention in palliative care. Based on these findings, we suggest ways in which animal companions and animal-assisted intervention may be incorporated into the practice of palliative care.

16.2 Extending palliative care through an integrative approach

Great strides have been made in the treatment of many diseases in recent decades to the extent that virtually half of persons who develop cancer can be cured. While the goal of medical practice is primarily battling the disease itself and the relief of symptoms is a secondary goal, the goal of palliative care is concerned with ameliorating symptoms, relieving suffering, and enhancing quality of life. Whether a disease can be cured—or whether one can hope only management of its progression or for limited remission—the patient most acutely feels the physical, psychosocial, and spiritual symptoms associated with the disease and its treatment. Do we think that the goals of fighting disease and palliative care are disparate? Absolutely not! Supportive or palliative, yes, but of lesser importance? Not to the patient who feels a great burden from a serious illness!

As has always been the case, the patient with chronic or life-threatening disease is often acutely aware of those symptoms that are under the rubric of supportive/palliative care. All too frequently physical symptoms are experienced such as fatigue and anemia, pain, nausea, constipation, oral mucositis, anxiety and depression. Patients experience not only physical symptoms, but also significant psycho-socio-spiritual issues that can weigh heavily on a patient and influence their health. For example, even if a fortunate patient is not currently suffering from symptoms listed above, they may actively fear them. Their fear can exacerbate undesirable symptoms, complicate treatment, and have a detrimental effect on the quality of life of both the patient and the patient's family.

There are many promising new disease treatments—Alzheimer's, cardiovascular, cancer, HIV, to name a few—both in development and on the horizon. No matter what these new treatments will offer in terms of curing the illness or prolonging life, many are likely to retain their reputations as devastating diseases, not only for the affected patients but for their families, the community, and health care providers. One always hopes to cure a patient, but even with cure, one hopes for the patient to be *healed* in the process—to enjoy a more meaningful quality of life. And certainly when a person cannot be cured, one can still die healed—having a sense of wholeness as a person. As health care professionals we often feel a clear responsibility to ensure that the patient with a chronic or life-threatening illness has a chance of being both cured *and* healed! We may not always be able to add days to lives, but we can add life to days.

16.2.1   Healing versus curing—an unnecessary either/or dilemma

Those patients who come to… medical experts for the most advanced treatment of their disease have a right to expect far more than mere technological efforts. There is no inconsistency between the ability to achieve great diagnostic and therapeutic victories and the ability to provide comfort when those victories are beyond reach.

(Nuland, 2000)

(Dan) Frimmer's favorite saying in the last months of his life was, "You can't die cured, but you can die healed." What did he mean? Explained his rabbi, Arnold Gluck: "Healing is about a sense of wholeness as a person, and that wholeness includes understanding our mortality, our place in the world…"

(Rutherford, 2000)

Living in a harmonious and supportive environment is desirable in any part of the lifespan, including the end of life. Palliative care is characterized as care that helps people live fully until they die (see Table 16.1). The World Health Organization (WHO, 2010) defines palliative care as "An approach that improves the quality of life

Table 16.1 Goals of palliative care (WHO, 2005)

1. Provides relief from pain and other distressing symptoms
2. Affirms life and regard dying as a normal process
3. Intends neither to hast nor postpone death
4. Integrates the psychological and spiritual aspects of patient care
5. Offers a support system to help patients live as actively as possible until death
6. Offers a support system to help the family cope during the patient's illness and in their own bereavement
7. Uses a team approach to address the needs of patients and their families, including bereavement counseling, if indicated
8. Will enhance quality of life, and may also positively influence the course of the illness
9. Is applicable early in the course of illness, in conjunction with other therapies that are intended to prolong life, such as chemotherapy or radiation therapy, and includes those investigations needed to better understand and manage distressing clinical complications

of patients and their families facing the problem associated with life-threatening illness, through the prevention and relief of suffering by means of early identification and impeccable assessment and treatment of pain and other problems, physical, psychosocial, and spiritual." According to the National Hospice and Palliative Care Organization (2010), palliative care extends the principles of hospice care so that a broader population of people can receive beneficial care earlier in their disease process prior to the last six months of life when hospice typically begins. In addition to enhancing the quality of life, applying palliative care early in the course of illness in conjunction with other therapies may also positively influence the trajectory of the patient's illness.

Since the introduction of end-of-life hospice/palliative care in the USA, its delivery to patients (and their families) has typically been subject to the bureaucratic restrictions of Medicare reimbursement regulations and life expectancy projections. The choice of medical services is often seen in "either/or" terms: "either" aggressive treatment (often fragmented) attempting to cure, "or" integrative interdisciplinary comfort care *only after* all curative efforts have failed.

Why not deliver both attempts (to cure and to comfort) at the same time? Both research and clinical literature report high patient and caregiver satisfaction with the interdisciplinary, integrative approach—not only in end-of-life care but in symptom management at all phases of health care. However, in most settings there are restrictions on the delivery of health care services that result in reimbursement for the interdisciplinary, integrative approach not being allowed until curative efforts have stopped. Statistics reveal that this situation has significantly impacted willingness to utilize this scope of service, since it imposes on patients an "either/or" financial decision that often compromises their need to obtain comfort and retain hope for a possibly prolonged prognosis or even a cure.

All health care providers have the ethical responsibility to "first do no harm." This includes alleviating the burden of the patient's dilemma—having to choose between aggressive treatment or comfort care. Supporting a patient's need for hope, their need for healing, their need for a sense of wholeness—these are so vital to a humane practice of medicine. Humanism in health care can be initiated by incorporating the proven principles learned by clinical experience in palliative care (a very successful model of integrative care) into mainstream general practice and across all specialty settings. Valuing the comfort and healing of a patient should not wait until the end of life. It should be implemented from the onset of a chronic disease diagnosis, fitting in quite naturally with the management of chronic pain. It should be continued throughout every day that the patient lives with the illness—just as aggressively as the efforts made to cure the patient.

Patients require both "high tech" and "high touch" care throughout their disease trajectory and sometimes beyond. The integrative, multidimensional, interdisciplinary approaches used in palliative care (or, more broadly, supportive care) can meet the patient's clinical, scientific, and functional needs with compassion. By utilizing the principles of palliative care, including the back-to-basics of "bedside care" approach to treating individuals with chronic pain, a patient with pain may or may not be cured yet he/she can have the resources that fully support his/her healing.

16.2.2 What should be regarded and treated as chronic pain?

Pain is a huge quality of life issue. Its prevalence and inadequate control is well documented in patients with cancer pain as well as in patients with chronic pain not related to cancer. There are many consequences of pain: depression, decreased socialization, increased agitation, impaired mobility, slowed rehabilitation, malnutrition, sleep disturbances, more visits to the doctor and hospital, and others.

Pain is a mental experience that can have a wide range of significance within a patient's medical condition. The total pain experienced by a patient is made up of more than just physical pain (see Figure 16.1). Total pain can involve a physical component as well as a suffering component. Suffering includes psychological and coping factors, social support, loss issues, fear of death, financial concerns, and spiritual concerns (such as the understanding and meaning of this difficult part of a patient's life). Understandably, most patients with chronic pain have both physical pain and suffering.

Optimally, a team of care providers should be involved as needed to help relieve suffering. Most notably the team should include doctors and nurses who are familiar with pharmacological approaches to pain relief as well as those who work with non-pharmacologic approaches to relieving pain, such as social workers, pet therapists, spiritual care counselors, recreation therapists, art therapists, body work therapists (e.g. massage and Reiki therapists), music therapists, and volunteers (including family and friends). To treat total pain, pharmacologic and/or invasive approaches are needed to relieve physical symptoms and non-pharmacologic approaches are needed to relieve suffering.

Following the World Health Organization (WHO) guidelines for pain relief significantly reduces the severity of pain but it is clear that the published guidelines are not being followed. Many scientific research studies have made it clear that our society needs to make major changes in the way we recognize and treat different forms of pain. Recently, the Joint Commission on Accreditation of Healthcare Organizations (JCAHO) has required that all hospitals and nursing homes assess pain as a fifth vital sign, on par with blood pressure or pulse. The inability to relieve pain, even when we have the tools to do so, suggests that professional and patient education has been inadequate.

16.2.3 A provocative care structure that works

Care more particularly about the patient than for the special features of the disease.
(Sir William Osler) (Madison, 1997)

People who are dealing with any chronic illness, including chronic pain, experience various degrees of suffering. The way people deal with their suffering is mostly influenced by their own inner resources: their personality, coping styles, cultural background, and their personal meaning of life (Frankl, 1984). While pain has been described in the literature for centuries, it has been one of medicine's greatest mysteries. It still remains a challenge for health care professionals to provide the best

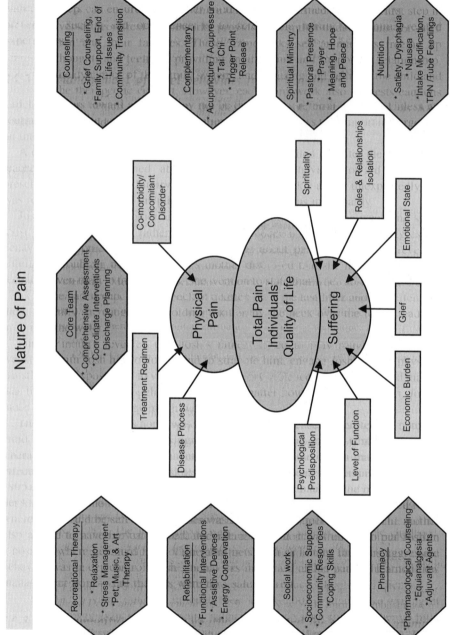

Figure 16.1 Total pain experienced by a patient

of care for the patient and his/her family. To treat suffering, we try to nudge the patient's inner resources—much more through personal caring than through the impersonal procedures of illness treatment—to take them in the direction of healing. Whether it is through the patient's own pets or through animal-assisted intervention (AAI), appropriate animals can strongly convey the caring that is so fundamental to opening the patient's inner avenues of healing.

Several approaches are necessary to treat patients with chronic pain and alleviate suffering. First and foremost, we as health care providers need to recognize that we need to drop the barriers of our respective roles in order to communicate effectively with our patients on the human level of both caring and suffering. We need to understand that we are not all that different from our patients and that we, too, can have chronic pain and can understand their suffering. Of course, those barriers are often much less of an issue with pets. Second, we need to enter the patient and family system, comfortably, so that suffering can be understood and taken in the right context. Third, it is essential to validate the various feelings and emotions experienced by the patients as well as their family members as normal when facing a challenging situation such as chronic pain. Pets and animals can often bring out feelings in a patient, and thus make it easier for human care givers to validate and reinforce those positive feelings.

Palliative care and supportive care should involve the collaborative efforts of an interdisciplinary team. This team must include the patient with a chronic or life-threatening illness, his or her family, caregivers, as well as the group of involved health care providers. "Out of the box" creativity can be used as a provocative and wonderfully constructive structure within an integrative, palliative care model of relieving chronic pain. Recent advances in complementary, behavioral and pharmacologic therapies call for a renaissance in pain and palliative care medicine. The integrative, palliative care model is a holistic view with the patient and family always in the forefront. As an example, serving "high tea" (typifying tea for royalty) creates a comfortable milieu for the patient to shift away from suffering and share a happier, more desirable moment with family, friends and health caregivers. This offers a setting to converse, verbalize wishes and concerns or reminisce. Always remembering flexibility and hospitality for patients, families and other health care providers will help to break down sterile barriers and lighten the intensity level. We use team theme days such as "sun-fun," "mardi gras," signature hats and boas as a diversion patients welcome from white coat attire. Spontaneous celebrations of life such as setting the TV channel to a game played by an inpatient's favorite football team, or sending an outpatient to a performance by his/her favorite musician, have reminded patients that their life is more than suffering.

16.3   Meeting the challenges of research on healing in palliative care

16.3.1   The need for strengthening evidence in psychosocial research

Behavioral research increasingly involves assessment of phenomena that are influenced by multiple dimensions: psychological, social, spiritual, and physical. A good example is the measurement of pain. The consensus among members of the Initiative on Methods, Measurement, and Pain Assessment in Clinical Trials (IMMPACT) is that six core domains should be considered in chronic pain clinical trials (Turk et al., 2003): (1) pain, (2) physical functioning, (3) emotional functioning, (4) participant ratings of improvement and satisfaction with treatment, (5) symptoms and adverse events, and (6) participant disposition. The large oval in the upper part of Figure 16.2 represents the set of all features of the target phenomenon (e.g. pain), the smaller internal ovals represent features within the phenomenon (e.g. subjective experience of pain, physical functioning, emotional functioning).

Quantitative assessments enable the use of scales for precise comparisons. However, phenomena, features, structures, ranges and interactions are fundamentally identified and described in terms of qualities or properties. Therefore qualitative description is the core of any theory of a psycho-socio-spiritual phenomenon. The remainder of this section on meeting the challenge of research on healing in palliative

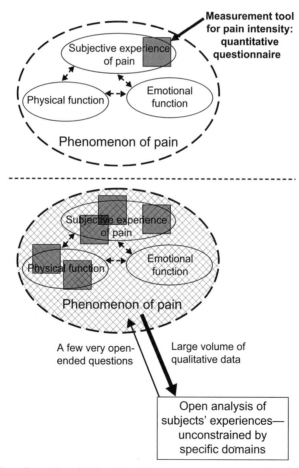

Figure 16.2 Core dimensions in chronic pain

care is concerned with some specifics of why and how to strengthen empirical evidence by combining qualitative and quantitative methodologies.

Quantitative assessment questionnaires (instruments or tools) and the items within them are typically associated with specific constructs. The ability to discriminate construct from non-construct (discriminant validity) gives the instrument specificity and meaning. However, this generally means that an existing, well-validated tool does not completely cover the phenomenon of interest. The challenge is apparent in Figure 16.2 (upper part): a typical quantitative tool can provide substantial strength of evidence for a feature (e.g. pain intensity) within its focus (e.g. the subjective experience of pain) but much of the target phenomenon of pain can be omitted. Depending on the nature of the pain (sharp and localized vs. non-specific; unvarying vs. widely varying), the nature of the patient's illness (acute vs. chronic or even life-long), and on the relationship between physical pain and physical activity and emotional experiences, some patients have difficulty assigning a single position on a scale or a single number to their pain intensity. The problem of incomplete coverage is compounded because even the best of quantitative pain intensity measures is silent about what pain features and descriptors it has not captured, and no degree of statistical control in a quantitative study design will avoid silent omissions.

A study using a multi-assessment approach is designed to have greater strength of evidence than a study using a single tool, all other factors being equal (see lower part of Figure 16.2). However, there is still the problem that even the best group of standard, validated quantitative measures will be silent about any omitted features and interactions (e.g. pain intensity and emotional function). If the target phenomenon has any insufficiently explored or unique features (often the very thing that makes the phenomenon of interest to the researcher), the assessment obtained by the multi-assessment approach is not sure to uncover them.

16.3.2   Including open examination of a target phenomenon

An open examination of all discernible features of a phenomenon can substantially help identify any insufficiently explored or unanticipated features. Open examination aims to capture the entire range of first-hand experience that can be reported by the research subjects. This generally adds to the strength of any study, from a small isolated study to a large research program.

Not surprisingly, open examination is likely to involve a distinctly different methodology than that used for hypothesis testing. Qualitative methods are particularly appropriate when the research focus is on ensuring that we know the *process* of a phenomenon and not on a measurement of the *outcome* (Smith, 1996). In reflecting on her very substantial experience with performing well-recognized quantitative and qualitative studies, Beck (1997) comments, "... their vision of their research program should not be blinded by their lack of expertise in particular research methods ... the investigator may need to cross over from inductive to deductive methods or vice versa at certain points in the research trajectory." As a brief introduction to the tools of qualitative research, Beck describes six of the most common qualitative research designs and includes some examples from her own research to illustrate them (Beck, 2009).

The schematic diagram in the lower part of Figure 16.2 illustrates the complementary roles of these two sets of tools. The solid black rectangles represent well-validated quantitative assessment tools. The span of the target phenomenon's feature set can be more fully covered by qualitative open examination (cross-hatched area). One of the great advantages of open qualitative data (e.g. narrative data) is that the researcher is not required to have prior knowledge or understanding of the features of the phenomena that may be evidenced in the narrative data. It is the complementary situation to quantitative assessment, for which the responses must always be pre-determined through expert understanding. Inclusion of qualitative data in a study as a major component alongside quantitative data and analysis can also provide well-grounded corroborating evidence. This is represented by the areas in Figure 16.2 where quantitative (solid black rectangles) and qualitative analyses (cross-hatched entire domain of pain) overlap with each other. Some key features of combined research programs are summarized in Table 16.2.

16.3.3   Comparing basic features of qualitative and quantitative research

Combined research programs not only gather both quantitative and qualitative data, they also perform both quantitative and qualitative analyses. An understanding of their differences in analyses helps the research team gain the full advantages of both. The primary objective may be to achieve a comprehensive phenomenological model that is empirically grounded (generated only from the interview data itself), that is complete (contains all aspects of the phenomenon), that is self-consistent (all the parts fit together), and that forms a well-delineated construct (minimal ambiguity about where the construct of interest is bounded with respect to other constructs). Categorization of qualitative data is a systematic discovery process that is somewhat analogous to putting together a complete picture (the desired model) from jigsaw puzzle pieces (coded data) coming from several puzzle boxes (different constructs in

Table 16.2 Strengthening evidence by combined studies

Quantitative only	Combined: Quantitative + Qualitative
Multiple quantitative assessment instruments	Overlap of qualitative data with quantitative data adds corroboration obtained by independent methodology
Silent omission of features not targeted by multiple assessment tools	Open examination can capture features for which there is no measurement tool (e.g. phenomenological study)
Partial capture of model dynamics in uncontrolled settings	Open examination can capture dynamics for which there is no measurement tool (e.g. grounded theory study)
Uncontrolled settings contribute to limitations of study	Additional empirical data provide more information and may reduce limitations of study

the subject's experience: healing, coping, etc.). As pieces are individually fitted together, objects in the picture (categories) start to become recognizable (left side of Figure 16.3). These recognizable objects in the picture (categories) can then speed up assembly. Some of the pieces are duplicates, and they are kept as reinforcements. Other pieces may belong to another picture. Their inconsistencies with respect to the picture need to be recognized, and they need to be saved in the appropriate box (not discarded) rather than trying to force those pieces into the picture (ignoring inconsistencies, or mixing constructs). As the puzzle is assembled, one constantly checks for missing pieces (gaps in the model)—the picture is not complete until there are no holes or irregular edges. In the end, it is much more the recognizable objects (categories) than the shape of the individual pieces (coded data) that make the picture (the model).

The number of individual interview and analysis processes is sufficient when category saturation has occurred. Category saturation means that the data from the most recent subjects are not generating new categories of experience or substantively adding to the model (right side of Figure 16.3). In this diagram, white space represents undiscovered qualitative categories, gray patterned squares represent partially-filled distinct categories, and black-and-white patterned squares represent filled distinct categories. The diagram also illustrates that inconsistent categories (ones that belong to another construct) are removed or replaced as the model is developed iteratively.

Recognizing valid empirical categories, inconsistencies and gaps in the model are all critical aspects of the analysis. This is one reason why qualitative analysts perform immediate analysis of interviews as they are performed (individual interview and analysis processes), so that the selection of the next subject can be guided by the further information they need to complete the picture or model. Performance of qualitative analysis and model revision after each interview is a very useful design feature from grounded theory methodology (Charmaz, 2006). Concurrent qualitative data acquisition and analysis can take the form of a cycle for each individual subject consisting of an individual subject session, qualitative analysis, conclusions, revisions, and planning for next subject (purposeful selection for the sake of data completeness and study validity). The analysis benefits from a high degree of familiarity and insight with respect to the phenomenon of interest (just as a quantitative investigator needs these to design and carry out valid quantitative experiments),

Qualitative Model Development

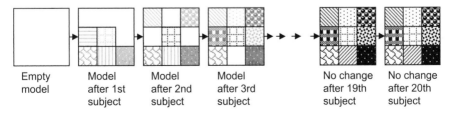

| Empty model | Model after 1st subject | Model after 2nd subject | Model after 3rd subject | No change after 19th subject | No change after 20th subject |

Figure 16.3 Qualitative model development

yet also requires an ability to put one's own experience, ideas, and even the theories of one's field of expertise into the background.

Patient interviews are a typical primary source of empirical data in a multiple-methodology research plan. The purpose of an open qualitative interview may be to generate a deep conceptual grasp of the target construct, whereas the purpose of a closed quantitative interview may be to make a specific measurement or assessment. Both types of interviews may be conducted sequentially in the same research session with a subject, often with the open qualitative interview first so as not to prime the subject with the content of the quantitative assessments.

Utilizing both forms of interview enables a research team to see the target phenomenon from different sides. Selection in phenomenological research is aimed at finding subjects whose collective first-hand experience most fully and authentically represents the phenomenon of interest (Wertz, 2005). An open interview aims to elicit each subject's concrete experiences—including unanticipated features of the phenomenon—rather than interpretations, opinions or beliefs. The corresponding analysis goes well beyond mere content analysis into interpretation, and its validity depends on remaining fully grounded in the subjects' data. The closed quantitative assessment represents much more focused measurements framed by an expert's perspective (e.g. current theory of established constructs). Thus the contents of the two forms of interview are substantially different yet highly complementary views of the same target phenomenon (see Table 16.3). Ways to reconcile these differences will be seen in the following two examples of research programs that have very successfully combined quantitative and open qualitative methodologies to strengthen their evidence.

16.3.4 Beck's research on postpartum depression

Rather than just adding to the proliferation of assessment tools, a more definitive instrument can be developed through well-planned qualitative and quantitative coordination. As an example, a combined qualitative and quantitative research program

Table 16.3 Comparing subject selection and enrollment

Quantitative	Qualitative
Randomize subjects into groups for the sake of test validity	Hand pick the subjects most likely to yield data to flesh out the model, or use convenience sampling
Subject selection is separate from data acquisition, and both are separate from data analysis	It is advantageous to base selection of each subject on the analysis results from all previous subjects
Enrollment in a quantitative study is governed by the desired statistical power, and the number of subjects is set before the study begins	Enrollment is continued until category saturation has occurred—the number of subjects is not determined until saturation has occurred

begun in the mid-1990s by Cheryl Tatano Beck developed both a comprehensive understanding of postpartum depression (PPD) and widely used clinical tools for predicting, measuring and providing relief from PPD (Lasiuk, 2005).

Prior to Beck's research, postpartum depression was assessed using standard inventories of general depression. Her first experimental study examined the relationship between maternity blues and postpartum depression (Beck et al., 1992), using two standard quantitative tools: the Stein Maternity Blues Scale and Beck Depression Inventory (BDI; developed by Aaron T. Beck et al., 1988). Apparently C. T. Beck was sufficiently aware of what the subjects in her study were experiencing (informal qualitative data) to suspect that the BDI was not capturing the full scope of experiences or symptoms of depression that were occurring in the target population. The situation is the same as depicted in the upper part of Figure 16.2.

She was also well versed in the maternal-newborn research literature (Beck, 1989, 1991a, 1991b), and realized that there were no phenomenological research studies in the literature. Postpartum depression was at a nascent stage of development. A nascent construct does not have an established theoretical framework or phenomenology to guide the selection and application of quantitative research tools. This meant that there was no way to assess how well the BDI instrument was matched to the phenomenology of PPD—an empirically well-grounded list of experiential or symptomatic themes.

At this point, Beck made the first critical choice among several options that led her research to becoming definitive instead of incremental. One option was to accept the BDI assessment as perhaps incomplete yet sufficient to accomplish the requirement of a quantitative assessment of depression. A second option was to do further study using a variety of measures of depression. Beck (1997) chose a third option to obtain the needed coverage, which was to switch completely from a quantitative study to a qualitative one: a phenomenological study of PPD. This was the option with the greatest opportunity to capture the full picture of PPD. It is an inquiry that is open-by-design to all that may be part of that full picture. A well-performed phenomenological study provides an empirically grounded list of features that may be compared to the questionnaire items in related assessment tools. This comparison provided the first strong indications of the degree of coverage of PPD provided by each available assessment tool.

Following the phenomenological study she performed a grounded theory study to identify and understand the stages in the progression of PPD—the trajectories or pathways that women tended to follow through the course of PPD. Once she had both the features of PPD and its stages, Beck was in a good position to pursue further studies that could develop quantitative screening tools for PPD. Table 16.4 (after Beck, 1997) lists some key steps by which Beck produced two definitive quantitative measures: one for assessing the potential for PPD in a patient's future, and one for screening patients to detect active PPD.

The design of a phenomenological study is to start with an open-ended question (e.g. "What are the categories or themes of experience of women who have PPD?") and then fill in the picture by collecting, thoroughly considering, and sorting elements of the experiences of different women who have PPD. It is not first to make an

Table 16.4 Quantitative and qualitative steps in Beck's postpartum depression research program

Quantitative	Qualitative
Literature review (1991b) "Maternity blues research: a critical review."	
Do existing quantitative tools capture the PPD phenomenon? (1992a) "Maternity blues and postpartum depression."	
	Phenomenology—what are the categories of experience in PPD? (1992b) "The lived experience of postpartum depression: a phenomenological study."
	Grounded theory—how does PPD begin and progress? (1993) "Teetering on the edge: a substantive theory of postpartum depression."
Screening tool development (1995) "Screening methods for postpartum depression."	
Screening tool development (2000; with R. K. Gable) "Postpartum depression screening scale: development and psychometric testing."	
Screening tool development (2001; with R. K. Gable) "Comparative analysis ... PPD screening scale with two other depression instruments."	
	Metasynthesis of qualitative PPD theory (2002) "Postpartum depression: a metasynthesis."

educated guess about those categories of experience, and then test whether the women have those categories—that may simply be another closed experiment that is silent about whether features of PPD are being missed. The silence about omitted features can be substantially reduced by letting the subjects' narratives (the voices of actual experience) be the source of information.

When circumstances favor combined data acquisition rather than separate qualitative and quantitative studies, even a single combined data acquisition can identify new features and substantially strengthen the evidence compared to a study only utilizing quantitative data. Folkman's work is an example of this.

16.3.5 Folkman's combined research on caregiver coping in the AIDS epidemic

PPD may be viewed as a unitary construct representing a relatively well-delimited challenge. In contrast, coping refers to all the various types of "cognitive and behavioral efforts to master, reduce, or tolerate the internal and/or external demands that are created by the stressful situation" (Folkman, 1984). Coping refers to a general process that has a number of pathways (Folkman, 1997), and it also refers to various "ways of coping" (Folkman and Lazarus, 1980) and may be employed along pathways within that general process—the *process* of coping is not the same as the *ways* of coping. An individual may dynamically switch from one distinct *way* of coping to another or combine ways of coping (Folkman and Lazarus, 1985) without switching their *process* pathway. Coping has therefore been called a category construct and multidimensional, but even these descriptors may fail to convey all that is grouped under the term coping. This complex structure makes coping research a natural candidate for combined quantitative-qualitative study designs.

We will focus on Folkman's work to further elucidate a model of coping *beyond* what Carver et al. (1989) have called the landmark contribution of the Ways of Coping questionnaire and its eight empirically constructed scales (confrontive, distancing, self-controlling, seeking social support, accepting responsibility, escape-avoidance, planful problem-solving, and positive reappraisal). The original eight scales were viewed in terms of two categories: emotion-focused coping and problem-focused coping. In this example (covering a period of more than two decades after Ways of Coping was released), Folkman used some of the combined qualitative-quantitative research program features seen in Beck's work to arrive at a major revision of the Transactional Model for the general process of coping. At the same time, there are important differences between Folkman's and Beck's approaches which are highly instructive.

Folkman et al. (1992, 1994) had the opportunity to study personal caregivers during the AIDS epidemic in San Francisco before anti-retroviral therapy—a substantially unique and limited time period of high stress in the subject population's relevant history—as part of the UCSF Coping Project. She knew from prior experience what data (both qualitative and quantitative) would be useful to gather in a highly stressed population, yet based on preliminary qualitative input from some of her subjects (Folkman et al., 1994; Folkman, 2009) she also incorporated additional probes for *positive* outcomes (both quantitative measures and qualitative interview questions) in this highly stressed population (see Figure 16.4). It was the data from those additional probes that led to an unexpected discovery and a major revision of the theoretical framework for coping (Folkman, 2009).

In the UCSF Coping Project, a large number of qualitative interviews were conducted before substantive analysis was begun. Folkman therefore lost one advantage

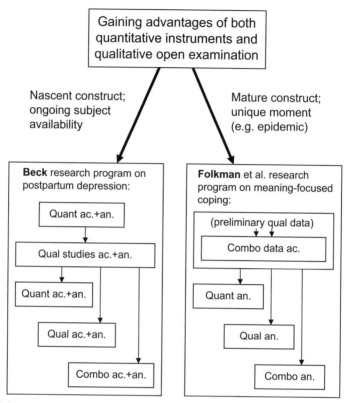

Figure 16.4

of a combination research program by sacrificing simultaneous qualitative data acquisition and analysis. However, she was able to compensate for this by gathering qualitative data from all subjects in the quantitative portion of the study—a far greater number of subjects than would be interviewed in a typical qualitative study. Folkman and coworkers could then perform qualitative analysis studies and combination studies by using a modified "purposeful selection," or apply other selection criteria from within the large number of subjects who were interviewed. (If one takes large volumes of narrative data from large numbers of subjects selected at random, it is typically unrealistic to expect the research team to do a labor-intensive phrase-by-phrase coding analysis on the narrative data from all subjects.)

Results of these complementary methodologies produced two major revisions in Folkman's Transactional Model (Folkman, 1997, 2009). One is the addition of a third category, meaning-focused coping, having four scales: dwelling on what makes some moments positive, goal revision, reflecting on deeply held values, and benefit-finding. Meaning-focused coping was added to address what Folkman calls a "coping gap"— an omission from the original coping model. The *content* of these four scales comes primarily from qualitative data and analysis. Folkman's use of a combined qualitative-quantitative design was necessary for the identification and definition of these scales.

The other addition to the model is the co-occurrence of positive and negative affect in coping, with positive emotions based on underlying meaning. Folkman designed the caregiver coping research program to assess positive and negative affect both qualitatively and quantitatively. Either methodology (qualitative or quantitative) was sufficient by itself to determine that positive and negative affect were occurring together in the same individual. When both methodologies pointed to the same phenomenon, it strengthened the evidence. In addition, the qualitative data gathered by Folkman's research team gave the strongest evidence of the link between meaning and positive affect: that positive emotions were possible because of the underlying meaning that the subjects found in highly difficult circumstances.

Recognition of meaning within coping theory precedes the development of Ways of Coping in the theories of several workers. Meaning is implicit in Richard Lazarus' central concept of appraisal (Lazarus, 1966). Bandura (1977) included discussion of the role of meaning in his theory of behavioral change. Pearlin and Schooler (1978) identified three main components of protection from stress in his theory of coping: problem-management, controlling meaning, and emotional management. Folkman (2009) used complementary data and analyses to generate stronger evidence that could demonstrate experimentally and explain theoretically how meaning is not just an element of coping, but is at the basis of durable positive outcomes (e.g. maintaining well-being) in the midst of major long-term challenges (e.g. bearing the burdens of serious chronic disease).

To summarize, qualitative data and analyses played several important roles in Folkman's study of personal caregivers during the AIDS epidemic. First, preliminary qualitative data provided guidance regarding the unexpected co-occurrence of positive and negative outcomes. Second, the results from qualitative and quantitative analyses yielded substantive corroboration for each other. Third, the qualitative data were key in the interpretation of quantitative results, and led to an important revision of Folkman's coping model and also new ways of coping (qualitative phenomenology).

16.3.6 *Psycho-socio-spiritual healing in palliative care—design of a combined research program*

Psycho-socio-spiritual healing (PSS healing) in the context of chronic or life-threatening illness is a patient-reported outcome consisting of growth or benefit in psychological, social and/or spiritual dimensions *representing improvement well above the patient's pre-morbidity baseline*. Empirical observation by clinical staff of the Pain and Palliative Care Service (PPCS) at the NIH Clinical Center and other palliative care providers has often demonstrated that there are some patients who progress beyond the experiences of trauma, coping and acceptance. Health care providers report that in some way patients can feel changed for the better or stronger mentally compared to the way they were before their disease was diagnosed. This phenomenon of patients ending up stronger mentally than they were before the onset of their illness has most often been called "healing" in palliative care. Health care providers also report that the phenomenon has apparent psychological, social, and spiritual dimensions, therefore we are presently referring to it as "psycho-socio-spiritual healing" or "PSS healing."

Increased incidence and efficacy of PSS healing could reduce suffering and enhance the quality of life of palliative care patients, who often face intense emotional as well as physical challenges of a chronic or life-threatening illness. The feature of becoming "better than before" psychologically, sociologically, or spiritually is a key criterion in this concept of healing. This positive outcome often occurs despite substantial suffering during the illness, and is observed in cases with terminal outcome as well as those patients who experience cure or remission (Kearney, 2000).

The following deficiencies limit the practical application of PSS healing, and have motivated this research program:

1. Well-validated outcome measures of PSS healing are not presently available.
2. The descriptions of PSS healing in the health care literature have not been structured in categories that enable quantitative measures to be developed from them, despite hundreds of good-quality phenomenological studies (suffering, healing, quality of life, etc.) of patients who have chronic or life-threatening illness.
3. The relationship of PSS healing to other psychometrically measurable constructs such as post-traumatic growth, resilience, coping, and acceptance is not yet clear. One of the main tasks of research on healing is to determine which features of PSS healing are unique, and which are adequately captured by existing assessment tools of other constructs. For example, the co-occurrence of positive and negative affect has long been known anecdotally as one of the indicators of healing in palliative care (Saunders, 1977), but, more recently, Folkman (1997) has interpreted similar phenomena as "meaning-focused coping." Furthermore, Tedeschi (1996) has interpreted similar phenomena as "post-traumatic growth."
4. Several grounded-theory (Charmaz, 2006) descriptions of the process of PSS healing have been published (Denz-Penhey and Murdoch, 2008; Fleury, 1995; Koithan et al., 2007; Landmark and Wahl, 2002; Swatton and O'Callaghan, 1999) yet there is no widely accepted theory of PSS healing: how and why it happens.
5. Although supportive care is well known to reduce obstacles to PSS healing, the process of PSS healing is substantially unmeasured and uncontrolled in clinical practice (Kearney, 2000).

PSS healing is a nascent construct—it does not have a widely accepted theoretical framework or specific phenomenology to guide the selection and application of quantitative research tools. Therefore, it is appropriate to follow the research program design of Beck. However, PSS healing may involve not only a process but also a number of different ways of healing that may be active within that single fundamental process, much like coping. Therefore, it may be appropriate to incorporate some features of Folkman's research design.

The first protocol in our PSS healing research program has a qualitative, open-examination design. NIH IRB approval was obtained for the current protocol, and as of this writing, the study is actively under way. The study is retrospective, using an eligibility criterion requiring that PSS healing must be established for at least six months. A specific aim of this protocol is to provide a taxonomy of PSS healing that is structured in phenomenological categories suitable for the development of a quantitative psychometric instrument to measure PSS healing in the context of life-threatening or chronic illness. We expect to incorporate both quantitative and qualitative methodologies during each of the development stages for the sake of developing a clinically meaningful and robust instrument.

16.4 The role of pet companions and animal-assisted interventions in supporting persons with chronic and terminal illnesses

Straub (2007) highlights that one of the strongest aspects of social supports is the emotional concerns that seemed to get conveyed. This is often observed in homes where a pet companion is intricately involved in the family. For example, animals often provide their human family members with loving greetings when they come home and often shower them with attention throughout the day. In regards to people with illnesses, McNicholas et al. (2003) identify that relationships with pets seem to have a positive impact in coping with the early stages of bereavement as well as after the treatment for breast cancer. They conclude by noting that, although support from an animal should not be considered as a sole alternative to help received from other people, pets have some certain advantages and are more likely to demonstrate consistency in their relationship.

Pets are also often used by people of various ages as a strong outlet for feelings and emotional refuge (Fine and Eisen, 2008; Melson, 2001). It is not uncommon to hear of people who feel isolated to turn to their animals for company as well as an excuse to leave the house. In Bill's case, his devotion to his cats has helped him cope with living in isolation. Bill (not his real name) has been battling AIDS for several years. In a recent interview with one of the writers, Bill confesses his cats were his major source of company in his life. He stated: "They pick up on my feelings of loneliness and comfort me in a way I could not imagine. When they know I am sad, they are more attentive to me; almost to the point of annoyance because they won't leave me alone. I somehow find a spiritual connection with them; the process of petting them and taking care of them allows me to take a break from my own mental anguish. Many times I sing with them and find this as an outlet to relieve some of my anxiety." In many ways the cats seem to inoculate him for his debilitation and provide him with outlet of joy. Schwarzer and Leppin (1991) hypothesized that positive social supports may inoculate people from the negative impacts of stressors, such as the loneliness just described in this previous case example.

Straub (2007) argues that people who perceive a high level of social support may experience less stress and cope more effectively, even in times of great need. He reported that social supports have been attributed as promoting faster recovery in people from numerous illnesses including childhood leukemia, strokes and rheumatoid arthritis. Research by Spiegel and Kato (1996) would agree with this finding. Their research highlighted that patients with cancer with the fewest contacts each day were 2.2 times more likely to die of cancer over a 17-year period than those with greater social support. Bryant (2008) proposes that most humans seek out social support to help them adapt to difficult situations. She believes that social supports are an important foundation for healthy functioning and that pet companionship needs to be considered as an excellent alternative for people.

The authors are in absolute agreement. It is critical to conceptualize and recognize the importance that an animal may have or had in the life of a person coping with his/her illness. Pets may often symbolically represent some aspect of the person's life experience or need (McNac, Personal conversation, Aug. 16, 2009). For example, personal pets may be representative of a past relationship, where the animal was obtained during a time in the individual's life that is remembered as a source of comfort and happiness. Pets can also represent children or grandchildren that the individual never had or does not have access to on a continual basis. For some, pets seem to represent some aspect of their personality or fear, as in persons who adopt and nurture an animal who has been rejected or abandoned because of its age, appearance, or behavior. Understanding the potential of symbolism in a relationship with pets can serve as an extension of an individual's ability to choose how to live and who to love. As the end of life approaches, many people lose more and more of their autonomy as they become increasingly dependent on caregivers. When these individuals have a strong attachment to their pets and a deep symbolic meaning to those relationships, removal of their beloved pet from their presence can trigger a deep grief reaction or separate them from the very comfort and companionship they need most. Ultimately, the professional community needs to understand that, for some people, the animals in their lives are every bit as important as other family members' support on their end-of-life journey.

There are several hypotheses that explain how social supports benefit our health. The buffering hypothesis promotes the notion that social supports mitigate stress indirectly by helping us cope more efficiently (Straub, 2007). On the other hand, the direct effect hypothesis suggests that social supports produce beneficial effects in both stressful and non-stressful times by enhancing the body's responses. Perhaps social supports provide people with greater immunity and resistance to health and psychological challenges. Nevertheless, too much of anything may not be helpful and may actually increase a person's stress (Straub, 2007). For example, sometimes getting too much advice and support, especially differing ideas, may become counterproductive.

16.4.1   Quality of life and the roles of animals

The authors would argue that personal pets and animal companionship may be one positive source that could enhance an individual's quality of life when either battling or accepting a terminal illness. A case in point would be the findings from the Muschel (1984) study that examined the effects of an animal contact program on a group of patients with terminal cancer. The study involved 15 patients taking part in a 10-week, 90-minute weekly session with visiting dogs. The results of the study significantly showed that the contact with the visiting dogs decreased anxiety and despair in the individuals. McCabe et al. (2002) also demonstrated similar findings that highlighted the psycho-social impact of visiting therapy dogs to a nursing home for people with Alzheimer's. The results showed that the long-term presence of the dog boosted social behaviors of the patients and decreased their agitation.

Dr. Edward Creagan (2002), a professor of medical oncology at the Mayo Clinic, argues that there is an indisputable mind/body connection that is anchored by pets. He believes that pets create a balance between one's mind and body. He stated while presenting at the PAWSITIVE INTERACTIONS Conference that "I prescribe pets to a third of my cancer patients to help them cope with the rigors of their terrible disease. I consider getting a pet to be one of the easiest and most rewarding ways of living a longer, healthier life" (Creagan, 2002).

Phear (1996) prepared a report that surveyed the attitudes to companion animals in a day hospice in the United Kingdom. The primary purpose of the study was to determine how important companion animals were in the lives of the terminally ill as well as how animals contributed in palliative care. The report suggested that all hospice patients enjoyed the companionship and interaction from visiting animals. Within the report, Phear (1996) noted that 77% of hospices in the United Kingdom showed a strong interest in having companion animal visits. Almost 89% of the hospices had resident animals—mostly fish and cats. Close to 40% of the hospices had visiting dog programs. The staff concurred with the value of the animals and believed that the visits helped relax the patients with the benefits of touching and petting them. Phear (1996) concluded that one of the strongest benefits derived from the animals was the fact that the animal was an attentive audience to individual patients and provided the needed affection.

In another exploratory study in the early 1990s, Chinner and Dalzeil (1991) pointed out that the use of a therapy dog in a hospice setting appeared to enhance the patient – staff relationship and enhanced the morale of the living environment. Chinner and Dalzeil (1991) also observed that the dog had a relaxing and comforting effect on the patients. Nevertheless, they did report that those patients who felt isolated or alone had less affection for the therapy animal. Chinner and Dalzeil (1991) believed that this outcome could occur because of the distancing reaction which is a common mechanism for those particular patients who were struggling with their coping with death. This finding could be an important consideration for AAI in palliative units in considering which patients may be the most amenable to the intervention. However, caution is also given to recognize that, for some clients, there may be other factors which rekindle their drive for life and indirectly leave them feeling more hopeful.

16.4.2   Bronfenbrenner's eco-system model of support

The authors have considered many models in an attempt to describe how companion animals and animal-assisted activities can be understood as an important dimension of support. A theoretical "eco-system" model developed by Bronfenbrenner (1989) seems applicable in describing the support mechanisms that people use for overcoming the stresses of having a chronic and/or terminal illness (see Figure 16.5). This model consists of a series of nested contexts called a microsystem, exosystem and macrosystem. The original model has been utilized to describe many significant challenges confronting families, including divorce, and child abuse (Belsky, 1980).

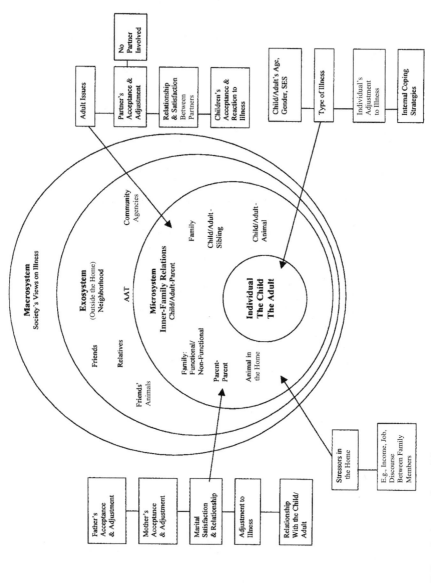

Figure 16.5 Bronfenbrenner's model

This model views a person's life as a social unit embedded within various formal and informal social units (Shea and Bauer, 1991).

Bronfenbrenner's model explains behavior similarly to the way a naturalist would view nature. An individual's ecosystem may be visualized as a series of layers that are all connected. The most central layer is what he called the microsystem. This system incorporates all the variables that either can support or contaminate the growth of an individual within his or her home. A child or adult who has a functioning support system at home may adapt more effectively to his/her illness. The impact of the medical challenge on any family appears dependent on the number of factors imposed by the condition. These factors may include the family resources (e.g. financial, job), the relationships within the family and the social support system within both the family and the community.

The exosystem consists of all other support systems found outside the home. Financial, medical and emotional supports found in formal and informal neighborhood opportunities can make the life of a person with a chronic illness more livable or less of an ordeal. These options may be found formally at a work site, clinics, various religious institutions, as well as numerous community social service agencies. Informally, a person's sense of well-being may be lifted as a direct result of the contributions made by extended family members and close friends. Having good neighbors and family members who will frequently visit or call can tremendously impact one's perceived quality of life. Also, support groups, social clubs and churches can help enlarge one's support from the person's exosystem.

Finally, the macrosystem is the outermost layer of a human being's ecosystem and incorporates the larger culture of the world in which we all live. This macrosystem may represent the culture's bias and reaction to various illnesses and conditions; it is within the cultural macrosystem that the stigma of an illness is developed. According to the tenets of an ecosystem model, there is a positive correlation with the resources secured and an individual's ability to function and adapt more effectively.

Bronfenbrenner urges mental health professionals to view the psychological health of any individual as a direct result of the forces operating within the systems that he or she lives within. The model permits simultaneous consideration of numerous factors within the microsystem, the exosystem and the macrosystem which can help an individual adapt to illness.

16.5 Practical suggestions for AAI within palliative care and concluding remarks

Whether a disease can be cured or whether one can hope only management of its progression, the patient has the burden of the physical, psychosocial, and spiritual symptoms associated with the disease and its treatment. The goal of palliative care is to minimize such negative burdens and to maximize positive aspects of a patient's quality of life. Pets can connect with patients emotionally and significantly improve their quality of life when the patient might otherwise be somewhat withdrawn from other persons around them.

The following synthesizes some of the findings previously discussed and provides some suggestions for clinicians to consider for their clients who have an affinity for animals in their lives. Several of these suggestions were identified in an interview conducted with Rev McNac, who is the Director of Spiritual Care at a Hospice in Oklahoma (personal interview Aug. 16, 2009). Rev McNac, who is also a veterinarian, has some valuable insights about the value of the human/animal bond.

McNac points out that one of the major challenges that exist today is the lack of awareness and sensitivity by many palliative and hospice care workers on the role that pet companions have in the lives of several of their patients. Many professional care providers may exclude pets from their assessment of the patient's psychosocial needs and potentially miss an important aspect of the patient's support system.

Some health care professionals may also miss the importance of an individual's sense of responsibility for the safe keeping of a pet, especially as they become more ill. For example, many patients may be reluctant to voice concerns about needing assistance to care for their pets out of fear their pet will be taken away. When understanding this process, health care providers may be able to support clients by finding people in the community that can help them take care of the animal, so the animal's welfare is preserved. In the upcoming chapter, the authors will provide some insight on how programs such as PAWS can provide dynamic resources and support for animals and their families. Such support for pet care allows people to continue to have their pets at home when they may not be well enough to take care of their basic needs. Here again, there is an opportunity to document the efficacy of the intervention through practice-based research.

Some professionals may also miss the opportunity to connect with their patients on an alternative level, and to talk with and explore with them the importance of their pets in their daily life. By validating the relationships they have with pets, palliative care workers are given the opportunity to model their care and compassion for their clients through positive interaction with their pets.

Furthermore, hospice and palliative care workers can encourage animal visitation programs with all patients that do not have contraindications to animals. Whenever possible, a client should have the opportunity to continue his/her relation with his or her own pet. Guidelines will need to be established on the overall hygiene of the pet, but these details can be worked out.

Additionally, there should be opportunities made available for animal visitation programs. These visitations will allow people who have a love of animals to continue to have opportunities to be visited by them: even if on a more limited basis. Material in various chapters of this book discusses some of the guidelines for implementing and designing both AAT and AAI programs that definitely can be applied to this population.

Ultimately, the most important outcome that can occur is a shift in the mindset of educators and health care workers, so they incorporate AAI in educational and care plans as a recognized integrated modality in palliative care with a positive track record under accepted guidelines. Once this mindset becomes more accepted, there are numerous resources that are available to help those interested in implementing services that meet individuals' needs. However, it is less likely that such a shift in understanding and health care practice will take place without widespread evidence to support it. AAT and AAI professionals can supply practice-based evidence with thoughtful planning and record-keeping, especially if this is coordinated between a significant number of practitioners. Rather than relying on randomized, controlled trials—which are most often time consuming and costly—a better strategy may be to pursue a wider base of practice-based evidence that is strengthened by incorporating both qualitative and quantitative data. Evidence can speak more powerfully to professional care providers than many ideas and suggestions. Such evidence may be in the form of first-hand experience, opinions from other professionals they respect, or research studies. The most effective strategy may be to utilize all three.

Providing suitable research studies is a particular challenge due to very limited funding available for pet-related research, palliative care research, or any research that is not aimed at curing a disease or disorder. Such disciplines may need to adopt a strategy that gets the most research value out of the very limited funding available. One such strategy is to increase the strength of evidence in any formal controlled research study by utilizing both quantitative and qualitative data. This strategy is especially important for integrative therapies for which quantitative tools are not yet well developed.

An additional strategy is to complement formal research studies with less controlled practice-based research. Practice-based research has a dual benefit. First, it can provide an additional source of evidence to professional care providers who otherwise "just don't get it." Second, it provides a fertile pool of data from which more formal research studies might draw preliminary data to use in proposals, thus strengthening their bid to win research funding. This interactive, complementary structure of uncontrolled practice-based research and controlled formal research is a way in which full-time practitioners and full-time researchers can mutually benefit each other. Evidence collected by a practitioner from their own client base can be both qualitative and quantitative to increase the strength of the data. Formal controlled research gives reliable, widely respected evidence to practitioners. The main thing is for practitioners (including associations of practitioners) to simply yet systematically begin gathering, organizing, and presenting the data that is already present in one's practice, with an option to increase the sophistication of the practice-based research as one gains experience.

Hippocrates once stated "healing is a matter of time," but it is sometimes illnesses that confront many of our patients. Rather, the care will provide opportunities for healing and quality of life for the time that they have remaining. Animal-assisted interventions, supported by both researchers and practitioners, may be a viable ingredient for some in their own recipe for healing.

References

Bandura, A. (1977). Self-efficacy: toward a unifying theory of behavioral change. *Psychological Review, 84*(2), 191–215.

Beck, C. T. (1989). Maternal-newborn nursing research published from 1977 to 1986. *Western Journal of Nursing Research, 11*(5), 621–626.

Beck, C. T. (1991a). Early postpartum discharge programs in the United States: a literature review and critique. *Women and Health, 17*(1), 125–138.

Beck, C. T. (1991b). Maternity blues research: a critical review. *Issues in Mental Health Nursing, 12*(3), 291–300.

Beck, C. T. (1992b). The lived experience of postpartum depression: a phenomenological study. *Nursing Research, 41*(3), 166–170.

Beck, C. T. (1993). Teetering on the edge: a substantive theory of postpartum depression. *Nursing Research, 42*(1), 42–48.

Beck, C. T. (1995). Screening methods for postpartum depression. *Journal of Obstetric, Gynecologic, and Neonatal Nursing: JOGNN/NAACOG, 24*(4), 308–312.

Beck, C. T. (1997). Developing a research program using qualitative and quantitative approaches. *Nursing Outlook, 45*(6), 265–269.

Beck, C. T. (2002). Postpartum depression: a metasynthesis. *Qualitative Health Research, 12*(4), 453–472.

Beck, C. T. (2009). Viewing the rich, diverse landscape of qualitative research. *Perioperative Nursing Clinics, 4*(3), 217–229.

Beck, C. T., & Gable, R. K. (2000). Postpartum depression screening scale: development and psychometric testing. *Nursing Research, 49*(5), 272–282.

Beck, C. T., & Gable, R. K. (2001). Comparative analysis of the performance of the postpartum depression screening scale with two other depression instruments. *Nursing Research, 50*(4), 242–250.

Beck, C. T., Reynolds, M. A., & Rutowski, P. (1992). Maternity blues and postpartum depression. *Journal of Obstetric, Gynecologic, and Neonatal Nursing: JOGNN/NAACOG, 21*(4), 287–293.

Beck, A. T., Steer, R. A., & Garbin, M. G. (1988). Psychometric properties of the Beck Depression Inventory: twenty-five years of evaluation. *Clinical Psychology Review, 8*(1), 77–100.

Carver, C. S., Scheier, M. F., & Weintraub, K. J. (1989). Assessing coping strategies: a theoretically based approach. *Journal of Personality and Social Psychology, 56*(2), 267–283.

Charmaz, K. (2006). *Constructing Grounded Theory: A Practical Guide Through Qualitative Analysis*. Los Angeles: SAGE Publications.

Chinner, T., & Dalziel, F. (1991). An exploratory study on the viability and efficacy of a pet-facilitated therapy project within a hospice. *Journal of Palliative Care, 7*(4), 13–20.

Denz-Penhey, H., & Murdoch, J. C. (2008). Personal resiliency: serious diagnosis and prognosis with unexpected quality outcomes. *Qualitative Health Research, 18*(3), 391–404.

Fleury, J., Kimbrell, L. C., & Kruszewski, M. A. (1995). Life after a cardiac event: women's experience in healing. *Heart Lung, 24*, 474–482.

Folkman, S. (1984). Personal control and stress and coping processes: a theoretical analysis. *Journal of Personality and Social Psychology, 46*(4), 839–852.

Folkman, S. (1997). Positive psychological states and coping with severe stress. *Social Science and Medicine, 45*(8), 1207–1221.

Folkman, S. (2009). Stress, coping, and well-being: integrative medicine meets behavioral science. Presented on Dec. 8, 2009 at "NCCAM's 10th Anniversary Research Symposium: Exploring the Science of Complementary and Alternative Medicine", Retrieved Dec. 12, 2009 from http://videocast.nih.gov/Summary.asp?File=15484

Folkman, S., Chesney, M. A., & Christopher-Richards, A. (1994). Stress and coping in caregiving partners of men with AIDS. *Psychiatric Clinics of North America, 17*(1), 35–53.

Folkman, S., Chesney, M. A., Pollack, L., & Phillips, C. (1992). Stress, coping, and high-risk sexual behavior. *Health Psychology, 11*(4), 218–222.

Folkman, S., & Lazarus, R. S. (1980). An analysis of coping in a middle-aged community sample. *Journal of Health and Social Behavior, 21*(3), 219–239.

Folkman, S., & Lazarus, R. S. (1985). If it changes it must be a process. Study of emotion and coping during three stages of a college examination. *Journal of Personality and Social Psychology, 48*(1), 150–170.

Frankl, V. (1984). *Man's Search for Meaning*. New York: Simon & Schuster.

Kearney, M. (2000). *A Place of Healing: Working with Suffering in Living and Dying*. USA: Oxford University Press.

Koithan, M., Verhoef, M., Bell, I. R., White, M., Mulkins, A., & Ritenbaugh, C. (2007). The process of whole person healing: "unstuckness" and beyond. *Journal of Alternative and Complementary Medicine, 13*(6), 659–668.

Landmark, B. T., & Wahl, A. (2002). Living with newly diagnosed breast cancer: a qualitative study of 10 women with newly diagnosed breast cancer. *Journal of Advanced Nursing, 40*(1), 112–121.

Lasiuk, G. C., & Ferguson, L. M. (2005). From practice to mid-range theory and back again: Beck's theory of postpartum depression. *Advances in Nursing Science, 28*(2), 127–136.

Lazarus, R. (1966). *Psychological Stress and the Coping Process*. New York: McGraw-Hill.

Madison, D. L. (1997). Osler: inspirations from a great physician (book review). *New England Journal Medicine, 337*, 1324–1326.

McNicholas, J., Gilbey, A., Rennie, A., Ahmedzai, S., Dono, J., & Ormerod, E. (2005). *British Medical Journal, 331*, 1252–1254.

Melson, G. (2001). *Why the Wild Things Are: Animals in the Lives of Children*. Cambridge: Harvard University Press.

National Hospice and Palliative Care Organization. (2010). What is Hospice and Palliative Care? Retrieved May 13, 2010 from http://www.nhpco.org/i4a/pages/index.cfm?pageid=4648

Nuland, S. B. (2000). *Time* magazine. Retrieved from the article's page 2 on Oct. 20, 2009. http://www.time.com/time/magazine/article/0,9171,997988–2,00.html

Pearlin, L. I., & Schooler, C. (1978). The structure of coping. *Journal of Health and Social Behavior, 19*(1), 2–21.

Phear, D. (1996). A study of animal companionship in a day hospice. *Palliative Medicine, 10*, 336–339.

Rutherford, M. (2000). *Time* magazine. Retrieved from the article's page 7 on Oct. 20, 2009. http://www.time.com/time/magazine/article/0,9171,997969–7,00.html

Saunders, C. (1977). On dying and dying well. *Proceedings of the Royal Society of Medicine, 70*(4), 290–291.

Smith, J. A. (1996). Qualitative methodology: analyzing participant's perspectives. *Current Opinion in Psychiatry, 9*(6), 417–421.

Spiegel, D., & Kato, P. (1996). Psychosocial influences on cancer incidence and progression. *Harvard Review of Psychiatry, 4*, 10–26.

Straub, R. (2007). *Health Psychology*. New York, NY: Worth Publishers.

Swatton, S., & O'Callaghan, J. (1999). The experience of "healing stories" in the life narrative: a grounded theory. *Counselling Psychology Quarterly, 12*(4), 413–429.

Tedeschi, R. G., & Calhoun, L. G. (1996). The posttraumatic growth inventory: measuring the positive legacy of trauma. *Journal of Traumatic Stress, 9*(3), 455–471.

Turk, D. C., Dworkin, R. H., Allen, R. R., Bellamy, N., Brandenburg, N., Carr, D. B., et al. (2003). Core outcome domains for chronic pain clinical trials: IMMPACT recommendations. *Pain, 106*(3), 337–345.

Wertz, F. J. (2005). Phenomenological research methods for counseling psychology. *Journal of Counseling Psychology, 52*(2), 167–177.

WHO. (2010). World Health Organization Definition of Palliative Care. Retrieved May 13, 2010 from http://www.who.int/cancer/palliative/definition/en

17 Human/animal support services: the evolution of the San Francisco model and pet-associated zoonoses education

Ken Gorczyca*, Aubrey H. Fine†, Stephanie Venn-Watson‡, Laura Nelson*, Andrea Brooks*, John L. Lipp*, C. Victor Spain§, Ilana Strubel¶, Jane Irene Kelly, Belinda Wong¶, Dana O'Callaghan**, Lori Popejoy††

*Pets Are Wonderful Support, †California State Polytechnic University, ‡National Marine Mammal Foundation, §Merck & Co., Inc., ¶SFCCC VET SOS, ¶University of California, **National University and Palomar College, ††University of Missouri

People come to visit, but they can only stay an hour and then they have to go; my cat, she's always there.

Bob, pet owner with AIDS

Afraid of infection, I fear the birds (Tuberculosis), the cats (Toxoplasmosis), my dog, my horse (Mycobacterium avium), and people. For weeks, I was reluctant to leave the house. I didn't ride my horse for several months. Walking in the park or at the beach was unpleasant because of the birds. My doctors gave contradictory advice—Dr. (A) said to get rid of all animals. Dr. (B) said it didn't matter and enjoy what life I had left. My cousin asked if I couldn't get a bubble like the bubble boy.

Stephen Yarnell, MD, When Doctors Get Sick, 1987

PAWS Keeps "Families" Together

Cecil, Charlie and Butter

Cecil Baker says he doesn't know how he would take care of his "family"—his beloved feline companions, Charlie and Buttermilk Johnny—if he couldn't rely on

Handbook on Animal-Assisted Therapy. DOI: 10.1016/B978-0-12-381453-1.10017-0

help from the volunteers and the vital services of San Francisco-based, non-profit, Pets are Wonderful Support (PAWS). PAWS was founded in 1986 by members of the San Francisco AIDS Foundation Food Bank—many living with AIDS themselves—who reached out to several food bank clients with HIV/AIDS who needed assistance caring for their companion animals.

Cecil, a diabetic who suffered a debilitating brain hemorrhage several years ago, has been a client of PAWS since 2005. His cats Charlie and Buttermilk Johnny (a.k.a. "Butter") receive monthly home delivery of cat litter, food and other supplies from the PAWS food bank. As of 2009, PAWS was serving about 800 clients in the San Francisco Bay Area through its Companion Animal Support Services (CASS) program.

All PAWS clients, like Cecil, live on a fixed income. Many struggle with disabling illnesses, such as HIV/AIDS. Some are elderly and frail. And all need the extra support from PAWS to keep together the precious "family" they have made with their companion animals.

"Charlie and Butter are such good company—and they make me laugh. I really love them," Cecil says with obvious pride. "But I don't know what we would do without help from PAWS. The volunteers are so nice. They always make sure we are doing OK."

Cecil adds that it puts his mind at ease knowing that if he needs to be hospitalized again, PAWS will be there to care for Charlie and "Butter." When a PAWS client must stay in the hospital for an extended period, the organization works to find a temporary foster home for the client's pet through the PAWS Foster Care Program. If no foster home is available, PAWS goes the distance to make other arrangements—even providing in-home care, if needed—until a foster home is found or until the pet can be reunited with its owner.

"It's just so comforting to know there is an organization that understands how important pets are to people like me," says Cecil. "Charlie and Butter are here to see me through both good times and tough times, and it's important to me that I keep them happy and healthy, too."

17.1   Introduction

People who suffer from chronic or terminal illness—and particularly those who also live at the poverty level—find their physical condition influences their quality of life and has a tremendous impact on their ability to accomplish everyday activities. For some, the physical and often psychological barriers manifested by their medical condition leads to a decrease, or even an end, to social opportunities and relationships previously enjoyed.

However, for many people facing these challenges, their relationships with their pets—their "companion animals"—offer a source of unconditional love and acceptance. These relationships also provide the opportunity for increased socialization, brought about by the need to take care of another living creature.

Human/animal support services (HASS) evolved during the AIDS pandemic to help keep people with disabling illness together with their animal companions for as long as possible in a mutually beneficial relationship (see Table 17.1). HASS provides

Figure 17.1 PAWS client Cecil Baker with Charlie and Butter. Photo credit: Michael Tedesco

financial, emotional, practical and educational assistance to the disabled and vulnerable pet owner.

The previous chapter uses an ecosystem model to explain how support systems and animals may contribute to an increased quality of home life for those who struggle with chronic disease, but are able to live at home or in transitional housing (see Table 17.4 Bronfenbrenner's definitions). (Note: Traditional animal-assisted therapy (AAT) programs and the benefits of animals in hospital-based programs are discussed elsewhere in this book.)

This chapter examines the history and intersection of the AIDS pandemic, the human/animal bond movement, public health education and veterinary medicine. There is a particular focus on the AIDS pandemic, as it helped to spawn the field known today as human/animal support services and pet-associated zoonoses education. Zoonoses (pronounced ZO-uh-NO-seez) are diseases that humans can catch from other animals. This background information will be followed by evidence of how animals can enhance the quality of life for people living with illness and disability.

The second part of this chapter will be practice oriented, focusing on the development of two successful San Francisco HASS organizations: Pets Are Wonderful

Table 17.1 Definitions of human/animal interactions (HAI) services

1. Human/animal support services (HASS) are programs that help keep a person with a chronic/terminal illness or disability together for as long as possible with their current animal companions in a mutually beneficial relationship. HASS services include financial, emotional, educational and practical assistance to the disabled pet owner. These programs can be independent, volunteer-run, non-profit organizations. They also can be programs under the umbrella of other organizations such as humane associations or societies, veterinary hospitals, schools or associations, AIDS organizations or other similar human or animal community service organizations.

2. Animal-assisted activities (AAA) are goal-directed activities designed to improve the patients' quality of life through the utilization of the human/animal bond. Animals and their handlers must be screened and trained, but are not guided by a credentialed therapist.

3. Animal-assisted therapy (AAT) utilizes the human/animal bond in goal-directed interventions as an integral part of the treatment process. Working animals and their handlers must be screened, trained, and meet specific criteria. A credentialed therapist working within the scope of practice of his/her profession sets therapeutic goals, guides the interaction between patient and animal, measures progress towards meeting therapy goals, and evaluates the process.

4. Hospital personal pet visitation (HPPV) provides patients who are critically ill (and sometimes unlikely to leave the hospital) the opportunity to visit with their own pets in their hospital room. All patients, excluding those in bone marrow units, are eligible for visits facilitated by trained volunteers as long as the animal companion passes a special screening process.

5. Companion Animal Support Services (CASS) are the services provided by HASS organizations. These include dog walking, pet care, food bank and delivery, veterinary care, in-home services, case management, behavioral assistance, pet-associated zoonoses education, client advocacy, emotional support and other services that help support the human/companion animal bond.

Support (PAWS—www.pawssf.org), founded in 1986, and SFCCC VET SOS (www.vetsos.org), founded in 2001. Also discussed is how other communities may benefit from these types of services and how to develop and implement similar programs and services in their own community. The goal of both animal-assisted therapy and HASS is to work in parallel, encouraging positive emotional and physical health benefits from human/animal interaction (see Table 17.1).

The AIDS pandemic brought about a movement of volunteer-based social services for both people and animals. Many people living with AIDS are also pet guardians, who, as their disease may progress, eventually may require help caring for their animals. Traditionally, social services supported the financial, physical, and emotional assistance these populations required. Over time in the early AIDS pandemic, the social services field evolved to include human/animal support services (HASS) designed specifically to help keep the vulnerable person and his or her animal companion(s) together for as long as feasibly possible in a mutually beneficial relationship or "family."

The San Francisco community, a leader in fighting the AIDS pandemic, also offers unique insights into the evolution and development of HASS organizations and programs such as PAWS and VET SOS. This has become known as the San Francisco model.

Additionally, the AIDS pandemic has provided opportunities for veterinarians, veterinary students and veterinary technicians to volunteer, participate, and make important strides in improving and enhancing benefits of animal companionship. In San Francisco, four veterinarians served as board presidents of PAWS, and many more have participated as board members, practitioners and volunteers. To date, 17 veterinary students have participated in the PAWS veterinary externship program. VET SOS also has a very active local volunteer veterinary program. By promoting pet-associated zoonoses education and the benefits of animal companionship, veterinarians continue to play a major role in public health and as members of the health care team. Current information and support is now easily available to the public and medical community on numerous websites (see Table 17.9). The medical and veterinary professions have recently started to collaborate together by forming the One Health Initiative (www.onehealthinitiative.com).

Early in the pandemic, many physicians recommended that their patients with AIDS get rid of their pets to avoid the risks of zoonoses. Veterinarians, understanding the importance of animal companionship and how to minimize the risk of zoonotic disease, took the lead to dispel these myths through outreach and education. Today, the American Veterinary Medical Association, the Centers for Disease Control, the Delta Society, Pets Are Wonderful Support and many other associations and organizations all continue to play a role in promoting the understanding of the human/animal bond and pet-associated zoonoses education.

17.2 AIDS: an overview

Acquired immunodeficiency syndrome (AIDS) is one of the more serious and complex health problems humanity has faced in recent history. AIDS is caused by the human immunodeficiency virus (HIV), which attacks the immune system and can reduce an infected person's ability to resist other infections and diseases. An estimated one million US citizens are infected with HIV, with as many as 56,000 new infections each year in the USA (Campsmith et al., 2008).

Although the epidemic has appeared to slow somewhat in the developed world, AIDS has reached pandemic levels in developing countries such as India and South Africa (United Nations AIDS/WHO, 2004). Worldwide, there were 2.5 million new infections in 2007 alone (see Table 17.2). Ninety-five percent of all HIV-infected people live in developing countries (UNAIDS/WHO, 1998). AIDS has killed at least 26 million people, orphaned more than 12 million children, and currently infects over 33 million people worldwide (UNAIDS/WHO, 2007).

HIV is transmitted in various ways: sexually, through contact with infected body fluids; from mother to child during pregnancy or breast-feeding; through the sharing or medical use of infected needles; or through blood transfusions. The progression from HIV to AIDS is usually a slow process. It may be 10 years or longer from the time of initial infection with HIV until symptoms of AIDS appear. Before the availability of effective treatments, a person with an AIDS diagnosis had an 8–10-month life expectancy. Once immunosuppression has occurred, people with

Table 17.2 Global summary of AIDS pandemic

People living with HIV in 2007	33,000,000
North America	1,200,000
Sub-Saharan Africa	22,000,000
Western and Central Europe	700,000
People newly infected with HIV in 2007	2,500,000
AIDS deaths in 2007	2,100,000

From UNAIDS/WHO 2007 report on the global AIDS epidemic, United Nations Program on HIV/AIDS (www.unaids.org).

AIDS (PWAs) become susceptible to "opportunistic" infections, cancers and meta-bolic illness. These opportunistic infections typically cause minimal disease in healthy persons but can lead to death in PWAs.

As more effective and less toxic treatments become available, AIDS is becoming more of a chronic condition. Many individuals who start appropriate therapy early are now able to have productive and healthier lives. However, many of the therapies used to treat AIDS are still relatively new and have unknown toxicities when used over a person's lifetime. Already, serious complications such as liver and kidney failure, heart disease and bone disease are on the increase in individuals using the AIDS treatments for long periods. In addition, these therapies are expensive and not generally available to populations in the developing world or to the uninsured or underinsured in the developed world. This obstacle has led to the evolution of two distinct epidemics, with 95% living in the developing world.

17.3   The psycho-social impact of illness: the AIDS virus

In 1986, when PAWS started providing its services in San Francisco, people living with AIDS/HIV were often isolated and typically suffered quick physical health declines. The psychological burden produced by AIDS and HIV infection exceeded that produced by any other medical condition at that time (Maj, 1991). PWAs are faced with the disease process as well as the psychological ramifications of this serious illness. Primary to these obstacles are HIV's incurability and the associated public hysteria and misunderstanding (Cherry and Smith, 1993). There is a wealth of information that suggests PWAs have been targets of stigmatization (Bennett, 1990). Individuals with AIDS often describe feelings of isolation, alienation and estrange-ment and loneliness (Carmack, 1991).

Two specific categories of loneliness have been described: emotional isolation and social isolation (Weiss, 1973). Emotional isolation appears to develop as a direct result of absence of an attachment figure, such as a partner or close friend. Social isolation, on the other hand, occurs when an individual lacks (or perceives a lack of) an effective social network. Research reported by Christ et al. (1986) suggests PWAs may be especially susceptible to the experience of loneliness. They reported that 75% of patients with AIDS have diminished social support from friends, family and significant others.

17.4 The role of pets

Pets are a large and integral part of American culture. The US Humane Society indicates that more than half of US households have pets (HSUS, 2003). Pets are more common in households with children, yet there are more pets than children in US households (HSUS, 2005). An estimated 45% of Americans infected with HIV own pets (Spencer, 1992) and many other PWAs have contact with animals through traditional AAT programs while hospitalized or in a hospice. It is in these situations, such as living with AIDS or another chronic illness or disability, that the importance of finding meaning and joy in life through the positive interactions with pets may be particularly beneficial.

It is not uncommon for a child or an adult to perceive an animal as a peer or family member (Nebbe, 1991). Pets provide a valuable source of comfort and companionship for many individuals, including children (Wilson, 1991). According to Veevers (1985), animals may act as surrogates when they take the place of people. He suggests that "almost all interaction with companion animals involves some anthropomorphism and can in some way be construed as a surrogate for human relationships." Serpell (1983) further suggests that animals can supply compassion in cases where humans are unable or unavailable to do so.

People with AIDS may perceive a companion animal to be a family member as well as a direct source of emotional support. (see Table 17.3). This is particularly important for someone who may feel isolated and perhaps neglected. In an article on companion animals for PWAs, Carmack (1991) notes that animal companions decrease feelings of isolation and provide a perceived reduction of stress. She also reports findings that suggest PWAs perceive that their companion animals help to reduce their stress levels. In turn, stress reduction can improve immune system function. Because animals require attention, affection and companionship, they can enhance feelings of being needed and valued—"I care for them, and that lets me forget about things."

Castelli et al. (2001) found that pet cats, but not dogs, offered comfort and companionship to people with AIDS, and enhanced their relationships with family and friends. They also found that people with advanced AIDS sometimes found the activity level of a companion dog to be stressful. In contrast, a calm cat was

Table 17.3 Benefits animal companions can provide to people
with chronic illnesses

Provide companionship
Decrease feelings of loneliness
Act as a surrogate for other relationships
Decrease stress
Provide a reason to exercise
Give the human caregiver a sense of purpose
Ease social interactions in public
Provide a sense of security to children and adults
Provide health benefits

comforting as their lives became more isolated. Similarly, Siegel et al. (1999) found that men with AIDS who had close attachments with their pets were significantly less likely to suffer from depression than those men with AIDS who did not have pets as companions.

Chinner and Dalziel (1991) found that a resident poodle in a hospice setting facilitated interactions between people and improved both staff and patient morale. However, attachment to the pet does seem to make a difference as to how much of an effect the animal has on the person. Those who were isolated or lonely did not develop affection for the poodle. Early work by Rynearson (as cited in Cookman, 1996) supports the importance of attachment and notes that the reciprocal nature of the relationship between pet and owner is crucially important. It is wise to keep in mind, however, that not all people desire to develop an attachment to an animal.

Alternatively, Volth (1985) indicates that there may be a biological predisposition for humans to develop a strong attachment bond to animals. It is not uncommon to see many companion animals that may, for example, sleep in their owners' rooms and accompany their owners on short trips and holidays. Many companion animals are recipients of special treats and gifts, just like other family members. Volth's research points out that both dog and cat owners can become equally attached to their animals. Jorgenson (1997) observes that pets are a constantly available source of direction of attention and affection.

Cohen (2002), in a recent study about pets functioning as family members, found that pets do function within the family circle and give back as much as they receive from their owners. Within the animal/human relationship, there is an unambivalent exchange between pet and owner that may not exist in other relationships. Pets may allow people to express deep feelings and offer them a way to nurture another living being (Cohen, 2002).

According to Siegel (1993), companion animals within the home appear to acquire the ability to bring forth positive emotional responses from their owners. Positive responses are initially elicited from the good feelings derived from tactile and emotional contact with the animal. This continued pairing usually leads the owner to view the animal as a source of comfort.

Interestingly, a social worker in England pointed out that companion animals appear to demonstrate some of the same attributes seen as being favorable qualities in social workers (Hutton, 1982). Companion animals, for example, tend to help people use their own strengths to help themselves. Animals tend to have the ability to form and establish relationships quickly; they also are sensitive to people's feelings and emotions, and thus are able to recognize those occasions when they are needed or wanted.

Cusak (1988) suggests that animals can function as human surrogates in a number of roles, including friends and confidants. Persons secluded within their homes may find the companionship of animals more meaningful. They can act as true friends, not only to pass time with, but also to engage in authentic relationships. Pets can bring laughter and tenderness into a home. They also can offer comfort at times of overbearing loneliness.

A good illustration of how pets support patients resulted from a study by Muschel (1985), who looked at the effects of animals on enhancing the quality of life of patients with cancer. Animals visited 15 hospitalized patients. Twelve of the 15 patients seemed very concerned about the "visiting" animals' welfare and would go out of their way to reassure the pets. They also seemed more content and outgoing in the presence of the animals and were observed to sing and play with them. Interestingly, Muschel also alluded to how the animals seemed to be valuable as companions while the patients were struggling with facing death: "The animal's quiet, accepting and nurturing presence strengthens, and frees the patient to resolve his or her final experience successfully." Much in the same way, having a companion animal in a patient's home would seem to elicit the same responses.

Companion animals in the home may also improve physical health by increasing the amount of exercise in which chronically ill people may engage (Meer, 1984). Pet ownership also has been shown to improve cardiovascular health by reducing anxiety, loneliness and depression (Friedman et al., 1983; Katcher, 1981; Wilson, 1984). Animals can be used to support and enhance healthier living patterns on many levels. However, PAWS clients were found to experience significant financial stress regarding veterinary care. Still, despite the financial stress, they found their lives more socially satisfying than people with AIDS who did not have PAWS assistance or those who did not have pets (ISAZ Poster, 2008).

In addition to benefits for chronically or terminally ill people, studies have shown that seniors with pets tend to be healthier than those without. They handle stress better, and are less lonely and more physically active. A relationship with a pet is especially important to seniors who live on their own and are responsible for the day-to-day tasks associated with pet ownership such as walking a dog, feeding a cat or simply brushing a pet. These activities give lonely and isolated seniors a sense of purpose and seem to contribute to significantly lower blood pressure and heart rates. Interaction with a beloved pet also helps to ease seniors' feelings of depression and isolation. Pets become important family members and, in some cases, can even lead seniors towards more social interactions with other humans—for example, through daily dog walking.

While the important role that companion and therapy animals can play for people with chronic illnesses should be recognized, these people may need assistance in caring for their animals from within Bronfenbrenner's exosystem (see Table 17.4). In most cases, research has been conducted addressing the importance of human

Table 17.4 Bronfenbrenner's definitions (see Chapter 16 for more details)

The individual:
    Type of illness, coping strategies
Microsystem:
    Inner-family relations, parents, partner, children, animal companion, home environment
Exosystem:
    Outside the home, neighborhood, friends, family, community agencies
Macrosystem:
    Society's view on illness

contemporaries and their relationships to enhance quality of life. Shea and Bauer (1991) point out that relatives, neighbors, friends, and community organizations may provide tremendous support to the individual.

An effective community can provide much-needed assistance and opportunities for an individual. There can be people outside one's immediate family who make life more meaningful and easier. Friends and relatives may make it possible for some people to continue living on their own by providing intermittent help with cooking, shopping, cleaning and pet care. Isolation may be prevented or decreased as a consequence of this external support system. Programs such as PAWS (Pets are Wonderful Support, described later in this chapter) or friends within the community can be viable resources for helping an individual keep a pet companion at home.

Close relationships outside the home may provide ongoing support as well as a sense of stability in the lives of PWAs (Jue, 1994). Supportive relationships, with friends or visiting animals, can contribute to an individual's quality of life. These connecting experiences indirectly and directly contribute to offsetting the effects of isolation and enhancing a sense of self-worth. These findings support the role of companion animals and visiting animal programs in decreasing a person's sense of social isolation.

In addition to the many benefits that animal companionship has to offer humans, it also should be understood that there are some risks, such as zoonotic disease and potential injury. The best interests of a pet should always be considered as well, as it is sometimes necessary to recommend and assist the person give up their animal companion. Following is a review of the historical significance of zoonotic disease and people with AIDS and the important role that veterinarians play as a member of the public health care team. The evolution of PAWS is also examined and the many companion animal support services (CASS) showcased. Finally, VET SOS, another San Francisco HASS program that helps the growing human homeless population and their animal companions is reviewed.

17.5   The historical significance of zoonoses and AIDS

Several million people in the USA have compromised immune systems, including an estimated one million people living with HIV (CDC, 2005). Other immunosuppressive illnesses and treatments include chemotherapy, some cancers, dialysis, congenital diseases, and others (see Table 17.5). Immunosuppressed persons are susceptible to a number of opportunistic infections including zoonoses, which are diseases that can be transmitted to humans by other vertebrate animals or shared by humans and other vertebrate animals. Angulo (1994) reported that about 45% of immunosuppressed individuals might own pets, but few are offered information about zoonoses prevention by health care providers. Although AIDS helped create the need for pet-associated zoonoses education, the information is important for all immunosuppressed populations (see Table 17.5).

AIDS was first identified in 1981, when a cluster of case reports in New York City emerged describing a rare pneumonia in young, previously healthy homosexual

Table 17.5 Immune system-compromising diseases/
conditions

Alcoholism/liver cirrhosis
Cancer (some)
Chronic renal failure
Congenital immunodeficiencies
Diabetes mellitus
HIV/AIDS
Immunosuppressive treatments for:
    Autoimmune diseases
    Cancer
    Transplant recipients
Long-term hemodialysis
Old age
Malnutrition
Pregnancy
Splenectomy

males. This specific infection, caused by an opportunistic parasite known as *Pneumocystis carinii*, had previously been seen only in patients with immune system dysfunction, cancer, or undergoing chemotherapy treatments. Suddenly, because of AIDS, a large number of people were developing previously rare opportunistic infections, including some considered zoonotic. The swift spread of the virus and the large number of deaths in previously healthy individuals were unprecedented in modern medicine.

Although it was known that companion animals could not transmit AIDS, at the time many questions about the risks of other infections remained unanswered. The medical community in general was not prepared to answer esoteric questions about catching diseases from "Fluffy" the cat. Veterinarians knew about animal-borne diseases and the benefits of animal companionship, but little about the degree of increased risk to immunosuppressed humans. Many physicians, unfamiliar with the details of zoonotic transmission, often chose to err on the side of caution and simply advised their immunosuppressed patients to relinquish their pets to minimize any possible risks.

Was there a real risk? Or was there an overreaction by overzealous physicians? In the mid-1980s, there was very little information in veterinary or medical literature about the increased risk of zoonoses to immunosuppressed individual pet owners. What made this situation so controversial and complicated was that there was a concurrent cerebral toxoplasmosis epidemic occurring in PWAs. PWAs were developing symptoms of this infection at previously unknown rates. In addition, infected cat feces were known to be one source of transmission of this infection to people. Toxoplasmosis is a parasitic infection mostly "associated" with cats, but it is now more generally understood that humans typically acquire this illness from food, the environment or it is a reactivation of an old infection when the person's immune system deteriorates. Companion cats were not the culprit in a vast majority of cases, and can be made safer through diet, proper litter box care and veterinary care.

Because most physicians were unfamiliar with zoonoses (Gorczyca, 1989), a real crisis of misinformation about AIDS and zoonoses developed within the health care system. Unfortunately, in the early days of the AIDS epidemic, the risks were not clear or understood. Many physicians, playing it safe, recommended that their patients have reduced contact with pets—or to give them away. Myths were created in the community and media.

The recommendation for PWAs to find their pets a new home created an entirely new dilemma. People with HIV typically face many losses—employment, friends and family. They also often feel isolated, rejected and stigmatized. However, it can be the special relationship they have with their pets that provide them with constancy, love and affection. Now, these people were being separated from their beloved pets, often due to medical advice. Unfortunately, many of these individuals were the very people who most needed the emotional and psychological benefits provided by their animal companions.

Soon, veterinarians began taking the lead in educating the public and health care fields about zoonotic risks for PWAs. These veterinarians questioned the value of separating animal companions from the people who seemed to need that companionship the most. Veterinarian Malcolm Kram, for example, moved the New York Veterinary Medical Association to develop the first recommendations in 1986 on how to minimize the risks of transmitting zoonoses from animals to people.

However, not all veterinary organizations were ready or willing to assume responsibility for educating the public and health care professionals. In some cases, it was the AIDS support organizations, such as the Shanti Project in San Francisco, that were willing to help (Gorczyca, 1991). These efforts eventually led to the publication of PAWS's *Safe Pet Guidelines* in 1988. These were the first published guidelines that explained how to minimize zoonotic risks and support the importance of the human/ animal bond for people with AIDS.

Today, there is still little evidence in the literature to support the idea that people can contract diseases from their companion animals, except for reptiles and some other exotic animals (Wong, 1998). In fact, for many physicians who treat AIDS patients, zoonoses have become a non-issue relative to other concerns about treatment and survival (D. Abrams, personal communication, 1998). However, there is still confusion and misinformation about pet-associated zoonoses. But is it the physician's or the veterinarian's role to educate? Veterinarians are taught public health and about zoonotic diseases. They are not allowed to attend humans, unless during an emergency. However, veterinarians are highly trained to be a vital player on the public health care team. Thus, physicians should be encouraged to consult with a patient's veterinarian if there is any question of zoonotic or undiagnosed chronic illness (see Table 17.9 and Appendix 1).

Today, information about zoonoses in immunosuppressed populations is now more readily available on the Internet. The Healthy Pets, Healthy People (HPHP) project was created in 1998 by Tuft's veterinary student Stephanie Wong under the mentorship of Michael McElvaine, DVM (as president of the Lesbian and Gay Veterinary Medical Association). The Lesbian and Gay Veterinary Medical Association (LGVMA) then took the lead, sponsored the HPHP initiative, and published the recommendations on their website (www.lgvma.org). Ms. Wong, as the first PAWS veterinary extern, was sent to the International AIDS Conferences in Geneva (1998) and Durban (2000) to present her project. Today, the Centers for Disease Control (CDC) now officially sponsors and hosts the initiative at www.cdc.gov/healthypets.

17.6   How PAWS developed to provide support for PWAs with pets

Around the same time zoonoses emerged as an issue for pet guardians with AIDS, the San Francisco community recognized there were many other unfulfilled needs that had to be met in order to keep the human and companion animal(s) "family" together. Individuals coping with the devastating effects of AIDS found it increasingly difficult to feed and care for their pets. For example, PWAs who chose to keep their pets often faced financial burdens and physical constraints (see Table 17.6). Many of these people lacked family support. As was previously highlighted within Bronfenbrenner's model, these individuals' microsystems were no longer functioning in ways to help them with pet care. Thus, community programs evolved in the exosystem to fill this void and help keep people and pets together by maintaining the existing relationship for those who already had pets in the home.

Initially, existing animal-oriented, social services or AIDS support organizations were not set up to provide the kind of in-home services PWAs needed to care for their pets. No single group was prepared to cope with this particular dilemma. Clients of the San Francisco AIDS Foundation (SFAF) Food Bank began to request pet food. Unfortunately, pet food was not initially available, and some clients were forced to use their human rations to feed their animal companions. In response, the food bank began carrying pet food in 1985.

While the financial needs associated with veterinary care and pet food were obvious, it soon became apparent that pet owners required other services, including assistance with dog walking, boarding services if the person became hospitalized, and adoption services if the person died. Except for providing pet food at the San Francisco AIDS Food Bank, other AIDS or animal-oriented organizations in San Francisco were not equipped to put resources toward the care of clients' companion animals. The AIDS epidemic quickly overwhelmed social services in San Francisco.

Table 17.6 Problems vulnerable populations face in caring for their pets

Vulnerable people may have limited ability to care for their companion animals because of:
Limited financial resources
Limited family and/or social support
Impaired physical ability
Dementia or mental illness
Risk of zoonotic disease
Misinformation on zoonotic disease
Loss or lack of housing
Lack of "reasonable accommodations"

In 1986, a group of people, including founding veterinarian Ken Gorczyca, banded together to help PWAs keep their pets for as long as possible. In recognition of the importance of the human/animal bond, they called their group "Pets Are Wonderful Support," nicknamed "PAWS." Since its founding, many courageous and dedicated volunteers, clients, staff members and donors have helped the organization to fill in the gaps between other AIDS service- and animal-related organizations to address the particular problems and questions faced by immunosuppressed pet owners. Utilizing the terminology discussed in our previous applied model, PAWS is an example of how a contributing member within the exosystem can help keep the companion animal and person together. In comparison to traditional AAT programs in which animals are brought into the hospital or home for short periods, PAWS' services allow, in essence, 24-hour therapy utilizing an individual's own companion animals. PAWS evolved to keep existing "families" together. The gay, lesbian, bisexual, transgender and the allied San Francisco community were the pivotal early pioneers and activists in the HASS movement.

PAWS became an independent not-for-profit, volunteer-based organization in 1987. The main Companion Animal Support Services (CASS) evolved to include financial, emotional, practical and educational assistance. Services today include veterinary care; a pet food bank providing flea medications and pet supplies; foster care for clients who are hospitalized; case management; volunteer support, including in-home pet care and pet transportation; and housing advocacy for people facing discrimination because of their service animals (see Table 17.7). PAWS also remains a leader in education on both the human/animal bond and pet-associated zoonoses.

PAWS' purpose has been to deliver support services to keep PWAs and their animal companions together for as long as possible in mutually healthy environments. Over the past two decades, similar organizations and programs have developed in

Table 17.7 HASS services

Veterinary care (preventive health and emergency care)
Pet food/supply bank
Foster care
Adoption planning
Grooming and flea control
In-home pet care (dog walking; aquarium, bird cage and cat litter box cleaning)
Pet transportation
Administration of medication
Pet-associated zoonoses education (brochures, talks, education booths, referrals)
Veterinary student externship program
Public health externship program
Housing advocacy
Education on service animal rights
Hospital pet visitation program (such as Personal Pet Visitation offered by PAWS Houston)
Seniors program (with Meals on Wheels)
Homeless human populations (with VET SOS)

Table 17.8 PAWS client categories

The breakdown in the categories of non-AIDS/HIV clients compared to those with AIDS/HIV is currently as follows (PAWS, 2009):
AIDS 404
Seniors 188
Other* 174
Homeless** 20

*Includes mental illness, diabetes, cancer and other disabling illnesses.
**This does not reflect the true numbers of homeless PAWS clients, as we do not currently track the number of clients living in marginal housing such as single room occupancy (SRO) hotels. Residents in such hotels are considered homeless.

Table 17.9

Current information about Pet-Associated Zoonoses Education and prevention guidelines can be found at:
Pets Are Wonderful Support, San Francisco: http://www.pawssf.org
The Centers for Disease Control and Prevention: http://www.cdc.gov/healthypets
The American Veterinary Medical Association's zoonoses updates: http://www.avma.org/avmacollections/zu/default.asp
Lesbian and Gay Veterinary Medical Association's Healthy Pets, Healthy People project: http://www.lgvma.org
One Health Initiative—One World, One Medicine, One Health: http://www.onehealthinitiative.com

other communities to fill this "niche." The authors will use PAWS of San Francisco as a model to describe the various services offered by HASS. Each community is diverse, and the services offered vary among the different programs, depending on the local funding, volunteer base, community need and macrosystem/exosystem support.

Some HASS organizations, including PAWS, have expanded their services to include other disabled or elderly populations as well as PWAs. In 2002, PAWS expanded its services to qualifying low-income people with disabling conditions including AIDS in the PAWS Expansion Program (PEP) (see Table 17.8). In 2007, PAWS expanded its services further to include low-income seniors over the age of 60. Additionally, PAWS partners with VET SOS to help the growing human homeless populations and their pets.

17.7 Services provided by Pets Are Wonderful Support (PAWS)

17.7.1 Veterinary care

The Veterinary Care Program is one of the most important functions of PAWS because keeping a pet healthy is essential to keeping the human companion healthy.

The program provides an annual physical examination and vaccinations to each client's animal. The visit with a veterinarian also allows for the client to ask questions about zoonoses and other public health issues. The annual exam, vaccines and advice are provided free of charge by Pets Unlimited, a local veterinary hospital and shelter. Under the guidance of veterinarian Kathy Gervais, Pets Unlimited Veterinary Hospital and Shelter works in partnership with PAWS to provide a significant share of PAWS' veterinary services.

To help defray the costs of emergency or other essential medical treatments, PAWS offers an annual veterinary (vet) fund to each client. Vet fund amounts are determined each year in the budgeting process ($200 per client in 2009). Local veterinary hospitals also help by offering discounts to PAWS clients. If the client is unable to take his or her pet to the veterinarian, PAWS arranges for volunteers to help transport the animal. In addition, PAWS encourages and helps to pay for spay/neuter surgeries.

PAWS also provides additional funding for urgent care that exceeds the annual vet fund. This is determined on a case-by-case basis. The maximum allotment per client is based on the current annual budget. This fund makes it possible for clients to access critical veterinary services for their companion animals including specialist care, crucial dental care, and lifesaving or life-altering surgery.

17.7.2 Pet Food Bank

The PAWS Pet Food Bank continues to be an important and popular service for clients. It provides monthly allotments of pet food, litter, flea treatments, and pet accessories. The pet food bank is open every weekend and may be accessed once a month by PAWS clients; delivery is provided for homebound clients and is handled by volunteers. Some of the products are donated by pet food manufacturers and distributors, local supermarkets, or by individual donors. Veterinary clinics also offer discounts on "special diets" for pets with specific dietary needs. Additional food is purchased through wholesale distributors with funds raised by PAWS development staff and volunteers. Additionally, PAWS recently partnered with Meals on Wheels in San Francisco to help provide pet food and CASS services to needy elderly.

17.7.3 Foster care

Often, it is a family member or friend who will take care of a companion animal if a PAWS client goes into the hospital or is unable to care for his or her pet. However, early in the AIDS epidemic, it was not unusual to find pets unattended in an owner's home when that person went unexpectedly into the hospital. Through the years, there have been many instances in which individuals refused necessary hospital care until they were absolutely sure that their animal would receive proper care while they were away.

PAWS Foster Care Program was created to fill this need. For example, if a client requires hospitalization, PAWS attempts to find a temporary foster home for their pet. If no foster home is available, PAWS will make arrangements with local kennels, veterinary clinics, or shelters to board the animal until a foster home can be provided, or until the pet can be returned to its owner. If appropriate, and when foster care is not immediately available, PAWS will also attempt to provide in-home care for the animal.

17.7.4   In-home services

PAWS volunteers—over 400 in 2009—provide services such as litter box cleaning, dog walking, aquarium and aviary cleaning, administration of pet medications, pet grooming and flea control. In addition, volunteers help bathe animals and trim their nails. PAWS also coordinates with local groomers to donate their services to PAWS clients' animals.

17.7.5   Case Management

PAWS professional Case Management staff work with clients individually to help address their many needs, often making referrals to other providers who can help clients deal with issues outside of PAWS' scope of services. Two case managers divide the client base equally and handle most aspects of service delivery and coordination. Clients have the ability to request access to services, discuss any concerns, and find comfort in simply knowing that someone is looking after their well-being as well as that of their companion animal. This one-on-one system allows PAWS to provide much-needed emotional support in addition to the practical support clients rely on.

The Case Management staff also can provide help with end-of-life issues surrounding the future of a client's companion animal by making an adoption plan, which includes developing a living will. The living will addresses clients' fears by identifying and securing a good home for the pet if and when the owner cannot provide one. Individuals are asked to notify PAWS of the future adopting "parent" to ensure the pet will be transferred to the appropriate person in the event of the pet guardian's death. If an individual is isolated and has no family or friends willing to adopt their companion animal(s), PAWS helps to identify possible alternative sources for adoption of the pets. PAWS has extensive networks within the animal welfare system and local animal adoption programs, most of whom have screening policies for new "adoptive parents" to help prevent mismatching.

17.7.6   Behavioral assistance

As PAWS strives to allow prospective clients to fill out their application at home, there is greater exposure to the home environment of clients. While doing an in-home intake, the case manager may notice animal behavioral problems that need to be addressed. In addition, clients can call the office for advice with different behavior issues they need help solving. PAWS staff work with trainers and behaviorists who donate their time to visit these clients and create an action plan designed to target specific behavioral problems.

17.7.7   Pet-associated zoonoses education: Safe Pet Guidelines

From the inception of PAWS, public health and pet-associated zoonoses education has been a priority. In response to the lack of information on the risk of contracting zoonoses for immunosuppressed individuals, PAWS' Education Committee developed the *Safe Pet Guidelines*, which were first presented at a Delta Society meeting of humane educators in 1988 (www.pawssf.org/library_safepetguidelines.htm). The first challenge was to educate physicians treating AIDS about the benefits of animal companionship, the "small" risk of zoonoses, and how to make pets even safer for their patients with AIDS. Veterinarians took the lead as community educators. In the 1990s, many other veterinary organizations and schools, humane societies and the Centers for Disease Control (CDC) published guidelines modeled after those published initially by PAWS. The Healthy Pets, Healthy People project, now run by the CDC, brings together current resources (see www.cdc.gov/HealthyPets/).

All PAWS clients receive a copy of the *Safe Pet Guidelines* brochures at intake. These guidelines are written to help educate individuals to better understand which animals and animal-handling behaviors are risky and learn how to reduce those risks through proper diet, good hygiene and appropriate veterinary care. Consultations with veterinarians also allow for questions about zoonoses to be answered. A primary goal of PAWS is preventive health education, which has led to continued outreach to physicians, veterinarians, and other health care workers about the important benefits and minimal risks of animal companionship for PWAs and other immunocompromised populations (see Table 17.9 and Appendices 1, 2 and 3).

17.7.8   Volunteers

Although larger organizations require paid staff to function and thrive, volunteer opportunities are numerous and essential for PAWS and other HASS organizations. In addition to pet care and the food bank and delivery options, there are the rides to the veterinarians, office support, fundraising events, and the board of director positions to choose from. Volunteering offers individuals an opportunity to get out, meet new people and experience community and service.

17.7.9   The PAWS externship program

The PAWS veterinary extern program was developed in 1998. The program allows interested veterinary students the opportunity to gain experience working in the public health field and with non-profit organizations, and to witness firsthand the benefits of the human/animal bond. In turn, externs help the PAWS education program to evolve. The first extern, Stephanie Wong, helped establish the Healthy Pets, Healthy People (HPHP) project in 1998 (see previous section on zoonoses).

The PAWS veterinary externship program continues to help PAWS publish booklets and informational materials. Recent publications that externs have assisted with include *The Health Benefits of the Human-Animal Bond*; *Updated Safe Pet*

Guidelines; *The Immunocompromised Household: Informing Clients about Pets and Zoonotic Disease*; *A Guide for Veterinarians*; *Smoking and Pets*; *Bedbugs and Pets* and *Dental Care and Pets*. PAWS has hosted 17 veterinary students over the past 11 years. HASS organizations can also offer externship opportunities for students of other professions (see http://www.pawssf.org).

17.7.10   National conference series

PAWS has sponsored two national conferences, "The Healing Power of the Human-Animal Bond: Lessons Learned from the AIDS Epidemic" in 2000 in San Francisco and "The Healing Power of the Human-Animal Bond: Companion Animals and Society" in 2005 in Los Angeles. The conference proceedings are available from PAWS.

17.7.11   Client advocacy program

Many disabled, low-income San Franciscans with service animals (including emotional support animals) face housing problems such as eviction or lack of reasonable accommodation. All of these individuals have animals that meet the Americans with Disabilities Act definition of a service animal: an "animal individually trained to work or perform tasks for an individual with a disability" (49 CFR 37.3).

The legal right to emotional support from animals was decided in a 2002 case before the California Department of Fair Employment and Housing and upheld in a 2004 ruling by the Court of Appeals. For many people who are homebound, isolated, and critically ill, the emotional support animals provide may be the only companionship they receive on a daily basis.

The Client Advocacy Program provides consultation, direct advocacy and access to pro bono legal assistance to low-income, disabled San Francisco residents who are having housing-related difficulties because they have a service animal. The program also educates service organizations and community leaders about housing and service animals.

17.7.12   Emotional support

Perhaps one of the most important functions of PAWS is the provision of caring emotional support. Both staff and volunteers often provide friendship and guidance to clients in the most difficult of times, such as following the loss of a beloved companion animal. Often, clients relish the opportunity to simply share a heartwarming story about their animal to someone who understands their intense bond. They know their connection to their animals will always be taken seriously. A PAWS study (Wong, 2005) asked clients what they thought was the best thing about PAWS. Clients revealed (in this order) the food bank, the organization itself, veterinary care fund, staff, and volunteers.

17.7.13   Personal pet visitation

PAWS Houston provides a unique program that enables hospital patients to receive visits from their own animal companions on a case-by-case basis. After many years of education and outreach, most hospitals in Houston now participate in this program. PAWS Houston arranges and coordinates the hospital administration logistics and necessary pet transportation for these visits. Pets are allowed in all areas of the hospitals except bone marrow transplant units.

Many medical professionals are trying to install these programs into other hospitals as well because of the tremendous research supporting the positive health benefits of having a pet close by. This is different than AAT or HASS programs described in the rest of the *Handbook*. This program can also be used to help people in hospices that can no longer keep their pet with them.

17.7.14   Meals on Wheels collaboration

In 2008, PAWS began actively planning a collaboration with Meals on Wheels (MOW) of San Francisco to offer a full cadre of PAWS services to homebound MOW clients and their companion animals. This new initiative was launched in January 2009. Since then, PAWS has brought on 54 new MOW/PAWS clients. PAWS' Director of Volunteer Services trains MOW volunteers to support this transition and a PAWS case manager conducts client intakes for MOW clients, covering their pet-related needs and an orientation to all of PAWS' services. MOW is continuing to provide the transitioned clients with non-pet-related services.

17.8   Examples of human/animal support service programs

Since the mid-1980s, the HASS movement has provided public health education, service and emotional support to marginalized members of the community. Each community has its own resources and needs and produces its own unique response. Various examples of programs have evolved nationwide to include independent not-for-profit organizations to programs of existing animal or human service organizations (see www.pawssf.org/ for current organizations).

PAWS in San Francisco started out as an initiative in 1986 to help pet guardians with AIDS/HIV. In 2002, after extensive planning and feasibility studies, PAWS expanded its services to include other needy members of the community. PAWS was careful to create the new program in a way that would not affect its original client base and level of services.

Many programs have closed down due to the changing nature of the AIDS pandemic and the availability of community resources, while new HASS programs have started with broader missions and services. Subsequently, PAWS also has led to the development of other innovative programs to help other marginalized members of our community, such as low-income elderly, and to assist VET SOS with homeless pet guardians. Many populations can benefit from HASS services (see Table 17.10).

Table 17.10 Leading causes of death in 2006 in the USA

Total deaths	2,426,264
Diseases of the heart	631,636
Cancer	559,888
Cerebrovascular diseases	137,119
Chronic lower respiratory diseases	124,583
Accidents (unintentional injuries)	121,599
Diabetes mellitus	72, 449
Alzheimer's disease	72,432
Influenza and pneumonia	56,326
Nephritis, nephronic syndrome, and nephrosis	45,344
Septicemia	34,234

Source: Centers for Disease Control and Prevention/National Center for Health Statistics hppt://www.cdc.gov/nchs/FASTSTATS/cod.htm

17.9 Getting started

PAWS believes there should be a HASS organization in every city across the country. In support of that vision, PAWS produces a HASS start-up kit to assist individuals and organizations with launching similar services. If an individual or group is interested in starting a human/animal support program in their own community, a great deal of planning is required.

Each community typically has resources to help developing non-profit organizations. Additionally, existing human and animal service organizations, including other HASS organizations, may offer assistance for the initiative. PAWS offers a start-up packet which was updated in 2009 for individuals and communities wanting a blueprint (www.pawssf.org). Staff members are available to answer questions about how the PAWS organization functions and how to address challenges that may arise with creating new services.

17.10 VET SOS: homeless people and pets

The initial San Francisco community's response to the AIDS pandemic helped lead to the development of the human/animal support service (HASS) movement and development of pet-associated zoonoses education. Although originally focused on individuals living with HIV/AIDS, the San Francisco PAWS model has shown to be effective for other populations. Indeed, PAWS now provides services to low-income individuals with all disabilities and the elderly. And PAWS' initial education efforts were always focused on all compromising immune disorders, including HIV.

In addition to reaching out to other communities to develop their own HASS models, PAWS indirectly prompted the development of Veterinary Street Outreach Services (VET SOS), which helps the human homeless population in San Francisco and their animal companions.

Based on an idea of a formerly homeless PAWS client, San Francisco Community Clinic Consortium (SFCCC)'s Street Outreach Services (SOS) program partnered in 2001 with former PAWS board president and volunteer veterinarian, Ilana Strubel, DVM, and four highly respected San Francisco-based animal welfare agencies to begin offering veterinary care once a month to homeless animals as a way to reach out to their homeless pet guardians.

The project, now called Veterinary Street Outreach Services (VET SOS), currently serves more than 900 homeless animals in San Francisco annually and links over 250 homeless pet guardians to human health services.

VET SOS provides critically needed quality veterinary care directly to companion animals of homeless people in San Francisco. The VET SOS team provides health care information and referrals to homeless individuals as well as free basic veterinary care and vaccinations for their pets; arranges spay/neuter surgeries for companion animals at no cost; educates homeless pet owners about animal health and responsible pet ownership; and distributes medications, pet food and supplies, including collars and leashes.

The goals of VET SOS are to improve the health of homeless San Franciscans and their companion animals, decrease the spread of infectious and zoonotic diseases, reduce pet overpopulation, foster the human/animal bond, provide human health care information and referrals, and champion the welfare of homeless pet guardians and their companion animals.

VET SOS services are provided by volunteer veterinarians, veterinary technicians, and outreach workers through the use of a specially equipped mobile outreach van (Figure 17.2 and Table 17.11). The van carries veterinary vaccinations, medications, medical charts, animal food, leashes, collars, halters, and other necessary supplies that are dispensed on-site by volunteers. VET SOS visits select areas of San Francisco

Figure 17.2 VET SOS outreach van at San Francisco's Project Homeless Connect Event. Photo credit: Mark Roger's Photography

Table 17.11 VET SOS 2009 service statistics

During 2009, VET SOS increased by 41% its free services to the companion animals of homeless San Franciscans and their humans:

905 animals received urgent and preventive veterinary care

65 animals were tested on-site for infectious diseases

661 animals received vaccinations

415 animals received medication

102 animals were spayed/neutered

8 animals received emergency medical transport and care

900 animals received food and/or pet supplies

378 animals received flea and tick preventive medication

124 animals received microchips

269 homeless San Franciscans with companion animals received human health referrals

once or twice monthly and provides its services at the city of San Francisco's six annual Project Homeless Connect events.

17.10.1 Why VET SOS?

There are many studies documenting the health benefits of the human/animal bond. Studies in "vulnerable" populations demonstrate that these benefits are especially pronounced when subjects face life challenges including bereavement, physical disability, poor social support system, and homelessness.

Homeless individuals often face multiple life challenges and are especially vulnerable; their pets serve as a significant source of support (Figure 17.3). Two studies performed in California demonstrate the great need for activities supporting the human/animal bond in homeless families. In one, performed in Oakland, 74% of homeless men and 48% of homeless women with pets reported that "pets were their only source of companionship and love," and 67% of pet owners said people treated them better than homeless individuals without pets (Kidd and Kidd, 1994). However, in the same study, the majority of subjects said finding veterinary care and feeding their pets were problems. And most feed their pets before feeding themselves.

In another study performed in Davis, homeless pet owners were found to be significantly more attached to their pets than a standard pet owner population. They also had depression and hopelessness scores equal to "normal" scores despite homelessness, suggesting a possible protective role for pets (Singer et al., 1995).

In a study performed in Texas that evaluated strategies for coping with loneliness among homeless adolescents, 40% of homeless youth interviewed said that having a dog was a main means of warding off loneliness. It was determined that pet dogs provided unconditional love, improved health status, and increased the desire for jobs and responsibility (Rew, 2000).

VET SOS recognizes that keeping pets of homeless people healthy also sustains the physical and mental well-being of their human guardians. Often, these pets serve as a sole source of emotional support, promote responsibility, and act as social catalysts for interactions with other people. By combining the efforts of animal health

Figure 17.3 VET SOS client holds his beloved animal companion close during a veterinary exam. Photo credit: Mark Roger's Photography

care providers and human health care providers to reach out to this often-wary population, VET SOS builds trust, enabling further outreach and education.

Supporting the human/animal bond in homeless families also promotes public health. In addition, by ensuring all companion animals are altered, VET SOS helps to decrease pet overpopulation in San Francisco. By providing vaccines, parasite prevention, and routine veterinary care, VET SOS reduces the spread of infectious disease. By distributing pet food, VET SOS reduces the amount of human food fed to pets and increases the amount of food available for their human guardians.

The city of San Francisco is struggling with one of the highest number of homeless persons in the country. The 2008 homeless count estimated that there were approximately 6,514 homeless people within city limits at any given time. Of this figure, 2,709 were considered "unsheltered" (e.g. sleeping on the street). By offering care to the companion animals of San Franciscans challenged by homelessness, VET SOS offers an additional means for the SOS program to reach out to this population in need.

Many clients who are reluctant to seek care for themselves will seek care for their companion animals, which creates a point of entry for the SOS team to offer its services to the homeless. The project has been very successful in getting homeless clients linked with needed health and social services, which is the first step to turning their lives around and becoming productive citizens.

VET SOS serves as a model, offering training opportunities to ensure that future veterinarians, vet techs, non-profit workers, and human health care providers have the practical skills to support homeless families. Equally important, however, is the experience of being part of a collaboration that recognizes the integral connection between human and animal health, the importance of giving back to the community, the support provided to the community's most vulnerable members, and the feelings of empathy and awareness that all these things engender. VET SOS is operated by a human health care private not-for-profit agency, San Francisco Community Clinic Consortium (SFCCC), in collaboration with four highly respected animal welfare agencies: Pets Are Wonderful Support (PAWS), San Francisco Department of Animal Care and Control (SF/ACC), San Francisco Society for the Prevention of Cruelty to Animals (SF/SPCA) and Pets Unlimited. VET SOS is also supported with funds and by veterinary community volunteers from the San Francisco Veterinary Medical Association.

San Francisco, the city of St. Francis, has been a pioneer and leader with animal and human support services. Over the past 25 years, a generous and giving community made up of volunteers, sponsors, not-for-profit organizations, government agencies and businesses has worked together to promote services for both people and pets. Together, San Francisco organizations, volunteers and donors continue to benefit needy and vulnerable animal guardians and their animal companions in their community. Other communities can use the San Francisco model as a template for improving their own HASS and Companion Animal Support Services (CASS) facilities.

17.11   Conclusion

Companion and therapy animals reach people on many life-enhancing levels. Companion animals have been used in community and health care settings to "reach" those who have a reduced capacity to interact with others (Fine, 2002). PAWS and VET SOS make it possible for people with chronic or terminal illnesses, the elderly, and those who also may be coping with unfortunate living situations, to stay together with their valued animal companions for as long as possible in a mutually beneficial relationship.

Animals provide affection and companionship that is not dependent on cognitive or physical capacity (Baun and McCabe, 2003). For those who have and care for pets, this special relationship can truly provide a method to enhance physical and emotional healing.

The HASS models presented in this chapter represent guidelines and provide blueprints designed to assist persons with chronic/terminal illnesses with caring for their pets and to enhance the quality of life while they live within their homes (or the homes of others). Clinicians, veterinarians and community members interested in enhancing the lifestyles of these individuals may consider using the San Francisco HASS model as a starting point to build upon.

References

Angulo, F., & Glasser, C. (1994). Caring for pets of immunocompromised persons. *Journal of American Veterinary Medical Association, 205*(12).

Baun, M., & McCabe, B. (2003). *Companion Animals and Persons with Dementia of the Alzheimer's Type. Therapeutic Possibilities*. University of Nebraska Medical Center.

Bennet, M. J. (1990). Stigmatization: experiences of persons with acquired immune deficiency syndrome. *Issues in Mental Health Nursing, 11*, 141–154.

Bronfenbrenner, U. (1977). Toward an experimental ecology of human development. *American Psychologist, 32*, 513–531.

Bronfenbrenner, U. (1979). *The Ecology of Human Development*. Cambridge, MA: Harvard University Press.

Campsmith, M. L., Rhodes, P., Hall, H. I., et al. (2008). HIV prevalence estimates—United States, 2006. *Morbidity and Mortality Weekly Report, 57*(39), 1073–1076.

Carmack, B. J. (1991). The role of companion animals for persons with AIDS/HIV. *Holistic Nursing Practice, 5*(2), 24–31.

Castelli, P., Hart, L. A., & Zasloff, R. L. (2001). Companion cats and the social support systems of men with AIDS. *Psychological Reports, 89*, 177–187.

CDC (n.d.) Retrieved May 1, 2005, http://www.cdc.gov/hiv/topics/aa/resources/factsheets/aa.htm

Cherry, K., & Smith, D. (1993). Sometimes I cry: the experience of loneliness for men with AIDS. *Health Communication, 5*, 181–208.

Chinner, T. L., & Dalziel, F. R. (1991). An exploratory study on the viability and efficacy of a pet-facilitated therapy project within a hospice. *Journal of Palliative Care, 7*, 13–20.

Christ, G., Wiener, L., & Moynihan, R. (1986). Psychosocial issues in AIDS. *Psychiatric Annals, 16*, 173–179.

Cohen, S. (2002). Can pets function as family members? *Western Journal of Nursing Reserch, 24*, 621–638.

Cookman, C. A. (1996). Older people and attachment of things, places and pets and ideas. Images. *Journal of Nursing Scholarship, 28*, 227–231.

Cusack, O. (1988). *Pets and Mental Health*. New York: The Haworth Press.

Delongis, A., Carpreol, M., Holtzman, S., O'Brien, T., & Campbell, J. (2004). Social support and social strain among husband and wives: a multilevel analysis [Electronic version]. *Journal of Family Psychology, 8*(3).

Fine, A. H. (2002). Animal assisted therapy. In M. Herson & W. Sledge (Eds.), *Encyclopedia of Psychotherapy* (pp. 49–55). New York: Elsevier Science.

Fine, A. H., & Fine, N. M. (1996). *Let Me in, I Want to Play*. Springfield, IL: Charles C. Thomas Publisher Ltd.

Friedman, E., Katcher, A. H., Thomas, S. A., Lynch, J. J., & Messent, P. R. (1983). Social interactions and blood pressure: influence of animal companions. *Journal of Nervous and Mental Disease, 171*, 461–465.

Garrett, L. (July/Aug. 2005). *The Lessons of HIV/AIDS. Foreign Affairs*.

Glasser, C., & Angulo, F. (1994). Animal-associated opportunistic infections among persons infected with human immunodeficiency virus. *Clinical Infectious Diseases, 18*, 14–24.

Gorczyca, K. (1991). Special needs for the pet owner with AIDS/HIV. In Latham Foundation Staff (Ed.), *The Bond Between All Living Things* (pp. 13–20). Saratoga, CA: R & E Publishers.

Gorczyca, K., Abrams, D., & Carmack, B. (1989). Pets and HIV disease: a survey of provider's knowledge and attitudes. *V International Conference on AIDS Proceedings*.

Gortmaker, S. L. (1985). Demography of chronic childhood diseases: prevalence and impact. *Pediatric Clinics of North America, 31*, 3–18.

Grant, S., & Olsen, C. W. (1999). Preventing zoonotic diseases in immunocompromised persons: the role of physicians and veterinarians. *Emerging Infectious Disease*, Jan.–Feb. 5(1), 159–163.

Healthy, Pets & Healthy People. (1998). *Healthy Pets, Healthy People Resource Guide*. San Francisco: Ed. S. Wong.

Hoffman, C., & Rice, D. (1995). *1997 National Medical Expenditure Survey*. San Francisco: University of California. Institute for Health and Aging.

Humane Society of the United States (HSUS). (2003). US pet ownership statistics. Retrieved on Feb. 21, 2005 from http://www.hsus.org/pets/issues_affecting_our_pets/ pet_ over-population_and_ownership_statistics/us_pet_ownership_statistics.html

Hutton, J. S. (November 1982). Social workers act like animals in their casework relations. *Society for Companion Animal Studies Newsheet, 3*, 30.

International Society for Anthrozoology (ISAZ) poster 2008.

Jackson, P. L., & Vessey, J. A. (2000). *Primary Care of the Child with a Chronic Condition* (3rd ed.). St. Louis: Mosby.

Johnson, R. (2003). Human animal interaction, illness prevention, and wellness promotion. *Editorial. Animal Behavioral Scientist, 47*(1), 5–6.

Jorgenson, J. (1997). Therapeutic use of companion animals in health care. *Journal of Nursing Scholarship, 29*, 249–254.

Judson, L. (2004). Global childhood chronic illness [Electronic version]. *Nursing Administration Quarterly, 28*(1), 607.

Jue, S. (1994). Psychosocial issues of AIDS long-term survivors. Families in society. *Journal of Contemporary Human Services, 43*, 324–332.

Katcher, A. H. (1981). Interactions between people and their pets: Form and function. In B. Fogle (Ed.), *Interactions between People and Pets* (pp. 46–47). Springfield, IL: Thomas.

Keresh, W., & Cook, R. (July/August 2005). *The Human-Animal Link. Foreign Affairs*.

Kidd, A. H., & Kidd, R. M. (1994). Benefits and liabilities of pets for the homeless. *Psychological Reports, 74*, 715–722.

Meer, J. (1984). Pet theories. *Psychology Today, 18*, 60–67.

Muschel, U. (1985 October). Pet therapy with terminal cancer patients. Social casework. *Journal of Contemporary Social Work*, 451–458.

Perrin, J. M., & MacLean, W. E., Jr. (1988). Children with chronic illness: the prevention of dysfunction. *Pediatrics of North America, 35*, 1325–1337.

Pets Are Wonderful Support. (June 2005). *Healing power of the human-animal bond*. Hollywood, CA: conference proceedings.

Pets Are Wonderful Support. (2005). *Safe Pet Guidelines* (3rd ed.). [Brochure]. San Francisco: Ed.

Pets Are Wonderful Support. (1998). *Questions You may Have about Your Cat and Your Health* [Brochure]. San Francisco: Ed. Blount and Spain.

Pets Are Wonderful Support. (1998). *Questions You may Have about Your Bird and Your Health*. [Brochure]. San Francisco: Ed. Blount and Spain.

Rew, L. (2000). Friends and pets as companions: strategies for coping with loneliness among homeless youth. *Journal of Child and Adolescent Psychiatric Nursing, 13*(3), 125.

Seniornet (n.d.). Chronic conditions. Retrieved May 10, 2005, from http://www.seniornet.org/ php/default.php?PageID=5541&Version=0&Font=0

Serpell, J. A. (Spring 1983). Pet psychotherapy. *People-Animals-Environment*, 7–8.

Sharkin, B. S., & Knox, D. (2003). Pet loss: issues and implications for a psychologist [Electronic version]. *Professional Psychology: Research and Practice, 34*(4).

Siegel, J. M. (1993a). Companion animals: in sickness and in health. *Journal of Social Issues, 49*, 157–167.

Siegel, L. J. (1993b). Psychotherapy with medically at-risk children. In T. R. Kratochwill & R. J. Morris (Eds.), *Handbook of Psychotherapy with Children and Adolescents* (pp. 472–501). Boston: Allyn and Bacon.

Siegel, J. M., Angulo, F. J., Detels, R., Wesch, J., & Mullen, A. (1999). AIDS diagnosis and depression in the multicenter AIDS Cohort Study: the ameliorating impact of pet ownership. *AIDS Care, 11*(2), 157–170.

Singer, R. S., Hart, L., & Zasloff, R. (1995). Dilemmas associated with rehousing homeless people who have companion animals. *Psychological Reports, 77*, 851–857.

Spencer, L. (1992). Study explores health risks and the human/animal bond. *Journal of American Veterinary Medical Association, 201*(11), 1669.

Thompson, R. J., Jr., & Gustafson, K. E. (1996). *Adaptation to Chronic Childhood Illness.* Washington, DC: American Psychological Association.

United Nations AIDS/World Health Organization. (1998). *Report on the Global HIV/AIDS Epidemic.*

UN AIDS (2004). Regional HIV and AIDS estimates 2004. Retrieved May 1, 2005, from http://www.unaids.org/EN/default.asp

UN AIDS/WHO (2007). Retrieved December 1, 2009, from UN AIDS/WHO 2007 report on the global AIDS epidemic. United Nations Program on HIV/AIDS. www.unaids.org

United States National Center of Health Statistics (n.d.). 2004 *National Vital Statistics Reports* [Electronic version]. Vol. 53(17). Retrieved June 15, 2005, from http://www.cdc.gov/nchs/data/dvs/nvsr53_17tableE2002.pdf

Veevers, J. E. (1985). The social meaning of pets: alternate roles for companion animals. In M. B. Sussman (Ed.), *Pets and the Family* (pp. 11–30). New York: The Haworth Press.

Volth, V. L. (1985). Attachment of people to companion animals. *Veterinary Clinics of North America, 15*, 289–295.

Weiss, R. S. (1973). *Loneliness: The Experience of Social and Emotional Isolation.* Cambridge, MA: MIT Press.

Wong, B. (December 2005). Role of pets in health promotion: a PAWS case study. Poster session presented at the 133rd annual meeting of the American Public Health Association. Philadelphia, PA.

Wong, S. (1998). Report from World AIDS Conference in Geneva. *Lesbian and Gay Veterinary Medical Association's Good News, 6*(3).

Wrongdiagnosis.com (n.d.). Statistics about chronic illness. Retrieved May 10, 2005, from http://www.wrongdiagnosis.com/c/chronic/stats.htm

Appendices

Appendices 1, 2 and 3 can be found at the PAWs website (www.pawssf.org) under the Library Tab in the Education section.

Appendix 1. *Educating People About Pet-Associated Zoonoses* by Stephanie Venn-Watson, DVM, MPH.

Appendix 2. *Guidelines for Preventing Zoonotic Infections When Conducting AAT with Immunocompromised Persons* edited by Vic Spain, DVM and adapted with permission from "Safe Pet Guidelines for Immunocompromised Animal Guardians," Pets Are Wonderful Support.

Appendix 3. Printable versions of the *Safe Pet Guidelines* are available at www.pawssf.org/library_safepetguidelines.htm

18 Animal abuse and developmental psychopathology: recent research, programmatic and therapeutic issues and challenges for the future

Frank R. Ascione*, Marie S. McCabe[†], Allie Phillips[†], Philip Tedeschi*

[*] University of Denver, [†] American Humane Association

18.1   Introduction

As animals become a more significant component of therapeutic interventions with children and adolescents, greater attention is being paid both to the benevolent and the problematic relations that exist between animals and young people. The field of animal welfare has a long history of attempts to enhance children's attitudes toward and treatment of animals (see Ascione, 1997, 2005b for overviews). But as society focuses on the persistent challenge of violence in human relationships, renewed attention is being given to animal abuse as a correlate of and potential precursor to human mental health problems (Ascione and Maruyama, in press; Green and Gullone, 2005; McPhedran, 2009a; Petersen and Farrington, 2007). The roles of animals in preventing and treating mental health dysfunction in children and adolescents are also receiving increased scrutiny (Ascione and Shapiro, 2009) as are animal welfare issues implicated in elder adult maltreatment (Peak and Ascione, in press).

This chapter provides (a) an updated overview of research on the relation between animal abuse and interpersonal violence (Ascione), (b) a discussion of efforts by animal and human welfare organizations to use this information to expand their scope to areas of common interest (McCabe and Phillips), and (c) an illustration of the unique role animals may play in assessment and therapeutic intervention with young people who are psychologically at risk (Tedeschi). Each of us approached this project from our own varying perspectives of developmental psychology, child and animal welfare, and child clinical intervention and animal-assisted social work. Yet a common thread in all of our work is the belief that collaboration among professionals is the most fruitful avenue to solving complex human (and animal!) problems.

Handbook on Animal-Assisted Therapy. DOI: 10.1016/B978-0-12-381453-1.10018-2

18.2   The confluence of animal maltreatment and interpersonal violence

18.2.1   How do we define animal abuse?

Throughout this chapter, we will refer to non-human animals as "animals" for simplicity. Defining animal abuse is a challenging endeavor due to the variety of statuses that animals acquire in different human cultures (Kaufmann, 1999). When we define animal abuse, are we referring to farm animals that provide food for humans, animals used in research (in human and veterinary medicine), wildlife, animals maintained in zoological parks, assistance animals, or companion animals? As cultures, we condone or condemn various practices depending on which status an animal occupies. Clearly, we are faced at the outset with a task more difficult than defining human abuse and one in which international and cross-cultural comparisons must be approached with caution (Pagani et al., 2007, in press).

Agnew (1998) has suggested that attempts to define animal abuse share a number of features—"...the harm inflicted on animals should be (1) socially unacceptable, (2) intentional or deliberate, and/or (3) unnecessary (see Ascione, 1993; Baenninger, 1991; Kellert and Felhous, 1985; Vermuelen and Odendaal, 1993)." Animal abuse may include acts of commission or omission, paralleling types of child maltreatment such as child physical abuse and neglect of a child's nutritional needs. In fact, we can easily borrow classifications of child maltreatment and apply them to animals (Munro, 1996; Munro and Thrusfield, 2001a,b,c,d)—physical and sexual abuse, neglect, and emotional abuse (see Beetz and Podberscek (2005) for an extensive exploration of the sexual abuse of animals, Blevins (2009) for a related and informative case study, and McMillan (2005) for an analysis of the emotional maltreatment of animals).

In judging the significance of animal abuse by young people, we must always determine whether the youth's behavior violates community and cultural standards and whether sufficient cognitive maturity is present to indicate that the behavior was intentionally harmful. Both of these factors are relevant for clinical assessment and may also be related to legal statutes pertaining to the treatment of animals.

How have scientists attempted to measure animal abuse, especially since this behavior often occurs secretively?

In some jurisdictions, especially those where animal abuse may be a felony offense, one could examine official records to determine the incidence of animal abuse reported to authorities. However, animal abuse misdemeanor offenses may not be recorded separately or cannot be extracted from official criminal records (H. Snyder, personal communication, Jan. 22, 2001). Animal welfare organizations also vary widely in their tracking of animal abuse cases. The current situation is similar to our inability to track the incidence of child maltreatment before mandatory reporting became law.

In cases where official records are available, checklists of different types of maltreatment can be used for categorization, a method employed in South Africa by

Vermuelen and Odendaal (1993). A similar process can be applied to the clinical case records of children and adolescents. However, as will be noted later, it is only in the past decade that animal abuse has been highlighted as a symptom of certain psychiatric disorders in young people. Prior to this, clinicians may not have asked about the presence of animal abuse in a child's history. A clinical history that does not contain animal abuse may reflect that no one asked about this symptom as distinct from its actual absence.

Structured interviews about animal abuse have also been used with respondents old enough for verbal questioning. This method has most often used retrospective reporting and been applied to adult clinical and criminal samples (e.g. Felthous and Kellert, 1987; Merz-Perez and Heide, 2004; Schiff et al., 1999). As with all self-report methods but especially with sensitive topics, issues of social desirability, reluctance to disclose, or false disclosure to enhance one's reputation for violence must be considered in evaluating such reports. These cautions also apply to the use of a structured interview protocol for children and adolescents developed by Ascione et al. (1997a)—the Cruelty to Animals Assessment Instrument (CAAI).

The CAAI is designed to elicit reports of abusive and kind treatment of pet, farm, wild, and stray animals either observed or performed by children at least five years of age. A rating system based on CAAI responses attempts to quantify a child's animal abuse in terms of frequency, severity, chronicity, and level of empathy. However, it has yet to be applied to large samples of young people at risk for psychological disorders.

More recently, three questionnaires based, in part, on the CAAI have been developed by Australian researchers (Dadds et al., 2004; Guymer et al., 2001; Thompson and Gullone, 2003). These assessments show great promise for the more efficient and standardized assessment of animal abuse as well as the positive treatment of animals (see also Baldry, 2003).

We especially recommend that therapists and researchers (and those wearing both these hats!) consider use of the Dadds et al. instrument for assessing animal abuse since it has been shown to have excellent psychometric properties and correlates with other antisocial behaviors such as fire setting (Dadds and Fraser, 2006).

Unstructured interviews and qualitative methods (Fitzgerald, 2005) have also been applied to assessing animal abuse. Examples include a police interview of a pedophile who admitted to repeatedly trying to suffocate and then revive a cat by sealing it a plastic garbage bag and the 1998 Herbeck case where the convicted perpetrator said he used animal abuse to soothe himself. (Jones, 1998).

The most commonly used clinical checklist that contains information, albeit meager, on animal abuse is the Child Behavior Checklist (CBCL) developed by Achenbach and Edelbrock (1981). One form of this assessment is administered to parents/guardians and asks about a number of symptoms, including "physical cruelty to animals" over the past six months. Respondents rate children on whether each symptom is never, sometimes, or often true of their child. Unfortunately, a youth self-report and a teacher report form of the CBCL do not ask about cruelty to animals. This makes assessment of correspondence between parent and child reports problematic. Offord et al. (1991) found poor correspondence using a variation of the CBCL. One factor that may account for the lack of correspondence is that animal abuse may occur covertly, especially for older children, and parents may be unaware of such acts (the Dadds et al. instrument may be valuable here since it includes both a parent report form and a child self-report form). In addition, since "cruelty" is not defined for respondents, we do not know the standards they use in making their judgments. Teachers may not see animal abuse but may hear reports of it from their students.

A cruelty to animals item is also included in Kazdin and Esveldt-Dawson's (1986) interview for antisocial behavior and responses to this item differentiate conduct-disordered (see description below) from non-conduct-disordered children.

Two other instruments have been developed specifically for assessing animal abuse in domestic violence situations. The Battered Partner Shelter Survey (BPSS; Ascione and Weber, 1997a) and the Children's Observation and Experience with Pets (COEP; Ascione and Weber, 1997b) assessment were designed for use with women and children who have entered a shelter for women who are battered. These structured interviews allow assessment of threatened and actual animal abuse as well as other information about pet care. A recently released assessment of children's exposure to intimate partner violence also includes one item related to exposure to pet abuse (Edleson et al., 2008).

How prevalent is animal abuse in adults?

Since national records on animal abuse are not available, we must rely on clinical case control studies to estimate its prevalence (i.e. any incidents of abuse within a partic-ular time frame) in adult samples. Felthous and Kellert's (1987) review suggests that in psychiatric and criminal samples, animal abuse is reported by up to 57% of respondents in contrast to near zero rates for respondents in normative comparison groups. In a study of serial sexual homicide perpetrators, prevalence rates approached 70% for men who said they themselves had been sexual abuse victims (Ressler et al., 1988). These estimates must be viewed with caution since definitional and measurement variations between studies may affect self-reports (Vaughn et al., 2009). The MMPI also contains some items related to the treatment of animals but we are not aware of any investigations on animal abuse using this instrument.

How prevalent is animal abuse in children and adolescents?

Ascione (1993) reported that between 14 and 22% of adolescent delinquents at facilities in Utah admitted to torturing or hurting animals in the past year. Using norming data from the Child Behavior Checklist (CBCL; Achenbach and Edelbrock, 1981), children and adolescents seen at mental health clinics display rates of animal cruelty between 10 and 25%, depending on the sex of the child. Comparable rates for non-clinic children are under 5%. Recall that animal abuse is not measured on the self-report form of the CBCL. That these percentages may be underestimates is suggested by data from Offord et al. (1991) in which maternal reports of cruelty to animals in a non-clinic sample of 12–14 year olds was 2% but the children's self-reports yielded a prevalence rate of 10%. Again, definitional issues, reduced parental surveillance as children get older, and parental reluctance to admit their children's animal abuse may all contribute to such discrepancies.

International data are now available on animal abuse perpetrated by young people, both from normative samples in Japan, Australia, and Malaysia (Mellor et al., 2009) and a sample of Japanese youth residing at correctional facilities (Tani, 2007).

Do children and adolescents "outgrow" abusing animals?

Behaviors that emerge and then "disappear" with increasing age are usually the result of complex interactions between maturational and experiential processes. Animal "abuse" by an older infant or toddler may be a matter of poor motor and impulse control that can easily be dealt with by parental monitoring and intervention. More recalcitrant animal abuse by a child may require more intensive assessment and treatment. An important theoretical analysis of adolescent antisocial behavior may be applicable here. Moffit (1993) suggested that adolescents who engage in antisocial behavior likely fall into one of at least two groups—adolescence-limited and life-course persistent. In the former group, acting out only becomes prominent during the adolescent period and might even be considered normative. When adolescents leave this period of development, they also leave their antisocial behavior behind. In the latter group, antisocial behavior emerges early in childhood and, if untreated, may persist into adolescence and adulthood (Eme, 2009). This categorization may also be true for animal abuse as a specific form of antisocial behavior. It should be noted that abusive behavior could shift from an animal to a human victim and/or may become more covert as a child gets older.

When a young child abuses animals, it may allow for early intervention but may also be an indicator that a child may be on a life-course persistent path for antisocial behavior. Therefore, early detection is critical both for separating normative from pathognomic animal abuse and for targeting scarce intervention resources.

What is the significance of animal abuse as a symptom of the childhood and adolescent psychological disturbance known as conduct disorder?

Although animal abuse has been considered potentially symptomatic of psychiatric disturbance for centuries (see Pinel, 1809), it is only within the past 12 years that animal abuse has been included in standard psychiatric classification manuals. "Cruelty to animals" made its first appearance in the revised third edition of the *Diagnostic and Statistical Manual of the American Psychiatric Association* (DSM-IIIR) in 1987 and has been found to be one of the earliest symptoms of conduct disorder to appear in childhood (Frick et al., 1993). At that time, it was unclear whether animal abuse, as a symptom of conduct disorder,[1] was more similar to

---

[1] Conduct disorder, "...is a repetitive and persistent pattern of behavior in which the basic rights of others or major societal norms or rules are violated..." (American Psychiatric Association, 1994, p. 85).

property destruction or interpersonal violence. This confusion was resolved in DSM-IV and DSM-IV-TR (American Psychiatric Association, 1994, 2000) in which physical cruelty to animals is listed among the symptoms in the heading "aggression toward people and animals." This change makes intuitive sense since animal abuse involves harm to sentient creatures capable of experiencing pain, distress, and death and speaks to potentially impaired capacity for empathy in the perpetrator. Animal abuse is also listed as a correlate of antisocial behavior in the International Classification of Diseases (World Health Organization, 1996). Recently, Gleyzer and colleagues (2002) reported that criminal defendants who abused animals were more likely to receive a diagnosis of antisocial personality disorder (37%) than those who did not abuse animals (8%). The relation between animal abuse, conduct disorder, and antisocial personality disorder was also explored by Gelhorn et al. (2007). Dadds et al. (2006) also report that animal abuse is related to callous and emotional traits in children, traits that may be implicated in more serious forms of conduct disorder.

These developments now make it more likely that clinicians and other mental health professionals will attend to this symptom during assessment and diagnostic work. Although research has not specifically addressed how often animal abuse is one of the symptoms present in diagnoses of conduct disorder, one estimate suggests that animal abuse may be present in 25% of conduct disorder cases (Arluke et al., 1999). This estimate received confirmation in a study by Luk et al. (1999).

What biological factors appear related to animal abuse?

Although no research, to our knowledge, has been specifically addressed to physio-logical and biochemical processes that may underlie animal abuse, the importance of such research should not be overlooked (see an instructive case study reported by Kruesi (1989)). As noted by Lockwood and Ascione (1997), "...we will need to attend to brain-behavior relations as we seek a better understanding of the phenom-enon of cruelty to animals" (p. 151). Even in cases where young people's genetic vulnerability for risk behaviors may be present, prevention may nevertheless be successful (Brody et al., 2009). Information on physiological and biochemical processes that may underlie animal abuse will be valuable for both diagnosis and intervention and would also help identify circumstances when engaging in animal abuse causes significant biochemical change in the perpetrator or cases where phar-macological agents may prompt animal abuse (Jimenez-Jimenez et al., 2002). Pharmacological interventions for violent behavior in general should also be exam-ined for their effectiveness in reducing animal abuse.

How is animal abuse specifically related to the physical and sexual abuse of young people?

Although attention to the overlap between animal abuse and child maltreatment is increasing, few existing studies have addressed this issue. DeViney et al. (1983) found a 60% pet abuse and neglect prevalence rate in a sample of families with substantiated child maltreatment. Friedrich (cited in Ascione, 1993) found that 27 to 35% of female and male child sexual abuse victims displayed cruelty to animals (the rate was less than 5% in the non-abused samples). More recently, Ascione and colleagues (2003) reported a study of 1,433 children 6 to 12 years of age some of whom were victims of sexual abuse and others who were psychiatrically disturbed. Subsamples of these children had also been physically abused and exposed to domestic violence. In these cases, cruelty to animals was as high as 60%. Duncan et al. (2005) reported that among conduct disordered youth, those with animal abuse as a symptom (in contrast to those not displaying animal abuse) were more likely to have been maltreated or exposed to intimate partner violence. These data support anecdotal reports of the overlap and case study examples (see Tapia, 1971 and Section 18.4 below) as does recent retrospective research with incarcerated sex offenders (Simons et al., 2008). Animal abuse has also been implicated in cases of severe inter-sibling abuse (Khan and Cooke, 2008).

What might motivate a young person to abuse animals?

Understanding the motivations underlying animal abuse will be essential for designing effective prevention and intervention programs. Ascione et al. (1997a) discovered a variety of motivations in a sample of at-risk children. These included identification with the aggressor and imitation, modifying one's mood (animal abuse creating excitement), peer-facilitated and forced animal abuse, and sexually-reactive animal abuse. The question, "why is the child doing this?" cannot be answered using behavioral checklists (Pinizzotto, 2008; see Ascione, 2005b for an extensive discussion of both adult and child/adolescent motivations for abusing animals). More in-depth assessment will be required as illustrated in the case study in Section 18.4.

What role does empathy play in preventing animal abuse?

We are only beginning to explore human capacity for empathizing with other species (Westbury and Neumann, 2008). The development of empathy between humans is believed to have its roots in early infancy (Eisenberg, 1992; Goleman, 1995) and be dependent on the quality of relationships a child experiences. It is believed that empathy enables humans to help each other and that its absence makes harming others easier. We must explore these phenomena and their applicability to human/animal relations. For example, Magid and McKelvey (1987) note that children with distortions in their attachments may lack empathy and be likely to abuse animals; the relation between empathy and a lower likelihood of violence toward others has been documented by developmental psychologists (Hastings et al., 2000). Two recent studies confirm an inverse relation between empathy toward humans and propensity to engage in animal abuse (Dadds et al., 2008; Thompson and Gullone, 2008). Empathy to people and empathy to animals are not identical but are sufficiently correlated to command our attention (Ascione, 2005b;

Pagani, 2000; Weber and Ascione, 1992). McPhedran's (2009b) review explores these issues in greater detail.

Is there a relation between domestic, or family, violence and animal abuse?

Research on the overlap between violence between intimate partners and animal maltreatment is still in its infancy (Ascione, 2005a,b, 2007; DeGue and DeLillo, 2009). Despite numerous anecdotal references to this overlap, Renzetti's (1992) research was the first to document the overlap in a study of violent lesbian relationships. In this study, 38% of abused respondents reported that their pets had been hurt by their partners. Ascione (1998) studied this phenomenon in 38 women seeking safety at a shelter for women who are battered. Nearly three-quarters of the women had pets (currently or in the past year) and over half of these women reported that their pets had been hurt or killed by their partner (similar results were reported in studies from Wisconsin and Colorado (Arkow, 1996)). A recent replication with 101 women who were battered (see Ascione et al., 2007) and a comparison group of women who did not report intimate partner violence (all of whom had companion animals) found similar results. In the replication study, over 60% of the children in these homes had witnessed animal abuse suggesting one mechanism by which some children might acquire and imitate animal abuse. However, it is also important to note that many children tried to intervene on behalf of their pets when violence erupted in their homes. More information about the potentially deleterious effects of exposure to animal abuse can be found in papers by Ascione (2009), Currie (2006), and Thompson and Gullone (2006).

Volant et al. (2008) have also completed a replication of the Ascione et al. (2007) study with similarly sized samples of abused and non-abused Australian women and documented that 52.9% of abused women reported harm to their pets. (For more extensive discussions of animal abuse and domestic violence, see the volume edited by Ascione (2008) especially chapters by Flynn, by Faver and Strand, and by Gullone and Clarke, and recent articles by Simmons and Lehmann (2007) and Strauchler et al. (2004).)

Why is information about animal abuse as a form of domestic violence important for the welfare of animals as well as the welfare of women and children?

The studies just described suggest that women, children, and animals are at risk in families experiencing domestic violence. In fact, Ascione et al. (2007) found that nearly one-quarter of the women reported that concern for their pets' welfare had kept them from seeking shelter sooner. In some cases, women may be forced to endanger themselves and their children because they do not know how to insure their pets' safety if they decide to leave a violent partner. This issue is reinforced by the inclusion of pet abuse on a number of instruments used to assess risk of danger from a violent partner (Walton-Moss et al., 2005).

Is the information about domestic violence and animal abuse being applied and, if so, how?

The results cited above have prompted a number of animal welfare agencies to collaborate with domestic violence programs to provide free or low-cost pet sheltering (either at the shelter facility or with foster caretakers) when a women decides to leave an abusive partner. The degree of need for such programs is still difficult to determine since only a minority of domestic violence shelters may ask women clients about pet abuse (Ascione et al., 1997b; a replication of this study is needed to determine if this is still the case).

As these sheltering programs emerge, a number of practical, programmatic, and ethical issues arise (Ascione, 2000; Ascione et al., 1997b; Kogan et al., 2004). For example, funding such programs may become problematic if pets are left for significant periods of time (e.g. months), designating personnel to direct these programs may divert animal shelters from other missions, and animal welfare/human welfare conflicts may arise such as: how long should sheltering last before adoption or euthanasia is considered? What if a woman is reclaiming her pet but is returning to her abusive partner who had harmed the pet? How does the animal shelter deal with reports that the children in these homes have abused pets?

Other animal-related issues have yet to be addressed. Although we know that children growing up in violent homes may display behavior disorders, how are the pets affected by such an environment? Are these pets less adoptable if given up by their owners? Will domestic violence shelters accept an assistance animal if a client has a handicap such as blindness? Since many battered women will return to their partners, can we assist them in developing a safety plan that will keep the women and their children's welfare paramount but also consider pet safety? Howard Davidson (1998) noted that an animal abuse history was used in a parental rights termination case. Is such information relevant for a woman if she is considering a permanent break from her partner but hopes to retain custody of the family pet(s)? Should she have on file a detailed complaint against her partner that could be used at a later time? Are there ways of easing the pain of separation from their pets when women and children must enter a shelter (see Section 18.3)? A strategy developed by the Baltimore Police Department was to take photos of the pets as a reminder that the pets will be well cared for (Ascione, 2005b, p. 146). Can animal welfare programs assist women to find transitional housing that allows pets? What is the extent of training about domestic violence issues such as confidentiality and safety factors that should be provided to animal shelter personnel and foster caretakers?

When children and adolescents abuse animals, what steps should be taken to address this behavior?

We recommend that animal abuse by young people be addressed like any of the other serious symptoms of conduct disorder. Comprehensive and developmentally sensitive assessment will help determine the context of the abuse and its seriousness as well as the child's level of culpability (Hindman, 1992). One could model animal abuse interventions on programs for dealing with childhood fire setting (Kolko, 2002). Curiosity fire setters will likely respond to educational interventions and humane education can be effective with some children who maltreat animals. Pathological fire setters require more intensive therapy similar to the therapy for animal abuse illustrated by the case study described at the end of this chapter (see Section 18.4). Interventions will need to consider exposure to family and community violence as well as a child's possible victimization (physical, sexual, emotional) by parents, other caretakers, and siblings.

Faver (2010) has recently made a case for humane education as a violence prevention strategy. Correlations between bullying and animal abuse have also been reported (Gullone and Robertson, 2008); it would be of interest to determine if effective bullying prevention and intervention programs could be adapted to reduce animal abuse.

What are the continuing needs for the assessment and tracking of the problem of animal abuse?

In the USA, the child welfare movement benefited dramatically from public acknowledgment of child maltreatment and legislative attention. We can now obtain documentation of the number of child maltreatment cases reported each year and the percent that are substantiated. Similar data are unavailable, on a national basis, for animal abuse cases. Without such data, we will never know if animal abuse is becoming more or less prevalent and we will lack a baseline against which to measure the effectiveness of prevention and intervention programs.

Congressional legislation resulted in a national system for reporting child maltreatment including designation of mandated reporters. This model is currently absent for animal abuse. Likewise, the Uniform Crime Report tracks incidents of juvenile perpetrated crimes, such as vandalism, but does not track animal abuse. Thus, those interested in animal welfare cannot use these reporting systems to assess animal maltreatment.

It would be an advantage if animal welfare professionals such as veterinarians and organizations such as animal shelters, at a minimum, were required to keep nationally comparable records on animal abuse reports and investigations. Other sentinels who may note animal abuse include groomers, postal workers, meter readers, and other neighborhood workers. Their watchfulness could also be used to document cases of animals at risk. The standard inclusion of questions about animal abuse on all risk of danger assessments for domestic violence cases would also be valuable. Since research on animal abuse and domestic violence has relied exclusively on the reports of women who are battered, there is a critical need for questioning batterers about their treatment of animals; to date, only one such study has been reported (Ascione and Blakelock, 2003).

In the area of research, the need for longitudinal analysis of animal abuse, especially in childhood and adolescence, is critical. We need to be able to differentiate transient from chronic animal abuse since animal abuse may only predict serious mental health disturbance when observations are aggregated over time (see Loeber et al., 1993). Recent retrospective research also suggests that the age of onset for animal abuse may be related to its seriousness and persistence (Henry, 2004a,b; Hensley and Tallichet, 2005).

Finally, despite the inclusion of animal abuse in the most current version of the *Diagnostic and Statistical Manual of the American Psychiatric Association*, there are indications that mental health professionals do not always ask about this symptom of conduct disorder (see Schaffer et al.'s (2007) exploration of this and related ethical issues in a survey of practicing psychologists). In a recent study by Nelson (2001), only 14% of clients were queried about animal abuse. Similar results have been reported by Bell (2001) when she surveyed child welfare and mental health agencies in England.

18.3   Programmatic responses to the "link" between violence to people and animals

In the USA, more than two-thirds of homes with children have pets and 98% of people consider their pets to be companions or family members (American Veterinary Medical Association, 2007). Recognition that families include both people and animals is causing researchers and practitioners to view animal abuse as a "red flag" for other harmful behaviors and may be the first clue that families are in need of intervention, services, and support. Many studies indicate that animal maltreatment is part of a complex constellation of family violence that often manifests in more ways than one creating overlaps among child maltreatment, domestic violence, elder abuse, and animal abuse. Today, this knowledge of The Link® (the potential overlap between animal abuse and other forms of interpersonal and family violence) informs a larger model of family violence prevention. Thorough family assessments are necessary to determine the potential risks to the safety and well-being of children, adults, and animals, and to ascertain whether one form of identified violence may be linked to another. It is important to incorporate questions about pets and their care and the behavior of family members towards animals, in intake forms and assessments. Such inquiries may provide useful information about the family and could help to identify patterns of violence that may exist, as well as other family members who may be at risk. Whenever possible, engaging the entire family to identify their needs and strengths can result in long-term positive change for all family members, including pets. Officials in child welfare, domestic violence, adult protective services, and animal care and control are coordinating their efforts. A model of this is American Humane's Differential Response and Family Group Decision Making program and can be accessed at www.americanhumane.org/protecting-children/programs/differential-response/and www.fgdm.org.

To achieve this, it is essential that communication and cooperation between all relevant agencies and organizations be developed and enhanced. In recognition of this need, a National Town Meeting on Strategizing The Link was convened by the American Humane Association, the Kenneth A. Scott Charitable Trust, and The

Linkage Project, a program of Youth Alternatives Ingraham. One hundred and eleven people came, as they say in Maine, "from away." They came to Portland, Maine, from 22 states, two Canadian provinces, and the United Kingdom as a "brain trust" of researchers, practitioners, and organizational leaders addressing The Link between animal abuse and human violence.

Their goal was to evaluate the current state of affairs and strategize future directions for Link research, public policy, and programming. A New England-style town meeting encouraged maximum input from all participants, with no breakout sessions, so the entire group could hear as one and grow in the knowledge. An overarching objective of the National Town Meeting was to invite representatives from as many community Link coalitions as could be identified to share their successes and challenges in order to identify strategies to improve coordinated community responses and enhance the sustainability of these groups. It was noted that there is no database of communities that have established Link coalitions or the status of coalition-building efforts. Representatives of coalitions from Arizona, Connecticut, Georgia, Maine, Massachusetts, New York, Ohio, and Texas provided an initial inventory of organizational issues. Another overarching goal of the National Town Meeting was to identify strategies that can overcome barriers affecting several professional groups whose level of engagement in Link activities has been sporadic. Two panels led audience discussions to address these issues (Summary Report of the "Strategizing the Link" National Town Meeting, June 8–9, 2008, Portland, Maine; http://www.americanhumane.org/assets/docs/human-animal-bond/HAB-Link-proceedings2008.pdf).

The town meeting was followed by an invitational summit of experts who synthesized the input from the field and set forth a pathway for the future to sustain and grow the movement. Participants represented national organizations, local agencies, and community coalitions. All brought a wealth of knowledge, experience, and interdisciplinary perspectives to address the challenge posed by the organizers. The group worked with a facilitator to identify critical issues and sow the seeds of a national coalition. With a steering committee appointed and critical issues identified, work began to create the National Link Coalition. It was determined that this coalition should be independent rather than part of an existing organization, with ad hoc coordinators representing both national organizations and local practitioners. A vision statement was created to read: *It is understood that there is a link between violence against humans and violence against animals. Through the recognition and integration of this understanding into policies and practices nationwide, people and animals are measurably safer.* The group worked to prioritize the most critical issues and to identify future directions. The five key strategic goal areas identified were:

- Building Public Awareness About The Link: Marketing, Messaging and Communications
- Overcoming the Fragmentation of Systems Through Network-Building
- Education and Training for Professionals
- Addressing the Root Cause: Prevention, Intervention, and Prosecution
- Engaging Academics for Research and Data Collection.

Today, we are seeing a growing number of publications, community programs, and national initiatives relating to The Link. These developments are no longer coming exclusively from the fields of animal and child welfare, but are also being generated by sociology, criminology, domestic violence, psychology, child development, criminal justice, veterinary medicine, adult protective agencies, and many other fields. Domestic violence agencies can work with local animal care agencies, veterinarians and rescue groups to establish temporary foster care support for clients' pets. These may be either off-site, in "Safe Haven"-type programs, or on-site in American Humane's Pets and Women's Shelters (PAWS™) facilities (http://www.americanhumane.org/assets/docs/human-animal-bond/HAB-LINK-paws-startup-guide.pdf). Professionals working with children can consider the use of trained and registered therapy animals with children who have experienced abuse or loss (http://www.americanhumane.org/assets/docs/human-animal-bond/HAB-TASK-manual.pdf). Children who have been harmed and/or have witnessed family violence are often more comfortable talking about their situations in the comforting presence of a therapy animal, and this technique is being used in many Children's Advocacy Centers. We can all encourage community and government leaders to support initiatives that include The Link and use a multidisciplinary approach to support families and end family violence.

18.3.1   Protecting pets from domestic violence

In recent years, there has been greater awareness for pets caught in the crossfire of domestic violence. American Humane's Link® program, and growing research on The Link, acknowledges that pets can become targets of domestic violence in order to exert silence and/or compliance on human victims. With over 71 million homes having companion animals (2009–10 National Pet Owner's Survey, American Pet Products Association) and approximately 1.3 million women being victims of physical assault by an intimate partner each year (NCADV Fact Sheet), it is logical that pets may get caught in the center of the violence, or be specifically targeted.

A 2007 study found that women seeking refuge at a family violence shelter were nearly 11 times more likely to report their partner had hurt/killed their pet and that shelter women were more than four times higher to report their pet was threatened (Ascione et al., 2007; Volant et al., 2008). Twelve independent surveys have reported that between 18 and 48% of battered women have delayed their decision to leave their batterer, or have returned to their batterer, out of fear for the welfare of their pets or livestock (Ascione, 2007).

As a result of this growing recognition linking domestic violence and animal abuse, there has been greater recognition for removing family pets from abusive homes when their victimized family members are fleeing for safety. American Humane's Pets and Women's Shelters (PAWS)® Program acknowledges this issue head-on and is the first and only national initiative to provide guidance on how to safely house family and pets together at domestic violence shelters. The PAWS Program is unique in that it acknowledges the human/animal bond of keeping people and their pets together during a time of crisis, and sets forth guidelines in the PAWS Start-Up Guide on how domestic violence shelters can make on-site accommodations for family pets. The PAWS Start-Up Guide is available from the American Humane website (http://www.americanhumane.org/).

The PAWS Program was launched in February 2008 with only four known shelters housing pets on-site. Two years later, the program has grown to 35 known PAWS shelters, with seven more in-progress. Twenty states are covered under the PAWS Program. Yet with approximately 2,500 domestic violence shelters in the USA, the PAWS Program must continue to expand until a PAWS shelter is within reach of any needy family member and pet.

The PAWS Program was created by co-author Allie Phillips, who, as an assistant prosecuting attorney in the mid-1990s, witnessed domestic violence victims return to their abusive homes in order to keep the family pet safe. Since its national launch, the PAWS Program has already assisted numerous family members and their pets. In Arizona, an abuser withheld food and water for two weeks from a dog named Tigger, and a cat named Kimba was used as BB-gun target practice by the abuser's son. The owner had fled once before for her safety, but was unable to take her pets. When she returned, knowing she and her pets would continue to be abused, she then learned of a PAWS shelter nearby. In late 2009, she fled the home with Tigger and Kimba and found safety at a PAWS shelter.

A PAWS shelter in California, which is expanding its on-site housing program to include doggie doors from two resident rooms to an outdoor run area, found the PAWS Program to be simple to implement. PAWS Program grantees, Meg's House in Greenwood, South Carolina and the Mt. Graham Safe House in Safford, Arizona, implemented their PAWS Programs in less than six months. A Community Safety Network shelter in Jackson, Wyoming, created their PAWS Program in just one month. The common theme among PAWS shelters is that they aimed to keep the process simple, as outlined in the PAWS Start-Up Guide, and therefore implementation was not time consuming or difficult.

The PAWS Program outlines three housing styles for family pets, and discusses various issues and concerns that should be addressed upfront, such as allergies, pet noises, zoning and permits. The first housing system involves placing the pet directly with its family in the sleeping quarters. Approximately 12 PAWS shelters house pets inside the resident's rooms. The second method involves creating an indoor kennel by utilizing a spare room within the shelter. The Shelter for Abused Women and Children in Naples, Florida, created an indoor kennel by changing a utility room into a kennel. With the placement of six large dog carriers in the room, the shelter is able to house animals of most shapes and sizes. The shelter expanded to an outdoor kennel area, with a dog run, to accommodate larger animals.

Lastly, many shelters are building outdoor shelters for animals so that allergies, noise or fear of animals are not an issue. Approximately 22 PAWS shelters have opted for the backyard kennel. Quigley House in Florida built an outdoor dog facility with ten dog runs. The runs have a grassy area around them, and this area is fenced in to enable families to let their dogs run and play with them. This grassy area includes benches, and a dog bath. Each run has a "licksit" system that enables the dogs to have fresh water on demand. The runs are covered, and are in a shaded area. There is metered mosquito control spray that is meant for kennels and barns to reduce the problem with pests. Their feline facility is climate controlled, and provides a place for the families to let the cats out of their cage and spend bonding time with their family.

The Community Safety Network shelter in Wyoming, a PAWS grant recipient, opened their outdoor PAWS kennel and dog run in Fall 2009 and immediately started helping families with pets.

Grander versions of the PAWS concept have been implemented in Las Vegas and Howell, Michigan, where larger animal shelters were built on-site. Through a capital campaign, Noah's House in Las Vegas opened in October 2007 and has 16 cat cages/condos and 15 dog kennels, six of which are indoor/outdoor. Most days, the shelter is at capacity.

Domestic violence shelters interested in the PAWS Program are guided through the process from start to finish. PAWS grants are available to help provide some start-up funds to approved shelters. The PAWS Program has been embraced by communities and is bringing together a variety of individuals and professionals because of its unique aspect of housing pets. Many PAWS shelters discover that local businesses and individuals offer their time, money and handy-work to help build their local PAWS shelter. The PAWS Program also engages local animal shelters, animal rescue organizations, and veterinarians to provide assistance and guidance to the domestic violence shelter.

The PAWS Program serves an important need for communities by providing clear and concise guidelines on how to effectively house pets on-site. The PAWS Program concept is reaching more domestic violence victims who know that options are available for being sheltered with their pets. Yet, PAWS shelters are out of reach for too many victims.

Complementing the PAWS Program is the Safe Havens concept for off-site housing of pets of domestic violence (Ascione, 2000). It is estimated that between 700 and 900 Safe Havens programs exist in the USA. The housing may consist of the domestic violence shelter establishing a foster care program where pets are housed in homes until they can be reunited with their family, housing pets at animal shelters, veterinary offices or boarding facilities through a cooperative agreement, or simply providing information to victims on where to place pets. Safe Havens is an important option for a community that has not implemented the PAWS Program. Yet, less than half of the domestic violence shelters offer any type of referral or off-site housing for pets of their clients.

Ahimsa House in Atlanta is an organization that works to safely house pets of domestic violence. Ahimsa House undertook the task of creating and maintaining a website of off-site housing programs throughout the country. This directory is invaluable since it often provides hope and options to a domestic victim who is too far from a PAWS Program, yet needs to get herself and her pet to safety. To read a comprehensive assessment and guide on the Safe Haven's concept, please visit the Ahimsa House website.

We are closer to the day when domestic violence shelters will either have a PAWS Program or Safe Havens Program out of recognition that families of domestic violence have pets that also need protecting. Great strides have been made in recent years to acknowledge this issue involving pets, yet more work needs to be done.

18.3.2 *Incorporating therapy animals with maltreated children*

For those professionals who work with maltreated children, providing a sense of safety and security to the child during the legal process can be challenging. The legal process can be frightening to adults, and particularly for children who may not understand what is happening. The concept of incorporating therapy animals to help these particular children is in its infancy, yet is growing in popularity in courtrooms, prosecutors' offices, and child protection agencies throughout the USA.

The bond between children and animals is undeniable. Animals are naturally a part of a child's world. Even if their family does not have a cat, dog or other companion animal, children are surrounded by animals from an early age. They have puppies, kittens, giraffes, monkeys, and teddy bears on their clothing and floating above their crib in a mobile; their books feature the Blue Clues dog, Clifford the Big Red Dog, Berenstain Bears, Dora the Explorer and her friends; and their TV shows and movies feature Big Bird, Simba and Nahla, Nemo, Winnie the Pooh, and many animated animal characters. As part of healthy growth and development, a child's bond with animals teaches empathy and compassion. When a child has been abused or traumatized, it can be the non-judgmental comfort from an animal that helps the child heal.

We often hear of the human/animal bond and people's personal bonds with their own family pets. However, the child/animal bond is something pure when witnessed. It can bring a withdrawn child out and provide emotional healing to a child that has been maltreated. Understanding this bond is essential to believing that animal-assisted therapy (AAT) can help children.

American Humane recognized the need for guidance in this sensitive area involving maltreated children being integrated with therapy animals. In August 2009, America Humane launched the Therapy Animals Supporting Kids (TASK)™ Program. The TASK manual was written to encourage professionals within the criminal justice and child welfare systems to incorporate trained and registered therapy animals into their programs. Children's advocacy centers (CACs), child protection service agencies, hospitals, prosecutors' offices, and courthouses are well suited to welcome a therapy animal. The TASK manual was written to set forth the proper handling of therapy animals around children who have been abused in a manner to keep both child and animal safe, as well as to avoid any unpleasant situations that may negatively impact on a civil or criminal case involving child abuse.

The manual emphasizes that incorporating an animal in therapy, particularly in the case of child abuse, is a specialized field which requires training in development and clinical application, animal handling skills and having an animal trained for therapy work. Without proper knowledge and experience in these areas, involving just any animal in a therapeutic setting could create issues of liability and compromise the child.

The TASK Program was created by co-author Allie Phillips and Diana McQuarrie, Director of Animal Assisted Interventions for American Humane. Together, Allie and Diana merge two important areas of expertise in co-authoring the TASK manual: the practical issues involving setting up an animal-assisted therapy program and safely working with therapy animals, along with the legal implications of how to effectively incorporate therapy animals to help children through an often difficult court process.

The TASK manual identifies six stages in which therapy animals can be beneficial to children, and thoroughly details the benefits and drawbacks to each stage as well as potential legal objections and responses. The six stages include: greeting children, the forensic interview or evaluation, the medical examination, individual or group therapy, court preparation and courtroom testimony. The manual features children's advocacy centers and prosecutors' offices that currently incorporate therapy animals to assist children. It also contains sample forms which can also be downloaded from American Humane's website.

The TASK manual was peer reviewed by nationally recognized leaders in child protection, prosecution and animal-assisted therapy, as well as agencies that have effectively incorporated therapy animals to benefit child victims and witnesses. It has also been endorsed by national leaders in child advocacy and prosecution.

The benefits of AAT with maltreated children are shown in stories like this. Isabelle is a Newfoundland therapy dog who helps with the Tarrant County (Texas) Kids In Court Program. In one instance, she was helping a 9-year-old girl prepare ready for court. The girl was shy, but warmed up especially after finding Isabelle's ticklish spot. Isabelle's handler told the girl one of Isabelle's stories about secrets and that it is okay to talk about secrets. The girl then disclosed to Isabelle more than she previously had about her abuse. As a result of her work, Isabelle was awarded the Volunteer of the Year Award in 2009 from the Alliance for Children, the children's advocacy center in Tarrant County, Texas.

The Harris County District Attorney's Office in Houston, Texas, created the *Paw and Order SDU: Special Dog Unit* Program in 2009. The program has six registered therapy dogs that accompany children and other witnesses to court twice monthly. The therapy dogs sit with children and other victims of domestic violence or abuse prior to having to testify. The therapy dogs keep the victims and witnesses calm during the process.

18.3.3   Training professionals on The Link between human violence and animal cruelty

Professionals assisting victims of familial crime are receiving training on The Link and how they can better work together to prevent family violence. Child protection, animal welfare, domestic violence, adult protective services, victim advocates, law enforcement and prosecutors are now working collaboratively in multi-disciplinary teams to address the dynamics of multi-occurrence violence in the home. Thirty-five states have passed laws that require some form of cross-reporting of child abuse, elder abuse, domestic violence or animal abuse.

In 2008, American Humane published a manual entitled *A Common Bond* which brought together information on The Link and its connection to animal abuse for child welfare professionals. The Link and other cross-training efforts are under way by American Humane at national, state and local child welfare, violence, animal protection, veterinarian, law enforcement and prosecution conferences. Training on The Link to these diverse multi-disciplinary audiences opens up awareness to consider all family members when investigating or assisting an abusive home. Education materials on The Link have also been published by American Humane to assist these multi-disciplinary professionals. Most recently, a Link guidebook has been published for teachers and parents, as well as specifically for prosecutors handling Link-related crimes.

18.3.4 Legislation that recognizes the linkage between people and their pets

In 2006, the first pet protective order bill was signed into law in Maine. Since that historic time, 14 states have followed suit, with dozens of bills being filed each year with anticipation of becoming law. A pet protective order is simply a mechanism by which pets are added to domestic violence orders. When a domestic violence victim is seeking court ordered protection, judges are allowed to add pets to those orders, even without the authorization of the law. Pets are deemed property in the USA and can be added to an order as property worthy of protecting. What pet protective order laws do is simply add a specific line item to the order to prompt judges to inquire as to whether there are any pets in the home needing protection. Eleven states protect "animals" in their law, whereas three states protect "pets" and one protects "domestic animals."

Pet protection laws are an important recognition of the linkage between domestic violence and animal abuse. With more states being added each year, this movement will undoubtedly spin off similar type legislative efforts. Efforts in 2008 and 2009 to have a Congressional Resolution recognizing Link Awareness Month did not receive the necessary vote, but a Congressional Briefing on The Link was hosted by American Humane in February 2008 to educate legislators on the importance of recognizing all family victims when addressing crime-related legislation. Since then several localities have recognized Link Awareness Days to promote awareness of the issue in their community.

Efforts are also under way to gain recognition of The Link in federal bills that provide funds to state and local agencies. Working through child welfare, domestic violence and juvenile justice federal coalitions, The Link is being discussed for possible future inclusion in the federal reauthorization bills.

18.4 Clinical implications

Social workers have historically documented the issue and relevance of both positive interactions with animals as well as animal abuse since the profession's origins. As a forensic social worker and member of the faculty at the University of Denver's Graduate School of Social Work, I find frequent opportunities to make relevant and examine the hypothesis that a person's abusive interactions with an animal may be indicative of their treatment of people. Sadly, this should not come as a surprise as it is frequently present in our everyday intervention casework. Modern social workers more than ever should have clinical training in the dynamics of cruelty to animals in the context of understanding individual child and adult interpersonal violence, intimate partner and family violence, as well as the correlation to child and adult protection. The presence of animal cruelty appears as a clinical indicator in the history of children who have been exposed to family violence, parental neglect, significant substance abuse problems, and exposure to violence and emotional, physical, and sexual trauma. Understanding the elements and the importance of accurate assessment of animal cruelty as a predictive correlate between animal abuse and early maltreatment or the development of future antisocial behavior has become more urgent as evidence seems to suggest that abuse of animals may be a reliable early manifestation (Arluke and Lockwood, 1997; Ascione, 1999; Quinn, 2000).

18.4.1   Why we need animal abuse-specific assessment

Forensic mental health evaluations require a unique set of skills and tools to assist in accurate differential diagnosis and intervention. Animal abuse-specific evaluations are no exception. Professionals who are requested to evaluate animal abuse behavior in either an adult or a child benefit from specialized training and are well served to utilize recognized protocols and tools designed to understand the specific domains that assist us in individualized understanding of each youth. An individualized assessment can assist in determination of cause, risk factors, mental health considerations, as well as differential diagnostic, treatment, and dispositional recommendations.

Too often, minimal or no formal evaluation is performed in animal abuse cases and intervention may amount to no intervention or a mild consequence such as a few hours of community service or a ticket. This is juxtaposed to the over-reaction that all animal abuse will lay a direct path to future serial murder or extreme violence. An example of this occurred in Colorado, when two high school students were arrested on animal cruelty charges after catching wild baby rabbits and bringing them into a school pep-rally where the animals were tossed across the gymnasium and eventually were severely injured, resulting in the death of the animals. Although the youths in this case had no significant history of antisocial behavior prior to this incident, the media referenced this behavior as a definitive precursor and likely trajectory of serial murder. This type of overexaggeration never assists with a useful or thoughtful response. At the other extreme, we have had frequent examples where a seriously disturbed child has begun to engage in major acts of animal cruelty including killing and where the behavior is so completely minimized that it is only well after the fact that the behavior is identified. The failure to import the details of animal cruelty into the formal assessment undermines accurate risk prediction.

The primary purposes in an animal abuse-specific assessment include:

- Identify behavioral, mental health, and trauma-based issues relevant to the emergence of animal cruelty behavior
- Provide an accurate estimation of the likelihood and circumstances for continued abuse behavior and community safety concerns
- Provide recommendations for intervention, disposition, and supervision.

Recognition that animal abuse is a potential signal of other serious coexisting mental health problems necessitates the use of sensitive, comprehensive and standardized methods for assessment in order to assist in the formation of appropriate recommendations (Boat, 1995).

The evaluator should be equipped with the following skills and information:

- A complete understanding of the incident including accurate police and animal control reports and referral information

- An unambiguous understanding of the federal, state, and local animal abuse laws
- Understanding of the potential legal and dispositional outcomes and intervention resources
- Fundamental knowledge about child and adult normative development and psychopathology
- Familiarity with child and adult mental health diagnosis and requisite assessment instruments
- Access to a clinical interview with the individual and his or her social support network including the family.

18.4.2   Assessment domains

A generalized label such as "animal abuser" does not provide clear diagnostic analysis of differences in either causation, risk, or intervention needs. Serious and chronic animal abuse is almost always symptomatic of other problems, which is different than saying animal abuse should be treated simply as a symptom of other problems. In Colorado and other states, cruelty statute language may erroneously orient the court to animal abuse as a feature of impulsivity or uncontrolled anger. This common misconception, although not always inaccurate, encourages premature assignment to anger management classes as a resolution for the problem. Without question, anger problems are prominent in some animal abuse cases but other problems are equally prominent. In youth, for example, low social competence factors or learned cruelty behaviors are probably more common. Comprehensive assessment is critical in making accurate decisions at every stage of the decision process including arrest, filing of cases, disposition, and consequences or interventions that are required. The primary domains that should be examined in the performance of an animal abuse assessment should include at least the following domains (Tedeschi, 2000):

- *Cognitive functioning.* This domain is used to determine if there is evidence of impairment in cognitive functions, processing difficulty, distorted belief systems, or the presence of a thought disorder
- *Personality and mental health.* This domain is intended to determine if there is an acute, chronic, or prior history of mental illness or emotional instability
- *Social/developmental history.* This domain is intended to elicit information relevant to understanding the individual's social and interpersonal functioning. It has been documented that significant social, attachment, and relational difficulties are often risk factors in the psychological profiles of animal abusers (Arluke and Lockwood, 1997)
- *Individual functioning/developmental competence.* Experts agree that it is important to distinguish between adults and children in assessing any problem behavior and this distinction should be made when assessing animal abuse behaviors. This domain will assist in making developmental sense of the actions of clients at different ages, developmental levels, and differing culpability levels. This domain will also assist in making appropriate age, culpability, and developmentally sensitive dispositional recommendations (Hindman, 1992)
- *Current family functioning.* This domain remains central to the client's ability to succeed in counseling and is important for an accurate assessment. Families who understand the severity of the issue and hold the individual accountable will improve prognosis and reduce the likelihood of further animal cruelty or abuse. Conversely, family systems denying the

relevance of the problem and normalizing the behavior may be dramatically increasing the likelihood of additional abuse activity. It is also critical to understand the client's worldview and cultural considerations as they relate to the behaviors being assessed. Behavior that is outside the cultural norm clearly carries different significance than behavior that is commonplace in the individual's cultural experience

- *Sexual and deviancy issues.* Evidence that animals are the victims of sexually abusive behavior necessitates that evaluators be prepared to evaluate the issues of sexual deviancy and sexualized abuse of animals
- *Employment/academic functioning.* This domain is important as an indicator of stability and functioning. In many cases where an individual is engaging in animal abuse, there are significant difficulties in their performance and relationship in either work or school environments
- *Delinquency, conduct, and antisocial behavioral issues.* This domain should review the presence of other antisocial and disruptive behavior. This may also include criminal and non-criminal deviant behaviors. This area is very important because one of the strongest risk predictors of any specific future behavior is past behavior. We should attempt to assess behaviors that the client was apprehended for as well as those behaviors that were not officially recorded
- *Assessment of risk.* Evaluators should spend special attention to this domain. There is not a validated instrument that can determine exactly which factors or criteria equate to a specific level of risk. However, expert rater screening tools based on widely recognized indicators from forensic assessment tools can effectively guide the determination of risk
- *Protective factors.* Risk assessment should be balanced and measured against the presence of health and protective factors. Protective factors are frequently dynamic variables and can be increased through effective treatment intervention and, conversely, individuals with few protective factors, significant isolation, and poor social support represent a substantially greater risk for poor outcomes and increased risk
- *Empathy and awareness of victim impact.* This domain is intended to examine the individual's ability to experience genuine emotion. Empathy and the capacity to understand other's experiences have been identified as an important inhibitor of abusive behavior
- *Substance abuse.* Substance abuse is a common contributor to the acceleration of all types of violence; it becomes very important to assess its role in animal abuse cases
- *Offense and abuse characteristics.* This domain is intended to provide clear, concise information about the nature, frequency, severity, and scope of the animal abuse behavior
- *Supervision and legal issues.* The supervision and legal factors domain is intended to assist in making clear decisions about the individual's responsibility, accountability, and need for supervision. All evaluations should attempt to have understanding of the client's social network because it is likely that those persons closest to the client may have the best ability to supervise the client and improve success.

18.4.3 How should the assessment be conducted?

Ideally, these evaluations allow for an in-depth structured clinical interview. It is appropriate for you as the interviewer to remain in control of the interview in order to gather the important information. When beginning the interview you should clearly state the reason why you are conducting this interview. These interviews should be performed as post-admission and pre-disposition assessments so that information can be made available to the court and treatment interventionist for consideration. This, however, should not be the end point of assessment because, prior to sentencing, individuals who are facing potential legal consequences are likely to withhold information relevant to accurate risk and treatment planning. Because of the potential repetitive nature of animal abuse and other interpersonal violence for some individuals and the contributions of fluctuating life stresses, level of risk may not be a static determination.

It generally improves the outcome of these assessments to be direct and confirm that the client understands all questions that are being asked of him or her. Every client should be treated with respect and generally approached non-confrontationally no matter how horrible the abuse behavior. If the client is expressing some form of discomfort and anxiety you should discuss it directly. If a client is refusing to answer questions or is unwilling to proceed with the evaluation, you should stop the interview and document the client's reason for terminating the interview.

It can be useful to monitor the non-verbal responses to interview questions. Do not agree to keep information secret unless this assessment is being done within the context of a purely confidential therapeutic relationship and even then withholding information regarding animal cruelty is almost never advisable. If a client states that he or she wants to tell you something "off the record," you should inform the client that you are unwilling to insure that this information will remain strictly confidential.

Because animal abuse can carry with it significant levels of social stigma we should present as non-judgmental and avoid expressing shock or disgust during the interview. This may take practice as many experienced examiners find the details of animal abuse very disturbing and have strong reactions. Consider planning ahead for debriefing with colleagues, and utilizing self-care to ensure avoiding secondary impact that these cases have on you.

When you ask questions, attempt to elicit details around the what, where, who, when, and how. Motivation for the behaviors should be asked directly without expressing opinion about the client's beliefs and attitude. Many clients will not accurately self-disclose the scope of their animal abuse behaviors. A careful review of collateral information and following up with others who know the client is critical. This means that clients will often under-report and minimize the scope of the frequency, intentionality, and harm done. Every effort should be made to find corroborating sources of information to compare against the client's self report.

18.4.4   Animal abuse typologies

There have been attempts to organize taxonomies for individuals engaging in animal abuse and there remains vigorous debate on the benefits and potential risks in placing labels on animal abuse behavior. The Anicare Model, drawn from conceptual models in the interpersonal violence field, has generally defined the likely typologies as falling into the recognized mental health related profiles such as personality disorders, mood disorders, and anxiety reactions (Anicare manual). Other widely publicized typologies include the animal abuse-related offense typologies defined by Dr. Randall Lockwood (Lockwood, 2006).

These include:

- Neglectors
- Collectors/hoarders
- Intentional abusers (most likely to be referred for psychological treatment)
- Ritualistic abusers
- Organized abusers (dog fighting, cock fighting)
- Sexual abusers
  - Opportunist/experimental
  - Fixated/primary
  - Domineering/sadistic (most likely to victimize).

It seems desirable to not unnecessarily define or label people as problems. However, for the sake of both humans and animals who share the need for safety, the seriousness associated with harming animals and people requires we prepare to accurately assess these behaviors. In this effort, examining typologies through the lenses of diagnostic and intervention priorities seems to make good sense.

Through the use of diagnostic screening, we can see the importance of making these types of diagnostic differential determinations. A diagnostic checklist generated from the criteria commonly associated with the *Diagnostic and Statistical Manual of Mental Disorders* (DSM- IV-TR 2000) (Diagnostic Typology Checklist, Nelson and Tedeschi, 2000) is an expert observer checklist designed to assist in the differentiation of youthful animal abuse offenders whose problem behavior emanates primarily from distinct underlying diagnostic categories of criminality, trauma-reactivity, or profound mental health problems. Originally developed by forensic evaluators Raymond Nelson and Philip Tedeschi, it provides information that can be clinically useful in treatment and case-management decisions. Though not intended to be a measure of risk prediction, this measure gives some indication of the relative level of severity of symptoms within the domains. Typology criteria include:

Criminogenic criteria:

- Presents as convincing or charming, with few indicators of vulnerability
- Presentation or history of manipulative or controlling behavior
- Displays jealousy, dislike, or animosity, low empathy towards victim
- Has been physically cruel, or caused physical pain or injury to persons or animals
- Bullies, threatens, or intimidates others
- History of fights, aggression, or property destruction
- Family history of aggression, criminal conduct, and/or chemical dependency
- Has used a weapon against others
- Illegal drug use or abuse, or early use of alcohol.

Traumagenic criteria:

- Has experienced, witnessed, or was confronted with an event or events that involve actual or threatened death, serious injury, or threats to physical or sexual integrity
- Reactive avoidance of stimuli that arouse recollections of traumatic events
- Intense psychological distress and/or behavioral reactivity upon exposure to internal or external cues that symbolize or resemble an aspect of traumatic events

- Noticeable regression from normally expected levels of personal, social, and intra-psychic stability and competencies, in response to stimulation of trauma issues
- Behavior may represent the re-enactment or resolution of traumatic events
- Reports images, thoughts, dreams, illusions, flashback episodes, or a sense of reliving the experience; or distress on exposure to reminders of the traumatic event
- Regression from normal levels of awareness and appropriate responsiveness to his or her surroundings when trauma issues are triggered
- Elevated anxiety symptoms, when compared to normal functioning, or increased arousal (restlessness, irritability, poor concentration, hyper-vigilance)
- Difficulties with sleep or appetite (excess or avoidance).

Psychogenic criteria:

- Low birth-weight or IQ (relative to siblings or peers)
- Diagnosis of developmental or autistic spectrum disorder
- Bizarre, or inappropriate affect (not including flat affect, or elective withdrawal/avoidance)
- Present or past intervention with psychotropic medications
- History of psychiatric hospitalization
- Family history of mental illness or psychiatric hospitalization
- History of unusually difficulty pregnancy or childbirth
- Inability to develop relationships due to perceptual inaccuracies around relationships and interactions with others (difficulties not due to emotional/traumatic resistance, or hostility)
- Social role as a scapegoat or outcast
- The youth is displaying significant difficulty or impairment in social, educational, family, or other important area of functioning.

Items on the checklist address diagnostic features of conduct and antisocial problems; post-traumatic and acute stress disorders, and pre-morbid predictors of chronic mental illness. Individuals generally score higher in one category on this measure, though elevated scores in two or three areas are not uncommon. More recent versions of these assessments are available at http://humananimalconnection.org/

The two cases in Boxes 18.1 and 18.2 exemplify and highlight the importance of utilizing such diagnostic instruments.

Box 18.1 Case study

In this case study, the individual took rabbits from his sister's rabbit hutch and proceeded to throw them into the air and then tried to catch them. This ultimately resulted in the death of eight rabbits. This individual was 17 years old, with a presenting IQ of 81, with notably impaired judgment and reasoning and difficulty with attention during neuropsychological testing. Academically, this individually has been placed in special education and testing indicates that he is reading at a grade level of 1.9 and writing at a 3.2 grade level. Based on formal diagnostic evaluation he had historically been diagnosed as having schizophrenia residual type. When applying the Typology Checklist diagnostic screening criteria he scores on 8 of the Psychogenic criteria, 4 of the Traumagenic criteria and 2 of the Criminogenic criteria.

Box 18.2 Case study

In this case study, the individual also killed rabbits, in the presence of another peer, stole the rabbits from the backyard hutch at a stranger's home in his neighborhood and proceeded to throw these animals against the side of a house killing five rabbits. This individual was 15 years old, with an IQ of 93, with impaired judgment revealed upon neuropsychological testing. His reading, writing, and math scores suggested that he was functioning at age appropriate grade levels in all areas. Based on history, he met the criteria for conduct disorder and, based on a review of collateral information, he displayed other conduct/criminal behaviors. Scoring him on the Typology Checklist diagnostic screening instrument criteria he scored 7 on the Criminogenic criteria, 1 on the Traumagenic criteria and 2 on the Psychogenic criteria.

An evaluator would want to gather many other detailed pieces of information to understand these cases but they serve as a lesson in why the type of animal cruelty behavior is not in and of itself useful to illuminate underlying causation or intervention needs. Diagnostic inference and insight can be extremely useful in the development of clinical intervention priorities and may be especially important given the public tendency toward under- and over-reaction to animal abuse behavior. This tool provides screening data that can be used to guide the evaluator toward the identification of the strongest diagnostic typological presence providing insight and guide recommendations for disposition. The tendency for inaccurate and misplaced diagnostic emphasis is exemplified in our continued efforts to consequence bi-polar disorder out of a youth or failure to identify and treat the acute impact of child maltreatment in a delinquent youth. The following might provide generalized treatment and intervention priorities:
Criminogenic needs

* Personal responsibility/accountability to others
* Cognitive behavioral learning
* Consequences (teach cause and effect)

Traumagenic

* Improved self-mastery/self-concept
* Empowerment/support
* Resiliency

Psychogenic

* Structured routines
* Medications
* Repetition/learning and life management.

18.4.5 The challenge of formal risk assessment

Although many risk prediction models attempt to orient themselves around a clinical theory that explains both the etiology and risk associated with given phenomena, actuarial risk prediction does not rely on a specific clinical theory and does not attempt to determine causality. Actuarial models may utilize very specific historical data or convenient variables that are commonly included in case history files, and attempt to predict recidivism based only upon statistical models of correlation. While no single variable will be sufficient to predict recidivism, through empirically identified predictor variables, the strength of correlation can be substantially improved. At this stage, development of stronger actuarial predictors would be beneficial as clinical predictions of risk (Hanson and Bussière, 1996). Violent animal cruelty behavior is a decision and the proximal cause(s) are influenced by a host of psychological, neurological, biological, and social factors. Managing animal abuse violence risk requires that we understand the following:

- Nature—what kinds of violent behavior can occur?
- Severity—how serious is the violent behavior?
- Frequency—how often does the violent behavior occur?
- Likelihood—what is the probability of the behavior occurring?

Risk assessment is not a perfect science and cannot know for certain what any one individual will do. However, by utilizing standardized psychometric testing along with expert administered animal abuse-specific screening tools, we may be able to estimate more accurately these risk factors and work toward actuarial risk prediction models and establish significantly more accurate risk profiles.

There are several approaches to completing a risk assessment in animal abuse cases. One of the most influential but dated models for the evaluation of youth with a history of animal cruelty was to reference the behavior as a recognized element of the so-called pathological triangle (Hellman and Blackman, 1966). This early framework of the "pathological or homicidal triad" originally articulated animal abuse as one of three factors found in individuals who were "destined" to engage in serious violence, especially serial murder. Animal abuse appears to often elicit opinions and reactions that range from extreme minimization to the serious and often inaccurate over-reaction. In the case of the "triad," it would seem that subsequent research brings into question the individual predictive power of the individual factors in the triad (Geddes, 1977). In numerous studies between 1951 and 2004, there was little support for the triad theory. It would appear that the presence is more predictive of social isolation, increased passivity, low social competence, and coexisting mental health concerns.

Although this model may misrepresent the implications of the triad behaviors, it also frames the actual behavior as consistent with the other triad behaviors, relegating animal abuse to a symptom of psychopathology. If used only as an equivalent symptom of pathology it distorts and serves to regularly minimize the potential for risk. This is especially true when current understanding of the roles and relationships of companion animals suggest that people have strong attachments to and view their animals as important companions and members of the family (Melson, 2003). If animals are included in risk prediction formulas as additional victims rather than symptoms of psychopathology, such as when equated to bed wetting, we have a more accurate understanding of the individual's capacity for interpersonal violence.

Several experts have pioneered animal abuse screening specific instruments:

- Randall Lockwood. *Factors in the Assessment of Dangerousness in Perpetrators of Animal Cruelty*—A comprehensive risk assessment checklist identifying relevant risks indicators
- Barbara Boat. *Boat Inventory on Animal-related Experiences*—This questionnaire introduces a tool that gathers information about specific areas related to animal abuse.

Box 18.3 Case study—animal abuse-specific evaluation

Steven was referred for an animal abuse-specific evaluation from the district attorney's office as Colorado law allows for an evaluation to be ordered. Animal control responded to a call of a dead cat hanging in a tree. While investigating the case, Steven was identified as having been seen in the area by a neighbor. Steven was interviewed at a youth detention center and his parents were asked to sign the required releases to allow for the interview. During the interview, Steven admitted to killing a cat, which he indicated was a stray he found in the alley near his home. He said that he was not sure why he decided to hang it in the tree but that he had killed the cat because it had looked sick and weak and he thought it should be put out of its misery. A forensic review of the deceased animal found that the animal had been beaten several times and strangled and it was unclear which abuse activity resulted in the animal's death. Steven was charged with a felony animal cruelty offense and, during advisement, the court requested that a pre-sentence evaluation be performed.

Name: Steven
Date of birth: (15)
Referral source: District Attorney's Office

Mental status/behavioral observation

Steven presents as a slightly odd young man, uncombed hair and unselfconscious about his appearance. He was cooperative, though non-assertive throughout the interview and testing. His mood remained upbeat, though slightly superficial, along with a generally positive though slightly restricted range of affect. Steven's speech was limited by his vocabulary and apparent memory deficits (having trouble remembering important people's names), though no gross speech abnormality was present. His thought patterns appear unaffected by perceptual distortions, and he denies experiencing hallucinations, delusions, or suicidality. Despite the absence of gross distortions, Steven's thinking appears childlike and concrete. Steven was consistently oriented to time, location, and person, though his insight into feelings, motivations, and interpersonal events appears substantially limited.

Offense characteristic

Steven was currently awaiting the dispositional hearing and his parents report they have been informed he will likely be placed on probation for this incident. Steven was charged and adjudicated for a felony animal cruelty offense after he was observed placing a dead cat in a tree near his home. During an interview with Animal Control he admitted that he had killed the cat. His parents were in attendance during the interview. His parents appear to be very concerned about his behavior and encouraged Steven to be honest during the interview. According to the report, it seems that Steven quickly admitted to the facts in the case. His parents have secured legal representation.

Under detailed interview, Steven admitted hitting the cat with a stick causing visible damage and likely death. When asked why he had done that, he reported that he believed the cat was weak and sick and was suffering so he wanted to end its suffering. Steven reported hitting the cat one time, although it appears that the animal was struck at least several times. Steven indicated he later discarded the stick. Animal control reports suggest that the cat was not particularly thin or unhealthy and appeared to be an owned cat from the neighborhood. He then stated that when the cat was stunned and not moving he placed a rope around the cat's neck to ensure it was dead.

Criminal history
Steven has no prior juvenile criminal record.

Multi-axial diagnosis
Based upon the data collected during this evaluation, the following diagnosis is offered for consideration:

Axis I Oppositional Defiant Disorder
   R/O Conduct Disorder
   Adjustment Disorder with Mixed Anxiety and Depressed Mood
   R/O Attention-Deficit Disorder
   R/O Reading Disorder
   R/O Disorder of Written Expression
   Axis II deferred
   Axis III deferred
   Axis IV deferred
   Axis V deferred

Typology assessment
The diagnostic typologies checklist indicates that Steven primarily requires intervention in the area of his psychological concerns then secondarily his acute trauma issues. He should continue to be assessed due to the fact that he recently has been escalating in school and engaged in some increased disruptive, conduct and behavioral problems and scoring indicates pronounced mental health concerns.

   Typology checklist results:
   Criminogenic—3
   Psychogenic—7
   Traumagenic—4

Cognitive functioning
Steven has been tested previously in the past, for educational purposes. Steven's mother reported to a previous evaluator that he had been on a respirator for three days at birth, and on oxygen approximately 6½ weeks at birth. Steven was delayed in developmental milestones such as sitting up, walking, talking, and speaking. Records indicate he was diagnosed with ADD at age 7, and was

prescribed Ritalin by his pediatrician. Prior WISC-R testing revealed a verbal IQ of 74 and performance IQ of 109, representing a significant discrepancy between the two and a full-scale score of 89. Previous testing revealed generally low average memory and learning strengths, with specific difficulties in tasks that demand sustained attention and the manipulation of abstract concepts. Academic reports also identify Steven's reading and written skills as areas of significant deficit and that he often will act out in class during these subjects causing disruption in the classroom.

Social/developmental history

Steven is a 15-year-old male who was born in Colorado. Reports indicate that Steven's biological father was an alcoholic who abused his mother. His mother moved out when he was three months old. But his mother remained in this relationship for another seven years. Steven's maternal grandparents helped to raise him, and when Steven was eight years old, his mother became involved with his stepfather. His stepfather and mother had a female child when he was nine years old. His mother expressed concerns that Steven learned this behavior because he has observed his biological father being very violent toward her on multiple occasions when he was young. She also reports that this individual was also abusive to a family dog that lived with them during his formative years (ages 0–5). His mother reports that the dog's whereabouts are unknown now, as it belonged to Steven's biological father and eventually was no longer around. She fears the animal was killed but does not have specific knowledge. Steven denies specific memory of this animal and generally reports he does not remember the abuse but does remember his father yelling and pushing his mother. He indicates that it never occurs with his stepfather.

Steven's stepfather and mother appear to be stable and committed to one another. Steven has always called his stepfather "dad" and has no contact with his biological father and has not seen him for over five years. Steven and his parents appear close and Steven reports feeling supported by both of his parents. It appears that his mother may be a bit overprotective of him and that has created conflict especially since this incident where his stepfather thinks that Steven needs significant consequences.

Steven has a low-average IQ and does have identifiable cognitive learning disabilities. Steven reportedly had trouble making friends and is still "picked on" by others. He apparently attends school regularly but struggles to pass grades. His middle school years showed some mild improvement, though his family is reported to have moved four times during this period. He generally obeyed the rules, and earned Cs and Ds with many late and incomplete assignments. He reports having no experience with drugs or alcohol. He does have a history of fighting from elementary through middle school (he was expelled from middle school in the 7th grade for four days due to fighting). When asked about this incident, Steven stated, "a kid pushed and tripped me and I beat him up." Steven has continued to have difficulty making and keeping friends in school and often is identified by teachers as disruptive and requires a lot of attention and redirection to keep him on task. This year he was placed in a special track designed for youth at risk. This program pairs him with a student teacher for half the day. Steven admits to shoplifting when he was 13 years old, stating that he was not caught. He has no additional criminal record.

His parents report that he is responsive and follows their direction well. They believe that his problems at school are due to "personality conflicts" with his teacher. He is also close to his grandparents since he spent his first four years of life in their home. Steven reports that he has no sexual experience but thinks about sex frequently and likes several girls at school but rarely have any of them talked to him.

Developmental competence

Steven generally presents himself as a friendly and easy-going youth. His teachers describe that during class he will often appear to feed off others' negative attention and then will escalate to becoming the class clown and become loud and disruptive. He laughs at inappropriate times and appears to be especially stimulated and escalated by teasing others. He is often immature and feeds into others' negative behaviors or can be prompted by other peers to engage in inappropriate behaviors.

His parents report that he has always played well with his sister and younger friends in their neighborhood. His parents shared that recently his sister stated that she wanted to be babysat by Steven. They were very surprised that his sister indicated that she was scared of him because they had always observed him playing with younger friends easily and appeared friendly and polite to these younger youth. He has never been on a sleepover except with cousins.

His parents reported that he has always needed structure and that when unexpected things happen, dinner is late or events do not happen as expected, he gets very upset and has difficulty settling down. They also reported that he had a lot of difficulty when he was bored and required some help finding things to do on his own. His parents have attempted to limit his TV watching because this appears to be his favorite activity. They stated that they have learned to be aware of his needs and it rarely causes a problem at home. He appears to respond most positively to his mother and grandmother.

Individual functioning

There do not appear to be any unusual changes in his functioning or acute stressors with the exception that his grandfather did have to undergo surgery two months before the offense and Steven appeared concerned and refused to go visit him in the hospital. He has also appeared to be very fearful of his transition into the 9th grade. He comes home from school angry and cries easily. He reports that other kids do not like him and he usually comes home immediately after school and does not leave the house unless initiated by his parents and grandparents. He has started to spend more time in his room and appears less communicative than last year. When he does express himself recently it has been through anger and he escalates quickly and has difficulty getting settled back down. During the family interview his parents both indicated that the entire family was motivated not to have him "blow up" because it generally ruined the remainder of the evening. It was described as a "tantrum."

Family functioning

Steven's family appears to have a sense of the seriousness of his behaviors. They have, however, failed to provide adequate supervision in some ways despite recognition and expressed concerns about his functioning. Both parents acknowledged that at the time of Steven's animal abuse behavior both parents were aware that he was appearing shut down, angry and more aggressive, especially with his sister. They, however, would continue to place Steven in a position of babysitting for her after school and often on weekends. In fact, Steven reported to this writer that he told his parents that he did not want to have to babysit for his sister and that he was told it was part of his job as an older brother in the family. Both parents work outside the home and would be home in the late afternoon—a consistent basis leaving Steven home alone often.

Delinquency and conduct/behavioral issues

Steven has no documented history of any prior delinquency problems or contacts with the law enforcement. He was expelled during 7th grade due to fighting and his teachers indicate that he can be disruptive in the classroom and that this behavior is escalating.

Assessment of risk

Based on assessment of risk factors, there is significant concern that Steven presents as a significant risk for continued cruelty behaviors and that his behaviors may be escalating. His risk level should be viewed as a moderate-high level for continued high-risk behavior.

Steven scores as follows on the risk assessment screening (see Table 18.1):
5/10—Low Risk Criteria
6/9—Moderate Risk Criteria
5/16—High Risk Criteria

Protective factors

Steven is a generally likeable young man, who has a good sense of humor. He appears to be gaining skills in the areas of self-sufficiency, and has demonstrated his ability to hold down a steady job (paper route) for at least four months. Steven states that he enjoys fishing, hiking, and shopping, and that he is good at fixing things. Steven has some realistic and attainable goals for the future including wanting to go to community college and become an auto mechanic. He does appear to be connected and trusting of both his parents and is also very attached to his maternal grandparents. He is able to express the seriousness of the behavior, though it appears to be information he has recently been told by his parents and attorney. The fact that he was caught and arrested appears to have stressed the seriousness of the event. His family is taking the issue seriously and appears to have started to examine the reality that Steven has significant problems. They have been forthcoming and already begun to seek psychological counseling. They have also indicated that they are making arrangements not to leave him unsupervised or alone with his sister.

Awareness of victim impact

Steven evidences inadequate levels of empathy at this time. He requires substantially more information related to animal abuse, the serious suffering that he inflicted on this animal victim. He appears to be intentionally in a defensive posture by explaining that he believed the cat was sick and suffering. When confronted about this not being the case, he replied that he "will need to learn a lot more about cats so that he knows the difference." This suggests that although he appears to be making himself receptive to change, he remains deceptive about his intent and he has not taken any real ownership for his abusive behavior.

Supervision

Both his parents and grandparents have voiced a willingness to participate in his counseling and his careful supervision. He requires a maximum level of informed supervision and should not be allowed to be unsupervised especially with vulnerable others such as his sister or other pets.

Amenability to treatment

Steven's amenability to treatment appears positive but will require specialized and integrated services in order to effect change in all the equally important treatment issues. His functional and learning deficits must be carefully considered when developing a treatment plan. Approaches that offer some promise might be those specially designed for special needs populations. Attempts should also be made to minimize his contact with antisocial peers.

Summary and recommendations

It is recommended that Steven be placed on supervised probation for the maximum time allowed under this offense. It is critical that he have meaningful consequence from his actions. His profile is consistent with youth who require extensive structure and routine. He will require ongoing psychological treatment and should have a psychotropic medical evaluation immediately. Although risk assessment is currently an inexact science, he should be viewed as a moderate-high risk for continued cruelty behavior. His risk is substantially elevated due to the extreme violence evidenced in his abusive behavior and his general mental health and unresolved trauma experience. The fact that he may be displaying the animal victim for others to see or to shock others suggests a disturbing need for attention. It is unclear if he is experiencing a level of sadistic pleasure from the behavior but it should continue to be evaluated. Clearly he is gaining a sense of control and power through very abusive means. He is a candidate for community-based treatment as long as he continues to have strong family involvement and supervision. He requires intensive individual therapy and may benefit from social skills groups and an animal abuse-specific intervention. He should be provided support to ensure that his school experience is allowing him to establish healthy peer relationships and should be encouraged to establish daily structured schedules after school that ensure his opportunities for increased self worth. Steven needs social skills, interpersonal competence and improved impulse control. His extreme violent behavior toward the cat he killed makes him currently a poor candidate for animal therapy but this should continue to be assessed. Prior to being allowed to work directly with a companion animal he should be able to demonstrate clear understanding of impact, demonstrate legal culpability, authentic emotional responsiveness, empathy associated with his actions and generally improved accountability and stability. At this point, indirect (non-hands on) experience learning about the emotional lives of animals and providing concerned response to animals could be valuable to improve capacity for empathy. Efforts should be made not simply to teach Steven to appear empathic but to make him actually feel more empathic.

18.4.6 Anicare Adult and Child Model

The Anicare Model provides a comprehensive approach to the assessment of and intervention for animal cruelty with a model designed for adults and the AniCare Child Model designed for youth under 18 (Randour et al., 2001). AniCare uses a cognitive-behavioral approach with direct interventions emphasizing the client's need to acknowledge accountability for their behavior. The program uses assessment activities to assist the clinician in determining the likely treatment priorities and make some determinations related to causation. The program also places emphasis on supervision, insight, and personal accountability. AniCare indicates that there are several import identifiers, including accountability, respect/freedom, reciprocity, accommodation, empathy, attachment, and nurturance. Ken Shapiro, the Executive Director of Animals and Society Forum, reports that since 2001, "there have been 12 cases in which the judge has included in the sentence of a person convicted of animal abuse the requirement that he (all have been male) undergo AniCare treatment." An informal analysis suggests that in the six states in which the cases occurred there are two factors in common: an animal-friendly prosecuting attorney and previously held AniCare workshops (http://www.psyeta.org/AniCare.html).

These models remain invalidated but have added significant specialized knowledge to the assessment process and are valuable tools for clinical screening and case planning. It seems important to view these existing tools as providing about the same prediction capacity as a seasoned clinical interviewer's ability to gather the most critical clinical information for determination about risk.

18.4.7 Should animal-assisted therapy (AAT), animal-assisted activities (AAA) or animal-assisted learning (AAL) be utilized as a modality for individuals who have engaged in animal abuse?

This issue generates diverse and often emotional reactions from the human/animal interactions field. The debate is understandable because, on the one hand, we have no greater responsibility in the facilitation of AAT/AAA than to ensure the physical and psychological well-being of the animals and the human participants. On the other hand, AAT has been defined as a widely excepted application for use with at-risk populations. There appears to be a good potential of reaching individuals with a history of conduct problems and antisocial behavior; on the other hand, we have a responsibility never to place an animal in a situation that could result in intentional

Table 18.1 Risk assessment screening scores

LOW RISK	MODERATE RISK	HIGH RISK
1. No patterned history of animal abuse	1. Escalating history of animal abuse (more than 1X)	1. Multiple victims
2. No evidence of premeditation	2. Increased harm to animal	2. Prior history of animal and human violent behavior
3. Less serious harm to animal	**3. Difficulty in interpersonal relationship and family problems**	3. Behavior suggests premeditation
4. Participates in getting animal medical care	**4. Inadequate remorse and empathy**	**4. Animal abuse activities achieve sense of pleasure**
5. Does not use abuse to achieve specific gain except attention needs	**5. History of family violence**	5. May be ritualized and patterned
6. Minimal denial	**6. Moderate denial**	**6. Behavior results in severe harm or death**
7. Client has capacity for remorse/empathy	7. Family endorses abusive belief systems—including hyper-masculinity	7. Complete denial
8. No other significant dysfunction	**8. Prior history of mental health problems**	**8. Sadistic**
9. Follows rules and accepts consequences	9. Prior and current history of criminal behavior	9. Fails to follow supervision and may be hostile to intervention
10. Family takes abuse seriously	**10. Other abusive behavior**	10. Significant lack of remorse/empathy
11. No criminal history		**11. Early onset**
		12. Serious history of other criminal activity
		13. Severe family dysfunction
		14. Personality disorder (psychopathy)
		15. Sense of aggressive entitlement
		16. Serious mental illness (especially paranoia and psychosis)
		17. Early exposure to violence

abuse or harm. In the life of an at-risk youth, every day presents new challenges and opportunities for learning. Youth who abuse animals can be taught new attitudes and ways of interaction with them. A well-planned animal therapy program with adequate supervision can reliably protect and advocate for the animal and, in turn, use the overt advocacy as an opportunity to have the child reinvestigate their own issues of safety and attachment (Parrish-Plass, 2008). If safety for the animal and persons involved cannot be assured, then it is not appropriate to include animals.

Youth's knowledge of their strengths and weaknesses allows them to intentionally and experientially learn by planning, monitoring and self-correcting when necessary, as well as reflecting on their own performance. Youth who lack this type of awareness and insight cannot be expected to effectively self-regulate. A key finding that has surfaced from studies of youth's cognition is that learning occurs best in the context of successful experiences rather than experiences of failure. This discovery implies that learning can be more productive when teaching approaches and activities are designed to ensure youth's achievement. Further research on childhood development has shown that the functional organization of the brain depends on and positively benefits from experience. Additional research is needed to determine which types of AAT and AAA experiences are linked to critical periods of development. Such information is critical to consider when designing animal-assisted interventions with at-risk youth, such as those who have endured abuse or neglect. These findings shed light on the importance of creating interventions that offer youth the potential to succeed.

If Steven were allowed to participate in an animal-assisted therapy program, the following might be an example of an early carefully supervised animal therapy plan that could be effectively incorporated into Steven's goals.

Animal-assisted intervention plan for Steven

In order to recommend that Steven be part of an AAT program, he would need to demonstrate significant improvement in his capacity for empathic regard, stability in school, impulse control and have taken full responsibility for his animal abuse behavior. If he demonstrates the ability to consistently follow directions and shows a genuine interest in learning about animals he might be interviewed and asked to complete an application to be involved in the marine fish tank group.

A fish tank is a practical intervention because the safety risks for both the youth and fish are manageable. These interventions require the involvement of and close communication with a fisheries specialist, who can work in tandem with the youth and therapist to ensure the well-being of the fish. Since the tank is self-contained and can be closely supervised, and the youth have limited direct contact with the marine animals, there is a low likelihood that the animals and/or youth will be harmed. In this group we utilize an aquarium or marine tank (approximately a 150 gallon tank, or one that is large enough to accommodate a variety of marine species). With proper guidance and supervision from the therapist, the youth in this group should be able to effectively engage in caring for the tank and enjoy the satisfaction of knowing that his or her role of caretaker has been successful. The tank can be used as a development and age-appropriate intervention that requires hands-on work that is both engaging and challenging. For example, the youth can check the temperature of the water, feed the fish, and use their hearts and minds to care for and learn about the marine life. Such an intervention should appeal to all types of learners: the visual, the auditory, and the kinesthetic. This intervention is premised on the notion that youth learn best through experience, specifically successful experiences (Bransford et al., 2000). Youth can visually see the reward of their work when equilibrium has been achieved within the tank and learn that their interest and concern for the well-being of the fish have allowed them to thrive.

Clinical rationale

Youth who have conduct disorder are persistently antisocial and repeatedly violate rules, age-appropriate societal norms, or the rights of others. They show aggression toward people or animals, destroy property, lie or steal, and defy adults. Youth who have oppositional defiant disorder are defiant and hostile to the point that school, work, and social relationships are impaired (Morrison and Anders, 2006). As a result, their social relationships at school and at home greatly suffer and they can become depressed, isolated and even more hostile. Consequently, they may have difficulty making and keeping friends. Growing bodies of research show that interaction with animals stimulates social growth and communication in youth (Rud and Beck, 2000). Additional evidence suggests that the mere presence of an animal can positively affect youth's attitudes toward themselves and their ability to relate to others. The presence of animals can also initiate youth to talk about their feelings and encourage social contact and the development of empathy (Beck, 1999).

The animals and environment found in a tank will be used metaphorically to demonstrate the social relationships among different animals, particularly relationships that are symbiotic in nature. Marine environments require equilibrium as every creature living in the tank has a role and a purpose upon which other creatures depend. For example, many fish form an important symbiotic relationship with certain green algae that reside in the animals' cells. The fish benefit and in turn the algae are given exposure to sunlight and protection from micro-feeders. Another example of a mutual relationship within a saltwater tank is that of marine plant life and the fish that use that habitat for protection. Even in an aquarium, where there are few predators, the clownfish will remain within 6 to 12 inches of the sea anemone for an entire lifetime (Campbell and Reece, 2002).

The sea anemone, green algae, and clownfish are examples of animals that might be utilized in Steven's intervention. These animals demonstrate that all types of living creatures, no matter how they differ, can learn to live together and they demonstrate the balance of relationships and the ways in which living beings can thrive or suffer according to the roles and choices of others. Another aspect of the tank is the delicate balance that must be sustained for each creature to live a healthy life. Placing different creatures together in a tank can initially be a stressful experience for them. Eventually, though, the creatures begin to adapt to each other and their new environment. The tank would serve as a valuable metaphor for the youth because the youth can likely identify with the feeling of being a "fish out of water," or feeling "displaced." Like the fish, however, the youth can learn to develop adaptive coping mechanisms that enable them to achieve symbiotic relationships with others. Through the development of social skills and an understanding of relationships and boundaries, the youth may realize that they *do* have a place among people and that they can peacefully coexist with others. These interpersonal questions offer Steven the opportunity to gain improved empathy for others.

Clinical objective

The intervention itself would involve asking the youth to work both individually and collaboratively toward a shared goal. This goal would be to care for and maintain the health of the tank. In the beginning, this would be the youth's primary role and purpose. Such a task would require learning the necessary components that create equilibrium within a tank. This would involve understanding the tank's filtration system and testing the water's pH, salinity, temperature, nitrogen levels, and so on. The youth would also need to learn the additional elements that go into creating a well-balanced, well-controlled tank, such as the kinds of lighting (fluorescent, wattage), the types of rocks (limestone, coral), and the types of plants (artificial, authentic). Even more importantly, though, the youth would begin to learn about themselves and each other through the process of working together and learning about marine animals. Although this intervention could be provided as an element of Steven's individual therapy, he may also benefit from working in a cooperative group environment. It is likely that this group will have youth with differing needs with a primary focus of communication with each other and improved social skills, responsibility, teamwork and improved empathy responses. Steven's evaluation also suggests that he has difficulty making age appropriate friendships and has difficulty taking others' perspective. He might learn how fish get along with each other and project how they feel.

Through an evaluation of the multiple elements required for the animals' health, comfort and safety, Steven can begin to evaluate what *they* need and desire in order to thrive and lead healthy, happy lives. Such dialogue would depend on the therapist's ability to elicit conversation about the link between animals and humans. In addition, the therapist would need to ask open-ended questions that encourage discussion and help Steven find appropriate terminology to identify and discuss his feelings, help him gain improved ability for self control and increase social competence.

Expected clinical outcomes

With practice, support, structure and peer-modeling, we would hope that Steven would begin to make connections between concrete behaviors and the ways in which others respond and feel about these behaviors. Over time, Steven may start to replace old coping behaviors with new, healthier social skills and social scripts that can be added to his cognitive repertoire and used when faced with challenges or stressors. These changes in the Steven's behaviors, and ability more effectively to talk about feelings, should be used as measures of progress.

Through this intervention, our hope specifically for Steven is that he finds a healthier and improved self-worth, purpose and strategies for a positive exchange of interaction with the animals and others compelling him to continue investing in safe and humane animal relationship and human friendships.

18.5 Conclusion

Animal-assisted therapy is a newly evolving field that holds great promise and potential for many populations. While research on this subject is limited, existing findings show that the human/animal bond is a powerful force that has the capacity to effect meaningful change when used appropriately. Animal cruelty and abusive behaviors are also a feature of the human/animal connection. These abuse behaviors are found pathologically embedded with other human cruelty problems. The new generation of social workers must recognize both sides of the human/animal connection, protecting both people and animals but also see the potential to utilize animals in therapeutic settings and channel these interventions to help our clients connect with themselves, each other, and the world at large. Such tasks require great effort, strong patience, and diligent documentation in our efforts to establish evidence-based practices.

References

Achenbach, T. M., & Edelbrock, C. S. (1981). Behavioral problems and competencies reported by parents of normal and disturbed children aged four through sixteen. *Monographs of the Society for Research in Child Development, 46*. Serial No. 188.

Agnew, R. (1998). The causes of animal abuse: a social-psychological analysis. *Theoretical Criminology, 2*, 177–209.

American Psychiatric Association. (1994). *Diagnostic and Statistical Manual of Mental Disorders* (4th ed.). Washington, DC: Author.

American Psychiatric Association. (2000). *Diagnostic and Statistical Manual of Mental Disorders* (4th ed., Text Revision—TR). Washington, DC: Author.

American Veterinary Medical Association. (2007). *U.S. Pet Ownership and Demographics Sourcebook*. Schaumburg, IL: American Veterinary Medical Association.

Arkow, P. (1996). The relationship between animal abuse and other forms of family violence. *Family Violence and Sexual Assault Bulletin, 12*, 29–34.

Arluke, A., Levin, J., Luke, C., & Ascione, F. (1999). The relationship of animal abuse to violence and other forms of antisocial behavior. *Journal of Interpersonal Violence, 14*, 963–975.

Arluke, A., & Lockwood, R. (1997). Understanding cruelty to animals. *Society and Animals, 5*(3), 183–193.

Ascione, F. R. (1993). Children who are cruel to animals: a review of research and implications for developmental psychopathology. *Anthrozoös, 6*, 226–247.

Ascione, F. R. (1997). Humane education research: evaluating efforts to encourage youth's kindness and caring. *Genetic, Social, and General Psychology Monographs, 123*(1), 57–77.

Ascione, F. R. (1998). Battered women's reports of their partners' and their youth's cruelty to animals. *Journal of Emotional Abuse, 1,* 119–133.

Ascione, F. R. (1999). The abuse of animals and human interpersonal violence: making the connection. In F. R. Ascione & P. Arkow (Eds.), *Child Abuse, Domestic Violence, and Animal Abuse: Linking the Circles of Compassion for Prevention and Intervention* (pp. 50–61). West Lafayette, IN: Purdue University Press.

Ascione, F. R. (2000). *Safe Havens for Pets: Guidelines for Programs Sheltering Pets for Women who are Battered.* Logan, UT: Author.

Ascione, F. R. (2005a). Children, animal abuse, and family violence—the multiple intersections of animal abuse, child victimization, and domestic violence. In K. A. Kendall-Tackett & S. Giacomoni (Eds.), *Victimization of Youth and Youth: Patterns of Abuse, Response Strategies* (pp. 3-1-3-34) Kingston, NJ: Civic Research Institute, Inc.

Ascione, F. R. (2005b). *Children and Animals: Exploring the Roots of Kindness and Cruelty.* West Lafayette, IN: Purdue University Press.

Ascione, F. R. (2007). Emerging research on animal abuse as a risk factor for intimate partner violence. In K. A. Kendall-Tackett & S. Giacomoni (Eds.), *Intimate Partner Violence* (pp. 3-1-3-17) Kingston, NJ: Civic Research Institute.

Ascione, F. R. (Ed.), (2008). *International Handbook on Animal Abuse and Cruelty: Theory, Research, and Application.* West Lafayette, IN: Purdue University Press.

Ascione, F. R. (2009). Examining youth's exposure to violence in the context of animal abuse: a review of recent research. In A. Linsey (Ed.), *The Link between Animal Abuse and Human Violence* (pp. 106–115). East Sussex, UK: Sussex Academic Press.

Ascione, F. R., & Arkow, P. (1999). *Child Abuse, Domestic Violence, and Animal Abuse: Linking the Circles of Compassion for Prevention and Intervention.* West Lafayette, IN: Purdue University Press.

Ascione, F. R., & Blakelock, H. H. (2003). *Incarcerated men's reports of animal abuse: a study of the perpetrator's perspective.* Portsmouth, NH: Paper presented at the 8th International Family Violence Conference. July 14.

Ascione, F. R. and Maruyama, M. (in press). Animal abuse and developmental psychopathology. In P. McCardle, S. McCune, J. Griffin, & V. Maholmes (Eds.), *How Animals Affect Us: Examining the Influence of Human-Animal Interaction on Child Development and Human Health.* Washington, DC: American Psychological Association.

Ascione, F. R., & Shapiro, K. J. (2009). People and animals, kindness and cruelty: research directions and policy implications. *Journal of Social Issues, 65,* 569–587.

Ascione, F. R., & Weber, C. V. (1997b). *Children's Observation and Experience with Pets (COEP).* Logan, Utah: Utah State University.

Ascione, F. R., & Weber, C. V. (1997a). *Battered Partner Shelter Survey (BPSS).* Logan, Utah: Utah State University.

Ascione, F. R., Friedrich, W. N., Heath, J., & Hayashi, K. (2003). Cruelty to animals in normative, sexually abused, and outpatient psychiatric samples of 6- to 12-year-old children: relations to maltreatment and exposure to domestic violence. *Anthrozoös, 16,* 194–212.

Ascione, F. R., Thompson, T. M., & Black, T. (1997a). Childhood cruelty to animals: assessing cruelty dimensions and motivations. *Anthrozoös, 10,* 170–177.

Ascione, F. R., Weber, C. V., & Wood, D. S. (1997b). The abuse of animals and domestic violence: a national survey of shelters for women who are battered. *Society and Animals, 5,* 205–218.

Ascione, F. R., Weber, C. V., Thompson, T. M., Heath, J., Maruyama, M., & Hayashi, K. (2007). Battered pets and domestic violence: animal abuse reported by women experiencing intimate violence and by non-abused women. *Violence against Women, 13,* 354–373.

Baenninger, R. (1991). Violence toward other species. In R. Baenninger (Ed.), *Targets of Violence and Aggression* (pp. 5–43). Amsterdam: North-Holland.

Baldry, A. C. (2003). Animal abuse and exposure to interparental violence in Italian youth. *Journal of Interpersonal Violence, 18,* 258–281.

Beck, A. M. (1999). Companion animals and their companions: sharing a strategy for survival. *Bulletin of Science, Technology and Society, 19*(4), 281–285, Sage Publications, Inc.

Beetz, A. M., & Podberscek, A. L. (Eds.), (2005). *Bestiality and Zoophilia: Sexual Relations with Animals.* West Lafayette, IN: Purdue University Press.

Bell, L. (2001). Abusing children—abusing animals. *Journal of Social Work, 1,* 223–234.

Blevins, R. O. (2009). A case of severe anal injury in an adolescent male due to bestial sexual experimentation. *Journal of Forensic and Legal Medicine, 16,* 403–406.

Boat, B. (1995). The relationship between violence to children and violence to animals: an ignored Link? *Journal of Interpersonal Violence, 10,* 229–235.

Bransford, J., Brown, A., & Cocking, R. (Eds.), (2000). *How People Learn: Brain, Mind, Experience and School.* Washington, DC: National Academy Press.

Brody, G. H., Beach, S. R. H., Philibert, R. A., Chen, Y., & Murry, V. M. (2009). Prevention effects moderate the association of 5-HTTLPR and youth risk behavior initiation: gene x environment hypotheses tested via a randomized prevention design. *Child Development, 80,* 645–661.

Campbell, N., & Reece, J. (2002). *Biology* (6th ed.). San Francisco: Pearson Education.

Currie, C. L. (2006). Animal cruelty by children exposed to domestic violence. *Child Abuse and Neglect, 30,* 425–435.

Dadds, M. R., & Fraser, J. A. (2006). Fire interest, fire setting and psychopathology in Australian children: a normative study. *Australian and New Zealand Journal of Psychiatry, 40,* 581–586.

Dadds, M. R., Hunter, K., Hawes, D. J., Frost, A. D. J., Vassallo, S., Bunn, P., Merz, S., & El Masry, Y. (2008). A measure of cognitive and affective empathy in children using parent ratings. *Child Psychiatry and Human Development, 39,* 111–122.

Dadds, M. R., Whiting, C., Bunn, P., Fraser, J. A., Charlson, J. H., & Pirola-Merlo, A. (2004). Measurement of cruelty in youth: the Cruelty to Animals Inventory. *Journal of Abnormal Child Psychology, 32,* 321–334.

Dadds, M. R., Whiting, C., & Hawes, D. J. (2006). Associations among cruelty to animals, family conflict, and psychopathic traits in childhood. *Journal of Interpersonal Violence, 21,* 411–429.

Davidson, H. (1998). On the horizon: what lawyers and judges should know about the Link between child abuse and animal cruelty. *ABA Child Law Practice, 17*(4), 60–63.

DeGue, S., & DiLillo, D. (2009). Is animal cruelty a "red flag" for family violence? Investigating co-occurring violence toward children, partners, and pets. *Journal of Interpersonal Violence, 24,* 1036–1056.

DeViney, E., Dickert, J., & Lockwood, R. (1983). The care of pets within child abusing families. *International Journal for the Study of Animal Problems, 4,* 321–329.

Duncan, A., Thomas, J. C., & Miller, C. (2005). Significance of family risk factors in development of childhood animal cruelty in adolescent boys with conduct problems. *Journal of Family Violence, 20,* 235–239.

Edleson, J. L., Shin, N., & Armendariz, K. K. J. (2008). Measuring children's exposure to domestic violence: the development and testing of the Child Exposure to Domestic Violence (CEDV) Scale. *Youth and Youth Services Review, 30,* 502–521.

Eisenberg, N. (1992). *The Caring Child*. Cambridge: Harvard University Press.

Eme, R. (2009). Male life-course persistent antisocial behavior: a review of neuro-developmental factors. *Aggression and Violent Behavior, 14*, 348–358.

Faver, C. A. (2010). School-based humane education as a strategy to prevent violence: review and recommendations. *Youth and Youth Services Review, 32*, 365–370.

Felthous, A. R., & Kellert, S. R. (1987). Childhood cruelty to animals and later aggression against people: a review. *American Journal of Psychiatry, 144*, 710–717.

Fitzgerald, A. J. (2005). *Animal Abuse and Family Violence: Researching the Interrelationships of Abusive Power*. Lewiston, NY: Edwin Mellen Press.

Frick, P. J., Van Horn, Y., Lahey, B. B., Christ, M. A. G., Loeber, R., Hart, E. A., Tannenbaum, L., & Hanson, K. (1993). Oppositional defiant disorder and conduct disorder: a meta-analytic review of factor analyses and cross-validation in a clinical sample. *Clinical Psychology Review, 13*, 319–340.

Geddes, V. A. (1977). *Enuresis, fire settings and animal cruelty—a follow-up study to review the triad hypothesis in reference to the prediction of violence*. Long Beach, CA: Dept. of Criminal Justice, California State University.

Gelhorn, H. L., Sakai, J. T., Price, R. K., & Crowley, T. J. (2007). DSM-IV conduct disorder criteria as predictors of antisocial personality disorder. *Comprehensive Psychiatry, 48*, 529–538.

Gleyzer, R., Felthous, A. R., & Holzer, C. E., III (2002). Animal cruelty and psychiatric disorders. *Journal of the American Academy of Psychiatry and the Law, 30*, 257–265.

Goleman, D. (1995). *Emotional Intelligence*. New York: Bantam Books.

Green, P. C., & Gullone, E. (2005). Knowledge and attitudes of Australian veterinarians to animal abuse and human interpersonal violence. *Australian Veterinary Journal, 83*, 17–23.

Gullone, E., & Robertson, N. (2008). The relationship between bullying and animal cruelty behaviours in Australian adolescents. *Journal of Applied Developmental Psychology, 29*, 371–379.

Guymer, E. C., Mellor, D., Luk, E. S. L., & Pearse, V. (2001). The development of a screening questionnaire for childhood cruelty to animals. *Journal of Child Psychology and Psychiatry, 42*, 1057–1063.

Hanson, R. K., & Bussière, M. T. (1996). *Predictors of sexual offender recidivism: a meta-analysis*. Canada: Cat. No. JS4-1/1996-4E, Public Works and Government Services.

Hastings, P. D., Zahn-Waxler, C., Robinson, J., Usher, B., & Bridges, D. (2000). The development of concern for others in children with behavior problems. *Developmental Psychology, 36*, 531–546.

Hellman, D. S., & Blackman, N. (1966). Enuresis, firesetting, and cruelty to animals: A triad predictive of adult crime. *American Journal of Psychiatry, 122*, 1431–1435.

Henry, B. C. (2004a). Exposure to animal abuse and group context: two factors affecting participation in animal abuse. *Anthrozoös, 17*, 290–305.

Henry, B. C. (2004b). The relationship between animal cruelty, delinquency, and attitudes toward the treatment of animals. *Society and Animals, 12*, 185–207.

Hensley, C., & Tallichet, S. E. (2005). Learning to be cruel? Exploring the onset and frequency of animal cruelty. *International Journal of Offender Therapy and Comparative Criminology, 49*, 37–47.

Hindman, J. L. (1992; 1999). *Juvenile culpability assessment, second revision*. Ontario, OR: Alexandria Associates.

Jimenez-Jimenez, F. J., Sayed, Y., Garcia-Soldevilla, M. A., & Barcenilla, B. (2002). Possible zoophilia associated with dopaminergic therapy in Parkinson disease. *Annals of Pharmacotherapy, 36*, 1178–1179.

Jones, M. (1998). Cat killings bring 12-year prison term: Animal rights activists pack court. Milwaukee Journal Sentinel Online, July (Document ID: 0EB82BC13A427074).

Kaufmann, M. E. (1999). The relevance of cultural competence to the link between violence to animals and people. In F. R. Ascione & P. Arkow (Eds.), *Child Abuse, Domestic Violence, and Animal Abuse: Linking the Circles of Compassion for Prevention and Intervention* (pp. 260–270). West Lafayette, IN: Purdue University Press.

Kazdin, A. E., & Esveldt-Dawson, K. (1986). The interview for antisocial behavior: psychometric characteristics and concurrent validity with child psychiatric inpatients. *Journal of Psychopathology and Behavioral Assessment, 8*, 289–303.

Kellert, S. R., & Felthous, A. R. (1985). Childhood cruelty toward animals among criminals and noncriminals. *Human Relations, 38*, 1113–1129.

Khan, R., & Cooke, D. J. (2008). Risk factors for severe inter-sibling violence: a preliminary study of a youth forensic sample. *Journal of Interpersonal Violence, 23*, 1513–1530.

Kogan, L. R., McConnell, S., Schoenfeld-Tacher, R., & Jansen-Lock, P. (2004). Crosstrails: a unique foster program to provide safety for pets of women in safehouses. *Violence against Women, 10*, 418–434.

Kolko, D. (Ed.), (2002). *Handbook on Firesetting in Youth and Youth*. New York, NY: Academic Press.

Kruesi, M. J. P. (1989). Cruelty to animals and CSF 5HIAA. *Psychiatry Research, 28*, 115–116.

Lockwood, R. (2006). *Animal Cruelty Prosecution: Opportunities for Early Response to Crime and Interpersonal Violence*. Alexandria, VA: American Prosecutors Research Institute.

Lockwood, R. L., & Ascione, F. R. (Eds.), (1998). *Cruelty to Animals and Interpersonal Violence: Readings in Research and Application*. West Lafayette, IN: Purdue University Press.

Loeber, R., Keenan, K., Lahey, B., Green, S., & Thomas, C. (1993). Evidence for developmentally based diagnoses of oppositional defiant disorder and conduct disorder. *Journal of Abnormal Child Psychology, 21*, 377–410.

Luk, E. S. L., Staiger, P. K., Wong, L., & Mathai, J. (1999). Children who are cruel to animals: a revisit. *Australian and New Zealand Journal of Psychiatry, 33*, 29–36.

Magid, K., & McKelvey, C. A. (1987). *High Risk: Children without a Conscience*. New York: Bantam Books.

McMillan, F. D. (2005). Emotional maltreatment in animals. In F. D. McMillan (Ed.), *Mental Health and Well-being in Animals* (pp. 167–179). Ames, IA: Blackwell Publishing.

McPhedran, S. (2009a). Animal abuse, family violence, and child wellbeing. *Journal of Family Violence, 24*, 41–52.

McPhedran, S. (2009b). A review of the evidence for associations between empathy, violence, and animal cruelty. *Aggression and Violent Behavior, 14*, 1–4.

Mellor, D., Yeow, J., Hapidzal, N., Yamamoto, T., Yokoyama, A., & Nobuzane, Y. (2009). Childhood cruelty to animals: a tri-national study. *Child Psychiatry and Human Development, 40*, 527–541.

Merz-Perez, L., & Heide, K. M. (2004). *Animal Cruelty: Pathway to Violence against People*. Walnut Creek, CA: AltaMira Press.

Moffit, T. E. (1993). "Life-course persistent" and "adolescence-limited" antisocial behavior: a developmental taxonomy. *Psychological Review, 100*, 674–701.

Morrison, J., & Anders, A. (2006). *Interviewing Children and Adolescents: Skills and Strategies for Effective DSM-IV Diagnosis*. New York: Guildford.

Munro, H. (1996). Battered pets. *Irish Veterinary Journal, 49*, 712–713.

Munro, H. M. C., & Thrusfield, M. V. (2001a). "Battered pets": features that raise suspicion of non-accidental injury. *Journal of Small Animal Practice, 42*, 218–226.

Munro, H. M. C., & Thrusfield, M. V. (2001b). "Battered pets": non-accidental physical injuries found in dogs and cats. *Journal of Small Animal Practice, 42*, 279–290.

Munro, H. M. C., & Thrusfield, M. V. (2001c). "Battered pets": sexual abuse. *Journal of Small Animal Practice, 42*, 333–337.

Munro, H. M. C., & Thrusfield, M. V. (2001d). "Battered pets": Munchausen syndrome by proxy (factitious illness by proxy). *Journal of Small Animal Practice, 42*, 385–389.

Nelson, P. (2001). *A survey of psychologists' attitudes, opinions, and clinical experiences with animal abuse. Unpublished doctoral dissertation.* Berkeley, CA: Wright Institute Graduate School of psychology.

Nelson, R. & Tedeschi, P. (2000). Juvenile Diagnostic Typology Checklist.

Offord, D. R., Boyle, M. H., & Racine, Y. A. (1991). The epidemiology of antisocial behavior in childhood and adolescence. In D. J. Pepler & K. H. Rubin (Eds.), *The Development and Treatment of Childhood Aggression* (pp. 31–54). Hillsdale, NJ: Lawrence Erlbaum Associates.

Pagani, C. (2000). Perception of a common fate in human-animal relations and its relevance to our concern for animals. *Anthrozoös, 13*, 66–73.

Pagani, C., Robustelli, F., & Ascione, F. R. (2007). Italian youths' attitudes toward and concern for animals. *Anthrozoös, 20*, 279–293.

Pagani, C., Robustelli, F., and Ascione, F.R. (in press). Investigating animal abuse: some theoretical and methodological issues. *Anthrozoös*.

Parrish-Plass, N. (2008). Animal-assisted therapy with children suffering from insecure attachment due to abuse and neglect: a method to lower the risk of intergenerational transmission of abuse? *Clinical Child Psychology and Psychiatry, 13*(1), 7–30.

Peak, T. and Ascione, F.R. (in press). Adult protective services and animal welfare: should animal abuse and neglect be assessed during adult protective services screening? *Journal of Elder Abuse and Neglect*.

Petersen, M. L., & Farrington, D. P. (2007). Cruelty to animals and violence to people. *Victims and Offenders, 2*, 21–43.

Pinel, P. (1809). *Traite medico-philosophique de la alientation mentale* (2nd ed.). Paris: Brosson.

Pinizzotto, A. J. (2008). Foreword. In F. R. Ascione (Ed.), *The International Handbook of Animal Abuse and Cruelty: Theory, Research, and Application* (pp. ix–x). West Lafayette, IN: Purdue University Press.

Quinn, K. (2000). Violent behavior-animal abuse at an early age linked to interpersonal violence. *The Brown University Child and Adolescent News Letter, 16*(3). March.

Randour, M.L., Krinsk, S., and Wolf, J. (2001). The AniCare child: assessment and treatment approach for childhood animal abuse.

Ressler, R. K., Burgess, A. W., & Douglas, J. E. (1988). *Sexual Homicide: Patterns and Motives*. Lexington, MA: Lexington Books.

Rud, J., & Beck, A. (2000). Kids and critters in class together. *Phi Delta Kappan, 82*(4), 313.

Schaefer, K. D., Hays, K. A., & Steiner, R. L. (2007). Animal abuse issues in therapy: survey of therapists' attitudes. *Professional Psychology: Research and Practice, 38*, 530–537.

Schiff, K., Louw, D., & Ascione, F. R. (1999). Animal relations in childhood and later violent behaviour against humans. *Acta Criminologica, 12*, 77–86.

Simmons, C. A., & Lehmann, P. (2007). Exploring the link between pet abuse and controlling behaviors in violent relationships. *Journal of Interpersonal Violence, 22*, 1211–1222.

Simons, D. A., Wurtele, S. K., & Durham, R. L. (2008). Developmental experiences of child sexual abusers and rapists. *Child Abuse and Neglect, 32*, 549–560.

Strauchler, O., McCloskey, K., Malloy, K., Sitaker, M., Grigsby, N., & Gillig, P. (2004). Humiliation, manipulation, and control: evidence of centrality in domestic violence against an adult partner. *Journal of Family Violence, 19*, 339–354.

Tani, T. (2007). Investigation of animal cruelty among youths: focusing on relationships between juvenile offenders and interpersonal violence. [Seishounen ni okeru doubutsu gyakutai no jittai: Hikoushounen to taijinbouryoku tono kanrenwo chushin to shite]. *Seishinigaku, 4*, 727–733.

Tapia, F. (1971). Children who are cruel to animals. *Child Psychiatry and Human Development, 2*, 70–77.

Tedeschi, P. (2000). *Animal Abuser Screening Interview and Risk Assessment Tool (ARRAT)*. Unpublished manuscript.

Thompson, K. L., & Gullone, E. (2003). The Children's Treatment of Animals Questionnaire (CTAQ): a psychometric investigation. *Society and Animals, 11*, 1–15.

Thompson, K. L., & Gullone, E. (2006). An investigation into the association between the witnessing of animal abuse and adolescents' behavior toward animals. *Society and Animals, 14*, 221–243.

Thompson, K. L., & Gullone, E. (2008). Prosocial and antisocial behaviors in adolescents: an investigation into associations with attachment and empathy. *Anthrozoös, 21*, 123–137.

Vaughn, M. G., Fu, Q., DeLisi, M., Beaver, K. M., Perron, B. E., Terrell, K., & Howard, M. O. (2009). Correlates of cruelty to animals in the United States: results from the National Epidemiologic Survey on Alcohol and Related Condition. *Journal of Psychiatric Research, 43*, 1213–1218.

Vermuelen, H., & Odendaal, J. S. J. (1993). Proposed typology of companion animal abuse. *Anthrozoös, 6*, 248–257.

Volant, A. M., Johnson, J. A., Gullone, E., & Coleman, G. J. (2008). The relationship between domestic violence and animal abuse: an Australian study. *Journal of Interpersonal Violence, 23*, 1277–1295.

Walton-Moss, B. J., Manganello, J., Frye, J., & Campbell, J. C. (2005). Risk factors for intimate partner violence and associated injury among urban women. *Journal of Community Health, 30*, 377–389.

Weber, C. V., & Ascione, F. R. (1992). *Humane attitudes and human empathy: relations in adulthood. Keynote address at the Sixth International Conference on Human Animal Interactions*. Canada: Montreal. July 23.

Westbury, H. R., & Neumann, D. L. (2008). Empathy-related responses to moving film stimuli depicting human and non-human animal targets in negative circumstances. *Biological Psychiatry, 78*, 66–74.

World Health Organization. (1996). *International Classification of Mental and Behavioral Disorders (ICD-10)*. Cambridge, UK: Cambridge University Press.

19 Animal-assisted activity as a social experience

Arnold Arluke

Northeastern University, Boston

19.1 Introduction

Violent behavior continues to be an uncontrollable problem in many societies, including America (World Health Organization, 2004). Most efforts have failed to prevent such behavior by intervening in the lives of children and adolescents at risk of incarceration. However, a few programs have had promising results by trying to change and improve the social, emotional, and cognitive skills of targeted groups (e.g. Beelmann et al., 1994; Schneider and Byrne, 1985).

Animal-assisted activities (AAA), which also target these skills, offer a novel and potentially more effective way to prevent violence (Kruger and Serpell, 2006) because of the unique ability of animals to appeal to children and adolescents (Arluke, 2004), to be highly responsive, and to provide many opportunities for interaction (Myers and Saunders, 2002). AAA provides participants with a variety of animal contacts, ranging from purely spontaneous and recreational to structured and instructional ones that are overseen by shelter workers, volunteers, animal trainers, and paraprofessionals who, rather than setting specific treatment goals, have more general objectives for participants, ranging from attendance and general comportment to caring for and training animals. Despite their variety, all AAA programs allow for and encourage participants to interact and perhaps bond with animals and people in a non-threatening and supportive environment.

Anecdotal and research data on program outcomes suggest that AAA can positively shape the attitudes and behavior of problem youth (Dalton, 2001; Rathmann, 1999). Program advocates, admittedly biased to see success among participants, nevertheless have countless personal reports, many quite convincing at face inspection, that point to AAA's ability to transform problem youth into happy, responsible, outgoing, verbal, and involved young adults who lead productive lives (e.g. Hill, 2003). Studies of the impact of AAA show more specific benefits of exposure to these programs, including teaching knowledge about animals to participating youth (Zasloff et al., 2003), reducing aggression and recidivism (Dalton, 1995, 2000; Merriam, 2001; Siegel, 1999), curbing anxiety and depression (Woolley, 2004), improving vocational skills (Dalton, 1993–1994, 2005), and enhancing social skills, such as empathy, decision making, patience, task concentration, and interpersonal

Handbook on Animal-Assisted Therapy. DOI: 10.1016/B978-0-12-381453-1.10019-4

communication (Dalton, 1993–1994, 2005; Merriam, 2001; Rathmann and Cohen, 2001).

Despite the encouraging, albeit small, literature on AAA outcomes, researchers have failed to examine why these programs may be so effective. However, some attempt has been made to explain the success of animal-assisted therapy (AAT). Since the latter is a related although not identical intervention, understanding why AAT works can shed light on why AAA also works. Katcher (2002), for one, speculates that AAT's efficacy stems from the liminality of the contacts between animals and people targeted by these interventions, the ability of animals to serve as transitional or projective objects, and the generalization of positive attributions from animals to humans that occur in these programs. While these psychological mechanisms may contribute to AAT's success, they cannot be easily manipulated, if at all, or deliberately designed into animal programs to bolster their efficacy.

However, interpersonal explanations offer greater opportunity to enhance the effectiveness of animal programs because they can be more easily created, influenced, and shaped by program designers and advocates compared to trying to change the built-in psychological dispositions or abilities of participants. McNichols and Collis (2006), for example, suggest one such relational explanation, stemming from the formation of human/animal relationships in these programs; namely, that therapy animals provide social support to participants. Although it is a start, this explanation may not do justice to the variety of relationships that participants can form in these programs. Research needs to specify what exactly about these relationships, or others that form between participants and their peers and participants and staff members, may contribute to the apparent success of these animal programs.

To understand how interpersonal relationships can contribute to the success of animal interventions, we need a baseline description of what these relationships look like in these programs. Only then can future researchers verify and weigh which, if any, relational features, alone or in combination, make for greater program efficacy with particular target groups. Establishing this baseline calls for a focus on participants' broad social experience in these programs. This experience includes, but goes beyond participants' contacts with program animals and whatever formal curriculum and structured plans they encounter.

The nature of this experience and the belief that it helps to transform participants into more civil, trusting, calm, empathic, confident, and responsible people stems from each program's informal culture, or what staff members believe is the right way for participants to regard and act toward animals, peers, and adults when they attend the programs. Since it is part of program culture, this staff perspective is not recorded but understood and enacted by those present, and passed on to new staff members and volunteers through observation or verbal instruction about how they should view and treat participating youth. Describing this cultural underpinning of AAA programs—the social experience that staff members want participants to have because of its presumed therapeutic benefit— is this chapter's focus.

19.2 Method

An ethnographic approach is uniquely suited for this descriptive, rather than explanatory, task. Naturalistically positioned to unearth data with a high degree of internal validity, the ethnographer immerses him- or herself in the everyday social world of the group under investigation and uses unstructured interviewing and observation, as well as document and record analysis, to discover the beliefs and group processes underlying the local culture (Harris et al., 1997). This approach is especially good at discovering cultural insights because the ethnographer's rapport with respondents and firsthand observation of their behavior as it unfolds makes it easier to examine and understand issues that are politically or emotionally sensitive as well as those that are hard to articulate, let alone quantify on survey questionnaires.

Using this approach, the author studied four AAA programs for at-risk children and adolescents with a wide range of behavioral and emotional problems and one AAA program for incarcerated young adults. Two programs had participants train service dogs for the disabled, two had participants train shelter dogs for adoption, and one had participants visit and care for farm animals. These sites were chosen because of their reputation for being the best of their kind (i.e. they were long established, internally evaluated, and well documented), according to leading scholars and practitioners having knowledge of specific animal programs across the country.

A total of 116 staff members and targeted youth were studied. The staff ($n = 35$) included program directors, treatment managers and supervisors, volunteers, interns, psychologists, school or facility administrators, and teachers. Children and young adults ($n = 81$) included those incarcerated ($n = 6$) and those deemed at risk ($n = 75$) because of emotional and behavioral problems, among who were 17 females, 64 males, 33 African Americans and Latinos, and 48 whites, ranging in age from three to 25 years.

The author was given full access to observe animal activities and to interview participants and staff members in all programs. Approximately 80 hours of observations were conducted between September 2004 and April 2005. Observations were general, describing the culture of each program, especially as it pertained to teaching participants, formally and informally, various social skills, attitudes, and knowledge. During class or activity time, participants were observed as they interacted with staff, played with peers and animals, practiced dog training, took animals for walks, and cleaned up after, groomed, and fed animals. Observations also were made of informal interactions among participants, and between participants and staff members, as the former arrived and departed programs, and during timeouts and food breaks.

Forty-nine taped interviews (including 28 staff members and 21 participants) were conducted along with countless untaped, impromptu conversations. Given their different perspectives and experiences, both staff members and participants were interviewed in order to cast a wide exploratory net that could tap into aspects of these program cultures that might underlie their presumed effectiveness. Staff members were treated as key informants who had an interest in understanding the perspective of children and adolescents in their programs and had extensive firsthand experience observing and talking with them; in addition, many had prior training in social work or psychology that equipped them to make insightful observations about program dynamics and participants' experiences. The interviews were unstructured and open ended, making it possible to probe respondents' perspectives while allowing them to take the interview in unplanned directions. This enabled the author to explore their beliefs about the programs—more specifically, how and why they believed that AAA "worked" to benefit participants.

Finally, program records were scrutinized for self-assessment forms and results, background information about participants, training manuals, publicity, news coverage, and written communications from former participants. In-house program evaluations, when available, were also inspected.

All data gathered through observations, interviews, and secondary sources were transcribed and subjected to grounded theory analysis (Glaser and Strauss, 1967), a technique that inductively reviews data to identify general group beliefs and experiences. The findings discussed below represent the major relational themes that resulted from this analysis.

There are two apparent limitations to the present study that turned out to benefit its exploratory goal. For one, program staff members were advocates for AAA and had a vested interest in seeing their programs "work." Their spirited interest in seeing what they regarded as positive changes in participants and their general interest in the operation of their programs hardly made them objective evaluators, but it did make them eager to help the author at every step of the way and, more importantly, to help the author gather insight into why their programs might benefit participants. For another, program participants were not randomly assigned to each program; they were often, but not always, selected by staff members for being ready and motivated to benefit from and function in these programs, selected by facility administrators because they exhibited "good" behavior in classes, and/or were self-selected because participants wanted to work with animals. As the "cream of the crop" they were not typical of their peers, but they offered the greatest likelihood of program success as variously defined by staff members and institutional administrators. If any AAA programs achieved sought-after changes in targeted youth, the ones studied here would do so, then making it possible to investigate and theorize why they might be effective.

19.3 Findings

Results reported in this chapter describe the kinds of social experiences encountered by participants in AAA programs. More specifically, in the programs studied, youth were exposed to close relationships with animals, close relationships with humans, softened hierarchies, new perspectives, easy successes, and manageable challenges. Also considered are the ways these experiences might benefit participants.

19.3.1   Close relationships with animals

Programs provided participants with opportunities to experience close relationships with animals (Sanders, 2003), whether this involved creating, sustaining, or releasing them. Before entering programs, many participants had pets, but these prior connections were emotionally shallow compared to those established with their new animals. Most who reported having owned dogs had instrumental, rather than affective, relationships with pit bulls or Rottweilers where the animals were treated more like objects than conventional pets. Their new animal relationships, unlike their former ones with pets, were intrinsically rewarding, relatively long term, and involved considerable emotional stake; unlike their former relationships with humans, these animal connections were unambivalent and unabusive.

Qualities unique to animals help to build these close relationships with participants. Many participants touch or are touched by animals very quickly and very often, compared to their experiences with humans where touch is awkward, rare, or unwelcomed. One staff member noted: "Even if the teacher develops a relationship in time with the kids, they'll start to get closer to you, talk to you, and they might touch you, but they're still not touchers. So the fact that they touch dogs is really a remarkable accomplishment in a short time. By the second week of school you start to see kids touching dogs." In return, participants allow the dogs to touch them (e.g. being licked, pawed, jumped on, or leaned against). Participants also "get something immediately back" from most dogs that they define and experience as positive, such as attention or affection. If nothing else, dogs at least respond in some way to the child's presence. This is not true, though, with most farm animals. Sometimes, there is no response, as with a sleeping pig or indifferent horse, and signs of outward or undeniable affection are even harder to come by. For children with boundary problems, this reticence may allow them to establish relationships when that is problematic for them with humans. Also, the reticence to be demonstrative can be an advantage to those with histories of being emotionally overwhelmed by people who appear to invade participants' own boundaries.

Fostering close relationships, some participants identify with the animals' plight and future. Unlike the service dog programs where animals do not have troubled medical or social histories, the farm animal and dog obedience programs use abandoned, abused, or otherwise mistreated animals. One staff member observed: "They all were abandoned or something terrible happened. It's so appropriate because here are these kids that are all misplaced and here are these animals that are misplaced." "They all have stories," said one program psychologist. Histories of animals are part of the oral cultures of these programs. Participants may ask where animals come from, why they are injured, or how they learn such bad behavior, at which point staff members explain their histories. "If kids ask, 'How did Carmen get here?' then the story will be told, if the person knows the story." In one program, the staff posted each animal's "story" on its stall for the children to read.

By connecting these animal stories to their own histories, staff members expect participants to take comfort in their own situations and have hope for the future. For example, a staff member talked about a girl in her program, saying: "With Diane, she can see that Honey's (abused horse) life got better from the situation that it was in. And that gives Diane hope. That just hits a nerve. She had a horrible background just like Honey, and she can have some hope that things will get better for her too…some sense of future, which abused kids don't have." Another staff member added, "They are troubled dogs who will work with troubled kids, where they can help each other have a good future." Participants see that staff members do not give up on these animals until they are safe and cared for, and that perhaps they will be protected and loved too. In the words of one program director, "I won't give up on finding them homes, 'See, we didn't give up!' We can find good homes for them and they now have good lives. And it is a lesson I want the kids to get—we don't give up on troubled animals or troubled kids."

Many participants connect their own abused, homeless, or abandoned backgrounds to those of program animals. A participant in one of the farm programs articulated these parallels, saying: "The thing I liked the most when I came here, you have these animals around you that I kind of identified with. Like it's a place where they live and I lived in a children's home. So it's kind of like a children's home and an animal's home. So I just kind of see similarities—they live here and they get taken care of by Michelle and all the other people, the helpers and staff. And then at the children's home, you get taken care of by adults as well." Participants also see similarities between the behavior of their animals and their own behavior. For example, it is common for shelter dogs to need "calming down." One youth made this connection with a dog he was training: "Molly loves to bolt, she loves to run and jump, and she's getting worse. She gets really hyper and excited. She does it right when you open her cage. And you've got to be ready to hold onto that leash or she's going right by you. So she is a behavior problem because I can't get her to calm down immediately. I need her to focus. That's a challenge, but it will be fine. You know, when I started here I guess I gave everybody a hard time too. I flew off the handle really easy, but people tell me I don't do it so much anymore."

The result is that very close, even intense, relationships often develop between participants and their program animals, an intensity particularly revealed when participants let go of animals when they leave programs or when animals are placed with clients or adopters. The head of the juvenile detention center connected to one program recalled: "There was a young man here who was detached from his family and he got involved in the dog program. After about four months of training a dog for adoption the family came to take the dog away and the kid broke down in tears. And we had never seen any kind of emotion like that nor had his family. It goes back to that relationship between the youth and his dog."

19.3.2 Close relationships with humans

Most participants have a history of relationships with friends or family members that often or almost always lacked nurturing, support, trust, caring, and open communication. Although AAA programs are ostensibly about human/animal interaction, as much or more of the interaction in these programs is between humans. These human contacts offered participants a chance to form and maintain satisfying and consistent close relationships with program peers and adults, making it possible to sample the emotional benefits that come with such connections and perhaps seek similar relations in the future.

Participants commonly develop relationships with peers in their programs. Dog programs encourage participants to help each other train animals by pointing out and correcting peers' mistakes; teamwork and joint problem-solving behavior often result. Particularly in programs with older youth, dog training provides challenges that test problem-solving ability and often lead to joint solutions among peers. For example, on one occasion, three participants mulled over how to lessen a dog's aggressiveness, sharing their thoughts about what the dog's perspective was and why it was so aggressive. As part of a team, participants also learn to sanction peers who do not work hard in their programs. Such sanctioning rarely became divisive. More typically, they understood peer sanctioning as a sign of mutual respect and regard for the program, the animals, and the staff; in other words, it was a sign of fellowship rather than a symptom of social breakdown and distance. Peer relations also flower in these programs because participants are allowed to socialize with each other by talking, playing, teasing, or roughhousing. Whatever their impetus, these program-based peer relationships sometimes lead to strong friendships between two or more participants that carry over to their dorms.

Participants also can form close relationships with staff members. The latter believe that they relate better to participants than do most other adults in the facility. Because of this presumed special connection, many participants appear to develop a strong rapport with the staff. One of the older youths singled out how trust between peers and staff allowed the former to depend on the latter. He claimed: "Personal relationships are really important. There is a trust level here. We are kind of a tight family, I guess you can say. They rely on us, and I like that. [The program] gives me lots of confidence. And I've never had those feelings before." Once established, a trusting relationship allows participants to feel that the staff understands them and will do the right thing by them. This rapport permits participants to reveal things to staff members that they cannot tell other teachers or administrators; doing so will get them into trouble (e.g. having a gun) or be too personal (e.g. having girlfriend problems).

Close relationships with staff members are often forged indirectly by teaching participants interpersonal and emotional skills, such as nurturing. As staff model these roles, their relationships with participants often become more intimate. The latter may realize that they, and not just the animals, are being nurtured. Participants get the "message that they (staff) are going to take really good care of you (participants)," just as they do with program animals. Participants also see staff members nurturing them, which increases the sense of trust between them. They see that staff members are "human beings, not just teachers, who care for the kids." Consequently, many participants "feel like they can open up to the adults, ask questions or just feel more comfortable because there is a lot of anger about the authority stuff" (i.e. staff in their group homes). One girl experienced so much conflict in her group home that she did not want to leave the program, preferring to stay there where she felt more comfortable and safe. Unsurprisingly, many staff members claim they function as substitute parents for participants. In this role, the staff is viewed as "family," with participants sometimes staying in touch with them long after leaving their programs.

19.3.3   Softened hierarchies

Participants in AAA programs are used to being the hierarchical bottom rung, whether their subordinate role was in a classroom, residential facility, or correctional center. In these settings, there is usually a striking gap between participants and the age, class background, education, and authority of teachers, counselors, dorm directors, and criminal justice figures. The culture of AAA programs provides participants with a less hierarchical and formal experience so they can have an opportunity to be assertive, take responsibility, and feel self worth.

One way to soften program hierarchies is to teach a skill to participants that may be learned so well, it puts participants nearly on a level with some staff members in terms of this special competence. When participants first enter dog programs they know nothing about animal behavior, care, and training, while staff members know everything. This knowledge gap quickly closes as staff members freely share information and skills with participants, a few of whom gain sufficient expertise to rival and even challenge the staff's authority and decision making regarding the training of dogs. For instance, one young man with two years' experience in a shelter-dog program sometimes disagrees with the director and trainer about how best to train the dogs. In one case, he strongly opposed their approach to paper training dogs; he explained: "I despise wee-wee pads because they are for the lazy person. I told them that what they are doing is teaching the dog that it is okay to pee on paper indoors when essentially you can teach the dog the same thing outside. It's just cutting corners to me. And then you come home and discipline him, they are going to be confused about where to go." In another case, he did not want to use a "halty" to stop a dog's jumping behavior, although the director and trainer suggested this to him. The director did not want to tell him that he had to use the halty because she wanted the young man to decide on his own. She feels that such an approach allows youths to make some independent decisions—something which most of them, she believes, are never allowed to do.

Another way that program hierarchies are softened is that animals add a hierarchical level below participants. In classrooms, for instance, the hierarchy is simply teacher versus student, but the presence of animals in AAA programs creates a tier below participants in terms of authority and power. For once, the participants have someone below them. In addition, sometimes participants appear to develop stronger bonds with individual animals than they have with staff members. When this happens, animals show greater interest in or responsiveness to participants than staff. These emotional connections can create an informal hierarchical alliance that couples and distinguishes participants and their animals from the staff, blurring the adult/child, teacher/student distinction.

The presence of animals also softens hierarchical differences by increasing the informality of program settings compared to more formal settings, such as classrooms. Animals facilitate informal conversation where it might otherwise not occur, as happens when dogs are walked in public and strangers are encountered (Robins et al., 1991). Participants also can interact easily with adults through the animals. They can, for example, ask questions about animals or jointly find humor in what animals do. And adults can easily initiate conversation with participants through animals, when talking to them might otherwise be hard. Communication encouraged by this informality likely fosters closer relationships and mutual identification between staff and participants. Also, animals bark, snore, hee haw, defecate, urinate, vomit, attack, run uncontrollably, kick, or act out. Doing this drowns out staff members' words, breaks their concentration, or otherwise stops them from conducting the usual routine. When this happens, their authority is reduced and programs become more informal and relaxed.

Animals also soften the hierarchy because staff members often piggyback or ride the coattails of the rapport created by animals. By being connected to animals in this way, staff members are perceived by participants not as single individuals but as part of a unit or couple, or what Sanders (1990) calls a "human/animal with." In other words, they see staff members as "together" with animals or co-members in the ongoing activities of programs. Once seen as a unit, staff members share the halo of uncritical acceptance attributed to animals. This borrowed rapport softens how participants perceive the staff, just as strangers initiate encounters with unfamiliar dog owners because of the "interactional vulnerability" of humans with dogs in public places (Robins et al., 1991).

Some programs also take steps to reduce overt signs of hierarchical differences that can further the individuality of participants. For example, one program director dresses participants in clothing that does not resemble the uniform, drab clothes worn by other youth in the facility (i.e. gray sweat pants and T-shirts). Instead, they wear non-gray shirts bearing the program's name, blue jeans, and blue Columbia rain slickers. Additionally, the institutional clothing often does not fit well and hangs unappealingly on many youth, compared to the better fitting clothing given to them by the director. Staff members do not take these steps to soften the hierarchy, according to the director; they are to enhance and make more effective the youth's presentation to outsiders coming to adopt or kennel animals. Whatever their stated aim, attempts to modify individual appearance can soften hierarchical distinctions, especially in institutions where clothing is a scare and restricted commodity.

Finally, sometimes staff members deliberately withhold their own decision making, such that participants themselves become decision makers. Although this abdication of control does not happen around urgent or dire matters, it does provide an important opportunity for role playing and learning. For example, one program had a mouse problem that the director used to encourage problem solving by youth. She said that one unit supervisor at her institution handled his mouse problem by stomping them to death and encouraging his boys to follow suit. Instead, she wanted to be compassionate and not even use traps, so she privately considered trying more humane alternatives. Rather than continuing, she let participants come up with their own solution as part of her larger goal of allowing them to think through problems and to feel empowered, softening her program's hierarchy, to some degree.

19.3.4 New perspectives

Staff members believe that participants have weak or no perspective-taking skills because they are not encouraged, taught, and rewarded for such thinking. To address this assumed cognitive failure, AAA programs provide many opportunities for participants to observe, practice, become accustomed to, and be lauded for seeing and taking others' perspectives when they work with clients, staff members, and animals. Through these experiences, participants are urged to trust and apply this new kind of thinking not only when they attend the programs but afterwards with others in their facilities, families, and general communities.

The first perspective they learn is that of the animals with which they work, both as individuals and species. For example, to train dogs successfully, participants are encouraged to "think like a dog." One child illustrated this type of thinking: "You start to know what they want. Like with Sara, she was sniffing around me, so I was like thinking what she was thinking in her head." They need to practice this skill because many opportunities arise when empathy is needed to help dogs that have trouble learning new commands. Once participants become comfortable interpreting the dog's perspective, they invariably conclude that their animals care about them. This increases their attachment and encourages them to use and trust their newly learned empathic skills. One student, for example, said that dogs sensed when he was in a "bad mood" and took actions to make him happier. "They are going to be like, yeah, there's something wrong with him. Let me do something that will make this guy happy." Another said, "If you are mad, the dog would know. She knows that you are mad, she can see it in your face. She would stay away from you. Like, she's 'oh man, oh, man, he's mad at me. I should stay away.' "

Learning to think like an animal may enable participants to make emotional deductions to humans. One staff psychologist observed: "They learn to see that when this dog's tail drops and she is averting her head that she is telling you she is frightened. Or she is upset because she does not understand what you are telling her. That this means this in dog language. And sometimes the light bulb goes on for the kid. And the student will say, 'I saw that in Rosy when I was training her yesterday and I can see that in my friend Johnny. Johnny has the same sad face on today that Rosy had on yesterday, so something must be bothering him.' "

Staff members encourage participants to make these emotional deductions to adult groups, such as parents or teachers, by using animals as metaphors to teach lessons about human relationships. In one case, the behavior of a program's beloved mascot allowed the staff to teach students important lessons about good parenting. Sky, the good-natured, aging retriever, allowed several very frisky puppies to jump on her without stopping them or getting angry with them. The program director suggested to students that Sky was being a good parent by putting up with all this commotion and annoyance from her "kids." In another case, a staff member compared a student's frustration when teaching his dog to the frustration he created for his reading teacher. "One student last year, he had difficultly with reading. And he would describe how frustrating it was to teach his dog each step and how long it took. And I was then able to make the analogy about his teacher and him and his reading. 'Do you understand that when she is trying to speak to you and you are not paying attention to her, do you see how frustrating that might be for your teacher?' It can click." This metaphorical lesson did appear to click; the child at least articulated the teacher's point, as he generalized from his dog's behavior to that of his own behavior to grasp the problem he created for others: "If you tell the dog to sit and they don't sit or something and they are being disobedient, it would be like, oh this is like how I am and how frustrated my teacher gets with me. So I don't want that. I don't like being frustrated either."

Staff members also hope that program youth will generalize the animal's perspective to their peers. In one case, dogs were used to teach participants how to get along with their classmates and friends by first appreciating the dog's perspective. One volunteer gave an example of how the program director did this by comparing human behavior to dog behavior: "She was trying to show the kids the dog's behavior and how it correlated with human behavior. Like, who would be the bully dog or have the pack mentality, and show dominance and eye contact. She was trying to translate that into their peer relations."

Participating youth also learn to see things from an adult perspective. In two programs, participants use wheelchairs in class and on field trips to role play their client's disability. At these times, they learn that "some people have it worse than they do," or they directly observe clients' limitations. In one case, for example, the staff attributed a boy's empathy for a disabled client to his experience in the program. The client was a 30-year-old woman whose car was rear ended, leaving her with a stroke and limited balance that required her to use a walker. She was staying in a building near the dog program. One day she was having a difficult time during heavy rain cutting across the grass between the two buildings. Charles, a boy in the program, ran over to her with an umbrella, held her around the shoulders, and walked with her across the grass. When asked if his kindness resulted from the program, a staff member explained. "Exposure to this arena. Exposure to this part of the world. You know, he knew what his dog could do. He was glad to give it to her. He was concerned about her falling. That was something that happened to him...he became very aware of disabled people. He said to me, 'You know, I really like helping disabled people. Is there a job in that?' And I said, 'Absolutely. You'd be very good at it and you don't need to go to college.'"

Service dog programs also have built-in rituals that celebrate prosocial behavior and give participants further practice in and validation for learning new perspectives. At the end of their training in one program, students pass the dogs to someone with a physical disability. This passage starts with "boot camp" where students train their disabled clients how to use the dogs. Staff members hope that students learn many things about their clients, as a result. One director explained: "The goal is for them to understand that this is a person with a disability, they have feelings and goals like you, they want the same things that you want, instead of seeing that disability over there and not recognizing the person behind it. I have seen students come out of working with a person with a disability being more empathetic and more understanding toward people who don't have the same issues that they do."

19.3.5   Easy successes

Most participants have a history of poor academic performance, little if any experience volunteering or working in the community (sometimes because they were so young), and tarnished self-concepts from years of being negatively labeled as emotionally troubled or even criminal children. These prior experiences make participants feel alienated from the mainstream community and ill equipped to succeed at new challenges at home or at school. Programs make it easy for participants to feel accomplished and competent as they acquire new skills, see positive results, gain new roles, and learn to speak of their own success and progress.

Staff members believe that participants need a "timeout" from being judged negatively by teachers, counselors, family members, and criminal justice authorities whose evaluations of participants constantly batter their already fragile sense of self. One way this is done is for staff members not to label participants. Doing so is quite easy because little if any such damaging diagnostic or disciplinary history circulates in programs. This lack of knowledge is deliberate. Program directors are not usually given such information and, even if available, the sentiment is that knowing participants' prior labels could adversely affect the staff by biasing their interactions with participants or making them worry about their well-being once they leave the program. One program director elaborated this problem: "A couple of instances have come up when the volunteers knew about the kids, and it is very difficult then for them to work with the kids because it is hard to normalize the situation when you are so worried about what's going on with the kids and they are worried about what's going to happen to the kids when they go." Also, staff members learn not to ask participants to talk about their former mental health diagnoses or criminal histories. As one staff member said, "It's like a place where they can be free from it (negative labeling) for a while. And they get to experience a happy, nurturing, loving, positive experience for that hour without having to think about it or talk about it."

When carrying out many animal-assisted activities, it is hard for participants to fail. One farm animal program, for example, has no end points to complete or behaviors to assess; participants simply visit and watch animals if they choose. And if there are tasks to perform, they tend to be easy, such as throwing a few handfuls of hay into a horse's stall. In dog programs, most participants can train animals, whether they are for the disabled or general community. Service dogs, according to staff members, are not that difficult to train because the commonly used breed—retrievers—are good natured and relate well to children, even if training takes many repetitions. Obedience training of shelter dogs can be somewhat more challenging, but most youths are able to see significant changes in their charges' behavior over time.

When students fail to complete animal-related tasks it is not necessarily due to incompetence. For example, the few students who did not finish the service dog programs failed to do so because of allergies, lack of interest in working with dogs, or inability to do well in their other classes. In another program, some participants left to make more money elsewhere in their facility. Although exceedingly rare, an occasional participant was asked to leave a program because of inappropriate attitude or behavior; for example, one sharply pinched a dog's ear and another refused to take suggestions for training his dog.

More important than making it hard to fail, it is easy for participants to see clear, positive benefits resulting from their work with animals. In the case of shelter dog programs, participants could see that their efforts helped animals in need or "saved" them from death by providing them with an adoptive home. In both service dog and shelter dog programs, many spoke about how their trained animals provided adopted families with new companions or enabled disabled clients to function more independently. Their efforts to help people outside the institution also distracted them, even if briefly, from some of their own worries and concerns. As one youth pointed out, "On a general level you are helping a family out by giving them an actual dog that hopefully won't hurt or bite them, and will give them a nice long-lasting relationship. It really inspired me to strive to help the dog more and stop worrying about all the other problems I have with people. Instead, I focus on how I am going to get this dog in and out of here."

Participants actually see the successful results of their training when adopters or clients return with dogs that appear well placed in their new homes. One youth explained: "It's a really great feeling. It makes me feel good that I did something for the community. I have customers come back that adopted my dogs." Continuing, he gave an example of one of his successful dogs. "I had Don. He was a white Great Dane mix. And we had him for a long time. So he finally went to this home. We put lots of training into the family. A month later, he comes back, he's got fifteen pounds on him. And it just made me feel so good that he's doing good and he's comfortable in his home. And he comes back, and of course he remembers you. It's a good feeling to know that that dog succeeded."

Programs also were set up to push participants to assume new roles that signaled success to them and others. Those in dog training programs can potentially earn a living by becoming obedience trainers, kennel workers, dog groomers, or animal caretakers. One program deliberately prepared its youth for future work by treating them as employees: they recorded their time on the job, got paid for their time, and sometimes had their work performance assessed. They also were expected to "give and take orders" as well as appear and speak professionally with outsiders who came to kennel a dog, receive dog training, or consider a dog for adoption. Also, in this program, students were constantly reminded about the parallels between their work with dogs and the kinds of job skills they will need after release, such as being polite and reliable when dealing with the public. One youth spoke about how his communication skills seemed to improve by being involved with the program: "You have to do an interview with the person you are adopting the dog out to. And you have to communicate very well. My first time wasn't so hot. So the staff helped me make out a list of where to start and how to explain things, you know, brief summaries of what I needed to cover so I could get it next time. I was never a very good speaker. When the pressure is on I choke. You get tons of practice here."

Participants also could assume other roles that indicated competence. For one, they could become teachers—whether that is to teach disabled clients, adopters, or peers. For example, staff members look for and applaud instances when children on their own teach a skill they have mastered to another child. By doing this, they become role models. In one such case, "Amber is with the chickens all the time. She feels empowered enough to go to the smaller children and put the chickens with them. Amber can go into the place where the chickens are, catch the chickens and bring them out. She feels comfortable that she can do that where the little kids don't." For another, participants could assume a role of responsibility where they felt needed or relied on by several parties, including the animals, disabled clients, adopters, or the staff. One participant said of the program: "Project Pooch makes you feel like you are part of something that is good, and a lot of us haven't been involved in that kind of stuff. It's like a club, almost, you know. And clubs make me feel good because you feel wanted. Project Pooch kind of brings that to you."

Finally, feeling successful was built into program cultures by teaching participants to speak about and label their own improvement. They hear adults in the programs who are quick to verbalize presumed changes in participants, no matter how subtle or ambiguous. For example, staff members often pointed to changes in facial expression as evidence of alleged change. In one case, a volunteer said, "I see the healing that animals can give to children. You can see it on their faces. You just see the light in their faces. It touches them and that's really neat to see." At least some participants learn to parrot and see in themselves these presumed changes. Although sometimes genuine, their ability to articulate such change is also part of their socialization into these programs. "They're just talking. They know you want to hear that," said one staff member. One child, for instance, said that he had "anger management problems" before starting the program, but now claimed to keep his anger "under control," even though the staff did not see a significant change in this regard. A supervising staff member used the same language to describe this child's success. In a similar vein, many participants spoke about feeling much "calmer" because of their program experience, again a change commonly pointed out by staff members.

Feeling successful, according to staff members, gave participants new-found confidence. For example, in one program a student allegedly entered the facility with very "guarded" behavior, unwilling to take any risks, even with peers. "Opening himself in any way was not something he was comfortable with." Contact with the dog-training program "made a huge difference in his life…he was more willing to participate in a game, rather than sit off on the side. He would participate in a way that was sort of risky. For a kid who isn't willing to take any risks at all, to participate in a game that is somewhat competitive was a huge step for this particular student." When asked what it was about the program that made this difference, the staff member replied: "He could see that he could make a difference in this dog's life—that he could teach the dog something that he couldn't do before—a self confidence builder."

19.3.6 Manageable challenges

Many participants find it difficult to handle frustration, easily becoming angry when facing everyday problems in their schools, facilities, and homes. Although AAA programs are built for participants to feel successful, various kinds of frustrations are inevitable and welcomed by staff members who see these as teachable moments. Staff members believe that the most important gains in self-control happen when children and young adults face frustrating situations, become aware of their control problems, and then take steps to stop this behavior. By becoming more aware of actions that "set them off" or that "pull their trigger," participants then realize that they do not have to "give in" to their anger in the future.

Working with animals can be frustrating and sometimes even challenging. Staff members do not eliminate these animal-related problems because they are thought to be manageable and to offer opportunities for youth to practice and experience self-control, patience, calmness, and self-awareness. Dog training can be challenging for both novice and experienced participants, especially those with anger control and attention deficit disorders. Almost all new participants get frustrated with the basics of animal training, as one recalled: "When I first started here, I didn't know what was going on. I would get frustrated like this. I would say, heel Betsy, and she wouldn't listen to me. She just sat there and looked at me. And Jane (volunteer) had a smile on her face; she said that's what she does when she doesn't listen to you." However, even experienced participants can find it frustrating to train new dogs. One teen with three years of dog-training experience said: "Once you train them to a point, like you got Alley Cat and Molly, then it is easy. You can fly through all the commands and everything. But then when you have to start at the beginning with these guys they don't listen...You say, 'stay,' they look at you. You walk away and when you come back they are way over there and stuff. They run around. So it gets frustrating." Another student went so far as to describe dog training as a "battle." He said: "It's a constant battle for you and the dog because you are just trying to get the dog to listen to you and do what it is supposed to. And it's sitting there trying to spite you and say that it is in charge. I mean, it gets a little annoying at times."

Most participants learn to manage the frustrations posed by animal training and care. They learn, in a practical sense, not to let their aggravation get the best of them because it just makes animal training that much harder. For instance, one boy who had a "big struggle" with patience learned to "stop himself" from getting angry by realizing that "it's just a dog, calm down. It doesn't know any better." Some students say that if they are angry when they try to train their dogs, the dogs will sense this and "shut down and not want to work for you." Instead, they learn to be patient with their charges because teaching an individual behavior to dogs often takes many repetitions.

Participants also learn to manage frustration by drawing on their relationships with animals. One boy claimed that by simply looking at his dog's face "you are like, how in the heck I am supposed to get mad at him. Like with Drifter, to me, he always looked like he was smiling. So any time I would get mad at him, he would just look at me with a smile. Then I would start hugging and kissing him and I would automatically calm down." Beyond a "look" in the dog's face, several children acknowledged that relationships with their charges helped them "control" their frustration. One teen commented about how "love" for his dog helped him. "Like, I will get frustrated, but I won't get highly frustrated, like I did when I first started in this class. Especially my first dog, he was hyper because of me because I was hyper too. He would not stay on the box. He was like all over the place. And so, like, we got to know each other. Then he would listen to me and he became more mature. Yeah, I used to get frustrated with him, but I loved him."

Staff members believe that participating youth are also better able to cope with frustration because they are in an environment that has a general calming influence. One program psychologist said, "It's hard for the kids to learn things—like responsibility, being on their own, teamwork—when they are in a hypervigilant state, which a lot of them are, except when they are out here. This is fabulous learning that is hard to teach in a schoolroom. When they get here, they immediately relax. The relaxation allows them to take in those things." Staff claim that the programs allow participants to "chill" with animals, peers, and teachers, who over time are seen as "understanding" the youth. "It's a comfort." This "chilling" is thought to result from human/ animal interaction in these programs. For one, it is "relaxing" for participants because the dogs do not expect them to do anything. For another, "the dogs accept them no matter what, when their peers might be cursing at them and calling them names." In addition, according to staff, an environment of acceptance that is part of program culture "calms down" participants. Several say that this calming down, whatever its source, enables participants to "get through" their days.

Staff members in service dog programs also believe that certain rituals help participants cope with frustration. After participants train disabled clients to use their assistance dogs in "boot camp," there is a formal "graduation" ceremony to celebrate the passage of dogs from the programs to clients. The graduation commemorates the students' sacrifices, acknowledging that their altruism can have emotional costs to them. Relinquishing their attachment, despite the frustration and emotional pain it causes, is seen by the staff as a way to learn selflessness. (While lacking such formal group rituals to deal with it, shelter dog programs also could involve considerable frustration for participants who bonded to their animals only to give them up when adopted.) Graduation encourages participants to articulate these feelings, as one staff member noted: "Every kid can talk about how that feels to them. Instead of shutting down—'this makes me sad, this hurts me, I am angry that I spent eight months with Annie, and now I have to give her to this other person.' And being able to say, 'I know this is Annie's job and I know this is why I trained her, it's still hard for me to watch her go to another person.' The majority of the kids say 'the graduation is so much harder than I thought it would be, but I want to do it again. Even though it hurts, it feels good and I am helping.'"

Students frequently articulated the latter sentiment—that helping others helped them cope with the loss. As one said, "Like with my dog, I had an awesome, remarkable bond. Then I was crying my eyes out when he was leaving. But then I thought about it. And I was like, wait a minute. Yeah, we had like the most perfect bond, but now it is his turn to bond with somebody else. Somebody who really needs him. I am going to see him on TV, and I will be like, I trained that dog." Another youth claimed that by seeing the "bigger picture" he could give up a dog with whom he was very attached: In his words: "You've just got to think of the bigger picture. It can't be a selfish act…it can't be this dog is mine. When the dog leaves, it's like, at least it will be happy and in a better home. You've got to look at the positives, you can't ever look at the negatives or else you won't want to do the program."

Participating youth and staff members claim to see many benefits from learning to manage the frustrations encountered in these programs. For one, becoming more patient with animals seems to transfer to becoming less frustrated with people. One boy, for instance, spoke about how he felt more patient with his own young child, instead of quickly becoming frustrated with its difficult behaviors. Another felt that learning patience with dogs helped him get along better with difficult peers in his unit: "You've got to just back up if someone's getting to you...this is something I learned to do with my dogs when I was getting nowhere." And another participant attributed his improved coping ability to the dog program in general. "Now, when I get mad and stuff in the cottage [student residence], I don't walk out any more. I just think of the good times I had with my dog, or the funny things that Ron [program director] did or says." In this manner, one student felt that being responsible for his dog deterred interpersonal problems at school: "In the school, if you think you are going to get yourself into trouble, you think, boy, I have to be with the dogs, it is my responsibility to be with my dog. There's nobody to work with the dog. I need to be over there and be with my dog, or what would happen if I got into trouble. It's not fair to my dog." Staff members add that learning to be patient makes youth in their programs more civil in general, allegedly using fewer profanities and being friendlier and more engaging.

19.4   Discussion

This chapter describes the kinds of social experiences created for participating youth in reputably effective AAA programs. Overall, these experiences may chip away at the selves of these participants, at least during their stay in these programs, by stimulating their ability to form attachments with others, both human and animals, and by forcing them to look at themselves and others in new, prosocial ways. Perhaps in the end, participants are learning much more than how to care for and train animals; they are discovering and trying out new ways of thinking, feeling, and acting that may transfer or generalize to their future relationships after leaving these programs.

The next step is for researchers to verify the extent to which, if at all, these experiences are linked to specific positive outcomes in targeted youth and, if so, whether these changes are carried over into the youth's lives outside AAA programs at their schools, homes, or workplaces. Of course, researchers will have to consider that some participants may bring a readiness to try on new experiences in programs that may make them better candidates for personal change; some of this readiness will come from their prior relationship history, or lack thereof, with both humans and animals. Armed with this knowledge, those designing or implementing AAA programs could train staff members to allow, foster, and encourage those experiences having special therapeutic benefit for their target populations.

Acknowledgments

Thanks to the Laura J. Niles Foundation, Inc. and the Humane Society of the United States for supporting this project. The author also wishes to thank Andrew Rowan for his valuable guidance.

References

Arluke, A. (2004). *Humane education as violence intervention: Immunizing children against future aggression*. Washington, DC: Unpublished report prepared for the Humane Society of the United States.

Beelmann, A., Pfingsten, U., & Losel, F. (1994). Effects of training social competence in children: a meta-analysis of recent evaluation studies. *Journal of Clinical Child Psychology, 23*, 260–271.

Dalton, J. (1993–1994). *Project Pooch: student outcomes*. Unpublished chart.

Dalton, J. (1995). Project Pooch. *Presented at the International Conference on Human-Animal Interactions*. Geneva, Switzerland. Sept. 6–9.

Dalton, J. (2000). *Project Pooch: a juvenile corrections dog project*. Unpublished report.

Dalton, J. (2001). How they bring hope to those whose future may have otherwise been lost. *Interactions, 19*(2).

Dalton, J. (2005). Personal communication. Dec. 2.

Deltasociety.org., n.d.

Glaser, B., & Strauss, A. (1967). *The Discovery of Grounded Theory: Strategies for Qualitative Research*. New York: Aldine.

Harris, K., Jerome, N., & Fawcett, S. (1997). Rapid assessment procedures: a review and critique. *Human Organization, 56*, 375–378.

Hill, N. (2003). Second chances, Sept. 1.

Katcher, A. (2002). Animals in therapeutic education: guides into the liminal state. In P. Kahn, Jr., & S. Kellert (Eds.), *Children and Nature: Psychological, Sociocultural, and Evolutionary Investigations* (pp. 179–198). Cambridge, MA: MIT Press.

Kruger, K., & Serpell, J. A. (2006). Animal assisted interventions in mental health: Definitions and theoretical foundation. In A. Fine (Ed.), *Handbook on Animal Assisted Therapy: Theoretical Foundations and Guidelines for Practice* (pp. 21–38). New York: Academic Press.

Lockwood, R. (2005). Personal communication. June 12.

Merriam, S. (2001). *Discovering Project Pooch: A special program for violent incarcerated male juveniles*. Discover N' Education Research and Consulting. (based on PhD dissertation, Pepperdine University).

Myers, O., Jr., & Saunders, C. (2002). Animals as links toward developing caring relationships with the natural world. In P. Kahn, Jr., & S. Kellert (Eds.), *Children and Nature: Psychological, Sociocultural, and Evolutionary Investigations* (pp. 153–178). Cambridge, MA: MIT Press.

McNicholas, J., & Collis, G. (2006). Animals as social supports: insights for understanding animal-assisted therapy. In A. Fine (Ed.), *Handbook on Animal Assisted Therapy: Theoretical Foundations and Guidelines for Practice* (pp. 49–71). New York: Academic Press.

Rathmann, C. (1999). Forget Me Not Farm: teaching gentleness with gardens and animals to children from violent homes and communities. In F. Ascione & P. Arkow (Eds.), *Child Abuse, Domestic Violence, and Animal Abuse: Linking the Circles of Compassion for Prevention and Intervention* (pp. 393–409). West Lafayette, IN: Purdue University Press.

Rathamann, C., & Cohen, M. (2001). *Results of the child behavior checklist*. Santa Rosa, CA: Forget-Me-Not Farm. Unpublished study.

Robins, D. M., Sanders, C. R., & Cahill, S. (1991). Dogs and their people: pet-facilitated interaction in a public setting. *Journal of Contemporary Ethnography, 20*, 3–25.

Sanders, C. (1990). Excusing tactics: social responses to the public misbehavior of companion animals. *Anthrozoös, 4*, 82–90.

Sanders, C. (2003). Actions speak louder than words: close relationships between humans and nonhuman animals. *Symbolic Interaction, 26*, 405–426.

Schneider, B., & Byrne, B. (1985). Children's social skills training: a meta-analysis. In B. Schneider, K. Rubin, & J. Ledingham (Eds.), *Children's Peer Relations: Issues in Assessment and Intervention* (pp. 175–192). Springer: New York.

Siegal, W. (1999). *Does learning to train dogs reduce the noncompliant/aggressive classroom behaviors of students with behavior disorders?* New Orleans, LA: University of New Orleans. PhD dissertation.

Woolley, C. (2004). *Changes in child symptomatology associated with animal-assisted therapy.* Logan, UT: Utah State University. PhD dissertation.

World Health Organization. (2004). *World Report on Violence and Health.* Geneva, Switzerland: World Health Organization.

Zasloff, R., Hart, L., & Weiss, J. (2003). Dog training as a violence prevention tool for at-risk adolescents. *Anthrozoös, 16*, 352–359.

20 Assistance animals: their evolving role in psychiatric service applications

Philip Tedeschi*, Aubrey H. Fine†, Jana I. Helgeson†

* University of Denver Graduate School of Social Work, † California State Polytechnic University

Heaven goes by favor; if it went by merit, you would stay out and your dog would go in.

Mark Twain

20.1 Introduction

Emerging human/animal interaction therapies and applications call for re-definition in the field of assistance animals and a re-examination of previous conceptualization of use, terminology, training guidelines and formal designations. Specifically, this chapter explores the participation of specialized assistance, service and support animals in their application to social, emotional and psychiatric issues. Of major concern to the authors of this chapter are the new demands on service animals, especially as applied to patients with serious mental health concerns. The benefits for the people who are psychiatric service animal recipients are more obvious. They include:

- Increased social interaction
- Reduced feelings of avoidance and stigmatization
- More empowering conversations focused on their abilities and their dog's abilities rather than disabilities
- Feelings of improvement in general health
- Emotional and psychological support from their dog resulting from sharing their emotions, concerns, and engaging in contact with the dog when upset or sad (Lane et al., 1998).

Box 20.1 Case study

A 74-year-old widower contacted the Psychiatric Service Dog Society (PSDS) explaining that his panic disorder with agoraphobia had rendered him reclusive to his home for most of the last 15 years. He said that he used to have friends, but they eventually stopped calling, because of his refusal to leave his home for

---

(Continued)

Box 20.1 Case study—*cont'd*

friendly outings. He was too afraid to go out because he did not want to risk having a panic attack in public. So he turned down the friendly invitations, which eventually tapered off. He stayed home with his four-year-old German shepherd dog named "Maggie."

He explained that many years ago he used to be a puppy raiser for a guide dog training school. He had trained his German shepherd dog to a high standard of obedience both on- and off-leash. After some discussion, he decided that he would like to train his dog to be a psychiatric service dog.

Several months after completing his training, he called very excited to share some news. He said, "I decided to take Maggie with me to a restaurant for a cup of coffee. The people at the restaurant were so pleasant and they welcomed Maggie, that I decided to order a sandwich with my coffee!" He went on to explain that he hadn't been in a restaurant for 15 years! "Training Maggie to be my psychiatric service dog has allowed me to do the things that I used to do before I became so disabled by panic disorder. I can't thank you enough for giving me back my life through Maggie."

20.2 Labels, definitions and controversy

Throughout this chapter definitions will clarify new terminology in the emerging field of psychiatric assistance animals. Attempts will be made to provide distinction for the applications between service, emotional support and therapy animals. There are three types of assistance applications as identified by organizations such as Assistance Dog International. They include: (1) guide dogs for the blind and individuals with seeing impairments, (2) hearing dogs for the deaf and individuals with hearing impairments and (3) service dogs specially trained for persons with other recognized disabilities (http://www.assistancedogsinternational.org/aboutAssistanceDogs.php)

Assistance Dog International (ADI) defines Service Dogs as follows: "Service Dogs assist people with disabilities other than vision or hearing impairment. With special training these dogs can help mitigate many different types of disabilities. They can be trained to work with people who use power or manual wheelchairs, have balance issues, have various types of autism, need seizure alert or response, need to be alerted to other medical issues like low blood sugar, or have psychiatric disabilities. These specially trained dogs can help by retrieving objects that are out of their person's reach, by pulling wheelchairs, opening and closing doors, turning light switches off and on, barking to indicate that help is needed, finding another person and leading the person to the handler, assisting ambulatory persons to walk by providing balance and counterbalance, providing deep pressure, and many other individual tasks as needed by a person with a disability" (ADI, 2009).

Confusion continues to exist on formal definitions for service animals and there are frequent reports of misuse of classifications and labeling by those who wish to achieve public access with an animal who is strictly assigned as a companion animal or pet. The Americans with Disabilities Act (ADA) (P.L. 101–336) is the most far reaching and comprehensive civil rights legislation adopted to address the discrimination against persons with disabilities. Public and private entities as well as federal, state and local entities offering public accommodations, services and transportations are required to comply with the law. Because there is no single universally defined certification or proof required for public access with a service animal, inaccurate use of the label adds to the confusion and increased likelihood of conflicts. In an attempt to establish best practices, ADI provides a "model law" (http://www.assistancedogsinternational.org/ modellaw.php) to assist in the definition of accepted standards that are consistent with ADA guidelines (1990). The ADA indicates a service animal must be individually trained to "do work" or "perform tasks" of benefit to a disabled individual in order to be legally established from companion animal to service animal status. The ADA defines a "disability" as a "mental or physical condition, which substantially limits a major life activity."

20.3   The history of assistance animals

The earliest use of modern assistance animals emerged from the use of canines as messengers during World War I and their capacity to work effectively under difficult combat circumstances. These dogs' heroic efforts quickly established their effectiveness and capacity to find wounded soldiers, as an article from *The Literary Digest* written in 1917 stated:

> *These army, or Red-Cross, or sanitary dogs, as the Germans call them, are first trained to distinguish between the uniform of their country and that of enemies. Then the dog must learn the importance of a wounded man as being his principal business in life. News of the wounded must also be brought to his master. He must not bark, because the enemy always shoots. There are various ways in which the dog tells his master of his discovery. One method is, if no wounded have been discovered, to trot back and lie down, whereas if he has found a wounded man he urges the master to follow.*

These skills soon resulted in the further use of dogs to assist veterans in a number of ways, most notably those whom had lost their eyesight.

On November 5, 1927, Dorothy Harrison Eustis introduced America to the concept of using dogs as guides for the blind in a historic article in *The Saturday Evening Post*. By 1929, she had founded The Seeing Eye, which became the first group in the USA to breed, raise, and train guide dogs.

Over the decades, the consistency and trustworthiness of assistance animals resulted in their use for many additional human support purposes. By the middle of the twentieth century, service dogs were accepted as an important and effective alternative to support citizens with disabilities. Over the past century, the roles of service animals have been expanded to extensive support for an ever-widening list of disabilities. Canine Companions for Independence (CCI), founded in 1975 in Santa

Rosa, California, pioneered the concept of the specialized service dog, a highly trained canine used to assist people who have disabilities through performing specific tasks to support already existing human services. Service dogs may be trained for people with many different types of disabilities and can perform many tasks that a person with a disability may not be able to accomplish independently. Some of the tasks might include picking up dropped articles, pulling wheelchairs, assisting walkers, turning lights on and off, opening and closing doors, carrying school books, alerting their owners and pulling their owners out of bed. CCI uses specially trained golden retrievers, Labrador retrievers, and crosses of these two breeds. As of 2009, CCI had established over 3,000 graduate teams (CCI History, 2008).

In 1977, Roy Kabat, who began as a trainer for animal actors in movies and television, founded Dogs for the Deaf, an organization which believed that dogs from shelters and humane society dogs could be trained to help the deaf. They now train over 100 dogs a year, including service dogs for persons with autism. As was discussed in an earlier chapter by Grandin et al., they frequently provide dogs that are trained to work with children with autism by acting as an anchor to prevent the child from bolting into dangerous situations. These dogs often have a calming effect on the child and possibly improve the child's ability to communicate and establish relational attachment.

20.4 Therapeutic benefits of contact with animals: the possible psycho-social benefits of service animals

Studies show that simply interacting with animals, and interacting with dogs in particular, has a strongly ameliorative effect on people with a range of psychiatric disorders, increasing evidence that despite differing designations, all assistance dogs convey psychosocial benefits. Animal-assisted therapy (AAT) reduces anxiety (Barker and Dawson, 1998), improves social contact (Villatra-Gil et al., 2009), can decrease use of psychotropic medication (Geisler, 2004), and improve overall quality of life for the patient. In these studies, the extent of the therapeutic relationship has been limited to an interaction between the patient and the animal such as clients voluntarily stroking (Geisler, 2004; Kovacs et al., 2004) or talking to the animal or talking about the animal to a handler (Barker and Dawson, 1998; Geisler, 2004). When the animal is asked to perform a task, it is often a basic obedience command such as "sit" or "down" or a "trick" such as "shake hands" (Barker and Dawson, 1998). Namely this requires dogs to be housebroken, have mastered basic and frequently advanced obedience training, and not to have undesirable behaviors such as nuisance barking, aggressive behavior, or inappropriate sniffing, licking, or other forms of intrusion into a client's personal space (Froling, 2003). Since animals do have such strong, positive effects on people with psychiatric and psychological disorders, and the standard of conduct for animals working in a therapeutic capacity by necessity must be strict, there is a legitimate need for new, expanded definitions and guidelines for what defines and differentiates a service animal and what comprises "work" or a service "task," especially as it relates to psychiatric disabilities.

20.5   Psychiatric service animals

The most common applications in mental health situations for service animals are the major DSM-IVTR Axis I disorders that include: mood and anxiety disorders, including post-traumatic stress disorder, panic reactions, agoraphobia, and acute trauma reactivity. Psychiatric service animals are also widely used to mitigate the negative impact of mood disorders, most specifically severe depression. That said, there is widely recognized endorsement for the use of these specially trained service dogs to support persons with psychiatric disabilities. However, there appears to be in the professional circles a disagreement about the appropriateness of the term "psychiatric service dog." It seems that persons living with chronic mental health disabilities generally favor the term "psychiatric service dog" but persons who do not live with such disabilities appear to be uncomfortable with the term proffering that it unfairly labels or identifies the owner as a person with a psychiatric disability. This might be easily addressed by simply vesting the animal with a designation as a service animal without need for diagnostic labeling or further definition.

As greater specificity has been required to support public access and the application to psychiatric conditions, practitioners have established legitimacy by defining the "work" or "tasks" of psychiatric service dogs for identified psychiatric conditions as a function of the handler's diagnoses. A service dog, even when solely interacting with patients or helping an individual to cope with the effects of a debilitating psychiatric disorder, is performing an identifiable set of tasks providing assistance, despite the fact that these tasks may appear different from those forms of assistance traditionally associated with a service dog assisting for persons with physical disabilities.

Joan Froling focuses on the performance of "tasks" and outlines four areas where service dogs might be trained in specific tasks for individuals with psychiatric conditions:

1. Assistance in a medical crisis
2. Treatment-related assistance
3. Assistance coping with emotional overload
4. Security enhancement tasks.

Examples offered for each of these areas include: A dog might be trained to retrieve a bag holding medication upon command, or even backpacking medication or medical supplies on an ongoing basis. In order to provide support, a dog may be trained to bring a telephone or even dial 911 or a suicide hotline on a specialized k-9 rescue phone. In order to support a person with treatment, a dog can be trained to alert someone to take medication at a certain time of day or alert someone to provide assistance or be alerted to signals, sounds or doorbells. For those persons with extreme startle reflexes, being alerted to the presence of someone approaching can be helpful in managing these anxiety reactions. Froling also describes tasks that could assist consumers with emotional overload. For example, a dog that is trained to provide significant tactile contact in order to assist in "reality affirmation" can greatly improve a sense of control and grounding. This has been reported as highly effective in managing fear reactions, loss of orientation, nightmares and terrors. In some situations an animal's trained insistent interaction with their owner can be used as a legitimized reason for an individual to leave stressful or threatening situations. Security and safety remain one of the more challenging psychiatric issues for service providers, as for example, in the case of combat veterans struggling with the disabling experience of hypervigilance. Froling suggests that a service dog can be trained to assist in identification of safe situations, turning on lights, checking the environment and leading the patient to a safe place or choosing an exit strategy. Patrons utilizing psychiatric service dogs also widely report feeling improved confidence in dealing with public outings (Joan Froling, Service Dog Tasks for Psychiatric Disabilities, July 30, 2009 http://www.iaadp.org/psd_tasks.html).

Esnayra (2009) emphasizes the importance of "work" relative to psychiatric service dogs; whereas persons with physical disabilities are supported by service animals in a physical manner, those that have mental health disabilities are supported either mentally or cognitively. It is evident that the work of psychiatric service dogs will look somewhat different to the work of service dogs for persons with physical disabilities. Unfortunately, many of the tasks performed for people with psychiatric disabilities fall under the heading of "coping skills" and, as such, are not permissible as a service that mitigates a disability (Froling, 2003). In many ways, the lack of understanding related to the experience of coping with a chronic mental heath condition, sometimes referred to as the "invisible disability," is found in these restrictive criteria of the ADA guidelines as they relate to service animals.

Esnayra defines the "work" of psychiatric service dogs as "...assistance that engages the handler's cognitive behavioral skills (i.e. dog alerts to the onset of hypomania when handler has Bipolar Disorder); or, assistance that leverages the dog's natural response to its immediate environment for the purpose of reality-testing (i.e. hallucination discernment when handler has Schizophrenia); or assistance that prompts the handler to engage mind/body regulatory approaches (i.e. controlled deep breathing exercises with the dog when handler has Panic Disorder)." Many persons in the service dog world who are unfamiliar with subtleties of mental health and psychiatric applications frequently refer to these diverse forms of work as "emotional support." This is an unfortunate erroneous attribution that oversimplifies the complex, non-verbal, therapeutic interactions between handler and dog that serve to stabilize and restore a mentally ill handler's ability to function.

The United States Department of Justice, which oversees the enforcement of the Americans with Disabilities Act, states in a Notice of Proposed Rulemaking published in the Federal Register in June 2008, had been petitioned and encouraged to define that "performing tasks" should form the basis of the service animal definition, that "do work" should be eliminated from the definition, and that "physical" should be added to describe tasks. Tasks by their nature are physical, so the Department does not believe that such a change is warranted. In contrast, the phrase "do work" is slightly broader than "perform tasks," and adds meaning to the definition. For example, a psychiatric service dog can help some individuals with dissociative identity disorder to remain grounded in time or place. As one service dog user stated, in some cases "critical forms of assistance can't be construed as physical tasks," noting that the manifestations of "brain-based disabilities," such as psychiatric disorders and autism, are as varied as their physical counterparts. One commenter stated that the current definition works for everyone (i.e. those with physical and mental disabilities) and urged the Department to keep it. The Department has evaluated this issue and believes that the crux of the current definition (individual training to do work or perform tasks) is inclusive of the varied services provided by working animals on behalf of individuals with all types of disabilities and proposes that "this portion of the [service animal] definition remain the same" (http://www.ada.gov/NPRM2008/titleiii.htm. Accessed Feb. 9, 2010)

The Psychiatric Service Dog Society (PSDS) has collected over 12 years of documentation from a wide range of mental health consumers who were reclusive to their homes, sometimes for years, due to panic disorder with agoraphobia but who are now able to leave their homes accompanied by their PSD. There are numerous examples from veterans who report how important their PSD is to them. An example from one specific war veteran with traumatic brain injury (TBI) and post-traumatic stress disorder (PTSD), explained that he was not able to sleep at night because when he heard a noise, he believed it was an insurgent or an IED. With the support of his PSD, he was finally able to sleep at night, because he learned to trust that his dog would alert him to the presence of other people outside his apartment. Some veterans utilize their PSD in order to manage hypervigilance, a hallmark symptom of PTSD. They have learned how to read their dog's body language in order to ascertain whether or not there is a threat in their immediate environment.

Sexual assault-induced PTSD is another area in which dogs seem to be the primary tool in a study focused on adult women. The clinician utilized both working dogs and pets in the intervention focusing on a number of different activities. Exposure was a major component of two key ways in which the therapists utilized dogs masterfully (Lefkowitz et al., 2005, pp. 287–289). The first was an exercise in which the client talked through a rape and re-imagined the incident vividly. A therapy dog was utilized as a buffer, listener, and focal point during this exercise. The second was a homework assignment designed to have the client revisit the site of the rape or other triggering environment with a dog with which they felt comfortable (Lefkowitz et al., 2005, pp. 287–289). The ability of the client to select his or her own animal in the second exercise seems highly logical to support a feeling of empowerment.

The detailed treatment plan developed by Lefkowitz et al. seems to be very aware of animal selection in their formulation. The authors state evidence that people are often anxious around new dogs and acknowledge the fact that clients might be more comfortable with a dog they have known longer or feel protected by in this intense exercise. It appears obvious that the authors made a conscious effort to incorporate empirically supported practices in working with the human/animal dynamic. Offering the client a choice in the second assignment shows a conscious effort to be flexible in a situation where the client might need to be more self-directed in order to achieve an outcome that truly impacts their progress favorably. The subtle changes found in a sense of empowerment, self-confidence and social support, although subtle, are often significant factors in positive outcomes in management of that mental heath issue.

20.6   Emotional support animal (ESA)

An emotional support animal (ESA) is an animal that provides companionship and comfort. This designation, however, has created confusion because it is often assumed that emotional support animals are the equivalent of psychiatric service animals, which is not generally accurate. A psychiatric service animal may also serve as an emotional support but an emotional support animal is not by definition an approved service animal.

As assistance dogs and specifically service dogs are increasingly recognized for their value in mental health, new classifications and framework as well as ways of selecting, training and pairing individuals with these dogs are emerging. Wood et al. (2005) use the term "social capital" to describe the opportunities for increased communication and connections to others created by the presence of the dog. These psychosocial benefits increasingly are prompting health care providers to recommend an emotional support animal for psychological reasons. One of the most common supporting justifications is that animals, dogs in particular, are catalysts for increased social interactions by providing a social lubricant with their presence in both personal and public environments, which in turn facilitates the development of rapport and communication with others, significant psychosocial benefits. An example of this can be found in the case study in Box 20.2.

Box 20.2 Case study

In an interview with a soldier who served as a medic in the Iraq war, his health care provider encouraged him to adopt and train a cat to perform specific tasks to assist him in management of his post-combat trauma. His doctor at the VA clinic also recommended a cat after critically evaluating his case. Fortunately, the animal became pivotal in his recovery. The veteran believes that his experience with his cat is replicable for other veterans dealing with post-combat trauma. He commented during an interview that he knew himself to be an intimidating guy, got angry easily and had been involved in numerous physical altercations due to hypervigilance, paranoia and anger. His cat Wendy offered him a buffer in social situations and had a way of reducing potentially stressful situations that might have become physically violent. His cat was trained to accompany him into social environments and would jump on his shoulders and lick his ear relentlessly if he was escalating his behavior, raising his voice and breathing hard until he would leave situation or stop (J. W. Personal communication, 2008).

Another theoretical perspective argues that animals assist people in modifying their cognitive and social experience, allowing for improved self-esteem and to sustain a more positive and optimistic framework. Many persons report that the unconditional love, attention, companionship and affection of an animal promote increased confidence and self-control, thus encouraging an improved level of psychological health.

20.7 ADA guidelines for transportation and the Federal Air Carriers Act

The role of transportation and decisions made by the Federal Aviation Administration (FAA) has had significant impact on the field of service animals and related definitions. The FAA covers the rights of disabled people and their animals on airlines with the following statement: "Carriers shall permit a service animal to accompany a qualified individual with a disability in any seat in which the person sits, unless the animal obstructs an aisle or other area that must remain unobstructed in order to facilitate an emergency evacuation" (http://www.faa.gov). In May 2009, the updated Air Carrier Act regulations were put into effect. The Department of Transportation updated its original 1996 guidelines to include animals providing emotional support. Ironically, these guidelines were an attempt to limit and clarify which animals should be granted public access to travel with their owner on airlines. Recognizing that it is difficult for airline personnel to distinguish service animals from companion animals, five guidelines were issued:

1. Airline personnel have the right to obtain credible verbal assurances that the animal is a service animal and not a pet by asking how the animal is trained to assist the individual. If the passenger cannot provide a credible response that indicates individual training to perform some task or function, documentation can be requested.
2. Airline personnel are encouraged to look for visual indicators on the animal such as a harness, vest or backpack with markings that identify the animal as a service animal. It is, however, noted that the lack of such equipment is not to be construed as an indicator that the animal is not a service animal.
3. The law allows airline personnel to ask for documentation but not to require it as a condition for permitting travel in the cabin. Examples of documentation are a letter from a licensed professional who treats the passenger for a specific condition.
4. Airline personnel are encouraged to observe the behavior of the animal. Service animals are trained to behave in public by remaining beside their owner, refraining from barking, growling or jumping on others. Disruptive behavior by the animal can serve as an indication that the animal has not been trained to function as a service animal (Federal Register, Vol. 68, No. 90, May 9, 2003).

Those wishing to travel with an emotional support animal, which includes a psychiatric service dog, must notify the airlines 48 hours in advance. In addition, they are required to submit a letter on professional stationery from a licensed mental health professional affirming that the traveler is a current client in need of traveling with his or her animal. The mental health professional must state that the passenger has a condition listed in the DSM-IV (resulting in a public identification of the passenger as someone living with mental illness) and explain that the animal is needed as an accommodation for air travel or for activity at the individual's destination. The letter must be dated within the past year and contain the provider's state licensing number, state and date of issue. This new regulation has provoked outrage from many psychiatric service dog handlers, because no other service animal handlers are subjected to these specific stigmatizing and labeling requirements. The authors believe that there is an urgent need to educate the public as well as those involved in public

Table 20.1 Summary and distinguishing criteria for each type of assistance animal

Service animal	Registered/certified therapy animal	Emotional support/ companion animal
ADA protected	*Not ADA protected*	*Not ADA protected*
Animal is trained to "do work or perform a task" for an individual with a disability (mental or physical)	Visits and participated in animal-assisted therapy or animal-assisted therapy	No specialized training
Specialized training	Frequently requires CGC testing, specific certification and handler credentials and program-specific evaluation defined by program	No training required. Training maybe required by Air Carrier Act
ADA allows for public access	NOT covered under ADA public access rights	NOT covered under ADA access rights/potentially allowed by Air Carrier Act

policy in regards to the significant value of these service animals and the roles they play in the lives of persons with mental illness whose challenges may not be physically apparent but are invisible in nature. What is critical is that policy makers need to be assured that the same rigor in assessing the need for service animals will be put into place, so there will not be any abuse of this resource.

20.8   Psychiatric service animal selection and training

Significant variation exists in the selection of animals that may be incorporated as psychiatric service animals with increasing prevalence of cats and monkeys, but by far the most common remain dogs. Some of the most striking differences between animals that perform traditionally accepted service animal tasks and animals that serve as psychiatric service dogs are the type of dog used and where the dog comes from. Traditionally, service dogs are usually medium to large breed dogs such as Labradors, golden retrievers, and German shepherds. According to the Psychiatric Service Dog Society (PSDS), psychiatric service dogs may be trained using a variety of low to medium energy breeds. Size preference is another individual parameter with some handlers choosing large dogs such as Great Danes or mastiffs and others preferring tiny dogs such as Yorkies or chihuahuas (http://www. psychdog.org/faq.html). Purebred dogs and established breeding programs where the dog genetics, early socialization and initial training, may offer the advantage of increased predictability. If a breeder is familiar with the parents, some assumptions about the anticipated size and temperament of the resulting puppy may be made.

Benefits may exist as utilizing dogs of mixed parentage sometimes exhibit what is called "hybrid vigor," a genetic outcome that may allow an animal to live longer, free of the debilitating genetic disorders found in some purebred animals. If one decides to select and train a dog from a shelter, securing professional help to evaluate the dog's temperament and suitability to the service needs of the recipient is recommended.

Predicting a successful pairing between human and animal is highly difficult and unless a better theoretical or clinical model is developed, the health provider, and in some instances the recipient, will have to determine selection of the animal. Many studies that have been conducted seem keenly interested in the use of dogs and give little or no attention to other species.

There are also a number of approaches to ensure that the animal meets appropriate training expectations. Although there are numerous variations of evaluation and each dog has differing attributes that may make them either desirable or result in their elimination from selection, most organizations and trainers underscore the importance of having sufficient time in which to evaluate a dog, typically no less than 30 days. Some dogs improve and others exhibit less desirable behaviors over the course of an evaluation period. Temperament testing often includes body sensitivity, noise sensitivity and a retrieve test.

Currently, there are no federally established service dog training standards or regulatory oversight of service dog training. Agencies that certify service dogs do so privately and are not directly connected to any governmental agency. Most of the highly specialized agencies that train service dogs have their own detailed training protocols and evaluation criteria. Well-known organizations such as the Delta Society encourage handlers to carry identification that may be used if there is a question about their animal's status as a service dog and also to have them clearly designated by wearing a visible vest.

20.9   Training models

Some service animal training organizations, such as Assistance Dogs International (ADI), set standards which define individual training as "deliberately teaching the animal through the use of rewards and/or corrections to perform a task in response to a command or another stimulus such as the onset of a seizure" (ADI, 2009). Assistance Dogs International has developed an accreditation manual defining standards for training service dogs and by 2010 all programs that apply for membership in ADI must be accredited. The major difference, other than the breed and type of dog, between traditional service dogs and some psychiatric service dogs is how they are trained and who does the training. This can be illustrated by comparing traditional and psychiatric service dog training. Traditional training places an emphasis on predictability and control. If they control the breeding, selection, training, and finally the pairing of the dog with the service recipient, they can predict the results of that pairing. In general, puppies stay with their littermates until they are eight weeks old and then each puppy is sent to live with a trained puppy raiser. The puppy raiser keeps the dog for approximately 12 to 16 months and does the initial socialization of the dog and trains the puppy to respond to many basic commands. Following this socialization period, the dog is generally sent for formal training that includes Canine Good Citizenship (CGC) training and completion of public access training along with specified task training. In other words, the dog is completely trained prior to meeting its paired recipient handler. Then, team training assists the dog to learn to respond to the recipient, and for the recipient to learn how to handle the dog.

In contrast, PSDS advocates that recipients train their own psychiatric service dog with one-on-one assistance from a professional dog trainer. According to www. psychdog.org, there are numerous benefits to training one's own service dog. In an interview with the President of the Psychiatric Service Dog Society, Joan Esnayra discussed the various strengths and weaknesses of the owner-trainer model. She comments that the owner-trainer model is an empowerment model. In learning how to train one's own service dog, the handler learns to better communicate with the dog. This in turn leads to the creation of a stronger bond which sets the stage for keener alerting abilities (i.e. the ability of the dog to "cue" to the handler's physiology). She believes owner-training is the optimal way to train psychiatric service dogs because no one else can train the dog to *"cue" to changes in the handler's physiology*, which is what most PSD handlers need their animal to do. Esnayra (2009) also believes that when a handler learns the fundamental principles of dog training, s/he is better equipped to maintain a high behavioral standard with their service dog. Esnayra believes that these principles cannot be adequately learned in the two-week placement window of most traditional service dog training programs. Learning how to train one's own PSD also puts the handler into a behavioral mindset that focuses his/her attention on stimulus/response interactions in the environment, with the dog and within his/her own body.

Nevertheless, in our discussions, Esnayra (2009) points out that the owner-trainer model is not for all candidates. Lack of consistency in training produces a poorly trained and confused, even frustrated, dog. Since there is no established oversight for owner-trainers, it is easy for some to slip into bad handler habits and this can cause a dog's public decorum to slip in noticeable ways.

At best, basic obedience training teaches individuals how dogs learn and how a handler must act to achieve desired behaviors. Also, embarking on the training process together enhances the bond and builds trust between the handler/recipient and the service dog in training as well as offering therapeutic benefits as it teaches the handler to "think like a behaviorist."

As the handler learns to critically observe the behaviors of the service dog in training, he or she can learn how to observe his or her own behaviors. PSDS philosophy toward training can be partially summed up as follows: "the Psychiatric Service Dog Society is committed to the ongoing and empirical articulation of PSD work. Whether psychiatric symptoms are mitigated through the execution of trained physical tasks, or by subtle non-verbal interactions between dog and handler, does not matter to us. PSDS is focused quite singularly on the therapeutic effect of psychiatric service dog partnership, as well as how to leverage and sustain those effects over time." For PSDS, the training process is a very necessary part of achieving these therapeutic effects.

There are several models, most commonly related to dogs, of training service animals, all of which have advantages for the people who are recipients but may have limitations for the animals involved. Prison puppy raiser programs have also become popular as a way for young service dogs to be started, socialized and receive basic obedience training. The dual benefit to this model reportedly is that responsibility for training these young dogs offers psychosocial benefits for the inmate, and it remains unclear if this is a safe method of training for the animals involved.

20.10   Animal welfare considerations: impact on animals when placed with individuals with mental health concerns

The authors strongly endorse that the highest provisions need to be established for the welfare of all service animals, including psychiatric service animals. These issues must be considered a priority so that a service animal's quality of life is strongly preserved. For example, in a paper by Burrows et al. (2008), the authors identify lack of rest, recovery time, and opportunity for recreation, lack of structure in a daily schedule, and unintentional maltreatment as the primary concerns for the welfare of service dogs working with autistic children. These liabilities, among others, are legitimate concerns and very important ethical considerations that must be addressed by organizations that provide service animals to all people employing service animals but may have differing issues for animals working with persons with psychiatric disabilities and mental disorders. Difficult conditions not only affect the animal's welfare but also its performance as a service animal. How the individual came to the decision to seek a service animal has been reported as an important factor in predicting positive outcomes. Individuals who initially wanted the dog will likely experience more benefits and foster a healthy and care-driven relationship with their animal than do those who were persuaded by others.

20.11   Assessing for good fit with an animal

There is an ethical, safety and practical need for making sure that we have a good pairing and fit with each individual recipient. The following are recognized as best practices by numerous agencies and professionals involved in placing psychiatric service animals:

- Comprehensive interviews, references, and home visits to help assess for pairing
- Assessments of patients with PTSD, dissociative symptoms, and impulsivity/aggression, should be given at least two separate interviews to assess for fluctuations in behavioral/emotional patterns
- Changes in severity of symptoms have been shown to increase dangers of risky behavior (i.e. suicide, substance abuse).

Table 20.2 Exclusion criteria for potential PSD handlers

Life circumstances

Homelessness or risk of homelessness
Unreliable access to transportation
Unsupportive or destructive partner relationship
Unwilling to accept 24/7 PSD partnership
Unable or unwilling to exercise dog outside home on daily basis
Lack of financial ability to support ongoing mental health care
Lack of financial ability to support the needs of a dog
Lack of financial ability to hire private professional dog trainer when client has little or no dog
training experience

Individual characteristics

Does not like dogs
History of animal abuse
History of domestic violence perpetration
History of relinquishing numerous animals
Passivity or dependent personality
Those who are unable to handle confrontations without abusive volatility

Patient's clinical status

Those who do not have a DSM-IVR diagnosis
Those who are currently suicidal or who have been actively suicidal within the last three
months
Those who were hospitalized for psychiatric reasons within the last three months
Those who are not under the care of a mental health professional
Those who are non-compliant with their treatment plan
Those with a low degree of insight or those with a low potential for insight
Those who have a marked inability to apply cognitive behavioral skills
Repeatedly destructive or self-sabotaging responses to external stressors

In discussions with Esnayra (2009), we asked about her impressions of contra-indications for a service animal and her perceptions of how to safeguard the animal's integrity and welfare. Table 20.2 lists several of the concerns she noted as well as the exclusion variables for potential PSD handlers. The most critical aspect seems to be the monitoring and the support the individual has. The writers concur with these principles and also suggest that individuals who have service animals stay permanently connected with an organization so that the welfare of the animal is preserved and monitored. Agencies placing service animals must accept the responsibility to ensure the welfare of the animals they place by having regular contact with the consumer. The authors argue that this process needs to be in place for all service animals to make sure that they are being well looked after. In many organizations, certifications occur annually. Considerations should look closely at the physical and emotional well-being of the animal and review the consumer's stability. Continued research should be conducted to further address these concerns.

Often, a lengthy screening and application process as well as frequent follow-ups with newly matched teams address these concerns. Regular evaluation of the dog's health and mood should occur in order to monitor adherence to training as well as any evidence of resistance or mishandling such as toileting accidents or destruction in the home. A well animal checkup must also be scheduled with a veterinarian familiar with the expectations for that animal, within the first month at home and then ongoing. If the animal is trained in an owner-trainer model there is a question as to whom the veterinarian should report concerns. The graduate team (handler and dog) should also retest for public certification on a regular basis. Some service dog training agencies retain ownership of the dog throughout its working life and many reserve the right to remove the dog from the graduate at any time if they have reason to suspect the animal's well-being is suffering. Conversely, some PSD handlers would find the lack of permanence or inability to own the animal an unacceptable condition. At the end of the dog's working life (generally from eight to ten years of age) the graduate is "considered" as a possible caretaker for the retired service dog. The owner-trainer model may empower the handler to make these care and end-of-life determinations without the influence of outside organizations' expectations, this self-determination is an important quality in establishing efficacy for individuals with mental illness

Benefits to the teams being trained within the structure of a formal service dog training agency are things such a insurance coverage, free boarding, grooming, veterinary care, support to help graduates with training and behavior questions as well as home visits and one-on-one assistance. With every pre- and post-match, the precautions are as detailed above, but it remains less clear what the specific support structures will be for owner-trainer service dogs. PSDS appears to use online communication and a peer support training community to support its members as well as professional relationships with a trainer and mental health provider.

20.12   Screening for clients

Placing a dog with someone with a disability mental illness is a potentially risky activity if not done carefully. For service dog provider organizations a detailed application process can take over a year to complete. It begins with an initial application, which asks for personal information about the applicant and the other members of the home. It asks specific questions about the nature and severity of the client's disability. It asks for detailed schedules from the primary applicant and the other members of the home for weekdays and weekends. CCI asks applicants to present their plans for the next five to six years to ensure that they have factored in the addition of a dog to their lives. References must be provided attesting to the applicant's character and lifestyle. A letter from disabled applicants' primary physician must be included describing again the nature and severity of the applicant's disability. If the initial application is accepted, a home study is conducted—either in person if the applicant lives in the vicinity of a CCI office, or through photographs and contact with landlords and neighbors if the applicant does not. The home study is followed by a phone interview in which many of the areas above are discussed in greater detail.

20.13 Conclusions

The most striking issue in exploring the role of psychiatric service dogs is the profound and positive change in refractory symptoms expression, decreased medication usage, and restored functionality of the handler. As an added bonus, psychiatric service dogs may bolster handler confidence and facilitate social integration into the community. These new applications seem worthy of carefully established guidelines and planned intervention with skillful research on outcomes. It remains difficult to measure the value of relationship and the power of trustworthiness. Subtle changes such as sense of control or loyal companionship may yield significant changes in quality of life as does a handler's willingness to trust their dog when it offers timely biofeedback that from a spouse or friend might otherwise be rejected.

The future for the application and utilization of psychiatric service animals continues to evolve. Many questions still need to be answered on how they can be best applied and challenges resolved. There is a need for increased research on the efficacy of these applications as well as the need for understanding the best practices for training and animal well-being. Careful selection and training of animals can improve the consistency of outcomes. Psychiatric service animals can dramatically change the quality of life for someone with mental illness, providing a safe and reliable support, capable of enduring patience and responsiveness to the specific needs of the individual disability even under stressful circumstances. Animals can also be impacted, are sensitive to emotional and mental status changes in humans and can also experience trauma reactivity. The impact on animals can be dramatically remediated by ensuring thorough and accurate screening of clients to determine requisite stability and readiness of the handler or recipient. Impact on animals can also be managed by careful selection of the type of animals utilized to ensure proper aptitude supported by consistent training and standards of care.

In this chapter we have tried to encourage the reader to identify the unique potential that psychiatric service animals may have when properly paired and trained for their unique service applications. We also attempted to emphasize that the animal welfare concerns and related ethical care issues are not unique to being placed with someone with a mental illness. Instead, the emphasis must be placed on evaluating the unique individual situation in each case. Service animals are asked to perform on heroic and at times demanding levels. This is true for both physical and mental health applications. It would seem the industry and the laws and policy governing ADA supported public access are more familiar with the expectations and requirements for service applications for physically disabled clients, and guidelines for psychiatric service animals are less well recognized, misunderstood and, as a result, at risk of experiencing discriminatory treatment. Information and training for professionals working within the mental health field are needed to provide information on the potential and appropriate application of inclusion of a service animal, and organizations and trainers need greater understanding and examination of the clinical considerations of psychiatric illness. The information to ensure proper applications is available but it will remain for those in the field with expertise and understanding of mental illness and experience with screening and training of therapy animals to further develop a minimum set of national standards and best practices.

References

Assistance Dogs International (ADI). (2009). *Glossary.* Retrieved July 10, 2009, from www.assistancedogsinternational.org

Barker, S., & Dawson, K. (1998). The effects of animal-assisted therapy on anxiety ratings of hospitalized psychiatric patients. *Psychiatric Services, 49*(6), 797–802.

Beck, A., Seraydarian, L., & Hunter, G. F. (1986). Use of animals in the rehabilitation of psychiatric inpatients. *Psychological Reports, 58,* 63–66.

Burrows, K., Adams, C., & Millman, S. (2008). Factors affecting behavior and welfare of service dogs for children with autism spectrum disorder. *Journal of Applied Animal Welfare Science, 11*(1), 42–62.

Canine Companions for Independence (CCI). (2008). *History.* Retrieved July 10, 2009 from www.cci.org

Corson, S., Corson, E., Gwynne, P., & Arnold, E. (1977). Pet dogs: a nonverbal communication link in hospital psychiatry. *Comprehensive Psychiatry, 18*(1), 61–73.

Diagnostic and Statistical Manual of Mental Disorders DSM-IV-TR. (2000) (4th ed.). Washington. DC: American Psychiatric Association.

Esnayra, J. (2003). *Psychiatric Service Dog Tasks.* http://www.psychdog.org/tasks.html

Friedmann, E., & Son, H. (2009, March). The human-companion bond: How humans benefit. *Veterinary Clinics of North America Small Animal Practice, 39,* 293–326.

Froling, J. (2003). *Service Dog Tasks for Psychiatric Disabilities.* Retrieved July 10, 2009 from http://www.iaadp.org/psd_tasks.html

Geisler, A. M. (2004). Companion animals in palliative care: Stories from the bedside. *American Journal of Hospice and Palliative Medicine, 21*(4), 285–288.

Harra, M. O. (1979, March 18). *Ray Kabat trains dogs to "hear" for the deaf.* Ocalal Star Banner, p. 18.

Heimlich, K. (2001). Animal-assisted therapy and the severely disabled child: a quantitative study. *Journal of Rehabilitation, 67*(4), 48–56.

Klontz, B., Bivens, A., Leinart, D., & Klontz, T. (2007). The effectiveness of equine-assisted experiential therapy: results of an open clinical trial. *Society and Animals, 15,* 257–267.

Kogan, L., Granger, B., Fitchet, J., Helmer, K., & Young, K. (1999). The human-animal team approach for children with emotional disorders: two case studies. *Child and Youth Care Reform, 28*(2), 105–123.

Kovacs, Z., Kis, R., Rozsa, S., & Rozsa, L. (2004). Animal assisted therapy for middle-aged schizophrenic patients living in a social institution. A pilot study. *Clinical Rehabilitation, 18,* 483–486.

Lane, D. R., McNicholas, J., & Collis, G. M. (1998). Dogs for the disabled: Benefits to recipients and welfare of the dogs. *Applied Animal Behaviour Science, 59*(1), 49–60.

Lefkowitz, C., Paharia, I., Prout, M., Debiak, D., & Bleiberg, J. (2005). Animal-assisted prolonged exposure: a treatment of survivors of sexual assault suffering post traumatic stress disorder. *Society and Animals, 13*(4), 275–297.

Miller, M. (2007). *Helping Dogs.* NY: Chelsea House Publishers.

Parish-Plass, N. (2008). Animal assisted therapy in children suffering from insecure attachment due to abuse or neglect: a method to lower the risk of intergenerational transmission of abuse. *Clinical Child Psychology and Psychiatry, 13*(1), 7–30.

Parshall, D. P. (2003). Research and reflection: animal-assisted therapy in mental health settings. *Counseling and Values, 48*, 47–58.

Podberscek, A. P. (2000). *Companion Animals and Us: Exploring the Relationships between People and Pets.* Cambridge: Cambridge University Press.

Reichert, E. (1998). Individual counseling for sexually abused children: a role for animals and storytelling. *Child and Adolescent Social Work Journal, 15*(3), 177–187.

Smith, M., Esnayra, J., & Love, C. (2003). Use of a psychiatric service dog. *Psychiatric Services, 54*(1), 110.

Strom, S. (2006, October 31). *Trained by inmates, new best friends for disabled veterans.* The New York Times.

Villatra-Gil, V., Roca, M., Gonzalez, N., Cuca, Escanilla, A., Asensio, M., Esteban, M., Ochoa, S., Haro, J., & Group, Schi-Can (2009). Dog-assisted therapy in the treatment of chronic schizophrenia inpatients. *Anthrozoös, 22*(2), 149–159.

Wood, L., Gles-Corti, B., & Bulsara, M. (2005). The pet connection: Pets as a conduit for social capital? *Social Science and Medicine, 61*, 1159–1173.

Zapf, S. A., & Rough, R. B. (2002). The development of an instrument to match individuals with disabilities and service dogs. *Disability and Rehabilitation, 24*(1), 47–58.

Resources

Americans with Disabilities Act, Service Animals. US Department of Justice:

Association of Assistance Dog Partners: http://www.iaadp.org/psd_tasks.html

Canine Companions for Independence: www.caninecompanions.org

Canines for Combat Veterans: www.neads.org

"Facts you should know about service dogs:" www.deltasociety.org

Guide Dogs for the Blind: www.guidedogs.com

History (2008). Retrieved July 10, 2009, from Canine Companions for Independence: http://www.cci.org

http://www.assistancedogsinternational.org/aboutAssistanceDogs.php

http://www.assistancedogsinternational.org/assistancedogproviders.php

http://www.usdogj.gov/crt/ada/svcanimb.htm

Justice, U.D. (2008). www.ada.gov. Retrieved May 7, 2009, from Emotional Support Animals: http://www.ada.gov/NPRM2008/t3NPRM_federalreg.htm

Psychiatric Service Dog Society (PSD): http://www.pychdog.org

Sterling Service Dogs. (2007). *Service dog tasks for psychiatric disabilities: tasks to mitigate disabling illnesses classified as mental impairments under the Americans with Disabilities Act.* Sterling Heights, MI: Froling, J.

The Delta Society: www.deltasociety.org

Part Four

Special Topics and Concerns in Animal-Assisted Therapy

21 Loss of a therapy animal: assessment and healing

Susan Phillips Cohen, DSW

The Animal Medical Center

The first and necessary step of grief is discovering what you have lost. The next step is discovering what is left. What is possible.

John Schneider

21.1 Introduction

Although scholars have written much about animal-assisted therapy's (AAT's) benefits and techniques, few in the field have studied the loss of a therapy animal and its effect on the lives of patients and practitioners. AAT is a happy kind of therapy. In the care of thoughtful people and appropriate animals it can transform the lives of those who receive it and of those who practice it. Each party to the therapy enhances the effect on the others, giving the method an intensity and power that other systems may not achieve. Even observers and those who simply read about the approach are touched. For these very reasons, thinking of the day when the three-way relationship must end can be extraordinarily painful.

The author has been working in the field of animal loss since 1982, when she began practicing social work at the Animal Medical Center in New York City. When she started, there was almost nothing written on the topic. It became clear almost immediately that much of the standard literature on bereavement did not apply to pet loss, at least pet loss as found in a big urban veterinary teaching hospital.

Over time patterns emerged. The reasons people gave to explain why this loss was worse than others fell in three general areas: The role of this pet in their life, the way in which the pet died, and what else was going on at the time. Many of these patterns fit the relationship among practitioner, therapy animal and patient/recipient/consumer. Other issues affecting the experience of loss in these situations are different than those with pets. This chapter will help professionals assess anyone experiencing the loss of an important animal and suggest ways of easing the pain.

In the last 40 years, research has fleshed out a feeling that nature lovers have long held: interacting with animals helps people heal from a variety of ills. The pairing of scholarly investigation and clinical practice has driven our understanding of human/animal interaction, but it has also been a field in which ordinary people contribute.

Handbook on Animal-Assisted Therapy. DOI: 10.1016/B978-0-12-381453-1.10021-2

Animals may be family pets accompanied to the nursing home by friendly visitors, wild birds arriving solo to a feeder outside the windows of a hospice or highly trained horses working with skilled professionals to help a young woman with cerebral palsy develop muscle strength. All the people involved—professionals, handlers, consumers and observers—can become attached to the animals. That means everyone involved can suffer when these animals retire, disappear or die. As professionals in the field we need to recognize the potential for grief in a wide group of people. We must consider all that is lost when contact ends and learn to help clients, coworkers and ourselves get through the process in a way that strengthens each person.

21.2 Scholarly research

Other chapters in this book provide comprehensive reviews of evidence that contact with animals is good for people. This chapter contains a sample of that research, which illustrates some of the benefits to different populations. Those who care for therapy animals run the risk of losing the benefits if the animal dies or is lost in some other way.

Human/animal bond research often looks at how pet contact or animal-assisted therapy helps a specific population improve social contact or mental health. Numerous studies show that elderly people socialize more or have improved quality of life when pets are present (Fick, 1993; Johnson and Meadows, 2002; Kaiser et al., 2002; Mahalskie et al., 1988; McCabe et al., 2002; Raina et al., 1999; Rogers et al., 1993). The effect of dogs on social interactions is particularly strong (McNicholas and Collis, 2000; Rossbach and Wilson, 1992).

Other studies have shown that pet contact can attract or even break through to psychiatric patients (Barker and Dawson, 1998; Berget et al., 2008; Corson et al., 1975; Holcomb and Meacham, 1989) Some prison studies have shown positive effects when incarcerated individuals care for or train animals (Katcher et al., 1989; Lee, 1984; Moneymaker and Strimple, 1991). Several research efforts have looked at how assistance animals and pets help children with disabilities and adolescents in foster care enhance social relationships (Gonski, 1985; Mader et al., 1989; Martin and Farnum, 2002).

A second area of research has focused on physical health benefits, primarily on cardiovascular functioning. An early study finds that pet ownership is a strong predictor of survival after a heart attack. In that study, benefits are not limited to dog owners (Friedmann et al., 1980). A later study of people with severe heart arrhythmias, who had already had a heart attack, finds that having a dog improves survival, though there is no difference in the physiologic profiles of pet owners and non-pet owners. In other words, dog owners do not survive just because they were healthier in the first place (Friedmann and Thomas, 1995). Recently, a Minnesota study of 4,435 people finds that living with a cat, presently or in the past, is associated with a significantly reduced risk of death from cardiovascular disease, including stroke (Qureshi et al., 2009). Other research and practice experience demonstrating improved health is discussed later in the chapter.

21.3   Understanding loss

In many ways, the loss of a therapy animal is like losing any other important person or pet—it hurts. The ways in which it hurts depend on many factors: What role did the loved one play in your life? How did the loved one die? What other experiences in your life influence your response?

While cultures create beliefs and rituals to help mourners process the loss of human relationships, the loss of important non-humans is often ignored. In 1978, clinical support for pet loss began at the University of Pennsylvania when the dean of the School of Social Work recognized that clients at the veterinary hospital were showing the same signs of grief that she recognized from her work in human loss. Her work led to the hiring of Jamie Quackenbush, a doctoral student from Michigan, to support bereaved pet lovers (Quackenbush, 1981; Ryder and Romasco, 1981). Academic recognition began in March 1981, when New York City's Animal Medical Center and Foundation of Thanatology held a three-day conference on Pet Loss and Human Emotion (Kay et al., 1988). Since then, many veterinary colleges have developed counseling programs that include support for clients, instruction for students, community outreach and scholarly studies. Few if any programs exist specifically to support the friends and caretakers of therapy animals.

21.4   Loss of a special animal

21.4.1   Loss of a pet

Our knowledge about pet loss comes largely from clinical practice and from a few research studies. Many books have been written to help bereaved pet lovers. Lago and Kotch-Jantzer alert planners to the need for community programs to help both sides of the pet loss dyad: the impact of pet death on older adults and the effect of caretaker death on the fate of pets (1988). Cohen and Fudin outline the need for support from parents and professionals at the time of euthanasia (Cohen, 1985; Fudin and Cohen, 1988). Adams et al. (2000) highlight the harmful effects of a lack of understanding from friends and family. Field et al. (2009) have refined the concept of attachment in evaluating pet loss. Dunn et al. (2005) detail how to set up a pet loss support group.

Grief is not just for those who live with pets: people grieve for animals that do not even belong to them. Neighbors become fond of each other's pets (Casciato, 2010) and visitors grow attached to particular residents of the local zoo (Fire at the Philadelphia Zoo, 1995; Zongker, 2010). Animals in trouble, such as endangered birds that have been raised or rehabilitated for later return to the wild, can capture the attention of a nation (Zongker, 2010; Zoo condors to be released in Andes, 1997). Caretakers who work closely with such animals may be heartbroken when they are transferred or euthanized (Egan, 1999; Film star holds funeral for water buffalo, 2001; San Diego Zoo to euthanize pioneering monkey, 2003; Szita, 1988).

A few quotations from and about mourners serve to show that living with someone is not essential to loving someone. Any loss, including death, can hit hard and last a long time.

Casper was a longhaired tuxedo cat who became famous for catching the bus every day from his home town into Plymouth, England: After he died in a hit and run accident, many who had been captivated by his story expressed their sorrow. "The bus service, First Devon and Cornwall, said it was 'devastated' by the cat's death…The website for local newspaper *The Herald* said it had received tributes from around the world" (Casciato, 2010).

A woman at the farewell party for a Washington, DC panda said before his return to China, "I love Tai Shan so much, I don't know how I'm going to handle it" (Zongker, 2010).

Actor Bin Banloerit explained why his fellow cast member deserved a three-day funeral in the Buddhist tradition: "He could not just die like other regular water buffaloes because he had done so much for the movie" (Film star holds funeral, 2001).

A San Diego Zoo representative's account of reactions to the impending eutha-nasia of a twenty-three-year-old endangered monkey whose willingness to take insulin injections for his diabetes helped children overcome their own fears— "Everyone from the welders who made his cage to zoo regulars have stopped by to say their goodbyes…'It will be a regular trip to the hospital,' Killmar said, her voice breaking. 'He just won't come back'" (San Diego Zoo, 2003).

21.4.2 Role of the animal

Many therapy animals begin as pets/family members. Seeing the effect that their friendly, well-behaved cat, dog or bunny has on others, pet lovers begin to think about how to make the most of the therapeutic properties their animal companion already has. They join an animal-assisted activity program and visit nursing home residents or train as a volunteer with a group that certifies animals for a range of therapeutic work. Other people begin when they are already established in a career. Licensed in one of the helping professions, such as social work or physical therapy, they decide to incorporate domestic animals in their work. Though we think of therapy animals primarily as partners in healing, these roles developed for pet relationships apply equally to them.

- Companion—Most Americans choose pets for companionship, and much of animal-assisted therapy works for the same reason: Humans relax around calm animals, which allows them to stretch physically, mentally, and emotionally.
- Protector—Both urban dwellers and rural folk keep pets for protection. While many people tend to think only of dogs in this role, other pet lovers say their cats, birds and even bunnies alert them to sounds outside. Losing a pet leaves these people feeling vulnerable. While those receiving animal-assisted therapy may not feel unprotected, those who live with the animal co-therapist have a strong connection and may experience loss as ripping away a line of defense.

- Assistant—People with physical disabilities often use the terms "assistance" or "service" animal, while those who have animal companions for mental health and cognitive support tend to describe the dog, cat, rabbit or monkey as a "therapy" animal. Losing such a helper adds additional burdens beyond emotional ones. Those who depend on non-human support may become housebound from fear or slip back into the self absorption of autism. In addition, no matter how hard the person is grieving, he or she must acquire a new helper even before the pain has subsided.
- Trophy—For some people an important part of any possession is its rarity. Though many cringe at the notion of animals as property, they may still enjoy being seen with a beautiful horse or unusual cat. For both professionals and volunteers, training a therapy dog to meet certification standards or taking a llama for a walk enhances self-esteem, which loss may shatter.
- Bridge—Research and common sense demonstrate that friendly animals help humans bridge gaps of age, class and familiarity. Loss of a therapy animal can mean no more trips to the corral, no more reading sessions with the dog, no more chats about cats in the nursing home recreation room. In losing the animal, these participants in animal-assisted therapy lose their connection to other people.
- Family member—The feeling that one is in a family relationship reaches far beyond legal and genetic ties. Both the caretaker with whom a therapy animal lives and those receiving help may feel a specific animal is part of their family (Cohen, 2002). Loss of that tie can be devastating, in some cases causing greater pain than the death of human family.
- Significant other—For many people an animal companion can be the most important emotional tie in their lives. The handler often lives as well as works with a therapy animal, meaning the person's life and professional identity are intertwined with this other being.

In the case of therapy animals, another factor in their role in the lives of clients depends on the kind of animal and the nature of the intervention. For example, interacting with dolphins can relieve depression (Antonioli and Reveley, 2005). Dolphins are large animals that one meets in unfamiliar surroundings—large bodies of water. While dolphin programs may be an expensive treatment for mild depression, the setting and symbolism—being in the water eye-to-eye with highly intelligent "wild" creatures—make it a circumstance that will not be duplicated by any other approach, including other kinds of animal-assisted therapy.

Another different remedy involving animals and water is placing a fish tank in the dining room of an Alzheimer's disease (AD) facility. Gazing at the fish increases the appetite of AD patients, or at least their willingness to keep eating, leading to health-protective weight gain (Edwards and Beck, 2002). Unlike swimming with dolphins there is no physical contact or one-on-one relationship, but there is a physical effect, as well as an individual response.

21.5 Manner of loss

A second part of the loss experience is the way in which the loved one leaves or dies. The truth is, there is no easy way to lose a loved one, but some separations are more painful than others. For example, when a therapy animal retires, those left behind can enjoy thinking that the animal is enjoying his days in the sun. They imagine that Shep, the dog that visited them during their frequent hospital stays, is frolicking in the grass, and that they might meet again one day. The parting might be sad, but with it comes pleasure and hope.

Separation also comes from the actual loss of the animal. Although therapy animals are usually well supervised, volunteer therapy animals can slip out a door and become inadvertently lost. A therapist might move away or close down the program, taking one's favorite four-footed companion along. In these cases, the client or recipient loses contact without the buffering knowledge that the animal is happy and possibly available for a future reunion. The client and perhaps the therapist have no control over whether they can maintain contact with the therapy animal.

Separations through illness or death are difficult to bear. When a therapy animal becomes seriously ill, those who depend on it may cycle through a series of feelings, such as shock, fear, pain, and waiting to see whether the animal will survive the treatment and return to its role as healer. If the animal makes it through but can no longer work, both handler and consumer feel relieved that at least the animal is alive. If the animal does not survive, some individuals will find that their pain eases more rapidly because on some level, the mind began to work through the reality of impending loss. For other people, the idea that an animal who contributed to the health and well-being of many others might have suffered is a torment.

Sudden death carries its own agony, because there is no time to prepare. Life was good, and now it is unrecognizable. In severe cases, the shock is so great that it constitutes a trauma, an emotional wound that may last months or years. The unexpected death of a spouse puts a great strain on the survivor, a strain that family, friends and health care providers often underestimate (Rodger et al., 2006–2007; Wortman and Silver, 1989). Sudden death leads to greater depression in widowed individuals (Burton et al., 2006).

Losing a special animal without warning stuns survivors. In the author's experience, while many people feel surprised by the death of a loved one no matter how long they have been ill, the shock that follows sudden loss seems to last longer.

Whether it is a protection from dealing with our own fears of death or whether we just see human beings as responsible for whatever happens to them, we tend to blame people, at least a little, for their misfortunes. We told them to exercise and to quit smoking, but they did not listen. Now look what has happened. In the case of companion animals, which are seen as innocent and dependent (Bulcroft and Albert, 1987; Perin, 1986), caretakers often feel responsible in some way. They should have known the food was tainted, prevented the cat from ripping open the window screen, argued with the veterinarian about surgery or looked up from writing the Great American Novel long enough to notice the dog was losing weight. Some who lose a pet or therapy animal will feel deep guilt that may never quite resolve.

21.5.1 Life experiences (nine stories)

A third way of understanding what the loss of a therapy animal might mean depends on a person's life experiences before and during work with the animal. The author has found that nine stories told by clients often suggest that an individual will have difficulty when a particular pet dies or disappears. These stories, or accounts of the human's life, affect the experience of losing therapy animals as well.

- Other loss—No one can endure repeated blows from life without staggering. Often a special animal helps buffer the ups and downs of life, so when that support disappears, someone who has suffered other losses, especially recent ones, may feel as though the ground has dropped out from under them.
- Time spent with pet—Those who both live and work with an animal may become closer as many aspects of life intertwine. Neither the human therapist nor the recipient can go to the office and forget about the empty leash that now hangs by the front door. In addition, the author's research shows that for urban pet lovers the sheer number of hours spent together correlates closely with scores on the Poresky Human-Animal Bonding Scale (Cohen, 2002; Poresky et al., 1987).
- Rescue—Rescue can go in either direction. A stroller who scoops a discarded kitten from the garbage may feel especially connected to that animal. Similarly, an alcoholic who feels that his dog kept him from going under completely may feel that the dog rescued him. Therapy animals are designed to improve the health and functioning of people who may feel rescued from a life of social and physical hardship, perhaps even financial downturns.
- Mistake—While many mourners feel regret after the death of a loved one, those who care for animal companions may feel especially responsible because they see domestic animals as innocent and dependent. If, in addition, the person can point to an apparent mistake—picking the "wrong" pet sitter, accidentally injuring a pet—anguish can overwhelm a rational appraisal of what went wrong.
- Live alone—Someone who lives with only one other person or pet shares meals, activities, and even sleeps with the same companion. Years of shared routines can contribute to having all their emotional eggs in one basket.
- First pet/last pet—In modern urban life many young adults get their first pet with no childhood animal care experience to guide them. Losing a pet may be their first experience with the death of someone close. They have no bereavement skills to fall back on. Animal caretakers at the other end of life may not want another 20-year commitment to a new animal. Even if they are willing to take on the responsibility, their new living arrangements may make the keeping of pets or other animals impossible. Land needed for large therapy animals, like llamas, is sold, co-op apartment boards change their rules, forbidding pet keeping. The first serious loss in someone's life and the last, if it carries no hope of finding a new love, can be especially hard to bear.
- Shared life events—At times the most consistent relationship in one's life is an animal companion. Birds and horses may stay for decades. Cats and dogs see their caretakers through several love affairs, at least one romantic partnership, and jobs/apartments/and hair styles too numerous to mention. Whether a person and pet volunteer in a reading program or work side by side in therapeutic riding, the level of mutual understanding is high and the number of shared experiences rivals that of any other family member. Consumers of animal-assisted therapy also share life-changing events with four-footed catalysts. When a therapy animal dies or retires, caretaker and client lose a witness to history, a trusted companion who "knew them when."
- Tie to another—An animal companion can gain special significance when a person associates that Siamese cat, parrot or pony with someone who is no longer part of their lives. Inheriting Mom's dog allows one to keep a piece of the past alive.

- Identification with animal companion—People identify with animals because of similar physical characteristics and life circumstances. The author's clients have said they felt they and their pet were bachelors together, that they were both arthritic old ladies or that they shared a love of pizza and nature programs on television. The shared experience may involve a challenge, such as surviving cancer or abuse. In the Animal Medical Center's animal-assisted activity program, Pet Outreach, some of the most effective therapy animals have been missing a leg or part of an ear. Their unspoken message is that even those who look different can be productive and loveable. Depending on the depth of the identification, the loss of an animal can frighten someone who feels their lives are similar.

21.6   Differences between losing pet and therapy animal

To review, the loss of a pet and the loss of a therapy animal have many similarities based on the role of the animal, the way in which it is lost and the prior life experiences of the mourner. In addition, the special relationship that both clients and handlers have with therapy animals makes some effects of loss unique. When clients lose contact with a helping animal, they lose what they gained from the therapy. Whether developing physical strength from horseback riding or learning to connect by sharing conversations over a friendly dog, human beings can get benefits from interacting with a friendly animal and a therapist together that transcend either one alone. Part of that therapy may involve physical activity, which elevates mood as well as strength and flexibility. In addition, clients often lose social connections made through animal-assisted therapy. Hanging out at the stables or laughing with another resident about the cat's backflip as she pursues a toy allows people with disabilities to form friendships that they might not otherwise have had.

Practitioners and handlers also lose special experiences when they lose a therapy animal. Perhaps most important is the sense of oneself as a healer. Those with professional skills still have that capacity, but nearly all animal-assisted therapists choose this approach to healing, and often that choice has cost them time, effort, and money. Many therapists have battled their own institutions, insurance companies and colleagues for the right to practice a non-traditional method of alleviating human problems. Such therapists may see themselves as not only healers but as warriors, protectors of both people and domestic animals. Those who have invested themselves in a professional identity and then fought for the right to practice with an animal co-therapist may lose a piece of that identity when a therapy animal dies.

Another loss for professional therapists and AAT volunteers is a way of operating in public. The law grants some therapy animals privileges pets do not enjoy. They may travel on airplanes or other transportation systems. They can convey a certain status, in some of the same way a trophy animal does. For volunteers, having a therapy animal in their own home validates their personal affection and elevates the animal's status to friends and family: "This isn't just a pet, he's a working dog. Everyone at the nursing home loves him."

21.6.1 Type of relationship

The nature of different kinds of therapy animals leads to diverse relationships for people. Bunnies are soft to touch, cats curl up in laps, little dogs dance, big dogs sidle up and put their heads under hands, inviting a caress. Getting into the water with a dolphin who clicks its greeting can reach autistic children who have little speech. Enjoying the gentle movement of colorful fish in a tank relaxes anxious dental patients (Katcher et al., 1984) and may capture the attention of those with Alzheimer's disease long enough to encourage them to eat more (Edwards and Beck, 2002). All of these interactions have a physical consequence.

Perhaps no other therapeutic relationship with a non-human has more physical and emotional effects than that with a horse. This interaction goes by different names and has different goals. Some therapeutic riding programs focus on developing physical strength by teaching individuals with disabilities to hold their bodies erect and move in rhythm with the horse (hippotherapy). Others use riding to encourage academic skills and other learning, for example creating study stations around the paddock (equine facilitated learning). Still others draw on the horse's size, strength and temperament to heal psychological wounds.

Equine facilitated psychotherapy encourages the building of strong bonds with a horse. Riding a large animal that responds to one's cues enhances self-esteem. The client who masters the techniques of riding or driving develops a sense of safety and skill development. Many therapeutic riding and psychotherapy sessions end in grooming the horse. Not only can this make touch a pleasure for a person who grew up in a violent home, it teaches those who have been neglected to meet the needs of someone else. In addition, some therapists argue that because horses operate as members of a herd, they have evolved a heightened sensitivity to others, which makes them effective as co-therapists/catalysts (Bachi et al., 2008).

Emerging research is zeroing in on the biological basis of the human/animal bond. Odendaal identifies oxytocin, a peptide known for its role in parent/child bonding, as a factor in the pleasure humans find in the company of dogs. Stroking a friendly dog not only lowers blood pressure for both, it increases the amount of oxytocin (Odendaal, 2000). Recently, a Japanese research team found that gazing at one's own dog can also raise oxytocin levels (Nagasawa et al., 2009). Perhaps this effect partially explains the sense of dislocation and emptiness many mourners report when a loved one dies. Might the removal of this powerful hormone also reverse blood pressure improvement?

21.6.2 Surviving loss

As healing professionals we will have to face the loss of both pets and therapy animals in the lives of our clients and in our own. We owe it to others who have come to love the beings that encouraged them to sit up straight, or talk, or get past a childhood of abandonment to learn how to help them recover. The first step is to take the loss seriously. This might seem obvious, but grief frightens people. In an attempt to avoid it or at least minimize the damage, well-meaning friends and relatives downplay the impact of the death of loved ones. After a brief expression of sympathy, listeners urge the bereaved person to look on the bright side—grandpa had a long life, there will be other horses to ride, now you are free to take that trip—and then they change the subject. A true friend, a true counselor, needs to be the person who does not change the subject.

The next step is often to encourage the mourner to talk about the one lost. How did they meet? What drew them together? How did the person know this was the one? If both parties know the person or animal, they can reminisce, tell tales of times they shared and of experiences they did not. Throughout human history, storytelling has preserved our memories and shaped the narrative of our relationships.

Another necessary conversation is more difficult. The story of how someone died is a tale survivors need to tell repeatedly in order to grasp how it could be that their loved one is no longer here. Particularly when the death came rapidly, those left behind walk themselves and their listeners through every detail: "It was last Tuesday, no, it was Monday night. Buster didn't eat his whole dinner, and Buster loves to eat. I didn't think much of it, but then when we were taking our walk, he just wanted to go to the curb and back."

By this point many listeners have begun to squirm. Their eyes glaze over from the effort of trying to keep track of the plot; they want to flee from the outcome, the part where someone dies. Because of temperament or cultural difference some people believe dwelling on sorrow keeps mourners stuck. They tell the bereaved person to stop crying before they make themselves sick. Others who grew up in families that keep personal problems to themselves assume that even though the mourner is talking about their loved one's death, they wouldn't welcome questions.

One reason the average person becomes uncomfortable when a friend starts to talk about problems is that the recipient of this confidence does not know what to say. The listener feels called upon to do something, but death is impossible to fix. In their discomfort they create a reason why it is in the mourner's best interests to stop thinking about their problems and especially to stop talking about them.

The professional counselor understands that when someone in pain opens up, they hope the listener cares, or can at least tolerate the topic. They want to unburden themselves, figure out what this change in their life means and learn how to handle it. This process is essential to coming to terms with the reality of a new life, what Elisabeth Kubler-Ross called "acceptance." How well the mental health professional helps the bereaved person tell the story and make sense of it shapes whether the experience will help the client retreat or grow.

21.6.3 Case examples

Two stories illustrate how the death of an animal involved in psychotherapy can have either a negative or positive effect on clients. Both of these accounts are true, though some details have been changed to protect confidentiality.

Box 21.1 Case 1

A psychotherapist and his girlfriend, a nutritional counselor, lived together in a large house that also contained both of their offices. While they practiced separately, they often referred patients to each other. Although they did not volunteer the information that they were a couple, they did not deny it. There was a third healer in the home, Fritz the dachshund. He kept each of his human companions company during sessions, so that some patients felt they were part of a therapeutic family, complete with a mommy, a daddy and a kid brother.

In some ways this was a productive arrangement. Patients enjoyed the homey atmosphere and found Fritz a comfort as they discussed painful feelings about body and spirit. Prompted by the environment, patients explored their most hurtful family experiences, contrasting their own childhoods to the happier home of their therapists.

Difficulty arose when Fritz was diagnosed with cancer. The therapists could not conceal his weight loss or his frequent trips to the hospital for surgery and radiation therapy. Most patients offered their sympathy and then got on with their own work. Others were caught up in the drama. A few of these became sad and anxious about the future. A handful struggled with jealousy at the attention their pseudo parents might lavish on their four-footed "sibling." When Fritz died unexpectedly, the couple was forced to deal with intense reactions in some patients, while maintaining their own professional discipline in the face of personal heartbreak.

Box 21.2 Case 2

In contrast, the death of a therapy animal that is well handled from the beginning can spark new understanding and personal growth. During the early days of the HIV epidemic when the diagnosis was a death sentence, a therapist with an assistance dog began a group for men with AIDS. His dog was a large, friendly, yellow lab named Caesar. As in the previous case, Caesar became a routine part of the therapy milieu. Although he spent most of his time resting quietly beside the therapist, he seemed to know when one of the group members was particularly gloomy or angry. He would silently leave his post and move to the distressed man, leaning against his knee. At a time when the general public hesitated to even brush up against a person with AIDS, Caesar's acceptance and warmth made a powerful impact.

Sadly, like Fritz the dachshund, Caesar also developed cancer, which required months of treatment. As with Fritz, the reality of Caesar's illness could not be hidden, so the therapist told his patients and invited their response. Not surprisingly, the men identified with the dog's grim prognosis. They wrestled with the idea that no matter how hard doctors tried and no matter how much their companions loved them, both the men and the dog would die. After their death, friends and family would live on, sad, but free to create a new life, free to love again. When Caesar died, group members mourned him, watched the therapist recover and came to better terms with the cycle of life.

21.6.4   Pet loss experts

There are times when grief is so profound that the bereaved person needs a pet loss expert to help them through the experience. Many veterinary schools and a few large practices employ mental health professionals who provide counseling and communications training (Cohen, 1985, 2008). Some private psychotherapists include pet bereavement among their specialties. There are also online chat rooms for those who cannot find counseling in their communities.

There are several advantages to using a mental health practitioner who specializes in human/animal bond issues. The person will have heard many accounts of animal loss and can often reassure clients that what they are feeling is normal. These counselors may also have considerable exposure to animal illness and will be able to ask productive questions to help the client explore what happened, as this may be different from what the client suspects.

Working with a therapist who is based in a veterinary setting also allows the client access to information about how the doctors and the institution work. In addition, their counselor can facilitate conversations between client and staff, help make decisions on the spot and convey client's wishes and confusions to staff. While only veterinary colleges and very large veterinary practices have full-time counselors available, some practices have a therapist to whom they refer distressed clients. If the doctors and staff feel comfortable with this individual, they convey this when they make the referral, increasing the chance the client will accept help.

Another popular approach pet loss experts use is the support group. The Animal Medical Center in New York City began its group in early 1983, a time when confessing one's attachment to a dog or cat prompted snickers, stunned looks or outright disbelief. Facilitated by social workers based at the Center, the group brings together members of the community whose pets have died or are in life-threatening conditions. In the group, people tell their stories of pet illness and death uninterrupted. Members who begin as strangers offer insights that ring hollow when friends and family say them; fellow sufferers trust each other. Listening to others tell of their desperate efforts to save a loved one helps members absorb the reality that no matter how hard people try to prevent it, all lives come to an end.

Unfortunately, some of those affected by the death of a companion animal never find their way to counseling. Families with pets may overlook the pet's many friends; operators of therapy programs may not be able to reach all the patients working with a particular animal. Ideally, these bereaved persons will find help. The author has seen dog walkers and groomers at the pet loss group who seem more upset at a pet's death than the people to whom it belonged. Sadly, if an animal does not live with the mourner, grief may be disenfranchised in the way partners in unsanctioned love affairs must grieve alone (Weinbach, 1989)

Finally, one route to processing the loss of a special animal that is available to all is through spirituality and ritual. Studies of human bereavement offer mixed opinions on whether religious beliefs actually help to resolve pain faster (Becker et al., 2007; Walsh et al., 2002). Nevertheless, when someone leaves the family, many people turn to faith or to ceremonial practices for comfort. In the past, grieving animal lovers had difficulty finding clergy members who were willing to say prayers and blessings for animals after death. The new millennium seems to have ushered in a greater readiness for religious leaders to offer comfort to the person and care for the animal. For those who need guidance in creating a personal or communal ritual, Harris's (2002) book on spirituality is a good place to start. Rabbi Josh Snyder (2006) has created an excellent outline that those of any faith could use to craft an appropriate ceremony to mark the passing of a loved animal. Those seeking a practitioner to conduct a healing or funeral service might begin online with animalchaplains.com.

In conclusion, the power to heal that comes from combining practitioner, therapy animal and person-in-need leads to an intense bond. Much of animal-assisted therapy causes significant physical change, while other forms help individuals overcome psychological trauma and neglect. The loss of the animal catalyst can be devastating. When a special animal dies, those who practice AAT, as well as those who provide psychological support in more traditional ways, need to assess everyone who might possibly be affected. If they provide empathy and understanding, seeking expert help where needed, helping professionals can turn loss into an opportunity for growth.

References

Adams, C. L., Bonnett, B. N., & Meek, A. H. (2000). Predictors of owner response to companion animal death in 177 clients from 14 practices in Ontario. *Journal of the American Veterinary Medical Association, 217*, 1303–1309.

Antonioli, C., & Reveley, M. A. (2005). Randomised controlled trial of animal facilitated therapy with dolphins in the treatment of depression. *British Medical Journal, 26*, 1407.

Bachi, K., Terkel, J., & Teichman, M. (2008). *Equine facilitated psychotherapy for at-risk adolescents: the influence on self-image, self-control and trust.* Unpublished paper from MSW thesis, Tel Aviv University.

Barker, S. B., & Dawson, K. S. (1998). The effects of animal-assisted therapy on anxiety ratings of hospitalized patients. *Psychiatric Services, 49*, 797–801. http://ps.psychiatryonline.org/cgi/content/full/49/6/797.

Becker, G., Xander, C. J., Blum, H. E., Lutterback, J., Momm, F., Gysels, M., & Hgginson, I. J. (2007). Do religious or spiritual beliefs influence bereavement? A systematic review. *Palliative Medicine, 21*, 207–217.

Berget, B., Ekeberg, O., & Braastad, B. O. (2008). Animal-assisted therapy with farm animals for persons with psychiatric disorders: effects on self-efficacy, coping ability and quality of life, a randomized controlled trial. *Clinical Practice and Epidemiology in Mental Health, 11*, 4–9.

Bulcroft, K., & Albert, A. (1987). Similarities and differences between the roles of pets and children in the American family. *Delta Society 6th Annual Abstracts of Presentations Conference,* p. 12.

Burton, A. M., Haley, W. E., & Small, B. J. (2006). Bereavement after caregiving or unexpected death: effects on elderly spouses. *Aging and Mental Health, 10*, 319–326.

Casciato, P. (2010, January 21). Bus-riding cat Casper killed in hit and run. Retrieved 1/22/10, from http://news.yahoo.com/s/nm/us_cat_commuter/print.

Cohen, S. P. (2008). How to teach pet loss to veterinary students. *Journal of Veterinary Medical Education, 35*, 514–519.

Cohen, S. P. (2002). Can pets function as family members? *Western Journal of Nursing Research, 24,* 621–638.

Cohen, S. P. (1985). The role of social work in a veterinary hospital setting. *Veterinary Clinics of North America: Small Animal Practice, 15,* 355–363.

Corson, S. A., Corson, E. O., Gwynne, P. H., & Arnold, L. E. (1975). Pet-facilitated psychotherapy in a hospital setting. *Current Psychiatric Therapy, 15,* 277–286.

Dunn, K. L., Mehler, S. J., & Greenberg, H. S. (2005). Social work with a pet loss support group in a university veterinary hospital. *Social Work in Health Care, 41,* 59–70.

Edwards, N. E., & Beck, A. M. (2002). Animal-assisted therapy and nutrition in Alzheimer's disease. *Western Journal of Nursing Research, 24,* 697–712.

Egan, M. (1999, November 29). *Washington's giant panda Hsing-Hsing dies.* Retrieved 11/30/99.

Fick, K. M. (1993). The influence of an animal on social interactions of nursing home residents in a group setting. *American Journal of Occupational Therapy, 47,* 529–534.

Field, N. P., Orsini, L., Gavish, R., & Packman, W. (2009). Role of attachment in response to pet loss. *Death Studies, 33,* 334–355.

Film star holds funeral for water buffalo. (2001, January 8). Retrieved 1/8/01, from http://news.excite.com/news/r/010108/08/odd-buffalo-dc?printstory=1

Fire at the Philadelphia Zoo kills 23 primates. (1995, Dec. 25). *The New York Times,* p. 12.

Friedmann, E. S., Katcher, A. H., Lynch, J. J., & Thomas, S. A. (1980). Animal companions and one year survival of patients after discharge from a coronary care unit. *Public Health Report, 95,* 307–312.

Friedmann, E., & Thomas, S. A. (1995). Pet ownership, social support, and one-year survival after acute myocardial infarction in the cardiac arrhythmia suppression trial (CAST). *American Journal of Cardiology, 76,* 1213–1217.

Fudin, C., & Cohen, S. (1988). Helping children and adolescents cope with the euthanasia of a pet. In W. Kay, S. Cohen, C. Fudin, A. Kutscher, H. Nieburg, R. Grey, & M. Osman (Eds.), *Euthanasia of the Companion Animal: The Impact on Pet Owners, Veterinarians, and Society* (pp. 79–86). Philadelphia: The Charles Press.

Gonski, Y. A. (1985). The therapeutic utilization of canines in a child welfare setting. *Child and Adolescent Social Work Journal, 2,* 93–105.

Harris, J. (2002). *Pet Loss: A Spiritual Guide.* New York: Lantern Books.

Holcomb, R., & Meacham, M. (1989). Effectiveness of an animal-assisted therapy program in an inpatient psychiatric unit. *Anthrozoös, 2,* 259–264.

Johnson, R. A., & Meadows, R. L. (2002). Older Latinos, pets, and health. *Western Journal of Nursing Research, 24,* 609–620.

Kaiser, L., Spence, L. J., McGavin, L., Struble, L., & Keilman, L. (2002). Dog and a "Happy Person" visit nursing home residents. *Western Journal of Nursing Research, 24,* 671–684.

Katcher, A., Siegel, H., & Beck, A. (1984). Contemplation of an aquarium for the reduction of anxiety. In R. K. Anderson, B. L. Hart, & L. A. Hart (Eds.), *The Pet Connection* (pp. 171–178). Minneapolis, MN: Center for the Study of Human Animal Relationships and Environment.

Katcher, A., Beck, A. M., & Levine, D. (1989). Evaluation of a pet program in prison. *Anthrozoös, 2*(175), 180.

Kay, W. J., Cohen, S. P., Fudin, C. E., Kutscher, A. H., Nieburg, A. H., Gray, R. E., & Osman, M. M. (1988). *Euthanasia of the Companion Animal: The Impact on Pet Owners, Veterinarians, and Society.* Philadelphia: The Charles Press, Publishers.

Lago, D., & Kotch-Jantzer, C. A. (1988). Euthanasia of pet animals and the death of elderly owners: implications for support of community-dwelling elderly pet owners. In W. J. Kay,

S. P. Cohen, C. E. Fudin, A. H. Kutscher, A. H. Nieburg, R. E. Grey, & M. M. Osman (Eds.). (1988). *Euthanasia of the Companion Animal: The Impact on Pet Owners, Veterinarians, and Society* (pp. 148–156). Philadelphia: The Charles Press.

Lee, D. (1984). Companion animals in institutions. In P. Arkow (Ed.), *Dynamic Relationships in Practice: Animals in the Helping Professions* (pp. 229–236). Alameda, CA: Latham Foundation.

Mader, B., Hart, L. A., & Bergin, B. (1989). Social acknowledgments for children with disabilities: effects of service dogs. *Child Development, 60*, 1529–1534.

Mahalski, P. A., Jones, R., & Maxwell, G. M. (1988). The value of cat ownership to elderly women living alone. *International Journal of Aging and Human Development, 27*, 249–260.

Martin, F., & Farnum, J. (2002). Animal-assisted therapy for children with pervasive developmental disorders. *Western Journal of Nursing Research, 24*, 657–670.

McCabe, B. W., Baun, M. M., Speich, D., & Agrawal, S. (2002). Resident dog in the Alzheimer's special care unit. *Western Journal of Nursing Research, 24*(6), 684–696.

McNicholas, J., & Collis, G. M. (2000). Dogs as catalysts for social interactions: robustness of effect. *British Journal of Psychology, 91*, 61–70.

Moneymaker, J. M., & Strimple, E. O. (1991). Animals and inmates: a sharing companionship behind bars. *Journal of Offender Rehabilitation, 16*, 133–152.

Nagasawa, M., Kikusui, T., Onaka, T., & Ohta, M. (2009). Dog's gaze at its owner increases owner's urinary oxytocin during social interaction. *Hormones and Behavior, 55*, 434–441.

Odendaal, J. S. J. (2000). Animal-assisted therapy—magic or medicine? *Journal of Psychosomatic Research, 49*, 275–280.

Perin, C. (1986). Cultural implications of contemporary canine jurisprudence. *Unpublished paper, presented at Delta Society 5th Annual Conference*, p. 73.

Poresky, R. H., Hendrix, C., Mosier, J. E., & Samuelson, M. L. (1987). The companion animal bonding scale: internal reliability and construct validity. *Psychological Reports, 60*, 743–746.

Quackenbush, J. E. (1981). Pet owners, problems, and the veterinarian. *The Compendium on Continuing Education for the Practicing Veterinarian, 31*, 764–770.

Qureshi, A. I., Memon, M. Z., Vazquez, G., & Suri, M. F. K. (2009). Cat ownership and the risk of fatal cardiovascular disease. Results from the second national health and nutrition examination study mortality follow-up study. *Journal of Vascular and Interventional Neurology, 2*, 132–134, Retrieved 2/4/10, from http://jvin.org/V2N1/V2N1Qureshi.pdf

Raina, P., Waltner-Toews, D., Bonnett, B., Woodward, C., & Abernathy, T. (1999). Influence of companion animals on the physical and psychological health of older people: an analysis of a one-year longitudinal study. *Journal of the American Geriatric Society, 47*, 323–329.

Rodger, M. L., Sherwood, P., O'Connor, M., & Leslie, G. (2006–2007). Living beyond the unanticipated sudden death of a partner: a phenomenological study. *Omega (Westport), 54*, 107–133.

Rogers, J., Hart, L. A., & Boltz, R. P. (1993). The role of pet dogs in casual conversations of elderly adults. *Journal of Social Psychology, 133*, 265–277.

Rossbach, K. A., & Wilson, J. P. (1992). Does a dog's presence make a person appear more likable?: Two studies. *Anthrozoös, 5*, 40–51.

Ryder, E., & Romasco, M. (1981). Establishing a social work service in a veterinary hospital. In B. Fogle (Ed.), *Interrelations between People and Pets* (pp. 209–220). Springfield, IL: Charles C. Thomas Publisher.

San Diego Zoo to euthanize pioneering monkey (2003, June 16). Retrieved 6/16/03, from http://story.news.yahoo.com/news?templ+story&cid=570&ncid=753&e+6&u=/nm/20030616

Schneider, J. Quotation retrieved 5/26/04, from http://www.interluderetreat.com/thought.htm

Snyder, J. (2006). Creating a ritual for the loss of a companion animal. Retrieved 1/31/01, from http://www.ritualwell.org/lifecycles/sitefolder.2006–10-25.0669142154/Primary Object.2006-03-20.2059/view?searchterm=companion animal

Szita, B., & Kotch-Jantzer, C. A. (1988). Euthanasia in zoos: issues of attachment and separation. In W. J. Kay, S. P. Cohen, C. E. Fudin, A. H. Kutscher, A. H. Nieburg, R. E. Grey, & M. M. Osman (Eds.), (1988). *Euthanasia of the Companion Animal: The Impact on Pet Owners, Veterinarians, and Society* (pp. 148–163). Philadelphia: The Charles Press.

Walsh, K., King, M., Jones, L., Tookman, A., & Blizzard, R. (2002). Spiritual beliefs may affect outcome of bereavement: prospective study. *British Medical Journal, 324*, 1551.

Weinbach, R. W. (1989). Sudden death and secret survivors: helping those who grieve alone. *Social Work, 34*, 57–60.

Wortman, C. B., & Silver, R. C. (1989). The myths of coping with loss. *Journal of Counseling and Clinical Psychology, 3*, 349–357.

Zongker, B. (2010, Feb. 4). Superstar farewell for US-born, China-bound pandas. Retrieved 2/5/10, from http://news.yahoo.com/s/ap/20100204/ap_on_re_us/us_pandas_depart/print

Zoo condors to be released in Andes. (1997, Dec. 16). *The New York Times*, F8.

22 Animal-assisted interventions and humane education: opportunities for a more targeted focus

Phil Arkow

The Latham Foundation and the American Humane Association

22.1 Introduction

It has been taken for granted in the humane movement for a century and a half that children who are taught to respect animals will develop empathy, compassion, and grow up to be kinder to their fellow human animals (Arkow, 1990). It is widely accepted as axiomatic in the field of animal-assisted therapy and activities (AAT/AAA) that there is an "undeniable bond" between children and animals (Phillips and McQuarrie, 2009).

As these two disciplines have evolved, the worlds of AAT/AAA and humane education have occasionally intersected, with innovative practitioners continually discovering new applications to introduce the soothing powers of animals to children and youth. Demographic and market research (American Veterinary Medical Association, 2007) depicting households with children as overwhelmingly having pets, plus psychological research addressing the role of pets in healthy and abnormal child and adolescent development (Ascione, 2005; Kruger et al., 2004; Melson, 2001), fuel efforts to bring humane education and animal-assisted interventions (AAI) to young audiences.

The use of AAIs with at-risk, abused, and special-needs youth continues to proliferate and mature (DeGrave, 1999; Fine, 2006; Rathmann, 1999; Ross, 1999). A new generation of programs using animals to help students improve their reading skills and overcome behavioral disorders that impact their academic learning has emerged. As interest in AAT/AAA has grown, children and adolescents are finding increasing opportunities to experience beneficial animal contact.

The American Humane Association has developed the PAWS® program—Pets And Women's Shelters—to enable battered women and their children to keep their pets with them (American Humane Association, 2009b), and the TASK® program—Therapy Animals Supporting Kids—in which therapy animals in children's advocacy centers and courtrooms facilitate police investigations, forensic examinations, and courtroom testimony for sexually abused children (Phillips and McQuarrie, 2009).

Handbook on Animal-Assisted Therapy. DOI: 10.1016/B978-0-12-381453-1.10022-4

Families in Illinois, California and Pennsylvania have sued local school districts to allow their children's autism service dogs to accompany them to class and serve as calming influences, familiar links in new circumstances, and safety barriers to keep the children from running off (Associated Press, 2009).

At Susquehanna and Bucknell Universities and Gettysburg College in Pennsylvania, professors and school counselors bring their own pets to "Dog Days" for an hour of social interaction to help incoming freshmen overcome homesickness. "Students can't pick up their phones and call Sparky. Or text him. Or e-mail him," wrote a newspaper reporter. Added Susquehanna's associate dean of students and director of the counseling center: "The fact is that students miss their pets, sometimes more than they miss their families" (Snyder, 2009).

Programs like these are breathing new life into opportunities for animal-assisted humane education. Whereas traditional humane education emphasizes presentations to individual classrooms or entire school audiences to build community awareness of humane causes, a more strategic approach today specifically targets youth with special needs or who are at risk of violence, abuse, or committing antisocial behavior. These new approaches integrate AAT/AAA, animal behaviorism, and knowledge of The Link® between animal abuse and human violence into more focused animal-assisted educational interventions that may prove more effective, directly reaching those who are most at risk of being victims, or perpetrators, of violence.

22.2   The roots of humane education

Many philosophers and writers, including Ovid, St. Thomas Aquinas, Montaigne, John Locke, William Hogarth, Immanuel Kant, and Margaret Mead, have argued that harming animals is the first step down a slippery slope that desensitizes individuals against interpersonal violence. These writers have extolled the virtues of being kind to animals not just in consideration for animals' well-being, but out of concern for what animal maltreatment says about the human condition (ten Bensel, 1984; Wynne-Tyson, 1990).

Locke (1705), in particular, gave impetus to a robust philosophical construct promoting childhood kindness to animals as having significant implications on positive character development. *The History of Little Goody Two-Shoes*—one of the first full-length children's books in the English language—written by an anonymous author in 1765, accentuated this concept as heroine Margery Meanwell helps animals who have been mistreated. In what may be one of the earliest usages of the term "animal rights," Herman Daggett (1792) described an unfettered belief in what today would be called humane education to correct antisocial behavior:

> *Only let a person be taught, from his earliest years, that it is criminal to torment, and unnecessarily to destroy, these innocent animals, and he will feel a guilty conscience, in consequence of any injury which he shall do to them, in this way, no less really than if the injury were offered to human beings. The force of education, and of wrong habits, in setting aside natural principles, is amazing, and almost incredible.*

However, the use of the word "humane" in conjunction with animal well-being took considerable time to develop. While the word, derived from the Latin *humanus* and the French *humaine*, originated as a common earlier spelling of "human" (and even today one occasionally finds interchangeable usage of "inhuman" and "inhumane"), circa 1500 "humane" began to describe gentle, kind, courteous, friendly behavior as befits a human being, with no connotation of protecting animals. In Shakespeare's *Coriolanus*, written in 1608, starving plebeians say that if patricians gave them surplus food "we might guess they relieved us humanely" (I,i), and a senator recommends bringing Coriolanus to the market place for a public airing of all their grievances, rather than executing him, because "it is the humane way: the other course will prove too bloody" (III,i).

After 1700, the word came to describe sympathy with and consideration for the needs and distresses of others (Simpson and Weiner, 1989). Samuel Johnson's seminal *A Dictionary of the English Language* (1755) makes no association of the word with kindness to animals, rather defining humane as "kind, civil, benevolent, and good-natured."

The interpretation of "humane" as benevolence took on an entirely new human welfare meaning with the formation in 1774 of the Royal Humane Society in London for the recovery of persons who had apparently drowned. The London organization claimed in its first decade to have "restored to their friends and country" 790 out of 1,300 persons apparently dead from drowning (Humane Society of the Commonwealth of Massachusetts, 1786). This type of "humane society," which actually originated in the Netherlands in 1767, was soon replicated with similar lifesaving services in Paris, Venice, Hamburg, Milan, and eventually Boston in 1786.

This venerable organization, the third oldest charitable society in Massachusetts, was founded "for the recovery of persons who meet with such accidents as to produce in them the appearance of death, and for promoting the cause of humanity, by pursuing such means, from time to time, as shall have for their object the preservation of human life and the alleviation of its miseries" (Humane Society of Massachusetts, 1845). John Lathrop (1787) praised the nascent Humane Society of Massachusetts as being the first benevolent institution to address "the cries of the needy," "the fight of wretchedness," and "the relief to prevent misery" among those suffering from apparent death.

Early American humane societies in Boston, Philadelphia, New York, and elsewhere erected rescue sheds and boathouses along the Atlantic seaboard and published guidelines for the "reanimation" and resuscitation of persons who appeared to have died from drowning, heat prostration, hypothermia, lightning strikes, and other causes (Humane Society of Philadelphia, 1788). Other American humane societies fought for prison reform and the closing of "petty taverns and grog-shops" which, while necessary for the weary traveler, were seen as "the nurseries of intemperance, disorder and profligacy" among the laboring poor of New York City (Humane Society of the City of New York, 1810).

Other early American usages of "humane" were humanitarian in scope but with no reference to kindness toward animals. The term is commonly found in early calls for penal reform, such as advanced by William Penn who, in 1681, created "a more humane house of correction based on labor," and by Benjamin Franklin who in 1790 advocated for "humane treatment of inmates" in the Walnut Street Jail by using solitary cells (Dickinson, 2008). "Humane Fire Companies" were established in Philadelphia, Easton and Norristown, PA, and Bordentown, NJ, as early as 1797 (Underwood, n.d.; Burlington County Firemen's Association, 1922).

The first attempt to start a federated fundraising drive was undertaken in Philadelphia in 1829 by one Matthew Carey, who entreated 97 "citizens of the first respectability" to sign an appeal entitled, "Address to the Liberal and Humane" (Cutlip, 1990). In an 1829 letter directing the infamous "Trail of Tears" forced relocation of five American Indian tribes from Mississippi and Alabama, President Andrew Jackson told Native American leaders that the relocation plan was the only way by which "they can expect to preserve their own laws, & be benefitted [sic] by the care and humane attention of the United States" (Colimore, 2009). An 1840 morality tale describes how a couple in 1745 "humanely" took it upon themselves to care for the three children of neighbors who were imprisoned and executed during Scottish insurrections (Mrs. Blackford, 1840). Other uses of "humane" include the description of weapons or implements which inflict less pain than others of their kind, and the branches of study or literature which tend to refine.

At some unknown point, "humane" came to include showing compassion and tenderness towards "the lower animals" (Simpson and Weiner, 1989). An unnamed "humane society" was cited by Thoreau in *Walden* (1854) as being the greatest friend of hunted animals (p. 211). "No humane being, past the thoughtless age of boyhood, will wantonly murder any creature which holds its life by the same tenure that he does," Thoreau wrote (p. 212), although elsewhere he apotheosized Nature when the winds sigh "humanely" (p. 138) and described philanthropy as a "humane" pursuit (p. 73). In *Cape Cod* (1865), he described the "Charity or Humane Houses" erected on the beaches of Barnstable County where shipwrecked seamen may look for shelter; in mentioning an incident where a little boy had poached 80 swallows' eggs from their nests, Thoreau wrote, "Tell it not to the Humane Society." How such a human-centric organization with a mission of reanimating drowning victims came to adopt animal protection as a cause remains unclear.

The earliest usage of "humane" in an extant animal welfare organization appears in the first annual report of the Pennsylvania SPCA (1869), in which a fundraising appeal is made to the "humane" citizens of Philadelphia for financial and membership assistance. The Oregon Humane Society was founded in 1868, and the Missouri Humane Society in 1870, but it is unknown whether these were the original names for these organizations or subsequent name changes.

About this time, the nascent animal protection movement in the USA began to identify "humane education" as the intervention of choice for guiding wayward youths into a righteous path in which animals were well regarded, respected and cared for—not just for the animals' welfare, but to improve human behavior. George Angell, founder of the Massachusetts SPCA, argued that although animal abuse should be a concern in its own right, society should heed animal abuse as an omen of violence among people (cited in Ascione, 2005). Three of the founders of the early animal welfare movement—Angell in Boston, Henry Bergh in New York, and

Caroline Earle White in Philadelphia—outspokenly believed that the focal job of an authentic humane society should be moral education and public advocacy rather than rescuing and sheltering animals (Animal People, 2009).

Angell stressed humane education's utility for ensuring public order, suppressing anarchy and radicalism, smoothing relations between the classes, and reducing crime: it would be a valuable means for socializing the young (especially of the lower socioeconomic classes) and the solution to social unrest and revolutionary politics. This promotion of humane education as an antidote for depraved character and a panacea for societal ills aligned the fledgling animal protection movement with other social reform and justice movements concerned with cruelty, violence and the social order (Arkow, 1992; Unti and DeRosa, 2003). Child welfare and animal welfare work often overlapped: pioneering and muckraking social reformer Jacob Riis (1892) described the American Humane Association as protecting "the odd link that bound the dumb brute with the helpless child in a common bond of humane sympathy" (p. 150). By 1922, 307 of the 539 animal protection organizational members of the American Humane Association devoted their work to the protection of abused children as part of the same humanitarian continuum of care (Shultz, 1924).

Humane education was seen as a means of insulating youth, and boys in particular, against tyrannical tendencies that might undermine civic life were such violent natures left unchecked. Animals were nicely suited for instruction and became important vehicles for inculcating standards of gentility including self-discipline, Christian sentiment, empathy, and moral sensitivity. Societal class stratification was an underpinning of humane education as well, as advocates saw the teaching of "kindness to animals" as a way to separate refined, urbane, middle- and upper-class youth from the coarser, rustic behaviors of lower classes and immigrants who were considered the sources of much brutality (Ritvo, 1987; Saunders, 1895; Unti and DeRosa, 2003).

Throughout the Victorian era, moralistic tracts filled with lofty sentiments about animal cruelty being a precursor to antisocial behaviors were mainstays of childhood education:

A worm, a fly, and all things that have life, can feel pain: if we learn to be cruel while boys, we shall not grow up to be good men.

(Cobb, 1832)

One who is cruel to a cat or a dog, a bird or a fish, will be cruel to his fellow-man, and such cruelty dulls all those finer feelings which make a true gentleman or lady.

(Johnson, 1900)

The humane education movement is a broad one, reaching from humane treatment of animals on the one hand to peace with all nations on the other...It implies character building. Society first said that needless suffering should be prevented; society now says that children must not be permitted to cause pain because of the effect on the children themselves.

(Eddy, 1899)

The Latham Foundation, founded in 1918 for the promotion of humane education, still exemplifies this paradigm. A poster from the 1930s, widely used today, depicts two children with a puppy approaching a set of steps leading to "world friendship." The first step up this hill is "kindness to animals," which will subsequently take the voyagers to kindness to each other, other people, our country, other nations, and the world (Forman, 2007).

A century later, advocates still promote humane education as a virtue that can solve all societal ills and achieve global peace. Weil (2004), for example, hyperbolically described humane education as offering a solution to war, bigotry, cruelty, environmental disaster, terrorism, species extinction, human oppression, ecological degradation, racism, sexism, homophobia and global warming. Antoncic (2003) declared, "Humane education can offer society hope for an active, independent, self-thinking future citizenry."

It is significant to note that from its inception, the philosophical and moral underpinnings for humane education are based as much upon what cruelty to animals says about the human condition as upon the adverse impact upon the animals themselves. The premise that kindness to animals has a benefit to human beings and the psychological and social development of children is a natural opportunity for AAIs to be added to more traditional humane education offerings.

22.3   The role of animals in the lives of children

The American Veterinary Medical Association (2007) estimated that pets are present in 67.7% of US households with children under the age of six, and in 74.6% of households with children aged six or over; 49.7% of pet owners consider their pets to be family members and 48.2% consider them to be companions. Foer (2006) reported that significant numbers of children routinely include pets in lists of the most important individuals in their lives and spontaneously mention their pets when asked to identify whom they turn to when feeling sad, angry, happy, or wanting to share a secret.

Even if families do not have pets, children are surrounded by animal images from an early age, in such forms as stuffed toys, mobiles above their cribs, pictures in their books, characters in their TV cartoons, and imprints on their clothing. Most children learn their numbers by counting animals and learn to read from picture books filled with animals (Doris Day Animal Foundation, 2005).

Melson (2001) observed that *dog, cat, duck, horse, bear* and *bird* are among the first 50 words that most American toddlers say, and that more children say these words than any other words except *mama* and *daddy* or their equivalents (p. 84). Fairytales have more animals in them than fairies (p. 139). Pets are more likely to be a part of children's growing up than are siblings or fathers (p. 34). And 80 to 90% of American children first confront the loss of a loved one when a pet dies, disappears or is abandoned (p. 62). But traditional education renders animals as objects to be analyzed apart from the texture of daily experience (p. 74), with few studies on the impact of classroom animals on young children (p. 75). School educators often overlook opportunities for learning presented by the sheer ubiquity of pets in the lives of children: "The average school child seems to know more about dinosaurs and fictitious creatures than those with which it may interact on a daily basis" (Mills and De Keuster, 2009).

When attachments between children and animals are nurtured, many positive benefits ensue. However, when the bond between children and animals is broken by real or threatened violence or neglect in the family, children pay a high price, often with short- and long-term consequences. These children are at higher risk of developing behavioral problems, failing academically, and engaging in delinquent and criminal behavior, and are more vulnerable to physical and psychological problems. Strong consensus now exists among researchers and policy makers that animal abuse, child maltreatment, domestic violence, and elder abuse are potentially co-occurring elements of family violence. Paying attention to the situation of animals in families may provide early opportunities to redirect the trajectory of a child's antisocial development into more positive directions (Arkow, 2003, 1996; Ascione and Arkow, 1999; Randour and Davidson, 2008).

It is not the mere presence of animals in a family, but rather the degree of the bond or attachment to those animals that may encourage a child's positive development (Poresky, 1990). A child's attachment to pets has the potential to teach empathy and compassion, and animals can bring a withdrawn, abused or traumatized child out of his or her shell. The non-judgmental comfort offered by a pet can help a child heal (Phillips and McQuarrie, 2009). A wide range of institutional settings for children with special needs—children's advocacy centers, juvenile and adolescent mental health and correctional institutions, children's hospitals, child protection agencies, schools for emotionally disturbed youth, private consulting rooms and many others— incorporate AAIs. Schools where humane education is offered may be added to this institutional list.

Childhood cruelty to animals is one of the earliest reported symptoms of conduct disorder, manifesting at 6.75 years of age (Frick et al., 1993). Children who are cruel to animals exhibit more severe conduct disorder problems than other children (Luk et al., 1999). Findings such as these provide empirical credence to the largely anecdotal data that have directed humane education activities for decades, and lend support to more strategic approaches in which humane education is coordinated with AAIs targeted to reach at-risk, delinquent, or academically challenged youth.

22.4   AAIs with youth

Research detailing the benefits of AAIs with children who have been abused, or who are at risk of behavioral or antisocial disorders, though relatively sparse and recent (Phillips and McQuarrie, 2009), appears emotionally intuitive and convincing. Melson and Fogel (1996) reported that after only five minutes of contact with an unfamiliar dog, 76% of children believed that the dog knew how they felt and 84% indicated they would confide secrets to a dog. The presence of animals in a child's therapeutic environment makes the therapy seem friendlier and less threatening, helps build rapport with children, expedites a sense of trust, and has a calming effect (Fine, 2006; Nagengast et al., 1997). Parish-Plass (2008) reported two significant variables that differentiated those who survived childhood abuse as well-adjusted adults from those who did not: the presence of an adult who inspired confidence in them and encouraged them, and responsibility for caring for a younger sibling or pet.

Emotional support—the sense of being able to turn to others for comfort in times of stress and the feeling of being cared for by others—may be enhanced by even relatively brief interactions with animals (Kruger et al., 2004). Dimensions of emotional support cited in AAIs with abused or at-risk children include animals' seeming abilities to: build rapport with the adult professional; promote engagement with the child; reduce anxiety and stress; provide nonjudgmental acceptance and attention; provide a sense of safety, friendliness and normalcy; allow children to role play, project, transfer, and re-enact experiences; improve children's self-esteem; allow children to practice social and communicative skills; reduce feelings of social alienation; learn about appropriate and inappropriate touching; and improve morale (Phillips and McQuarrie, 2009). While this phenomenon is more commonly utilized in therapeutic settings, it has applications as well in humane educational contexts.

22.5 Making humane education more relevant

Although history offers a long, irrepressible, and largely unproven faith in the power of humane education to effect positive changes in children's character (Arkow, 2006), and researchers (Bjerke and Ostdahl, 2004; Kellert, 1989) have correlated higher levels of education with support for moralistic, humanistic and ecologistic attitudes consistent with animal rights, animal welfare and environmental causes, humane education has not been institutionalized in public education systems. Despite more than 140 years of classroom programming, support from national parent/teacher organizations (Arkow, 1990; Wishnik, 2003), and at least 12 states mandating its inclusion in school curricula (American Humane Association, 2008; Antoncic, 2003), humane education remains a largely marginalized activity.

Humane educators often have difficulty in gaining access to schools where teachers resist adding instruction to already crowded curricula and state mandates. Guides for educators about how to nurture humaneness in a school environment describe it as reflecting enlightenment, compassion, or self-actualization, but fail to mention kindness to animals (Scobey and Graham, 1970). Meanwhile, instructional programs of "values education" and "character education" are flourishing with federal dollars flowing to school districts across the USA.

Traditional humane education is often conducted as a shelter tour or classroom presentation covering such topics as responsible pet care, pet overpopulation, safe interactions with animals, and ethical human/animal concerns. Although developing a sense of empathy for animals is assumed to be a bridge to caring about human beings and make children more resilient, more socially competent, more popular with their peers, and less aggressive (Doris Day Animal Foundation, 2005), this premise and the effectiveness of humane education have been difficult to assess (Ascione,

2005; O'Brien, n.d.). With a 45-minute presentation representing only 4/10,000ths of 1% of classroom contact exposure over a student's 12-year school career (Arkow, 1990), the long-term impact of such a program would appear to be minimal, even more so when the influence of students' peers, family and the media are factored in. In communities marked by high incidence of gang-, gun- and drug-related crime, humane educators may particularly wonder how they can go into a classroom and teach children to be kind to animals when these students are afraid to go to school because of drive-by shootings (Arkow, 2006). Animal welfare organizations that should consider the educational imperative to be mission-critical often fail to support it with adequate financial and human resources (Senechalle and Dunn, 2004) and even the venerable ASPCA in 2009 discontinued classroom and teacher training presentations.

Still, professional and volunteer humane educators soldier on, nobly attempting to teach children a sense of responsibility, respect and compassion for animals and their needs, in hopes of developing good character, self-awareness, and greater respect for all living things (Yao, 2003).

Perhaps greater respect for, and inclusion of, humane education in school curricula can be obtained by emphasizing the positive, therapeutic benefits of animals and improved social capital attendant with responsible pet husbandry. Children who have pets have greater self-concept and self-esteem, are better integrated socially, have wider social networks, and are more popular with their classmates (Endenburg and Baarda, 1995). High school students who have pets perform better on college entrance examinations and have higher grade point averages (American Pet Products Manufacturers Association, 1999). Because attachment to pets is a gender-neutral expression of caring, pets may be especially important for the development of empathy among young boys (Melson, 1988). The presence of pets can counteract the erosion of what Putnam (1996, 2000) called "social capital" and enhance community networks, norms and trust. Pets were reported to facilitate civic engagement, communications, and the social connectivity that is vital for healthy communities (Wood et al., 2005).

22.6 Overcoming challenges to traditional humane education: "new wine in an old bottle"

In an earlier version of this chapter (Arkow, 2006), I identified issues that have kept traditional humane education marginalized and undercapitalized as compared with more established character initiatives:

- Inadequate definitions of "humane education" and "cruelty to animals"
- Marginalization of animal cruelty vis-à-vis crimes against human members of society
- Insufficient knowledge of the etiology of acts of violence against animals
- Inadequate prioritization within the animal welfare and philanthropic sectors
- Insufficient statutory authority mandating the inclusion of animal welfare curricula
- Lack of processes to evaluate whether such programming results in behavioral changes and whether such messaging carries into adulthood

- Lack of cultural diversity within humane organizations, making it difficult to implement culturally relevant programming
- Competition from more established special interest groups seeking to have their curricula included
- Absence of systemic training, professional development, and certification for humane educators
- Lack of public and parental support
- Resistance from teachers opposed to additional instructional mandates
- Bureaucratic stasis
- Incomplete understanding of how children react to the messaging and what meets their needs.

In that chapter, I referred to efforts to modernize humane education as "old wine in a new bottle," a repackaging of age-old concepts into more contemporary language acceptable to educators. The field of education is not unique in marginalizing, or even trivializing, animal welfare issues. Professionals in such fields as law enforcement, prosecution, social services and government frequently ask, "Why should I focus on animal problems when there are so many more pressing human welfare concerns?"

In reality, animal welfare issues are human welfare concerns as well. American animal protection laws are the oldest in the world, dating to 1641, historically enacted because of the impact that animal maltreatment is perceived to have on the human condition (Animal Welfare Institute, 1990; Frasch et al., 1999; Lacroix, 1999). This attitude was exemplified in 2009 by the US Solicitor General's Office in a brief to the US Supreme Court arguing that commercial trafficking of videotapes of dogfights is illegal and not protected by the First Amendment's rights of free speech. "Illegal acts of animal cruelty result in great suffering to defenseless animals, as well as injuries to human beings, and the erosion of important public mores," the brief stated (Kagan, 2009).

Given growing recognition that addressing humane causes has benefits for humans, that animal abuse is linked to other forms of human violence, that 98% of Americans consider pets as "members of the family" or "companions" (American Veterinary Medical Association, 2007), and that AAIs can be beneficial for youth, perhaps a new description is indicated. Perhaps the integration of animal-assisted education into traditional humane education is more appropriately "new wine in an old bottle."

22.7   Strategies for overcoming the challenges

Much as the field of AAT/AAA has developed professional standards and training for animals and handlers, the field of humane education has become more professional in its development of personnel and innovative in its delivery systems. Guidelines have been developed to ensure that humane educators meet the highest standards of practice (Association of Professional Humane Educators, 2006). An online Certified Humane Education Specialist program is available from the Humane Society of the United States. Weeklong camps, vacation workshops, service learning opportunities, civic engagement at universities to benefit animal shelters, curricula that meet state education standards, adult education classes, animal-behavioral programs for new adopters, outreach programs in children's museums, interactive kiosks in animal shelters, and positive-reinforcement dog training programs for at-risk youth are some of the new humane education developments (Jane Deming, personal communication, Oct. 19, 2009).

Additional progress is being achieved through recognition of the links between animal abuse and interpersonal violence as the rationale for introducing humane education into school curricula. With educators, school psychologists, parents and community leaders seeking ways to reduce the incidence of bullying (Henry and Sanders, 2007) and school violence, research that links animal abuse to child abuse, criminal behaviors and the development of conduct problems is relevant to educators (Arluke and Luke, 1997; Ascione, 1998, 2005; Ascione and Arkow, 1999; Ascione et al., 2000; DeViney et al., 1983; Gullone and Clarke, 2008; Randour and Davidson, 2008). Risk factors associated with children's committing acts of animal abuse include fire setting, bullying, other criminal acts, decreased empathy, corporal punishment, physical and/or sexual abuse, exposure to domestic violence, exposure to animal abuse, and other psychiatric disorders such as antisocial personality disorder (Ascione, 2009).

The American Psychiatric Association (1994) includes cruelty to animals as an indicator for a diagnosis of conduct disorder. With the median age of onset of animal abuse occurring in the child's sixth year, acts of cruelty to animals are often noticed before other indicators of conduct disorder are manifest, and may forecast major dysfunction in adulthood. Identifying animal abuse early and intervening before a child is seven years of age may be a way to stop maladaptive behavior (Ascione, 2005). Preliminary evidence also indicates that animal-based interventions in mental health settings for adolescents have many potential benefits (Kruger et al., 2004).

On the basis of the assumption that children exposed to violence are at an elevated risk of committing violence (Currie, 2006), many advocates view humane education as an applicable tool for violence intervention and prevention (Merz-Perez and Heide, 2004). Animal-assisted humane education interventions may prevent further abuse to animals and humans by fostering respect, responsibility and empathy in youth towards all forms of life and the environment. Several studies validate humane education as a deterrent to violence (Antoncic, 2003).

AAIs should be a crucial component of a humane education curriculum. Educators and counselors can use humane education to help identify youth at risk of perpetrating violence and as a remedial strategy following adverse human/animal interactions (Thomas and Beirne, 2002).

Childhood offers a brief window of opportunity to intervene with a violent child at a critical juncture, and childhood acts of animal cruelty have been called "the Rosetta Stone of predatory psychopathology" (Vachss, 2005). It is no longer acceptable to excuse acts of animal cruelty as youthful indiscretions: violent boys have a great risk of becoming dangerous men. When animal maltreatment becomes culturally unacceptable, real, lasting changes—including integrating humane education into standard school curricula—will be made.

22.8   Animal-assisted humane education

While the mere presence of pets is neither necessary nor sufficient for children to develop empathy (Arluke, 2003), if animals are present and especially if there is attachment to those animals, there is an opportunity for children to develop a healthy sense of compassion for others (Ascione, 2005), higher measures of social competence and empathy (Poresky, 1990), greater orientation toward social values and greater likelihood of entering a helping profession (Vizek-Vidovic et al., 2001), greater empathy towards people (Ascione and Weber, 1996), higher self-esteem (Bierer, 2001), and less aggression (Hergovich et al., 2002).

Consequently, traditional humane educational programs are being augmented by targeted interventions in juvenile offender facilities, schools for emotionally disturbed and behaviorally challenged students, and classes for at-risk youth. Many of these AAIs are based upon recognizing the links between animal abuse and human violence, returning to the humane movement's original premise that stopping childhood violence against animals can head off future antisocial behaviors (San Diego Humane Society and SPCA, 2005; Soltow and Shepherd, 1992).

For example, the Alberta SPCA obtained Canadian federal funding to publish a guide to resources and curriculum design for teachers based upon the link between animal abuse and other violent behaviors. This guide, used in the Alberta Teachers' Association's Safe and Caring Schools Project, includes the symbiotic relationship between children and animals, and offers recommendations for teachers whose students disclose incidents of animal abuse (Battle, 2003). An extensive *Humane Education Guidebook* is predicated upon the connections between animal abuse and child maltreatment (Federated Humane Societies of Pennsylvania, 2000). In South Africa, promotion of the link between violence towards women, children and animals resulted in widespread distribution and enthusiastic support by provincial Departments of Education for a multi-lingual humane education curriculum and the establishment of student "ubuntu" clubs that promote "better life for all living beings" (Humane Education Trust, 2003). The Latham Foundation has published a handbook for therapists, humane educators and teachers using the animal abuse/human violence link as the keystone for humane education and AAT interventions (Loar and Colman, 2004).

The targeted use of AAIs to mitigate violent behavior among at-risk youth evolved, in part, from programs for adult offenders in correctional facilities in the USA, Canada, England, Scotland, Australia, and South Africa (Correctional Service of Canada, 1998). Prison programs utilize a variety of domestic, livestock and wild species in attempts to rehabilitate inmates, provide them with vocational training, and train homeless animals to become assistance dogs (Granger and Kogan, 2006; Strimple, 2003).

Some of these prison programs are affiliated with local humane organizations. It was a natural extension of this concept to adapt such programs to youthful offenders and to children and youth at risk of antisocial behaviors. Such synergies create a natural linkage between animal welfare and social services advocates with "a shared interest in providing humane care to all living creatures, despite their offenses, [and] the potential for a powerful alliance to influence reformation of care for sheltered dogs and for incarcerated individuals" (Davis, 2007).

In these targeted interventions, which incorporate the principles of humane education, animal behaviorism, and awareness of the intersections of animal cruelty and other forms of human violence, homeless animals and incarcerated youths share commonalities: both need to be cared for, rehabilitated and integrated into a community while sequestered in a secure facility. Both are "throwaway populations," discarded by a society that does not care what happens to them (and prefers they be kept out of sight). Having inmates and animals help each other in a symbiotic relationship results in a win-win-win situation, with not only the inmate and animal benefiting but the larger community as well (Davis, 2007; Furst, 2006).

A pioneer in this arena has been Project POOCH (Positive Opportunities, Obvious Change with Hounds) that has paired incarcerated youths at the MacLaren Youth Correctional Facility in Woodburn, Oregon, with homeless shelter dogs since 1993 (www.pooch.org). Youths, guided by professionals, learn to train dogs using positive reinforcement and behavior modification techniques, groom them, and find them new adoptive permanent homes. The dogs leave the program ready to be great pets, while their trainers re-enter the community with new vocational and personal skills, increased compassion and respect for all life, and techniques to manage their own behavior. Project POOCH participants demonstrate a reduced incidence of interpersonal aggression, growth in leadership skills, and improvement in their ability to work with others (Davis, 2007). Studies have reported marked behavior improvements among participants in respect for authority, social interaction, leadership, honesty, empathy, nurturing, social growth, understanding, confidence level, and pride of accomplishment (Merriam-Arduini, 2000).

For some students, this relationship is their first experience of unconditional love and emotional support that helps them develop self-confidence. Davis (2007) observed that animal behaviorists know that a dog engaged in purposive work and interaction, whether it is being companionable or chasing sheep, is likely to display fewer behavioral difficulties. Humans also seem to need a level of engagement in meaningful, self-directed activity to meet maximum potential.

Another residential AAI program is based in Albuquerque, NM, where the Youth Diagnostic and Development Center's Project Second Chance program partners with the Animal Humane Association of New Mexico to pair teenage offenders with homeless shelter dogs who, like them, are "serving time" for a variety of offenses. The youth learn empathy, community responsibility, kindness, an awareness of healthy social interactions, and basic dog grooming; the dogs, many of whom were surrendered for such behavioral problems as hyperactivity, jumping, house soiling, chewing, and separation anxiety, learn basic obedience commands (Beyke, 2002; Harbolt and Ward, 2001).

The Shiloh Project in Fairfax, VA, is another early pioneer in using AAIs to teach compassion to juvenile offenders and at-risk youth. Focusing primarily on teens, the group teaches respect and responsibility toward animals and others through socializing and interacting with rescued dogs, promoting the adoption of homeless pets, understanding the links between animal abuse and human violence, and encouraging healthy and positive human/animal bonds (www.shilohproject.org).

Other AAIs in which at-risk and incarcerated youths work with homeless dogs to develop empathy, personal awareness, responsibility and vocational training include Urban Tails (www.urbantails.org) ("helping save dogs and the youth who save them"), a new program in South Florida that offers opportunities for self-discovery and the vulnerability of self-expression; and Teacher's Pet: Dogs and Kids Learning Together (www.teacherspetmichigan.org) in Rochester Hills, MI, that pairs at-risk or court adjudicated youth with hard-to-adopt shelter dogs for a workshop on basic obedience training. This program is also offered through two weeklong summer camps for middle school students.

Cisco's Kids is an AAI addressing behavioral and social difficulties that have negatively impacted the academic learning of incarcerated youth at the Rhode Island Training School. Created through a partnership involving clinical social workers within the school system, the program's goals include helping students to improve their behavior, social skills, self-esteem, and non-violent conflict resolution skills within the academic program by learning to respect animals (Cournoyer and Uttley, 2007).

The pioneering prototype in targeted humane education interventions with emotionally disturbed, behaviorally challenged and at-risk students is the residential treatment program at Green Chimneys in Brewster, NY, which is described elsewhere (Ross, 1999) and in this book (see Chapter 8) and needs no elaboration here.

AAIs can serve for prevention as well as for intervention, and humane organizations have augmented traditional broad-spectrum classroom presentations with specialized animal-assisted preventive programs for at-risk youth (Arkow, 2003). The Los Angeles Society for the Prevention of Cruelty to Animals (www.spcala.org) developed TLC (Teaching Love and Compassion), a volunteer workshop for at-risk youths aged 11 to 13 with histories of disruptive or violent behavior. The youths attend a four-week workshop offered four times a year during the school intercession break or in prime-risk after-school hours. Teams consist of a boy and a girl working collaboratively with a dog using positive reinforcement behavioral techniques and non-violent resolution of conflicts (Randour and Davidson, 2008; Yao, 2003).

In Milwaukee, the Wisconsin Humane Society (www.wihumane.org) launched People and Animals Learning (PAL), now a nationally recognized violence prevention program for at-risk youth, in 1993. Teachers and school social workers nominate students as candidates who, under the supervision of a professional dog trainer, work in teams to train shelter dogs to become well-mannered companions for adopting families. Participants also learn to care for injured birds and other wildlife as a way of carrying forward the humane ethic (DeGrave, 1999).

Forget-Me-Not Farm was started in 1992 at the Humane Society of Sonoma County, CA (www.sonomahumane.org), to expand traditional humane education efforts and break the intergenerational cycles of violence among abused children. Representatives of the humane society, the YWCA of Sonoma County, and the San Francisco Child Abuse Council collaborated to design and implement a program that teaches gentleness and non-violent conflict resolution techniques through animal care and gardening. The program incorporates AAT, horticulture therapy, and educational programming among students with special needs, disabilities and histories of abuse/ neglect, and children residing in women's, foster care and substance abuse recovery shelters (Arkow, 2004; The Latham Foundation, 1993, 2004; Rathmann, 1999).

In Ft. Lauderdale, FL, the Humane Society of Broward County (www. humanebroward.com) created Pet Clubs in nine Boys and Girls Clubs in high-risk neighborhoods where children are regularly exposed to feral cats and dogs who are chained and trained to be dangerous. Because few of these children have had positive experiences with animals and many are terrified of dogs, the Pet Clubs provide AAT/ AAA visits that allow children to interact in positive ways while learning the correct ways to approach, handle and care for pets. The Humane Society also developed a "No Bones About It" badge for local Girl Scouts (Katz, 2004).

East Coast Assistance Dogs (www.ecad1.org) of Dobbs Ferry, NY, which trains and places assistance animals to help the disabled, created Pet Assisted Learning Services (PALS) in 1999. The goal was to help children improve their ability to focus, set and reach manageable goals, practice self-control, and increase self-esteem through mastering measurable skills by interacting with dogs. In 2005 they added the Best Friends recreation program to allow residential school boys to exercise dogs, visit nursing homes and senior centers, and eventually work at the canine training center. The Work Appreciation for Youth (WAY) Program is a job readiness program that offers boys a chance to be employed in either service dog training or kennel management.

The Reaching Hands Ranch (www.reachinghandsranch.org) in Powell, WY, matches rescued horses who need refuge and rehabilitation with children aged 9 to 18 in a hands-on mentoring experience that gives both children and horses a second chance. The organization aids in the prevention of abuse and neglect through a caring and learning environment (Cramer and Crawford, 2009).

Wayside Waifs (www.waysidewaifs.org) in Kansas City, MO, augments such traditional humane education programs as pet care and responsibility, safety around strange dogs, and shelter tours with several programs with AAI themes. "Service Dogs in Action" introduces service animals to children. "No More Bullies" teaches children the principles of compassion, responsibility, self-control, integrity, and respecting the rights of others, including pets. "Ready, Pet, READ" provides practice opportunities for children in schools and libraries to improve their literary skills by reading aloud to companion animals.

Perhaps the most widely acclaimed AAI in an educational context is the use of dogs as literacy mentors in reading enrichment programs. Conducted in schools and libraries, animals serve as compliant listeners while children read stories aloud to them to help overcome speech, language and reading difficulties. One of the oldest such programs, Reading Education Assistance Dogs (R.E.A.D.) (www. therapyanimals.org) was launched in 1999 by Intermountain Therapy Animals in Salt Lake City, Utah. Today, thousands of registered R.E.A.D. teams work in the USA, Canada, the UK, and elsewhere.

Reading enrichment AAIs have proliferated rapidly. Tony La Russa's Animal Rescue Foundation (www.arf.net) in Walnut Creek, CA, initiated the All Ears Reading experience to improve children's reading skills, self-esteem and empathy by creating a supportive environment for children. Pets help foster an eagerness to read because they are attentive, non-judgmental and comforting. Noting that traditional humane educators are having difficulty gaining entrance into schools due to teachers facing increases in state mandates, benchmarking assessments and testing procedures, and decreases in time available for enrichment activities, Hart (2009) reported the All Ears Reading program is an appealing alternative. In one study of the program's effectiveness, significant gains were measured in students' reading fluency and accuracy, self-perception, and perceptions of their relationships with animals. Similar successes have been reported in other reading interventions in which visiting dogs are a good complement producing a less stressful process than traditional oral classroom reading; dramatic reductions in fear associated with reading aloud, and notable increases in students' enjoyment of reading, have been reported (Alden, 2009; Kurtz and Leger, 2009).

Many reading programs for children are conducted by Delta Society Pet Partners. The Paws and Tales Program at two Asheville, NC, elementary schools targets first-graders who have trouble reading or problems with confidence or self-esteem. Pictures of the children reading to the dogs are added to the covers of books of the first grade vocabulary list. In Macon, NC, a similar program resulted in all 18 first-graders achieving accelerated reading program target goals. A bunny named Oreo is a Pet Partner visitor to a reading program at El Marino Language School in Burbank, CA. One little girl's father said, "I never thought it would work. I don't know how it works, but it does. She was never interested in reading before. And now she is. I can't get over it!" (Delta Society, 2009).

School-based AAIs may be conducted with counselors as well as in classrooms. In Highwood, IL, school social worker Marci Morrison and her Pet Partner dog Bailey provide goal-directed interventions for K-8 students individually and in group sessions. These goals include improving attention skills, listening, cooperation skills, empathy training, socialization, respect, responsibility, and reducing anxiety (Delta Society, 2009). Nebbe (2009) identified ways to blend AAI with a school counseling program:

- counselors bringing their own animals to school
- visiting pets from AAA/AAT or humane organizations
- visiting therapy animals working under the counselor in specialized programs, such as R.E.A.D.
- students bringing their own pets to school
- children talking about their pets at home, which can be a useful assessment tool for the counselor
- working with wildlife rehabilitators to rescue fallen birds
- service learning opportunities with animal organizations
- using posters, pictures, stuffed animals, and puppets of animals.

The South African Red Cross Society launched a unique program in Strandfontein, Western Cape Province, that trained school dropouts in first aid skills for animals. The program took at-risk youth off the streets and away from crime, drugs and dogfighting to become part of an Animal Ambulance Service, rescuing animals in distress and providing transportation to veterinarians for the pets of economically disadvantaged families (*Animal Voice*, 2005).

A Jane Goodall Institute Roots & Shoots service learning component is working with the Santa Fe, NM, Animal Shelter and Humane Society Youth Board to provide leadership opportunities. One group of students in the "Saturdays at the Shelter" project chose the connection between domestic violence and animal abuse as the theme for their service project (Ray Powell, personal communication, June 25, 2009).

Other humane education programs use animal behavior awareness to reach high-risk children who are most likely to experience dog bites. American Humane's KIDS (Kids Interacting with Dogs Safely) curriculum, created for 4-to-7 year olds, is focused on six pillars of character education and teaches safety through empathy rather than fear (American Humane Association, 2009a).

22.9 Conclusion

Mankind's earliest known works of art, dating back 32,000 years, are cave paintings of animals (Associated Press, 2001). Our earliest ancestors had primeval affinities with the animals that shared their environment. Over the last 32 millennia we have feared animals, worshipped them, domesticated them, and brought them indoors as members of our families. Today, we partner with them to bring healthful interventions to targeted populations. In the future, we may take them with us as companions into outer space to mitigate the loneliness of interplanetary travel (Levinson, 1984).

Animals can often capture children's attention, imagination, and emotions in ways that people-focused subject matter cannot. Teaching abstract concepts like character and compassion can be easier, more engaging, and more fun when animals are the springboard for discussion. As AAA/AAT practitioners have long known, animals are catalysts for communication (Arkow, 2004): people often find it easier to talk about animals than about other topics—particularly if the other person is a stranger, an authority figure or if the subject is uncomfortable. Even beauty parlors use therapy dogs to sit with children with special needs (Adorn Beauty Center and Spa, 2009).

Despite the rich heritage and deep emotional connectivity of human/animal interactions, however, humane education continues to be a good idea that has not quite caught on (Alberta SPCA, 2004). Unlike similar movements such as environmental education, character education, values education, interpretive displays in zoos, wildlife conservation and animal husbandry, whose principles border or sometimes overlap those of humane education, efforts to institutionalize the teaching of humane treatment of animals systemically within the educational establishment have had only sporadic success.

Those seeking to impart humane education values to school audiences are poised at a fortuitous juncture. While continuing to offer such traditional programming as responsible pet care, careers with animals, safety around dogs, animal behavior, pet overpopulation, and discussion of community animal issues, humane organizations are beginning to introduce curricula focused on the benefits to human well-being by the human/animal bond and on the links between animal abuse and interpersonal violence. Meanwhile, animal-assisted reading enrichment and violence prevention interventions are bringing the world of AAA/AAT into classroom contexts.

For example, the Dumb Friends League (2009) of Denver, CO, offers school programs in "Bully Prevention," "Animal Abuse and the Violence Connection" and "Dog Fighting: A Community Challenge" that teach "leading and winning through character" and that meet state model content standards for civics. The Los Angeles SPCA (www.spcala.org) augments traditional classroom presentations with programs about the link between animal cruelty and human violence; its internationally renowned Teaching Love and Compassion (TLC) violence-prevention program works with at-risk youth and is being taught in California, Oregon, New York, Arizona, Missouri, Georgia, Indiana, Colorado, England and Australia. Chicago's Anti-Cruelty Society (www.anticruelty.org), whose educational offerings reach 40,000 students annually, has produced several videos and classroom presentations depicting the cycles of violence that meet state learning standards goals. The Society also offers a Teen Anti-Violence After-School Program, "Exploring the 'Link,'" to help students gain insight into how violence and cruelty affect their community, themselves, and animals. The Hinsdale, IL, Humane Society (www.hinsdalehumanesociety. org) offers three middle and high school-level classes on the links between conduct disorder and animal abuse and ways to stop the cycle of abuse.

A number of humane organizations provide animal-assisted reading enrichment programs in schools. These include: the Hinsdale, IL, Humane Society's PALS (Pet-Assisted Literacy Skills); the Pasadena, CA, Humane Society's Barks and Books; the Santa Fe, NM, Animal Shelter and Humane Society's Pet Outreach; the Hudson Valley, NY, Humane Society's Paws for Reading; and the R.E.A.D program of Lollypop Farm, the Humane Society of Greater Rochester, NY. These shelters have joined the ranks of AAA/AAT groups' literacy programs with such names as Reading with Paws (Tallahassee, FL), Hawaii Fi-Do (Haleiwa, HI), Paws and Effect (Des Moines, IA), Book Hounds (Helena, MT), Bona Fide Readers (Omaha, NE), and Reading with Rover (Seattle, WA) that bring therapy into schools and libraries.

Dogs have been found to contribute to overall emotional stability and to more positive attitudes towards school among elementary school students diagnosed with severe emotional disorders. Students also tend to be more attentive, more responsive, and more cooperative with an adult when a dog is present in the classroom. The infusion of AAIs into classrooms offers humane educators exciting and as-yet-unexplored areas for research and practice in how AAIs might benefit all children emotionally and socially in classrooms (Friesen, 2009).

Widespread concern about rates of violence and bullying are energizing preventive measures through classroom instruction that make humane education especially relevant (Unti and DeRosa, 2003). Evolving research into the human/animal bond and AAIs should lead to a renaissance of humane education programs based upon concrete data rather than abstract moral philosophies.

Given this growing recognition that addressing humane causes has benefits for humans, that animal abuse is linked to other forms of human violence, and that AAIs can be beneficial for youth, the integration of animal-assisted education into traditional humane education is an area of untapped potential that can be considered "new wine in an old bottle."

References

Adorn Beauty Center and Spa. (2009). *Specializing in Special Needs*. Bordentown, NJ: Author. [Brochure].

Alberta, S. P. C. A. (2004). Humane education: an idea whose time has come. *AnimalWise, 5* (2), 4–5.

Alden, A. (2009). *Canine interventions: dogs assist a reading program for children*. Kansas City, MO: Presentation at 18th Annual Conference, International Society for Anthrozoology. Oct. 20–23.

American Humane Association. (2008). *States Humane Education Laws*. Alexandria, VA: Author.

American Humane Association. (2009a). *KIDS: Kids Interacting with Dogs Safely Curriculum Set*. Englewood, CO: Author.

American Humane Association. (2009b). *Pets and Women's Shelters (PAWS) Program: Startup Guide*. Englewood, CO: Author.

American Pet Products Manufacturers Association. (1999). *Cited in Time*, Nov. 8.

American Psychiatric Association. (1994). *Diagnostic and Statistical Manual of Mental Disorders* (4th ed.). Washington, DC: Author.

American Veterinary Medical Association. (2007). *U.S. Pet Ownership and Demographics Sourcebook*. Schaumburg, IL: Author.

Animal People. (2009, June). *Elizabeth Morris and Annie Waln introduced hands-on humane work*, p. 6.

Animal Voice. (2005, Autumn). *Red Cross launches first ambulance for animals in Africa*, p. 1.

Animal Welfare Institute. (1990). *Animals and their Legal Rights*. Washington, DC: Author.

Antoncic, L. S. (2003). A new era in humane education: how troubling youth trends and a call for character education are breathing new life into efforts to educate our youth about the value of all life. *Animal Law, 9*, 183–213.

Arkow, P. (1990). *Humane Education*. Englewood, CO: American Humane Association.

Arkow, P. (1992). Humane education: an historical perspective. In M. E. Kaufmann (Ed.), *Progress in Humane Education* (pp. 2–3). Englewood, CO: American Humane Association.

Arkow, P. (1996). The relationships between animal abuse and other forms of family violence. *Family Violence and Sexual Assault Bulletin, 12*(1–2), 29–34.

Arkow, P. (2003). *Breaking the Cycles of Violence: A Guide to Multidisciplinary Interventions*. Alameda, CA: Latham Foundation.

Arkow, P. (2004). *Animal-assisted Therapy and Activities: A Study, Resource Guide and Bibliography for the Use of Companion Animals in Selected Therapies* (9th ed.). Stratford, NJ: Author.

Arkow, P. (2006). "Old wine in a new bottle": new strategies for humane education. In A. H. Fine (Ed.), *Handbook on Animal-assisted Therapy: Theoretical Foundations and Guidelines for Practice* (2nd ed.). (pp. 425–452) San Diego, CA: Academic Press.

Arluke, A. (2003). Childhood origins of supernurturance: the social context of early humane behavior. *Anthrozoös, 16*(1), 3–27.

Arluke, A., & Luke, C. (1997). Physical cruelty toward animals in Massachusetts, 1975–1996. *Society and Animals, 5*(3), 195–204.

Ascione, F. R. (1998). Battered women's reports of their partners' and their children's cruelty to animals. *Journal of Emotional Abuse, 1*, 119–133.

Ascione, F. R. (2005). *Children and Animals: Exploring the Roots of Kindness and Cruelty*. West Lafayette, IN: Purdue University Press.

Ascione, F. R. (2009). *Animal abuse: an overview of current research for human and animal welfare professionals. Presentation at Cruelty/Crime Connection: Breaking the Chain Symposium.* Edmonton: Alberta SPCA. Oct. 8–9.

Ascione, F. R. & Arkow, P. (Eds.), (1999). *Child Abuse, Domestic Violence and Animal Abuse: Linking the Circles of Compassion for Prevention and Intervention.* West Lafayette, IN: Purdue University Press.

Ascione, F. R., Kaufmann, M. E., & Brooks, S. M. (2000). Animal abuse and developmental psychopathology: recent research, programmatic and therapeutic issues, and challenges for the future. In A. H. Fine (Ed.), *Handbook on Animal-assisted Therapy: Theoretical Foundations and Guidelines for Practice* (2nd ed.). (pp. 325–354) San Diego, CA: Academic Press.

Ascione, F. R., & Weber, C. V. (1996). Children's attitudes about the humane treatment of animals and empathy: one-year follow-up of a school-based intervention. *Anthrozoös, 9* (4), 188–195.

Associated Press. (2001, July 12). Prehistoric engravings found in France. *The Philadelphia Inquirer,* p. A1.

Associated Press. (2009). Schools fight families over autism service dogs. Retrieved Oct. 4, 2009, from http://www.msnbc.com

Association of Professional Humane Educators. (2006). *Professional Guidelines for Humane Educators.* Alameda, CA: Author.

Battle, T. (2003). *Learning to Care through Kindness to Animals: A Guide for Teachers.* Edmonton: Alberta Teachers' Association.

Beyke, A. (2002). Project Second Chance: kids helping animals, animals helping kids. *The Latham Letter, 23*(4), 6–7.

Bierer, R. E. (2001). The relationship between pet bonding, self esteem, and empathy in preadolescents. *Dissertation Abstracts International, 61*(11-B), 6183.

Bjerke, T., & Ostdahl, T. (2004). Animal-related attitudes and activities in an urban population. *Anthrozoös, 17*(2), 109–129.

Blackford, Mrs. (1840). *The Scottish Orphans: A Moral Tale Founded Upon a Historical Fact and Calculated to Improve the Minds of Young People.* Philadelphia: John B. Perry.

Burlington County Firemen's Association. (1922). *Historical Issue: Sketches of Fire Companies of Burlington County.* Mount Holly, NJ: Author.

Cobb, L. (1832). *Cobb's Juvenile Reader No. 2 Containing Interesting, Moral, and Instructive Reading Lessons Composed of One, Two, and Three Syllables.* Philadelphia: Thomas L. Bonsal.

Colimore, E. (2009, Sept. 16). How Jackson moved nations: letter found that led to tribes' "Trail of Tears." *The Philadelphia Inquirer,* pp. A1, A17.

Correctional Service of Canada, Office of the Deputy Commissioner for Women. (1998). *Literature Review: Pet Facilitated Therapy in Correctional Institutions.* Ottawa: Author.

Cournoyer, G. P., & Uttley, C. (2007). Cisco's Kids: a pet assisted therapy behavioral intervention program. *Journal of Emotional Abuse, 7*(3), 117–126.

Cramer, J., & Crawford, T. (2009). Reaching Hands Ranch. *The Latham Letter, 30*(4,6), 12–13.

Currie, C. L. (2006). Animal cruelty by children exposed to domestic violence. *Child Abuse and Neglect, 30*(4), 425–435.

Cutlip, S. M. (1990). *Fund Raising in the United States.* Piscataway, NJ: Transaction Publishers.

Daggett, H. (1792). *The Rights of Animals: An Oration Delivered at the Commencement of Providence College, September 7, 1791, by Herman Daggett, Candidate for the Master's Degree.* Sagg Harbour, NY: Frothingham.

Davis, K. (2007). *Perspectives of Youth in an Animal-Centered Correctional Vocational Program: A Qualitative Evaluation of Project POOCH*. Baltimore, MD: Presentation at National Technology Assessment Workshop on Animal- Assisted Programs for Youth at Risk. Dec. 6–7.

DeGrave, J. (1999). People and Animals Learning: the PAL program. In F. R. Ascione & P. Arkow (Eds.), *Child Abuse, Domestic Violence, and Animal Abuse: Linking the Circles of Compassion for Prevention and Intervention* (pp. 410–423). West Lafayette, IN: Purdue University Press.

Delta Society. (2009). Pet Partners—state by state. *Interactions, 27*(2), 11–24.

DeViney, E., Dickert, J., & Lockwood, R. (1983). The care of pets within child abusing families. *International Journal for the Study of Animal Problems, 4*, 321–329.

Dickinson, E. E. (2008). The future of incarceration, and a brief history. *Architect, 97*(8), 66–71.

Doris Day Animal Foundation. (2005). *The Empathy Connection*. Washington, DC: Author.

Dumb Friends League. (2009). *Humane Education Programs*. Denver, CO: Author.

Eddy, S. J. (1899). *Friends and Helpers*. Publisher unknown.

Endenburg, N., & Baarda, B. (1995). The role of pets in enhancing human well-being: effects on child development. In I. Robinson (Ed.), *The Waltham Book of Human-Animal Interaction: Benefits and Responsibilities of Pet Ownership* (pp. 7–17). Exeter: Pergamon.

Federated Humane Societies of Pennsylvania. (2000). *Humane Education Guidebook*. New York: ASPCA.

Fine, A. H. (2006). Incorporating animal-assisted therapy into psychotherapy: guidelines and suggestions for therapists. In A. H. Fine (Ed.), *Handbook on Animal-assisted Therapy: Theoretical Foundations and Guidelines for Practice* (2nd ed.). (pp. 167–206) San Diego, CA: Academic Press.

Foer, J.S. (2006, Nov. 27). My life as a dog [Op-Ed]. *The New York Times*, p. A6.

Forman, G. (2007). Teach your children well: how animals make kids better human beings. *The Latham Letter, 28*(1), 4.

Frasch, P. D., Otto, S. K., Olsen, K. M., & Ernest, P. A. (1999). State animal anti-cruelty statutes: an overview. *Animal Law, 5*, 69–80.

Frick, P. J., VanHorn, Y., Lahey, B. B., Christ, M. A. G., Loeber, R., Hart, E. A., et al. (1993). Oppositional defiant disorder and conduct disorder: a meta-analytic review of factor analysis and cross-validation in a clinical sample. *Clinical Psychology Review, 13*, 319–340.

Friesen, L. (2009). *A review of the literature: animal-assisted therapy with children. Presentation at 18th Annual Conference, International Society for Anthrozoology*. Kansas City, MO, Oct. 20–23.

Furst, G. (2006). Prison-based animal programs: a national survey. *Prison Journal, 86*(4), 407–430.

Granger, B. P., & Kogan, L. R. (2006). Characteristics of animal-assisted therapy/activity in specialized settings. In A. H. Fine (Ed.), *Handbook on Animal-assisted Therapy: Theoretical Foundations and Guidelines for Practice* (2nd ed.). (pp. 263–286) San Diego, CA: Academic Press.

Gullone, E., & Clarke, J. P. (2008). Animal abuse, cruelty, and welfare: an Australian perspective. In F. R. Ascione (Ed.), *International Handbook of Animal Abuse and Cruelty: Theory, Research, and Application* (pp. 305–334). West Lafayette, IN: Purdue University Press.

Harbolt, T., & Ward, T. H. (2001). Teaming incarcerated youth with shelter dogs for a second chance. *Society and Animals, 9*(2), 177–182.

Hart, E. (2009). *Assessment of the All Ears Reading Program. Presentation at 1st Human Animal Interaction Conference, Research Center for Human-Animal Interaction*. Kansas City, MO, Oct. 22–25.

Henry, B. C., & Sanders, C. E. (2007). Bullying and animal abuse: is there a connection? *Society and Animals, 15*(2), 107–126.

Hergovich, A., Monshi, B., Semmler, G., & Zieglmayer, V. (2002). The effects of the presence of a dog in the classroom. *Anthrozoös, 15*(1), 37–50.

Humane Education Trust. (2003). *Why Humane Education is Crucial to Society.* Cape Town, South Africa: Author.

Humane Society of the City of New York. (1810). *A Report of a Committee of the Humane Society Appointed to Inquire into the Number of Tavern Licenses; the Manner of Granting Them; their Effects Upon the Community; and the Other Sources of Vice and Misery in this City; and to visit Bridewell.* New York: Collins and Perkins.

Humane Society of the Commonwealth of Massachusetts. (1786). *The Institution of the Humane Society of the Commonwealth of Massachusetts.* Boston: Author.

Humane Society of Massachusetts. (1845). *History of the Humane Society of Massachusetts.* Boston: Samuel N. Dickinson.

Humane Society of Philadelphia. (1788). *Directions for Recovering Persons, Who are Supposed to be Dead, from Drowning, also for Preventing & Curing the Disorders Produced by Drinking Cold Liquors, and by the Action of Noxious Vapors, Lightning, and Excessive Heat and Cold, Upon the Human Body.* Philadelphia: Joseph James.

Johnson, I. T. (Ed.), (1900). *Young People's Natural History: A Popular Story of Animals, Birds, Reptiles, Fishes and Insects, Describing their Structure, Habits, Instincts and Dwellings, with Thrilling Stories of Adventure and Amusing Anecdotes of Wild and Tame Animals.* Chicago: A.B. Kuhlman & Co.

Johnson, S. (1755/1983). *A Dictionary of the English Language.* Reprinted London: Times Books.

Kagan, E. (2009). In *U.S. vs. Robert J. Stevens, on writ of certiorari to the U.S. Court of Appeals for the Third Circuit: Reply brief for the United States No. 08-769.* Washington, DC: Office of the Solicitor General.

Katz, L. (2004). Join the club! Humane society shares a wealth of knowledge. *ASPCA Animal Watch, 24*(3), 40.

Kellert, S. R. (1989). Perceptions of animals in America. In R. J. Hoage (Ed.), *Perceptions of Animals in American Culture* (pp. 5–24). Washington, DC: Smithsonian Institution Press.

Kruger, K. A., Trachtenberg, S. W., & Serpell, J. A. (2004). *Can Animals Help Humans Heal? Animal-assisted Interventions in Adolescent Mental Health.* Philadelphia: University of Pennsylvania School of Veterinary Medicine Center for the Interaction of Animals and Society.

Kurtz, M., & Leger, H. (2009). *The use of animal-assisted therapy in reading intervention programs. Presentation at 18th Annual Conference, International Society for Anthrozoology.* Kansas City, MO, Oct. 20–23.

Lacroix, C. A. (1999). Another weapon for combating family violence: prevention of animal abuse. In F. R. Ascione & P. Arkow (Eds.), *Child Abuse, Domestic Violence, and Animal Abuse: Linking the Circles of Compassion for Prevention and Intervention* (pp. 62–82). West Lafayette, IN: Purdue University Press.

The Latham Foundation. (1993). *Garden Therapy.* Alameda, CA: Author. [Motion picture].

The Latham Foundation. (2004). *Breaking the Cycles of Violence.* Alameda, CA: Author. [Motion picture].

Lathrop, J. (1787). *Discourse Before the Humane Society in Boston, Delivered on the Second Tuesday of June.* Boston: E. Russell.

Levinson, B. (1984). Foreword. In P. Arkow (Ed.), *Dynamic Relationships in Practice: Animals in the Helping Professions* (pp. 1–20). Alameda, CA: Latham Foundation.

Loar, L., & Colman, L. (2004). *Teaching Empathy: Animal-assisted Therapy Programs for Children and Families Exposed to Violence—A Handbook for Therapists, Humane Educators, and Teachers.* Alameda CA: Latham Foundation.

Locke, J. (1705). *Some Thoughts Concerning Education.* London: A. and J. Churchill.

Luk, E. S. L., Staiger, P. K., Wong, L., & Mathai, J. (1999). Children who are cruel to animals: a revisit. *Australian and New Zealand Journal of Psychiatry, 33*, 29–36.

Melson, G. F. (1988). *Attachment to pets, empathy and self-concept in young children. Presentation at 7th annual conference, the Delta Society.* Orlando, FL, Sept. 29–Oct. 1.

Melson, G. F. (2001). *Why the Wild Things Are: Animals in the Lives of Children.* Cambridge, MA: Harvard University Press.

Melson, G. F., & Fogel, A. (1996). Parental perceptions of their children's involvement with household pets: a test of a specificity model of nurturance. *Anthrozoös, 9*, 95–106.

Merriam-Arduini, S. (2000). *Evaluation of an experimental program designed to have a positive effect on adjudicated violent, incarcerated male juveniles age 12–25 in the state of Oregon.* Unpublished doctoral dissertation. Pepperdine University.

Merz-Perez, L., & Heide, K. M. (2004). *Animal Cruelty: Pathway to Violence against People.* Walnut Creek, CA: AltaMira Press.

Mills, D. S., & De Keuster, T. (2009). Dogs in society can prevent society going to the dogs. *Veterinary Journal, 179*(3), 322–323.

Nagengast, S. L., Baun, M. M., Megel, M., & Liebowitz, J. M. (1997). The effects of the presence of a companion animal on physiological arousal and behavioral distress in children during a physical examination. *Journal of Pediatric Nursing, 12*(6), 323–330.

Nebbe, L. (2009). *Animals as part of the school counseling program. Presentation at 1st Human Animal Interaction Conference, Research Center for Human-Animal Interaction.* Kansas City, MO, Oct. 22–25.

O'Brien, H. (n.d.). *An Annotated Bibliography of Research Relevant to Humane Education.* East Haddam, CT: National Association for the Advancement of Humane Education.

Parish-Plass, N. (2008). Animal-assisted therapy with children suffering from insecure attachment due to abuse and neglect: a method to lower the risk of intergenerational transmission of abuse? *Clinical Child Psychology and Psychiatry, 13*(1), 7–30.

Pennsylvania Society for the Prevention of Cruelty to Animals. (1869). *Annual Report.* Philadelphia: Author.

Phillips, A., & McQuarrie, D. (2009). *Therapy Animals Supporting Kids (TASK) Program: Program Manual.* Englewood, CO: American Humane Association.

Poresky, R. H. (1990). The young children's empathy measure: reliability, validity and effects of companion animal bonding. *Psychological Reports, 66*, 931–936.

Putnam, R. D. (1996). The strange disappearance of civic America. *The American Prospect, 7*, 1–18.

Putnam, R. D. (2000). *Bowling Alone: The Collapse and Revival of American Community.* New York: Simon and Schuster.

Randour, M. L., & Davidson, H. (2008). *A Common Bond: Maltreated Children and Animals in the Home—Guidelines for Practice and Policy.* Englewood, CO: American Humane Association.

Rathmann, C. (1999). Forget Me Not Farm: teaching gentleness with gardens and animals to children from violent homes and communities. In F. R. Ascione & P. Arkow (Eds.), *Child Abuse, Domestic Violence, and Animal Abuse: Linking the Circles of Compassion for Prevention and Intervention* (pp. 393–409). West Lafayette, IN: Purdue University Press.

Riis, J. A. (1892). *The Children of the Poor.* New York: Charles Scribner's Sons.

Ritvo, H. (1987). *The Animal Estate: The English and Other Creatures in the Victorian Age.* Cambridge, MA: Harvard University Press.

Ross, S. B. (1999). Green Chimneys: we give troubled children the gift of caring. In F. R. Ascione & P. Arkow (Eds.), *Child Abuse, Domestic Violence, and Animal Abuse: Linking the Circles of Compassion for Prevention and Intervention* (pp. 367–379). West Lafayette, IN: Purdue University Press.

San Diego Humane Society and SPCA. (2005). Teaching children to respect animals has far-reaching effects. *Animal Fare, 40*(2), 1.

Saunders, M. (1895). *Beautiful Joe: The Autobiography of a Dog.* London: Jarrold and Sons.

Scobey, M.-M. & Graham, G. (Eds.), (1970). *To Nurture Humaneness: Commitment for the '70's.* Washington, DC: Association for Supervision and Curriculum Development.

Senechalle, J. A., & Dunn, R. M. (2004). University of Illinois students evaluate use and effectiveness of humane education materials. *The Latham Letter, 25*(3), 6–8.

Shultz, W. J. (1924). *The Humane Movement in the United States, 1910–1922.* New York: Columbia University Press.

Simpson, J. A., & Weiner, E. S. C. (1989). *The Oxford English Dictionary* (2nd ed.). Oxford: Clarendon Press.

Snyder, S. (2009, Oct. 2). A freshman's furry friend: nothing like a canine visitation to ease the loneliness of moving to campus. *The Philadelphia Inquirer*, p. B7.

Soltow, W. A., & Shepherd, J. (1992, November). Justifying humane education as a means to prevent child abuse and other violence. *Shelter Sense*, p. 3.

Strimple, E. O. (2003). A history of prison inmate-animal interaction programs. *Animal Behavior Scientist, 47*(1), 70–78.

ten Bensel, R. (1984). Historical perspectives of human values for animals and vulnerable people. In R. K. Anderson, B. L. Hart & L. A. Hart (Eds.), *The Pet Connection: Its Influence on our Health and Quality of LIFE* (pp. 2–14). Minneapolis: University of Minnesota/CENSHARE.

Thomas, S. C., & Beirne, P. (2002). Humane education and humanistic philosophy: toward a new curriculum. *Journal of Humanistic Counseling, Education and Development, 41*, 190–199.

Thoreau, H. D. (1854). *Walden.* Princeton: Princeton University Press. Reprinted 1971.

Thoreau, H. D. (1865). *Cape Cod.* Princeton: Princeton University Press. Reprinted 1993.

Underwood, T. (n.d.). The History of the Easton Fire Department. Retrieved Oct. 4, 2009 from http://www.easton-pa.gov

Unti, B., & DeRosa, B. (2003). Humane education past, present, and future. In D. J. Salem & A. N. Rowan (Eds.), *The State of the Animals II 2003* (pp. 27–50). Washington, DC: Humane Society of the US.

Vachss, A. (2005). Foreword. In F. R. Ascione (Ed.), *Children and Animals: Exploring the Roots of Kindness and Cruelty* (pp. xiii–xvi). West Lafayette, IN: Purdue University Press.

Vizek-Vidovic, V., Arambasic, L., Kerestes, G., Kuterovac-Jagodic, G., & Vlahovic-Stetic, V. (2001). Pet ownership in childhood and socio-emotional characteristics, work values and professional choices in early adulthood. *Anthrozoös, 14*(4), 224–231.

Weil, Z. (2004). *The Power and Promise of Humane Education.* Gabriola Island, BC, Canada: New Society Publishers.

Wishnik, Y. (2003). *Humane Education Learning Community: A California Public Charter School Proposal Presented to the Governing Board of the San Juan Unified School District.* Citrus Heights, CA: California Teachers Association Humane Education Learning Community Charter School Development Team.

Wood, L., Gills-Corti, B., & Bulsara, M. (2005). The pet connection: pets as a conduit for social capital? *Social Science and Medicine, 61*, 1159–1173.

Wynne-Tyson, J. (1990). *The Extended Circle: An Anthology of Humane Thought.* London: Sphere Books.

Yao, S. (2003). A valuable lesson: SPCALA's humane education department works to break the cycle of violence and abuse. *The Latham Letter, 24*(4), 18–19.

23 Welfare considerations in therapy and assistance animals

J.A. Serpell*, R. Coppinger[†], A.H. Fine[‡], J.M. Peralta[§]

* University of Pennsylvania, [†] Hampshire College, [‡] California State Polytechnic University, [§] Western University

23.1 Introduction

Throughout history, people have used animals—whether for food, fiber, sport, adornment, labor or companionship—as a means of satisfying human ends and interests. But animals also have interests—in avoiding pain, fear, distress or physical harm, and in pursuing their own needs, desires and goals (DeGrazia, 1996). Relations between human and non-human animals become morally problematical where there is a conflict of interests between the two: where the human use of the animal either causes the latter pain, fear or harm, or it in some way thwarts or prevents the animal from satisfying its own needs and goals.

During the last 20 years, purveyors and proponents of animal-assisted interventions (AAI)[1] such as the Delta Society have made concerted efforts to professionalize the "industry," and establish selection and training standards that aim to minimize the risks of harm to all concerned, including the animals (Hines and Fredrickson, 1998). However, the field has experienced explosive growth in recent years and, in many cases, these standards have been established in the absence of any systematic or empirical evaluation of the potential risks to animals imposed by current practices. Indeed, the general but unsubstantiated feeling across the industry is that these are "good" activities for animals to be engaged in. The fact that a large number of animals fail to respond to the nurturing and training they receive has not generally been taken as evidence that they do not want to, or are unable to, participate. Instead, practitioners tend to respond to failure by changing the selection or the training procedures, as if the animals are theoretically capable of responding positively to any demands made of them. Indeed, with the laudable exception of some contributions to this volume, it is unusual to find more than a passing reference to animal welfare concerns in any recent review of risk factors in the AAI field (see, e.g., Brodie et al., 2002).

---

[1] Animal-assisted interventions are defined here as, "any therapeutic intervention that intentionally includes or incorporates animals as part of the therapeutic process or milieu" (see Kruger et al., 2004).

Handbook on Animal-Assisted Therapy. DOI: 10.1016/B978-0-12-381453-1.10023-6

Much of the rest of this *Handbook* has been devoted to demonstrating how the use of therapy and assistance animals significantly enhances human health and well-being. The primary question we address in this chapter is whether this end morally justifies the means of achieving it. Specifically, our goal is to re-examine the animal/human partnership from the animal's viewpoint to see what the benefits might be for the animal, or to see if the raising, training, and use of therapy and assistance animals is causing significant degradation in their welfare. In doing so, however, we recognize that there is a serious shortage of reliable scientific evidence to reinforce some of our claims and suggestions.

Behnke (2005) points out that the ability to use ethical judgment and discretion are defining features of the helping professions, and that arriving at an ethical course of action implies weighing and balancing the values of professional knowledge and realizing that complex situations do not necessarily result in simplistic solutions. With these observations in mind, we urge practitioners and clinicians to examine their ethical responsibilities for the welfare of their therapeutic adjuncts, and insure that the safety and well-being of these animals are safeguarded at all times.

23.2   General welfare considerations

The term "animal welfare" generally refers to the state of an animal, and the extent to which it can be said to be faring well or ill in a particular situation or at a particular point in its life. Different animal welfare experts tend to give priority to different aspects of an animal's state when assessing its welfare: some emphasize unpleasant or pleasant subjective feelings (Boissy et al., 2007; Dawkins, 1980; Duncan, 1993), while others focus on the animal's ability to express "natural" or species-typical behavior (Rollin, 1995), or its capacity to adapt to, or cope with, the demands of its environment (Broom and Fraser, 2007). An animal's welfare can also be said to be broadly synonymous with its quality of life (Duncan and Fraser, 1997). For the purposes of this review, we will consider welfare as comprising all of these different ideas and concepts.

23.2.1   The Five Freedoms

Although different kinds of welfare problems attend the specific roles and activities performed by different classes of therapy or assistance animal, there are some basic welfare considerations that tend to apply to all of them regardless of how they are used. Most authorities accept that these basic considerations are reasonably well summarized by the "five freedoms," originally formulated by the so-called "Brambell Report" (Command Paper 2836, 1965). This original report described the need to provide animals with the opportunity or freedom "to stand up, lie down, turn around, groom themselves and stretch their limbs." The Five Freedoms were further refined and expanded by the Farm Animal Welfare Council in the early 1990s to take their most current form (FAWC, 2009):

1. *Freedom from thirst, hunger and malnutrition*—by ready access to fresh water and a diet to maintain full health and vigor.

2. *Freedom from discomfort*—by providing a suitable environment including shelter and a comfortable resting area.

3. *Freedom from pain, injury and disease*—by prevention and/or rapid diagnosis and treatment.

4. *Freedom from fear and distress*—by ensuring conditions that avoid mental suffering.

5. *Freedom to express most normal behavior*—by providing sufficient space, proper facilities and company of the animal's own kind.

Of these "freedoms," the fifth is the probably the hardest to define and the easiest to overlook or ignore. While it is obvious to most people that animals have physical requirements for adequate food, water, protection from the elements, and so on, it is much less widely acknowledged that animals also have social and behavioral needs (Dawkins, 1983; Hughes and Duncan, 1988), and that these needs differ markedly between species (Mason and Mendl, 1993). Understanding animals' social and behavioral needs by primary caregivers is part of the ethical obligation attending animal ownership and use. It is of some concern, therefore, that few practitioners in the AAI field receive adequate ethological training on such matters. Judging the value of a particular behavior or social interaction to an animal may sometimes be difficult. However, in general, if an animal is strongly internally motivated to perform a particular behavior or social interaction, and if its motivation to perform appears to increase following a period of deprivation, it is an indication that the activity or interaction is probably important to the maintenance of that animal's welfare. Common indications of deprivation include animals performing abnormally high frequencies of displacement or vacuum[2] activities, repetitive or stereotypic behavior, apathy and prolonged inactivity, and/or self-mutilation (Broom and Johnson, 1993; Dawkins, 1988).

Conversely, and in contrast to free-living animals, most therapy and assistance animals are trapped in systems where they have little control over their social lives, and where they cannot avoid or escape unwelcome or unpleasant social intrusions. Denying animals control over their physical and social environment is also known to have adverse effects on their physical and mental well-being (Hubrecht, 1995). Animals need to have an opportunity to habituate to the environment and to the activities in which they are involved. This allows them to adapt to the situation and cope with potential sources of distress or discomfort. If a stressful situation overwhelms the animal, the animal's welfare will be dramatically compromised. Fine and Eisen (2008) reveal a case study where they discussed a few occasions where therapy dogs were integral in the treatment of an extremely active child diagnosed with ADHD. Close attention needed to be given to assure that the animals were not overwhelmed or became anxious at times where the stimulation was high (loud noises or over-petting). They recommended that clinicians must be cognizant of what occurs within therapy and its impact on their therapy animal. If any signs are noticed, there needs to be an opportunity for respite or refuge for the animal.

---

[2] Displacement activities involve the performance of seemingly irrelevant acts, such as grooming, scratching, yawning or feeding, out of context in situations that excite conflicting motivational tendencies, thwarting or frustration. A vacuum activity is the performance of a particular behavior pattern in the absence of its normal eliciting stimulus: e.g. sham feeding in the absence of food (Hinde, 1970).

For service and therapy animals, problems of basic welfare are most likely to arise in circumstances where animals are either residential within health care settings, or spend large amounts of time in holding facilities such as kennels or stables. In the former context, inadequate advance planning, selection, and staff commitment and oversight can lead to animals being improperly cared for (Hines and Fredrickson, 1998). Small mammals, birds and reptiles that are caged or confined are probably at greater risk of neglect or improper care, and non-domestic species that tend to have more specialized requirements than domestic ones are also likely to be at greater risk. "Improperly cared for" in these contexts should have the broadest definition. Most often it is defined as animals that are inadequately fed, watered or cleaned. However, any failure to attend to individual needs should be regarded as improper care. Overfeeding animals to the point of obesity is just as negligent as underfeeding. Giving an animal the opportunity to exercise or interact with conspecifics is not enough without insuring that the individual takes advantage of the opportunity.

23.2.2 Aging and retirement issues

Further welfare challenges arise when therapy and assistance animals begin to age. Many dogs, for instance, display clear evidence of progressive cognitive as well as physical impairment associated with aging, including disorientation, failure to recognize familiar individuals, restlessness, and house-soiling (Neilson et al., 2001). Naturally, under these circumstances, an animal's schedule for therapeutic involvement will need to be curtailed. This may cause some disruption and adjustment for both the clinician and the animal, although careful planning may help to mitigate this. Each case should be handled individually to ensure that the needs of the animal are best met. In some cases, it may be ideal to stop using the elderly animal altogether. However, if the animal has grown accustomed to participating in therapy sessions for many years and finds a sudden and radical change in schedule or activities this too may be stressful. It is imperative for the therapist to appreciate the animal's age and physical health. Adjustments need to be made, and the first priority should be the welfare of the animal. If in doubt, it may be a good idea to consult with an impartial third party, such as the animal's veterinarian or an animal behaviorist.

Based on observations when his first therapy dog (Puppy) began aging and slowing down, one of the present authors noted that, despite her decline in energy, she remained eager to go to work. Every day, Puppy would be found next to the door when it was time to leave for work. Curtailing her work schedule had been a consideration for a few months, since she appeared tired and deserving of a break. However, when left at home, she seemed unhappy and would just lie next to the door. This was a dog that was used to being on the go. Altering her activities without any proper planning appeared to be devastating, especially because it modified her daily routine (Fine, personal observation). A transition plan was therefore formulated that allowed Puppy to have an adjusted schedule, with plenty of opportunities for respite and sleep. A day bed was set up for Puppy in one of the conference rooms. When she was tired, Puppy quickly learned that she could retreat to the room and nap for as long she needed. Whenever she rested, the clients were told that she was not to be disturbed. Some of the children just wanted to stick in their heads and see her. We eventually shortened her day at the office, which did not seem to bother her. She would just be picked up earlier in the day and went home and relaxed. Puppy lived until the ripe age of 14. She passed away on a weekend, actually working a few days before her death. By planning for retirement and making provisions for her, Puppy was able to preserve her sense of integrity. Attention was given to her health as well as her emotional well-being. Throughout her final years of therapy, Puppy received frequent health checks by a veterinarian to assess her health and to monitor her capabilities of continuing her therapy role. This process has now been followed with several of the writer's older animals. The approach seems to be the most humane for all parties involved and is strongly recommended for older therapy animals.

23.2.3 The problem of stress

As originally defined by Hans Selye (1957), stress is the body's natural physiological response to environmental stressors. The processes underlying this stress response are now reasonably well understood: when humans and other animals are subjected to unpleasant or painful stimuli, their bodies respond by secreting a group of hormones from the hypothalamus, and the pituitary and adrenal (HPA) glands. These hormones ordinarily serve to prepare the body for so-called "fight or flight" reactions, and, once the emergency is over, hormone secretion generally declines to a normal baseline level. However, under certain circumstances, particularly when the source of pain, anxiety or distress cannot be readily avoided or controlled, the stress response of the HPA system may become prolonged or "chronic," thereby producing a number of deleterious consequences for the health and welfare of the individual. It is essentially impossible to know precisely what levels of stress an individual is experiencing at any given moment. Instead, we are reliant on various indirect measures or "indicators" including levels of stress hormones (cortisol, catecholamines, etc.) in body fluids— blood, saliva, urine, etc.—and outward manifestations of stress involving overt changes in behavior. Behavioral indicators of stress vary greatly between species, and in many they have never been studied or described in any detail. In the dog, studies and anecdotal observations suggest that sweating paws, salivating, panting, muscle tension, restlessness, body shaking, paw lifting, yawning, aggression, hypervigilance, and intensified startle reflex may all be behavioral manifestations of stress (Beerda et al., 1998, 1999; Butler, 2004), while in cats, alert inactivity, tense muscle tone, crouching posture, and pupil dilation may be indicative (McCobb et al., 2005). In horses, signs of stress can be characterized by vocalization, pawing, increased inci- dence of head movements, increased aggression, sweating, and increased respiratory and heart rates (Kay and Hall, 2009; Stull, 1997). Unfortunately, in other species of animals that can be used in therapy, such as reptiles or fish, the signs of stress may be harder to identify. In general terms, attempts by the animals to escape or increased propensity towards aggressive behaviors can be perceived as signs of discomfort, distress or stress. Therapists must pay close attention to the animals and be aware of stressful signs. Beyond that, detailed attention to the animals and their actions, supported by a precise knowledge of the species characteristics and behaviors, both normal and abnormal, is required to make an adequate assessment.

There are many potential sources of chronic stress in the lives of therapy and assistance animals. Trainers, practitioners and end-users of these animals should be educated to recognize the warning signs and act accordingly. It is ideal if stressful situations are anticipated and corrected before the animal shows signs of being affected. Planning for regular breaks in between therapy sessions in which animals are given an opportunity to rest and are given positive human contact, if appropriate, can alleviate the effects that potentially stressful situations may have on them. If a stressful situation presents, prompt action to ameliorate its impact on the animal's welfare is required. This may result in the removal of the animal from the stressful environment, giving time for the animal to fully recover.

23.2.4 Use of non-domestic species

Most domestic animals have been selected to show a higher degree of tolerance of stressful situations and stimuli compared with non-domestic species, even those reared entirely in captivity (Hemmer, 1990). The implications of this are that, if a particular animal-assisted intervention or activity is stressful or potentially stressful for a domestic species, such as a dog, cat or horse, it is likely to be even more so for a non-domestic one. The majority of wild animals kept in captivity also have more specialized nutritional and husbandry needs than their domestic counterparts and, in many cases, their specific needs and requirements are not as well known, greatly increasing the likelihood that they will receive inadequate care unless practitioners, staff, and consulting veterinarians are properly versed in their particular species-specific requirements. Clinicians should become educated on proper handling, nutrition and care of these animals so that they are not inappropriately interacted with. These unsuitable actions could lead to behavioral and physical challenges. Non-domestic species are also harder to train, and their entrained responses extinguish more quickly in the absence of appropriate reinforcement. Some species, such as parrots and many non-human primates, are also highly intelligent and socially manipulative (Cheney and Seyfarth, 1990), and this tends to make them potentially unreliable or disruptive as social companions. All of these factors render non-domestic species less suitable for use in AAA/T and assistance animal programs, and more likely to experience welfare problems if used.

Among therapy animals, this point is well illustrated by the increasing use of parrots in residential settings, such as hospices, long-term care facilities, and correctional institutions. Recent advances in avian medicine, nutrition, and behavior reveal that most of these birds have highly specialized needs relating to air quality, nutrition, lighting, housing, sleep, and both environmental and social enrichment. Since avian wellness and welfare is difficult to maintain in institutional contexts due to a lack of centralized, informed, and consistent care, it should be questioned whether it is ethically appropriate to place birds in these settings at all (Anderson et al., 2005).

Similar concerns are raised by recent efforts to train and use capuchin monkeys (*Cebus* sp.) to assist profoundly disabled people. In most cases, these programs have found it necessary to neuter and surgically extract the canine teeth from the monkeys before they can be used safely with such vulnerable human partners. Monkeys may also be required to wear remotely controlled, electric shock-collars or harnesses in order to provide the user with a means of controlling the animal's potentially aggressive and unreliable behavior. Clearly, the necessity of using of such extreme and invasive measures raises doubts about the practical value of such programs, as well as serious ethical questions concerning the welfare of the animals involved.

23.3   Animals used in therapy

Although the boundary may at times seem blurred, particularly with respect to so-called "emotional support animals" (ESAs),[3] a reasonably clear distinction exists between therapy animals and service (or assistance) animals, at least in the USA. However, whereas service animals are relatively strictly defined under federal law (Americans with Disabilities Act, 1990), therapy animals form a heterogeneous category that can encompass everything from pet visitation to swim-with-dolphins programs (Iannuzzi and Rowan, 1991). The particular welfare issues confronting therapy animals are therefore correspondingly diverse.

23.3.1 Animal visitation programs

The majority of therapy animals are personal pets (usually dogs) that, together with their owners, provide supervised visitation programs to hospitals, nursing homes, special-population schools, and other treatment centers (Duncan, 2000). Such animals (and their human partners) are typically certified as being suitable for the task of visiting based on their responses to simplified temperament tests. However, while most such tests evaluate the animal's reaction to acute stressors, and their willingness to tolerate intimate or invasive handling by strangers, rarely if ever do they attempt to ask the animal if he or she is actually motivated to interact socially with unfamiliar humans given the choice. As one author on the subject points out, the distinction is a crucial one:

> Nothing else dogs do compares to the kinds of intrinsically stressful social interactions that take place when they visit clinical, educational, or post-trauma situations. No other canine-related event, no sport nor competition requires a dog to enter the intimate zones of unfamiliar humans and remain there for several minutes of petting and hugging...Most dogs have been bred for generations to distinguish between outsiders and the family, and to act accordingly. There has never been a breed of dog designed to enjoy encroachment from strangers. Dogs who actually enjoy interactions in clinical and educational settings are very rare, and the uniqueness of their talent should be appreciated.
>
> (Butler, 2004, p. 31)

[3] See Grubb (2005). http://www.gdui.org/cado.html, Dec. 6, 2005. http://www.bazelon.org/issues/housing/infosheets/fhinfosheet6.html, Dec. 6, 2005.

Even if this last sentence might be considered exaggerated by some, the fact remains that visiting animals rarely enter therapeutic settings of their own volition, and many of them are likely to find the experience of being constantly approached and handled by strangers—often strangers with abnormal behavior or demeanor—stressful and/or anxiety-provoking. If this is the case with dogs, it is reasonable to conclude that the other species occasionally used in visitation programs are even more likely to experience welfare problems.

Signs of stress-related fatigue are commonly reported in visiting therapy animals, leading some practitioners to conclude that such visits should be limited to one hour or less (Iannuzzi and Rowan, 1991). As one author notes, "[E]thical handlers develop time frames and environmental policies that allow their dogs to visit only within environments that are comfortable for them, and they leave before, not after, their dogs develop major symptoms of stress" (Butler, 2004, p. 37). Unfortunately, many handlers appear oblivious to the stress signals emitted by their animals, perhaps because they enjoy the social aspects of visitation more than their dogs do. In these cases, it is important that the handler or the therapist be responsible for the animal participating in a visitation therapy program and actively assess the animal's status for changes in behavior. This will allow for the anticipation of situations that may cause stress to the animal. This problem-solving process should lead to the establishment of the necessary modifications to the visit or to the prompt removal of the animal from the stressful environment before clear signs of discomfort appear. A good knowledge of the individual animal's behavior is required to pick on the subtle cues that the animal gives to show its discontent or tiredness. For example, bringing a therapy dog on a unit for youth with psychiatric disorders, the therapist must be aware of unusual behaviors that the dog may emit which may be demonstrative of various stressors. When this occurs, the animal should be removed from the situation and plans must be made to avoid further discomfort. Even if the handler has no precise knowledge of the dog, the presence of some general signs of stress, such as body stiffness, lowered tail, whining or increased panting, without any other obvious reason, should lead to an assessment of the animal and, even if in doubt, to its removal from the specific situation.

23.3.2   Residential programs

Although reliable evidence is lacking, the potential for stress-related fatigue or "burnout" in therapy animals is probably greatest among residential programs—prisons, nursing homes, inpatient psychiatric hospitals, long-term care facilities, etc.—where the animals are potentially "on duty" all day, every day of the year (Iannuzzi and Rowan, 1991). Animals housed in residential settings must therefore be provided with adequate "downtime" as well as access to comfortable and safe havens where they can escape entirely from the attentions of residents should they wish to. A minimum number of opportunities for resting need to be included in the daily schedule and planned to be of appropriate length and as often as required depending on the potential for stress associated with the specific animal use. Unfortunately, none of the associations representing therapy animals have prescribed a protocol to identify a realistic length of time that an animal should be in therapy sessions without a break.

This must be considered, and prescribed breaks and respite should be implemented. However, due to individual differences in animals and various species, adjustments must be made on an individual basis. The authors urge the readers to take this into strong consideration to assure that ample time is given to animals to relax. It is better to do it this way rather than wait until the animal shows signs of being fatigued.

While the goals of therapy or rehabilitation may be enhanced by encouraging inmates and residents to participate in the care and training of such animals, it is essential that these activities are appropriately supervised, and that one of more staff persons is fully committed to accepting primary responsibility for insuring the welfare and well-being of the animals. The lack of a clear "chain of command" with respect to animal care responsibilities is the most frequently cited reason why animals' needs are sometimes neglected in residential facilities. Regular, routine veterinary examinations should also be required both to monitor the animals' health and to evaluate their stress status (Iannuzzi and Rowan, 1991).

The potential for serious animal abuse and cruelty is probably also greatest in residential programs, particularly those based in correctional or psychiatric facilities. Although thankfully rare, occasional cases of outright cruelty to therapy animals have been reported or alluded to in the literature, usually in situations in which the human/animal interactions have not been closely supervised (Doyle, 1975; Levinson, 1971; Mallon, 1994a,b). Once again, this speaks to the necessity of establishing clear and careful guidelines regarding staff oversight and control of all animal-based interventions.

23.3.3 *Animals in individual counseling and psychotherapy*

As in most animal visitation programs, the animals used in individual counseling and therapy are usually the therapist's own pets. The ethical responsibilities and obligations attending this type of AAI are therefore comparable to those attending pet ownership, although with additional risks associated with exposure to potentially unpredictable clients. For obvious reasons, most clinicians would be ill-advised to employ any animal as a co-therapist unless they are already very familiar with, and confident about, its particular characteristics and temperament, and possess sufficient knowledge, time and resources to insure that its welfare needs can be accommodated at all times.

There is also an additional concern associated with animals used in therapy, which will likely lead to a financial gain for the therapist. Pet owners have an ethical obligation to ensure the well-being of their animals in a manner that serves not only the owner's interests but also those of the animal. If this is done in a way that is fair to both owner and animal, it should lead to the meeting of the basic needs of the animals and the provision of a good quality of life. In cases where a therapist gains financially from the use of a therapy animal, this could potentially lead to the animal's quality of life being compromised. For example, utilizing an ailing or elderly animal because it is a favorite of the clients, may place the welfare of the animal at risk. The therapist may be inclined to continue using this animal because that pleases the client, but consideration needs to be given to the impact that these visits may have on the animal regardless of what may be good for the practice or even the clients. In these cases, it is the responsibility of the therapist to ensure that such conflicts of interest do not arise.

Animal-assisted therapists should also be cautious about how animals are introduced to their clients. They should make a special point at the outset of therapy to discuss with patients the importance of demonstrating kindness to the animals, and of avoiding behavior that might disturb or frighten them such as sudden or erratic movements, loud noises, or overvigorous physical interactions. Animals should never be placed in any situations where they could be at risk either physically or emotionally. This kind of orientation sets the stage for proper integration of the animal in a safe therapeutic partnership based on mutual respect.

It is also important to plan for what to do with the animals when not in use. Appropriate accommodations and supervision need to be provided to ensure the animal is safely and comfortably housed. A comfortable site to rest and, if outdoors, access to shelter from the environment must be provided. Dogs can be comfortable in a crate, but they should be taken out often, not confined for hours on end, as space may be too restrictive to allow for the necessary exercise and normal behaviors to take place. Ad libitum access to water is nearly always essential and food may be required depending on the nutritional needs of the animal. Tethering should be avoided unless for a very short period of time and while the animal is under proper supervision to prevent accidents. For social species, as dogs are, concerns about placing them in isolation need to be taken into consideration.

23.3.4 "Ecotherapy"

Along with the expanding popularity of ecotourism, the idea of restoring human health through contact with nature—or "ecotherapy"—is acquiring a growing following among alternative and complementary therapists. While in many such programs therapy involves contributing directly to wildlife rehabilitation or conservation projects, others promote recreational contact with wild animals, chiefly dolphins and other cetaceans, in natural, semi-natural or captive settings (Burls and Caan, 2005). So-called "dolphin-swim" programs of various kinds are proliferating worldwide at an alarming rate and, since the majority are based in developing countries, they are largely unregulated from an animal welfare perspective.[4] Several detailed studies have recently documented serious risks to the welfare and survival of cetaceans involved in these programs, particularly those involving captive animals that must be captured in the wild and, in some cases, transported for thousands of miles to established aquaria (Samuels and Bejder, 2004; Samuels et al., 2000). Capture is stressful, as is the grouping of dolphins in new pods. Additionally, these animals are forced to interact with humans, which often leads to chronic stress and to a higher prevalence of disease and injuries. Captive dolphins are often housed in small tanks and have little opportunity to retreat to a safe area away from people. Even if dolphins born in captivity are used, it is difficult to find any ethical justification at all

[4] http://www.onevoice-ear.org/english/campaigns/marine_mammals/victory_caribbean.html, Dec. 6, 2005. http://csiwhalesalive.org/csi05303.html, Dec. 6, 2005.

for supporting these kinds of interventions given the high costs and limited evidence of therapeutic efficacy of dolphin-swim programs (Humphries, 2003; Marino and Lilienfeld, 1998).

23.4 Service/assistance animals

The Americans with Disabilities Act (1990) defines a service animal as any guide dog, signal dog, or other animal individually trained to provide assistance to an individual with a disability. If they meet this definition, animals are considered service animals under the ADA regardless of whether they have been licensed or certified by a state or local government. Service animals typically perform some of the functions and tasks that the individual with a disability cannot perform for him- or herself: for example, guiding people with impaired vision, alerting persons with hearing impairments to sounds, pulling wheelchairs, carrying and picking up things for persons with mobility impairments, and assisting persons with mobility impairments with balance. Because of their relatively specialized functions, assistance animals are subjected to a more refined level of "processing" (e.g. controlled breeding, rearing, selection, training, etc.) compared with the average therapy animal, and this creates a set of particular welfare problems that are more or less unique to this class of animal.

23.4.1 Changes in social and physical environment

The lifecycle of the typical assistance animal generally involves a series of relatively abrupt changes in its social and physical environment. For such sociable and sensitive animals as dogs, these disruptions may give rise to welfare problems—a good example being the practice of rearing guide and service dogs in the enriched environment of a human foster home, and then kenneling them individually for months at a time as part of their final training (Hubrecht and Turner, 1998). At the end, when they are no longer useful to assist the person in need, they are often adopted out, which means they are uprooted from the environment where they had lived in most cases for several years and placed in a new home. Even though the physical care provided along the way may be appropriate, the psychological effects of all these changes are generally ignored or not properly mitigated. Such sudden and extreme changes in the animals' social and physical milieu appear to be highly stressful for some individuals (Coppinger and Zuccotti, 1999), not only affecting their immediate welfare but also potentially fostering obnoxious behaviors that may preclude successful training and placement later in life.

Assistance animals may also be at risk because of the changing nature of their relationships with successive human owners and handlers throughout their lives. Most of these animals are picked because they seek out social interactions with others, and because they form strong bonds of attachment for their human partners. Having to endure a succession of different handlers with different characteristics, experience, and motivations for "ownership" is likely to be particularly stressful for these individuals. Unfortunately, many assistance animal practitioners have little first-hand knowledge of animal needs other than hygienic, veterinary or training considerations, and with many agencies there is confusion as to who is responsible for the animals' social requirements. The organizations keeping and rearing these animals should recognize their ethical obligations by doing everything possible to minimize the distress caused by these difficult transitions.

24.4.2 Selecting and breeding animals for assistance work

Not all domestic animal species are practical for becoming assistance animals. Without belaboring the point it would be difficult to conceive of a guiding cat, or a hearing ear donkey. In practice, dogs may be the only domestic species that can be reliably trained to perform a wide variety of household tasks for a disabled person, but within the dog population as a whole there is considerable individual variation in the suitability of dogs for this type of work.

Some assistance dogs, such as the hearing ear dogs, are often obtained from animal shelters, partly out of a desire to rescue some of these otherwise forsaken animals. Recycling animals relinquished to shelters clearly has a beneficial welfare impact. Some practitioners, however, doubt the reliability of these reconditioned pets, fearing that latent, unacceptable behavior will emerge and cause injury to the person using the animal (Weiss and Greenberg, 1997). About half of all assistance animal agencies currently rely on shelter dogs, although identifying suitable dogs among the four to five million relinquished each year is a major problem. Hearing ear and therapy dogs are perhaps the easiest to locate since there are no size restrictions, but it is important to identify the animal before the abandonment and confinement process has a permanent damaging effect on its personality (Coppinger and Coppinger, 2001). Agencies using these dogs often have a prescribed test which the dog is required to pass in order to be accepted into a program (e.g. Weiss and Greenberg, 1997). However, personnel vary widely in their ability to interpret test results, and few of the tests have been properly validated (Weiss, 2002). Given the industry's need for qualified dogs, and the ethical benefits of using shelter animals, there is considerable room for improvement in the identification and distribution of serviceable animals from shelters.

In-house breeding programs are favored by guide dog and wheelchair dog organizations. Both kinds of agencies will also purchase dogs, and accept donated dogs. The primary reason for producing and buying dogs is to obtain animals of relatively uniform size, and of the desired temperament and behavioral characteristics. It is not necessarily that other breeds are temperamentally unsuited, but the task to be performed requires a dog with particular physical characteristics. Within the industry, most of the emphasis is on just three breeds: Labrador retrievers, German shepherds, and golden retrievers. Recently, more interest has also been shown in using cross-bred retrievers.

The vast majority of our modern sporting and working dogs originated from the results of random matings accomplished by the animals themselves, and accompanied by post-zygotic culling of unwanted animals. In the 19th century, a shift toward prezygotic selection began which has intensified ever since. Just prior to the beginning of the 20th century, breeds were created by hybridizing strains in order to achieve working excellence. The assumption behind this process is that excellence of form and behavior can be purified and preserved within a breed. Unfortunately, although such breeding practices do tend to produce uniformity of appearance and behavior within breeds, in the absence of periodic out-crossing, dogs generated by these systems tend to be more inbred and therefore more vulnerable to infectious disease, inbreeding depression, and the phenotypic expression of deleterious mutant alleles. These genetic defects may result in conditions that have a negative, possibly long-term, impact on the animals' welfare. Even if animals with genetic defects are not used for assistance and are placed in adoptive homes, the effect of the impairment on their welfare may last for the rest of their lives. This should remain a concern to those involved in these breeding programs. Overall, these kinds of issues raise doubts about the wisdom of maintaining exclusively pure-bred strains of dogs for assistance work.

In some agencies, there is considerable attention paid to inbreeding depression but it is mostly in terms of how to slow the rate, rather than discussions of how to prevent it. There has been some suggestion that sharing breeding stock between agencies could revitalize inbred stock. Progress made at one agency at eliminating genetic defects could then be helpful to other breeders.

23.4.3 The importance of early development

There is confusion among many assistance animal programs concerning the difference between genetic, environmental, and developmental effects. The embryological definition of development is the interaction between a gene and its environment (Serpell, 1987). Therefore, a dog with the condition known as hip dysplasia is a product of inherited (genetic) predispositions interacting with the environment at various stages in its development. Precisely the same is true of behavior. It is well established from research on canid development that early experiences have more profound and longer-lasting effects on behavior than those occurring at later stages of the lifecycle (Serpell and Jagoe, 1995). It is not difficult to understand why. When a German shepherd puppy is born, it has a brain volume of about 8 ccs, and at this stage it has all the brain cells it is ever going to have. By eight weeks its brain has grown to 80 ccs, and by 16 weeks the brain is approaching its adult size of 120 ccs. Since the brain increases 15 times in volume during this short period, but maintains the same cell number, most of the growth is clearly occurring due to the development of connections between the cells. This matrix of cells is constructed during the first 16 weeks in response to electrical stimulation and activity patterns. How the animal moves, what it perceives with its senses, and the kinds of stresses it endures all determine the pattern of growth of the connective matrix. Human children growing up in orphanages have not only smaller brains (not as many connections) than "normal" children but they do not show the same electrical patterning, even though they presumably have the same number of brain cells. This is what is meant by a developmental effect—a synergism between genes and the environment.

In the sense that they tend to insulate puppies from varied stimuli, many breeding kennels for assistance dogs may be equivalent to orphanages. Although kennel workers are very good at keeping puppies clean and healthy, it would probably be fair to say that few are familiar with the profound effects of early environment on brain development. Why is it that a substantial proportion of agency-bred dogs are unable to perform the tasks assigned to them? Is it because of genetic flaws, or is it because of the developmental effects of spending the first eight weeks in an impoverished environment? If the latter, then the "industry" may be predisposing puppies to be ill-equipped to cope with the demands made on them later in life. The behavioral result of environmental impoverishment during this critical period is relatively permanent. Depending on how the dog was wired in those early sensitive periods largely predetermines how it will behave as an adult.

Agencies and programs raising animals for service have a duty to insure that the animals they produce are correctly prepared for their adult roles. At every stage of growth and development, dogs should be shaped and molded to perform their adult tasks. If particular tasks are required of an assistance dog—i.e. turning on a light—then the puppy's developmental exposure should prepare it for such a task. Food boxes could require similar tasks in such a way that the dog achieves a cognitive awareness of what is being performed. How dogs handle novel situations and stimuli is another major cause of rejection. A fearful dog cannot be trained to deal with novelty. For example, sidewalk grates that are common in cities may be an insurmountable problem for a dog. Many such problems might be eliminated by paying attention to the early (4–16 week) developmental environment.

If done properly, a dog might even learn to enjoy performing its work simply because it has developed the cognitive ability to transcend operant conditioning and understand what it is doing, and why. On the other hand, the "industry" may also have to face the morally uncomfortable possibility that the only way to raise a "good" assistance dog is to raise it in a deprived environment. It may be that the most successful dogs are products of particular kinds of environmental impoverishment; that the more cognitively developed animals are actually ill-suited to perform this kind of repetitive and tedious daily work (Coppinger and Coppinger. 2001).

23.4.4   Use inappropriate or aversive training methods

The underlying assumption of operant conditioning is that any animal can learn any performance by external reward or external punishment. For example, a moving animal is rewarded for going in the correct direction and punished for going in the wrong direction. There is a lengthy and complex literature on when, how much, and how often the animal should be rewarded or punished, and about what is actually reinforced. This is essentially the learning paradigm used to train many assistance animals, but two important elements are often missing: First, one of the reasons dogs have been so successful as companions is that they are prepared to work for the reward of social interaction with people. Second, because particular dog breeds innately "like" to search for game or to herd sheep, it is not essential to reward such performances. Working dog specialists generally consider it impossible to train an animal that does not show the internal motivation to perform the specific task. Furthermore, most traditional working dog trainers do not use aversive conditioning as the primary training strategy. Nor do they need to. Dogs tend to "sour" with aversive conditioning, and since many performances depend on stamina and willingness to work, dog trainers avoid associating performance with any form of punishment. On a sled dog team severe punishment might be used to stop dogs fighting, but no experienced driver would attempt to persuade a dog to run by punishing it (Coppinger and Coppinger, 2001).

In contrast, aversive conditioning is the primary method of instruction for many assistance dogs. It may be the only method that is practical since many assistance dog tasks are not discrete; nor is the significance of the task necessarily understood by the dog. "Find the bird" is a discrete task, regardless of how long it takes. It has a beginning and an end of which the dog is aware. Pulling a wheelchair is fundamentally different because there is no intrinsic reward, nor is it socially facilitated in the manner, say, of a sled dog performing with other dogs. Tasks like these are difficult to reward because performance is an ongoing event. You cannot reward the cessation of activity at the end of the pull, and punishment is equally inappropriate (Coppinger et al., 1998). There has recently been some interest in "click and treat" training methods using a variation of Pavlovian conditioning. This is a useful approach for "civilizing" assistance dogs, and works reasonably well on hearing ear and therapy dogs. Unfortunately, it has not yet been demonstrated to work as a viable system for training wheelchair or guide dogs. Clearly, greater efforts could and should be devoted to developing non-aversive alternatives to current training methods for these animals, as aversive methods are detrimental to the animals' welfare by inducing fear, anxiety and other forms of psychological stress (Hiby et al., 2004; Overall, 2007; Schalke et al., 2007; Schilder and van der Borg, 2004).

23.4.5 Unrealistic expectations

Assistance animals are expected to obey complex commands and perform relatively challenging physical activities that also create a potential for welfare problems. In one study, Coppinger et al. (1998) were critical of the unrealistic expectations that some assistance dog programs have of their protégés. Superficially simple activities, such as pulling a wheelchair or opening a swing door, may impose excessive physical strains on a dog that could result in physical injury over time. Furthermore, since the tasks themselves are potentially aversive, and because the dogs have not been specifically selected for performing these tasks the way most traditional working dogs have, they lack any internal motivation to perform, and may, as a consequence, have difficulty meeting the goals of conventional reward-based training, or retaining responses once they have been entrained (Coppinger et al., 1998).

Additionally, assistance animals are oftentimes expected to "work" for extended periods of time, frequently in highly stressful environments, with little opportunity for resting while "on the job." They work in busy streets, in crowded areas, among unfamiliar people and other animals, navigating through complicated pathways, performing challenging tasks. When this is anticipated, appropriate plans need to be made to ameliorate the effect that such demands have on the animals' welfare. If unexpected conditions arise that lead to stressful situations, the status of the animal must be assessed and the necessary changes implemented to ensure that their effect on the animal is mitigated and that its needs are met. There are always opportunities to improve the working conditions for assistance animals and to ensure that they have minimal impact on their well-being, even if just by giving the animal time to relax, play, run, etc., along the way.

23.4.6 Use of poorly designed equipment and facilities

By analyzing the "physics" of some of the tasks that service dogs are asked to perform, Coppinger et al. (1998) drew attention to inherent design flaws in some of the equipment used by disabled persons that may result in discomfort or injury to the dogs. Harnesses, for example, suggested that the designers did not understand the basic principles of harness design. Some had pulling webs crossing moving parts, thus chafing the dog badly as it moved. Trying to get a dog to pull a wheelchair that is designed to be pushed forces the dog into awkward positions, thereby increasing the difficulty of the task. And some of the tasks, such as pulling a wheelchair or pulling open a door with the teeth, reach the limits of what a dog is physically able to perform.

Various studies have also been critical of conventional kennel-housing for dogs, most of which has been designed to reduce labor costs and facilitate hygiene rather than with the welfare of the animals in mind. Kennels used to house service dogs during training are often cell-like in appearance with opaque barriers separating adjacent pens. Dogs are usually housed singly or, less often, in pairs, and often there is little in the way of toys or other forms of enrichment to relieve the tedium of kennel existence. Dogs housed in these sorts of conditions for long periods display a range of abnormal, repetitive or "stereotypic" behavior, such as circling, pacing, "wall-bouncing" and barking (Fox, 1965; Hite et al., 1977; Hubrecht et al., 1992; Hughes et al., 1989; Sales et al., 1997). Noise levels from barking in some facilities may also be sufficiently loud to cause permanent damage to dogs' hearing (Sales et al., 1997).

23.5 End-user problems

Although there have been few systematic studies of the problem, anecdotal observations suggest that some therapy and assistance animal users may have negative attitudes to animals, or be insufficiently experienced with handling or training them. As a consequence, the people are likely to derive less satisfaction and therapeutic benefit from the animal (Lane et al., 1998), and the animals may be ignored or neglected, given inappropriate or ill-timed commands, punished for failing to respond to these commands, rewarded at inappropriate times, and so on (Coppinger et al., 1998; Iannuzzi and Rowan, 1991). Any of these actions is obviously detrimental to the animals' physical or mental well-being and should be corrected promptly. Otherwise, and not surprisingly, animals may become confused and apathetic as a result of such inept handling, and the problems are likely to multiply with the use of less trainable and more socially manipulative species such as non-human primates.

Some agencies provide refresher courses for their clients, or can send a trainer to the person's home to correct special problems. However, greater continuing education efforts by agencies would certainly help to insure improved quality of life for animals used in this way.

The issue of continuing education is also a significant concern for clinicians applying AAA/T in their own practices. As stated in earlier chapters, although clinicians may be very cognizant of treatment goals with their clients, they may be in need of further training on how to incorporate animals into their practice (therapeutically and safely). Hines and Frederickson (1998) point out that without training on how animal interactions impact various user groups, therapists may incorporate inappropriate animals and procedures that fail to maximize treatment outcomes. The "Pet Partners Program" developed by the Delta Society includes in-service training on a variety of areas including an awareness of health and skill aptitude of the animals as well as strategies to incorporate the animals with the clients. The Pet Partners Program should be considered as a valuable introductory course for practitioners in this field. Educational programs should be interdisciplinary in nature, and must combine sound theory along with good practical training. Topics that ought to be covered include ethology and human/animal interactions, the psycho-social benefits of animals as social support providers, and risk management concerns, a review of the basic behavioral and social needs of the specific animal species used, a practicum on how to identify signs of stress and distress, and suggestions on how to avoid or alleviate the effects of stressful conditions commonly encountered in the assistance or therapy settings (Turner, 1999).

Clinicians will also be able to find continuing education opportunities at conferences and workshops sponsored by organizations such as the International Association of Human-Animal Interaction Organizations,[5] the International Society for Anthrozoology,[6] and the Delta Society.[7] Further opportunities may also be available at conferences and workshops sponsored by local and regional humane societies, as well as many other professional organizations interested in the therapeutic utility of human/animal interactions.

23.6 Conclusions and recommendations

The concept of using trained and socialized animals to assist people with disabilities, or as therapeutic adjuncts, has great intrinsic appeal, exemplifying, as it does for many people, the ultimate in mutually beneficial animal/human partnerships. Nevertheless, while the advantages to the humans in these relationships may be obvious, the benefits to the animals are by no means always self-evident. Indeed, the use of animals for animal-assisted activities and therapy imposes a unique set of stresses and strains on them that the "industry" has only recently begun to acknowledge.

[5] http://www.iahaio.org/
[6] http://www.isaz.net
[7] http://www.deltasociety.org/

In this review, we have tried to identify a number of potential sources or causes of animal welfare problems in AAA/T and assistance work. In doing so, it is not our intention to criticize particular programs or practitioners, but rather to focus attention on specific practices that may give rise to ethical concerns, and which ought therefore to be subjected to further scrutiny and study. This is after all a new field of animal exploitation, and a certain number of "growing pains" are only to be expected.

While it is still early days, and much of what can be said is necessarily somewhat speculative, the following preliminary recommendations are appropriate:

1. Those involved in preparing or using animals for service and therapy need to educate themselves regarding the particular social and behavioral needs of these animals, both to avoid the consequences of social and behavioral deprivation, as well as to permit animals a degree of control over the levels of social and environmental stimulation they receive.

2. AAI practitioners need to understand that close physical contact with strangers may be inherently stressful for many animals, and recognize the signs of stress when they appear. Ideally, visitation and therapy sessions should be terminated before, rather than after, such symptoms are manifested.

3. In residential programs, one or more staff persons should be held primarily accountable for the care and welfare of any therapy animal, and for supervising all interactions with inmates/residents. No animal should be left unsupervised in a situation where its welfare might reasonably be considered at risk.

4. Non-domestic species should not be used for AAA/T or assistance work except under exceptional circumstances (e.g. wildlife rehabilitation), and where appropriate care can be guaranteed.

5. On the basis of current evidence, so-called "dolphin-swim" programs cannot be ethically justified.

6. During the process of rearing and training assistance animals, transitions between successive handlers or owners should be carried out in such a way as to cause minimal distress due to the disruption of pre-existing social bonds.

7. Efforts and resources should be dedicated to developing methods of accurately identifying and distributing suitable assistance animals from among those relinquished to animal shelters. These efforts should include research into appropriate behavioral screening methods.

8. The present level of assistance dog "failure" is ethically unacceptable and needs to be reduced. The "industry" should be more aware of the problems inherent in the use of closed, pure-bred populations of service and assistance dogs. The potential benefits of out-crossing to other populations and of cross-breeding should be explored to reduce the prevalence of deleterious genetic diseases, as well as improving infectious disease resistance.

9. The "industry" should give more attention to insuring that assistance and service animals are adequately prepared during development for the tasks and roles assigned to them as adults.

10. Alternatives to the use of aversive conditioning in the training of assistance animals need to be investigated and developed wherever possible, particularly with respect to the training of wheelchair dogs. If necessary, the "industry" should consider discontinuing the use of animals for particular purposes, if alternatives to aversive conditioning cannot be found.

11. More attention should be given to the design and construction of animal-friendly equipment and holding facilities for AAA/T and assistance animals.

12. Continuing education programs for animal practitioners and end-users should be available to insure that animals are correctly handled, cared for and used throughout their working lives.

To assist in organizing some of our thoughts pertaining to the psycho-social concerns and needs of therapy animals, Appendix 1 has been formulated to identify specific guidelines for consideration. These guidelines are pertinent to both services provided in large-scale institutionally based programs as well as small clinical practices.

References

Anderson, P. K., Coultis, D., & Welle, K. R. (2005). Avian wellness: consideration of birds in institutional settings. *Journal of Applied Animal Welfare Science.* (in press).

Beerda, B., Schilder, M. B. H., Van Hooff, J. A. R. A. M., De Vries, H. W., & Mol, J. A. (1998). Behavioural, saliva cortisol and heart rate responses to different types of stimuli in dogs. *Applied Animal Behaviour Science, 58*, 365–381.

Beerda, B., Schilder, M. B. H., Van Hooff, J. A. R. A. M., De Vries, H. W., & Mol, J. A. (1999). Chronic stress in dogs subjected to social and spatial restriction. 1. Behavioral responses. *Physiology and Behavior, 66*, 233–242.

Behnke, S. (2005). Reflecting on how we teach ethics. *Monitor of Psychology, 36*, 64–65.

Boissy, A., Manteuffel, G., Jensen, M. B., Moe, R. O., Spruijt, B., Keeling, L. J., Winkler, C., Forkman, B., Dimitrov, I., Langbein, J., Bakken, M., Veissier, I., & Aubert, A. (2007). Assessment of positive emotions in animals to improve their welfare. *Physiology and Behavior, 92*, 375–397.

Brodie, S. J., Biley, F. C., & Shewring, M. (2002). An exploration of the potential risks associated with using pet therapy in healthcare settings. *Journal of Clinical Nursing, 11*, 444–456.

Broom, D. M., & Fraser, A. F. (2007). *Domestic Animal Behaviour and Welfare* (4th ed.). Wallingford, Oxford: CABI.

Broom, D. M., & Johnson, K. G. (1993). *Stress and Animal Welfare*. London, UK: Chapman Hall.

Burls, A., & Caan, W. (2005). Human health and nature conservation. *British Medical Journal, 331*, 1221–1222.

Butler, K. (2004). *Therapy Dogs Today: Their Gifts, Our Obligation*. Norman, OK: Funpuddle Publishing.

Cheney, D. L., & Seyfarth, R. M. (1990). *How Monkeys See the World*. Chicago: Chicago University Press.

Command Paper 2836. (1965). *Report of the technical committee to enquire into the welfare of animals kept under intensive livestock husbandry systems*. London, UK: Her Majesty's Stationery Office.

Coppinger, R., Coppinger, L., & Skillings, E. (1998). Observations on assistance dog training and use. *Journal of Applied Animal Welfare Science, 1*, 133–144.

Coppinger, R., & Zuccotti, J. (1999). Kennel enrichment: exercise and socialization of dogs. *Journal of Applied Animal Welfare Science, 2*, 281–296.

Coppinger, R., & Coppinger, L. (2001). *Dogs: A Startling New Understanding of Canine Origin, Behavior and Evolution*. New York, NY: Scribner.

Dawkins, M. (1980). *Animal Suffering: The Science of Animal Welfare*. London: Chapman and Hall.

Dawkins, M. (1983). Battery hens name their price: consumer demand theory and the measurement of behavioural needs. *Animal Behaviour, 31*, 1195–1205.

Dawkins, M. S. (1988). Behavioural deprivation: a central problem in animal welfare. *Applied Animal Behaviour Science, 20,* 209–225.

DeGrazia, D. (1996). *Taking Animals Seriously: Mental Life and Moral Status.* Cambridge: Cambridge University Press.

Doyle, M. C. (1975). Rabbit—therapeutic prescription. *Perspectives in Psychiatric Care, 13,* 79–82.

Duncan, I. J. H. (1993). Welfare is to do with what animals feel. *Journal of Agricultural and Environmental Ethics, 6*(Suppl. 2), 8–14.

Duncan, I. J. H., & Fraser, D. (1997). Understanding animal welfare. In M. C. Appleby & B. O. Hughes (Eds.), *Animal Welfare.* CAB International.

Duncan, S. L. (2000). APIC state-of-the-art report: the implications of service animals in health care settings. *American Journal of Infection Control, 28,* 170–180.

FAWC. (2009). Farm Animal Welfare Council—5 Freedoms. Retrieved July 7, 2009. Website: http://www.fawc.org.uk/freedoms.htm

Fox, M. (1965). Environmental factors influencing stereotyped and allelomimetic behavior in animals. *Laboratory Animal Care, 15*(5), 363–370.

Hemmer, H. (1990). Domestication: The Decline of Environmental Appreciation, *trans. Neil Beckhaus.* Cambridge: Cambridge University Press.

Hiby, E. F., Rooney, N. J., & Bradshaw, J. W. S. (2004). Dog training methods—their use, effectiveness and interaction with behaviour and welfare. *Animal Welfare, 13,* 63–69.

Hinde, R. A. (1970). *Animal Behaviour: A Synthesis of Ethology and Comparative Psychology* (2nd ed.). London: McGraw-Hill.

Hines, L., & Fredrickson, M. (1998). Perspectives on animal-assisted activities and therapy. In C. C. Wilson & D. C. Turner (Eds.), *Companion Animals in Human Health* (pp. 23–39). Thousand Oaks, CA: Sage.

Hite, M., Hanson, H., Bohidar, N., Conti, P., & Mattis, P. (1977). Effect of cage size on patterns of activity and health of beagle dogs. *Laboratory Animal Science, 27,* 60–64.

Hubrecht, R. (1995). The welfare of dogs in human care. In J. Serpell (Ed.), *The Domestic Dog: Its Evolution, Behaviour, and Interactions with People* (pp. 179–195). Cambridge: Cambridge Press.

Hubrect, R., Serpell, J., & Poole, T. (1992). Correlates of pen size and housing conditions on the behaviour of kenneled dogs. *Applied Animal Behaviour Science, 34,* 365–383.

Hubrecht, R., & Turner, D. C. (1998). Companion animal welfare in private and institutional settings. In C. C. Wilson & D. C. Turner (Eds.), *Companion Animals in Human Health* (pp. 267–289). Thousand Oaks, CA: Sage.

Hughes, B. O., & Duncan, I. J. H. (1988). The notion of ethological needs, models of motivation and animal welfare. *Animal Behaviour, 36,* 1696–1707.

Hughes, H. C., Campbell, S., & Kenney, C. (1989). The effects of cage size and pair housing on exercise of beagle dogs. *Laboratory Animal Science, 39*(4), 302–305.

Humphries, T. L. (2003). Effectiveness of dolphin-assisted therapy as a behavioral intervention for young children with disabilities. *Bridges, 1,* 1–9.

Iannuzzi, D., & Rowan, A. N. (1991). Ethical issues in animal-assisted therapy programs. *Anthrozoös, 4,* 154–163.

Kay, R., & Hall, C. (2009). The use of a mirror reduces isolation stress in horses being transported by trailer. *Applied Animal Behaviour Science, 116*(2–4), 237–243.

Lane, D. R., McNicholas, J., & Collis, G. M. (1998). Dogs for the disabled: benefits to recipients and welfare of the dog. *Applied Animal Behaviour Science, 59,* 49–60.

Levinson, B. M. (1971). Household pets in training schools serving delinquent children. *Psychological Reports, 28,* 475–481.

Mallon, G. P. (1994a). Cow as co-therapist: utilization of farm animals as therapeutic aides with children in residential treatment. *Child and Adolescent Social Work Journal, 11*(6), 455–474.

Mallon, G. P. (1994b). Some of our best therapists are dogs. *Child and Youth Care Forum, 23* (2), 89–101.

Marino, L., & Lilienfeld, S. O. (1998). Dolphin-assisted therapy: flawed data, flawed conclusions. *Anthrozoös, 11*, 194–200.

Mason, G., & Mendl, M. (1993). Why is there no simple way of measuring animal welfare? *Animal Welfare, 2*, 301–320.

McCobb, E. C., Patronek, G. J., Marder, A., Dinnage, J. D., & Stone, M. S. (2005). Assessment of stress levels among cats in four animal shelters. *Journal of the American Veterinary Medical Association, 226*, 548–555.

Neilson, J. C., Hart, B. L., Cliff, K. D., & Ruehl, W. W. (2001). Prevalence of behavioral changes associated with age-related cognitive impairment in dogs. *Journal of the American Veterinary Medical Association, 218*, 1787–1791.

Overall, K. (2007). Considerations for shock and "training" collars: concerns from and for the working dog community. *Journal of Veterinary Behaviour, 2*, 103–107.

Rollin, B. E. (1995). *Farm Animal Welfare: Social, Bioethical and Research Issues.* Ames, IA: Iowa State University Press.

Sales, G., Hubrecht, R., Peyvandi, A., Milligan, S., & Shield, B. (1997). Noise in dog kennelling: is barking a welfare problem for dogs? *Applied Animal Behaviour Science, 52*, 321–329.

Samuels, A., Bejder, L., & Heinrich, S. (2000). *A review of the literature pertaining to swimming with wild dolphins* (Contract Number T74463123). Bethesda, MD: Marine Mammal Commission.

Samuels, A., & Bejder, L. (2004). Chronic interaction between humans and free-ranging bottlenose dolphins near Panama City Beach, Florida, USA. *Journal of Cetacean Resource Management, 6*, 69–77.

Schalke, E., Stichnoth, J., Ott, S., & Jones-Baade, R. (2007). Clinical signs caused by the use of electric training collars on dogs in everyday life situations. *Applied Animal Behaviour Science, 105*, 369–380.

Schilder, M. B. H., & van der Borg, J. A. M. (2004). Training dogs with the help of the shock collar—short and long term behavioural effects. *Applied Animal Behaviour Science, 85*, 319–334.

Selye, H. (1957). *The Stress of Life.* London, UK: Longmans, Green & Co.

Serpell, J. A. (1987). The influence of inheritance and environment on canine behaviour: myth and fact. *Journal of Small Animal Practice, 28*, 949–956.

Serpell, J., & Jagoe, J. A. (1995). Early experience and the development of behaviour. In J. A. Serpell (Ed.), *The Domestic Dog: Its Evolution, Behaviour, and Interactions with People* (pp. 80–102). Cambridge: Cambridge University Press.

Stull, C. L. (1997). Physiology, balance, and management of horses during transportation. In *Proceedings of the Horse Breeders and Owners Confefence.* Alberta, Canada: Red Deer. Jan. 10–12, 1997.

Turner, D. (1999). The future of education and research on the human-animal bond and animal assisted therapy. In A. H. Fine (Ed.), *Handbook on Animal Assisted Therapy.* New York: Academic Press.

Weiss, E. (2002). Selecting shelter dogs for service dog training. *Journal for Applied Animal Welfare Science, 5*, 43–62.

Weiss, E., & Greenberg, G. (1997). Service dog selection tests: effectiveness for dogs from animal shelters. *Applied Animal Behaviour Science, 53*, 297–308.

Appendix 1

Ethical guidelines for the care and supervision of animals while utilized in AAT or AAA

Goal: Incorporating animals therapeutically to assist human clients.

Issue: How to balance the needs of human clients with respect for the needs of the animal.

Basic ethics principles for use of the therapy animal:

1. All animals utilized therapeutically must be kept free from abuse, discomfort, and distress, both physical and mental.
2. Proper health care for the animal must be provided at all times.
3. All animals should have access to a quiet place where they can have time away from their work activities. Clinicians must practice preventive health procedures for all animals.
4. Interactions with clients must be structured so as to maintain the animal's capacity to serve as a useful therapeutic agent.
5. A situation of abuse or stress for a therapy animal should never be allowed except in such cases where temporarily permitting such abuse is necessary to avoid a serious injury to, or abuse of, the human client.

Procedures for ethical decision making regarding therapy animals:

1. Identify the human needs:
   What does the client need from the therapy animal?
   How much time does the client need to spend with the animal?
   What is the nature of the contact/time spent with the animal?
2. Identify the animal's most basic needs:
   Proper care
   Affection
   Quiet time
3. Compare the human and animal needs:
   Only the most compelling of human needs (e.g. avoiding serious mental or physical injury) should ever be allowed to take priority over the basic needs of the animal.

Implications of procedure for ethical decision-making regarding therapy animals:

1. If the intervention is unduly stressing the animal, the clinician should suspend the session or the interaction.
2. Therapists using therapy animals must provide "downtime" for the animal several times a day.
3. Animals that due to age or other reasons become unduly stressed should have their service scaled back or eliminated entirely. Attention should also be given to transition the animal as s/he begins to retire. This will help with the animal's sense of wellness.
4. In a situation where a client, whether intentionally or unintentionally, subjects a therapy animal to abuse, the basic needs of the animal must be respected, even if this means terminating the animal's relationship with the client. In a case where a therapist suspects that a client may be likely to abuse the animal, a therapist must take precautions to protect the

animal's welfare. When any evidence of stress or abuse becomes evident the therapist must terminate the animal's relationship with the client. If there are concerns that a client may pose a risk of abuse to other animals or humans, the therapist should notify the proper authorities.

5. Clients who severely abuse a therapy animal may thereby destroy the animal's capacity to help others. Clients in this situation thus violate Principle 4 (above).

24 The role of the veterinary family practitioner in AAT and AAA programs

Richard Timmins DVM *, Aubrey H. Fine[†],
Richard Meadows DVM, DABVP[‡]

[*] Association for Veterinary Family Practice, [†] California State Polytechnic University, [‡] University of Missouri

24.1 The origin of veterinary family practice

The evolution of the relationship between humans and companion animals has had a marked effect on the practice of veterinary medicine during the past few decades. A prime indicator of the changing role of pets in human society is the extent to which humans have welcomed companion animals into their homes. In a survey of Canadian pet owners conducted in 2001, 83% of the respondents indicated that their pets were part of the family—including 26% of respondents who described the pet as the baby in the family (IPSOS-REID, 2001). In a more recent survey of US pet owners, 86% of participants declared that their pets were part of the family, with 50% claiming that the pet is just as much a part of the family as any other person in the household (GfK Roper Public Affairs and Media, 2009).

Historically, the legal status of animals reflected society's perception of animals as chattel, considered only in terms of their economic value. That perception is changing. Some communities seek to alter that status through statutes—for example, replacing the term "pet owner" with the word "guardian," or outlawing certain procedures perceived to be inhumane (Fiala, 2005; Sapperfield, 2002). Although courts have occasionally confirmed the non-economic value of animals by issuing awards to pet owners for suffering and loss of companionship (Fiala, 2004; Lofflin, 2004), cases seeking emotional damages are being denied (Whitcomb, 2009). Bills have been introduced in a number of state legislatures in 2009 (Hawaii, Massachusetts, Mississippi, New Jersey, New York, Oregon, Rhode Island, and Washington, DC) which change laws to award non-economic damages in cases where a pet is wrongfully injured or killed (Whitcomb, 2009). The legal status of companion animals continues to be a hotly contested issue.

With the strengthening of the bond between humans and their pets, veterinary clients demand technologically advanced health care for their pets, and they show an

Handbook on Animal-Assisted Therapy. DOI: 10.1016/B978-0-12-381453-1.10024-8

increasing willingness to spend more money to maintain the health of their animal companions (Grieve et al., 2003). The veterinary profession has responded with a revolution in medical and surgical technology and knowledge. In urban and suburban America, the number and type of veterinary specialty services offered have grown dramatically in the past few decades. Enhanced technology and scientific knowledge, however, will not meet all of the needs generated by the evolution of the human/animal bond. Over 30 years ago, psychologist Boris Levinson (1987) predicted that the "...veterinarian will become involved in the emotional life of the family whose pet he treats. He will become aware of the meaning of the pet to its owner." There are additional sets of skills and knowledge required to advocate for the well-being of animals in the context of their roles in the human family (see Table 24.1) and to interface with the emotional bond between human and pet. Enhanced interpersonal skills are essential, including client communication, emotional intelligence, leadership, teamwork, conflict management, human psychology and media interaction. The discipline of veterinary family practice (http://www.avfp.org) seeks to define and teach the skills and knowledge necessary to meet the objectives of veterinary family practice, as described in Table 24.2.

It has been well established that companion animals in a home exert a positive influence on the health and well-being of the human family members. Coronary patients who are pet owners have a greater survival rate than non-pet owning coronary patients (Friedmann et al., 1980). Pets decrease loneliness and depression in people with inadequate social support, including elderly, single women, and people with disabilities or chronic diseases (Garrity et al., 1989; Siegel et al., 1999; Zasloff and Kidd, 1994). Pets can lower their human companions' blood pressure (Friedmann and Thomas, 1995). Mayo Clinic oncologist Edward Creagan stated: "I prescribe pets to a third of my cancer patients to help them cope with the rigors of their terrible disease. I consider getting a pet to be one of the easiest and most rewarding ways of living a longer, healthier life" (Creagan, 2002).

Schwabe (1984) reflected on how the impact of pets on human well-being presented a challenge to the veterinary profession: "There has been great reluctance...

Table 24.1 The roles of companion animals in human families

- Providing emotional support (unquestioning)
- Offering companionship (being there)
- Serving as a playmate for children (or adults)
- Teaching children responsibility
- Competing (canine sports, show)
- Encouraging and enhancing physical exercise
- Serving as social facilitators
- Protecting
- Promoting mental and physical health of the humans
- Entertaining
- Working (search and rescue, police and immigration duties, service and therapy animals)
- Relieving stress

Table 24.2 Objectives of veterinary family practice (VFP)

- Serve as a community resource for information about the well-being of animals
- Advocate for the physical health and the emotional well-being of companion animals in the context of their roles in the family and in society, providing information and resources to help clients manage the health and well-being of their animal companions
- Develop a life-long health plan for individual patients, taking into account genetics, environmental exposures, and functional expectations
- Provide preventive and therapeutic medical and surgical services to patients, referring to specialists when appropriate
- Embrace the role of the VFP as a member of a multidisciplinary professional network supporting the health and well-being of both human and non-human members of the community

to suggest that veterinarians may have, in fact, even more significant and perhaps unique social roles to play *vis à vis* the emotional and even the closely related physical well-being of animals' owners than of the animals themselves." Schwabe's insight has given birth to the concept of One Medicine, espoused by the American Veterinary Medical Association. This concept acknowledges and embraces the overlap of veterinary, human and environmental health. It is now quite obvious that a veterinary practice is far more than a repair shop for dogs and cats. The fact that approximately 75% of human diseases emerging in the last three decades have been zoonotic places veterinarians in the front lines in their detection and prevention (Taylor, 2001). Signs of animal abuse suggest a potential for violence towards humans, imbuing a greater responsibility for the veterinarian to be alert for and to respond to any such indication (Flynn, 2000). It is not unlikely that the veterinarian will be the first to witness evidence of spousal, child or elderly abuse and, in many states, they are mandatory reporters of any suspicions of abuse. Because of the trust that develops in a veterinary family practice, the practitioner may become aware of specific needs of elderly or disabled clients and have the opportunity to direct them to appropriate social services or other resources. Ormerod (2008) proposed the formation of a multidisciplinary professional network (MPDN), consisting of veterinarians, police, child protection officers, medical practitioners, community mental health workers, teachers, social workers and humane society officers. This network could be an excellent resource for the veterinarian encountering zoonotic, novel or emerging diseases, suspected animal or human abuse, or clients in need of social services.

An area that is very ripe for collaboration with mental health providers relates to pet loss. The intense bond between owner and pet increases the grief at the loss of the shorter-lived species, and requires the veterinary practice team to skillfully counsel clients about end-of-life issues. Unfortunately, the loss of a pet has not been given significant attention by most mental health professionals in the past. This is now changing because most realize the importance of animals in the lives of their patients. The loss of an animal can be hard for most people, both young and old. Research has found that the grieving process is exceptionally more difficult for people who live alone or those who have a more limited social support and spend a great deal of time with their pets (Planchon and Templer, 1996). Furthermore, for families who have to decide if they need to euthanize their pet, the grieving process can be arduous. Sharkin and Knox (2003) point out such decisions may be very difficult to grapple with, especially when evaluating the quality of life for the animal or a person's desire to have more time with his /her beloved pet. Feelings of guilt may also arise in people who feel they need to euthanize the animal because of the financial burdens of keeping the animal alive. It is within these types of scenarios, as well as others, that a closer relationship with veterinary family practitioners and health providers needs to exist. A viable relationship between mental health practitioners and practicing veterinarians can be very beneficial in this time of need. Providing supports such as grief and loss support groups would be a positive collaborative option. Veterinarians could develop community referrals to send some of their clients that seem to be struggling significantly with the loss. The concept of One Medicine seems to be a logical fit within this area. And the role of the veterinarian is truly vital.

24.2   The role of veterinary family practitioners in AAT/AAA

Animal-assisted interventions provide an opportunity for the veterinary family prac-titioner (VFP) to work closely with owners of animals with specific functions outside the family. This interface provides an excellent model for an MPDN. Often, the most important role identified for veterinarians in AAT/AAA programs is "…the need for careful behavioral and medical (zoonotic) screening of animals…" (Johnson and Meadows, 2000). The American Veterinary Medical Association expands this role in the Wellness Guidelines for Animals Used in Animal-assisted Activity, Animal-assisted Therapy, and Resident Animal Programs (American Veterinary Medical Association, 2001). These guidelines recommend that the veterinarian should work closely with the individual with primary responsibility for the animal, the therapist and a qualified behaviorist to develop a wellness plan that will enhance the health and welfare of the animal. The Guidelines also state that "Total wellness encompasses the physical and behavioral attributes of the animal, as well as the characteristics of interaction between people and animals participating in the program." This is in accordance with the concept of veterinary family practice, in which the veterinarian is an active member of a team that includes the hospital staff, the pet owner and area specialists, all of whom are focused on the well-being of the pet. A major aspect of well-being is enabling the pet to perform a particular function effectively without stress or discomfort. When the function is participation in an animal-assisted therapy or animal-assisted activity program, the VFP can be a valuable partner with the therapist and the individual responsible for the care of the animal. The following discussion will assume that the therapist is the individual responsible.

24.2.1   Animal selection

The first opportunity for the VFP to facilitate the work of the therapist is to counsel the therapist on the species or breed of animal appropriate for the therapeutic objectives. It is important that the therapist be specific about the work expected of the animal during therapy. A discussion of these expectations will lead to identifying the characteristics which are essential to therapeutic success. A list of possible expectations can be found in Table 24.3.

Mental, social or physical qualities of the patient or client may determine the appropriateness of a given species or breed. Is the patient immunocompromised? Does the patient have allergies or phobias? Are there aspects of the patient's history that suggest a positive or negative value of a particular choice of species or breed? Are there limitations due to a physical disability or the patient's age?

If the therapist is seeking a relaxing environment, fresh or salt-water aquariums have been shown to have calming and other beneficial effects on humans (Katcher et al., 1984). Although there are now veterinarians specializing in aquaculture, it is likely that a VFP will refer the therapist to a local store specializing in fresh water or tropical fish for supplies and information. Although reptiles may be interesting to certain patients, in general they are non-interactive, are the object of some phobias, and may carry a high risk of zoonotic disease (see below). Reptiles are usually not recommended as therapeutic animals (Hess et al., 2005). However, should a therapist determine that a reptile could contribute to a superior therapeutic outcome, precautions need to be put into place. Fine (2005) notes that antiseptic hand wash needs to be available, at all times, especially after the client handles the animal. There are several

Table 24.3 Possible expectations of animals employed in AAT

1. Provide an atmosphere of acceptance
2. Offer a non-judgmental social interaction
3. Reinforce a sense of responsibility and accountability in the patient
4. Induce a calm, non-stressful environment
5. Provide reassurance to patients in difficult moments
6. Follow directions from therapist to interact with patients in specific ways
7. Act as a model of positive behavior
8. Act as a sounding board to some clients
9. Assist the therapist in developing rapport with the client
10. Support the therapist in establishing limits in a session. The animal will act as a calming agent
11. The animal will need to follow very simple directions and commands. It is imperative that the animal/human team is in tandem, so the attention will be given to the client(s)
12. The animal's behavior must be reliable. Younger animals and those that are active will have a hard time in a therapeutic setting
13. Some animals will be involved in taking therapeutic walks with clients. The behavior of the selected animals must be reliable. The animals have to be able to handle the sounds and be comfortable navigating throughout the community
14. When involved in group settings, a therapy animal should be comfortable moving among groups of people, as well as being handled. It is imperative that the clinician safeguard the safety of the animal, so inappropriate handling and treatment are prevented
15. The animal should be accepting of all humans it is in contact with

gentle species of reptiles which may be appropriate to incorporate. Bearded dragons tend to be gentle animals and are very comfortable in being handled. Therapists who consider utilizing reptiles need to be in contact with a specialist who can explain the physical needs of the animal.

It is becoming more common for birds of various species to be used as therapeutic assistants. With the exception of cockatiels, love birds and budgerigars, most of the parrot species should be considered wild animals in the process of becoming domesticated. Certain individual birds of other species may be appropriate for patients who benefit from interaction and visual stimuli. But it is important that these birds be carefully evaluated to ensure that they are tame, easily handled by a variety of people and are predictable. Risks to the patient include unintentional scratches or intentional bites associated with inexperience in handling pet birds. In spite of the increasing popularity of birds as pets and the rapidly growing veterinary specialty of avian medicine and surgery, our knowledge about the behavior and the emotional and physical well-being of these creatures is still limited. Many of the species of birds chosen to be pets (Amazons, African grays, cockatoos) are very social and highly intelligent. They are curious, but easily startled and instinctually seek to escape a situation perceived as threatening. Conditions of domestication are at odds with the instinctual behavior of these birds. Confinement in cages and deprivation of inter-action with conspecifics leads to considerable frustration and stress. Therapists considering using birds need to be aware of the special behavioral challenges that could arise as a consequence of the therapeutic interaction. Fine (2003) noted the strong commitment therapists must consider when they utilize larger birds. Clinicians need to be aware of the lifespan of these animals as well as their needs for special care. Unfortunately, many people do not realize that the attention that one gives a bird early in its life is the same amount required when it ages. Therefore, careful planning needs to be instituted, so one will be able to live harmoniously with a bird over time. It is highly recommended that, if birds are to be considered, appropriate and thorough training of both human and avian partners be implemented.

Rabbits and "pocket pets" such as small mammals like guinea pigs, hamsters, mice and rats, offer a visual and tactile experience that may have therapeutic benefit. But they also have an element of unpredictability and are somewhat fragile because of their size.

Cats are a popular therapeutic animal because their soft fur and audible purr in response to petting can have a very positive effect on patients. Care must be taken, however, to choose animals with a docile disposition and their claws must be managed in order to prevent accidental or intentional scratches. The claws can be clipped short on a regular basis or protected with a covering such as Soft Paws® (Soft Paws Inc., Lafayette, LA).

Dogs are certainly the most common therapeutic animals and the subject of the majority of research on the subject. This is undoubtedly a result of their trainability, sociability and predictability. The latter is a result of years of breeding for specific traits, which allows the VFP to make recommendations depending on which personality characteristics will help achieve therapeutic objectives.

It is important to remember that selection of a particular species is just the first step. If a dog, cat or even a guinea pig or rabbit is chosen, an appropriate breed should be identified. Years of selective breeding offer some consistency in physical characteristics, personality and behavioral tendencies within breeds. This does not, however, guarantee identical performance by individual members of a given breed. Mixed breed dogs (and cats) may also be considered. In this case, determining the breed influence and applying a temperament test might help suggest whether an individual animal might have the desired traits. For dogs, some well-established screening tests exist, such as the PALS Behavior Evaluation Form for Dogs (Bustad, 1980) and the AKC Canine Good Citizen® Program (http://www.akc.org/events/cgc/). These instruments can be of value if used in a consistent and thorough method.

24.2.2   Developing a health maintenance plan

Following the selection of an appropriate therapeutic animal, the VFP can develop a lifestage health maintenance plan for the animal. In order to function effectively in AAT, the animal must maintain optimal physiological and psychological health. The plan must be based on a thorough risk assessment that takes into account genetic and environmental factors, zoonotic potential, behavior requirements, nutritional needs and special demands of the therapeutic job the animal is to perform. It also must take into account the personality of the animal.

Genetics

Certain breeds of dogs and cats have a greater risk of suffering from a genetic disease. Persian cats, for example, are at risk for polycystic kidney disease, which can lead to kidney failure. Doberman Pinschers and Papillons may be afflicted with von Willebrand's disease, which prolongs bleeding time. Labrador retrievers and miniature poodles may suffer from progressive retinal atrophy (PRA), which can result in vision deficits. There are tests for these and many other genetic diseases affecting a wide range of breeds. Mixed breed animals whose ancestry includes one or more of these breeds may also be at risk. The VFP can recommend appropriate tests for the individual animal and propose actions based on the result of those tests. Certain diseases may result in a shortened lifespan or disability that may interfere with the desired AAT function. Affected animals would not qualify for AAT. Other diseases may require careful monitoring, but may not interfere with the AAT function. The VFP and the therapist together can determine if the benefit of using a specific individual in an AAT program outweighs the risk of the disease.

Some diseases, like hip dysplasia, have both a genetic and a non-genetic component. A long-term study compared Labrador retrievers whose daily calorie consumption from the age of eight weeks to eight years was restricted to 75% of that of paired littermates with littermates who were allowed to eat *ad libitum*. The calorie-restricted dogs suffered from a significantly lower incidence of hip dysplasia and other types of arthritis (Kealy et al., 2002). In this case, nutrition apparently affects the expression of the genes for hip dysplasia. There is very little known about genetic diseases in other species (besides the mouse) that may be considered for AAT.

Environmental exposures

Control of infectious disease in small mammals is usually managed by maintaining high standards of husbandry, including cleanliness and strict regulation of the environment. Usually these animals are restricted to cages or other small areas and are not exposed to unknown animals or environments, reducing the possibility of encountering an infectious disease. The VFP can advise the therapist on the appropriate husbandry to minimize disease potential, while promoting quality of life.

Birds are generally confined and exposure to unfamiliar animals is restricted. Although there have been vaccines developed to protect birds from certain diseases, their risks and effectiveness have been controversial and their use is generally not recommended for pet birds who are the only birds in the household or who share it with a small number of other birds. Cleanliness, good nutrition, attention to social and environmental needs and regular health examinations comprise a major part of disease prevention for pet birds.

For many years, annual vaccinations had been the cornerstone of disease prevention in dogs and cats. However, recently, it was determined that the immunity conferred by some vaccines was much longer than one year, and the wisdom of vaccinating all dogs or all cats according to the same "one size fits all" protocol has been questioned. It has become apparent that vaccine protocols must be customized for each individual animal based on a careful risk vs. benefit assessment. The VFP can work with the therapist to determine the appropriate vaccines and vaccination schedule for the therapy dog or cat, based on the animal's likelihood of exposure. Particular attention should be given to providing protection against diseases, such as Leptospirosis, that may be spread from animals to people (zoonoses).

Zoonoses

Zoonoses (discussed in Chapter 14) are diseases that can be transmitted from animals to humans. The VFP can develop a program of diagnostic tests, therapies and preventive measures (e.g. frequent bathing or cleaning of the animals hair coat and frequent hand washing) to minimize or eliminate the potential of disease that might spread to humans involved with the AAT. The program should take into account the species, age, and origin of the animal, the environmental exposures of the animal, the degree of interactivity with the patient/client, and the age and health of the patient/client. The program should become part of the health maintenance plan for the animal.

Behavior

Therapists must understand what constitutes normal behavior for the species considered for involvement in the AAT. The VFP can help the therapist identify which behaviors will support and which will interfere with therapeutic objectives. Then a behavioral protocol can be designed that will promote appropriate behaviors and discourage those that are inappropriate. Many animals, for example, can be taught through positive reinforcement to sit quietly and to tolerate handling by strangers. Some species of birds can be taught to "step up" onto a proffered finger or arm, and to speak various phrases. Of all the potential AAT partners, dogs are probably the most trainable.

All dogs should undergo basic obedience training, and the VFP can recommend an appropriate local training facility. It is important for the VFP and the therapist to discuss in detail the concept of "behavioral wellness" (Hetts, 2004), which is a proactive approach ensuring that the pet is well adapted to its role in the family, in the AAT program and in society. At a minimum, AAT dogs should receive Canine Good Citizen certification through the American Kennel Club or be certified through Delta Society's Pet Partners® (Fine and Stein, 2003). Dogs may then be taught additional behaviors that may be helpful to the therapy. The training can be arranged either through the veterinary family practice or through a recommended trainer or veterinary behaviorist.

Occasionally, a dog develops some unacceptable behaviors that may threaten the success of the therapy. It is essential to differentiate signs of stress or discomfort from aberrant behavior. (See the discussion of stress in the Quality of Life section below.) If the VFP and the therapist agree that it is not an indication of stress or an indication of a health problem, it may be appropriate to consult with a behaviorist in order to determine the cause of the problem and to create a program that will eliminate the problem behavior. If, however, a health problem is causing the undesired behavior, it should be addressed immediately. If the animal is showing signs of stress, the cause must be identified and eliminated or the animal must be given appropriate training to deal with it. If the therapy work itself proves to be too stressful for the animal, he or she must be removed from the program.

Nutrition

An important part of the health maintenance plan is nutritional management. Nutritional needs of the therapy animal will change according to life stage, state of health and types and degrees of activity. Young animals require more calories per body weight than older animals. Animals in active training also require more calories than those who are not. Food intolerance is not uncommon in dogs and cats. It may require testing to identify the offending food and research to find an acceptable food. Large and giant breed dogs require fewer calories and a more calcium-restricted diet than medium and small dogs. Older animals may benefit from increased antioxidants. Prevention of obesity is extremely important. The VFP will help identify the specific nutritional needs of each AAT animal, and work with the therapist to develop a nutritional program to meet those needs. Raw foods are not recommended by the authors due to the increased risk of zoonotic disease transmission (e.g. Salmonellosis). Attention needs to be given to the treats animals may receive during a therapy day. Clinicians should consider allocating a portion of the animal's food each day that may be given as treats to help reduce the risk of obesity.

Quality of life

Maintaining or enhancing the quality of life (QOL) of the therapy animal is a shared goal of the VFP and the therapist. Many medical judgments are made based on how the result will affect the patient's QOL. Exactly what is meant by "quality of life" is often very subjective and personal. When veterinarians think of QOL, they generally associate it with freedom from disease, hunger, thirst and pain—especially the latter. Pet owners may consider other behaviors or attitudes of the animal as indicators that may suggest the QOL of their pet. Schalock (1996) points out that there are two approaches to measure QOL. The objective approach assesses external, objective, social indicators such as health and safety. The subjective represents a perception of life experiences that include areas such as physical well-being. When evaluating an animal's QOL, the primary areas would include health and wellness, safety, and nurturance and care the animal receives. However, there is often a risk that anthropomorphism will invalidate the assessment (Wojciechowska and Hewson, 2005). MacMillan (2000) points out that, although QOL is often an important factor when evaluating outcomes of therapeutic interventions or when making decisions about therapy or euthanasia, there is no accepted definition of QOL and there are no validated criteria to measure it.

MacMillan (2000) proposes that affect (subjective feelings) about a physical or emotional state defines the QOL in animals. The challenge is to identify those feelings. He also suggests that QOL is a "continuum of feeling, ranging from comfort to extreme discomfort." Recently, instruments have been developed attempting to define QOL in dogs. Wiseman-Orr et. al. (2004) describe an instrument in the form of a questionnaire designed to measure QOL in dogs afflicted with chronic pain due to osteoarthritis. By identifying behavioral domains and verbal descriptors (terms used by owners to describe aspects of behavior), the authors were able to construct a questionnaire that may be appropriate for a proxy measurement of chronic pain and quality of life. Clinical application of this questionnaire has not been reported. Wojciechowska et al. (2005) evaluated a different questionnaire for pet owners that was designed to demonstrate a difference in QOL between sick and healthy dogs visiting a veterinary teaching hospital. The QOL questionnaire did not, unfortunately, differentiate sick from healthy dogs. Inherent methodological factors may have been responsible for the failure of the questionnaire, but the study confirmed the difficulty of trying to objectify QOL.

These studies attempted to define the QOL of one individual in comparison with the QOL of a larger population. MacMillan (2000) notes that "Quality of life is a uniquely individual experience and should be measured from the perspective of the individual." Perhaps a better approach would be to construct an instrument that would essentially involve a longitudinal study of an individual that monitors an animal's affect under varying environmental and physiological conditions.

Until such an instrument is developed, the VFP and the therapist must jointly determine what characterizes an excellent quality of life for the therapy animal. Specifically, what behaviors can be identified that confirm that the animal is comfortable, and what appears to increase the animal's pleasure? Conversely, what behaviors communicate discomfort, and what does the animal perceive as unpleasant. The answers to these questions will serve as guidelines to evaluating the therapy animal's QOL. These factors will change as the animal ages and has more varied experiences.

As a part of this exercise, the therapist must learn to identify signs of stress in his or her therapy animal. Signs of stress vary across species and among individuals. Although stress assessment tools have been developed, they have been shown to have weaknesses and they are not entirely reliable (cf. McCobb et al., 2005). Together, the VFP and the therapist can ascertain what signs will indicate that the therapy animal is suffering from stress, and therefore discomfort.

24.3   Selection of an appropriate veterinary family practitioner

Selection of an appropriate veterinarian is of paramount importance to anyone who has a therapy animal in their household. Although veterinarians are becoming more aware of the increasing use of animals in therapy and other types of service, they may or may not have any experience with the various types of therapy work. What is most important is that the veterinarian has an interest in and experience with the species, and be knowledgeable about that species' behavior and physical needs. Table 24.4 lists veterinary associations or boards, a membership in which indicates a strong interest or specialty training in designated areas. Although membership in one of these associations does not guarantee expertise, it suggests that the veterinarian has a strong interest in the area and that there is likelihood that he or she has sought additional relevant training.

The veterinarian and hospital staff must be willing to work closely with the therapist to accomplish all of the work described in previous paragraphs. It would be of value for the therapist to schedule a preliminary appointment with the veterinarian to see if the veterinarian and hospital appear to be a good fit. A tour of the hospital should be arranged to observe the staff, watching for signals that they are friendly and happy to be there. Some questions that could be asked of the veterinarian are listed in Table 24.5.

Table 24.4 Veterinary associations with interests in selected species or practice areas

- American Board of Veterinary Practitioners (www.abvp.org)
- Association of Avian Veterinarians (www.aav.org)
- American Association of Feline Practitioners (www.aafponline.org)
- Association of Reptilian and Amphibian Veterinarians (www.arav.org)
- Association of Veterinary Family Practitioners (www.avfp.org)
- Association of Human-Animal Bond Veterinarians (www.aahabv.org)

Table 24.5 Questions an owner of a therapy animal may ask during an interview with a veterinarian

- What is your experience with AAT/AAA (describe specific type)?
- What suggestions and guidance can you provide on best practices for the care of therapy animals?
- What is your experience with the particular species to be used in AAT/AAA (if other than a dog or cat)?
- Do you have a special interest in a particular area of veterinary practice?
- Do you have any credentials or certifications (e.g. Board Certification in any of the specialties, Credential in Veterinary Family Practice, Academy of Veterinary Dentistry, etc.; these are not essential, but may suggest special expertise)?
- Are you a member of any veterinary associations (such as local and national veterinary medical associations and those listed in Table 24.4)?
- Are you a member of any other human/animal bond organizations (e.g. Delta Society, local Humane Society)?
- What courses do you attend for continuing education? (Ideally, courses related to the species of interest including behavior, nutrition and genetics, in addition to general medicine, surgery and dentistry.)
- What do you recommend for vaccinations? (Answer should be that it varies depending on the animal's exposure, age, function, etc.)
- Are behavior training services offered by the hospital, or can you recommend a reputable local trainer?
- Do you refer to veterinary specialists? Which ones?
- Do you offer emergency services or refer to an emergency hospital?
- What are the key factors you consider when developing a life maintenance plan for an animal? (The answer should include the role of the animal in the family, any functional demands on the animal, the environment, species, age, sex, breed, etc.)
- What suggestions can you provide to enhance the QOL of the therapy animal?
- Can you provide sound medical guidelines that should be considered for the daily routine of specific therapy animals?
- How frequently should a therapy animal be examined by the veterinarian, and what is involved in the examination?

24.4 Conclusion

In order for the therapy animal to perform optimally, it must be in good health, behave appropriately, and receive pleasure from the work. These conditions can best be achieved by choosing an appropriate animal for the AAT and developing a plan for life-long health maintenance. This plan can be implemented through the joint efforts of the AAT clinical team, the veterinary family practice staff and the primary care-taker of the therapy animal. Establishing a life-long plan will offer an animal the best opportunity to achieve healthy QOL while providing support to humans who are in need.

References

American Veterinary Medical Association. (2001). Wellness guidelines for animals used in animal-assisted activity, animal-assisted therapy, and resident animal programs. Retrieved Aug. 22, 2005 from http://www.avma.org/noah/members/policy/wellness_guidelines.asp

Bustad, L. (1980). *Animals, Aging and the Aged.* Minneapolis, MN: University of Minnesota Press.

Creagan, E. (2002). A scientific look at the human-animal bond. PAWSitive Interaction 2002 White Paper. Retrieved Aug. 11, 2009 from http://www.pawsitiveinteraction.org/background.html

Fiala, J. (2004). CVMA covets heightened legal status for pets. *DVMNewsmagazine, 35,* 36–39.

Fiala, J. (2005, April 1). CVMA sues city over declaw ban. *DVMNewsmagazine.* Retrieved Aug. 20, 2005 from http://dvmnewsmagazine.com/dvm/article/articleDetail.jsp?d=1555735

Fine, A. H. (2005, May 2). Animal assisted therapy and clinical practice. Psycho-Legal Associates CEU meeting, San Francisco, CA.

Fine, A. H., & Stein, L. (2003, Oct. 25). Animal assisted therapy and clinical practice. Psycho-Legal Associates CEU meeting, Pasadena, CA.

Fine, A. H. (2003, Nov. 1). Animal assisted therapy and clinical practice. Psycho-Legal Associates CEU meeting, Seattle, WA.

Flynn, C. P. (2000). Woman's best friend: pet abuse and the role of companion animals in the lives of battered women. *Violence, 6,* 162, Retrieved Aug. 11, 2009 from Sage Journals Online.

Friedmann, E., Katcher, A. H., Lynch, J. J., & Thomas, S. A. (1980). Animal companions and one year survival of patients after discharge from a coronary care unit. *Public Health Reports, 95,* 307–312.

Friedmann, E., & Thomas, S. A. (1995). Pet ownership, social support and one-year survival after acute myocardial infarction in the cardiac arrhythmia suppression trial (CAST). *American Journal of Cardiology, 76,* 1213–1217.

Garrity, T. F., Stallones, L., Marx, M. B., & Johnson, T. P. (1989). Pet ownership and attachment as supportive factors in the health of the elderly. *Anthrozoös, 3,* 35–44.

GfK Roper Public Affairs and Media. (2009, May 28–June 1). The AP-Petside.com poll. Retrieved Aug. 2, 2009 from http://www.ap-gfkpoll.com

Grieve, G., Neuhoff, K., Thomas, R., Welborn, L., Albers, J., & Parone, J. (2003). *The Path to High-quality Care: Practical Tips for Improving Compliance.* Lakewood, CO: American Animal Hospital Association.

Hess, L., Crimi, M., New, J., Orosz, S., & Pitts, J. (2005). The veterinarian's role in preventing and controlling disease in exotic animals in assisted-care facilities. *Journal of Avian Medicine and Surgery, 19,* 46–55.

Hetts, S., Heinke, M., & Estep, D. (2004). Behavioral wellness concepts for general veterinary practice. *Journal of the American Veterinary Medical Association, 225,* 506–513.

IPSOS-REID. (2001). Paws and claws. Retrieved Jan. 8, 2008 from http://www.ctv.ca/generic/WebSpecials/pdf/Paws_and_Claws.pdf

Johnson, R., & Meadows, R. (2000). Promoting wellness through nurse-veterinary collaboration. *Western Journal of Nursing Research, 22,* 773–775.

Katcher, A. H., Segal, H., & Beck, A. M. (1984). Contemplation of an aquarium for the reduction of anxiety. In R. K. Anderson, B. L. Hart, & L. A. Hart (Eds.), *The Pet*

Connection: Its Influence on Our Health and Quality of Life (pp. 171–178). St. Paul, MN: Globe Publishing.

Kealy, R. D., Lawler, D. F., Ballam, J. M., Lust, G., Biery, D. N., Smith, G. K., & Mantz, S. L. (2002). Evaluation of the effect of limited food consumption on radiographic evidence of osteoarthritis in dogs. *Journal of the American Veterinary Medical Association, 217,* 1678–1680.

Levinson, B. (1987). Foreword. In P. Arkow (Ed.), *The Loving Bond Companion Animals in the Helping Professions.* Saratoga, CA: R&E Publishers, Inc.

Lofflin, J. (2004). The changing status of pets. *Veterinary Economics, 45,* 33–38.

McCobb, E., Patronek, G., Marder, A., Dinnage, J., & Stone, M. (2005). Assessment of stress levels in cats in four animal shelters. *Journal of the American Veterinary Medical Association, 226,* 548–555.

McMillan, F. (2000). Quality of life in animals. *Journal of the American Veterinary Medical Association, 216,* 1904–1910.

Ormerod, E. J. (2008). Bond-centered veterinary pactice: lessons for veterinary faculty and students. *Journal of Veterinary Medical Education, 35*(4), 545–552.

Planchon, L., & Templer, D. (1996). The correlates of grief after the death of a pet. *Anthrozoös, 9,* 107–113.

Sapperfield, M. (2002). In San Francisco, pet owners recast as "guardians." *The Christian Science Monitor.* Retrieved Aug. 20, 2005 from http://www.csmonitor.com/2002/1220/p01s02-usgn.html

Schalock, R. (1996). The quality of children's lives. In A. Fine, & N. Fine (Eds.), *Therapeutic Recreation for Exceptional Children.* Springfield, IL: Charles C. Thomas.

Schwabe, C. (1984). *Veterinary Medicine and Human Health* (3rd ed.). Baltimore, MD: Williams and Wilkins.

Sharkin, B., & Knox, D. (2003). Pet loss: issues and implications for psychologists. *Professional Psychology, Research and Practice, 34*(4), 414–421.

Siegel, J. M., Angulo, F. J., Detels, R., Wesch, J., & Mullen, A. (1999). AIDS diagnosis and depression in the multicenter AIDS cohort study: the ameliorating impact of pet ownership. *AIDS Care, 11,* 157–170.

Taylor, L. H., Latham, S. M., & Woolhouse, M. E. (2001). Risk factors for human disease emergence. *Philosophical Transactions of the Royal Society B: Biological Sciences, 356,* 983–989.

Whitcomb, R. (2009). Court denies emotional damages for pet's loss. *DVMNewsmagazine, 40*(9), 1.

Wisemann-Orr, M., Nolan, A., Reid, J., & Scott, E. (2004). Development of a questionnaire to measure the effects of chronic pain on health-related quality of life in dogs. *American Journal of Veterinary Research, 65,* 1077–1084.

Wojciechowska, J., & Hewson, C. (2005). Quality of life assessment in pet dogs. *Journal of the American Veterinary Medical Association, 226,* 722–728.

Wojciechowska, J., Hewson, C., Stryhn, H., Guy, N., Patronek, G., & Timmons, V. (2005). Evaluation of a questionnaire regarding nonphysical aspects of quality of life in sick and healthy dogs. *American Journal of Veterinary Research, 66,* 1453–1460.

Zasloff, R. I., & Kidd, A. H. (1994). Loneliness and pet ownership among single women. *Physiological Reports, 75,* 747–752.

25 Methodological standards and strategies for establishing the evidence base of animal-assisted therapies

Alan E. Kazdin

Yale University

25.1 Introduction

Psychotherapy is defined broadly to encompass interventions that use psychosocial techniques (e.g. interpersonal interaction, learning experiences, role playing, practice, coping skills) to reduce distress, maladaptive behavior, and psychological and psychiatric problems and to enhance adaptive functioning and positive experiences in everyday life. The therapist provides conditions (e.g. support, encouragement, acceptance) through which these techniques are applied. Key concepts that are addressed or emerge in therapy include the patient/therapist relationship and bond, support, attachment, and friendship (e.g. Norcross, 2002; Schofield, 1986; Wallin, 2007). Also, the benefits of therapy are considered to include developing awareness, empathy, and increased interpersonal sensitivity, making individuals feel better, reducing stress, and improving the quality of life. Each of the concepts and benefits central to psychotherapy figures prominently in writings of human/animal relationships (e.g. Anderson, 2008; Olmert, 2009; Salotto, 2001). Thus, the systematic use of animals in the context of therapy is reasonable, intuitive, and consistent with core concepts of traditional psychotherapy.

Outside of the context of therapy, the benefits of close contact with animals are widely recognized. This can be attested to in part by pet ownership, which encompasses 63% of all households in the USA, based on 2005–06 data (www.americanpetproducts.org/). The number of pets (≈ 350 million) in the USA actually exceeds the number of people (≈ 303 million). The benefits of animal contact are evident from personal experience with pets, observation of the experience of others, and reliance on pets among many cultures currently and throughout history, as well as from scientific research on health and well-being. The challenge is to harness these benefits so they can be systematically applied in the context of therapy.

The appeal, widespread belief, and everyday experience of the benefits of human/animal contact are at once a strength and liability for developing the science

Handbook on Animal-Assisted Therapy. DOI: 10.1016/B978-0-12-381453-1.10025-X

base of animal-assisted therapy (AAT). The strength draws on the keen interest in these benefits and extending these benefits to many whose lives might be improved with animal contact. The liability stems from the almost universal acceptance of the benefits of animal/human contact. One might ask: Do we need research when all signs point to the huge impact of animals on human experience? Is it not obvious that animals and people help each other? That animals are subjectively valued and improve the quality of life are easily evaluated by just asking people. It is quite another matter to raise the empirical question of whether AATs can ameliorate social, emotional, behavioral adjustment problems and diagnosable psychiatric disorders (e.g. autistic spectrum disorders, anxiety, depression, conduct disorders) and mitigate the impairment with which these are associated. Claims have been made that AATs can effect change in these latter domains. Given the public health implications of advocating and delivering interventions, scientific scrutiny is essential.

The goal of this chapter is to foster further scientific evaluation of AATs in contexts in which the goal is to improve the social, emotional, behavioral adjustment or adaptive functioning or to ameliorate some psychological or psychiatric condition among children and adolescents. This chapter highlights the current status of psychotherapy (non-animal assisted) for children as a backdrop to convey current methodological standards for intervention research. The discussion moves from conceptual underpinnings of an investigation, to the specific question that is asked about treatment, and to control and comparison conditions pivotal to AAT research. Common methodological practices in AAT research that interfere with drawing conclusions about the effects of treatment are highlighted. The chapter concludes by proposing next steps for research; these are intended to advance both the conceptual understanding of AATs and the conclusions about their impact on child functioning.

25.2   Context: current advances in psychotherapy outcome research

AATs are often designed to improve adjustment and functioning of individuals and to decrease various sources of social, emotional, cognitive, and behavioral problems. Psychotherapy shares these goals but of course without the use of animals. The status and accomplishments of psychotherapy research are relevant because they convey a body of literature to which AAT research will be compared and integrated. Although most psychotherapy research focuses on adults, let me highlight progress by referring to psychotherapies for children and adolescents.[1]

There has been enormous progress in child therapy research in the past few decades (see Kazdin, 2000b; Weisz and Kazdin, 2010). First, the quantity of controlled therapy outcome studies is remarkable. The last formal estimate of such studies in 1999 placed the number at 1,500 (Kazdin, 2000a). The number continues

---

[1] "Children" in this chapter refers to children and adolescents, unless a specific distinction is required.

to increase in light of a constant stream of journals in which therapy studies are routinely published. It is difficult to evaluate that number without some comparison. It is useful to mention in passing that a recent review of AATs identified six studies of children and adolescents in which there were control or comparison groups (Nimer and Lundahl, 2007). There are hundreds of child and adolescent clinical problems and sources of impairment (e.g. anxiety, depression, oppositional defiant disorder, autistic spectrum disorders) (e.g. American Psychiatric Association, 1994). A large number of studies are needed to test variations of treatment across a range of dysfunctions.

Second, the quality of child psychotherapy research has improved over the years. Several methodological practices currently guide psychotherapy research and they are listed in Table 25.1. Randomized controlled clinical trials (RCTs) are the rule rather than the exception and many other practices listed in the table raise the methodological bar even higher. Not all studies include all of these practices, but it is difficult to obtain funding for treatment research or to publish the results of a psychotherapy outcome study in the scientific literature without including most of these features.

Third, quantitative (meta-analytic) reviews of the research consistently conclude that many forms of psychotherapy for children are effective (Weisz, 2004). These reviews place diverse outcome measures from the individual investigations on a common metric (effect size) so that studies can be combined and conclusions can be reached about different treatments, clinical problems, patient samples, and other characteristics spanning the studies. Improvements among children in treatment groups surpass the changes made by children in control-group conditions.

Table 25.1 Methodological practices that guide psychotherapy outcome research

1. Random assignment of participants to conditions
2. Careful specification of the client sample and the inclusion and exclusion criteria required for participation
3. Use of strong control or comparison groups (e.g. treatment as usual or another viable treatment rather than or in addition to no treatment or wait-list control groups)
4. Use of treatment manuals to codify procedures and practices so as to permit training of therapists and replication of treatment by other investigators
5. Assessment of treatment integrity, i.e. the extent to which the intervention was carried out as intended
6. Use of multiple outcome measures with multiple assessment methods (e.g. self-report, parent report, direct observation) and measures of multiple domains of functioning (e.g. symptoms, prosocial functioning)
7. Evaluation of the clinical significance of change, i.e. whether the changes at the end of treatment make a difference in returning individuals to adaptive functioning
8. Evaluation of follow-up weeks, months, or years after post-treatment assessment of child functioning.

Moreover, the magnitude of the effects of treatment is reasonably large (effect size $\approx .70$).[2]

Fourth and related, there are now several evidence-based psychotherapies. These refer to psychotherapies that have controlled studies to support them, where the effects of treatment have been replicated, and where several of the methodological practices noted in Table 25.1 have been included (Christophersen and Mortweet, 2001; Nathan and Gorman, 2007; Weisz and Kazdin, 2010). As an illustration, consider the treatment of aggressive and antisocial behavior among children (current psychiatric diagnosis is conduct disorder). Aggressive and antisocial behavior among children is the most commonly referred clinical problem to child inpatient and outpatient services (33–50% of all referrals in the USA). There are now at least seven evidence-based treatments. The treatments encompass young children through adolescents and mildly oppositional and aggressive behavior to severe and repetitive antisocial behavior that has led to adjudication.[3] This is a remarkable accomplishment in relation to a serious clinical problem. This is one example. Evidence-based psychotherapies are available for many other clinical problems, as reviewed in the previous citations.

My comments highlight advances in psychotherapy research. In passing, it is important to acknowledge the current status of child therapy as carried in clinical practice. There has been a huge lag in disseminating treatments that have a strong empirical base to clinical practice or to training programs in the mental health professions (e.g. clinical psychology, psychiatry, social work, and nursing). In clinical practice with children, more than 550 techniques are in use (Kazdin, 2000b). Most treatments in use have never been investigated empirically; many treatments known to be effective are *not* in widespread use; some treatments in widespread use are known not to be effective; and well-intentioned efforts to help children (e.g. horticulture therapy, smudge art therapy, wilderness camps) continue to emerge with no empirical evidence to support them.

For the purposes of this chapter, it is relevant to refer to a large and actively used set of treatments in clinical work that have little evidence to support them. Historically, unevaluated psychotherapies have had little scrutiny or accountability. Currently, the absence of evidence for a given intervention provides a sharp contrast

---

[2] Effect size (ES) refers to the magnitude of the difference between two (or more) conditions or groups and is expressed in standard deviation units. For the case in which there are two groups in the study, effect size equals the differences between means, divided by the standard deviation:

$$ES = \frac{m_1 - m_2}{s}$$

where m_1 and m_2 are the sample means for two groups or conditions (e.g. treatment and control groups), and s equals the pooled standard deviation for these groups.

Cohen (1988) has provided us with an admittedly arbitrary but now commonly used metric to judge the magnitude of effect sizes. Small, medium, and large ESs correspond to 0.2, 0.5, and 0.8, respectively.

[3] The seven treatments include: parent management training, multisystemic therapy, multidimensional treatment foster care, cognitive problem-solving skills training, anger control training, brief strategic family therapy, and functional family therapy. For a description and review of these treatments other sources are available (Kazdin, 2007b; Weisz and Kazdin, 2010).

to many other interventions now available. Scrutiny by state and federal agencies and third-party payers increasingly will influence what interventions are administered and reimbursed. Consequently, unevaluated treatments or poorly researched treatments will have renewed pressure to justify their use.

The progress I have highlighted conveys there is now a large outcome literature on psychological treatment for children. While the substantive gains have advanced, the methodological standards have evolved as well. Those standards reflect a broader movement in intervention research and health care. The standards for clinical trials across many disciplines have become higher and more explicit. As a prominent illustration, the Consolidated Standards of Reporting Trials (or CONSORT) have emerged to guide how clinical trials are conducted and reported. A checklist for investigators is available to address critical facets of the trial, such as how the sample was identified, how they were allocated to conditions, how many started in the trial and completed treatment, and whether they received the intended treatment (please see www.consort-statement.org/). The standards have been adopted by hundreds of professional journals from many disciplines and countries (see www.consort-statement.org/about-consort/supporters/consort-endorsers—journals/) in an effort not only to improve reporting of trials but also to increase their quality.

The implications of progress in psychotherapy research and explicit standards (e.g. CONSORT) for conducting intervention trials are clear. Methodological standards are in place and evolving; these standards convey what is required of any intervention for it to be added to the body of knowledge. Any newly proposed treatment or treatment that has been available for some time but has not undergone careful empirical evaluation has a methodological template to follow in order to gain the attention of the scientific community.

25.3   Conceptualizing the study and its focus

The preceding comments provide a backdrop for AAT by conveying advances in developing a list of evidence-based psychotherapies and in setting the methodological standards for adding less well-studied or evaluated interventions to that list. The context is useful but, by itself, is not very helpful in beginning or designing a study to evaluate an AAT. Development of a specific study begins with conceptualization of the study, treatment, and therapeutic change. Conceptualization of a study is discussed here at three levels proceeding from the more general to the specific issues that guide the design of a study and how the treatment is evaluated.

25.3.1   Small theory: the investigator's view of animal-assisted treatments

The design of a study begins with making explicit the theory that one has about the treatment. This has been referred to as a "small theory" or "treatment theory" to convey that it is confined to the particular study and need not be something grandiose to explain all therapy or all clinical problems (Lipsey, 1996). This theory specifies the clinical problem, what the treatment is, how or why that treatment can be expected to have impact on the problem, what the critical components of treatment are, and what outcomes best reflect therapeutic change. This small theory makes explicit the rationale for the treatment, its application, and evaluation. As I discuss later, common methodological problems in AAT research often emerge from not clarifying the rationale for the intervention or how the intervention might be expected to help participants.

The small theory proposes how the therapy works, i.e. through what processes. For example, what facet of the animal's presence in the session is responsible for or contributes to therapeutic change? Is it the presence of an animal, the inter-actions of the child with the animal, or the bond or relationship of the child to the animal that leads to or is likely to lead to change? Of course, it could be all of these and many more alternatives than those I am using for illustrative purposes. The processes are important to specify. Once specified, the investigator knows what to measure during treatment to ensure that in fact the process was altered. This might include evaluation of the extent of direct interaction or the bond the child reports.

Apart from assessment, specifying the process through which change occurs can guide the activities of the therapy sessions. Thus, if the child/animal relationship is important, the treatment procedures ought to maximize that. If direct contact and interaction are important, the sessions should be structured to ensure these occur at a high rate. One would expect the critical process(s) to relate to therapeutic change but the first task is to ensure that the process itself was invoked or occurred as intended.

Our small theory also directs attention to the outcome of treatment, i.e. assess-ments administered at the end of treatment (and perhaps follow-up) to evaluate efficacy. We might propose that the process of therapy reduces arousal in the session, perhaps because of the calming effect of direct physical contact with an animal. For outcome assessment, perhaps a measure of arousal also would be good to include in light of our small theory about what therapy is likely to accomplish. Arousal may be the primary measure and, in light of our view, and more likely than some other measure of anxiety (e.g. teacher ratings) to reflect change. Multiple measures might be included to evaluate treatment but the small theory conveys clearly what is likely or expected to happen and, at the very least, guides us in selecting some of the outcome measures to ensure our focus connects the problem, processes in treatment, and therapeutic change.

In short, a small theory guides the investigator in what to emphasize during the sessions and what to measure both during treatment (process measures) and after treatment (outcome measures). The absence of a small theory can foster a weak test of treatment and weak outcome effects. The small theory of why treatment works and what to emphasize might well be wrong, but remains a good place to begin in deciding what treatment to provide and how to deliver the treatment in ways likely to maximize its impact.

25.3.2 Questions to guide animal-assisted treatments

Another way to guide the design is to make explicit the specific question that may serve as the impetus for the study. Studies of psychotherapy (or other psychological, educational, and health care interventions) usually focus on one or more of several questions. These questions codify the substantive focus but in the process also influence many methodological decisions such as what the control or comparison groups will be. Table 25.2 lists several treatment strategies that encompass specific questions and control or comparison conditions required for their evaluation. These are frequently asked questions that guide intervention research and apply to AATs.

The first and most fundamental question is whether treatment is effective and surpasses changes over time that might otherwise occur without treatment. This is not an easy study to carry out in many situations because of ethical issues alone raised by withholding treatment for a no treatment or wait-list treatment control condition. From a methodological standpoint, a comparison of treatment versus no treatment is the most basic of the studies to show that treatment is effective. Also, this is the study most likely to show an intervention effect. Effect sizes (the magnitude of change) usually are stronger for treatment versus no treatment studies than treatment versus some other treatment condition. When two treatments are compared (e.g. AAT vs. treatment as usual), the differences between means of the groups and the effect sizes are smaller and a much larger sample size is needed for statistical power (Kazdin and Bass, 1989).[4] In principle, the comparison of treatment versus no treatment is a place to begin to establish the efficacy of treatment. In practice, withholding treatment makes this difficult to do with clinical samples. Also, now with many viable (evidence-based psychotherapies) the treatment/no treatment comparison is of diminished interest in many contexts (e.g. treatment of anxiety, depression, disruptive behaviors). There are already effective treatments and, in such cases, there is interest in showing some benefit or advantage in relation to one of these (e.g. lower cost, broader impact, less attrition from treatment, stronger maintenance of changes). An alternative is comparing a treatment (AAT) with a treatment that is routinely used (referred to as "treatment as usual").

The second question in the table, what components contribute to change, may be of special relevance to AATs. In evaluating and establishing the effectiveness of AATs, we take almost as a given that use of an animal in therapy contributes to therapeutic change. A study in which an AAT is compared to no treatment does not provide evidence that the animal made a difference to treatment outcome. There is strong evidence that meeting with a client and establishing a relationship contributes to therapeutic change when no animal is present. These influences are called the *non-specific treatment factors* or *common factors* of therapy and they alone seem to effect change. The factors are referred to as common because they characterize many even if not all therapies (Wampold, 2001). Among the elements are attending sessions, meeting with a therapist, expecting improvement, and having others (e.g. parents,

---

[4] Statistical power refers to the extent to which a study can detect a difference between groups when a genuine difference exists. It is quite possible that treatments have different effects and that one is in fact superior to the other but no differences are obtained on statistical evaluation. Such studies are likely to have insufficient power.

Table 25.2 Questions that guide psychotherapy research

Treatment strategy	Question asked of treatment	Control and comparison conditions required
Treatment package	What is the impact of treatment relative to no treatment?	Treatment vs. no treatment or wait-list control
Dismantling strategy	What components contribute to change?	Two or more treatment groups that vary in the components (or ingredients) of treatment they receive—some components are "subtracted" from the main treatment to see if they are needed
Constructive strategy	What treatments can be added (combined treatments) to optimize change?	Two or more treatment groups that vary in components. New components are added to the basic treatment to see if they enhance outcome
Parametric strategy	What parameters can be varied to influence (improve) outcome?	Two or more treatment groups that differ in one or facets of the treatment. A component central to treatment is varied (e.g. amount of contact with the animal; type of animal)
Comparative treatment strategy	How effective is this treatment relative to other treatments for this problem?	Two or more different treatments for a given clinical problem (could be two different models of AATs or AAT vs. some entirely different treatment)
Treatment moderator strategy[a]	What patient, therapist, treatment, and contextual factors influence (moderate) outcome, i.e. affect the magnitude or direction of impact	Treatment as applied separately to different types of cases or as administered by different types of therapists to see what variables influence the effectiveness of an AAT
Treatment mediator/ mechanism strategy[b]	What processes within or during treatment influence, cause, and are responsible for outcome (therapeutic change)?	Treatment groups in which processes during the course of treatment are evaluated to identify critical constructs on which therapeutic change depends

[a]A *moderator* refers to any variable that changes the magnitude or the direction of a relationship. For example, if an AAT is more or less effective with boys rather than girls (or younger rather than older children), then sex (or age) is considered be a moderator.

[b]A *mediator* refers to a statistical relation between an intervening variable and the relationship between an independent variable (e.g. AAT) and dependent variable (treatment outcome). A *mechanism* is the underlying basis for the effect and identifies the processes or events that are responsible for the change and how these changes come about (see Kazdin, 2007a for further discussion).

other relatives) who may also expect change. If an AAT were more effective than no treatment, the most parsimonious interpretation is that the effect was due to the impact of common factors. Another parsimonious interpretation would be that treatment with a human therapist led to change, again without suggesting the animal made a special contribution. These are plausible and parsimonious interpretations because they explain larger sets of studies in a uniform fashion in which animals (other than humans) were not present.

To test whether the animal contributes to therapeutic change requires that one group receives an AAT and another group receives a very similar treatment but without the animal present. From my perspective, of all the questions listed, question two is the highest priority for AAT research. There is a firm belief that presence of the animal makes a difference. I am not challenging that. Yet, I do not believe there is a strong body of empirical research in the context of child treatment to make the case persuasively, i.e. to the standards mentioned previously (see Table 25.1).

I mentioned that treatment versus no treatment control group studies are difficult to do with clinical samples and individuals in need of services. In contrast to that, question two is more feasible and user (clinician, administrator, and client) friendly. Among the groups needed for the study are two variations of treatment, one with and one without the presence of an animal. Because the vast majority of psychological treatments do not involve non-human animals, a comparison intervention without an animal is not likely to raise ethical concerns. The question is whether the animal makes an addition to treatment outcome and that can be readily addressed by a study comparing two genuine treatments.

The questions in Table 25.2 provide a broad portfolio of research. A well-designed study addressing any of the questions would be an excellent contribution. I have favored question two; other questions might be equally compelling. For example, the question of moderators addresses various conditions (e.g. type of children, type of animal, and child/animal combinations) that might influence therapeutic change. The investigator may have a view that some children (e.g. older versus younger; boys versus girls; individuals with anxiety versus other types of problems) will respond better or that one type of animal (or breed of a given animal) is better for a specific problem or age group. One could begin with a test of one of these hypotheses and not only evaluate the efficacy of treatment but also whether efficacy varies as a function of some other variable (moderator). There is no *a priori* reason to begin with one question rather than another. Yet, as one moves down the list of questions in Table 25.2, the experimental designs, assessment procedures, and data analyses can be increasingly complex and demanding.

25.3.3   Control and comparison conditions

Arguably, the two most fundamental questions for AATs are: Does the presence of an animal improve the effectiveness of therapy? and if it does, What is it about the animal contact that makes a difference? These questions nicely illustrate the control and comparisons needed in research and move to a more helpful level of specificity than enumerating the broad portfolio of treatment questions.

The first question about the contribution of the presence of an animal is relatively easily addressed. It is helpful to begin by recognizing that there is a large therapy literature of children interacting with animals where that animal is a human. We know that child/human contact can lead to therapeutic change. AATs propose that therapeutic change is enhanced when an animal is added and new experiences are built around that addition. It would be important to include a control condition in which an AAT is compared with the same or as similar as possible treatment with just the therapist. Support for the first question is easily tested by showing the AAT leads to greater therapeutic change or is better in some other way (e.g. subjective evaluation of the session by the child, better participation of the child in the treatment process) when compared to that treatment or very similar treatment without the addition of an animal. In brief, to show that the non-human animal makes a difference requires controlling for the influence of the human animal (therapist) in the session. That study is not difficult to do.

Let us assume that in fact the above comparison, treatment by a therapist with an animal leads to greater therapeutic change than that same or similar treatment without the animal. We move to the second question: What is it about the animal/child contact or about introducing an animal in the session that makes a difference? Is it the use of a *live* animal (e.g. dog) in the session or would a non-living substitute (e.g. stuffed animal) do just as well? We know that children use stuffed animals to cope with fear and anxiety (e.g. Muris et al., 2001) and hence these "animals" too might be reasonable therapeutic aides. Tinkering with stuffed animals so they can be heated (Weiner, 2001) and perhaps warm and cozy might make their utility in therapy even more plausible to some. Presumably, most of us believe strongly that there is something very special about the live animal/child bond that is therapeutic. From a methodological standpoint, all we need to do is to specify that feature or set of features and ensure that any comparison or control group does not receive that part. Again, this is precisely where the small theory of the investigator not only dictates the therapy group but also the appropriate control group.

Based on that small theory, a credible control condition might be based on robotic pets, especially since robotic pets are becoming increasingly sophisticated in terms of their response to children, their ability to acquire information (learn) and patterns of interaction, and their ability to "see" and react (through small cameras). For example, the robotic dog, named AIBO™ (by Sony), has been subjected to careful research pertinent to the discussion of AAT.[5] After a period of interacting, children accord AIBO mental states (e.g. AIBO can feel happy, tries to obtain a nearby toy) and biological characteristics (e.g. can grow, breathe, feel pain). Also, children ascribe to AIBO the ability to establish social rapport (e.g. AIBO likes the child, can be a friend, wants to spend time with the child) (Kahn et al., 2006). Children at different ages view the capacities and social attributes of a robotic pet, stuffed animal, and live animal

---

[5] AIBO is a robotic dog developed by Sony and marketed as a social companion. "AIBO" is taken from the name of the software that controls its action. The robot has the shape of a dog (see photo at http://en. wikipedia.org/wiki/AIBO) and is capable of engaging in several activities including locating a ball, butting it, kicking it, and more. The robot acquires a repertoire of behavior (learns), goes through stages of development, and interacts with the child.

differently, however, the similarities are striking (see Melson et al., 2009). Differences in child interactions with AIBO and a live dog favored AIBO on some measures (e.g. social interaction, touching) and a live dog on others (e.g. stroking, participation in the sessions) (Ribi et al., 2008). AIBO has been suggested as an alternative to use in AAT. Indeed, AAT research using AIBO has increased activity and social behavior among the elderly and surpassed the impact of a control condition using a stuffed animal (Tamura et al., 2004).

The purpose here is not to advance the use of robotic pets in the context of treatment. Yet, the notion of robotic animals and their increased sophistication can help sharpen our view and research on AATs. Precisely what is it about the child/animal contact or connection in AAT that is an aid to therapeutic change? This question refers to the process of treatment and what an AAT may uniquely provide. Can robotic animals in the session, stuffed animals, or other means (e.g. virtual animals and pets on a computer screen) be used to provide the benefits of animals in therapy? Many, if not most of us, believe that the live animal (and indeed live pet) are without peer in what they provide for human interaction. In everyday life all we need to support that belief are subjective reports of individuals from surveys. However, the AAT professional literature has a more sophisticated agenda and challenge, namely, empirical demonstration that live human/non-human interaction has effects that are unique. That agenda requires demonstration against strong control conditions that omit the unique components of live animal/human interaction.

I have made the assumption that most professionals interested in AATs would view live animal/human interaction as critical. It is possible that many would view animals in all of their living and non-living forms (e.g. robotic pets) as potential therapeutic aids. That view would greatly change the nature of a treatment study. If a live animal is conceived as critical, then contact with a stuffed or robotic animal is a possible control condition. If animal contact in any form is critical, then stuffed and robotic animals become two viable and possibly equally effective treatments. Again, the methodology, in this case what might be a control condition, stems from the small theory about a given AAT and the facet(s) of child/animal contact critical to therapeutic change.

25.4 Common methodological problems

From reviews and perusal of several AAT studies, I have identified a set of issues and practices that limit the conclusions reached about AAT. These issues and practices encompass general points already made but more concretely convey potential problems and what might be done to solve them.

25.4.1 Conceptual issues

I mentioned the importance of a small theory to guide research. The reason is that without this theory it is easy to have assumptions that are likely to misguide the project or limit the effects of treatment. Consider two such issues that emerge in the AAT literature.

Etiology and change theories

In specifying the rationale for AATs, it is important to distinguish theory of etiology and theory of change. Etiology refers to the causes or origins of the problems the child is experiencing. Change refers to what can be done to overcome or alleviate the problems. A common view is that one must get at the "putative" root of the problem and that unless one undoes the cause, there will be no improvement or amelioration of the problem. There are many examples in which this is quite true (e.g. rabies, strep throat). Whether in medicine, psychology, or counseling, we always want to know the cause(s) and once we do, effective treatment and preventive efforts become much more feasible. However, we do not have to know the cause to have effective interventions. For example, in medicine many problems varying in severity and consequence (e.g. headaches, blood pressure, childhood leukemia, and many cancers) can be effectively treated. Similarly, in clinical psychology, psychiatry, and social work, anxiety, depression, conduct disorder, and sexual dysfunction, to mention a few areas, can be effectively treated. In each instance, we do not know the causes. Indeed, there are likely to be many causes. A specific outcome (e.g. anxiety disorder) might be arrived at in any number of ways.

I mention this in the context of AAT research because more attention is needed on articulating why and how the presence of animals can enhance or lead to change. Occasionally, one finds pressure of the investigator to explain how the problem comes about and then to connect that to why the focus is important and justified. As I illustrate later, trying to explain etiology and change and connecting them often is forced or departs from what is known about a clinical problem. We would profit from a theory of change for AATs or theories of change for various problem domains (e.g. anxiety or depression).

Consider an illustration from an area in which I work. In the treatment of children with severe aggressive and antisocial behavior, altering how parents interact with their children (parent management training) is an evidence-based therapy (Kazdin, 2005). Some parents engage in interactions (e.g. use of harsh corporal punishment) that may well play an etiological role in the child's problems and here changing the interaction patterns might be relevant to etiology and change. However, more commonly, we have no clear idea why the child engages in the antisocial acts leading to his or her referral; aberrant parenting practices are not evident. Even so, changing parent/child interaction patterns to promote prosocial behavior can make a significant difference in child functioning. Research on learning has generated principles and concrete practices known to change behavior (parent and child), and these practices serve as the basis for the intervention. The focus is on change and the processes leading to that. And so with AAT, it would be useful to make explicit the change theory and processes likely to be involved in therapeutic change.

Questionable or unsupported assumptions

The blending or confusion of etiology and change is often evident when an investigator selects a characteristic of the child that he or she considers to be the basis of a problem (etiology) and believes the goal of AAT as altering that characteristic (change). In many instances, the very premise can threaten the credibility of the study. As an illustration, youth might be identified for inclusion in a study because of behavior problems or lack of impulse control. The rationale for using a particular AAT may be that the treatment will build self-esteem. Self-esteem may be assumed to be the culprit responsible for the children's problems (etiology) or the basis for redressing the problems (change). Improving self-esteem becomes the focus or goal of treatment. Yet, self-esteem has no clear connection to behavioral or other mental health problems either via etiology or change processes (see Baumeister et al., 2003). (An exception is that low self-esteem can accompany and be part of clinical depression.) There is no strong reason to focus on self-esteem to change disruptive behavior, anxiety, poor academic performance, or social skills deficits and, indeed, empirical reasons to avoid this focus. One might focus on self-esteem as an end in itself. That is, if the children are identified because of low self-esteem and the goal is to build self-esteem, obviously the means and goals are aligned. It is the notion that self-esteem is an important target to accomplish some other goal (e.g. changing a clinical problem) that is difficult to support.

My comments are not about self-esteem *per se*. Rather, the target of treatment or what the treatment is trying to change must have a connection to the outcomes. Many studies begin with the premise that if the children had a better understanding, if they showed more empathy, if they knew better, if they developed a caring relationship with an animal, or if they took responsibility for an animal, they would no longer have the problems or would be significantly improved in some specific domain (e.g. symptoms, academic performance, social skills). From my understanding, each of these views has little empirical support.

Three lines of evidence are relevant to support the focus on such characteristics as self-esteem, empathy, understanding, and other constructs that might guide treatment: (1) that children with clinical dysfunction or social, emotional, and behavioral problems have deficits of some kind (e.g. in understanding, self-esteem, or empathy); (2) that changing self-esteem (empathy, understanding or other constructs) leads to change in the target focus (e.g. disruptive behavior, anxiety); and (3) that working with animals changes that specific focus (understanding or other constructs), which then leads to improvement in clinical outcomes.

Children with clinical problems (e.g. anxiety disorder, conduct disorder, autistic spectrum disorder) often have deficits or special characteristics in multiple domains of functioning (e.g. in affect, cognition, behavior, family life). When such characteristics are measured concurrently, i.e. at the time the diagnosis is made, these are correlates. If these characteristics are measured in advance of the onset of the problem or diagnosis, they are referred to as risk factors. There is extensive research on correlates and risk factors and hence support for (1) is readily available for many clinical disorders.

Evidence for (2) is more difficult to find in relation to AATs or many other therapies for that matter. That research is needed because attempting or succeeding at altering correlates and risk factors may not have impact on the outcome. (I return to this point in the discussion of risk factors.) Question (3) is particularly demanding and asks about the role of the animal in changing the construct (self-esteem) and whether the animal contact contributes to therapeutic change. I could not find evidence for (3), but of course that does not mean it does not exist.

If the goal of an AAT is to teach knowledge about animals, to build self-esteem, to develop empathy, to develop responsibility, to overcome loneliness, to provide social support, to improve human/animal relations and bonding, and to reduce cruelty to animals, then an AAT may be a very reasonable means of accomplishing these goals. The gap between the goals of therapy (e.g. developing responsibility) and the means through which they are achieved (e.g. taking care of an animal) is relatively narrow. A small theory may more easily bridge the goals and means to achieve them. In contrast, if the goal is to reduce violence, aggression, anxiety or to improve inter-personal relations and academic performance, the gap to bridge may be larger. The goals may be reasonable but their connection to the means is less clear. The small theory has more demands placed on it to convey the link between what the AAT does and accomplishes and how that leads to changes in clinical dysfunction. The over-arching question is why would one expect the addition of animals in treatment to make a difference in a particular outcome domain?

25.4.2 Sampling issues

Ambiguous samples and treatment foci

AAT studies occasionally focus on "at-risk" individuals. There are so many children exposed to untoward conditions early in life. Examples of these conditions include natural disasters (e.g. hurricanes, tsunamis, drought), human-made disasters (e.g. war, crime, trafficking of children), other life calamities (e.g. loss of parents, homelessness from parent lack of resources), and experiences in the home (e.g. neglect, abuse, and exposure to violence). Children with such exposure form a vast group who are at increased risk for some or usually multiple untoward outcomes. Preventing and alleviating these outcomes are enormously important.

That said, research practices within the AAT literature can impede progress in developing the scientific base of treatment without better clarifying the samples. In AAT intervention studies with "at-risk" children, often it is unclear what the children are at risk for. This has multiple implications for the study and what the results might yield. First, if "at-risk" children are identified for inclusion in a study, what makes them at risk (what characteristics or variables) and how were those variables measured? Sometimes the measures are easily obtained, available, or obvious (e.g. age, family socioeconomic standing, medical or psychiatric diagnosis). Interpretation and replication of the results require knowing who was studied, their key character-istics, and how these characteristics were assessed.

Second and related, when possible it is useful to quantify the degree of risk. It is quite possible that the effectiveness of the intervention will vary; some children will respond well, some perhaps less well, and some not at all. Degree of risk is a reasonable dimension to evaluate in relation to outcome. Was the AAT effective across all levels of children at risk? That would be very useful to know and represents one of the questions (treatment moderator strategy) included in Table 25.2.

Third, the outcome measures ought to be closely connected to the domain for which the children are at risk. For example, if the youth are at risk for delinquency or academic failure, it is important to evaluate the extent to which the treatment reduced risk for these specific outcomes. That is, how did the AAT change the risk status of individuals? If the focus were on children at risk for depression and treatment tried to increase self-esteem that might be a reasonable focus because low self-esteem is associated with depression. Here is a case where measures of self-esteem would be appropriate at pretreatment to ensure the children were really at risk and to operationalize this in a way so the study could be replicated. Also, at post-treatment, self-esteem too would be relevant to show that changes in fact were made.

As I mentioned, a risk factor is an antecedent correlate of a later outcome. Often malleable risk factors are targeted for intervention for preventive purposes. However, it is critical to bear in mind that altering (reducing) risk factors has no necessary relation to effecting change in relation to preventing a particular outcome (Kraemer et al., 1997). From the standpoint of designing an AAT study, it may be sufficient to show that the children were at risk for an outcome and that risk was reduced at the end of the treatment. However, the connection between how the sample was selected (what they are at risk for), the focus of treatment (what is done within AAT sessions), and the measures used to evaluate outcome ought to be explicit.

Heterogeneous samples

Another issue that emerges in selecting an unspecified "at-risk" population warrants separate comment. The selection of such a population without further specification is likely to lead to a heterogeneous sample for a given study. That is, children will have a wide range of experiences that place them "at risk" and a wide range of outcomes for which they are at risk. At first blush, there seems to be an advantage of selecting a heterogeneous sample. After all, we want to know about children as they really are or as they are in a particular institution or setting. Yet, in conducting a treatment outcome study, one would like to begin with a relatively homogeneous sample, that is, children who are similar in age and who present roughly similar problems. The initial task of research is to evaluate unambiguously if there is an effect and whether the AAT makes a difference. The more diverse the sample in the study, the greater the variability (individual differences) they will show on any outcome measure. The greater the variability, the more difficult it can be to demonstrate a treatment effect. The high variability resulting from a very diverse sample usually will require a much larger sample size to ensure that there is sufficient statistical power to detect an intervention effect. Even with that increased power, the success and failure of the intervention for multiple subgroups within the study could obscure genuine treatment effects.

As a place to begin, it is usually advisable to establish the effectiveness of the intervention with a relatively homogeneous sample. Once treatment is established as effective, next steps can include evaluating the effects with various samples (e.g. types of clinical, social, or educational problems), conditions of administration (e.g. individual, group; daily, weekly), and other variables (e.g. therapist or animal characteristics, matching animals to children) that might influence outcome. This beginning point might begin with the question: With what sample is one likely to see the effects of an AAT? That is, we want to design the study to reveal if there are effects under circumstances that we believe provide our strongest test. Early research is a test of principle to see if the treatment has therapeutic effects, rather than an effort to see if the intervention can be generalized to most people, with most problems, and under most circumstances. Homogeneity and heterogeneity of a sample or other conditions (e.g. settings) under which a given treatment is tested are a matter of degree. From the standpoint of demonstrating whether an intervention is likely to effect change, it is usually advisable to err on the side of homogeneity of the sample early in a program of research.

25.4.3 Design and procedural issues

Single-group pre-post-only design

The number of AAT studies for children and adolescents is small although no doubt larger than the 16 identified by meta-analysis a few years ago (Nimer and Lundahl, 2007). Most of the studies omit control groups. Rather, they include one group in which the children's presenting problems (e.g. anxiety, disruptive behavior) or some other characteristic are assessed before and after completion of an AAT. In the demonstration, the results may indicate improvements from pre- to post-treatment assessment. These improvements may be statistically significant and interpreted as evidence that treatment led to change.

In meta-analyses of psychotherapy outside the context of AATs, pre-post evaluations of an intervention are rarely permitted (see Weisz, 2004). The reason is that these are not considered as research studies in which conclusions about treatment can be drawn. Changes from pre- to post-treatment can occur for a variety of reasons that are well codified in research methodology.[6] The impact of history (events during the treatment period), maturation (processes within the individual), repeated testing, statistical regression, and changes in the measuring instrument or how that instrument is interpreted are often plausible and parsimonious explanations of such changes (see Kazdin, 2003). These influences (e.g. history, maturation) are readily ruled out as explanations of the basis for the change once a control group (e.g. no treatment, wait list) or another treatment group (e.g. treatment as usual without animals) is used and children are randomly assigned to conditions. Pre-to-post change of one group allows the researcher to say there was a change but from a methodological standpoint one cannot attribute that change to the intervention.

---

[6] In methodology, these influences are referred to threats to internal validity. They consist of extraneous influences in the study that might explain the effects attributed to the intervention. There are other categories of threats that focus on the generality of a finding (threats to external validity), on interpretation of what is responsible for therapeutic change (threats to construct validity), and aspects of the data analyses and evaluation that can mislead in relation to the conclusions that are drawn (threats to statistical conclusion validity). These are beyond the scope of the present chapter but selected issues they raise (e.g. interpretation of AAT effects, statistical power) are raised here (see Kazdin, 2003).

Let us assume for a moment that we used a pre-post test, single-group study and found improvements at the end of treatment. Let us say further that all those influences I mentioned (e.g. history, regression) could not explain the findings. Even at that point, we cannot attribute the changes to the AAT. There is no evidence that the animal/child interaction had any role in the improvements. The influence of common factors of therapy mentioned previously is one plausible explanation of why change occurred. The influence of a human therapist alone, without the need for an animal in the session, is yet another plausible interpretation. Both these interpretations have parsimony on their side because they can explain many other findings as well as those of this hypothetical demonstration. Again, I am not asserting that these other interpretations really do explain the change. I merely note the methodological point the results of a single-group, pre-post demonstration do not provide support for the impact of an AAT. The changes cannot be unambiguously attributed to the intervention, leaving aside the use of an animal as part of that intervention. Single-group, pre-post tests are an excellent way to begin pilot work before a study is conducted. Pilot work allows one to explore ways to implement and improve the intervention, to evaluate if the measures are feasible and reflect change, and to master other details of running a study. However, the work is not sufficient to draw conclusions about the effects of the intervention.

Single therapists, single animals

As a general rule, evaluation of an AAT in a given study requires at least two therapists administering the intervention and at least two animals (e.g. two dogs). For example, if an AAT is compared with no treatment and a dog is the animal of choice, it is important to have at least two therapists administer treatment and at least two dogs. The dogs can be similar and so can the therapists!

The reason for at least two is that the effects of treatment must be separable (procedurally and statistically) from the conditions of administration (which therapist, which dog). If only one therapist (therapist A) and only one dog (dog A) were used and the AAT were effective, a conclusion cannot be reached that the AAT was responsible for the effects. Rather the conclusion has to be discussed as the combination of AAT + therapist A + dog A. It might be that this special combination was responsible for the change and concluding that it was the AAT (without acknowledging the connection to one therapist) is not appropriate. Adding one more therapist and one more dog to the study allows one to separate the impact of these influences statistically and reach a clearer conclusion.

Ideally, therapist A sees several children and works with dog A for half of the children she sees and with dog B for the other half of the children she sees. Therapist B sees several children and works with dog A and dog B in the same way. At the end of the study, the investigator can evaluate the effects of treatment (when compared to some control group) and see or show that AAT is effective whether administered by therapist A or B and whether a child received treatment with dog A or B. One could then conclude that the AAT works independently of which of the two (or more) therapists and which of the two (or more) dogs were used. That demonstration is much stronger than if only one therapist or one dog was used.

It might well be that treatment is more effective with one of the therapists or one of the dogs. That is not necessarily a problem. The differential effectiveness of some therapists, some animals, and some therapist/animal combinations may even generate useful hypotheses for further study. Using only one therapist or one dog (or other animal) in a study is a problem because it does not allow discussion of the impact of the AAT apart from the very narrow and possibly non-replicable treatment/therapist/animal combination.

Codifying the intervention

Treatment manuals are written descriptions of the intervention and are used in research to codify treatment procedures and how they are implemented. Treatment manuals usually serve four functions. First, they provide materials that can be used to train therapists. They provide guidelines for what therapists should do and provide a tool, but not necessarily the only tool, to train therapists. Second, they provide guidelines for evaluating adherence to treatment. The extent to which therapists did what they were trained to do and followed the intended treatment are significant issues in treatment research (Perepletchikova and Kazdin, 2005). Third, manuals permit the accretion of experience and research findings. Experience with treatment and overcoming obstacles in applying the treatment can lead to revisions in a manual. Without a manual, the benefits of experience and clinical applications are more likely to be lost. Fourth and critical for establishing the scientific base of AATs is that manuals permit replication by others.

Treatment manuals vary from a list of general principles with illustrations of how these are applied (e.g. Henggeler et al., 1998) to overly compulsive word-for-word, session-by-session scripts to guide therapists (e.g. Kazdin, 2005). AATs, when manualized, might vary greatly from this one extreme to the other. One codifies all that one can and usually that is not all that is done in the treatment sessions. Training surgeons, airline pilots, and snipers involves specifying and then teaching all one can but in the actual context with an individual patient, flight, or battle, invariably there are actions that could not have been fully codified or anticipated. And so it is on the battlefield of clinical work. That all clients are different or need to be considered individually is not a firm basis for omitting a well-specified plan. Research asks that the plan be made explicit so it can be replicated.

Codifying treatment does not mean that individual differences of the children or the animals are ignored. Bypass surgery and appendectomies have many standard features, even though every operation varies as a function of the patient and the surgeon. Here, too, in AATs, a study ought to codify key procedures, what kinds of interactions are important among the therapist, child, and animal, what is likely to be discussed, what activities will be performed, and what roles the therapist, child, and animal will have. The treatment manual is a place where the small theory that guides the study is translated into more concrete procedures. What activities, statements, procedures, or other facets of treatment ought to guide the therapist? These form the manual with the level of specificity that the intervention allows.

Actually, the task of developing a treatment manual for an AAT is slightly greater than for a similar treatment without an animal. The role of the animal (e.g. any desirable activity, any contact with the child, approximately how much) ought to be described. Guidelines describing the activities and role of the animal, apart from describing the equivalent for the therapist, are essential.

Treatment manuals become odious to ponder if one views them as recipe books with ingredients and their amounts precisely specified. Treatments are not rigid recipes. However, for therapy research the other extreme is not permissible either, namely, free-wheeling, idiosyncratic therapist delivery of an intervention in which we have no way of knowing what was done and no way of replicating that specific intervention. Those days are long past in light of the progress of therapy research I highlighted previously. Treatment manuals or guidelines are critical both for the scientific and clinical application of treatment. We want treatment not only to be replicable in research but also for training therapists in clinical work.

25.4.4 Assessment issues

Multiple measures of outcome

Outcome measures refer to those indices that will assess the effectiveness of the intervention. The measures are connected closely to the reasons why the children were selected to participate. For example, if the children have behavioral problems, the measures would be selected to reflect these problems. In any given study it is important to have more than one measure of the outcome and more than one method of assessment (e.g. self- and other-report, direct observation, ratings, physiological measures). We are interested in the construct (or domain), such as behavioral problems (or anxiety, depression, for examples), rather than in any single measure. The measure is one index to operationalize the construct but the construct is better represented by more than one measure.

As an example, parent and teacher ratings on standardized and well-validated measures such as the Child Behavior Checklist are commonly used to evaluate psychotherapy for children (Achenbach, 1991a,b). They both sample multiple domains of functioning (e.g. symptoms of many types, positive social behavior) and yield different perspectives on how well the child is doing. Sometimes, direct observations of behavior or samples of child behavior in the treatment setting often are assessed as well. The point here is that more than one measure and use of more than one rater or method of assessment are advisable. Multiple measures and methods of assessment strengthen the conclusion that the domain of interest was altered.

The use of more measures or many measures does not always need to be onerous. Not all outcome measures are time consuming or client unfriendly. There are validated measures that have been used with adults and children in clinical settings to evaluate progress of ongoing treatment. A prominent example is a family of measures referred to as Outcome Questionnaires with versions that vary by age group (see www.oqmeasures.com/site). For each version, patients (or for children, their parents) can rate several items that assess multiple symptom domains (e.g. depression, anxiety, interpersonal problems, and others). The measure can be completed weekly (or each session) and takes approximately 5 minutes to complete. Some of the versions have been well tested and validated (e.g. >10,000 patients) and shown to be useful in evaluating and predicting response to treatment (e.g. Lambert et al., 2003).

I write not to lobby for any particular measure but rather to convey that valid assessments are available that are compatible with the exigencies of ongoing clinical work and research. In therapy research, multiple outcome measures are now the rule rather than the exception. The measures often reflect the primary focus (e.g. aggression, anxiety). In addition, the measures may be used to evaluate the scope of treatment impact as discussed next.

Scope of assessment

I have emphasized outcome assessment which focuses on the problem domains that served as the impetus for providing an AAT in a given study. Yet, one might also want to evaluate more domains than the primary problem. As an illustration, at the clinical service in which I work, our treatments (parent management training, cognitive problem-solving skills training) lead to reductions in aggressive and antisocial child behaviors at home, at school, and in the community (www.yale.edu/childconductclinic/index.html). The children are referred to the service for such problems. Consequently, those problems are the emphasis of our interventions and outcome assessment battery. However, psychosocial treatments are not usually surgical in their impact, that is, the benefits are likely to be reflected in other domains. In our work, we find that reducing aggressive and antisocial child behavior is associated with reductions in mother depression and stress in the home and improved family relations (Kazdin and Wassell, 2000; Kazdin and Whitley, 2006). We do not specifically focus on these latter domains but it is helpful to document broader effects beyond the treatment goals.

For a given application, it might well be that an AAT is equally effective as some other treatment in improving child functioning. Yet, an AAT might be viewed as more acceptable to children and parents, have less stigma associated with it than some other form of treatment, or have lower rates of dropping out, when compared to a more traditional form of therapy. The benefits of treatment and the relative benefits in relation to other treatments do not necessarily derive from the impact on the clinical problem alone. For example, medications for depression often do not differ very much in their impact on the disorder, but some vary markedly in their side effects (e.g. loss of interest in sex) that influence their use. It is likely that an AAT would have broad as well as specific effects and including measures of these, to the extent feasible, could be very useful.

25.4.5 General comments

I have highlighted several concrete practices that relate to the quality of an investigation and the conclusions that can be drawn. Many of the practices make concrete the more general conceptual issues I noted previously about the theory behind the study, the specific question(s) that will be asked, and the control and comparison conditions to be included. Methodological practices fundamentally are influenced by what the investigator wishes to say and is entitled to say at the end of the investigation. Once one is clear on precisely what one wishes to conclude, many facets of the how the study ought to be carried out fall into place.

I gave special attention to control and comparison groups because they relate directly to the conclusions one wishes to reach. I provided that emphasis because of the strong interest in demonstrating that human/animal interaction and experience contributes to therapeutic change, which is easily addressed with suitable control conditions once an investigator specifies a bit about what of that interaction is critical.

25.5   Possible next steps

My comments directed toward developing a stronger scientific base of AATs focus on treatment and therapeutic change. Well-designed treatment trials in keeping with current standards for such research are obviously important. Yet, there are additional options for next steps for AATs that are arguably as or more valuable in developing the strong empirical base. Let me highlight three.

25.5.1   Quality of life and subjective experience

It would be excellent to add one or several AATs to the list of evidence-based psychotherapies for changing anxiety, depression, or conduct problems to mention just three clinical domains for which such treatments exist. However, there is much more to life and to AATs than therapeutic change for clinical disorders. Readers of this chapter are likely to believe that animal contact makes human life better and improves the quality of everyday experience. For children who receive contact with animals whether in an institution, outpatient service, or at home, we presume that life is better.

It is hardly trivial to show that children's lives are improved whether or not they are getting better in relation to some problem they experience. For any population in need of care, consider that they may not improve therapeutically with a particular medical or psychological procedure. Animal contact might prove to be an oasis for one's emotional life in situations in which there might not be changes for some condition that cannot be controverted therapeutically. For any population not in need of care (e.g. children functioning well in everyday life) it would also be great to elaborate further the benefits of animal contact, their scope, and for whom, and under any special circumstances.

In my opinion and as an outsider to this field, demonstrations that show reliable and replicable effects that systematic (or unsystematic) contact with animals improves subjective experience, alters mood (transient states), increases joy, improves feelings of physical health (whether health was affected or not), and makes the quality of life better would be an enormous contribution. If there are controlled studies that already show and elaborate these effects, it would be worth bringing them to better light. If such studies are rare, programmatic research on the topic would be worth doing.

The requisite research to evaluate quality of life and subjective experience might include surveys and self-report, but certainly other measures (e.g. social interaction after contact with pets, behavioral measures of enjoying oneself) could enrich the demonstrations. Also, special opportunities could be seized to convey how subjective experience and adaptation and coping are enhanced during difficult times. For example, are children with pets functioning better after trauma (e.g. exposure to loss, natural disaster such as a hurricane, divorce of parents) than those without pets? These are studies that require careful evaluation (e.g. to control for all sorts of variables with which pet ownership can be confounded) but could help color the larger canvas of systematic research that conveys the contribution of animals to the quality of life.

25.5.2 Laboratory studies of human/animal contact

It is likely that contact with animals can exert significant impact on affect, behavior, and cognition, and responses to stress, to mention a few domains. It would be quite useful to conduct laboratory studies to elaborate this impact. By laboratory work, I mean sessions where a child and animal come to a room and specific tasks are presented. The goal is to codify the impact of animal presence or contact on such domains as measures of concentration, measures of sociability, facial expressions (e.g. smiles, joy), stress reduction when given a challenging task, biological measures (e.g. cortisol), and neuroimaging (e.g. fMRI). There are studies that show that the presence of animals affects performance in some spheres (e.g. speed of performance on motor tasks, compliance with instructions; Gee et al., 2007, 2009). Other studies evaluate the types of contact with animals and whether the benefits of contact exceed the benefits with stuffed or robotic animals (e.g. Kahn et al., 2006; Stanton et al., 2008). These include free play and laboratory types of activities in which children are observed and their reactions are recorded.

Studies demonstrating the benefits of animal contact could advance AAT significantly. Moreover, mounting such demonstrations is much more feasible than an RCT. The research could provide underpinnings for later treatment trials as the benefits of animal contact among different domains of functioning begin to be elaborated. This elaboration would include at least these three steps: (1) showing that there are benefits, (2) elaborating the scope or breadth of the benefits (e.g. social, emotional, cognitive, experiential), and very importantly (3) attempting to understand why or how these benefits occur (e.g. what happens biologically and how those processes might explain the benefits). This research, all out of the context of therapeutic applications, would provide a strong base for treatment research.

The careful control that laboratory studies provide maximizes the likelihood of demonstrating effects of various manipulations of type and dose of animal contact. Also, within the laboratory, understanding mechanisms of action can begin to be addressed, i.e. through what processes do contacts with animals exert their influences. For example, it would not be difficult to begin to elaborate the neurological underpinnings (e.g. via neuroimaging) of contact with animals. Such work could greatly advance therapeutic applications by suggesting how animal contact exerts impact and what systems (e.g. neurotransmitters, brain circuits) might be affected. This work might interface with other studies of clinical dysfunction already available in which similar systems are implicated.

25.5.3 Expanding the methodologies to study animal-assisted treatments

My comments regarding methodological requirements and guidelines for therapy research were all in the tradition of quantitative research. Quantitative research refers to the methods in which most researchers are trained. Familiar features of the methodology include null hypothesis testing, comparison of groups that are exposed to separate conditions or interventions, and use of statistical significance testing to draw inferences about the impact of an intervention or experimental condition. Within this research tradition, RCTs are considered to be the "gold standard" for intervention research, whether those interventions are medical (e.g. vaccines, chemotherapy), educational (e.g. special curriculum), or psychosocial (e.g. psychotherapy, AAT). The development of evidence-based psychotherapies I highlighted previously was based on RCTs.

RCTs are the Esperanto of the sciences and therefore a language with which AAT research must be fluent. Such trials can be difficult and expensive to mount in light of many requirements (e.g. administering, collecting, coding assessments; protecting client rights through informed consent and procedures to assure privacy and confidentiality of the clients and their data; monitoring the delivery and integrity of treatment; and entering, checking, and analyzing the data). In AAT research, there are additional requirements to ensure the safety, care, and appropriate treatment of the animals.

In addition to RCTs, three other strategies could play a pivotal role in developing the research base of AATs. First, within the quantitative research tradition there are more options than just the RCT. *Quasi-experiments* include studies in which individuals cannot be assigned randomly to conditions (Shadish et al., 2002). Individuals from different groups in an institution or from different institutions can be exposed to different treatments (e.g. an AAT) or control conditions (e.g. wait list that serves as a temporary no treatment control group or treatment as usual). There are ways to draw inferences about the impact of treatment by taking into account characteristics of the samples and by matching samples using statistical techniques (e.g. propensity score matching, instrumental variable techniques, trajectory modeling). In recent years, these matching techniques have become better understood and greatly strengthen the quality of inferences that can be drawn when random assignment is not possible. Quasi-experiments often are much more feasible than RCTs, and their yield can be very strong.

Second, beyond the quantitative tradition, other design strategies are available and feasible. *Single-case experimental designs* can readily permit drawing valid inferences about the impact of an intervention (Kazdin, 2010). The designs are infrequently taught but are just as powerful in demonstrating causal relations as are RCTs.

Among the key characteristics of these designs is assessment of functioning on multiple occasions over time under different conditions (e.g. pretreatment baseline and then during the intervention).

For example, in one of the designs, an AAT could be introduced to different children or different programs or groups at different points. The staggering of when the intervention is introduced, against a backdrop of continuous assessment (e.g. daily or several times per week), permits causal statements to be drawn about the impact of the interventions (e.g. Esteves and Stokes, 2008). Single-case designs provide many design options that could be very useful in establishing the efficacy of AATs because they can be used in a single facility (clinic, institution) where such programs are already ongoing and do not require random assignment or withholding treatment. The designs do not require finding a comparison group. A single subject, classroom, group, or institution can be used. The way assessment is conducted (continuous over time) and the intervention is implemented surmounts the problems of the single-group, pre-post design mentioned previously.

Third, *qualitative research* would be quite useful as well. Qualitative research is a rigorous method of study that meets the desiderata of science; the methods are systematic, replicable, and cumulative (e.g. Denzin and Lincoln, 2005). The unique feature is the in-depth evaluation and richly detailed information about how individuals represent (perceive, feel) and react to their situations and contexts. The methods provide a rigorous way to codify experience and analyze the resulting data.

For example, qualitative research can examine the experiences of those who go through an AAT and thematic ways in which their lives are changed. The information could be very useful for understanding how treatment works and the changes that are produced and in generating hypotheses to be tested in other types of studies. Previously I mentioned systematically elaborating the subjective experience and benefits of human/animal interaction. Qualitative research would be quite valuable in this context too and could generate as well as test hypotheses about what that interaction does and the scope of impact of that interaction.

I have highlighted methodological approaches with broad strokes. The overarching point may be more critical than attempting to convey these approaches. No single research approach must be followed exclusively to build the empirical base of AATs. RCTs are essential, but so many questions including the efficacy of treatment can be addressed in multiple ways. Also, other types of research that elaborate processes involved in human/animal interaction could provide strong underpinnings for clinical research.

25.6 Conclusions

AAT is rich in opportunity because of the potential breadth in impact in physical and mental health and general well-being. This chapter focused on AAT as a form of therapy and directed toward social, emotional, and behavioral problems, psychiatric disorders, and overall adjustment and adaptive functioning. These domains are addressed by several evidence-based psychotherapies. It would be excellent to add AATs to that group of treatments.

The chapter highlighted several methodological standards now in place for establishing evidence-based psychotherapies. RCTs are a beginning point and regarded as the "gold standard." But a study begins long before the first client is recruited or assigned. I emphasized the investigator's small theory that connects the sample, the focus of the intervention, and the measures to evaluate treatment. Many different questions are asked in treatment studies. I highlighted these to clarify the options and control and comparison conditions needed in any given study. Several methodological problems of AAT research were also highlighted. Many of them derive from the failure to connect client problems, treatment processes, and outcome measures in a cohesive fashion.

Two key questions dominated the chapter: Does the presence of an animal improve the effectiveness of therapy? and if so, What is it about the animal contact that makes a difference? Systematic and well-controlled research on these questions would advance AATs greatly. They could occupy careers too given the range of populations that might profit from AATs and the range of options (e.g. animals, settings) for providing the treatments.

Progress might be accelerated if we could begin in an area or two where AATs are believed to be especially likely to have therapeutic impact with children. What youth and with what problems or areas in need of care are most likely to respond to treatment? And what variation of AAT is likely to be the most effective? We are building a literature empirically, but it is useful to draw on our strongest clinical experience and theory to guide research.

This chapter conveys the need for rigorous studies of AAT and this need has been voiced before (see Fine, 2006; Nimer and Lundahl, 2007). The message is worth repeating in the context of non-AATs, i.e. those therapies in which only human therapists (and no other animals) are involved. Research on many forms of psychotherapy that share the goals with AATs continues and often with rigorous studies that show changes on significant clinical problems. AAT research is needed that matches the current standards in place for outcome studies.

Advances can be made with other strategies to complement RCTs. I highlighted quasi-experiments, single-case experiments, and qualitative research as options that could test and generate theory, elaborate the broad benefits of child/animal interaction, and provide the underpinnings that could enhance therapeutic applications. I also mentioned other lines of research than therapeutic applications to advance AATs. Elaborating the impact of AATs, whether or not these include therapeutic change, was one line of work. Laboratory studies on basic tasks where affect, cognition, and behavior might be influenced by animal contact is yet another. These lines of work are not necessarily instead of therapeutic applications, but are likely to develop a body of basic findings from which applications more readily follow. Perhaps the guiding questions for research are: What are we trying to accomplish with AATs, what are the special strengths of these treatments, and for whom and under what conditions are they likely to effect change? In relation to treatment, the public is likely to be very sympathetic to AATs; many therapists are enthusiastic already. To bring others on board (e.g. practitioners trained in more traditional therapy, researchers, third-party payers, and grant funding agencies), we need to build the evidence base.

References

Achenbach, T. M. (1991a). *Manual for the Child Behavior Checklist/4-18 and 1991 Profile.* Burlington, VT: University of Vermont, Department of Psychiatry.

Achenbach, T. M. (1991b). *Manual for the Teacher's Report Form and 1991 Profile.* Burlington, VT: University of Vermont, Department of Psychiatry.

American Psychiatric Association. (1994). *Diagnostic and Statistical Manual of Mental Disorders* (4th ed.). Washington, DC: Author.

Anderson, P. E. (2008). *The Powerful Bond between People and Pets: Our Boundless Connections to Companion Animals.* Westport, CT: Praeger.

Baumeister, R. F., Campbell, J. D., Krueger, J. I., & Vohs, K. D. (2003). Psychological science in the public interest: does high self-esteem cause better performance, interpersonal success, happiness, or healthier lifestyles? *Psychological Science in the Public Interest, 4,* 1–44.

Christophersen, E. R., & Mortweet, S. L. (2001). *Treatments that Work with Children: Empirically Supported Strategies for Managing Childhood Problems.* Washington, DC: American Psychological Association.

Cohen, J. (1988). *Statistical Power Analysis for the Behavioral Sciences* (2nd ed.). Hillsdale, NJ: Erlbaum.

Denzin, N. K., & Lincoln, Y. S. (Eds.), (2005). *The SAGE Handbook of Qualitative Research* (3rd ed.). Thousand Oaks, CA: Sage.

Esteves, S. W., & Stokes, T. (2008). Social effects of a dog's presence on children with disabilities. *Anthrozoös, 21,* 5–15.

Fine, A. H. (Ed.), (2006). *Handbook on Animal-assisted Therapy: Theoretical Foundations and Guidelines for Practice* (2nd ed.). San Diego, CA: Academic Press.

Gee, N. R., Harris, S. L., & Johnson, K. L. (2007). The role of therapy dogs in speed and accuracy to complete motor skills tasks for preschool children. *Anthrozoös, 20,* 375–386.

Gee, N. R., Sherlock, T. R., Bennett, E. A., & Harris, S. L. (2009). Preschoolers' adherence to instructions as a function of presence of a dog and motor skills task. *Anthrozoös, 22,* 267–276.

Henggeler, S. W., Schoenwald, S. K., Borduin, C. M., Rowland, M. D., & Cunningham, P. B. (1998). *Multisystemic Treatment of Antisocial Behavior in Children and Adolescents.* New York: Guilford.

Kahn, P. H., Jr., Friedman, B., Perez-Granados, & Freier, N. G. (2006). Robotic pets in the lives of preschool children. *Interaction Studies, 7,* 405–436.

Kazdin, A. E. (2000a). Developing a research agenda for child and adolescent psychotherapy research. *Archives of General Psychiatry, 57,* 829–835.

Kazdin, A. E. (2000b). *Psychotherapy for Children and Adolescents: Directions for Research and Practice.* New York: Oxford University Press.

Kazdin, A. E. (2003). *Research Design in Clinical Psychology* (4th ed.). Needham Heights, MA: Allyn & Bacon.

Kazdin, A. E. (2005). *Parent Management Training: Treatment for Oppositional, Aggressive, and Antisocial Behavior in Children and Adolescents.* New York: Oxford University Press.

Kazdin, A. E. (2007a). Mediators and mechanisms of change in psychotherapy research. In S. Nolen-Hoeksema, T. D. Cannon & T. Widiger (Eds.), *Annual Review of Clinical Psychology, 3* (pp. 1–27).

Kazdin, A. E. (2007b). Psychosocial treatments for conduct disorder in children and adolescents. In P. E. Nathan & J. M. Gorman (Eds.), *A Guide to Treatments that Work* (3rd ed.). (pp. 71–104) New York: Oxford University Press.

Kazdin, A. E. (2010). *Single-case Research Designs: Methods for Clinical and Applied Settings* (2nd ed.). New York: Oxford University Press.

Kazdin, A. E., & Bass, D. (1989). Power to detect differences between alternative treatments in comparative psychotherapy outcome research. *Journal of Consulting and Clinical Psychology, 57,* 138–147.

Kazdin, A. E., & Wassell, G. (2000). Therapeutic changes in children, parents, and families resulting from treatment of children with conduct problems. *Journal of the American Academy of Child and Adolescent Psychiatry, 39,* 414–420.

Kazdin, A. E., & Whitley, M. K. (2006). Comorbidity, case complexity, and effects of evidence-based treatment for children referred for disruptive behavior. *Journal of Consulting and Clinical Psychology, 74,* 455–467.

Kraemer, H. C., Kazdin, A. E., Offord, D. R., Kessler, R. C., Jensen, P. S., & Kupfer, D. J. (1997). Coming to terms with the terms of risk. *Archives of General Psychiatry, 54,* 337–343.

Lambert, M. J., Whipple, J. L., Hawkins, E. J., Vermeersch, D. A., Nielsen, S. L., & Smart, D. W. (2003). Is it time for clinicians to routinely track patient outcome? A meta-analysis. *Clinical Psychology: Science and Practice, 10,* 288–301.

Lipsey, M. W. (1996). Theory as method: small theories of treatments. In L. Sechrest & A. G. Scott (Eds.), *New Directions in Program Evaluation: Understanding Causes and Generalizing about Them (Serial No. 57).* New York: Jossey-Bass.

Melson, G. F., Kahn, P. H., Jr., Beck, A., & Friedman, B. (2009). Robotic pets in human lives: implications for the human-animal bond and for human relationships with personified technologies. *Journal of Social Issues, 65,* 545–567.

Muris, P., Merckelbach, H., Ollendick, T. H., King, N. J., & Bogie, N. (2001). Children's nighttime fears: parent–child ratings of frequency, content, origins, coping behaviors and severity. *Behaviour Research and Therapy, 39,* 13–28.

Nathan, P. E., & Gorman, J. M. (Eds.), (2007). *Treatments that Work* (3rd ed.). New York: Oxford University Press.

Nimer, J., & Lundahl, B. (2007). Animal-assisted therapy: a meta-analysis. *Anthrozoös, 20,* 225–238.

Norcross, J. C. (Ed.), (2002). *Psychotherapy Relationships that Work: Therapist Contributions and Responsiveness to Patients.* New York: Oxford University Press.

Olmert, M. D. (2009). *Made for Each Other: The Biology of the Human-Animal Bond.* Cambridge, MA: De Capo Press.

Perepletchikova, F., & Kazdin, A. E. (2005). Treatment integrity and therapeutic change: issues and research recommendations. *Clinical Psychology: Science and Practice, 12,* 365–383.

Ribi, F. N., Yokoyama, A., & Turner, D. C. (2008). Comparison of children's behavior toward Sony's Robotic Dog AIBO and a real dog: a pilot study. *Anthrozoös, 21,* 245–256.

Salotto, P. (2001). *Pet Assisted Therapy: A Loving Intervention and an Emerging Profession: Leading to a Friendlier, Healthier, and More Peaceful World.* D.J. Publications.

Schofield, W. (1986). *Psychotherapy: The Purchase of Friendship.* Piscataway, NJ: Transaction Publishers.

Shadish, W. R., Cook, T. D., & Campbell, D. T. (2002). *Experimental and Quasi-experimental Designs for Generalized Causal Inference.* Boston: Houghton Mifflin.

Stanton, C. M., Kahn, P. H., Jr., Severson, R. L., Ruckert, J. H., & Gill, B. T. (2008). Robotic animals might aid in the social development of children with autism. *Proceedings of the 3rd ACM/IEEE International Conference on Human Robot Interaction 2008* (pp. 97–104). New York City: Association for Computing Machinery.

Tamura, T., Yonemitsu, S., Itoh, A., Okawa, D., Kawakami, A., Higashi, Y., et al. (2004). Is an entertainment robot useful in the care of elderly people with severe dementia? *Journal of Gerontology Series A: Biological Sciences and Medical Sciences, 59A*, 83–85.

Wallin, D. J. (2007). *Attachment in Psychotherapy*. New York: Guilford Press.

Wampold, B. E. (2001). *The Great Psychotherapy Debate: Models, Methods, and Findings*. Mahwah, NJ: Lawrence Erlbaum.

Weiner, G.A. (2001). Heated stuffed animal. United States Patent Application 2002/0028627 A1. (http://www.google.com/patents/about?id=h9-OAAAAEBAJ&dq=stuffed+animals+ and+comfort).

Weisz, J. R. (2004). *Psychotherapy for Children and Adolescents: Evidence-based Treatments and Case Examples*. Cambridge, UK: Cambridge University Press.

Weisz, J. R., & Kazdin, A. E. (Eds.), (2010). *Evidence-based Psychotherapies for Children and Adolescents* (2nd ed.). New York: Guilford Press.

26 The future of research, education and clinical practice in the animal/human bond and animal-assisted therapy

Dennis C. Turner*, Cindy C. Wilson, PhD, CHES[†],
Aubrey H. Fine[‡], Jeffery Scott Mio*

[*]Institute for Applied Ethology and Animal Psychology, [†]Uniformed
Services University of the Health Sciences, [‡]California State Polytechnic
University

A The role of ethology in the field of human/animal relations and animal-assisted therapy
Dennis C. Turner

26.1 Introduction

As pointed out over 25 years ago (Turner, 1984), the multidisciplinary fields of human/animal relations[1] and animal-assisted therapy (AAT) lacked quantitative, controlled observations on behavior and interactions between owners and their pets and between patients and therapy animals. Without intending to belittle the importance of other disciplines involved or interested in this field, the role that ethology has, and could continue to play in research and education on the human/animal relationship and AAT should not be underestimated.

"Ethology" can be defined as the observational, often comparative study of animal and/or human behavior. While in the long run, ethologists are mostly concerned with the biological basis of behavior, their methods and results are not without consequences for the applied fields of human/animal interaction and AAT. As a significant example, one may consider the early studies on dog and cat socialization toward conspecifics and humans (for an excellent summary, see McCune et al., 1995): both species exhibit a sensitive phase of socialization early in life, during which contacts

---

[1] Most recently called "anthrozoology" and defined as "the study of the relationships between humans and domesticated and/or feral animals" (*Cambridge Dictionary of Human Biology and Evolution*, 2005).

Handbook on Animal-Assisted Therapy. DOI: 10.1016/B978-0-12-381453-1.10026-1

with members of their own species and/or other species (including humans) influence the social inclinations of individuals for the rest of their lives. In dogs, this sensitive phase occurs from four to 10 or 12 weeks of age depending on the author (see Serpell and Jagoe, 1995), in cats from two to eight (towards humans) or 10 weeks of age (toward conspecifics) (Karsh and Turner, 1988; Schaer, 1989; Turner, 2000a). Certainly in cats (Hediger, 1988), probably also in dogs (Reichlin, 1994), socialization can take place simultaneously and independently toward members of the same species and toward humans. That dogs and cats involved in visitation and residential therapy programs are socialized toward both is of crucial importance for both risk management and outcomes, not to mention the welfare of the animals themselves (Hubrecht and Turner, 1998; Turner, 2005a).

Animal welfare laws in many countries require that animals be housed and treated in such a way that all of their species-specific needs can be satisfied and that they are not subjected to stress or pain. Therapy animals are no exception. Regarding behavioral and psychosocial needs, ethological studies provide the necessary background information (Rochlitz, 2005a; Turner, 1995a, 2005b); regarding stress and pain avoidance, studies from both ethology and veterinary medicine (e.g. Broom and Johnson, 1993; Casey and Bradshaw, 2005; Haubenhofer et al., 2005; Haubenhofer and Kirchengast, 2006) are usually the sources of factual information. Hubrecht and Turner (1998), for dogs and cats, and Rochlitz (2005b), for cats, have provided the most recent reviews on companion animal welfare in private and institutional settings, but more work is needed in this area. The International Association of Human-Animal Interaction Organizations, IAHAIO, has emphasized the importance of the welfare of therapy animals in its "IAHAIO Prague Guidelines on Animal-Assisted Activities and Animal-Assisted Therapy."[2]

There have been relatively few ethological studies of the interactions between pets and people, most of these on cats and many from the research team surrounding the author (Bradshaw and Cameron-Beaumont, 2000; Cook and Bradshaw, 1996; Day et al., 2009; Goodwin and Bradshaw, 1996, 1997, 1998; McCune et al., 1995; Meier and Turner, 1985; Mertens, 1991; Mertens and Turner, 1988; Rieger and Turner, 1999; Turner, 1991, 1995b, 2000b; Turner and Rieger, 2001; Turner et al., 1986, 2003). These have provided information on: the "mechanics" of human/cat interactions; differences between interactions involving men, women, boys and girls and involving elderly persons vs. younger adults; differences in interactions between several breeds of cats; and the influence of housing conditions on such interactions. Many of these results (should) have consequences for animal visitation and (especially psycho-) therapy programs.

As appropriate in any interdisciplinary field, advances in our knowledge about the human/animal relationship and its therapeutic value can also be secured by combining the methods and results of other disciplines with those of ethology. James Serpell (1983) was the first researcher to consider aspects of a companion animal's behavior in the interpretation of results from a non-ethological study of the human/dog relationship. He found associations between owner affection towards the dog and such

---

[2] See www.iahaio.org for the full text.

dog behavior and character traits as welcoming behavior, attentiveness, expressiveness and sensitivity. Over the years, Turner and his research team have borrowed and expanded upon the methodology of Serpell's first study to examine the ethology *and* psychology of human/cat relationships (Kannchen and Turner, 1998; Rieger and Turner, 1999; Stammbach and Turner, 1999; Turner, 1991, 1995b, 2000b, 2002; Turner and Rieger, 2001; Turner and Stammbach-Geering, 1990; Turner et al., 2003). Most recently, Kotrschal et al. (2009) have combined ethological observations of interactions between dogs, respectively cats (Kotrschal, pers. communication), and their owners with personality assessments of their owners and of the animals and discovered many interesting interactions between the two. These types of studies have many consequences for therapeutic work with animals but their potential has not yet been exploited.

What have ethological studies of human/animal interactions and relationships provided us so far? A few examples, based upon the literature cited above, are called for.

From the cat research group of Turner, we now know that: domestic cats show no spontaneous preference for a particular age/sex class of potential human partners, but indeed *react* to differences in human behavior toward the cats between the different age/sex classes and, therefore, show behavior that would lead us to believe they have preferences. Women and girls tend to interact with cats on the floor while men often do this from a seated position. Children, especially boys, tend to approach a cat quickly and directly, and are often first rejected by the animal for this. Adults usually call the cat first and allow the cat to do the approaching. Women speak with their cats more often than men and the cats also vocalize more often with them than with men. Women are also more frequently approached by cats and the animals are generally more willing to cooperate with them than with men. Retired persons show more tolerance or acceptance of the cat's natural behavior and desire less conformity by the cats to their own lifestyles than younger adults. When they interact with their cats, elderly persons do so for longer periods of time, often in closer physical contact with the animals, than younger adults, who nevertheless speak more often with/to their cats from a distance.

Differences in cat behavior related to the animals' sex have been sought but rarely found, although most studies (as well as most cats kept by private persons) were of neutered or spayed animals in past studies. However, Kotrschal et al. (pers. communication) have found a first indication of differences between male and female cats. Individual differences in behavior between cats are always statistically significant and these have had to be accounted for in any analysis of other parameters postulated to affect their behavior. Nevertheless, various personality types, e.g. cats that prefer playing while others prefer the physical contact of stroking, have been discovered (also statistically) among domestic non-purebred animals. Astonishingly, very few observational studies have been published comparing the behavior of pure breed cats. Turner (1995b, 2000b) compared Siamese, Persian/Longhair, and non-purebred cats in their interactions with humans. Differences relevant to potential therapy work with cats were found. Non-observational studies comparing the character traits of many different dog breeds have been conducted with highly significant results for AAA/AAT work (Hart, 1995; Hart and Hart, 1985, 1988). But ethological studies along the same lines are lacking with the possible exception of Schalke and colleagues (2005). Nevertheless, Prato-Previde et al. (2006) have observed gender differences in owners interacting with their pet dogs.

What have studies that combine observational data with indirect, subjective assessments of cat traits and relationship quality by their owners provided? Turner and Stammbach-Geering (1990) and Turner (1991) found correlations that help to explain the widespread popularity of cats, as well as one key to a harmonious relationship between a person and his or her cat: Cats are considered by their owners to be either very independent and unlike humans (who consider themselves, in this case, "dependent") or they are dependent and human-like. Some people appreciate the independent nature of the cat; others, their presumed "dependency" on human care. The authors also discovered that the more willing the owner is to fulfill the cat's interactional wishes, the more willing the cat is to reciprocate at other times. But the cat also accepts a lower willingness on the part of the owner and adapts its own willingness to interact to that. This "meshing" of interactional goals is one indication of relationship quality.

More recently, Stammbach and Turner (1999) and Kannchen and Turner (1998; see also Turner, 2002) combined psychological assessment tools measuring human social support levels, self-perceived emotional support from the cat and attachment to the cat with direct observations of interactions between women and their cats. Emotional attachment to the cat was negatively correlated with the amount of human social support the owner could count on and positively correlated with the self-estimated amount of emotional support provided by the cat. Attachment to the cat was found to be the more predominant factor governing interactional behavior rather than amount of human support available to the owner.

Most recently, Rieger and Turner (1999), Turner and Rieger (2001) and Turner et al. (2003) have used psychological tools and ethological observations to assess how momentary moods, in particular depressiveness, affect the behavior of singly living persons toward their cats, respectively, persons with a spouse. They emphasized that these persons, who had volunteered for the studies, were not necessarily clinically depressive. They discovered that the more a person was depressed, the fewer "intentions" to interact were shown. However, the more a person was depressed, the more he or she directly started an interaction. This means that depressed persons had an initial inhibition to initiate that was compensated by the presence of the cat. People who became less depressed after two hours owned cats that were more willing to comply with the humans' intents, than those of people whose "depressiveness" had not changed or became worse. When not interacting, the cat reacted the same way to all moods of the humans. This neutral attitude possibly makes the cat an attractive pacemaker against an inhibition to initiate. Within an interaction the cats were indeed affected by the mood: they showed more head and flank rubbing toward depressive persons. But apparently only the willingness of the cat to comply was responsible for reducing depressiveness. The authors interpreted their results after a model of intraspecific communication between human couples, in which one partner is clinically depressed (Hell, 1994) and found striking similarities. The potential of these findings for AAT sessions involving cats is obvious.

While Rieger and Turner (1999) and Turner and Rieger (2001) found that cats were successful in improving "negative" moods, but not increasing already "good moods" among single persons, Turner and colleagues (2003) found that a spouse was indeed capable of the latter. Nevertheless, they also found that a companion cat was about as successful as a spouse at improving negative moods.

26.2   Unanswered research questions

Despite the above-mentioned relevant results from ethological studies and those from investigations combining the methods and interpretations of other disciplines with those from direct observations, we have only begun to "scratch the surface" in the ethological analysis of human/pet relationships. This is true for human/cat, but especially so for human/dog relationships. Given the heavy involvement of dogs in AAA/AAT programs, it would be prudent to encourage similar studies of dog behavior and human/dog interactions. In particular, the breed differences in behavior and character traits reported in studies using only indirect methods (Hart and Hart, 1985, 1988) are extremely relevant to therapy work and should be substantiated by independent analysis of observational data. Further work on behavioral differences between cat breeds is also called for as this would be particularly useful for animal-assisted psychotherapists.

Another reason to promote comparative ethological studies of dog/human interactions is the reported difference in general *Gestalt* of the human/dog vs. the human/cat relationship (Turner, 1985, 1988): dog social life is organized around dominance/subordinance relationships, whereas cat sociality (assuming socialization toward humans in the first place) is based upon "give and take," mutuality/reciprocity and respect of their independent nature (Turner, 1995c). This basic difference must be considered especially in psycho-social therapy. Sex differences in dog behavior toward humans have been found (Hart and Hart, 1985, 1988; Sonderegger and Turner, 1996), but these need to be further examined in intact (non-spayed and non-neutered) cats. More detailed work on the communication signals used by dogs and cats in intra- and interspecific interactions is also required, in particular comparative studies to assess whether the same signals have the same meaning when directed to another species and how that other species interprets them. Mertens and Turner (1988), Goodwin and Bradshaw (1996, 1997, 1998), and Bradshaw and Cameron-Beaumont (2000) have made a start, but we have much more to discover in this area.

The study of Rieger and Turner (1999; see also Turner and Rieger, 2001; Turner et al., 2003) showed for the first time that moods of cat owners affect their interactional behavior and that the cats can indeed help persons out of a momentary depressive mood. The mechanism through which this probably occurs was postulated, but still needs to be tested; then trials with clinically depressed persons must be conducted. This study also produced the rather surprising (and difficult to defend in front of cat enthusiasts!) result that the cats did not react measurably to the different moods of their owners from the outset, only within an ongoing interaction. However, it is probable that humans (and cats) send out very fine signals (e.g. gaze, see

Goodwin and Bradshaw, 1998) not picked up by the ethogram used in this first study. Again, a finer analysis of communication between cats and their owners using video to record facial mimicry, etc. would be helpful.

Other species than dogs and cats are involved in some AAA/AAT programs, reportedly with positive outcomes, e.g. the effects of watching caged birds or aquarium fish in lowering blood pressure and pulse rate are well documented (Katcher et al., 1983) and their presence can significantly improve the quality of life of residents in institutions (Olbrich, 1995). Nature programs (also involving animals) have reported good results in the treatment of ADHD and CD children (Katcher and Wilkins, 2000). Rabbits, guinea pigs, hamsters, etc. are involved in some programs, but also sometimes improperly housed and/or handled. More ethological studies on proper housing of these species and *better education* of the AAA/AAT specialists using them are urgently needed (see below). Again comparative ethological studies of human interactions with these species would be useful: Turner (1996, 2005c) has postulated differences in the benefits accrued depending upon whether the therapy animal species is interactive and initiative (i.e. establishes contact with the patient of its own volition, such as dogs and many cats do) or simply present during the therapy session as an "ice breaker" (bridge to the therapist) or topic for therapeutic discussion. Presumably many rodent species, caged birds and fish serve this function.

To summarize, it is clear from the above-mentioned studies that ethology and ethological methods have much to offer the field of human/companion animal relations and potentially animal-assisted therapy, but that much remains to be done. We have or can expect information on: how to ensure the socialization of the animals involved in therapy programs or to assess the degree of socialization in animals up for selection; how to properly house, handle and care for the animals involved to minimize stress and ensure their health and welfare, thus maximizing potential benefits to the recipients of therapy; differences in interactive behavior between healthy women, men, girls and boys and between different species and breeds of intact, neutered or spayed male and female therapy animals, which provide baseline information for therapeutic work with less fortunate human beings; matching the animal and recipient of the therapeutic activities; assessing changes—improvement—in interspecific (human/animal) relationship quality which could (should) parallel changes in interpersonal relationship establishment and quality; and the mechanisms explaining why animals work as (co-)therapeutic agents.

It is equally clear that the combination of theories, methods and interpretations from different disciplines can lead to major advances in our understanding of those relations. Therefore, any educational program on human/animal relationships and animal-assisted therapy must, of necessity, be interdisciplinary.

26.3 Setting standards

Equally important as the distinction between animal-assisted therapists, animal-assisted pedagogues, and specialists for animal-assisted activities is the need for these persons to be professionally trained to involve animals in their work. To check the

Table 26.1 Curriculum requirements* for approval and recommendation for full membership in ISAAT

- Human/animal communication; theoretical explanations of somatic, social, and psychological effects of animal-assisted activities, animal-assisted pedagogy and animal-assisted therapy
- Methods of pedagogical and therapeutic work (prevention, rehabilitation, salutogenesis) with companion animals and farm animals typically used in different fields of practice
- Methods of (process and outcome) evaluation
- Animals and ethics; animal welfare; animal care
- Ethology; animal behavior, normal development and behavior of species frequently involved in animal-assisted activities, animal-assisted pedagogy, and animal-assisted therapy
- Methods and theories of animal learning
- Hygiene: Setting and observing standards of hygiene for humans and animals in animal-assisted activities, animal-assisted pedagogy and animal-assisted therapy; plans for the prevention of risks of infections, allergies, zoonoses, and general risk management
- Organization of professional pedagogical and therapeutic work with animals; basic economic and administrative knowledge
- At least 40 hours of practical work in venues offering animal-assisted activities, animal-assisted pedagogy or animal-assisted therapy, including a written report a report on observations/experiences

*A total of at least 225 hours of formal course work and supervised activities.

uncontrolled growth in this field and the misusage of terminology, the International Society for Animal-Assisted Therapy, ISAAT,[3] was founded in 2006 by representatives of universities and private institutions in Japan, Germany, Luxembourg and Switzerland. The goals of ISAAT are: (1) quality control of public and private institutions offering *continuing* education in AAT, AAP, and as specialists in AAA, through establishment of an independent "accreditation" board[4]; (2) the official recognition of AAT, AAP and AAA as professional disciplines; and (3) the official recognition of persons who have completed continuing education in an ISAAT member institution either as animal-assisted therapists, animal-assisted pedagogues or specialists for animal-assisted activities.[5]

The independent accreditation board of ISAAT is charged with controlling: admission criteria for the continuing education program; qualifications of the teachers; the curriculum for its interdisciplinary, theoretical, and practical content and duration; thesis (final report) requirements; examination rules; conditions of study

[3] Secretariat: D. C. Turner, Secretary of ISAAT, Dept. of Animal Behavior, University of Zurich-Irchel, Winterthurerstrasse 190, CH-8057 Zurich. E-mail: dennis.turner@ieu.uzh.ch. Home page: www.aat-isaat.org
[4] Since use of the word "accreditation" is also restricted by laws in various countries, those institutions applying for membership which meet the high standards of ISAAT will become full members of the organization and allowed to state in their documentation "This course (or program) was examined by the International Society for Animal-Assisted Therapy and is offered according to its standards."
[5] Documentation/application forms are available from the website.

and certification. The interdisciplinary curriculum is expected to adequately cover the items listed in Table 26.1.

At the time of writing, four institutions/programs have been accepted into full membership in ISAAT (=accreditation) and other applications are currently being examined by the board. Quite a large number of programs claim to follow the ISAAT standards; however, they have not been controlled and accepted for membership unless they are listed on the official ISAAT home page. Nevertheless, it is encouraging for the interdisciplinary field of HAI and AAT/AAP that more attention is being paid to standards and quality control and the future looks bright.

B   Human/animal interactions (HAIs) and health: the evidence and issues—past, present, and future

Cindy C. Wilson, PhD, CHES

26.4   Introduction

For the second edition of the *Handbook on Animal Assisted Therapy*, I was asked to set the direction for the research agenda for the human/animal interaction (HAI) field. As I reviewed that paper in preparation for a new chapter in the third edition, the recurring themes, issues, and conundrums surprised me. At the same time, there have been some positive, forward thinking, and moving events that are certainly milestones in the history of the field. My intent is to give a brief overview of research themes and issues that researchers and practitioners currently face in this field. Then, given changes in the field since the last edition, I will

1. review how HAI and health may currently fit into the expectations of an evidence
2. summarize strategic research decisions that must be made and operationalized by both researchers/practitioners and funding agents; and last
3. suggest where we should go from here if we are to improve the health of those research participants we serve through human/animal interactions protocols and programs and our own health.

The field of HAIs remains at an early stage of its development—currently estimated by this author at "late childhood or early adolescence." The topic of HAIs and health moved from being perceived as "non-mainstream" research to having two major funding initiatives (private and public) directed towards HAI and health. First, the Waltham Centre for Pet Nutrition/Mars™ (i.e. Waltham Centre) and the American Association of Human-Animal Bond Veterinarians (AAH-ABV) issued a request for funding in 2007. In 2009, the Waltham Centre partnered with the International Society of Anthrozoology (ISAZ) and again provided funding for select, peer reviewed proposals. Both of these calls for research proposals were to stimulate new research in the area of human/animal interactions, with particular interest in the impact of pets on the physical well-being of children, the role of pets in the lives of elders, and the impact of culture on the human/animal bond.

Concurrently, substantive experts from a variety of fields (e.g. psychology, sociology, ethology, child and human development, child abuse, clinical medicine, aging, veterinary medicine, nursing, and public health, etc.) were meeting in conjunction with representatives from the Waltham Centre/Mars™ and the National Institute for Child Health and Human Development to define research areas relevant to both organizations as well as to the HAI field at large. A series of substantive workshops led to the second funding initiative by the National Institute for Child Health and Human Development and a request for funding applications (RFA) entitled "The Role of Human-Animal Interaction in Child Health and Development (R01)." The purpose of this funding opportunity is to build an empirical research base on how children perceive, relate to and think about animals; how pets in the home impact children's social and emotional development and health (e.g. allergies, the immune system, asthma, mitigation of obesity); and whether and under what conditions therapeutic use of animals is "safe and effective." The NIH/Mars™ funding opportunity "supports both basic and applied studies that focus on the interaction between humans and animals and the impact of HAI in three major areas: (1) foundational studies of the interaction itself and its impact on typical development and health, including basic research on biobehavioral markers of suitable behavioral traits for HAI and for using domesticated companion animals as models for identifying gene-behavior associations in humans; (2) applied studies (to include but not limited to clinical trials of the therapeutic use of animals); and (3) population level studies of the impact of animals on public health (prevalence/incidence studies, etc.), social capital, and the cost-effectiveness of using pets/animals in reducing/preventing disease and disorders (RFA HD09-031, 2009)." Review of submissions for this RFA is currently under way and there is tremendous excitement within the research community regarding this commitment to the science of human/animal interactions.

The HAI field *has* moved forward as evidenced by the national and international attention being focused on building partnerships for funding initiatives and continued interaction across disciplines. However, the question remains whether the quality of the science has progressed alongside these initiatives. Several critical papers have been written that have reviewed the evidence supporting HAI. Table 26.2 briefly identifies the studies and notes their conclusions.

26.5   The physical evidence

Continued evidence mounts regarding the impact of companion animals (CAs) on health. Benefits of pet ownership (PO) are consistent with the goals and objectives of many leading health indicators for diabetes mellitus, physical activity and fitness, mental health, disability, HIV, and heart disease outlined in the national report, Healthy People 2010 (US Department of Health and Human Services, 2005). Of the 28 focus areas identified in Healthy People 2010 (US Department of Health and Human Services, 2005), seven areas (diabetes mellitus, disability and secondary implications, heart disease, HIV, physical activity and fitness, nutrition and overweight, and mental health) are positively influenced by PO. We now know that

Table 26.2 Reviews of the evidence

1. Wilson and Netting (1983) reviewed HAI studies related to older persons. They conclude that the early call for evidence-based interventions has largely gone unheeded by HAI researchers

2. Beck and Katcher (1984) reviewed animal-assisted therapy studies, and went one step further and divided the existing literature by the types of research design used. The majority of studies on animal-assisted therapy fell into the category of hypothesis generating studies

3. In 1988, the Working Group Summary from the National Institutes of Health Technology Assessment Conference on the Health Benefits of Pets concluded that, although future research *could begin* without explicit hypotheses, investigations must proceed from descriptive studies (i.e. observational) of representative, random samples to cross-sectional and retrospective studies and finally to prospective, longitudinal studies (National Institutes of Health, 1988)

4. Barba (1995) reviewed 52 research papers from the period of 1988 to1993. Barba concluded that there was increased knowledge of the impact of HAI even though most studies were non-experimental

5. In 1998, Garrity and Stallones (Garrity and Stallones, 1998) identified 25 empirical HAI studies from scientific literature between 1990 and 1995. Sixteen of the 25 studies (all noted in the bibliography) were correlational research and generally cross-sectional in nature while only five were experimental in nature with appropriate designs to address causation

6. Friedman, Thomas, and Eddy (2000) reviewed health and wellness and the relationship animals play in these dynamic processes. Friedman (2000) suggested that future studies should address potential interactive factors such as gender and other demographic variables in determining the health effects of human/animal interactions (e.g. Risley-Curtis, Holley, and Wolf, 2006)

sedentary behaviors not only contribute adversely to the health burden of PO but also to their animal companions (US Department of Health and Human Services, 1996, 2005). The Humane Society of the USA recommends twice daily walking to improve canine health and fitness ("Caring for your dog: the humane society of the United States," 2005) while the US Surgeon General recommends 30 minutes of exercise/day or approximately 10,000 steps per day. With approximately 65 million dogs in US households (American Pet Products Manufacturers Association, 2006), walking a dog may benefit a large proportion of the US population by increasing their physical activity (PA) and cardiovascular fitness (Kushner et al., 2006). This augmented level of PA may also have significant health benefits for their canine companions (Ham and Epping, 2006). Older dog walkers have been shown to have better health practices and mobility than geriatric non-dog walkers by reaching the US Surgeon' General's recommended weekly goal for PA (Thorpe et al., 2006).

The National Household Travel Survey (NHTS), a cross-sectional survey of personal transportation by the civilian, non-institutionalized population in the USA, was conducted by the Department of Transportation. A random sample of households ($n = 1,282$) was selected based upon the responses to categories of "walking trips for the purpose of pet care" (Ham and Epping, 2006). Among dog walkers (DW), 80% walked at least one or more times for at least 10 minutes and an estimated 59%

engaged in two or more walks a day. Nearly half of the adults in the sample who walked their dog two or three times a day easily accumulated 30 minutes or more of walking in a day. This PA contributes to the overall fitness of both the dogs and their owners and improves overall wellness.

In addition to the benefit of purposeful activity, dog walking may also support social aspects of PO health when identified as an effective behavioral mechanism to increase physical activity (Bryant, 1985; Serpell, 1991; Woods et al., 2005). Long-term adherence to walking was reported by many respondents as an obligation to provide their dog with needed exercise. Based upon the dog walker's logic, the dog is a "buddy" as well as a motivational factor for being physically active. In contrast to other forms of exercise, dog walking is convenient, requires no special equipment, and *can* be done at any time. This is important because convenience is a consistent predictor of regular exercise for many people (Bautisa-Castano, 2004; US Department of Health and Human Services, 2005).

26.6   Selected psychosocial evidence

A large body of research supports the positive health effects of human companionship (Allen et al., 2002; Friedman, 1983–2009; Parslow and Jorm, 2003; Wells, 2004). The benefits of having a companion, a spouse, or a "buddy" (Cain, 1983; Ham and Epping, 2006) to provide physical and emotional support (Cohen, 2004; Risley-Curtis et al., 2006a,b) are well described. Pets also continue to serve as a source of human social support (Peretti, 1990; Serpell, 1991; Wells, 2005) and emotional support; they also serve as part of a friendship network, bolster their companion's sense of competence and self-worth, serve as a opportunity for nurturance and love, as well as provide the opportunity for shared pleasure in spontaneous recreation and relaxation (Jennings, 1997; Wilson et al., 1998, 2001; Collis and McNicholas, 2001; Woods, 2004).

There is little doubt that companion animals, especially dogs, have an impact on the health of their companions. Yet, based upon the studies to date, there remains the question of whether these health effects will be found in all individuals regardless of the type of pet, the ethnic group of the owner, or across all age groups. Additional concern remains about these positive outcomes because of a variety of design and methodological issues.

26.6.1   *Building the evidence—standards and quality control in research*

Defining relevant terms and issues

The use of the term "human/animal interaction" is the best-known term for all relevant research in this area. Within that label would be familiar terms (e.g. animal-assisted therapy, animal-assisted activities, human/animal bond, etc.). All therapies, intervention, and assistance involve "interactions." However, in the databases of "evidence (e.g. PubMed, Cochrane)" that term does not occur. In fact, the most commonly used database in the USA for health-related topics is Medline and there still is no Mesh heading for human/animal interactions. The closest approximation to

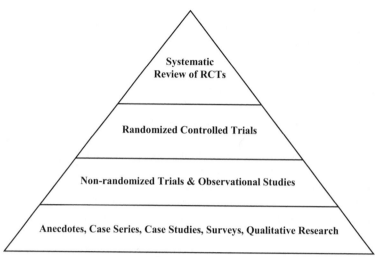

Figure 26.1 The hierarchy of evidence[6]

access journals remains "bonding-human-pet" (Spitzer, 2009). In Europe, in addition to Medline, another commonly used database for health-related inquiries is Embase. As in Medline, there is no key search term for human/animal interactions.

Defining the evidence hierarchy

In order to take its place as "evidence-based," HAI research must advance in the hierarchy. As shown in Figure 26.1, the "evidence" goes from less causal research methods (case reports/studies, case series, surveys, qualitative research, and anecdotes) to increasingly more sophisticated research methods—non-randomized trials and observational studies—to what is considered the "gold standard," the randomized controlled trials (RCTs). At the top of this pyramid is the most sophisticated of causal research methods, the systematic review of randomized controlled trials—more commonly known as the "meta-analysis."

Establishing the challenges to HAI research

There are many challenges to HAI research and to building the evidence base. Five of these areas are briefly described:

Challenge 1. Establishing and applying high quality standards of research

HAI research, like all scientific pursuits, attempts to identify outcomes of a particular relationship. To this end, there are six steps of the research process that require the same scientific standards regardless of the area of research.

[6] Adapted from Summerskill, W. S. M. (2001). The hierarchy of evidence. In McGovern, D., Valori, R. M., Summerskill, W. S. M., and Levi, M. (Eds.), *Key Topics in Evidence Based Medicine* (p. 15). Oxford, UK: BIOS Scientific Publishers Ltd.

Step 1: Problem identification and formulation. A research question is posed and its inherent concepts are progressively refined to be more specific, relevant, and meaningful to the field of HAI. As this is done, the feasibility of implementation is considered. Ultimately, the purpose of the study is finalized and the individual aspects of the research project, including hypotheses, independent and dependent variables, units of analysis, operational definitional units of analysis are described, and a robust literature review across *all* relevant disciplines is completed.

Step 2: Designing the study. The term research design deals with all of the decisions we make in planning a study. Decisions must be made not only about the overarching type of design to use, but also about sampling, sources and procedures for collecting data, measurement issues (internal and external validity and reliability), selection of instruments if appropriate, data analysis plans, as well as a plan for dissemination of outcomes/results. Decisions made in this step are guided by the original problem formulation, the feasibility of the plan, and the purpose of the research. For example, studies designed to address causation require logical arrangements that meet the three criteria of establishing causality (Lazarsfeld, 1959): (1) the cause must precede the effect; (2) the two variables being considered must be empirically related to one another; and (3) the observed relationship between two variables cannot be explained away as being a result of some third variable that causes both of them. This often requires an experimental design. Other questions require other designs; for example, questions about change over time generally require a longitudinal approach.

Step 3: Data collection. Once a study or program is designed, the structure of its implementation is planned in advance. Deductive studies that attempt to verify hypotheses or descriptive studies that emphasize accuracy and objectivity require more structured data collection procedures than will studies using qualitative methods to better understand meanings of certain phenomena or those that are intended to generate hypotheses rather than investigate hypotheses.

Step 4: Data processing. This step of the research process involves the classification or coding of observations in order to make them more interpretable.

Step 5: Data analysis. Processed data are analyzed for the purpose of answering the research question. Commonly, the analysis also yields unanticipated findings that reflect on the research problem but go beyond the specific question asked.

Step 6: Interpreting the results of the analyses. There is no single, "correct" way to plan a research study appropriate to HAI and/or animal-assisted therapy and no way to plan a study that ensures the outcome of data analysis will provide the "correct" or anticipated answer to the research question. Specific statistical procedures may provide the best interpretation of data, but cannot eliminate the need for sound judgments regarding the meaning of the findings. A thorough discussion of alternative ways to interpret the results, of what generalizations may be made based on them, and of methodological limitations and delimitations that could impact the meaning and validity of the results must be presented.

Challenge 2. Adapting to the evolving nature of science in HAI research

As time progresses, as does the sophistication of the research studies of health benefits of HAIs, the evidence will evolve. In clinical medicine, treatments and interventions have improved as scientific evidence supported change. In fact, medicine has adapted to the concept of "the evidence base" in medical practice and evaluates all research data by the "rules of evidence."

Based upon this approach, in the studies I reviewed earlier in this chapter, there would be "evidence" of: positive effects of human animal interventions ~22.5% of the time, insufficient evidence of effects ~21.3% of the time, "no effect" ~20% of the time, and actual harmful effects (e.g. allergies, scratches, negative responses to animals) ~6.9% of the time. Unfortunately, it was impossible to conduct a systematic review as expected in both the Ovid and Cochrane databases. Current change in patient care is based upon the type of "evidence" that is available. Hopefully, future clinicians and scientists can turn to the Ovid and Cochrane databases to determine what the evidence says about the effects of human/animal interventions based upon the causal hierarchy of studies. Unfortunately, the only systematic review currently found is the study by Forbes (Forbes, 1998) reviewing strategies for managing behavioral symptomatology with Alzheimer's dementia. As new concepts emerge, there will be more opportunities to assess the effectiveness of HAIs.

One of the common techniques in basic science is to determine assay sensitivity. One of the issues that we have yet to address, as seen by the number of "little to no effect" outcome studies, is *how we measure* HAI's impact on health but this may not be sensitive enough to detect the effect. Our measures may not be robust enough to identify an actual effect.

Challenge 3. Accommodating the diverse nature of human/animal interaction models

Prior studies that had insufficient or no effects are categorized as such on the basis of statistical significance without attempting to assess or capture the clinical significance. We need to conceptualize a framework in which these data may be useful to programs and individuals. An example from medicine would be studies whereby "me-too" drugs for hypertension or cholesterol do not have statistically significant effects upon a patient sample. Yet, they lower blood pressure, heart rate, or cholesterol in a clinically significant amount and without the side effects of the original drug. Non-significant findings, upon more critical review, may well be clinically significant.

As we look again at the hierarchy of evidence, we must consider the overlay of "users" of the evidence. For example, if we are to look at the effect(s) of an intervention, Figure 26.2 shows we would have basic scientists, clinical researchers, and regulators of the use of animal interventions. In fact, these user groups are already in place and in the area in which we are most comfortable. On the other hand, there is also the area of "use" (or usefulness) testing where the outcome is the actual use of the intervention in the context of the public's health, its use to practitioners, and to patients/clients. Figure 26.2 shows how this again builds the evidence. Examples of this type of study would be the Siegel's Maxicare study, or the Australian Heart Study by Anderson et al. (1992), or Thorpe's (2007) work with the Baltimore ABC study.

We cannot ignore the ethical issues of how the "evidence" is collected. Again, it matters where we are going, so we must have a plan of how to get there. Institutional Review Boards (IRBs) and Institutional Animal Care and Utilization Committees

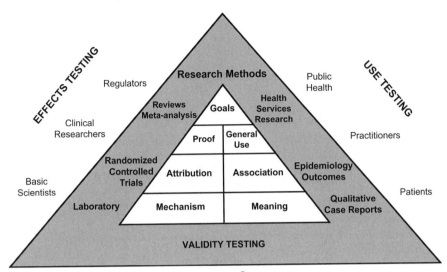

Figure 26.2 The evidence hierarchy and its users[7]

(IACUC) are self-regulating entities that, according to US federal law, must be established by institutions that use humans or laboratory animals for research or instructional purposes. The IRB and the IACUC oversee and evaluate all aspects of the institution's human and animal care and use program. Decisions made about how to conduct the research are carefully reviewed as well as the infinite possibilities of "what if this happens?"

Once we have the evidence, there is the expectation that the research quality must be measured. How likely is it that the effects reported are due to the independent variable (the animal/pet/companion)—i.e. what is the internal validity of the study? We can insure the internal validity of the study through randomization (subject assignment to groups in a random manner), baseline comparability (balanced demographics and prognostic factors), change of intervention (loss to follow-up, contamination, poor compliance), blinding (did patients/clients, investigators know who got the treatment?), outcomes analysis (was the objectivity, sensitivity, and reliability assessed? Was the number treated large? were p values significant? Were there multiple outcomes and were they all measured?) At the same time, the questions of how likely it is that the observed effects would occur outside the study and in different settings or the external validity of the study must be considered.

Not only must internal and external validity of the study be measured but also the generalizability of the data (is there a wide enough range of patients/clients/subjects to represent the field of actual practice use of the outcome?) must be assessed. Is this study reproducible (i.e. is what was done clear? Is the treatment intervention

---

[7] Adapted from Summerskill, W. S. M. (2001). The hierarchy of evidence. In McGovern, D., Valori, R. M., Summerskill, W. S. M., and Levi, M. (Eds.), *Key Topics in Evidence Based Medicine* (p. 15). Oxford, UK: BIOS Scientific Publishers Ltd.

transferable?). Was the outcome clinically significant? Was adherence good? Was there feedback for the participants and is the intervention practical in your practice setting? Were the outcomes of the study clinically relevant as well as important to the patients for whom it is intended?

Last in the list of accommodation is the evaluation of model validity. Within that evaluation, was thought given to using a model that was *representative* of the concept? Was the use of the animal intervention strategy adequate? Was the intervention clearly described? Did the researchers classify participants, determine the intervention and assess the outcomes according to the system (i.e. model) being assessed? Moreover, were participants believers in the intervention? Was the intervention adapted to the culture of the participants and what was the impact of informed consent?

Challenge 4. Addressing the underlying assumptions of human/animal interaction

Time for reflection on the underlying assumptions about this area of inquiry is past due. Are we making too much of a natural phenomenon? Are the potential benefits of human/animal interactions found only in Western science? Are there alternative outcomes of benefit that we should be considering? Are these "pieces of evidence" just novelty effects? Are there limits to the scientific level of inquiry in the field?

"So many questions—so little time," as the Rabbit said to Alice in Wonderland (Carroll, 2000). How *do* we progress in a meaningful manner as a field of scientific inquiry? I've just outlined a rigorous approach to sound studies in the field. Yet this is not new nor is it revolutionary. What I would like to propose as a possible solution is a change in professional roles and behaviors. Changes that I as well as many of my colleagues need to make.

Challenge 5. Providing quality education for investigators and program developers

We continue to need an international working group composed of key researchers and program directors in the HAI field to assist their colleagues in determining educational strategies most productive to building the hierarchy of evidence. Principles of evidence-based HAIs are equally applicable to allied health care providers/workers. This would also help to build interdisciplinary alliances with shared vocabulary and evidence building strategies. This working group could lobby the appropriate database professionals to include human/animal interactions as key search terms. This would address the issues of common definitions and terms. For the PubMed/Medline database, this could be accomplished through negotiations with the staff at the National Library of Medicine (http://www.nlm.nih.gov/mesh/staff). For the European sector, lobbying for a change in Embase terms would also be appropriate since there is even less specificity in search terms than in Medline with "pet therapy" used only in text but not as a key term (Spitzer, 2009). The closest term to human animal interactions found by a reference librarian was "animal use."

Practitioners/researchers must recognize that the evidence comes from a broader perspective than their own discipline. Indeed, the interdisciplinary nature of the HAI field is actually a benefit in seeking external funding. Translational research is the name of the game—from basic science to the patient…from applied science to the recipient. We need to build these relationships across disciplines and then incorporate or blend our research questions into the larger studies. This will address many of the validity issues that I posed while providing investigators with a greater potential for extramural funding.

We must re-evaluate our existing studies and program evaluations in light of validity and also extrapolation issues. We must integrate our research questions into large population studies to gain the same credibility as studies such as Framingham, the Australian Heart Study, the women's initiative, etc. Keep in mind that the largest sample size in the world does not help us if there is little or no comparability to the patients/ participants that we need to serve or that significance is found as a function of the sample size itself. In other words, we have not met the rules of evidence-based research.

In summary, HAI practitioners/researchers should know how to build systematic evidence as well as search for the evidence in the literature. We should be able to differentiate between good evidence, limited evidence, and wishful thinking. We then need the ability to evaluate the clinical applicability, relevance, and significance. Everything that is measurable is not necessarily important and everything that is not measureable should not be dismissed. As evaluators of the evidence as well as advocates for the timeless health benefits of companion animals we must know how to build the evidence for that which is measureable and be able to differentiate the value of that which is not. Solid design and research project development with attention to all of the challenges set forth in this chapter will move the state of the field to a higher level of evidence.

We must help build the evidence, guide the development of the hierarchy, as well as obtain the funding to support these endeavors. We must take what is "known" and fix the weaknesses we've identified, and develop an ongoing strategy to communicate the timeless impact of human/animal interactions. We cannot continue to critique the field of efforts without undertaking to help make the changes needed.

C The role of AAT in clinical practice: the importance of demonstrating empirically oriented psychotherapies

Aubrey H. Fine, Jeffery Scott Mio

26.7 Introduction

We are both frequently asked, whenever we give presentations for clinicians, questions that require simple solutions for therapy cases which by their nature are complex. For example, when Dr. Mio makes a presentation on the use of metaphors in politics, he often gets a question from a therapist asking something like, "What kind of metaphor works with someone who is depressed?" Similarly, Dr. Fine is commonly asked what kinds of dogs work best with specific kinds of illnesses, or perhaps what is the best approach to utilize the animals with specific groups of people. These kinds of questions imply that the questioner is looking for the "magic bullet"—a phrase or statement that would instantly lead to therapeutic cure of a disorder.

26.8 Skill of the therapist

While these kinds of questions might seem naive to the outside observer, we have found that when talking about AAT, quite often inexperienced therapists—or for that matter, some patients—have unreasonable expectations for the modality. They do not seem to appreciate the complexity for delivering such a therapeutic intervention. Writers have argued for decades that special attention needs to be given to the skills of the therapist in implementing such therapies. Draper et al. (1990) stress that the therapist "must possess appropriate competence in a definable therapy in absence of the animal" (p. 172). They believe that a therapist's competence and knowledge is the most important aspect of the therapeutic team. Others have investigated exactly what these therapist values are. For years, Strupp (1960, 1973, 1986) had examined factors that therapists bring into therapy. He concluded that the two major components of psychotherapy are (1) psychotherapy occurs within an interpersonal context (the therapeutic context or a therapeutic alliance), and (2) psychotherapy involves learning, be it learning new skills or unlearning unsuccessful patterns of behaviors. In order for therapists to create a therapeutic context, they need to be theoretically grounded and be competent or skillful in the therapeutic process. "As we have seen, the therapist's skill is significantly manifested by an ability to create a particular interpersonal context and, within that context, to foster certain kinds of learning" (Strupp, 1986, p. 126).

Stiles et al. (1986) would agree with Strupp's analysis. They contend, "Most of the proposed general therapist factors [of good psychotherapy] fall into two broad groups: (a) warm involvement with the client and (b) communication of a new perspective on the client's person and situation" (p. 172). Similarly, McMullen and Conway (1996) discussed how metaphors can be therapeutic when they are co-created by the client and therapist. This underscores both the therapeutic alliance and the meaning that emerges from the co-created metaphor.

Applying these concepts to AAT, one might see that a gentle, loving animal, such as a golden retriever, may enhance a warm therapeutic environment, whereas an enigmatic animal, such as a bird, may help stimulate a discussion in a new and interesting direction. However, the animal itself cannot "cause" therapeutic change; it can only assist in this change. Again, therapists need to be *skilled* therapists in order to providently use animals in treatment.

For example, skilled therapists might use AAT as one of the tools they have at their disposal, and with the sensitive use of animals, may very well achieve a therapeutic breakthrough. There are times that the animal makes breakthroughs that may be very difficult for the therapist to immediately achieve. Draper et al. (1990) suggest that the animal contributes by acting as a "prosthesis" to help establish and sustain the therapeutic relationship by the therapist. Pomp (1998) points out that the animal's presence encourages clients to readjust their boundaries of social comfort. Most clients appear more willing to disclose and to open up as a consequence of being surrounded by animals. Others point out that the presence of the animals enables the patient to begin feeling more comfortable and safer, thus leading to a stronger therapeutic alliance. However, Bowers and MacDonald (2001) stress that a skilled therapist needs to be in charge of the therapy to interpret the interactions in order to go beyond and to establish therapeutic gain. It is not necessarily the *fact* of using animals in therapy that leads to the breakthrough but the understanding of *how* an animal may lead to a positive result.

It has been reported that, since the 1960s, the number of psychotherapy approaches and theories has increased approximately 600% (Miller et al., 1996). Garfield and Bergin (1994) suggest that there are an estimated 200 therapy models today, including strategies such as AAT. Although some may believe that this expansion of theories has merit, others fiercely disagree. The opponents seem to be concerned with the dilution of what is considered effective therapy rather than just "pop" therapy. We believe that pop therapies negatively bias the public about the merits of psychotherapy.

26.9   What constitutes good therapy?

Hubble et al. (1999) edited a provocative book on what contributes to the therapeutic process. Many of the contributors reviewed what they saw as the common positive factors in therapy. Assay and Lambert (1999) synthesized the research findings and determined that, regardless of a therapist's theoretical orientation and techniques (e.g. biofeedback, systematic desensitization) (p. 31), all forms of therapy seem to have common therapeutic factors which enhance their success. These factors can be divided into four broad areas, including extra therapeutic changes, therapeutic relationships, techniques, and expectancy effects. Assay and Lambert referred to a paper by Lambert (1992) which highlighted the effects of each of these categories. According to Lambert (1992) as much as 40% of the improvement gained in psychotherapy is due directly to client variables (extra therapeutic changes), such as the severity of the disturbance, motivation for change, psychological health and the ability to identify the problem. On the other hand, research has consistently highlighted the importance of expectancy and placebo effects. Lambert sees this dimension contributing to 15% of the variance of change. Thus, expectancy for change and the hope demonstrated by the client that therapy will make a marked difference contribute 55% to the therapeutic change. Ironically, only about 15% of the variance of therapeutic change is attributed to the superiority of one approach over another.

The last major component Lambert (1992) addresses is the relationship factors that support therapeutic alliance. Factors such as warmth, affirmation, kindness are the backbone of this component. Researchers such as Najavitis and Strupp (1994) and Gatson (1990) as well as Lambert (1992) suggest that about 30% of the variance to the therapeutic outcome is directly impacted by therapeutic relationships. An inference can be made from this finding that could lead to an important question in the needed research agenda for AAT. Does having a trained therapy animal enhance the therapeutic alliance and relationship?

Although this initial information is relevant, the debate on what actually constitutes best practice in therapy continues to elude many professions including psychology. A major thrust over the past decade in many health care environments including medicine has been the quest to secure and develop evidence-based practices (as previously discussed in Chapter 4 by Katcher and Beck). Hitt (2001) in an article in the *New York Times Magazine* pointed out that evidence-based medicine is one of the breakthrough ideas of 2001. Although the field of medicine has portrayed itself as the discipline that is led by science, surprisingly there are not as many best practice treatments in medicine as the consumer is led to believe

According to the Institute of Medicine's (2001) definition of quality health care for the 21st century, "Evidence-based practice" is the integration of best research practice with clinical expertise and patient values. The impetus of evidence-based practices in mental health became a highly discussed topic since the early 1990s. In 1993, APA's (American Psychological Association) Division 12 (Society of Clinical Psychology) began developing and elaborating on a "list of empirically supported, manualized psychological interventions for specific disorders. The list was developed on the basis of randomized and controlled studies" (Norcross et al., 2006, p. 5). Since Division 12's benchmark efforts, several other divisions in APA have also issued their own preliminary guidelines for empirically supported interventions.

The attempt to empirically verify the effectiveness of psychotherapy has been an elusive pursuit for a while. For a period of time, the American Psychological Association (APA) encouraged therapists to use only those therapies that were empirically supported. This movement (EST—empirically supported treatments) proved to be ultimately too restrictive, in that it required that various elements in therapy be quantified to an exacting degree (Norcross, 2001). Consequently, APA loosened its requirements of ESTs to a bit more realistic set of requirements—evidenced-based practice in psychology, or EBPP (APA, 2006). While ESTs are the gold standard of EBPP, there are other elements that can be taken into consideration under EBPP, such as informed theoretical practice, expert opinion, and personal experience. Moreover, according to Kazdin (this volume), there are multiple acceptable kinds of empirical studies beyond the double-blind, random assignment to treatment standard of which we are all familiar.

The challenge that many of these divisions and organizations are now wrestling with is how does one accurately measure and determine treatment efficacy and what constitutes evidence (Goodheart, 2004)? Norcross et al. (2006) have edited what appears to be a seminal book that addresses the numerous variables that should be considered in conceptualizing evidence-based research as a whole. We will synthesize and report on some of their findings and use them as a springboard for our discussions. They suggest the following:

A. Clinical expertise, patient values and the need for scientific research on techniques are the areas where evidence is definitely needed.

B. Scientific research is the benchmark for evidence-based treatment. Research consists of a variety of methodologies and designs. Random clinical designs seem to have the most merit and are considered the gold standard for all disciplines. However, qualitative research (including ethnography, phenomenology, family analysis, ethnomethodology, case studies, single-participant designs) are all appropriate methods to also assess and gather evidence.

Qualitative research could be valuable for taking insights and comments made by patients or clinicians and studying them in a more systematic manner.

C. The treatment method, the impact of the individual therapist, the therapeutic relationship and the role of the patient are vital dimensions worthy of more clarity and investigation.

D. The available research needs to demonstrate that psychological treatments that eventually have empirical support are superior to no treatment or placebo treatment.

26.10   How best to study AAT?

Using Norcross et al. (2006) as our catalyst for how to best research AAT, clinical research with small sets of individuals has been accepted practice for social sciences for several years (Chambless, 2005; Chambless and Ollendick, 2001; Roth and Fonagy, 1996). Those interested in advancing AAT into more accepted evidence-based intervention must consider the steps that need to be taken to document its efficacy (Katcher and Beck, this volume; Wilson, this volume). According to the American Psychological Association, there are criteria used to judge evidence-based interventions. The following are some of the variables reviewed: (1) between-group designs demonstrating superiority to wait-list controls; (2) between-group designs demonstrating superiority to psychotherapy placebo; (3) between-group designs demonstrating superiority to some other forms of psychotherapy; (4) a large series of single-case designs demonstrating therapeutic efficacy; and (5) findings from at least two different investigators. These were general criteria used by a major task force examining empirically supported treatments (ESTs) commissioned by Division 12 (Chambless and Ollendick, 2001).

Clearly, the gold standard for research of this type is to have a random assignment to an AAT format and a traditional therapy format, then to determine which format led to better therapeutic outcome. Another variation on this is to have three groups, with the third group using an animal surrogate, such as a stuffed animal or a large pillow. While this methodology may be a theoretical gold standard, one must also carefully choose what one's measure of therapeutic success is. For example, measures for anxiety or depression (e.g. Beck Depression Inventory (Beck, 1967); Brief Depression Rating Scale (Kellner, 1986); Costello-Comrey Depression and Anxiety Scales (Costello and Comrey, 1967); Zung Self-Rating Anxiety Scale (Zung, 1971); and Zung Self-Rating Depression Scale (Zung, 1965)) tend to be global measures that are insensitive to subtle changes. Thus, if AAT is only subtly effective, then it will not yield statistically significant results on these global measures.

AAT can particularly benefit from the loosened stance of EBPP, as many elements of AAT may not necessarily be quantified to exacting standards. However, this does not absolve those in favor of AAT from *attempting* the gold standard of EST examination. While not investigating psychotherapy *per se*, Gee and her colleagues (Gee et al., 2007, 2009) have attempted to empirically measure the efficacy of using animals (certified therapeutic dogs to be exact) in modeling motor activities for preschool children. They have measured the effectiveness of dogs to model behavior in comparison with humans, stuffed animals manipulated by humans, and no-model controls and have found that the use of live dogs seems to be superior to the other conditions. Such attempts at studying the efficacy of animals in this form of interaction are what are needed in AAT.

Another issue to consider is that of proof. Even if AAT proves to be statistically significantly different from normal therapy, it could be that there are consistently small differences that are not clinically significant. Alternatively, there could be those who clearly benefit from AAT, but these individuals can be counterbalanced by others who may do worse with AAT, especially those clients who have aversive reactions or fears towards animals, or AAT practices which are not clinically sound. Finally, a therapeutic animal can pass away during the course of treatment, so many gains that may have accrued during treatment can be eliminated or even result in negative effects. Unfortunately, as many realize, a majority of published studies only highlight behavioral changes in one direction or another. Those studies that do not demonstrate any differences or therapeutic impact are rarely published. Denmark et al. (1988) highlight this position and suggest that studies not finding any convincing outcomes are rarely published. They suggested that we may very well believe there to be greater differences between genders because studies that found no differences are not published, so *only* those studies that found gender differences were published. Applied to research on AAT, the void in publications does not allow for a clearer understanding of the potential uses and misuses of AAT.

26.11   Establishing levels of proof: the difference between epistemological and metaphysical evidence

To secure respectability as effective evidence-based intervention, a methodology needs to establish a track level of acceptable proof that supports its position. Thus, the most logical question that follows is what level of proof is needed in order to be satisfied that there is a true benefit from AAT. This is akin to the difference between metaphysical versus epistemological proof that is discussed in philosophy (Smith and Medin, 1981). From an epistemological perspective, we require empirical proof. From a metaphysical perspective, we may "know" that something exists. Over the years I (AHF) have witnessed so many remarkable changes as a result of AAI. In *Afternoons with Puppy* (Fine and Eisen, 2008), several case studies are reported which are viewed metaphysically to illustrate the phenomena of change. The case study about Seth will now be discussed.

Box 26.1 Case study

After working with Seth and conducting a thorough evaluation, I eventually diagnosed him with Asperger's syndrome; along with an obsessive-compulsive disorder because of his visible interest in the weather. As with other children with Asperger's, Seth had trouble keeping up with his studies at school and making friends. He was placed in a special day class for several years until his family urged that he become more integrated.

> Although Seth eventually connected with most of the animals in my office, it was this small brilliant green-feathered bird (Boomer) that captured his attention and seemed to make a difference. The animals seemed to help Seth relax, and over the course of months, he seemed more open to talk when surrounded by their company. Observing the two together, I began to consider how I could integrate Boomer more intimately into Seth's treatment. I also began to notice that Boomer's presence seemed to decrease the agitation and anxiety that Seth would traditionally display. Boomer's affection had a positive therapeutic effect on Seth. He noted early in therapy, "I cannot get mad when I hold her. She trusts me and I would never hurt her". That statement seemed to be the catalyst for our future efforts.

My impressions from this intervention led me to believe, at least metaphysically, that the intervention that included Boomer made a significant impact. Empirically, self-reports and reports from others would also concur. Nevertheless, the degree of "proof" that was established still leaves many other unanswered questions, and too many skeptics with a rationale for their apprehensions.

It might be difficult to construct empirical studies that will yield epistemological proof. Animals can be unpredictable. This unpredictability can be used to therapeutic advantage or can be an impediment to therapy. For example, a dog may shy away from a client, thus unintentionally reinforcing the client's self-image that she is unlovable. Alternatively, if this dog were to warm up to the client, she may discover that she has the capacity to be loved. In another example, I recall hearing about an inexperienced therapist attempting to apply AAT into her practice. She loved bringing her dog to the therapy sessions, but recognized that the dog would constantly growl at her male clients. She was embarrassed about these actions and would reassure all her male clients not to take the growls personally. She also would let them know that the growls would eventually stop once the dog got used to them. Although her perceptions were accurate, was the dog's presence more of a detractor than being helpful? These two examples vividly highlight how the animal's unpredictable behavior could actually be an impediment to therapy. Thus, the general notion of the effectiveness of AAT may not necessarily be dependent upon the paradigm of AAT but by the spontaneous reactions of the animal/client interactions.

26.12 Gaining respectability for AAT

Over the course of close to three decades, I (AHF) have incorporated animals as adjuncts to the therapy. I have observed first hand many of the benefits discussed throughout the book. Nevertheless, I too have become cautious and skeptical of those who make unreasonable comments about the power of this form of intervention. Therapists incorporating AAT may have to reconsider their therapeutic approach, so they more naturally integrate the animal into the process. More importantly, it behoves leading researchers and clinicians to come together to generate more rigid guidelines for utilization of animal-assisted interventions, to develop clearer expectations and protocols. For AAT to eventually gain respectability in the mental health arena there is a strong need for evidence-based research to document the interventions. The question that we must now ask is how can we move this type of intervention closer to respectability?

Many ideas come to mind. For example, in the spring of 2004, several leading authorities in the human/animal bond movement—specifically AAT—congregated at University of Pennsylvania to discuss suggested research agendas for applying AAT with specific psychiatric populations. This process was also repeated in the fall of 2008 and the summer of 2009 at a meeting sponsored by Waltham and NICHD investigating the various research agendas for AAT with children. Although the meetings were all brief, they provided a forum for leading scholars and clinicians to meet with their counterparts applying and studying AAT. We believe that these types of venue are good places to begin wrestling with agendas for research and methods to implement the process. It is suggested that a possible mission of some of the university centers studying the human/animal bond (throughout the globe) could be to act as a clearinghouse of efficacy-based studies. If funding could be secured, scholars at various institutions could spearhead various evidence-based studies. It seems that a major area for evidence-based research could be on the area of how AAT enhances therapeutic alliance. Numerous studies could be established with clinician's providing guidance for the research team. With appropriate coordination, studies could be initiated that measured many of the dimensions that advocate AAT/AAI impacts. If an appropriate timeline could be established, within several years, there could be more respectable evidence-based studies generated in this area. Furthermore, the organizations involved in promoting all animal-assisted interventions need to clarify the terms used to describe various interventions. We strongly urge that these organizations raise the public's awareness by delineating what should be classified as therapy and by whom these services should be rendered. It is imperative for the general community to recognize that there is a difference in services rendered in animal-assisted activities in comparison to animal-assisted therapy. When these treatments are more clearly defined, it may make it easier for mental health practitioners and those not familiar with AAT to understand the spectrum of interventions made available.

26.13   Epilogue

What needs clarification is how frontline clinicians can support researchers in documenting therapeutic gains using AAT. There are daily procedures that therapists utilize (e.g. clinical notes) that if put to use, could be applied to document changes. This documentation may also include self reports, surveys and questionnaires completed by the client and significant others. Perhaps a website or discussion board can be developed where therapists can post successful and unsuccessful uses of AAT. We can then evaluate these posts to determine if trends can be detected. Utilizing some of these alternatives for documenting change could also be quite revealing.

As most researchers know, one cannot make statistical inferences from single case studies. However, a group of single case studies can point towards a trend and help researchers generate hypotheses to examine. Moreover, a collection of single case observations can help investigators determine the answers to various issues, including: (a) if there are protocols in using animals that work better with specific disorders; (b) if there are contraindications for AAT with specific disorders; and (c) if animals should be involved with every session.

For years, there has been an uneasy relation between researcher and clinician. The collaboration we suggest between these two groups of psychologists has the potential of contributing much to the field and may even become a desired, pet project. If the clinical community wants to increase the stature of AAT into a more critically accepted evidence-based approach, more scientific evidence is needed to make the skeptics more convinced that this is "more than just puppy love."

References

Allen, K. M., Blascovich, J., Tomaka, J., & Kelsey, R. M. (1991). Presence of human friends and pet dogs as moderators of autonomic responses to stress in women. *Journal of Personality and Social Psychology, 61*, 582–589.

Allen, K., Blascovich, J., & Mendes, W. B. (2002). Cardiovascular reactivity and the presence of pets, friends, and spouses: the truth about cats and dogs. *Psychosomatic Medicine, 64*(5), 727–739.

American Pet Products Manufacturers Association. (2006). In *Industry statistics and trends— pet ownership,* from http://www.appma.org/press_industrytrends.asp

American Psychological Association. (2006). Evidence-based practice in psychology. *American Psychologist, 61*, 271–285.

Anderson, W. P., Reid, C. M., & Jennings, G. L. (1992). Pet ownership and risk factors for cardiovascular disease. *Medical Journal of Australia, 157*, 298–301.

Assay, T., & Lambert, L. (1999). The empirical case for the common factors in therapy. In M. A. Hubble, B. Duncan & S. Miller (Eds.), *The Heart & Soul of Change* (pp. 20–34). Washington, DC: APA.

Barba, B. E. (1995). A critical review of the research on the human/companion animal relationship; 1988–1993. *Anthrozoös, VIII*(1), 9–14.

Bautista-Castano, I., Molina-Cabrillana, J., Montoya-Alonso, J. A., & Serra-Majem, L. (2004). Variables predictive of adherence to diet and physical activity recommendations in the treatment of obesity and overweight, in a group of Spanish subjects. *International Journal of Obesity and Related Metabolic Disorder, 28*(5), 697–705.

Beck, A. M., & Katcher, A. H. (1984). A new look at pet-facilitated therapy. *Journal of the American Veterinary Medicine Association, 184*(4), 414–421.

Beck, A. T. (1967). *Depression: Clinical, Experimental, and Theoretical Aspects.* New York: Harper & Row.

Blenner, J. L. (1991). The therapeutic functions of animals in infertility. *Holistic Nursing Practice, 5*, 6–10.

Bowers, M. J., & MacDonald, P. M. (2001). The effectiveness of equine-facilitated psychotherapy with at-risk adolescents. *Journal of Psychology and the Behavioral Sciences, 15*, 62–76.

Bradshaw, J., & Cameron-Beaumont, C. (2000). The signaling repertoire of the domestic cat and its undomesticated relatives. In D. C. Turner & P. Bateson (Eds.) *The Domestic Cat: The Biology of its Behaviour* (2nd ed.). Cambridge, UK: Cambridge University Press.

Broom, D. M., & Johnson, K. G. (1993). *Stress and Animal Welfare.* London, UK: Chapman and Hall.

Bryant, B. K. (1985). The neighborhood walk: sources of support in middle childhood. *Monographs of the Society for Research in Child Development, 50*(3), 1–122.

Cain, A. O. (1983). A study of pets in the family system. In A. H. Katcher & A. M. Beck (Eds.), *New Perspectives on Our Lives with Companion Animals* (pp. 351–359). Philadelphia, PA: University of Pennsylvania Press.

Cambridge Dictionary of Human Biology and Evolution. (2005). Cambridge, UK: Cambridge University Press.

Carmack, B. J. (1991). The role of companion animals with persons with AIDS/HIV. *Holistic Nursing Practice, 5*, 24–31.

Casey, R., & Bradshaw, J. (2005). The assessment of welfare. In I. Rochlitz (Ed.), *The Welfare of Cats*. Dordrecht, The Netherlands: Springer.

Chambless, D. L. (2005). Compendium of empirically supported therapies. In G. P. Koocher, J. C. Norcross & S. S. Hill, III (Eds.), *Psychologists' Desk Reference* (2nd ed.). (pp. 183–192) New York: Oxford University Press.

Chambless, D. L., & Ollendick, T. H. (2001). In S. T. Fiske, D. L. Schacter & C. Zahn-Waxler (Eds.), *Annual Review of Psychology. Empirically supported psychological interventions: controversies and evidence, Vol. 52.* (pp. 685–716). Palo Alto, CA: Annual Reviews.

Cohen, S. P. (2002). Can pets function as family members? *Western Journal of Nursing Research, 24*(6), 621–638.

Collis, G. M., & McNicholas, J. (2001). A theoretical basis for health benefits of pet ownership: attachment versus psychological support. In C. C. Wilson & D. C. Turner (Eds.), *Companion Animals in Human Health* (pp. 105–122). Thousand Oaks, CA: Sage.

Cook, S. E., & Bradshaw, J. W. S. (1996). *Reliability and validity of a holding test to measure "friendliness" in cats. ISAZ Conference, July 1996.* Cambridge: Downing College. (Abstract).

Costello, C. G., & Comrey, A. L. (1967). Scales for measuring depression and anxiety. *Journal of Psychology, 66*, 303–313.

Day, J. E. L., Kergoat, S., & Kotrschal, K. (2009). Do pets influence the quantity and choice of food offered to them by their owners: lessons from other animals and the pre-verbal human infant? CAB Reviews: Perspectives in Agriculture, Veterinary Science, Nutrition and Natural Resources, 4, Nr. 042 (doi: 10.1079/PAVSNNR20094042).

Denmark, F., Russo, N. F., Frieze, I. H., & Sechzer, J. A. (1988). Guidelines for avoiding sexism in psychological research: a report of an ad hoc committee on nonsexist research. *American Psychologist, 43*, 582–585.

Department of Health and Human Services. (2009). RFA-HD-09–031. 2009, from http://www.nichd.nih.gov

Deshriver, M. M., & Riddick, C. C. (1990). Effects of watching aquariums on elders' stress. *Anthrozoös, 4*, 44–48.

Draper, R. J., Gerber, G. J., & Layng, E. M. (1990). Defining the role of pet animals in psychotherapy. *Psychiatric Journal of the University of Ottawa, 15*, 169–172.

Forbes, D. A. (1998). Strategies for managing behavioural symptomatology associated with dementia of the Alzheimer type: a systematic overview. *Canadian Journal of Nursing Research, 30*(2), 67–86.

Friedmann, E. (1990). The value of pet for health and recovery. *Proceedings of the Small Animal Veterinary Association, 20*, 9–17.

Friedmann, E., & Thomas, S. A. (1985). Health benefits of pets for families. In M. B. Sussman (Ed.), *Pets and the Family* (pp. 191–203). New York: Routledge.

Friedmann, E., & Thomas, S. A. (1995). Pet ownership, social support, and one-year survival after acute myocardial infarction in the Cardiac Arrhythmia Suppression Trial (CAAST). *American Journal of Cardiology, 76*, 1213–1217.

Friedmann, E., & Tsai, C.-C. (Eds.), (2006) (2006). *The Animal-Human Bond: Health and Wellness*. San Diego, CA: Academic Press.

Friedmann, E., Katcher, A. H., Lynch, J. J., & Thomas, S. A. (1980). Animal companions and one-year survival of patients after discharge from a coronary unit. *Public Health Reports, 95*, 307–312.

Friedmann, E., Katcher, A. H., Thomas, S. A., Lynch, J. J., & Messent, P. R. (1983). Social interaction and blood pressure: the influence of animal companions. *Journal of Nervous and Mental Diseases, 171*, 461–465.

Friedmann, E., Locker, B. Z., & Lockwood, R. (1993). Perception of animals and cardiovascular responses during verbalization with an animal present. *Anthrozoös, 6*, 115–134.

Friedmann, E., Thomas, S. A. & Eddy, T. J. (Eds.), (2000). *Companion Animals and Human Health: Physical and Cardiovascular Influences*. New York, NY: Cambridge University Press.

Friedmann, E., Thomas, S. A., Cook, L. K., Tsai, C.-C., & Picot, S. J. (2007). A friendly dog as potential moderator of cardiovascular response to speech in older hypertensives. *Anthrozoös, 20*(1), 51–63.

Fritz, C. L., Farver, T. B., Kass, P. H., & Hart, L. A. (1995). Association with companion animals and the expression of noncognitive symptoms in Alzheimer's patients. *Journal of Nervous and Mental Diseases, 183*(7), 459–463.

Garfield, S., & Bergin, A. (1994). Introduction and historical overview. In A. E. Bergin & S. L. Garfield (Eds.), *Handbook of Psychotherapy and Behavior Change* (4th ed.). (pp. 13–18) New York: Wiley.

Garrity, T. F., & Stallones, L. (1998). Effects of pet contact. In C. C. Wilson & D. C. Turner (Eds.), *Companion Animals in Human Health* (pp. 3–22). Thousand Oak, CA: Sage.

Gatson, L. (1990). The concept of the alliance and its role in psychotherapy: theoretical and empirical consideration. *Psychotherapy, 27*, 143–153.

Gee, N. R., Harris, S. L., & Johnson, K. L. (2007). The role of therapy dogs in speed and accuracy to complete motor skills tasks for preschool children. *Anthrozoös, 20*, 375–386.

Gee, N. R., Sherlock, T. R., Bennett, E. A., & Harris, S. L. (2009). Preschoolers' adherence to instructions as a function of presence of a dog and motor skills task. *Anthrozoös, 20*, 267–276.

Goodheart, C. D. (2004, July). Multiple streams of evidence for psychotherapy practice. In C. D. Goodheart, & R. L. Levant, (Co-Chairs), Best psychotherapy based on the integration of research evidence, clinical judgment and patient values. *Symposium presented at the 112th Annual Convention of the American Psychological Association, Honolulu, HI.*

Goodwin, D., & Bradshaw, J. W. S. (1996). *The relationship between dog/dog and dog/human dominance interactions. ISAZ Conference, July 1996.* Cambridge: Downing College. (Abstract).

Goodwin, D., & Bradshaw, J. W. S. (1997). *Gaze and mutual gaze: its importance in cat/human and cat/cat interactions. ISAZ Conference, July 1997.* North Grafton: Tufts University School of Veterinary Medicince. (Abstract).

Goodwin, D., & Bradshaw, J. W. S. (1998). *Regulation of interactions between cats and humans by gaze and mutual gaze. ISAZ Conference, September 1998.* CZ: Prague. (Abstract).

Ham, S. A., & Epping, J. (2006). Dog walking and physical activity in the United States. *Preventing Chronic Disease: Public Health Research, Practice, and Policy, 2*(3). doi: http://www.cdc.gov/issuess/2006/apr/05_0106.htm

Hart, B. L. (1995). Analysing breed and gender differences in behaviour. In J. A. Serpell (Ed.), *The Domestic Dog: Its Evolution, Behaviour and Interactions with People*. Cambridge, UK: Cambridge University Press.

Hart, B. L., & Hart, L. A. (1985). *Canine and Feline Behavioral Therapy.* Philadelphia, PA: Lea and Febiger.

Hart, B. L., & Hart., L. A. (1988). *The Perfect Puppy: How to Choose Your Dog by its Behavior.* New York: W.H. Freeman.

Haubenhofer, D., & Kirchengast, S. (2006). Physiological arousal for companion dogs working with their owners in animal-assisted activities and animal-assisted therapy. *Journal of Applied Animal Welfare Science, 9*(2), 165–172.

Haubenhofer, D., Moestl, E., & Kirchengast, S. (2005). Cortisol concentrations in saliva of humans and their dogs during intensive training courses in animal-assisted therapy. *Tierärztliche Monatsschrift (Vienna), 92,* 66–73.

Hediger, A. (1988). *Die Freundlichkeit der Katze zum Menschen im Vergleich zur Freundlichkeit der Katze zur Katze.* MSc thesis, Zoology Institute, University of Zurich.

Hell, D. (1994). *Welchen Sinn macht Depression? Ein integrativer Ansatz.* Rohwolt: Reinbeck bei Hamburg.

Hirsch, A. R., & Whitman, B. W. (1994). Pet ownership and prophylaxis of headache and chronic pain. *Headache, 34,* 542–543.

Hitt, J. (2001, December 9). Evidence-based medicine. *New York Times Magazine,* p. 68.

Hubble, M., Duncan, B. & Miller, S. (Eds.), (1999). *The Heart & Soul of Change.* Washington, DC: APA.

Hubrecht, R., & Turner, D. C. (1998). Companion animal welfare in private and institutional settings. In C. C. Wilson & D. C. Turner (Eds.), *Companion Animals in Human Health.* Thousand Oaks, CA: Sage.

Humane Society of the United States. (2006). Legislation and laws, from http://www.hsus.org/legislation_laws

IAHAIO, the International Association of Human-Animal Interaction Organizations. December 2009. http://www.iahaio.org

Institute of Medicine. (2001). *Crossing the Quality Chasm: A New Health System for the 21st Century.* Washington, DC: National Academy Press.

Kannchen, S., & Turner, D. C. (1998). *The influence of human social support levels and degree of attachment to the animal on behavioural interactions between owners and cats. Abstract Book, 8th International Conference on Human-Animal Interactions, Prague: The Changing Roles of Animals in Society.* Paris: Afirac.

Karsh, E. B., & Turner, D. C. (1988). The human-cat relationship. In D. C. Turner & P. Bateson (Eds.), *The Domestic Cat: The Biology of its Behaviour.* Cambridge, UK: University of Cambridge Press.

Katcher, A. H., & Wilkins, G. G. (2000). The Centaur's lessons: therapeutic education through the care of animals and nature study. In A. Fine (Ed.), *Handbook on Animal-Assisted Therapy: Theoretical Foundations and Guidelines.* San Diego, CA: Academic Press.

Katcher, A. H., Friedmann, E., Beck, A. M., & Lynch, J. (1983). Looking, talking, and blood pressure: the physiological consequences of interacting with the living environment. In A. H. Katcher & A. M. Beck (Eds.), *New Perspectives on our Lives with Companion Animals.* Philadelphia, PA: University of Pennsylvania Press.

Kellner, R. (1986). The Brief Depression Rating Scale. In N. Sartorius & T. A. Ban (Eds.), *Assessment of Depression* (pp. 179–183). New York: Springer-Verlag.

Kidd, A. H., & Kidd, R. M. (1994). Benefits and liabilities of pets for the homeless. *Psychological Reports, 74,* 715–722.

Kotrschal, K., Schoeberl, I., Bauer, B., Thibeaut, A.-M., and Wedl, M. (2009). Dyadic relationships and operational performance of male and female owners and their***

Kushner, R. F., Blatner, D. J., Jewell, D. E., & Rudloff, K. (2006). The PPET Study: people and pets exercising together. *Obesity (Silver Spring), 14*(10), 1762–1770.

Lambert, M. J. (1992). Implications of outcome research for psychotherapy integration. In J. C. Norcross & M. R. Goldstein (Eds.), *Handbook of Psychotherapy Integration* (pp. 94–129). New York: Basic Books.

Lazarsfeld, P. (1959). Problems in methodology. In R. K. Merton (Ed.), *Sociology Today*. New York: Basic Books.

Loughlin, C. A., & Dowrick, D. W. (1993). Psychological needs filled by avian companions. *Anthrozoös, 6*, 166–172.

Loyer-Carlson, V. (1992). Pets and perceived family life quality. *Psychological Reports, 70*, 947–952.

McCune, S. (1995). The impact of paternity and early socialisation on the development of cats' behaviour to people and novel objects. *Applied Animal Behaviour Science, 45*(1–2), 111–126.

McCune, S., McPherson, J. A., & Bradshaw, J. W. S. (1995). Avoiding problems: the importance of socialisation. In I. Robinson (Ed.), *The Waltham Book of Human-Animal Interaction: Benefits and Responsibilities of Pet Ownership*. Oxford, UK: Pergamon Press.

McMullen, L. M., & Conway, J. B. (1996). Conceptualizing the figurative expressions of psychotherapy clients. In J. S. Mio & A. N. Katz (Eds.), *Metaphor: Implications and Applications* (pp. 59–71). Mahway, NJ: Erlbaum.

Meier, M., & Turner, D. C. (1985). Reactions of house cats during encounters with a strange person: evidence for two personality types. *Journal of the Delta Society* (later *Anthrozoös*), 2(1), 45–53.

Mertens, C. (1991). Human-cat interactions in the home setting. *Anthrozoös, 4*(4), 214–231.

Mertens, C., & Turner, D. C. (1988). Experimental analysis of human-cat interactions during first encounters. *Anthrozoös, 2*(2), 83–97.

Miller, D., Staats, S., & Partlo, C. (1992). Discriminating positive and negative aspects of pet interaction: sex differences in the older population. *Social Indicators Research, 27*, 363–374.

Miller, S. D., Hubble, M., & Duncan, B. (1996). *Psychotherapy is dead, long live psychotherapy*. Washington, DC: Workshop presented at the 19th Annual Family Therapy Network Symposium.

Najavitis, L. M., & Strupp, H. H. (1994). Differences in effectiveness of psychodynamic therapists: a process-outcome study. *Psychotherapy, 31*, 187–197.

National Institutes of Health. (1988). *Summary of Working Group: Health Benefits of Pets (No. DHHS Publication 1988-216-107)*. Washington, DC: US Government Printing Office.

Nielson, J. A., & Delude, L. A. (1994). Pets as adjunct therapists in a residence for former psychiatric patients. *Anthrozoös, 7*, 166–171.

Norcross, J., Beutler, L., & Levant, R. (2006). *Evidence-based Practices in Mental Health*. Washington, DC: American Psychological Association.

Norcross, J. C. (2001). Purposes, products, and products of the task force on empirically supported therapy relationships. *Psychotherapy: Theory, Research, Practice, Training, 38*, 345–356.

Olbrich, E. (1995). *Budgerigars in old people's homes: influence on behaviour and quality of life. Abstract Book, 7th International Conference on Human-Animal Interactions, Geneva: Animals, Health and Quality of Life*. Paris: Afirac.

Parslow, R. A., & Jorm, A. F. (2003). Pet ownership and risk factors for cardiovascular disease: another look. *Medical Journal of Australia, 179*(9), 466–468.

Peretti, P. O. (1990). Elderly-animal friendship bonds. *Social Behavior and Personality, 18*, 151–156.

Pomp, K. (1998). *Attachment Functions of Animal-facilitated Child Psychotherapy*. Unpublished manuscript. Topeka, KS: Karl Menninger School of Psychiatry and Mental Health Sciences.

Reichlin, B. (1994). *Begrüssungsverhalten vor dem Hundeferienheim in Abhängigkeit von früheren Erfahrungen.* Hirzel, Switzerland: Abschlussarbeit, I.E.T.I.E.T./I.E.A.P.

Rieger, G., & Turner, D. C. (1999). How depressive moods affect the behavior of singly living persons toward their cats. *Anthrozoös, 12*(4), 224–233.

Risley-Curtis, C., Holley, L. C., & Wolf, S. (2006). The human animal bond and ethnic diversity. *Social Work, 51*, 257–268.

Risley-Curtis, C., Holley, L. C., Cruickshank, T., Porcelli, J., Rhoads, C., Bacchus, D. N. A., et al. (2006). "She was family"—women of color and animal-human connections. *Affilia-Journal of Women and Social Work, 21*(4), 433–447.

Rochlitz, I. (2005a). Housing and welfare. In I. Rochlitz (Ed.), *The Welfare of Cats.* Dordrecht, The Netherlands: Springer Press.

Rochlitz, I. (2005b). *The Welfare of Cats.* Dordrecht, The Netherlands: Springer Press.

Rogers, J., Hart, L. A., & Bolt, R. P. (1993). The role of pet dogs in casual conversations of elderly adults. *Journal of Social Psychology, 133*, 265–277.

Roth, A. D., & Fonagy, P. (1996). *What Works for Whom? A Critical Review of Psychotherapy Research.* New York: Guilford Press.

Schaer, R. (1989). *Die Hauskatze.* Stuttgart: Verlag Eugen Ulmer.

Schalke, E., Mittmann, A., & Bruns, S. (2005). Assessment of behaviour of dogs of the pitbull-type and five other breeds by temperament testing according to the guidelines of the Dangerous Animals Act of Niedersachsen, Germany of July 5th, 2000 (in German). In *Aktuelle Arbeiten zur artgemässen Tierhaltung, KTBL-Schrift 437.* Giessen: Deutsche Veterinärmedizinische Gesellschaft e.V.

Serpell, J. (1991a). Beneficial effects of pet ownership on some aspects of human health and behavior. *Journal of the Royal Society of Medicine, 84*, 717–720.

Serpell, J. A. (1991b). Evidence for long term effects of pet ownership and human health. *Journal of the Royal Society of Medicine, 84*(December), 716–720.

Serpell, J., & Jagoe, J. A. (1995). Early experience and the development of behaviour. In J. A. Serpell (Ed.), *The Domestic Dog: Its Evolution, Behaviour and Interactions with People.* Cambridge, UK: Cambridge University Press.

Serpell, J. A. (1983). The personality of the dog and its influence on the pet-owner bond. In A. H. Katcher & A. M. Beck (Eds.), *New Perspectives on our Lives with Companion Animals.* Philadelphia, PA: University of Pennsylvania Press.

Siegel, J. M. (1990a). Human/Pet Relationships Measure. Stressful life events and use of physician services among the elderly: the moderating role of pet ownership. *Journal of Personality and Social Psychology, 58*, 1081–1086.

Siegel, J. M. (1990b). Stressful life events and use of physician services among the elderly: the moderating role of per ownership. *Journal of Personality and Social Psychology, 58*(6), 1081–1086.

Smith, E. E., & Medin, D. L. (1981). *Categories and Concepts.* Cambridge, MA: Harvard University Press.

Sonderegger, S. M., & Turner, D. C. (1996). Introducing dogs into kennels: prediction of social tendencies to facilitate integration. *Animal Welfare, 5*(4), 391–404.

Spitzer, L. (2009). MeSH search headings.

St Yves, A., Freeston, M. H., Jacques, C., & Robitaille, C. (1990). Love of animals and interpersonal affectionate behavior. *Psychological Reports, 67*, 1067–1075.

Stallones, L., Marx, M., Garrity, T. F., & Johnson, T. P. (1990). Pet ownership and attachment in relation to the health of U.S. adults, 21 to 64 years of age. *Anthrozoös, 4*, 100–112.

Stammbach, K. B., & Turner, D. C. (1999). Understanding the human-cat relationship: human social support or attachment. *Anthrozoös, 12*(3), 162–168.

Stiles, W. B., Shapiro, D. A., & Elliott, R. (1986). Are all psychotherapies equivalent? *American Psychologist, 41*, 165–180.

Straede, C. M., & Gates, G. R. (1993). Psychological health in a population of Australian cat owners. *Anthrozoös, 6*, 30–42.

Strupp, H. H. (1960). Nature of psychotherapist's contribution to treatment process: some research results and speculations. *Archives of General Psychiatry, 23*, 393–401.

Strupp, H. H. (1973). On the basic ingredients of psychotherapy. *Journal of Consulting and Clinical Psychology, 41*, 1–8.

Strupp, H. H. (1986). Psychotherapy: research, practice, and public policy (how to avoid dead ends). *American Psychologist, 41*, 120–130.

Summerskill, W. S. M. (2001). Hierarchy of evidence. In D. McGovern, R. M. Valori, W. S. M. Summerskill & M. Levi (Eds.), *Key Topics in Evidence-based Medicine* (pp. 15). Oxford, UK: BIOS Scientific Publishers, Ltd.

Thorpe, R. J., Jr., Kreisle, R. A., Glickman, L. T., Simonsick, E. M., Newman, A. B., & Kritchevsky, S. (2006). Physical activity and pet ownership in year 3 of the Health ABC study. *Journal of Aging and Physical Activity, 14*(2), 154–168.

Tucker, J. S., Friedman, H. S., Tsai, C. M., & Martin, L. R. (1995). Playing with pets and longevity among older people. *Psychology and Aging, 10*, 3–7.

Turner, D. C. (1984). Overview of research on human-animal interaction in Switzerland. *Journal of the Delta Society* (later *Anthrozoös*), *1*(1), 38–39.

Turner, D. C. (1985). The human-cat relationship: methods of analysis. In *The Human-Pet Relationship, Int'l. Symposium on the Occasion of the 80th Birthday of Nobel Prize Winner Prof. Dr. Konrad Lorenz, October 1983*. Vienna, Austria: IEMT and Austrian Academy of Sciences.

Turner, D. C. (1988). Cat behaviour and the human-cat relationship. *Animalis Familiaris, 3*(2), 16–21.

Turner, D. C. (1991). The ethology of the human-cat relationship. *Swiss Archive for Veterinary Medicine (SAT, in German), 133*(2), 63–70.

Turner, D. C. (1995a). Ethology and companion animal welfare. *Swiss Archive for Veterinary Medicine (SAT, in German), 137*, 45–49.

Turner, D. C. (1995b). *Die Mensch–Katze–Beziehung. Ethologische und psychologische Aspekte. Gustav Fischer Verlag*. Stuttgart: later, Enke Verlag.

Turner, D. C. (1995c). The human-cat relationship. In I. Robinson (Ed.), *The Waltham Book of Human-Animal Interaction*. Oxford, UK: Pergamon Press.

Turner, D. C. (1996). *Ethological aspects of the human-animal relationship—differences between animal species. Continuing Education Course on Pet Therapy*. WHO Research and Training Centre, Teramo, Italy: World Health Organization. June 10/11, 1996.

Turner, D. C. (2000a). The human-cat relationship. In D. C. Turner & P. Bateson (Eds.), *The Domestic Cat: The Biology of Its Behaviour* (2nd ed.). Cambridge, UK: Cambridge University Press.

Turner, D. C. (2000b). Human-cat interactions: relationships with, and breed differences between, non-pedigree, Persian and Siamese cats. In A. L. Podberscek, E. Paul & J. A. Serpell (Eds.), *Companion Animals and Us: Exploring the Relationships between People and Pets*. Cambridge, UK: Cambridge University Press.

Turner, D. C. (2002). The behaviour of dogs and cats. Points of contact between man and animal (in German). *Vierteljahrsschrift der Naturforschenden Gesellschaft Zürich, 147* (2), 51–61.

Turner, D. C. (2005a). Die beliebte Hauskatze—ein echtes "Heimtier". In M. Gäng & D. C. Turner (Eds.), *Mit Tiere leben im Alter*. München: Ernst Reinhardt Verlag.

Turner, D. C. (2005b). Human-companion animal relationships, housing and behavioural problems from an ethologist's view (in German). In *Aktuelle Arbeiten zur artgemässen Tierhaltung, KTBL-Schrift 437*. Giessen: Deutsche Veterinärmedizinische Gesellschaft e.V.

Turner, D. C. (2005c). A word about other species (in German). In M. Gäng & D. C. Turner (Eds.), *Mit Tiere leben im Alter*. München: Ernst Reihnardt Verlag.

Turner, D. C., & Rieger, G. (2001). Singly living people and their cats: a study of human mood and subsequent behavior. *Anthrozoös, 14*(1), 38–46.

Turner, D. C., & Stammbach-Geering, K. (1990). Owner assessment and the ethology of human-cat relationships. In I. Burger (Ed.), *Pets, Benefits and Practice. British Veterinary Association*. London: BVA Publications.

Turner, D. C., Feaver, J., Mendl, M., & Bateson, P. (1986). Variations in domestic cat behaviour towards humans: a paternal effect. *Animal Behaviour, 34*, 1890–1892.

Turner, D. C., Frick Tanner, E., Tanner-Frick, R., & Kaeser, I. (1998). *A curriculum for continuing education in animal-assisted counselling/therapy and animal-assisted activities. Abstract Book, 8th International Conference on Human-Animal Interactions*. Afirac, Paris: Prague: The Changing Roles of Animals in Society.

Turner, D. C., Rieger, G., & Gygax, L. (2003). Spouses and cats and their effects on human mood. *Anthrozoös, 16*(3), 213–228.

US Department of Health and Human Services. (1996). *Physical Activity and Health: A Report of the Surgeon General*.

US Department of Health and Human Services. (2005). Healthy people 2010: The cornerstone for prevention, from http://healthypeople.gov

Watson, N. L., & Weinstein, M. (1993). Pet ownership in relation to depression, anxiety, and anger in working women. *Anthrozoös, 6*, 135–138.

Wells, D. (2004). The facilitation of social interactions by domestic dogs. *Anthrozoös, 17*(4), 340–352.

Wilson, C. C. (1991a). A conceptual framework for animal interaction research: the challenge revisited. *Anthrozoös, 7*(1), 4–12.

Wilson, C. C. (1991b). The pet as an anxiolytic intervention. *Journal of Nervous and Mental Diseases, 179*(8), 482–489.

Wilson, C. C., & Netting, F. E. (1983). Companion animals and the elderly: a state-of-the-art summary. *Journal of the American Veterinary Medicine Association, 183*(12), 1425–1429.

Wilson, C. C., Fuller, G. F., & Cruess, D. F. (2001). *The emotional attachment of caregivers to companion animals. Paper presented at the 9th International Conference on Human-Animal Interactions*. Brazil: Rio de Janerio.

Wilson, C. C., Fuller, G. F., & Triebenbacher, S. L. (1998). *Human animal interactions, social exchange theory, and caregivers: a different approach. Paper presented at the the 8th International Conference on Human Animal Interactions*. Prague: Czech Republic.

Woods, L., Giles-Corti, B., & Bulsara, M. (2005). The pet connection: pets as a conduit for social capital? *Social Science and Medicine, 61*(6), 1159.

Zasloff, R. L., & Kidd, A. H. (1994). Loneliness and pet ownership among single women. *Psychological Reports, 75*, 747–752.

Zung, W. K. (1965). A Self-Rating Depression Scale. *Archives of General Psychiatry, 12*, 63–70.

Zung, W. K. (1971). A rating instrument for anxiety disorders. *Psychosomatics, 12*, 371–379.

Index